BRITAIN
IN TRANSITION

BRITAIN

IN TRANSITION
THE TWENTIETH CENTURY

Alfred F. Havighurst

THE UNIVERSITY OF CHICAGO PRESS
Chicago and London

Alfred F. Havighurst is Emeritus Professor of
History at Amherst College. His writings on
British History include *Twentieth Century
Britain* (2d ed. 1966); *Radical Journalist: H. W.
Massingham, 1860–1924* (1974); and *Modern
England 1901–1970* (Bibliographical Handbook),
1976.

The University of Chicago Press, Chicago 60637
The University of Chicago Press, Ltd., London

©1962, 1966, 1979 by The University of Chicago
All rights reserved. Published 1979

Printed in the United States of America
83 82 81 80 79   9 8 7 6 5 4 3 2 1

Library of Congress Cataloging in Publication Data

Havighurst, Alfred F
  Britain in transition.

  Revision of the work published in 1966 under title:
Twentieth-century Britain.
  Bibliography: p.
  Includes index.
  1. Great Britain—History—20th century.   I. Title.
DA566.H37 1979   941.082   78–16052
ISBN: 0-226-31968-7
ISBN: 0-226-31969-5 pbk.

For Miriam, my sister

Contents

Maps

Tables

Preface

This book is a very considerable extension and a thorough revision of my *Twentieth-Century Britain,* first published in 1962, and then reissued, with an additional chapter, in a second edition in 1966.

A new title seems amply justified on three counts. In the first place, there has been a change in tone and emphasis throughout the book. I have constantly had in mind the steady, sometimes even the inexorable change in Britain's fortunes—in the industrial basis of her economy, in her association with "Empire" and "Commonwealth," in her role as a great power in Europe and throughout the world, and in the nature of her social order. What was merely suggested in *Twentieth-Century Britain* is now asserted with emphasis and assurance. Indeed, in the course of the twentieth century Britain has faced a series of crises which indicate that this period will rank along with the Norman period, the Tudor and Stuart reigns, and the Victorian years as one of the formative eras in her history.

The second consideration is that since 1965, when the second edition of *Twentieth-Century Britain* was put together, the history of Britain in our time has been in considerable part rewritten. The circumstances are worthy of attention. By 1965 scholars were still barred by the fifty-year rule from examining official documents later than 1914. But in 1967 the Public Records Statute replaced this regulation with the thirty-year rule.

Suddenly was at hand a mass of new material on the period 1914–39, including the Foreign Office papers and the now indispensable documents of the Cabinet Office created in 1916. Similar relaxation of the bars at the British Library (until recently referred to as the British Museum) and other public depositories, together with more generous practice from private citizens with important manuscript collections, made accessible documentary material hitherto sealed against examination. Now the scholar and the student could investigate with far more assurance highly controversial areas and could more satisfactorily unravel the careers of politicians and statesmen, of editors and newspaper proprietors, of social scientists, labor leaders, and men of letters. While my own area of exploration of this new material has, of course, been selective, I have drawn heavily on the flood of monographs, biographies, and articles which have appeared in the past dozen years. I have modified, contracted, or expanded my treatment of the half century before 1950 as this new material has dictated.

The third point is that in *Britain in Transition: The Twentieth Century,* Britain's story has been brought down to the present, that is, to 1978. The chapters on the third quarter of the century have been entirely reorganized, largely rewritten, and extended in time. While archival material is restricted, the historian has been well served for the post–World War II period by autobiographies, published diaries and letters, as well as by an informed analysis of the contemporary scene by journalists and social scientists. Of course, as we approach the present we inevitably confront the limitations of instant history. Nevertheless, Britain's rapidly changing character and the transformation of her role in the world justify a narrative of historical events down to the present.

This book has been written primarily for the student and the general reader rather than for the scholar specializing in a particular aspect of the period. Nevertheless, it is hoped that as a synthesis the book will also prove useful to the historical profession. The degree to which I have drawn on the labors of others will be evident to anyone familiar with the literature on the subject; when possible I have sought to recognize this debt in the text. At the same time, I have not hesitated to reach my own conclusions, especially on matters on which scholars differ. And I do not consider it unimportant that at many points I have been able to supplement my reading from personal observation.

My greatest debt is to the many scholars on both sides of the water who have made of this period an exciting and rewarding area of study. I am especially grateful to Professor John C. Warren of Fairleigh Dickinson University, formerly a historian with the United States Air Force Historical Division, who read the chapter on World War II in its original form; his perceptive comments were very useful indeed to one not well schooled in military history. I am also greatly indebted to various libraries in Britain and in America: I should like to make special mention of the staff of the Robert Frost Library at Amherst College, who, for many years, have borne patiently my heavy demands on their services.

I am grateful to the following authors and publishers, whose material I have quoted: A. J. Youngson, *The British Economy, 1920–1957* (London: George Allen and Unwin, 1960); Winston S. Churchill, *The Second World War* (London: Cassell; Boston: Houghton Mifflin, 1948–53); H. G. Wells, *Mr. Britling Sees it Through* (New York: Macmillian, 1916); Geoffrey Keynes, ed., *The Poetical Works of Rupert Brooke* (London: Faber and Faber, 1946); William Sansom, *Westminster in War* (London: Faber and Faber, 1947); E. L. Woodward, *Short Journey* (London: Faber and Faber, 1942); Albert M. Imlah, *Economic Elements in the Pax Britannica* (Cambridge, Mass.: Harvard University Press, 1958); John Lehmann, *I am My Brother* (London: Longmans, Green; New York: Reynal, 1960); Siegfried Sassoon, *Collected Poems* (London: Faber and Faber, 1947); Siegfried Sassoon, *Siegfried's Journey* (London: Faber and Faber, 1945).

Grateful acknowledgment is made of permission from George Weidenfeld and Nicolson, Ltd., London, for permission to reproduce two maps taken from Nicholas Mansergh, *The Commonwealth Experience* (London, 1969).

A. F. H.
Amherst, Mass.

1

Beginnings

André Siegfried
England's Crisis
(1931), p. 13

To turn the corner from the nineteenth into the twentieth century, there, in a word, is the whole British problem.

G. M. Young
*Victorian
England: Portrait
of an Age* (1936),
p. 187

In the daily clamour for leadership, for faith, for a new heart or a new cause, I hear the ghost of late Victorian England whimpering on the grave thereof.

The Daily Mail,
January 1, 1900
(From Asa Briggs,
comp., *They Saw
it Happen: An
Anthology of Eye-
witnesses'
Accounts of
Events in British
History 1897–
1940* (1960),
p. 16

The nineteenth century is gasping out its breath—BOOM! The first stroke of midnight crashes through the frosty air and is hailed by an annihilating roar of jubilation. The succeeding strokes are almost unheard; they are all lost and drowned in the tumult of cheering. Hurrah! The twentieth century has dawned.

1900

Britain's story in the twentieth century has many beginnings; the last days of Queen Victoria, the advent of the Boer War, the
birth of the Labor Party, the decline of economic prosperity, the revolt
against the Victorian way of life—the alternatives are manifold and the
selection arbitrary.

A special meaning is sometimes associated with the transition from one
century to the next, as though mankind then pauses to contemplate
whence it has come and to gather strength and courage before venturing
further in search of its destiny. But we need not ponder mystically over
1900, for there is no occasion for magnetizing its historical significance
for the future.

The Death of Victoria

Nonetheless, particular events often do for a time have
an overriding impact upon the individual and may even briefly control
national consciousness. Certainly for those living in January 1901, the
death of Victoria in the eighty-second year of her life and the sixty-fourth
of her reign was high drama. Its impact was the greater for its suddenness. Though the queen had been failing, the public had little warning. As
Christmas approached in 1900, she had gone, as usual, to Osborne on
the Isle of Wight. On Friday, January 18, 1901, the Court Circular

1

disclosed that "she has not lately been in her usual health, and is unable for the present to take her customary drives." On the following Tuesday she died in the presence of her family, including the German emperor, who had interrupted preparations for the bicentennial celebration of the Prussian monarchy and had hurried to his grandmother's bedside. She was given a military funeral. As the cortege passed through London, the streets were packed and silent. Here, as in the final ceremonies at Windsor, the dominant impression from contemporary comment is that of three men in red cloaks who followed the gun carriage—the queen's two sons (King Edward VII and the Duke of Connaught), and her grandson (the Kaiser) in the uniform of a field marshal of the British Army.

After a stunned silence, emotion expressed itself in conventional terms. Osbert Sitwell recalled hearing people say, "What shall we do now?" On January 23 the lead article of the *Pall Mall Gazette* was headed, "The Glory of the Sunset," and of the *Daily Express*, "Peaceful End of the Greatest Reign in History—A World in Mourning—Universal Tribute to the Greatest of Queens and the Best of Women." In the House of Lords the prime minister, Lord Salisbury, attributed all the blessings of the nineteenth century to "the tact, the wisdom, the passionate patriotism and the incomparable judgment" of the late queen, while Balfour in the Commons initiated a phrase often repeated: "We feel that the end of a great epoch has come upon us."

Many a reign in English history, it would seem, has ended with a feeling of nostalgia for the past and of apprehension of the future. In 1901, no doubt, many were certain that something vital and irrevocable had departed from English life. For some the spell still held them in thrall years later. In 1936 Elinor Glyn could write: "I felt that I was witnessing the funeral procession of England's greatness and glory."

But on such an occasion it is hardly within reason to speak of "the nation's response." Each and every person had his own thoughts. Some quickly shook off any mood of melancholy. Craning his neck in a London crowd, Arnold Bennett, then more journalist than novelist, watched the funeral procession and recorded: "The people were not, on the whole, deeply moved, whatever journalists may say, but rather serene and cheerful." Others thought of the future. Though the public press vied in praise of the Kaiser, popular for a short time despite the Boer War, Wilfrid Scawen Blunt, then in Egypt, wrote of Victoria's death, "This is notable news. It will mean great changes in the world, for the long understanding among the Emperors that England is not to be quarrelled with during the Queen's lifetime will now give place to freer action. The Emperor William does not love his uncle, our new King."

Such perspective came more gradually to the nation as a whole. For some, Edmund Gosse, author and literary critic, broke the spell. Within three months his notable article on "The Character of Queen Victoria" appeared in the *Quarterly Review*. She had gradually "hypnotized the public imagination, so that at last . . . the nation accepted the Queen's view of her own functions and tacitly concluded with her that she ruled, a consecrated monarch, by Right Divine." But, Gosse added, she would have to be judged "not by what she seemed to be, but for what she actually was."

Long before her death, the world of affairs and of ideas had left her behind. Some historians would place the culmination of her reign in the Diamond Jubilee of 1897. So it would seem from reading her own account: "June 22 (1897). A never-to-be-forgotten day. No one ever, I believe, has met with such an ovation as was given to me, passing through those six miles of streets. . . . The crowds were quite indescribable, and their enthusiasm truly marvelous and deeply touching. The cheering was quite deafening, and every face seemed to be filled with real joy. I was much moved and gratified." But there was a vast difference between this jubilee—a tribute to her as an institution, a gesture of imperial defiance, a glorification of power which even then seemed like an ill omen—and the more homely Golden Jubilee of 1887, which was for Britain's own delight, a token of affection and esteem for the queen herself. G. M. Young suggests that the period between the two jubilees is the "epilog to one age, or the pre-history to another."

Queen Victoria's death, in itself, did not affect in any degree English society and politics. But it did dramatize the inevitability of change; it both focused attention on British achievement in the nineteenth century and underlined the transition from that which is called Victorian. With her death no one could any longer doubt it: the Victorian Age was past.

Uncertain Imperialism: The South African War

The South African War (1899–1902), commonly called the Boer War, tells us more about British life and spirit than any other event of its time. It led to a reorientation of British foreign policy; it brought to light the weaknesses of the British Army and eventually produced revolutionary change in the War Office; it stimulated jingoism and in time revealed the shallowness of imperialist doctrines which had warped the judgment of competent and well-intentioned men; it divided British leadership in time of war. Finally, the Boer War constituted a blow to self-confidence from which the country never fully recovered.

This conflict was the culmination of a protracted controversy between the British Cape Colony and the two Boer republics—the South African Republic (the Transvaal) and the Orange Free State. The original cause of the difficulty, as suggested at the time, was geological. With the discovery in the Transvaal of diamonds and then, in 1886, of a rich gold field on the Witwatersrand thousands of British rushed across the Cape Colony border. There can be no exact figures, for part of the population was floating, but by 1895 over half the population in the Transvaal was British, and in Johannesburg, hard by the Rand, the Uitlanders, as the Boers called the foreigners, were in the ascendancy at least three to one. The Boers in the Transvaal quite naturally resented this invasion, and feared for their institutions and for their independence. On the other hand, though the British paid the larger portion of the taxes, their schools and their language were relegated to second-class status. With only the greatest difficulty could rights of citizenship, particularly the franchise, be obtained. Of course, to the Boers it seemed that· a general grant of the franchise would soon mean a loss of the Transvaal. In the background was the moot question of whether the Transvaal was, in fact, a sovereign state—a point left uncertain in the Convention of 1884, which had terminated an earlier controversy with the British. It was this problem of Boer against Uitlander in the Transvaal after 1886 which led to war.

For our examination of the background of the war, it is well to keep in mind the roles of three individuals. "Oom Paul" Kruger had been president of the Transvaal from 1883—an elderly man, stubborn, dictatorial, and unprogressive. In appearance he was unprepossessing in the extreme—a fact unfortunate for his opponents, for the British failed to take sufficient note of him.

In Cape Colony, Cecil Rhodes, only forty-two years of age in 1895, was already a great man. In 1889 he was made managing director of the newly chartered British South Africa Company, and in 1890 he became prime minister of Cape Colony; thus, he was both the political and the economic chief. His immediate object was a federation of South Africa under the British; his dream was British hegemony in Africa generally. In 1895 the company, with London's blessing, occupied a strip of Bechuanaland bordering the Transvaal on the west. That state had already in 1890 been cut off from the sea by the diplomacy of Salisbury. A glance at the map shows a virtual British encirclement of the Boer republics.

In London Joseph Chamberlain was at the Colonial Office, his choice in 1895, though he might well have had the Exchequer. He became the chief spokesman for British imperialism and, as a biographer puts it, "had usually the power of a co-Premier and on some rare occasions more." In 1898 the *Revue de Paris* ran a series of articles on Chamberlain as "the man of Empire."

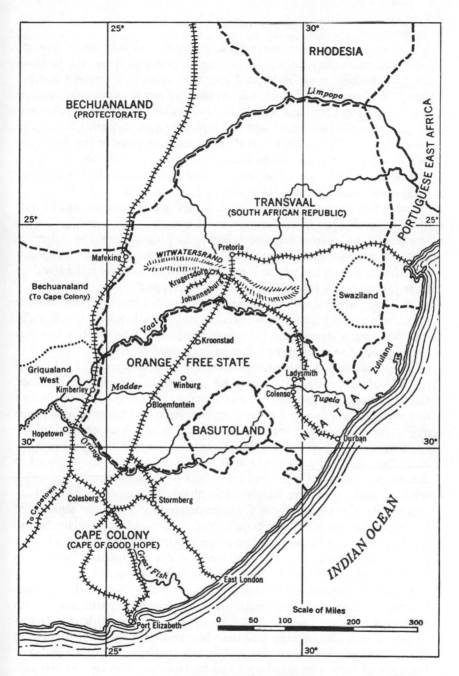

SOUTH AFRICA, 1899

The Jameson Raid

If any one incident produced the war, and if any one incident reveals the weakness in the English position, it was the Jameson Raid at the beginning of 1896. From that episode Winston Churchill dated "the beginning of these violent times" of our own century. So acute was the tension between Boer and Uitlander that the British in Johannesburg, inspired in part from Cape Colony, were now preparing for revolution. Once the Uitlanders revolted, Jameson, the agent of the South Africa Company in adjoining Bechuanaland, was to move into the Transvaal with a small force of mounted police and prevent the Boers in the rural areas from checking the rising in Johannesburg.

But in time, as preparations lagged, Jameson lost patience, and in spite of warning that the Uitlander movement was collapsing, and ignoring a last-minute order from the British high commissioner, on December 29, 1895, with some 470 men he dashed for Johannesburg, 180 miles distant. It was a complete fiasco; Johannesburg failed to rise, and a few days later Jameson and his men were in jail in Pretoria.

Had the British Government frankly accepted responsibility for the raid, there would probably have been an end to the incident, which might then have been salutary for the whole problem. Unfortunately this was not the case. Jameson, turned over to the British by Kruger, was tried in London and sentenced to fifteen months' imprisonment, of which he served only a portion. Popularly he was treated as a hero. In Cape Colony Rhodes resigned as prime minister, and the Cape Parliament, in a fair inquiry, held that he had been an accomplice to the general conspiracy within and without the Transvaal, but not to the actual raid. However, the parliamentary investigation in London was highly unsatisfactory. Even the leaders of the Liberal Party Opposition were disposed to defend the Colonial Office; and the report of the committee, July 1897, while severely censuring Rhodes, completely exonerated Chamberlain. Against Rhodes no penalty was recommended, not even the removal of his name from the list of privy councilors. And then Chamberlain, before the Commons, virtually repudiated the report to which he had been a party: "There has been nothing proved—and in my opinion there exists nothing—which affects Mr. Rhodes' position as a man of honor."

This investigation merely stimulated controversy. Not all the evidence had been presented to the parliamentary committee; in particular, certain telegrams between London and Capetown had been withheld. It was suggested that Chamberlain had been blackmailed into publc support of Rhodes. At the very least, many Liberals in Parliament thought their leaders had been victimized by Chamberlain. The contents of the suppressed telegrams are now known. While they do not support a clear case against Chamberlain, they would have been difficult to explain away had they been produced then.

Toward Intervention

If the responsibility for the raid is still controversial, there is little question of its consequences. Even the more progressive Boers were now suspicious of all aspects of British policy. President Kruger, heretofore in office only by a slender margin, was reelected in 1898 by polling more than two-thirds of all the votes cast. It is not easy to complete the story in a few lines. Both policy and opinion in Britain wavered, for the issues were never very clear. A cardinal mistake in British thinking was the persistent assumption that the Boers would never actually go to war. Furthermore, policy in London and in Capetown were often at cross purposes. The vigorous strain of imperialism in the outlook of the leadership of the Liberal Party blunted its effectiveness as the Opposition. Even in the press there was, in J. A. Hobson's phrase, "a false and artificial unanimity" in dealing with the South African question.

Chamberlain in these years was hardly the warmonger some of his critics have alleged, but he had small concern for Boer interests and was prepared to adopt only those solutions which would protect the Uitlanders. In the end he was not averse to playing a little of the game of bluff himself. In his Highbury speech, August 1899, he held Kruger responsible for the failure of negotiations. "The sands are running down in the glass. . . . The knot must be loosened . . . or else we shall find other ways of untying it." Diplomacy broke down completely; in September 1899 the Orange Free State officially announced support for the Transvaal; on October 9 Kruger issued his ill-advised ultimatum demanding that the British cease troop reinforcements in South Africa. The ultimatum was rejected and war began.

War and the Public Temper

The war itself in no manner enhanced Britain's reputation. If the "national character" included moderation, an instinct for fair play, and general good sense, it broke down. Most Englishmen never could understand the overwhelming sympathy in Europe for the Boers. It was no "capitalist war"; imperialism was not then a class issue. It was the nation's war. Public opinion was self-righteous, ill-formed, and superficial in judgment. It was hasty in celebration and easily overwhelmed by gloom. Alternating periods of "gratified and wounded pride" provide an unlovely parade of human emotions.

At the beginning, complacency was fairly general. No one seemed more sure of himself than Chamberlain as he defended his policy in the Commons. He had finally but reluctantly come to the conclusion that war had always been inevitable, so he said; full responsibility, he declared, rested on Kruger. "I say with all reverence and gravity, we accept the challenge, believing our cause to be just." The speech from the throne proroguing Parliament invoked divine blessing upon efforts "to vindicate the honor of this country." Imperial bombast reached new extremes in the press. The music halls rang with "We're not going to stand it."

An easy victory was expected against a farmer people "going to war in its everyday clothes." But a series of initial defeats culminated in a succession of disasters in "Black Week," December 11–16, 1899. Public incredulity changed to dismay, and dismay to hysteria. New leadership and new tactics reversed the early defeats, and one by one British strong points in Cape Colony and in Bechuanaland were recovered. Baden-Powell was relieved at Mafeking, May 17, 1900, after withstanding a siege of 217 days. Receipt of the news in London on the evening of May 18 was the signal for a celebration such as Victorian England had never witnessed. Through the night and on into the next day central London was one vast carnival of surging crowds.

This sudden frenzy for Mafeking, only an incident in the war, was followed by a decline in emotion just as abrupt. The prompt captures of Johannesburg and of Pretoria, the Transvaal capital, were far more important and yet attracted relatively little attention. When the taking of Johannesburg was announced, the derby at Epsom drew first billing on newspaper hoardings.

With the capture of Pretoria, Roberts proclaimed the annexation of the Boer republics. They would, of course, now surrender. "What reason is there to doubt," asked the Daily News on June 4, "that they will quickly realize that the blessings of self-government and free and equal rights under the British flag are to them the restoration instead of a deprivation of their genuine independence?" The guerrilla tactics, by which the Boers were to prolong the war another eighteen months, were not at first taken seriously.

But the conflict wore on, and the new century opened in an atmosphere of gloom. By this time the press was less complacent. "It may be that certain events have taught us a less confident and presumptuous note than heretofore" (Daily Mail, January 1, 1901) and "We have outlived the depressing and wildly exhilarating stages of the war and are now possessed by a disciplined determination to 'see it through'" (Pall Mall Gazette, January 3). Emotion, however, was not yet exhausted. There was still the charge of Boer atrocities ("Boers Behave like Brigands") and the vehement denial of inhumanity in the British "concentration camps" for rounded-up Boers.

The press generally reflected and stimulated these moods; often vacillating before the war on the issues in South Africa, each paper now took a strong position. In London the Liberal *Westminster Gazette* was the only influential paper which did not succumb to the jingo mood. But many an individual refused to be carried along. The novelist George Moore was a passionate pro-Boer. So was the young philosopher, Bertrand Russell, after a complete shift as war progressed. Henry W. Massingham, product as well as sponsor of the New Journalism, whose attitude toward the South African crisis before hostilities was indecisive, in November 1899 was forced from his editorship of the Liberal *Daily Chronicle* when he refused to stop criticism of the Government and the conduct of the war. Under new editorship, the *Chronicle* lined up with the *Daily Mail,* the *Daily News,* and the rest, in support of the war. There were pacifists like W. T. Stead, editor of the *Review of Reviews* and until the war one of Rhodes's strongest supporters. He and others formed a "Stop the War Committee" and later a "South African Reconciliation Committee."

Of the long-range effects of the Boer War on British morale there were some manifestations in 1900–1901. The *Annual Register* for 1900 reads: "The outlook at the end of the year which closed the nineteenth century could hardly fail to arouse misgivings as to the future in all but the imperviously self-satisfied." Support of the war was based more on pride and self-rightcousness than on issues and principles, and it may have disturbed the minds and consciences of more people than we know. How shall we interpret the endless discussion of the causes of the war? What was the explanation of the popular vote in the election of 1900, when nearly 47 percent of the electors voted against the Government? How shall we account for the sudden burst of pro-Boer sympathy on the issue of the concentration camps?

Challenge to Laissez-Faire

National budgets are not often of dramatic interest, but the budget of 1902 might well be taken by an economic historian as the starting point of twentieth-century Britain. In 1902 the chancellor of the Exchequer, in order to meet the financial demands of the Boer War, proposed a modest duty on imported wheat and flour. That may have been incidental, but a year later Joseph Chamberlain announced his conversion to general tariff reform, and one of the great battles of the century was on. Though protection as a general policy did not come until 1932, it may be said that free trade as an unchallenged tenet of economic theory had had its day.

A Weakened Economy

For explanation of these developments in 1902–3 we must look briefly at the British economy in the thirty years just preceding. The term "Great Depression" sometimes applied to the years 1873–96 is suitable only in reflecting the mood of contemporaries and the atmosphere in which several royal commissions carried on inquiry. On the other hand, it was a critical period because of a sharp decline in the rate of industrial growth from the mid-Victorian years and a weakening of Britain's economy relative to the more rapidly expanding economies of the United States, Germany, and France. British exports, by volume, continued to advance in the last quarter of the century, but at a much reduced rate and much less rapidly than imports. By 1898, when production and exports returned to what had been regarded as normal growth, Britain found that in key industries she was being outdistanced by Germany and the United States.

Table 1 | Imports and Exports of the United Kingdom during Selected Years, 1851–1912

Year	Imports	Exports
1851	£110,485,000	£214,388,000
1860	210,531,000	164,521,000
1870	303,527,000	244,081,000
1872	354,684,000	314,589,000
1873	371,287,000	311,005,000
1876	375,155,000	256,777,000
1883	426,892,000	305,437,000
1886	349,863,000	268,959,000
1890	420,692,000	328,252,000
1894	408,345,000	273,786,000
1898	470,545,000	294,014,000
1901	528,391,000	347,864,000
1906	607,889,000	460,678,000
1911	680,158,000	556,878,000
1912	744,641,000	598,961,000

Source: William Page (ed.), *Commerce and Industry: Tables of Statistics for the British Empire from 1815* (1919), pp. 71–72.

In 1851 the *Economist* had declared that the "economic superiority of the United States to England is ultimately as certain as the next eclipse." But the shift came sooner than most people anticipated. Both the American and the German economies expanded behind high tariff barriers, with the entire British market open wide to their products. By 1900 cotton textiles, the backbone of English industry, had lost most of the continental and American markets. In steel production England had dropped from first place to a poor third and by 1900 was actually importing steel.

Yet, for the sake of national well-being, Britain had to remain a frontrunning industrial nation and maintain a vast external trade. This is apparent from some figures by William Ashworth in *An Economic History of England, 1870–1939:* "On the basis of the first census of production it was estimated that in 1907 roughly one-quarter of the output of goods in the United Kingdom went for export, one fifth of the goods consumed came directly from imports and, allowing for home produced goods which incorporated other imports, the total retained imports equalled one-third of the total national consumption of goods."

Table 2   Quinquennial Increases in Volume of World and British Trade, 1876–1913

Periods Compared	World Trade in Manufactures	Total World Trade	British Exports	British Net Imports
1876–80 : 1881–85	24.4%	22.8%	27.1%	11.8%
1881–85 : 1886–90	12.9	15.5	12.1	13.2
1886–90 : 1891–95	1.7	10.2	−0.8	17.3
1891–95 : 1896–1900	4.7	12.9	13.1	21.6
1896–1900 : 1901–5	31.8	22.1	10.6	10.0
1901–5 : 1906–10	23.3	19.5	20.6	5.7
1906–10 : 1911–13	22.7	18.8	14.7	14.3

Source: William Ashworth, *An Economic History of England, 1870–1939* (1960), p. 148.

When we consider Britain's economy at the beginning of the century we have in mind the future. And, indeed, most of the losses are related to the future. What was happening did not seem as clear then as it does now. Most English industrial enterprise was doing well and exports were jumping ahead once more. The bill for imports could still be paid in part from British investments abroad, which accounted for about 15 percent of the nation's capital. Her ships were still carrying more than half the world's ocean-going cargo, and she was still launching 60 percent of the world's new tonnage. But there were weaknesses in the economy. Britain was importing more and more of her food. She was exporting machinery rather than finished goods, thus reducing the demand for her manufactured articles. Bulky coal was used as an outward cargo to balance bulky imports (cotton, timber, and wheat), but much of that coal could have been used to better economic advantage at home. In some industries British inventiveness and willingness to try new procedures, so prominent in the mid-Victorian period, were now lacking. This does not mean that British industry was generally inefficient; but it had weak spots, and these, combined with competition from strong nations possessed of abundant natural resources, in time brought Britain's economy to a critical stage.

The shift in the fortunes of agriculture during the last quarter of the nineteenth century is even more striking. Statistics tell a fantastic story. Until 1880 agriculture employed far and away more people than any other industry. But between 1871 and 1901 the number of agricultural laborers shrank by 33 percent, despite a general population increase of 43 percent. By 1901 in England and Wales the urban population comprised 77 percent of the whole. Whereas in 1851 one out of every four males was directly linked with agriculture, by 1911 it was less than one in twenty.

As late as 1840–45 England produced 90 percent of her food. However, by the end of the century 70 percent of Britain's wheat was imported, with the domestic price falling off roughly 40 percent. Agricultural rents declined on the average about 25 percent, much more than the decline in prices outside of agriculture. Land in the United Kingdom under cultivation fell from 17,000,000 acres in 1872 to 13,400,000 acres in 1913. These generalizations, of course, oversimplify what happened. They were not years of steady depression, year in and year out, and some areas were hardly affected at all. But agriculture as a whole declined markedly as a source of wealth and as a means of livelihood.

Again, it is not so much that British agriculture had intrinsic weaknesses as that its competitive power was greatly reduced. Enormous expansion of wheat-growing on the American prairies, construction of railroads, and a sharp drop in ocean-going freight charges meant disaster for British wheat. Surplus grain in Canada and Argentina also moved into the British market, though more slowly. Elsewhere in Europe, save in highly industrialized Belgium, native agriculture was protected by tariffs. But in Britain the price of wheat, which averaged about 55 shillings per quarter between 1850 and 1875, dropped to about 30 shillings in the late eighties, and then fell still lower, at one point in 1894 falling almost to 17 shillings. The British farmer also had a labor problem. Though agricultural wages, to meet industrial competition, rose considerably, farm labor became discontented and went to the cities, where real wages remained slightly higher and where life seemed brighter. The landed interest which had dominated English life and society since the Norman Conquest was losing its authority; the econoic basis of its position had been destroyed. The agricultural revolution of the last quarter of the nineteenth century completed the transition from rural England, from an agricultural to an industrial and financial state.

A Social Conscience and a Social Gospel

"The Advance Towards State Socialism" is the title of an article appearing in the *Economist* in 1894. "Cobden, if he were alive, would hardly recognize the world" was the unhappy comment of this organ of orthodox liberalism. The economic ideal of the mid-Victorian years was, of course, *laissez-faire* and Cobden was its chief spokesman. But new conditions in industry and agriculture, and in politics as well, brought new ideas. Labor, both rural and urban, became more articulate and more aggressive. Questions began to be asked about the distribution of the national income. Furthermore, periods of depression, particularly in the eighties, brought widespread unemployment and great distress.

The Victorian conscience was troubled. Complacent philanthropy gave way to social service agencies and to social literature which sought not only to alleviate distress but to get at the causes. It was the era of the Social Gospel. In 1888 "England practically spent the year with its conscience." The *Oxford Dictionary* records in this year the appearance of the word "unemployment." The evils of sweated labor were revealed in a Board of Trade report. Annie Besant, in her magazine the *Link*, and H. H. Champion, in his paper *Labour Elector,* exposed the poor working conditions of girls employed in the London match industry; the girls read them; some seven hundred of them went out on strike, a small affair in itself, but a strike which won general sympathy and financial support and was an indication of things to come. Social writings increased in significance. *In Darkest England and the Way Out,* a widely read study of poverty and vice, appeared in 1890. It was written by General Booth, the founder of the Salvation Army, with the assistance of W. T. Stead. Particularly important was the work of Charles Booth (no relation to General Booth), not a socialist but a wealthy ship-owner interested in social questions, who proposed a scientific investigation of poverty. In 1889 he began publishing the results of his investigation of the "Life and Labour" of the people of London, in which his object was to show "the numerical relation which poverty, misery and depravity bear to regular earnings and comparative comfort, and to describe the general conditions under which each class lives." There is perhaps no more significant statistic in the late nineteenth century than his conclusion that 30.7 percent of the people of London lived in a state of poverty, that is, at or beneath the level of bare subsistence; in some areas of the city, where families were crowded into wretched little buildings fronting twelve to fifteen feet on the street, the poverty figure reached 60 percent. Poverty had become "a national institution," to use Booth's own phrase, and his findings received sober attention.

The practice of state socialism has its roots deep in the nineteenth century; along with all the talk about *laissez-faire* in Victorian England went, if only for humanitarian reasons, a great deal of state intervention. Now, in the closing decades, this became more a part of conscious policy. In the Commons in 1891 Joseph Chamberlain, who gave his blessing to the work of Charles Booth, quoted with approval the statement of the economist Stanley Jevons that "the State is justified in passing any law, or even in doing any single act, which in its ulterior consequences adds to the sum of human happiness." A few years later came the oft-quoted remark of the Liberal leader Sir William Harcourt: "We are all Socialists now." The first statement was made with conviction, the second was intended as a slur, but both were recognition of a new outlook which had modified the operation of *laissez-faire* in the activities of government. One has but to scan the newspapers and periodicals of the eighties and nineties to realize how widespread were the discussions of social problems and of the responsibility of government. By 1900 it was generally recognized that state action, on a national level, was necessary to cope with the social evils which had developed with industrialization. But it took time for politicians to learn what the voters wanted. It also took time to reorient party philosophies. Above all, to embark on comprehensive programs of social security, to attack the slum areas and the problem of working-class housing, demanded funds far beyond the imagination of any chancellor of the Exchequer of the nineteenth century. This required a revolution in government finance.

Transitions in Politics

In party politics the answer to this question of the relation of government to society was not at all clear in 1900, certainly not in the parliamentary elections held in October of that year. For under the impact of changing economic and social problems, as well as the immediate issues of the Boer War, the pattern of politics was in process of transformation from lines familiar in the nineteenth century. Politics became increasingly identified with economic interests, a radical departure from the mid-nineteenth century, when it would have been exceedingly difficult to have guessed anyone's party affiliation on the basis of material self-interest. The new element in politics, the working class, now sought to advance its interest. Old parties painfully adjusted to new issues and new constituents.

Between the Reform Bill of 1832 and Gladstone's first Irish Home

Rule Bill in 1886 the Liberals had dominated the English scene. As the Whig Party they had, though with reluctance, accepted political change, including the participation of the middle class in government. As the Liberal Party they stood for "liberalism" of the nineteenth-century variety, a liberalism largely political in nature. "Freedom" was a key word, particularly in economics; they opposed, in principle, government restrictions on industry, and free trade was a cornerstone of their policy. They were not, generally speaking, imperially minded; some opposed colonialism on moral principle and others considered colonies economically unprofitable. The party drew its strength mainly from the remnants of the landed Whig aristocracy, from urban industrial and financial interests, and from the Nonconformists in religion. It included the self-styled Radicals—those particularly committed to "individualism," "freedom," and social change.

On the other hand, the Conservatives had recovered only gradually from their defeat as Tories back in 1832. They remained on the defensive, and their appeal to established institutions, especially to the Crown and to the Anglican Church, had insufficient attraction until the appearance in the seventies of Disraeli's glittering phrases, "the preservation of our institutions, the maintenance of our empire, and the amelioration of the condition of the people." The party's strength was concentrated in the rural areas, with the squirearchy and the parish clergy as chief supports.

Conservative Rejuvenation

In party fortunes, the parliamentary election of 1895 seemed to represent a great reversal. When the coalition of Conservatives and Liberal Unionists swept into power with 411 seats, as against 259 for the Liberal and Irish Opposition, it did seem that the turning point had finally come and that the rejuvenated Conservatives were in for a long lease of power.

A key to what was happening is found in the fact that much of the radicalism in Parliament became Conservative. The stormy petrel of these times was Joseph Chamberlain. First he built a fortune as a screw manufacturer, and then in the seventies he made a reputation as the radical mayor of Birmingham. His reordering of that city went far toward making public administration of municipal services a habit of life. He entered national politics as a Liberal and as a Radical; as a member of the Gladstone administration of 1880–85 he inaugurated a campaign of "doing for the nation what he had done for the town." He called for comprehensive reform: land reform to provide the farm laborer with a stake; free primary education; graduated taxation; alleviation of poverty; manhood suffrage and payment of members of Parliament; disestablishment of the Anglican Church in England, Scotland, and Wales. To many a working-class man he became an idol. The Whigs of his own party were shocked. The queen was horrified. It seemed that the new radicalism was about to capture the Liberal Party, that middle-class liberalism would be transformed into social democracy, and that Chamberlain would succeed to Gladstone's leadership.

Instead, Chamberlain bolted the party. On June 6, 1886, Chamberlain led some ninety-three fellow Liberals in revolt in the Commons to defeat Irish Home Rule, and the Gladstone Government collapsed. Save for the brief personal triumph of Gladstone in 1892, the Liberal Party remained in eclipse until 1905. Chamberlain, now committed to preserving the union with Ireland, became the "Radical Unionist," and with his supporters joined his erstwhile opponents, the Conservatives, in 1895, to form the coalition called indifferently "Conservative" or "Unionist." Salisbury, prime minister, represented the unprogressive wing of the party and had no passionate convictions about either the Empire or reform. Responsibility for initiative in both spheres fell on his colleague. But Chamberlain was more than busy in the Colonial Office, and the projected program of social reform was little advanced. There was an important Workmen's Compensation Act (1897) providing compensation for injuries while at work, an act then called "revolutionary" by socialists. In a much more publicized area, that of old age pensions, the Government was committed to action, but all schemes proposed seemed too expensive. By 1900 social reform was overshadowed by the Boer War.

Liberal Decline

In the end, the Liberal Party was to be just as strongly affected by the new formula of imperialism and social reform, but more slowly and more painfully. The last great victory of the Liberal Party, unified and self-assured, came in 1880. Gladstone's administration of 1880–85 cannot be regarded as a success. Foreign policy, while idealistic, was inept; the prime minister had to bear the brunt of the responsibility for the fate of Gordon, besieged at Khartoum and slain by the fanatical forces of the Mahdi. Gladstone's embrace of Irish Home Rule in 1886 brought defeat and further disintegration of the Liberal Party. The party lost control of urban constituencies; only the "Celtic fringe," especially Ireland and Wales, kept it in respectable numbers in the Commons.

As difficult as policy was the problem of leadership. To be sure, Lord Rosebery (the Fifth Earl) who succeeded Gladstone briefly as prime minister in 1894 was a nationally known figure—a prominent member of the House of Lords and foreign secretary under Gladstone. But he lacked qualities of leadership, and his government, 1894–95, was without "coherence, consistency and a clearly defined aim," declares a historian of the period. He divided Liberals when he repudiated "little Englandism" and sounded a call to Imperialism as "a larger patriotism." To compel Liberals to declare themselves on this issue he revived the term "Liberal Imperialism," originally used in the 1880s. In a fit of frustration Rosebery left the Liberal Party leadership in October 1896, to be succeeded by Sir William Harcourt who, as chancellor of the Exchequer, in 1894 had reformed the death duties with a graduated tax on capital wealth left by the deceased. Whether so intended or not, it was a revolutionary principle, for it implied a redistribution of wealth. In December 1898 Harcourt resigned, declaring that he did not wish to lead a divided party. Soon after, the Liberal members of the Commons elected as their leader Sir Henry Campbell-Bannerman, popular in all circles, but a man who had hitherto exercised little weight in party concerns. Indeed, he seemed a man quite without personal ambition; he had no clearly defined political philosophy. Neither Rosebery nor Harcourt thought of his leadership as more than temporary; yet in the end it was Campbell-Bannerman who restored the party's position in the Commons and with the electorate.

But before that, the South African War nearly finished the Liberals. In Parliament they had been generally critical of government policy toward the Boer states prior to the hostilities, but when war came the party found itself in disarray. There were a few pacifists and a few more pro-Boers. A substantial group of Liberal Imperialists backed the war without reservation and in April 1900 organized the Imperial Liberal Council, "deliberately provocative" (perhaps Rosebery's words) in name and purpose. And there was a middle group which had been critical of prewar policy but felt that in the end conflict had been forced upon the British and the war should be supported. This last group, the largest numerically, included Campbell-Bannerman. His task was somehow to develop among these diverse elements some common basis for opposition to the Government. But the slim prospect of regaining office offered little encouragement to unity, and intraparty fights on the floor of the Commons were prevented with difficulty.

The low point was reached in July 1900, when a motion very hostile to the Government sharply split the Opposition between the pro-Boers and the Liberal Imperialists. Campbell-Bannerman in desperation advised his whole party to abstain from voting. On the division, only 35 followed his lead, 31 voted for the motion, and 40 Liberal Imperialists voted with the Government. But shortly before, Campbell-Bannerman had shown his mettle when, within a few days after the capture of the Transvaal capital, he boldly committed himself to a policy of incorporating the Boer states, self-governed, into the British Empire. On this matter Campbell-Bannerman had the majority of his party behind him.

The "Khaki Election" of 1900

In 1900 the hard fact of life was the parliamentary election, the "khaki election" in October. The Conservatives were reelected to office. But the election was a sad commentary on the democratic process, for its meaning in terms of the popular will was obscure. It was waged with unusual bitterness on both sides—later reflected in its treatment in biographies of the principals written by celebrated journalists, in different camps in 1900—J. L. Garvin's *Chamberlain* and J. A. Spender's *Campbell-Bannerman*. The Conservative Cabinet deliberately exploited the war situation and called an election two years earlier than required by law. Chamberlain denounced the Liberal Imperialists with the rest, for they had never given Chamberlain personal support. A defeat for the Government would be construed as a disavowal of the war—the changes were rung on this theme. The pressure of events was too strong for the Liberals, and they never really expected to be more than "a good second."

But the Conservatives fell short of their expectations and returned to the new Parliament with their majority reduced by ten. Furthermore, their popular vote was only some 2,400,000, to 2,100,000 for the opposition. Apparently, criticism of the war and its conduct was much more widespread than had appeared. And what basis would there be for common action on social legislation between the unprogressive wing and the Radical wing of the Conservative-Unionist coalition? But for the Liberals, the perilous state of party ties was even more patent. In the course of the campaign, the Imperial Liberal Council sponsored a carefully selected list of Liberal candidates. And after the election they proposed to purge from the party "those whose opinions naturally disqualify them from controlling the action of the Imperial Parliament." In the face of such division, how could the Liberals possibly achieve unity?

The Birth of the Labor Party

In 1900 there was another political event, largely unheralded. On February 27 in Memorial Hall, Farringdon Street, London, 129 delegates from 65 trade unions and 3 socialist societies met to "devise ways and means for the securing of an increased number of Labour members in the next Parliament." To this end they established the Labor Representation Committee; in 1906 the name was changed to Labor Party.

The main sources of this development were trade unionism and socialism. At first they were quite distinct, and, indeed, often opposed, but eventually they established a common purpose and a common organization.

Trade Union and Socialist Origins. For trade unionism the Labor party was the outcome of a long and troubled process. In the course of the nineteenth century, trade unionism had achieved the formation of strong unions within skilled crafts, a national federation in the Trades Union Congress, and parliamentary legislation which brought legal safeguards. After 1875 the T.U.C. developed into an "aristocracy of labor," cautious and almost apologetic in political matters. It sought influence through the radical wing of the Liberal Party. By 1885 eleven working-class men were in the Commons, all sitting as Liberals. For the rest of the century this "Lib-Lab" alliance dominated political action of the T.U.C., which was unsympathetic toward socialist ideas and organization as likely to destroy the gains made.

Socialism—broadly, a criticism of the existing economic basis of society—did not, in Britain, originate with the worker. Its beginnings were intellectual, literary, and often utopian. Among the earliest influences was *Progress and Poverty* (1879) by the American Henry George. His magic phrase "unearned increment" soon became current in Britain. Though no socialist himself, his work stimulated socialist thought; it was, for example, the beginning of the socialist affiliation of George Bernard Shaw. There were also Edward Bellamy's *Looking Backward* (1888) and William Morris's *News from Nowhere* (1891) and many others. Simultaneously, small socialist societies appeared. Marxism was represented, in modified form, in the Democratic Federation (soon the Social Democratic Federation) founded in 1881 by H. M. Hyndman—hardly a member of the proletariat, for he had been educated at Trinity College, Cambridge. Morris and, briefly, Shaw were interested but the notion of class war never made much headway.

The Fabian Society dates from 1884. For the most part, its first members came from the middle class. It may be regarded as one of the formative influences of the time, for under its intellectual leadership British socialism rejected Marxism. The Fabians proposed a regeneration of society through cooperation and good will, the transformation of the State by parliamentary action into an agency which would promote the general welfare. For some years Bernard Shaw and Sidney Webb were the heart of the Fabian program of education, propaganda, and the "permeation" of all parties and all classes. Though almost ubiquitous in influence, the Fabian Society remained small in numbers, only 2,462 members by 1909.

Fabian ideas developed a persuasive and respectable quality because they were apparently grounded on information scientifically gathered and dispassionately presented. With Fabian research was soon identified one of the most remarkable Englishwomen of the past century. Beatrice Potter was the daughter of a wealthy timber merchant and railroad magnate. She became interested in the new field of social research; she assisted Charles Booth in his survey of London and in 1891 published her own *The Co-operative Movement in Great Britain,* often pronounced her most brilliant piece of scholarship. In 1892, after the death of her father, she married Sidney Webb; with her modest but adequate private income of £1,000 a year they were financially independent. Here began the famous partnership which in time produced a series of monumental studies of pure research on the history of local government, and other analyses, more tendentious, of trade unionism and socialist thought.

But socialism did not reach the masses through Fabianism. This was an object of the "Labor Churches," which placed social welfare ahead of salvation. A Lancashire journalist, Robert Blatchford, popularized socialist doctrine. His views first appeared in a socialist paper, the weekly *Clarion,* launched in 1891, which soon attained a sale of 100,000. It was unique. There was no dogma, no "middle-class unction," but only simple propaganda presented in everyday language. Blatchford unquestionably was a journalist of genius; his supreme triumph came in a little book, *Merrie England* (1894), which, offered as a gamble for one penny, promptly sold over a million copies. It would convince no intellectual, but it did appeal to most who read it. It merely states in simple, warm, and usually good-humored language and with lively and effective examples the conviction that society as constituted is unjust.

A Working-Class Movement in Politics. Various socialist societies developed ideas and kindled enthusiasm. But without organized labor it is doubtful that anything political would ever have been accomplished. The first step was the transformation of trade unionism into "industrial unionism." A mere 10 percent of labor was associated with unions federated in the early days of the Trades Union Congress. Now, in the eighties and nineties, the "new unionism" extended to unskilled labor—dock, gas, railway, road transport, coal mines. Relatively speaking, organized labor was still limited, comprising only about one-sixth of all wage earners.

Sentiment for a working-class movement in politics, independent of the established parties, was stimulated by the condition of unskilled labor unaffected by the increase of employment in the late eighties. A landmark was the London dock strike of 1889. One of the lowest grades of workers, dockers employed casually, sought a standard wage of sixpence per hour and hiring for not less than four hours at a time. Their strike became the topic of the day. Public sympathy was attracted, a considerable strike fund was raised, and in the end the strikers received virtually their full demands.

The dock strike was symptomatic. Union organization was being extended to the unskilled laborer. In 1888, it is estimated, trade unions had about 750,000 members, by 1892 more than twice that number. The leadership of this "new unionism" was socialist in doctrine, political in objective, and militant in tactics. The Trades Union Congress must be won over to socialist doctrine and to independent political action. The dominant personality in this endeavor was Keir Hardie from Scotland, who had gone to work in the mines as a "trapper" at the age of ten, and in time organized the Miners' Union. His break with the Liberal Party and defeat for Parliament in 1888 in a contest as a "labor candidate" against both a Liberal and a Conservative led to the formation in the following year of the Scottish Labor Party. Its object, to secure independent labor representation in Parliament, was soon shared by several local labor organizations. First success came in 1892 when three candidates, including Hardie, were elected.

But the T.U.C. at its 1892 conference by a close vote refused to support labor candidates independent of other parties. Consequently, in 1893 leaders of socialist societies met at Bradford, in the heart of industrial Britain, and established the Independent Labor Party. It proved a key development, for it brought together for the first time various socialist voices: the "new unionism," Hyndman's Social Democratic Federation, Morris's Socialist League, Blatchford's Clarionettes, Hardie's Scottish Labor party, the Fabians, and the Labor Churches. Though violently divided on some matters, they succeeded in establishing a common purpose, stated in socialist but not Marxist terms: "to secure the collective ownership of all the means of production, distribution and exchange." Parliamentary legislation was to be the means.

The I.L.P. continued the effort to capture the Trades Union Congress for independent political action. The atmosphere became more favorable when a series of court judgments jeopardized the legal position of trade unionism. It was an important step when, in 1896, an I.L.P. socialist, G. N. Barnes, was elected general secretary of the premier union, the engineers. Finally, in the Congress of 1899, "new unionism" carried a resolution advocating a conference of representatives of cooperative societies, socialist organizations, and trade unions. This conference met in London in 1900 and established the Labor Representation Committee, an event little noticed in the press.

The beginnings of the L.R.C. were not particularly auspicious. Compromise, on most matters, was inevitable. It was clear that trade unionism had not been really won over, for the trade union delegates represented less than two-fifths of the membership in unions affiliated in the T.U.C. The new organization did not call itself a "party." Its members sought merely to establish "a distinct Labour Group in Parliament

... to cooperate with any party which for the time being may be engaged in promoting legislation in the direct interests of Labour and ... to associate themselves with any party in opposing measures having an opposite tendency." In this there was no summons to action, not even a statement of policy. Neither here nor elsewhere did the word "socialism" appear. A relatively obscure member of the I.L.P., James Ramsay MacDonald, was elected secretary of the L.R.C., partly because of his known competence, partly because more prominent men did not desire the post. In the general election of 1900 only fifteen seats were contested and but two victories won.

The Labor Representation Committee was not Marxist; it was not even moderately socialist. It was not an intellectual society of the Fabian type. It was not a subsidiary of the Trades Union Congress. It was neither Lib-Lab nor a repudiation of Lib-Lab. It was merely a federation of working-class organizations with one purpose: to elect to Parliament men who would foster the interests and aspirations of labor. To this end an alliance of socialism and trade unionism had finally been achieved. And it might well have a future, even though then, in the *Clarion*'s words, it was only "a little cloud, no bigger than a man's hand."

"The New Search for Reality"

Historians of ideas have been intrigued with the rapid changes in thought in the closing decades of the nineteenth century. G. M. Young has remarked that the intellectual outlook of the English people changed more between 1865 and 1900 than between 1900 and 1935. Holbrook Jackson, in his brilliant study *The Eighteen-Nineties*, has told us that it was "the decade of a thousand 'movements.'" People "were convinced that they were not only passing from one social system to another, but from one morality to another, from one culture to another, and from one religion to a dozen or more!" But Jackson found in all the currents of thought of the latter years of the nineteenth century a common denominator in the reaction against the Victorian outlook rooted in evangelical piety and middle-class political and social morality. With the old faith shaken, there was a "new search for reality."

The Decline of Evangelical Religion

One thinks first of religion and the impact of natural science and biblical criticism. Here England in 1900 was at the end rather than in the midst of significant change. An elegant expression of a larger problem is found in Arthur Balfour's *A Defence of Philosophic Doubt* (1879), a denial of the necessity of absolute truth in either science or religion, and in his *Foundations of Belief* (1895). Popular interest is shown by the success of Mrs. Humphry Ward's novel *Robert Elsmere* (1888). Here an English clergyman, intelligent and wholly sincere, is confronted with scholarly criticism questioning the verbal inspiration of the Scriptures. Eventually he abandons faith in Christian dogma.

The results of this conflict of ideas were uneven. Many, particularly those of modest education, the controversy passed by. For example, George Lansbury, the socialist, was untouched and remained devoutly religious. So did a future prime minister, Stanley Baldwin. And Arthur Henderson, in time foreign secretary, first spoke in public as a Wesleyan lay preacher; his biographer attributes much of his character, "as strong as a rock," to his religious convictions. There were still powerful religious leaders, such as Henry Drummond (d. 1897), famous for his sermon, "The Greatest Thing in the World."

But for many intellectuals, the issues had lost relevance. There was growing tolerance of differences in creeds. The human element in the Bible was recognized and belief adjusted accordingly. Some abandoned dogma altogether and found salvation in social service; others became frankly materialistic. In general, religion had been separated from thought. It is interesting to examine attitudes toward religion of individuals who came to manhood in the last quarter of the nineteenth century. R. B. Haldane, the Liberal statesman, abandoned the Christian creed, though he continued to hold strongly to spiritual values. Beatrice Webb felt that service to God was replaced by service to man. Herbert Samuel tells us that when he was at Oxford in the early nineties the book which most affected his thinking was John Morley's *On Compromise*, a study of "the conflict between piety and conscience." John Maynard Keynes, as a student at Cambridge shortly after 1900, came to find in the ethics of a young philosopher, G. E. Moore, a substitute for formal religion. Headmasters of schools and fellows of colleges, hitherto generally clergymen, more and more ceased to take Orders.

Concurrently had come changes in church attendance. Churchgoing was ceasing to be a social convention. Available statistics for 1902–3 show only two persons out of eleven in attendance at church services in London, a distinct drop from 1886, though no close comparison is possible. Charles Booth demonstrated that the lowest classes in London, socially and economically, were almost untouched by formal religion. Outside London, church attendance held up better but was also declining. The practice of family prayers was fading. The Sabbath was changing, as evidenced by the opening of museums and art galleries on Sundays in 1896; the development of the Pleasant Sunday Afternoon (P.S.A.), a social gathering at a Nonconformist chapel; the general use of Sundays for working-class social and political meetings.

Artistic "Decadence" and Urbanity

In literary and artistic circles the "search for reality" took various forms. Briefly in the early nineties a *fin de siècle* mood was fashionable. Inspired from France, a group of writers and artists seized upon the term decadence as their symbol of merit. Most of them young, many of them precocious, and nearly all of them talented, they found themselves out of sympathy with a world which was passing more rapidly than they knew. They sought reality in the perverse, in the abnormal, in the bizarre, in the sensuous, in a pretended weariness of spirit—all rather affected and self-conscious. They had a horror of the obvious and the commonplace; they sought sensation; they were "the Bohemians" and were most at home in the famous Domino Room of London's Café Royal, so well preserved, as it was in 1893, by Max Beerbohm in his study of Enoch Soames in *Seven Men*. They were rebels only in their repudiation of old art forms; it was part of their code not to be "socially conscious." Still, they were aware of the complexities of their day, and their work is not to be dismissed. Perhaps its most arresting expression was in Aubrey Beardsley, a black-and-white illustrator of extraordinary talent. His work was grotesque rather than beautiful. His illustrations for *Salomé* depict "abstract spiritual corruption revealed in beautiful form, sin transformed by beauty."

The urbanity of the nineties is well expressed in Max Beerbohm—in Shaw's phrase of 1898, "the incomparable Max." He gently satirized the *fin de siècle* mood much as he did most everything else. In literary form the "realism" of the time is held to be best found in George Moore's *Esther Waters* (1894) and in Hardy's *Jude the Obscure* (1895). But just as representative were Rudyard Kipling's protest against aestheticism and intellectualism, his appeal to a vigorous patriotism, and the strong moral note in "Recessional." These constituted a reexamination of values. The Celt was "discovered," particularly in the work of W. B. Yeats. When Frank Harris, the British-American critic and editor, became editor of the *Saturday Review* in 1894, the staff from the universities made way for Beerbohm, Bernard Shaw, and H. G. Wells. For it was in the 1890s that Shaw and Wells entered the English literary scene. Their ideal was totally different from that of the Beardsley group; for them it was "art for life's sake." Shaw began asking his devastating questions, and incidentally writing and producing some of his most celebrated plays. Wells's social outlook developed more slowly; his writings before 1900 reflected speculation and imagination rather than conviction.

Wells's experience in "society" in the late nineties is an indication of another aspect of change. Particularly in London, but at the country houses as well, the atmosphere became less formal, less class-conscious.

Wells found himself attending the house parties of Lady Desborough at Taplow Court and those of Lady Mary Elcho at Stanway, so delightfully described in the memoirs of Lady Cynthia Asquith. On such occasions there might be present a galaxy of stars: John Morley, Arthur Balfour, George Curzon, Hugh Cecil, Maurice Baring, Professor Walter Raleigh, the Webbs. In London a rather self-conscious group of clever young men and pretty young women who called themselves "the Souls" brought together people of wide interests and varying backgrounds. For a time they lionized Oscar Wilde. Their leading spirit was the very clever Margot Tennant, who in 1894 married H. H. Asquith, who was later to become prime minister. Still another London group, collectivist but non-partisan, was the Rainbow Circle. Its membership included Charles Trevelyan and Herbert Samuel of the Liberals, Graham Wallas of the Fabians, James Ramsay MacDonald of the I.L.P., and J. A. Hobson, the economist. In these years we first hear of the intellectual *salon* of Sidney and Beatrice Webb at their home in Westminster, which brought together Haldane, Wells, Shaw, Graham Wallas, Herbert Samuel, Charles Trevelyan, Bishop Creighton, Bertrand Russell, and, of course, many others. Such cross-currents of men and ideas would influence the future.

The Fate of "Respectability"

The motorcar was barely in sight. Until 1896 a law required every "mechanical locomotive" on a highway to be preceded by a man on foot carrying a red flag. In the nineties England was caught up in the cycling craze. The bicycle had evolved from the boneshaker to the high bicycle (called the penny-farthing) and finally to the safety bicycle, chain-driven and with pneumatic tires. Cycling was an important factor in the increasing freedom of women. It influenced changes in dress styles; about 1890 the bustle was abandoned. The beginning of woman's emancipation from the home and from the legal domination of the husband constitutes one of the most important social changes of the end of the century. Ibsen's *A Doll's House* played to packed and absorbed houses.

Daily newspapers were changing character. The transformation was brought about not so much by the Education Act of 1870 (for there was a surprisingly high degree of literacy among the working classes in mid-Victorian England), as by the extension of the suffrage in 1867 and 1884. The working class became news-conscious and interested in political and economic affairs, domestic and foreign. The weeklies or semi-weeklies, published for working-class amusement and edification, were inadequate in providing information. The dailies, on the other hand, were produced primarily for the solid upper and middle classes. The standard organ was the one-penny morning paper, fairly responsible and generally accurate, which presented the news in long, unbroken columns of fine print and was generally stuffy, unadorned, and totally lacking in human interest.

On May 4, 1896, Alfred Harmsworth (later Lord Northcliffe), a young editor who had been extraordinarily successful with *Answers,* a lively, gossipy weekly, launched in London the *Daily Mail,* the first morning paper at a halfpenny and in the new style. Instead of detailed reporting, it had the "news story," with the plain facts rewritten, condensed, colored, and often presented out of context. "The paragraph supersedes the column, and the headline . . . becomes more important than the paragraph." Illustrations, serials, the "feature" story, reflect the purpose not so much to inform or to stimulate reflection as to amuse and to arouse sensation. And yet the paper's standards were superior to those of the working-class weeklies. The *Daily Mail* was successful because the working class, with gradually rising purchasing power, purchased it and the products it advertised. At the end of three years its daily sale stood at 543,000, more than twice that of any competitor. "Unionist and Imperialist," its influence for the Conservative Party was enormous. "Empire first and parish after" was its motto. Until 1900 it remained the only morning paper of its kind.

A similar popularization may be noticed in the amusement world, with the success of the variety shows in the music halls and their extension to the provinces. There was no Victorian reticence in the nonsense chorus "Ta-ra-ra-boom-de-ay," which dates from 1892 and which, starting from the red skirts of a music hall dancer, swept the country. In 1896 it was still vigorous; it was strident, rude, persistent, and ubiquitous. English respectability was shaken, annoyed, affronted, and defeated.

At the Turn of the Century

Historians studying the nineteenth century, with all its complexity, generally recognize in its middle years, particularly after 1848, a certain unity—a satisfaction in relative prosperity, a general rejoicing in the long years of peace, a feeling of security, a common outlook, an agreement on fundamentals, an utter confidence in the British way of life. To be sure, most of this was only the common property of the articulate minority—the aristocrats and the upper middle class; but it was part of the pattern, generally accepted, that they should rule Britain. This explains, at least in part, why such widely separated individuals as the historian W. E. H. Lecky, the churchman Dean Inge, and the man of letters G. M. Young have concluded that these were the years, above all others, when it would have been good to be alive in Britain.

One would probably search a very long time to find anyone making such a statement about the Britain of 1900. It is not difficult to see why. The key word to describe this period is not *unity* but *diversity*. The faiths of the nineteenth century had passed; no new set of common values or principles had developed. The 1890s were a period of an infinite variety of moods, the period of the poscur and of the reformer, of the idealist and of the materialist, of the evangelical and of the self-indulgent Bohemian, of art for art's sake and of art for life's sake. The phrase "splendid isolation" seems to have first appeared in 1896; yet two years later Chamberlain was making formal offer of alliance to Germany. It was a restless period, and self-consciously so. There were the New Unionism, the New Hedonism, the New Realism, the New Urbanity, and the New Woman.

But we must remember, as R. H. Gretton put it, that the people of Britain in 1900 were living in ignorance of the future. We cannot really see their world as they saw it. For some, there undoubtedly seemed more logic and consistency in events than we can now find. For others, there were only controversy, tension, frustration, chaos. For no one of them can the pattern of ideas and events which we construct and which is called history be his own story. But our endeavor must be to understand something of the world of the twentieth century as Englishmen, generally, experienced it, and to give that experience meaning in terms of that which Britain had been and was to be. And now as we enter the fourth quarter of the century, we are, rather suddenly, it would appear, acutely aware of the rapidly changing character of Britain in our time—profound changes in the character of English society and in Britain's role in Europe and in the world. As one reads the English press in the 1970s and as one reflects on the titles of much of the current writing—Martin Green, *Children of the Sun: A Narrative of "Decadence" in England after 1918* (1976); Stephen Haseler, *The Death of British Democracy* (1976); Paul M. Kennedy, *The Rise and Fall of British Naval Mastery* (1976)—one is constantly reminded that we in the twentieth century have been living through one of the great crises in English history. And as we approach the period historically we must ask ourselves: What factors brought about this crisis? To what extent did the English people and their leaders anticipate this crisis? To what extent did they meet it with industry and with informed intelligence? To what extent did they control events and shape the future? Questions of this nature will be our central concern as we examine Britain in transition.

2 Edwardian England

Harold Nicolson
Small Talk
(1937), p. 73

The Edwardian age will, we may presume, live in history as an age of comfort. *It was not.* It was an age of fevered luxury; at the same time it was an age of peculiar human ineptitude. People possessed false values ... It is time that the jade and lobster of the Edwardian epoch were exposed.

W. H. Mallock
Social Reform ...
(1914), p. 375

Conservatism is not a protest against change; it is a protest against change in the organic structure of society.

J. A. Hobson
The Crisis of Liberalism ...
(1909), p. xii

Liberalism is now formally committed to a task which certainly involves a new conception of the State in its relation to the individual life and to private enterprise.

1901–1914

If one believes in the power of ideas, there is no more significant approach to twentieth-century Britain than through an analysis of thought. It is in the crystallization of new attitudes toward mankind and society to replace the rapidly fading outlook which we call Victorian that the years from 1901 to World War I take on special meaning. For these years the term "Edwardian" is a useful convention, though to suggest, as has Samuel Hynes in his generally persuasive book, *The Edwardian Turn of Mind* (1968), that "few monarchs have so precisely embodied the spirit of their time" as did Edward VII, is at best only a half truth.

Edwardian thought was a complex of ideas; no two students today would reconstruct it in the same way and with the same results. In our approach we shall attempt, first, to distinguish the ideas which were then influencing action, and second, to emphasize those ideas which were persistent and which would influence practice in the future. Our special attention will be focused on seminal ideas, often more important for the future than for the present.

The Great Debate

If we stand within the period and look about us, and if we think of ourselves as of the aristocratic or even of the upper middle

classes, we can see validity in the phrase "Edwardian optimism." One
writer, viewing with nostalgia the life of his youth, regards it as an Age of
Plenty, an Age of the Golden Sovereign, an Age of Twenty Shillings in the
Pound. For those with wealth, even for those of more modest means but
able to buy the good things of life, it was a happy time in which to live.
Britain was still a tight little isle. Serious depletion of resources and trade
lay in the future, wealth was still accruing to men of property, the servant
class was still abundant and amenable, social distinctions were still clear.
"It was an age of boisterous wealth and prosperity for the upper and
middle classes. Life was incredibly free and comfortable for the well-to-
do, untroubled by passports, forms, and regulations. The postman delivered letters on Sunday morning; and if you had money in your pocket to
pay the fare, you took a cab to Victoria and boarded the continental train
without any tedious preliminaries." Violet Markham, the author of those
words, writes also in happy retrospect of the house parties, the garden
fetes, the London "season." The leisurely round of country house life
continued, and one can return to it in the pages of Lady Cynthia Asquith,
Hugh Walpole, Osbert Sitwell, Edward Marsh. Percy Lubbock's *Earl-
ham* evokes the memory of a timeless atmosphere in which nothing
happened. Ths shocked and whispered warning of "callers" was "as
though some blow unforeseen had suddenly fallen upon a peaceful family, shattering their security." At Ockham Park (Surrey), presided over by
the fabulous Lady Lovelace, hip baths and earth closets persisted, and
smoking was not permitted in her sight, even in the garden. In such
places the Victorian Age was merely extended into the early twentieth
century—that "remarkable afternoon of the British ruling class."

But quite different conclusions might come to an observer standing
apart in time. In two cartoons drawn in 1920 Max Beerbohm summed
up the Victorian and Edwardian ideas of progress. There was "the Future, as beheld by the Nineteenth Century"—a portly bourgeois pointing
complacently to a larger reproduction of himself. Then there was "the
Future, as beheld by the Twentieth Century"—an individual gaunt and
grim, a band of mourning on his arm, staring in disillusion at a question
mark in a lowering sky.

Nearly any age is too complex and too diversified to capsulate its spirit
or its outlook in a word, a phrase, or even an essay. But the right language often rings true. For the Edwardian years a word to linger over is
"decadence." The shift of mood from Kipling's *The Recessional* (1897)
to his *The Islanders* (1902) is a classic example. There was the widely
read anonymous pamphlet *The Decline and Fall of the British Empire*
(1905) which by reverse action stimulated the growth of the Boy Scouts
and the Girl Scouts. This information is provided by Samuel Hynes, (*The
Edwardian Turn of Mind*) who impressively develops this theme—the

atmosphere during the Boer War changing from jingoism to humiliation, diplomatic isolation becoming "less splendid and more lonely," the self-evident physical deterioration of the British. And just as challenging is the tone of Elie Halévy's volumes on the Edwardian period, which suggest that the verities of the nineteenth century have been left behind with nothing to take their place. But a term perhaps wider in its application than "decadence" has been suggested by C. H. Driver; the Edwardian period, he says, was not one of complacency or even of pessimism, but rather one of "disenchantment." Here is a link with the 1890s. Edwardian disenchantment was not so much with the present as with the past. "The world was never so emasculated in thought, I suppose, as it was in the Victorian time," wrote H. G. Wells in *The New Machiavelli* (1911). Few intellectuals felt either secure or complacent. To solve their problems they sought new ideas and fresh solutions.

Here then, perhaps, we have something of a unity in the ideas of the Edwardians. It may be briefly expanded: the nineteenth century had believed that progress was merely change for the better and that such progress was inevitable. Human nature as well as institutions would change; representative institutions, self-government under the elite— these would in time produce the "Parliament of Man, the Federation of the World." But by 1900 the complexity of the world and its problems were more fully realized. The gap between the real England and the ideal England seemed to widen; supremacy of land was being replaced by dominance of commerce, and on balance the shift did not always appear good. Edwardian society was often vulgar, and class distinctions based on wealth seemed more vicious than those based on birth. In an age of political democracy, even in the face of an industrial society which was raising the standards of living for the entire community, inequalities between rich and poor became more glaring, wealth more ostentatious, and the lot of many a human being mean beyond description.

There is also this in common among Edwardian thinkers: they repudiated the justification of existing society on biological grounds, a dominant idea in the late nineteenth century. Man is not to be limited by his accidental inheritance. "Freedom" and "liberty" are not static terms, but must be redefined and expanded. The function of the State is not only to preserve society but to serve it. But England will not muddle through to the good life. Only conscious thought and action, perhaps "collective" action, will accomplish it. Edwardians would have accepted Basil Willey's remark about the Victorian heritage: "We have rightly learnt from the nineteenth century that man must make himself, and be the changer as well as the product of his own environment."

We turn for an expression of these ideas to a variety of persons: to politicians and statesmen, to philosophers and scientists, to a group of scholars who taught, lectured, wrote books and articles (social scientists they were beginning to be called), and to men of letters. Each will respond in his own way.

The New Ethics

The problems were basically those of social ethics. The mid-Victorian approach through supernatural religion and the belief in the inevitability of progress still had able spokesmen. One of the most indefatigable and most articulate was W. H. Mallock (1849–1923), predestined a country gentleman, but one who spent his life in his study combating positivism in philosophy, materialism in religion, and socialism in politics. His work, in books and articles, was prolific and covered a long span, from 1877 (with his brilliant novel *The New Republic,* written as an undergraduate) through World War I. Much of his writing is in the Edwardian period. That he was widely read is certain. To many, particularly those past middle age, such books as *Aristocracy and Evolution* (1898), *The Reconstruction of Belief* (1905), *A Critical Examination of Socialism* (1907), and *Social Reform* (1914) provided refuge from the hazards of a rapidly changing intellectual atmosphere.

But we must look elsewhere for currents of thought which were influencing the younger generation. Intellectual leadership was now humanist rather than spiritual, and basic problems had become those of society rather than of cosmology.

In the preface to his *Principles of Mathematics* (1903) Bertrand Russell said that the doctrines of G. E. Moore at Cambridge were "quite indispensable to any even tolerably satisfactory philosophy of mathematics." Moore's *Principia Ethica* (1903)—Moore was then only thirty years of age—was barely mentioned in *The Times,* but was a work of "divine common sense" which influenced a generation. In the preface Moore says that two general questions usually confused by moral philosophers must be kept separate: "What kind of things ought to exist for their own sakes?" and "What kind of actions ought we to perform?"

To Moore, ethics is "the general enquiry into what is good"; and his questions now assume this form: "What is good in itself?" and "What is good as a means?" But first a preliminary question, "the most fundamental question in all Ethics," must be asked: "What is meant by 'good'?"

"Good," then, if we mean by it that quality which we assert to belong to a thing, when we say that the thing is good, is incapable of any definition . . .; "good" has no definition because it is simple and has no parts. It is one of those innumerable objects of thought which are themselves incapable of definition, because they are the ultimate terms by reference to which whatever *is* capable of definition must be defined.

As to the question "What is good in itself?"—or "To what things and in what degree does this predicate [good] directly attach?"—we can arrive at *an* answer by "intuition," but our verdict is capable of no direct proof or disproof. However, when we consider "practical ethics" and ask, "What is good as a means?"—or "What ought we to do?"—the answers, while difficult, are capable of some demonstration. Ethics "cannot hope to discover what kind of action is always our duty," but it may, Moore says, hope to decide which among a few such possible actions is better than others. "All moral laws ... are merely statements that certain kind of actions will have good effects."

This was all very exciting to an intelligent undergraduate; much of Moore's influence was through personal contact with students (particularly those who belonged to a select group known as "The Society" or "The Apostles") who passed his ideas on to others. John Maynard Keynes, one of the inner circle, wrote some years later: "It was exciting, exhilarating, the beginning of a renaissance, the opening of a new heaven on earth.... Nothing mattered except states of mind,... chiefly our own." And others—among them Lytton Strachey, Leonard Woolf, Clive Bell, and Desmond MacCarthy (all with reputations as writers and critics in the future) came within the range of Moore's thought. They carried his philosophy over into a wider circle which by 1906–7 was meeting frequently in Bloomsbury in London—the first recorded reference to the "Bloomsbury Group" seems to have been in 1910.

The intellectual atmosphere of "the Group" was dominated by revolt against dogmatism and authority in all areas: in politics, in religion, in morality, literary, and artistic standards. But, of course, the Bloomsbury Group is merely a fascinating example; the Edwardian scene was introducing a new world to intellectuals everywhere—to radical politicians and radical journalists, to "social scientists," to artists, and to men of letters. All sought liberation from the Victorian past.

The Inquiry of Social Science

Social critics confronting problems in "practical ethics" (Moore's term) usually painted a grim picture. C. F. G. Masterman (1874–1927), an M.P. (1906–14) and briefly (1914) a Cabinet minister, but better known as a Radical journalist, in his *In Peril of Change* (1905) raised the question of what was to replace a vanished landed interest, a rural life destroyed, evangelicalism on the wane, and an established church discredited. Was not England about to lose her soul?

Was the decline and fall of Rome to be reenacted? In a book which received wider notice, *The Condition of England* (1909), Masterman produced even darker exhibits: the triumph of materialism, rising class consciousness, the growth of suburbia, with its "vicarious sports and trivial amusements," the irresponsibilities of a leisure class without roots in the past. Masterman is sometimes characterized as a sentimentalist who did not translate his ideas into action, but it may be said with some assurance that his criticism of society is confirmed by the evidence. His readers found him provocative as well as brilliant. Something of Masterman's mood is found as well in *The Hindrances of Good Citizenship* (1909) in which James Bryce, ambassador to the United States, doubted the capacities of the ordinary citizen to solve the problems of life.

A more positive influence is found in Leonard T. Hobhouse (1864–1929). During the Boer War he was an important leader writer for the *Manchester Guardian* and later for the *Nation*. In 1907 he became professor of sociology in the University of London and henceforth was both teacher and journalist. Among his treatises is *Democracy and Reaction* (1904). It is a historic document—a powerful and memorable book which raised fundamental questions. How was one to explain the retreat from nineteenth-century liberalism: the reaction against self-government, against parliamentary institutions, against free trade, international peace, reduction of armaments, retrenchment in governmental expenditure? Why, above all, had the doctrine of force and the superman triumphed over humanitarianism and social justice? By way of answer, he asked other questions:

> Is it that the Democratic State, the special creation of the modern world, and the pivot of the humanitarian movement, has itself become an obstruction to progress? Does popular government, with the influence which it gives to the Press and the platform, necessarily entail a blunting of moral responsibility, a cheapening and vulgarisation of national ideals, an extended scope for canting rhetoric and poor sophistry as a cover for the realities of the brutal rule of wealth?

Hobhouse recalled democracy to its central aim, "that the political order must conform to the ethical ideal of what is just." He rejected Social Darwinism. Man and nature, he insisted, are not pitted against one another. *Laissez-faire* is not a principle fixed by nature. Progress is not conditioned by "the struggle for existence." Liberalism, he concluded, should absorb a considerable amount of collectivism, for social legislation is a necessary means to the fulfillment of liberal ideals. The liberal and socialist ideals are "complementary" and together must "make common cause against the growing power of wealth, which . . . is more and more a menace to the healthy working of popular government." The creed of Cobden's day can no longer be ours. "But it is only in proportion as we build up a new creed as logical, as sincere, as clearly reasoned out in relation to the experience of our own day, that we shall emerge from the chaos of recent years and present a united front to the forces of reaction."

The work of J. A. Hobson (1859–1940) was parallel in importance, though he never won the same sympathetic acceptance. Prior to 1900 Hobson developed his notions of the economics of distribution, his theories of taxation, and his doctrine of social spending, and thereby anticipated many of the contributions of John Maynard Keynes. But Hobson's real impact came with his *Psychology of Jingoism* (1901) and *Imperialism* (1902). Inspired by the Boer War, these works constituted an attack upon British imperialism as, in Hobson's words, "motivated, not by the interests of the nation as a whole, but by those of certain classes, who impose the policy upon the nation for their own advantage." Hobson found the explanation for colonialism in the search for overseas investments by private capital which, owing to the heavy concentration of the profits of industry in the hands of a few, could not find profitable investment in England. This was, of course, extremely controversial, and only the anti-imperialists greeted his books with delight.

By 1909 Hobson had returned to his earlier theme, and in *The Industrial System: An Inquiry into Earned and Unearned Income* he expanded his thesis that surplus income from industrial production accrued merely to those who owned capital and the means of production. In the distribution of the unproductive surplus, the "unearned and forced gains," he found the "prime cause of almost all the maladies of our industrial system."

This also was more than an academic matter. In the very year of publication of *The Industrial System* its essential idea was given official expression. The chancellor of the Exchequer, Lloyd George, introduced into Parliament his "People's Budget," with its more sharply graduated income tax and its levy on the unearned increment in land values. Also in 1909 appeared *Liberalism and the Social Problem,* a series of addresses by the rising young politician Winston Churchill, advocating in popular and nontechnical language much of the Hobson thesis. An American reviewer said: "Mr. Hobson has set out on the road to Socialism and does not seem to care whether he arrives or not. Mr. Churchill follows at a little distance protesting all the while that he is going in the other direction." In the writings of Hobson, the policy of Lloyd George, and the speeches of Churchill we have an illustration of the coming together of ideas and practice.

Elsewhere we find analysis of the irrational element in human behavior. Social psychology began to answer many questions hitherto not asked. Hobson was a part of this movement in his *Psychology of Jin-goism* and so was Hobhouse with his *Mind in Evolution* (1901). But the great work which changed the basic conception of the relation of man to society came in 1908 with publication of William McDougall's *Introduction to Social Psychology,* internationally recognized, and also with Graham Wallas's *Human Nature in Politics,* which provided a practical application of McDougall's ideas. Chapter 1 of the Wallas book is headed "Impulse and Instinct in Politics"; this sets its theme. To Wallas, instinct, sentiment, and habit were far more important than the formal structure of government in determining the responses of the individual and in explaining, for example, the failures of democracy and the limitations of education in producing intelligent action. His students testify to his great impact as a teacher at the London School of Economics from 1895 to 1923.

Literature as Social Criticism

To an unusual degree, literature during the Edwardian years was a vehicle for social criticism; women's rights, private property, marriage and the family, capital and labor, criminal justice, the penal code, were some of the areas it explored. It is interesting that most of the important writers were not trained in a great university tradition; most of them learned from their own observation and experience. A selection of significant writers is not arbitrary. Frank Swinnerton, born in 1884, has written: "The young men of 1909 and 1910 felt that with Shaw . . . and Galsworthy in the theatre, Bennett and Wells and in a lesser degree Galsworthy in the novel, and Chesterton and Belloc in the press, there was thrilling life in the intellectual world; and they were right."

It is of "the Big Four" that we first speak: H. G. Wells, George Bernard Shaw, John Galsworthy, and Arnold Bennett. Rebecca West writes, "All our youth they hung about the houses of our minds like uncles. . . . They have had more influence on innumerable young people than anybody else save their fathers and mothers." Artists all, they were also teachers, as in Beerbohm's cartoon: Beerbohm walks into an art gallery and all he sees are figures, of the "Big Four" among others, standing on tubs turned upside down and declaiming to the world.

Galsworthy, Bennett, and Shaw. Galsworthy (1867–1933) was no revolutionary and, in fact, never acknowledged any political affiliations. "Nobody can imagine the *Marseillaise* shattering our silence in response to Mr. Galsworthy's still and exquisite irony," stated the *Nation* for June 5, 1910. But his novels and his plays are primary sources for the period. Identification with vital issues is often close. The satire on Victorian attitudes represented in *The Man of Property* (1906) and its sequels assisted in the modification of the concept of private property. *Fraternity* (1909) exposed the artificiality of urban life and the decadence of upper-middle-class society. "A very dangerous and revolutionary book," said the *Saturday Review*.

Galsworthy was invariably sensitive to human suffering and injustice. His plays included *The Silver Box* (1909), concerned with the inequality of wealth and poverty before the law; *Strife* (1909), which dealt with the conflict between capital and labor; *Justice* (1910), a consideration of prisons and the evils of solitary confinement. These plays, though primarily dramatic productions, had a deep effect upon social attitudes. Reviewers recognized this as a consequence though they denied it as an object. Of a production of *Justice,* the *Spectator*'s reviewer wrote, "It would be easy to describe *Justice* as a tract in favor of prison reform, but the description would be false. It is merely a record of a series of events." We know, in fact, from the extensive correspondence between Galsworthy and Winston Churchill, then home secretary, that *Justice* was directly related to actual prison reforms.

The genius of Arnold Bennett (1867–1931) lay in his unsurpassed talent for portraying exactly what he saw. If one wishes to be instructed in the life of the provincial industrial towns, one should turn to Bennett's novels. Bennett was at his best in the group of novels dealing with the region of his youth, "the Potteries" in Staffordshire, popularly known as "the Five Towns," which soon became as a unit the borough of Stoke on Trent. *The Old Wives' Tale* (1908) made his reputation, but it was *Clayhanger* (1910) for which he made the more careful preparation and which he considered the more sociological. Bennett, it should be added, was not trying to set the world straight. He wrote about the Potteries because it was a region which he knew intimately and with which he was in sympathy. Most of his readers are not. Rather, they have something of the feeling articulated by J. B. Priestley, who describes the Potteries as a region of dingy little streets in dingy little towns, an embodiment of "Victorian industrialism in its dirtiest and most cynical aspect." And "you feel that nobody comes to the Potteries and nobody—except Arnold Bennett—has left them."

Then we come to Shaw (1856–1950). He likewise was really no revolutionary. He was, one might say, much too civilized. He was incorrigibly disarming. First and last he made his readers and his audiences laugh. To many, particularly in the Edwardian period, he appeared merely as a funnyman. He once remarked to Henry James, "Almost all my greatest ideas have occurred to me first as jokes." The upper classes, said a critic in 1909, found that "his preaching is no menace to their interests." That critic might have thought twice, for Shaw's influence was unpredictable.

Conventional persons were bewildered and sometimes shaken. "One really doesn't know what to think" was a remark certainly made more than once after a Shaw performance. The prime minister, A. J. Balfour, led the crowds in 1905 to see Shaw's latest sensation, *Major Barbara,* a blast at the sanctity of private property. C. E. M. Joad, a philosopher at the University of London, declared that it was Shaw who made him a socialist. Osbert Sitwell for a quite different reason can speak of Shaw as "the greatest European figure and writer since Voltaire."

Shaw's influence was so varied because he was limited by no dogma and no creed, religious, social, or political. His mind was completely free and he helped to release the minds of others. He was an enemy only to pretense, hypocrisy, intolerance, compromise. He ranged over the problems of society: property, wealth and poverty, militarism, marriage, the family, the legal status of women, medical science, penal institutions, and so on. And no matter what his vehicle—a play, an essay, a tract, an address, an argument—it was always Shaw talking to mankind. His influence on individuals has been remarked many times. But his effect upon his era was that he contributed to making thinking popular; he compelled men and women, particularly those in positions of responsibility, to consider his ideas and in so doing to reexamine theirs.

H. G. Wells. Like Shaw, H. G. Wells (1866–1946) was an extraordinary figure and can be discussed only in extraordinary terms. The distinction is that he was an active rebel. He was as nothing which had come before, for he stood for a complete break with the past. The years before the Great War were those of his exuberance, of his confidence in the future, of his passion for improving the world and mankind. His aim was complete social reconstruction—life was plastic and could be molded to meet the heart's desire. He was intensely alive. "One can lie awake at night and hear him grow," said G. K. Chesterton in those years.

Wells's point of view was that of a socialist, without qualification, and he propagandized for the world state. It was as a sociologist and as a novelist that he proclaimed his ideas. In several works in the opening years of the twentieth century he outlined his science for remaking society. Of the first, *Anticipations* (1901), he wrote later, "I take up contemporary pretensions of democracy and state the widely unspoken thought of the late Victorians, 'This will not work.'" Among his anticipations were some rather startling predictions about the nature of warfare in the twentieth century: trench warfare along a national frontier, tanks ("armored shelters for men, that will admit of being pushed over rifle swept ground"), submarine and aerial combat, the nation in arms. "The most remarkable book of the year," Beatrice Webb wrote in her diary in December 1901. And a few weeks later, "Altogether it is refreshing to talk to a man who has shaken himself loose from so many current assumptions and is looking at life as an explorer of a new world."

In *Mankind in the Making* (1903) Wells treated social regeneration as a task of education. The basic problem, he said, is simply this: Imagine "all our statesmen, our philanthropists, public men, our parties and institutions gathered into one great hall, and into the hall a huge spout, that no man can stop, discharging a baby every eight seconds. . . . Our success or failure with that unending stream of babies is the measure of our civilization."

In *A Modern Utopia* (1905) he offered a blueprint of his ideal world. With the reading public, skepticism turned to admiration. A reviewer in the impartial, critical, and authoritative *Athenaeum* said, "there has been no work of this importance published for the last thirty years." *New Worlds for Old* (1908) is a sober analysis of a socialist program: "the steady orderly resumption by the community, without violence and without delay, of the land, the apparatus of transit, of communication, of food distribution, and of all the great common services of mankind."

By 1906 Wells had arrived. An elaborate article on "Mr. Wells as a Sociologist" appeared in the *Fortnightly Review* in 1905, and another on "The Ideas of Mr. H. G. Wells" in the *Quarterly Review* in 1908. He was no longer a mere crank to be shrugged off. Of course, he disturbed some people. In the *Annual Register* for 1908 we find this representative comment: in *New Worlds for Old* "he seems to ignore the chief obstacle . . . the strongly marked individualism of his fellow countrymen, the keystone of our greatness." The *Spectator*'s reviewer called *Ann Veronica* (1909) "a poisonous book." Wells's novels generally won more favorable criticism. In *Kipps* (1905), concerned with the waste of human beings in modern life, he created one of the most convincing characters in modern fiction. *Tono-Bungay* (1909) was so brilliant many reviewers did not know what to make of it. In Wells's own words, he wrote of a "spectacle of forces running to waste, of people who use and do not replace, the story of a country hectic with a wasting aimless fever of trade and money-making and pleasure-seeking." *The History of Mr. Polly* (1910) is the story of another individual in conflict with his environment.

The books came forth, at this time at least one a year and sometimes two or three, and a steady stream of articles as well. By 1914 Wells had acquired a solid position among social thinkers. It was fashionable to read him and to discuss him. Many considered him irresponsible, his personality repellent; to others he was equally attractive. But always the impression was memorable. Upon the younger generation his influence in shaping attitudes toward morals and civilization was incalculable. The historian E. L. Woodward, a man of moderate social views, has written: Wells "disturbed me and widened my horizon; . . . he taught a lesson of fine and noble piety." And J. B. Priestley, a writer of the left: "At his worst he never diminished or hurt us. At his best, he made us feel, as he did, that we live on a star."

Counterrevolutionaries. In time a few years behind the Big Four were Hilaire Belloc (1870–1953) and G. K. Chesterton (1874–1936). They also adorn the opening years of the century.

Belloc—French-born, naturalized British subject, for a few years after 1906 a radical member of Parliament—was a writer of great gifts, whose essays, biographies, historical studies, and poetry were all written to propagate his ideas about the past and the present, views held with conviction and set forth with a scornful disdain for those of others. To Belloc it was inconceivable that his own ideas might be changed by more experience or more knowledge. To him there was always just one side to a question.

Chesterton, a more human person than Belloc, an incorrigible optimist (which in itself set him apart among intellectuals) and the master of paradox, wrote during his lifetime, we are told, more than a hundred books. At the same time, he was a contributor extraordinary to current periodicals, and more often than not was editing a paper of his own.

The activities and the ideas of the two were closely associated—so much so that Shaw invented a hybrid individual, "the Chesterbelloc," to represent their joint endeavor. Some of their writing was cooperative, and Chesterton frequently illustrated Belloc's books. Their doctrine may be summed up as counterrevolutionary. They were just as critical of society in the twentieth century as Shaw or Wells, but for different reasons. Their ideal was not in the future but in the past—in the Middle Ages. They were not only antisocialist but also anticapitalist, not only antiproletarian but also antibourgeois. In *Emmanuel Burden* (1904) Belloc was concerned with the decline of ethics in business. In *The Servile State* (1912) Belloc expounded his theory that loss of individual freedom is an accompaniment of both the capitalist and socialist states, and he predicted some of the developments in later totalitarian regimes. In subsequent writings, especially after World War I, he proposed a return to the society of the Middle Ages—the universal Catholic Church, the broad distribution of property, restoration of domestic industry and craft guilds.

As artists, Belloc and Chesterton were as gifted as most of their contemporaries, but as teachers they fought a losing battle. Their ideas were well known, but their books, relatively speaking, were not widely read. Counterrevolutionaries have not been popular in the twentieth century.

And ideas based on faith, inspired by the Middle Ages, and usually presented in paradox were not likely to convince an age dominated by science, nationalism, and industrialism. The world of H. G. Wells was more likely to come to pass than was the world of the Chesterbelloc.

Shapers of Opinion

During the Edwardian period many important decisions were being reached, and the heart of the process was discussion. Such terms as socialism, feminism, and imperialism evoked not so much outright enthusiasm or revulsion as curiosity and interest. There was a host of topics of immediate relevance—unemployment, education, disestablishment, old age pensions, taxation, home rule, House of Lords—which raised questions. Before these questions were answered opinion had to be formed.

In the formation of public opinion the chief medium was the English press, which reached the height of its influence in English life in the first quarter of the nineteenth century. With the daily papers were associated powerful editors, each of whom indelibly stamped his organ with his own personality and social and political outlook—among them, Alfred Harmsworth (later Lord Northcliffe) in the role of both proprietor and editor of the *Daily Mail* and *The Times;* A. G. Gardiner of the *Daily News;* J. L. Garvin of the *Observer;* J. A. Spender of the *Westminster Gazette;* C. P. Scott of the *Manchester Guardian.*

The great English journals also flourished—some old, like the *Contemporary Review,* the *Quarterly Review,* the *Westminster Review,* the *Fortnightly Review,* the free church *British Weekly*—and some new. A Radical weekly, the *Nation,* dates from 1907, and gave scope to another of the great editors of the twentieth century. Henry W. Massingham, who had been editor of the *Daily Chronicle* and then parliamentary reporter with the *Daily News,* assembled a group of brilliant writers: Leonard Hobhouse, J. A. Hobson, H. W. Nevinson, J. L. Hammond, F. W. Hirst, C. F. G. Masterman. The *Nation* exerted an influence far beyond its limited circulation. To its celebrated weekly staff luncheon came notable guests—politicians and statesmen, journalists, scholars, writers—from all parts of the world. And the *English Review,* "a periodical devoted to the arts, to letters and to ideas": was inaugurated in 1908. Its roster of contributors is a roll call of most of the luminaries in the world of books.

During the Edwardian years the endless debate and discussions on the platforms and in the press was a portent to some, an inspiration to others, an education to all. Shaw was inclined to take on all comers, but more especially Mallock, Chesterton, and Belloc. Private dining clubs were forums of discussion for matters political and social, where party lines were usually ignored. One of the best known was the "Coefficients," started in 1902 by Sidney Webb—its original purpose to find a meeting ground for all supporters of "Empire." The charter members, so one of them tells us, included R. B. Haldane and Sir Edward Grey of the Liberal Party leadership; Halford K. Mackinder, geographer and for several years director of the London School of Economics; W. A. S. Hewins, first director of the London School of Economics; Leo Maxse, editor of the ultrapatriotic *National Review*; L. S. Amery, a Fabian socialist in his youth and then a staunch Unionist of the Chamberlain school; Bertrand Russell; and H. G. Wells.

There were also the political clubs, led by the famous Carlton Club (Conservative) and the Reform Club (Liberal), both fashionably and elegantly housed in Pall Mall, as well as the steady succession of private dinner parties at the homes of statesmen, churchmen, businessmen. These were years in which there was a mingling of all sorts and conditions of men.

Economic Recovery

Of the British economy on the eve of the Great War a careful historian has written, "No honest man with a reasonably long and accurate memory, and some appropriate knowledge, could deny that it was a better order, if only by a little, than at any time in the modern industrial age." Professor Clapham was thinking in Victorian terms, and in such terms England achieved during the Edwardian years an economic stability and prosperity which more than matched the record of the mid-nineteenth century. Between 1896 and 1913 exports more than doubled in value and imports increased considerably more than 50 percent. The price rise in these years was about 30 percent.

Britain's entire economy and her general standard of living depended more than ever, as we have seen, on world trade. Coal, machinery, and manufactured articles were sent across the seven seas in exchange for food (over half her supply) and raw materials. Britain was now producing two-thirds of the world's export in textiles, four-fifths of the export in coal, a high percentage of the export in machinery. Such a volume of trade provided freight for the ever-expanding merchant marine, whose competitive position was apparently impregnable. The very favorable balance of trade made possible an export of capital to exploit new sources of raw materials and new markets. In 1911–12, 30 percent more capital was transferred abroad than in the entire decade of 1890–1900. All this activity was financed from London, the world's financial capital, and, because of the stability of the Bank of England and the supreme confidence of the British, it was accomplished with an astonishingly low gold reserve. The ideas of Adam Smith and Richard Cobden, set to work in industrialized England, had produced in the century between the Napoleonic Era and 1914 an increase in real income of 400 percent per capita.

Table 3   Foreign Investment of the United Kingdom and Average Rate of Return: In Single Years at Five-Year Intervals, 1862–1912

Year	Net Investment Abroad (Millions of Pounds)	Interest and Dividends: Average Rate of Return
1862	394	5.3%
1867	523	5.4
1872	764	5.8
1877	1,088	5.1
1882	1,255	5.0
1887	1,576	5.0
1892	2,005	4.7
1897	2,252	4.3
1902	2,431	4.5
1907	2,760	5.2
1912	3,568	5.2

Source: Albert H. Imlah, *Economic Elements in the Pax Britannica* (1958), p. 180. Imlah explains (p. 179): "The amounts shown under 'net investment abroad' are the net balances, that is after allowances for foreign investment in the United Kingdom, accumulated by the close of each preceding year." The rate of return in interest and dividends is figured on "the estimated net balance of this class of income, similarly after income allowance for foreign investment in the United Kingdom, for the year cited."

Demographic changes added, in some ways, to the complexity of the problem of England's standard of living. The birth rate declined after 1877, but that decline was more than offset by the sharp drop in infant mortality. Whereas between 1850 and 1900 the mortality in the first year of life was one in six or seven, by 1913, thanks to greatly improved urban sanitation and the control of infectious diseases, it was only one in nine; by 1923, it would be only one in thirteen. By 1911 the total population of the United Kingdom reached 43,300,300, an increase of nearly 4,000,000 in the years 1901–11, a larger increase than in any decennial period of the Victorian years. Eighty percent lived in England and Wales, an area approximately the size of the state of Illinois. In density this was 618 persons per square mile, as compared with 189 in France and 310 in Germany.

Judged solely by its own performance, the British economy was as sound in 1913 as it had been in 1870. Britain, of course, no longer occupied the enviable position she had in 1860. But she was still in the van in world trade; in 1913 she produced 27 percent of the world's exports of manufactured articles. She was not the decadent nation some of her competitors made her out to be. The real test would come after World War I.

Stability: Real or Illusory?

After the quarter century of "recession" (to employ a later term) just prior to 1900, this recovery is to be explained first of all by the general expansion of world trade, which increased the demand for British goods, coal, shipping, and capital. Wholly new markets were opened in South America (especially in the Argentine) and in the Far East (especially in Japan). Trade to the colonies and to the dominions increased, though the bulk of British trade was still outside the Empire. Competition, particularly that from Germany and the United States, was well met in textiles and steel goods (there had been a decided shift from iron to steel in the late nineteenth century), where the British kept pace with technological improvements and increasingly shifted over to quality goods. Concentration of the textile industry—83 percent of the cotton operatives were now in Lancashire and Cheshire—brought economies. If there was a slight decline, relative to other countries, in the export of cotton goods, this seemed more than compensated for by the increased production and export of coal. Even agriculture, such as it was, again was on a paying basis.

This situation brought satisfaction at the time to the factory owner, the shipbuilder, the coal mine operator, and the financier. But knowing the future, we see other circumstances just as significant. For one thing, the years 1900–1914 were uneven, with alternate periods of good years and bad. Industrial growth is evident, but not at the pace it showed during any other period of similar years in the nineteenth century. There was growing dependence on foreign lands for cotton, meat, petroleum. Since much of the new capital went abroad to be invested to advantage, capital gains were not plowed back in to British industry, did not create jobs for the British unemployed, did not produce goods for home consumption. During the lean years, English mercantile opinion was sensitive to the surplus of imports over exports. Was Britain merely living on capital? Was industry adapting itself to long-term needs? These were questions often asked. There was nothing ominous about exchanging coal and manufactured goods for food and raw materials, but it became increasingly apparent after 1900 that Britain was no longer "as much of an exporting monopolist manufacturer," in Clapham's phrase, and could no longer determine her own prices. In fact, she was now giving more exports to obtain the same amount of imports.

In her premier export industry, cotton goods, these years witnessed a gradual decline in the numbers employed and in the percentage of total export trade. Now it was coal by which Britain was paying much of her way—coal which as an industry had had fantastic growth since the mid nineteenth century. As an export, coal rose from tenth place in 1860 to third by 1900. Thereafter Britain exported more than one-fourth of the coal she mined, and by 1913 nearly one-third. Britain seemed favored—well-distributed fields lay under 12 percent of the surface of England and Wales, a larger percentage than in any other country. And the miners comprised an elite group in British labor. However, by 1900, conditions were changing. The best areas were exhausted. Little effort had been made to modernize the industry; in 1913 only 8 percent of the coal mined was extracted by machinery. And many of the still un-exploited fields consisted of inclined seams unsuitable for machinery. Costs of production, therefore, were rising; the average miner took out 403 tons in 1881, 340 tons in 1901, and only 300 tons in 1911. By that time, in comparison with 1901, 36 percent more miners brought out only 19 percent more coal. Well before 1914 the factors which would limit Britain's economic role between the world wars are plain to be seen.

The Standard of Living

There is, of course, a connection between national productivity and national welfare. From 1900 to 1913 the standard of living available to the average working man remained just about stationary—a marked change from the immediate past. During the last half of the nineteenth century, especially with the break in prices after 1875, the real income of the average worker, when employed, steadily improved. For a man doing similar work, real wages increased 75 percent. After 1900, though the price rise obscures the fact, the national income in real values did not rise per capita. Through unionization the unskilled worker somewhat improved his situation, but, in general, wages lagged behind the price rise; and only by 1913 had wages caught up to the purchasing power which they possessed in 1900. Terminology affords an interesting commentary. The business and financial world termed the years 1873–98 "the Great Depression" because of the drop in prices and profits; yet during those years real wages improved. On the other hand, 1898–1913 was by business standards, with expanding production, export, and profit, a period of recovery and prosperity; yet real wages were static or even depressed.

The explanation of this phenomenon is complicated. Some employers maintained it was the fault of trade unionism, with its rigid regulations limiting the output per man. *The Times,* in its columns in 1902, set out to demonstrate this point. Though exaggerated, the argument did have considerable basis, and this problem of obstacles to production under unionized labor contributed to the general controversy over the proper role of trade unions.

Others concluded that British industry had failed to develop more efficient methods of production and had failed to replace manual labor with machines. This was the argument in an authoritative report by the economist Alfred Marshall in 1903.

Still others found the explanation in the export of capital. The importation of goods did not keep pace with exports; thus the rising volume of trade and total profits did not bring a corresponding increase in consumer goods in England. Competition for world markets was keener. In order to keep prices down, costs of production, primarily industrial wages, had to be controlled; interest and dividend rates could not be lowered or an even larger proportion of capital would promptly flee overseas—or at least so this argument ran. Its exact weight is quite uncertain; for example, there appears to be no real parallel between fluctuations in real wages and fluctuations in capital exports. Yet Professor Clapham concludes, "It remains possible, even probable, that there might have been earlier improvement and more improvement, in real wages had there been less export of capital."

Whatever the explanation, it is generally agreed that the worker did not share in the economic revival of the years 1900–1914. To this conclusion one important qualification should be made: these were also, statistically speaking, years of "full employment." As a phenomenon and as a social problem, unemployment was attracting increasing attention, but its incidence in relation to trade union membership was not high. The average for the years 1901–13 was only 4.5 percent, and it was never more than 7.8 percent, which was well below the highs of 1879 and 1886. Unemployment among nonunionized casual labor was considerably higher, but in general it may be said that poverty and suffering among the working class at this time were not caused by unemployment. From the depressed or static condition of the artisan class stem much of the militant trade union activity, the rapid development of working-class political organization, and the pressure on all parties for social reform.

The Condition of the People

Just about 30 percent of the people of Great Britain (approximately twelve million) were living in a state of chronic poverty. This figure is close to Charles Booth's estimate for London published in 1889. In rather surprising fashion Booth's conclusion was supported by the results of a study of a smaller community, the city of York, selected "from the industrial standpoint" as "fairly representative of the average conditions which obtained in other provincial towns." B. Seebohm Rowntree in 1899 conducted a house-to-house canvass covering two-thirds of the total population of 75,000. In his report, published as *Poverty: A Study of Town Life* (1901), he concluded that 27.8 percent of the entire population, representing 43.4 percent of the working class, was living in a state of poverty, a condition defined as that without "the minimum necessaries for the maintenance of physical efficiency." Rowntree distinguished between "primary poverty," where the total earnings were insufficient, and "secondary poverty," where the total earnings would be sufficient to provide the minimum were not some portion absorbed by some other expenditure "useful or wasteful." Most of those in the latter class were living close to the "primary poverty" line, and 9.9 percent of the whole population was in primary poverty. The selected diets for minimum requirements were very conservative—less generous, for example, than those set down by the Local Government Board for the workhouses. Rowntree endeavored to get at the cause of poverty and concluded that while gambling, drink, and general shiftlessness were factors in many cases of secondary poverty, in the majority of cases of primary poverty the immediate cause was inadequate wages. Unemployment was almost negligible as a cause.

The extent to which the figures for London and York are representative of the country at large is not easy to determine. Any standard for "poverty" is arbitrary, and poverty figures for Britain, even for London or York, cannot be precise; but the findings of Booth and Rowntree and those of similar surveys in Reading, Northampton, and elsewhere indicated beyond doubt that a considerable minority of the population was destitute and miserable. In fact, the very poor, though proportionately fewer than in the nineteenth century, were worse off than ever. And the important consideration is that the British people generally were aware of it.

While unemployment did not explain the incidence of povery in York, it had been recognized before 1900 as a social evil demanding attention. Rowntree made specific inquiry (again in York) in 1910, published as *Unemployment: A Social Study* (1911). Every dwelling occupied by members of the working class was visited on June 7, 1910, to determine the extent of unemployment on that day. The results were carefully checked against other sources of information. A considerably lower proportion of unemployment was revealed in York than in the country as a whole. More important than its conclusions about York was the contribution which the book made to the general understanding of the problem.

Another line of development destined to bear fruit began with the appointment in 1905 of the Royal Commission on the Poor Law and the Relief of Distress Through Unemployment. To the commission was appointed Beatrice Webb, and to her attention had come the activities of William H. Beveridge. In 1905 he was in the employ of the *Morning Post,* a Conservative daily, where for several years he contributed leaders and special articles on social problems. Beveridge himself in *Power and Influence* lists the subjects: "unemployment, sweating, housing, old age pensions, the liquor trade, the feeding of school-children, infant mortality and so on." In 1909 he published *Unemployment,* with its suggestive subtitle *A Problem of Industry.* Without dogmatism, it soon established itself as a standard work.

"Sweated industries" had long been a subject of concern in political circles. The House of Lords had a committee back in 1888–91; it concluded that if "sweating" meant wages which were unfit for adult workers, there was a great deal of it. "The Report is that of surprised, simple-minded, honest men." In 1905 an Anti-Sweating League was formed, and in 1906 the *Daily News* organized a "Sweated Industries Exhibition."

Housing and Public Health

Legislation of the late nineteenth century had corrected the most glaring evils in urban living: minimum standards of sanitation had been set down and in particular the water supply had been improved; the most serious problems of overcrowding had been attacked. Nevertheless, in 1900, English industrial towns remained the most crowded in western Europe. Housing rapidly became a widely publicized area of social reform, but it soon became apparent that any radical transformation in the average industrial city, with its mean streets, its narrow cobbled courts, its "back to back" slum areas, would be a gigantic undertaking. Some indication of the character of the problem can be seen in the definition given to "overcrowding." It was a condition in which there were *more than two persons to a room.*

Conditions, of course, varied a great deal between towns and within towns. At their worst, particularly in the older industrial areas, conditions were little better than in the mid-nineteenth century. We have the most detail on the city of York, here again fairly average—by no means the most crowded nor the least. Rowntree's investigation, based upon his house-to-house canvass, revealed these results: Of 11,560 working-class families, dependent on wages, 26 percent lived in housing considered for one reason or another—overcrowding, lack of toilet facilities, unsatisfactory water supply—as quite inadequate. Many families shared the same water tap, many shared the same toilet facilities (nearly always apart from the house), and many had no bath facilities. Twelve percent of all working class families lived in "back to back" dwellings with no through ventilation; in 10 percent of the families people were living more than two to a room.

These figures compared very favorably with some. In Scotland, where the one- or two-room dwelling was standard and traditional, about 46 percent *of the entire population* in 1901 was living more than two to a room, 23 percent more than three to a room and about 10 percent more than four to a room. In London 16 percent of the population lived more than two to a room; in some areas of the city the figure reached 30 or 40 percent.

Only a slight improvement was indicated by the next census in 1911. The transportation revolution and the accompanying growth of suburban areas alleviated the situation somewhat in highly populated areas, particularly in London with the rapid extension of electric trams, the motor busses, and the tubes. But the general problem remained much the same. In 1911 the figures for overcrowding stood thus: for the entire population of England and Wales, 8.6 percent; in London 16 percent, in Halifax 12 percent, in Liverpool 10 percent, in Newcastle 37 percent, in Scotland 45 percent.

Housing was a matter of supply and demand. New construction was almost entirely the enterprise of private capital. The wage earners in these years could not afford improved housing. In 1900 an unskilled worker received eighteen or twenty shillings a week. A two-room, back-to-back slum dwelling cost around three shillings and sixpence per week; for a four-room dwelling, still in a mean area, he had to pay five shillings a week. Hardly anyone could ever afford to pay more. The skilled laborer, much in the minority, earning thirty to thirty-five shillings a week could have something only a little better. If labor could not afford better housing, private capital would not provide it; again, more profitable investment opportunities existed abroad. There could be no change until the real-wage scale was appreciably increased or until housing was taken over as a government responsibility. Town planning and housing legislation were not to come on any significant scale until well after World War I.

Statistics on general public health attracted attention. In 1904 the army issued a report covering the years 1893–1903. Of all those examined for military service, 34.6 percent failed to meet the minimum physical requirements, and a goodly number had been rejected without being troubled with an examination. Other surveys indicated that in Manchester in 1899 only 10 percent of those examined had been accepted for service in South Africa; in East London in 1900 eleven out of twelve were rejected. A special governmental Committee on Physical Deterioration, set up in 1903, publicized these and similar statistics. Municipal surveys indicated a correlation between conditions of urban living and general health.

"Riches and Poverty"

The surveys already mentioned and the bodies of statistics gathered were presented in no partisan or class spirit. They sought to determine conditions and not necessarily to advocate reform. Other presentations of social problems were more controversial. The work of L. G. Chiozza Money, a Fabian but a Liberal in politics, had great effect on opinion. In 1905 he published his *Riches and Poverty*. He concluded: one-third of all the income in Great Britain went to one-thirtieth of the people; one-half of the total income went to one-ninth; one-half of all the capital was in the hands of one-seventieth of the people. "In the aggregate we are wealthy, but the majority of our people are poor," he said. Chiozza Money generalized with less care than did Booth or Rowntree, but his book was more widely read; it went through three editions in the first six months, ten editions by 1910. To many, particularly of the younger generation, the book was a revelation.

Chiozza Money may have been sensational in tone and approximate in his statistics, but his general point was sound: not only were there rich and poor, but there were very rich and very poor. With social insurance in 1911 coverage was provided for all those with annual incomes of £160 or less. This group comprised practically the entire working class; most working-class incomes did not approach that level; an unskilled laborer was paid well under 50 percent of that figure. This may be contrasted with other representative incomes: the £1,000 annual income of Sidney and Beatrice Webb was considered "modest"; the provision in 1911 of a salary of £400 a year for members of Parliament was considered adequate only for those who came from the working class; a secretary of state received £5,000; judges of the High Court received £5,000 to £10,000; a successful barrister earned £15,000, £20,000, or even more; incomes of many living on capital investment were higher.

The relation of wealth and national income to human welfare was also studied. A young economist who was Alfred Marshall's successor at Cambridge, A. C. Pigou, developed the notion that such social evils as unemployment, inadequate wages, and poor housing constituted economic waste for which society should assume responsibility. In 1912 his *Wealth and Welfare* aroused discussion. Something of the same point of view is found in J. A. Hobson's *Work and Wealth: A Human Evaluation* (1914), in which the purpose is "to present a full and formal exposure of the inhumanity and vital waste of modern industry." To all such ideas

W. H. Mallock was moved to make answer in a work of which the full title runs *Social Reform as Related to Realities and Delusions: An Examination of the Increase and Distribution of Wealth from 1801 to 1910* (1914), and in which he argued that over this period an increasing proportion of the product of industry had gone to the laboring class.

An End to Complacency

The issue argued by Hobson and Mallock—which had been raised well back in the nineteenth century—becomes central in the twentieth century. It is an important question for the student of English history. It may be suggested that the standard of living had not kept pace with economic growth. But economic growth itself, to provide more goods and services, is essential if the life-style of people generally is to be improved. With this principle would soon be associated the necessity for more equitable distribution of the product of labor.

We may say without question that the Edwardian period was marked by a growing sensitivity to social problems and a recognition of the responsibility of government to deal with them. Scholars, journalists, and statesmen alike became increasingly aware of the close relationship of poverty, unemployment, casual labor, housing, wages, distribution of national income. There was a rapid increase of what Hobson termed "felt poverty." Arnold Bennett was overwhelmed by the vast contrast between the life of the rich and the life of the poor in London. A master of Balliol College told his students, "While you are at the University, your first duty is self-culture. . . . But when you have performed that duty and learned all that Oxford can teach you, then one thing that needs doing by some of you is to go and discover why, with so much wealth in Britain, there continues to be so much poverty and how poverty can be cured." Shaw's idea that there could be no improvement in morality and in intelligence without decent material surroundings won increasing acceptance.

Two further examples must suffice. In April and July 1910 the *Quarterly Review* ran an extensive article reviewing current books on socialism and social reform. Marxist ideas, says the writer, are no longer of significance for England. "But the great current of change, of which Socialism is the surface froth, will go on; let no one doubt it. It will more and more diffuse wealth and well being and in the process it may well be that the idle rich will gradually be shorn of some part of their idleness and riches. But the change will proceed by gradual and rational reforms or readjustment." It is doubtful whether such an article would have appeared in this periodical a dozen years before.

The other example comes from *The Times*, after 1908 enjoying rejuvenation under Lord Northcliffe. In January 1909 it carried a series of six articles on "The Socialist Movement in Great Britain," written by its industrial correspondent, Arthur Shadwell, a man of great knowledge and wide experience who sympathized with the aims of the working-class movements but had only contempt for catchwords and demagoguery. His presentation was moderate, fair, and accurate, distinguishing socialism from labor representation in Parliament and finding trade unionism in England generally opposed to doctrinaire socialism. Accompanying editorial comment rejected the principle of collective ownership and the methods of revolutionary socialism, but declared that the principle of *laissez-faire* had been too indiscriminately applied and "has left us the legacy of multitudes badly born, badly taught, badly fed, and finally robbed of employment." There must be "readjustment of values" and "a new basis of equilibrium" between capitalism and socialism. These articles and editorials marked the end of the complacent conservatism of *The Times*. Thereafter, while criticizing particular policies of the Government, it remained committed to a general policy of social reform.

3 Conservatism in Decline

H. H. Asquith
at a Liberal Party
dinner, July 19,
1901

What is the position, what is to be the future of the Liberal Party?

Joseph
Chamberlain at
Birmingham,
May 15, 1903, as
quoted in Julian
Amery, *Joseph
Chamberlain*,
5 (1969): 192

I believe in a British Empire, in an Empire which, although it should be one of its first duties to cultivate friendship with all the nations of the world, should yet, even if alone, be self-sustaining and self-sufficient, able to maintain itself against the competition of all its rivals ... And I do not believe in a Little England which shall be separated from all those to whom it should in the natural course look for support and affection.

Arthur Balfour
to Lord Knollys,
January 17, 1906,
quoted in Blanche
E. C. Dugdale,
*Arthur James
Balfour, 1906–
1930* (1936), p. 20

We have here to do with something more important than the swing of the pendulum or all the squabbles about Free Trade and Fiscal Reform. We are face to face (no doubt in a milder form) with the Socialist difficulties which loom so large on the Continent. Unless I am greatly mistaken the Election of 1905 inaugurates a new era.

C. F. G.
Masterman
*Nineteenth Cen-
tury and After*,
December 1906,
p. 715

Social Reform has not got beyond the rhetorical state.

1901–1906

In modern times the State, an organization of power for the control of social groups, has been the chief focus of the activity of man and of society. Political history is more than a recounting of the causes and results and incidents of international conflict, a narrative of monarchs, presidents, or dictators, or a statement of the decrees of government. It provides perhaps the most accurate reflection of "power and influence," to employ Lord Beveridge's happy phrase, the power of men and the influence of ideas, and their joint impact on the balance of forces in society. Through politics we can understand the changing character of Britain in the twentieth century.

After the death of Victoria in 1901, the next landmark is the general election of 1906, generally regarded as the most important parliamentary election between 1831 and 1945. The long rule of the Conservatives, undisturbed since 1886 save for the personal victory of Gladstone in 1892, ended in humiliation, and the newly formed Liberal Ministry was confirmed in office by an overwhelming majority. But the election marked also a general shift in social forces—in a democratization of the House of Commons. The most striking symptom was the appearance in Parliament of fifty-three members of the working class. John Burns, once a member of the Marxist S.D.F., became the first representative of the working class in the Cabinet. With him took office a group of statemen who controlled British policy, foreign and domestic, until 1915. The

stage was set for one of the most bitter periods of party politics and one
of the most important eras of social and political change in the history of
Britain.

The South African War in Politics

In 1902, after more than thirty-one months of
conflict, the war in South Africa finally came to an end. Peace terms
approved by Boer delegates at Vereeniging were formally signed at Pretoria, the capital of the Transvaal, on May 31. Lord Kitchener,
commander-in-chief since late in 1900, went down to Vereeniging to
address the Boers; they and the British who accompanied Kitchener
fraternized freely. Soon the British army was distributing rations, tents,
and farm equipment. In August the Boer generals went to England and
were received by the king.

The peace terms called for a full recognition of British sovereignty over
the Boer states but also the establishment as soon as possible of representative institutions as a prelude to self-government. Britain contributed
£3,000,000 toward the repair of war damage in South Africa. During
the war Britain employed 448,000 troops. Of these, 22,000 lost their
lives but only 5,774 directly from battle action. The Boers mobilized
about 80,000 men but the force actually in the field was never over
25,000. Their losses, for which no exact figures are known, were substantially less than the British. A new chapter opened in the history of South
Africa, and its problems ceased to be a factor in domestic British politics.

"Concentration Camps" and Peace Terms

But in 1901 South Africa overshadowed all other con-
cerns. Fiscal policy, education, old age pensions, and Ireland were all
relegated to the background. The war had not ended in 1900 as the
Conservatives had anticipated in the "khaki election" of that year. It had
merely changed character. The Boers, defeated in pitched battles and in
contests for key positions, turned to guerrilla warfare: ambushing convoys, raiding outposts, harrying communication and supply lines. With
these tactics they hoped to prolong the war indefinitely. To meet these
new conditions the British developed new tactics of their own: systematic
farm burning and devastation of areas where resistance persisted, the
establishment of a series of blockhouses connected by barbed wire to
protect key positions, the operation of a system of vast "drives" to sweep
all Boers in resisting areas into barbed-wire enclosures, and the establishment of camps to intern those rounded up.

These "concentration camps" became a chief war issue of 1901 in

England, particularly as reports, on the whole reliable, of their conditions—overcrowding, polluted water supply, widespread infectious disease, and inadequate medical care—began to circulate. The maximum population of the camps was 117,871. In fourteen months 20,117 died.

Miss Emily Hobhouse visited South Africa early in 1901 under the auspices of a private relief committee, and her unfavorable report was widely circulated. The Government, disquieted by the whole business, in the summer of 1901 dispatched a "ladies' committee," and its report pretty well confirmed the story of Miss Hobhouse. Milner himself recognized that the camps were indefensible, and Chamberlain had apparently been against them from the start. They were transferred to civilian control with an immediate improvement in conditions and a sharp drop in the death rate, and the camps were terminated by the beginning of 1902.

The other major war issue of 1901 concerned the nature of the peace which should end the war. Should it be a negotiated peace, or should the war end only with an unconditional surrender of the Boers? In the early months of 1901 peace negotiations broke down because of the British refusal to make outright grants for farm restoration and because of the failure of the combatants to agree on the status of the "rebels" from Cape Colony who had joined up with the Boers.

At first the Conservative press had remained jingoistic, justifying the concentration camps, and in turn accusing the Boers of war atrocities and declaring that it was impossible to negotiate with such a people. But the party leadership was not at all sure about the wisdom of farm burning or of the camps, and, in any case, neither provided much occasion for self-admiration. As usual there was contradiction in British policy in South Africa. This now took the form of serious conflict between the high commissioner (Milner), who was opposed to negotiation, and the commander in the field (Kitchener), who was anxious to end the war on any reasonable terms. By autumn much of the press, including *The Times*, had swung over to a position of criticism of the Government. But the Conservative Party, with its big majority in Parliament, was in no danger of losing control of the Government.

Liberal Party Crisis

The Opposition still faced the formidable task of finding common ground to unify the Liberal Imperialists, the moderates, and the pro-Boers. Early in 1901 the pro-Boers, under prodding from Lloyd George, strengthened their cause with the purchase of the *Daily News,* a London paper, with funds supplied in part by George Cadbury, chocolate manufacturer and ardent Quaker. From support for the Liberal Imperialists (on January 10 the paper proclaimed that "Sane Imperialism" and "Social Reform" should be the platform of the Liberal Party), the *Daily News* suddenly changed to outright support of the pro-Boers. When some Boer prisoners were reported to have desired to respect the hour of Queen Victoria's funeral, the paper on January 26 read, "The Boers are a brave and chivalrous people, with whom it is a great misfortune to be at war." With H. W. Massingham as parliamentary reporter, and with Harold Spender, J. L. Hammond, C. F. G. Masterman, and H. N. Brailsford on its effective staff, and with (a year later) A. G. Gardiner as its editor, the *Daily News* was set to play a prominent part in the revival of the Liberal Party, particularly its Radical wing.

The pro-Boers also captured the party leader, Sir Henry Campbell-Bannerman. On the war he had taken a middle-of-the-road position and had sought, above all, to preserve harmony in the party. Now, in the summer of 1901, he became a pro-Boer. In the second week of June he was interviewed by Emily Hobhouse, just returned from South Africa; a few days later, on the fourteenth, at a political dinner at the Holborn Restaurant in London he delivered one of the most significant speeches of his career. He denounced farm burning and concentration camps as "methods of barbarism." Several days later the phrase, in large print, was hurled back at him by the Conservative press.

But this speech precipitated another crisis in the Liberal ranks. Campbell-Bannerman would not retract the phrase, and he supported a Lloyd George motion (June 17) proposing a parliamentary discussion on the Hobhouse report. The Liberal Imperialists were almost as critical of Campbell-Bannerman as were the Conservatives, and on the division fifty Liberals abstained from voting.

The Liberals now indulged in a series of dinner speeches and replies referred to by Henry Lucy in *Punch* as "the war to the knife and the fork." Even H. H. Asquith, a Liberal Imperialist but one who usually enjoyed the confidence of the party leader, declared at a political dinner, June 20, at the Liverpool Street Station Hotel that the "methods of barbarism" speech did not represent the sentiment of his section of the party.

Campbell-Bannerman thereupon demanded a showdown. On July 9 he placed before the entire parliamentary party membership the question of his continuation as their leader. To the surprise of many, he won a unanimous vote of confidence. And in a subsequent dinner engagement (July 19) which he would happily have avoided, Asquith spoke only in broad terms, urging the Liberal Party to accept the Empire "as a fact" and welcome it "as a trust."

There was still Lord Rosebery, the leader of the Liberal Imperialists. In an open letter to the National Liberal Club, which appeared in *The Times,* July 17, he declared that unity in the Liberal Party was impossible and that he was therefore withdrawing from party politics. On July 19, the day of the second Asquith dinner, Rosebery addressed the City Liberal Club luncheon, reiterated the statement in his letter, and added the remark that was soon to become famous: "For the present, at any rate, I must proceed alone. . . ; but before I get to the end of that furrow, it is possible that I may find myself not alone."

Rosebery had not yet sprung his biggest surprise. After the crisis of July many Liberals hoped he would be able to resume leadership and rebuild a strong Opposition party. As a former prime minister he had immense prestige; he had a devoted personal following; his sporting interests (his entries had twice won the Derby) enhanced his appeal for many; he was an orator of renown; he was a scholar proud of his historical production; he stood firmly behind the Empire and was not tainted with the pro-Boerism which had captured Campbell-Bannerman. The Fabian Webbs, strongly influenced by their close friend, the Liberal Imperialist Haldane, hoped that Rosebery might be persuaded to lead the "progressive Liberals" and thus emancipate the party from Gladstonian doctrines and win the country to a program of "national efficiency," a combination of imperialism and social reform.

The Enigma of Lord Rosebery. Rosebery, as usual, was in no hurry to commit himself. Early in November, however, it became known that he had accepted an invitation to address the Liberal association at Chesterfield in Derbyshire on December 16. "The speech became an event a full month before it was delivered" (Spender). Politicians beat a path to Rosebery's door to offer advice, and the press was full of anticipation. When the great day finally came, there was snow on the ground as he delivered his speech, two hours long. Rosebery called for a negotiated peace with the Boers. He dissociated himself from the phrase "methods of barbarism," but favored immediate amelioration of conditions in the concentration camps. He asked the Liberals to "clean the slate" of "fly blown phylacteries." He scolded the Government for mishandling foreign affairs. Rosebery declared he was appealing not to the party but to the country. There was something in it to please everyone in the Liberal Party. Just what did Rosebery intend? Was he making a bid for party leadership? Was he offering himself as an alternate to Lord Salibury?

It did seem that Rosebery was prepared to abandon his "lonely furrow," but it was not at all clear on what terms. Campbell-Bannerman, encouraged by the editor of the *Westminster Gazette,* decided to try to find out. He waited on Rosebery but came away even more mystified and convinced that he had been snubbed. Fresh quarrels ensued. In February Rosebery expanded somewhat his Chesterfield phrase about a Liberal

Party "clean slate;" he had in mind particularly Irish Home Rule. Campbell-Bannerman promptly repudiated the doctrine of the clean slate and wanted to know whether "Lord Rosebery appeals to us from the interior of our political tabernacle or from some vantage-ground outside." The following day Rosebery answered, "I remain outside his tabernacle, but not, I think, in solitude." And he referred to the moment as one of "definite separation."

Anticlimactic to all this was the announcement soon after of the formation of the Liberal League, which was less provocative in name and intent than the Imperial Liberal Council which it replaced. Its leadership was the same—Rosebery, Asquith, Sir Henry Fowler, Sir Edward Grey—and it attracted much attention but did not challenge the official party organization or the leadership of Campbell-Bannerman, but its possible divisiveness was clear.

So as the war neared its close, the Liberals seemed as far from harmony as ever. The great enigma remained Rosebery himself, Rosebery whose every word, wrote H. W. Massingham a little later, (*Speaker,* January 24, 1903) was reported "as though he were a new soap or a new member of the royal family." Yet he had a salutary effect upon the divided counsels in all parties over the projected settlement in South Africa. His Chesterfield address gave an important stimulus to the efforts for a negotiated peace. As for Campbell-Bannerman, he had weathered all the storms which beset his party leadership. The pro-Boer policy which he finally embraced was to be an important element in the reconciliation of the Boers and in the establishment of a measure of stability. And in the end he would reunite the Liberal Party.

Challenging "the Favor of Destiny"

What the Liberals could not do for themselves the Conservatives soon accomplished for them. There was in 1902–3 a dramatic reversal of party fortunes. To all seeming still solidly entrenched, the Conservatives now developed new policies for which they had no electoral mandate, policies which rent asunder their coalition with the Unionists and which, in challenging traditional Liberal principles, served to reunite the Liberal Party and open the way for its victory in 1906.

Even as the war was grinding to a close, one could observe the first indications of change. On March 25, 1902, an Education Bill was introduced into the Commons which met opposition in all parties. And in May the chancellor of the Exchequer in his annual budget message proposed, for extraordinary revenue to meet war expenses, a new tax: a small levy on imported wheat and flour. An import duty! The Canadian prime minister promptly observed in Ottawa that in the forthcoming colonial conference in London he hoped for a policy of preference for Canada. Preference for Canada! A few weeks later, on May 16, Joseph Chamberlain declared that "old ideas of trade and free competition have changed," and closer ties within the Empire should not be prevented by "adherence to economic pedantry, to old shibboleths." The twentieth-century controversy of free trade versus protection had begun.

Soon after, Campbell-Bannerman and Asquith appeared together at the Eighty Club (commemorative of Gladstone's victory in 1880). As-quith declared, "Rarely, if ever, in the history of parties had any Gov-ernment at the same time challenged the favor of destiny and fired the zeal of its opponents by producing in one session two such measures as the Education Bill and the Corn Tax."

Both questions were temporarily pushed aside by the coronation of Edward VII and by a change in Downing Street. The coronation, delayed because of the king's sudden seizure with appendicitis, finally came off on August 9. Once the prime minister, Lord Salisbury, was assured of the king's recovery he resigned. He was himself in poor health and died a year later. He was the last peer to head a Government. He had become something of a legend; save for the interlude of 1892–95 he had been prime minister since 1886. But he held a rather loose rein over his Cabinet colleagues, particularly after his return to office in 1895, and the colonial secretary, Joseph Chamberlain, was permitted to extend his ac-tivities into the sphere of foreign affairs.

Since Chamberlain had so dominated the years of the Boer War, it might seem that he was the natural successor to Salisbury. But circum-stances prevented any possible Cabinet crisis, for on July 7 Chamberlain suffered severe injuries in a hansom cab accident and at the time of Salisbury's resignation was still confined to his home. Whether or not Chamberlain expected to be the new prime minister—he almost certainly had ambitions—one cannot say; his biographer asserts that he might well have secured the necessary support and that it would have been far better for the country as well as for the party if Balfour (who did succeed Salisbury) had given way to him. One can only speculate at the policies Chamberlain might have pursued as prime minister. But he was not trusted by the other leaders of his party—he had joined the Government in 1895 as an outsider. As it turned out it was the breach between Chamberlain and Balfour in 1903 which destroyed the commanding con-trol of the Conservatives.

Balfour's succession to the premiership was entirely normal, for he had been the party leader in the Commons since 1891. His premiership (1902–5) is fascinating to observe, even at this distance, and in large part because of Balfour's personality. Then fifty-four years of age, he had been long known in society as a brilliant and charming conversationalist and long recognized in intellectual circles as one of the finest minds of the day. But in public life he was another of the enigmas of this era. "He saw a great deal of life from afar," Ramsay MacDonald said in his eulogy in the Commons in 1930. Balfour in the early years of the century shared many of the premises of the new sociology and the new psychology, but nearly always emerged with different conclusions. He was a person of catholic interests and broad sympathies, yet he had few settled convictions— apparently he had serious doubts about the value of any and all human endeavor—he was in no sense a democrat, yet he was interested in social reform; he was quite worldly and yet religiously minded, with the detachment of the philosopher, which in fact he was. He had the reputation of the dilettante in public affairs, but proved to be one of the shrewdest of politicians.

The Education Act of 1902

As prime minister, Balfour's first test of strength was the Education Act of 1902, which has come to be regarded as one of the most constructive measures of this or any Government in the twentieth century. This legislation made possible for the first time a national system of education. For in it the vexed question of the relation of education to religion—the problem which in the nineteenth century had diverted attention from education itself—was squarely faced. The result—an act which shifted responsibility for education from the Church to the State—established the principles of all educational reform since. It was indeed "historic" though at the time few individuals, Balfour probably included, realized its full significance.

The problems are much too complex for brief explanation. The Education Act of 1870 had produced an ever increasing variety and number of institutions and educational authorities: the traditional "public schools;" the "voluntary schools," denominational but primarily Anglican, which were supported by sectarian funds assisted by state grants; the "board schools," set up by the 1870 act, financed from local rates, controlled by elected boards but actually dominated by Nonconformist religious interests; and finally the still newer technical schools which were developing under the authority of the new county councils. The results were competition for students, lack of uniformity in standards, gross inefficiency in many of the private institutions, financial difficulties for many of the "voluntary schools," and, in particular, an effective deterrent to the normal development of secondary education. New legislation became imperative in 1900–1901 when legal decisions jeopardized the continued existence of secondary schools which were fast developing, in extra-legal fashion, under the secular school boards.

The real framer of the bill of 1902 was a junior official in the newly created Board of Education who had made a deep impression on Balfour. Robert Morant was one of the outstanding civil servants of the twentieth century. Also prominent in the preparation of the bill was Sidney Webb, who with Graham Wallas controlled the London School Board, and both were anxious that education be recognized as a "public function." But it was Balfour who steered the bill through the long and difficult process of legislation.

The act as finally adopted in December 1902 abolished as unnecessary some 2,568 special school boards, replacing them with the newly established county councils. These and their counterpart in the cities (the county borough councils) were made responsible for all education, elementary and secondary, in all types of schools. Exactly 14,238 voluntary schools ceased to have direct access to Whitehall, which thereafter dealt with 328 Local Educational Authorities. Religious instruction was to continue in the "voluntary schools," with attendance optional.

Had it not been for the "religious difficulty" it is likely that the bill would have met little opposition. As it was, there was controversy hardly exceeded by any other legislation in the twentieth century. The Nonconformists led by Dr. John Clifford (Britain's leading Baptist clergyman and now minister of London's Westbourne Park Chapel) and stirred up by Liberal politicians (particularly Lloyd George) attacked the bill because (1) the "voluntary schools," mainly Anglican, would now be supported by local tax rates and (2) in many "single-school areas" children of Nonconformist families would be required to attend a sectarian school of some other denomination. Such criticism was based on principle, but on principle that had become outdated. Nonconformists were no longer the victims of discrimination. Their fears of the results of the act did not materialize. The act of 1902 and a similar act for London enacted in 1903 proved to be extraordinarily successful, made elementary education a right and not a charity, and made possible a systematic development of secondary education.

But in 1902 such legislation was political dynamite. Opposition frequently assumed the character of a crusade, with declarations that local taxes for education would not be paid. Himself a Unitarian, Chamberlain opposed the bill on both religious and political grounds and only reluctantly acquiesced in its passage. The Liberals, strangely enough, emerged stronger. Indeed, the Education Bill more than anything else reunited them. A by-election in North Leeds, fought squarely on the bill while it was before Parliament, brought a Liberal victory with much to spare in a constituency which the Conservatives had carried overwhelmingly in 1900. And in seven by-elections in 1903 the Liberal popular vote increased 37 percent.

The Tariff Question

Chamberlain's defeat within the Conservative Party on the Education Bill lends added importance to his great drive for imperial unity through colonial preference in trade.

The tariff question, thrust into politics by the corn duty in the budget of May 1902, was kept alive during the summer when the colonial conference passed resolutions favoring a system of reciprocal preference in trade relations of colonies and mother country. In the autumn Chamberlain was off to South Africa, in protest, some said, against the Education Bill's nearing passage. When he returned in March 1903 he was ready to make an issue of fiscal reform and imperial unity. Furthermore he was now sixty-six years of age. If he were to make a bid for party, and governmental leadership he could wait no longer.

Chamberlain's Challenge. The situation crystallized around the new budget introduced on April 23. This budget was entirely free trade—Ritchie, the new chancellor of the Exchequer under Balfour, had threatened to leave the Cabinet unless the corn duty was dropped. On this question Chamberlain met defeat in the Cabinet. So he turned to the country. In a momentous address to his constituents in Birmingham on May 15 he came out boldly for import duties on food and for preferential treatment for the colonies. These matters, he predicted, would be the dominant issues in the next general election. On the very same day, Balfour addressed the Commons in defense of the repeal of the corn duty. He used arguments directly contradicting those of his colleague. It was a simple matter for the Liberal press to print the two speeches side by side, a little game to be played more than once again in the next two years. The issue of fiscal reform was to destroy the unity of the Conservative Government and to ruin Balfour's career as prime minister.

Actually there was nothing very spectacular about Chamberlain's proposals. Certain interests had long clamored for protection, and tariff reformers had been propagandizing in the press. But this agitation had been kept out of politics. Politically, "free trade" was still a sacred phrase, much as "the freedom of the individual" or "the English character," and not to be tampered with. Therefore, Chamberlain's pronouncements were as startling to his Cabinet colleagues as they were to the Opposition. The press was full of rumors and so was the House of Commons lobby. What did it all mean? Had Balfour and Chamberlain consulted? Had they broken?

So far as was evident, they had done neither. In the next debate, May 28, both Balfour and Chamberlain insisted that their views did not conflict and that no change would be made in fiscal policy until after a general election. But on June 9, Ritchie (Exchequer) read aloud in the Commons a formal declaration reaffirming his commitment to free trade and disassociating himself from any proposal for reform. The next day Balfour, amid general astonishment, declared himself open-minded on the question. Of course, he said, any possible change in England's long-standing practice would require careful examination. But he himself could not "profess a settled conviction where no settled conviction exists." And this on a matter which had been regarded as a cornerstone of British policy for over fifty years. Strangest of all, he was probably sincere. He had avoided for the present any further discussion in Parliament—his main concern. But in an interview with the king he did not seem very hopeful of keeping the Cabinet together.

Now it was the turn of the Liberals to be jubilant; Campbell-Bannerman wrote at the end of May, "This reckless criminal escapade of Joe's is the great event of our time." But Campbell-Bannerman remained cautious; division in the Cabinet would not necessarily mean loss of control of the Commons.

But public discussion continued. In July 1903, rival organizations appeared, the Tariff Reform League and the Free Food League—the latter with fifty-four Unionist M.P.s in attendance at the initial meeting. In addition to Ritchie, those Conservatives who repudiated the Chamberlain proposals included the Duke of Devonshire (titular head of the Unionists and lord president of the Council), Lord Balfour of Burleigh (the Scottish secretary), Lord Goschen (once chancellor of the Exchequer), Arthur Elliot (a treasury official and editor of the *Edinburgh Review*), and young Winston Churchill, restless and impatient with a party in which he could see no future for himself, and soon to transfer allegiance to the Liberals. Eminent professors of economics signed an extended statement in *The Times* in criticism of protectionism; an equally eminent group, though smaller in number, issued a counterstatement—few people had realized that there were so many professors of economics. The *Fortnightly Review* carried a debate. In its July and August issues appeared, replete with citations from government reports, an article by J. L. Garvin outlining at length the Chamberlain position. J. A. Spender was given ten days to produce a reply; almost as fully documented, his defense of free trade appeared in the September issue.

Balfour's Answer. A Cabinet split, dissolution of Parliament, and a general election all seemed at hand. But such expectations did not take into account Balfour. August 5 he was able to formulate his position for the Cabinet; these were in part given to the public in a pamphlet, *Economic Notes on Insular Free Trade,* and reiterated as official policy at the annual meeting of the National Union of Conservative Associations. He proposed a tariff of retaliation to force down foreign duties considered detrimental to British trade.

But this was merely on the surface. It does little to explain what one historian has termed one of "the most drastic series of expulsions, resignations and reshuffles engineered by any Prime Minister in the twentieth century." Some of the details are enlightening. When the document, *Economic Notes,* was handed to the Cabinet in August, Balfour attached to it "a confidential Cabinet Memorandum," proposing imperial preference and food taxes as well as a tariff of retaliation. Thus, he appeared to accept the general principles of the Chamberlain program. Accordingly, Ritchie and the Duke of Devonshire reiterated their firm opposition.

But Balfour was reluctant to alienate Devonshire, whose loyalty he considered necessary for maintaining the Government; he told Chamberlain that it would not be politically safe to commit the Government to food taxes at just that time. Chamberlain, presumably to free himself for his own crusade to win the nation over to his cause, wrote Balfour on September 9, offering to resign from the Cabinet. This communication was not made public by Balfour, nor did he inform the other members of the Cabinet. Rather, within the following week, he accepted the resignations of the leading free traders in the Government—circumstances indicating that for Ritchie (Exchequer), Balfour of Burleigh (secretary for Scotland), and Lord George Hamilton (secretary for India) the resignations had been requested. They departed under the impression that Balfour had been won over to Chamberlain's principle of imperial preference. Consequently, Chamberlain's own letter of resignation, when published on September 17, was received with general astonishment. Devonshire, a confirmed free trader and very uncomfortable with the turn of events, despite Balfour's efforts to placate him, added his own resignation a few weeks later.

But Balfour had brought about the departure from his Cabinet of the leading tariff reform advocate and the chief spokesmen for free trade as well. No one could now say that the Cabinet was divided on free trade and thus violated the constitutional principle of collective responsibility. At the same time, the prime minister might commit the Government to a moderate policy of a tariff of retaliation. Chamberlain was not alienated. He and Balfour had agreed on a measure of fiscal reform, the free traders had been ejected, and Chamberlain's own son, Austen, became the new chancellor of the Exchequer.

The meaning of all this was not lost on Campbell-Bannerman. He wrote to Herbert Gladstone, "This whole plan of Joe outside and Arthur inside working in cooperation with 'our Mr. Austen' in charge of the counting house is too bare-faced for anything." *The Economist* spoke of elements "of tragedy, of comedy and of burlesque," and later, "One wonders how long this state of things is to be permitted to last. Have we a prime minister who means to lead and has a policy he means to carry out, or have we not?" *The Times,* which until 1906 sought to reconcile the Balfour position with the Chamberlain position, spoke only of the "consummate skill" of the prime minister, a judgment echoed by historians ever since.

Balfour held on for two more years. There was to be no dissolution, but also no change in fiscal policy, until after a general election, not due by law until 1907. Further discussion was therefore irrelevant, or so Balfour maintained. He sought to avoid a division in Parliament over the tariff issue, and somehow to hold together the restless band of Chamberlainites and the indignant free traders, and thus to keep the Government in being. And so by playing the role of politician and of the detached intellectual simultaneously, he made it seem almost improper for Conservatives to be all of the same opinion.

Chamberlain's tariff reform campaign began in October 1903 with his Glasgow address, reported in a Liberal paper under the headline "Cobden vs. Chamberlain." He came out as thorough-going protectionist, advocating duties on foodstuffs with preference to the Empire and a general tariff averaging 10 percent on imported manufactures. In the following four months he delivered seventeen major addresses. But, though an orator, he was no economist and no logician. He became less and less convincing, particularly when H. H. Asquith, possessed of great debating skill, began following him around, answering him point by point. Nearly always Asquith had the better of the argument.

Throughout Britain this controversy stimulated the consideration of related problems: the Empire, the role of agriculture, the condition of the working class. Defenders of free trade and proponents of fiscal reform alike appealed to labor and to the unemployed. There was much talk, with graphic illustration of the "Big Loaf," the "Big Teapot," and the "Big Sugar Basin."

If the Education Bill put the members of the Liberal Party on the road to unity, the threat to free trade just about took them to their destination. They exploited the division in the Government ranks and sought to compel a parliamentary vote on the fiscal question. To meet this challenge required all of Balfour's parliamentary skill. Once, when a direct question forced the issue, he and his followers walked out of the chamber; he permitted mere resolutions in favor of free trade to pass without opposition. Early in 1905, when he advocated a colonial conference to consider the Chamberlain proposals, he was asked how this squared with a pledge (to his supporters) that there would be no change in tariff policy without an election. He answered, "I cannot see how the announcement of a policy on this side of the House can be regarded as a pledge to the other side of the House." In such manner his Government continued to survive.

Coolie Labor in South Africa

Still another Conservative policy of 1904–5 weakened the position of the party; this was the introduction of Chinese coolie labor into South Africa, as recommended by Milner, the high commissioner. When emigration from the British Isles, predicted in some Government circles, did not materialize, mineowners induced the Balfour Government to authorize contracts under which the Chinese would be imported under indentures to insure payment of the costs of importation. Consequently, they were to live in compounds under severe restrictions; circumstances made it virtually impossible for families to emigrate together. By October 1905, 47,000 Chinese laborers were in South Africa.

Economically the idea was a success, morally it was vulnerable, and politically it was an error. Though the system had some precedent and its results were not as abhorrent as Liberals made out (Campbell-Bannerman exaggerated when he referred to it as a system almost indistinguishable from slavery), it was, it may be said, indefensible. Milner added another folly in sanctioning flogging of the coolies.

Conservative Accomplishments

These issues and the humiliating end of the Balfour Ministry have overshadowed the distinguished work which was accomplished in many fields. There was first of all the Education Act of 1902, which we have already discussed. Then in 1903 came the Irish Land Act—largely the work of George Wyndham, the imaginative chief secretary for Ireland—a constructive measure which was far more successful than any of its predecessors in stimulating outright ownership of land by Irish peasants. It encouraged the tenants to buy under easy terms of payment and a government bonus, and also encouraged the landlords to sell. Whereas previous legislation had been successful only in transferring ownership at a pace which would have required a hundred years to complete, under this new law by 1921 about two-thirds of the land had been transferred to the tenants.

The act was popular with all shades of Irish opinion; but the Irish Unionists (the natural allies of the Conservatives) were soon alienated once again, this time by a proposal for "devolution" in Ireland for which they held the Government responsible. The administration stood no chance of gaining Irish votes in the next election. A successful policy in Ireland? The fates seemed against it.

The Licensing Act of 1904 dealt with the problem of compensation to breweries (now often corporations) and public houses if licenses once granted were withdrawn. These licenses were considered by those who held them as a form of property, but a legal judgment in 1891 ruled that their legal limit was one year, after which they might be withdrawn by local authorities without compensation. In 1902 a number of licenses were canceled. This question revived older temperance attitudes and the sharp distinction between the village inn and the village pub. Through the years the brewing interests had found steady support from the Conservatives, while the temperance elements had been strong in the Liberal Party. The solution in the act of 1904 was ingenious. It restored the general assumption that licenses once granted would be renewed. If not renewed, compensation was to be provided out of funds of the brewery industry itself, for the surrender of certain licenses would obviously enhance the value of those which remained. The Opposition charged that the bill would "endow the Liquor Trade," and spirited parliamentary debate was terminated only under the drastic closure procedure.

An important Unemployed Workmen's Act (1905) empowered the Local Government Board to establish local committees to consider the general problem of unemployment, and regularized voluntary committees set up in 1904 as an experiment. These agencies were to maintain registers of unemployed; they might establish labor exchanges and assist emigration. They had no government funds, but a public appeal headed by Queen Alexandra secured £125,000 in less than two months. Just before leaving office in 1905, the Balfour Government announced the appointment of a Royal Commission on the Poor Law and the Relief of Distress through Unemployment. For this concern about social problems—unemployment and poor relief—Gerald Balfour, president of the Local Government Board, was chiefly responsible. In no sense a social reformer, he is representative of intelligent government officials in both parties before 1914 who, though themselves conservative in outlook, were conscious of the development of public opinion on social questions and were increasingly committed to governmental action.

Historians have enjoyed arguing over the meaning of "splendid isolation" and the departure therefrom, but whatever the language, the
Entente with France (1904) and other diplomatic ventures set Britain on
a new course in relation to the Continent and determined the general
character of British foreign policy down to 1914. As the nineteenth century came to an end, Britain had no part in the alliance system—the rival
military alliances of Germany, Austria, and Italy in the Triple Alliance on
the one hand and the Franco-Russian Alliance on the other. British leaders were acutely aware of their "isolation" during the Boer War; but
Salisbury himself seemed little disturbed and gave little support to
Chamberlain's abortive overtures to Germany for some sort of Anglo-
German alliance. But in November 1900, Salisbury, perhaps induced by
Cabinet criticism, relinquished the Foreign Office to Lord Lansdowne,
now anxious to redeem his reputation after an unfortunate sojourn in the
War Office. After some hesitation Lansdowne set out, to improve, by one
means or another, Britain's position among the great powers. His efforts
at an accord with Germany and then one with Russia on Far East policy
came to nought; a German prerequisite was that Britain join the Triple
Alliance, and on this matter Salisbury's opposition was probably decisive. With Japan Lansdowne was more successful. Despite some opposition from Salisbury, he obtained Cabinet sanction for a defensive alliance
with Japan, signed in January 1902. The two powers jointly guaranteed
the integrity of China and Korea. In defending this guarantee, if either
ally were attacked by two or more powers the other ally would provide
military assistance.

This step led to another. The Anglo-Japanese Alliance made possible
the Russo-Japanese War (1904–5), but an improvement in Anglo-French
relations was essential lest France be involved in a war by her alliance
with Russia, and Britain by her alliance with Japan. After some hesitation
negotiations began in earnest between Lansdowne and Paul Cambon,
French ambassador in London. A generally popular figure in France,
Edward VII in his state visit to Paris in May 1903 created a favorable
atmosphere even though his actual role in negotiations was slight. The
series of colonial agreements, with emphasis on French control in
Morocco and British predominance in Egypt, which constituted the
Entente, was signed in April 1904. At the time its full import was unclear.
The British Foreign Office held that the agreements had no European
significance, but Cambon and the French considered them as merely
introductory to a more formal alliance. To Germany the *Entente* seemed
a countermove to the German-dominated Triple Alliance. What in actuality it meant had to await the future.

The General Election of 1906

If Balfour's policy in foreign affairs was generally strong and secure, his position in domestic affairs had become untenable by the autumn of 1905. In vain he had counted on continued confusion within the Opposition. Grievances against his administration—the Education Act, the Licensing Act, tariff proposals, Chinese labor, parliamentary tactics—had piled up. By-elections indicated the rapidly waning confidence of the electorate.

Balfour was also finally losing control of the Conservative majority in the Commons. Compromise and vacillation on the tariff questions were wearing thin, and the breach between the tariff reformers and the free traders in the party was widening. At a meeting of party officials at Newcastle in November, Chamberlain carried resolutions in support of his proposals, and this in the face of a renewed Balfour plea for party unity. Soon after, Chamberlain demanded that the party accept his policy of a protective tariff. Even to Conservative journals this constituted a "party crisis." Only the Chamberlain-inspired *Pall Mall Gazette* ventured (November 25) to guess that Balfour would not resign. The Liberal *Daily News* declared, "As he [Chamberlain] behaved towards Mr. Gladstone, so he is now behaving towards Mr. Balfour." Indeed, there is good reason to believe that Chamberlain sought the dissolution of the Government in the hope that in opposition the Conservative Party would adopt his policy.

But the Conservatives had not solved all the problems of the Liberals. Their unity in defense of free trade called attention to a continued disunity on the Irish question, now the only major difference between the Campbell-Bannerman element and the Liberal Imperialists. Various pronouncements on the Irish question forced Campbell-Bannerman to speak. On November 23 before his own constituents at Stirling, he stated with great caution that the party viewed the Irish problem with sympathy, that the Irish should accept any measure of self-government as a step in the direction of home rule, but that in the event of a Liberal Government, more pressing problems would demand first attention. This moderate policy was generally acceptable within the party—but not to Lord Rosebery who wished to drop Home Rule altogether as a party principle. Two days later he treated the nation to a final political sensation. In an address at Bodmin he declared that the Liberal Party "has hoisted ... the flag of Irish Home Rule." This would injure the unity of the free trade party. "I will say ... emphatically and explicitly and once and for all that I cannot serve under that banner." Though this declaration at first seemed ominous, it soon became known that Rosebery had spoken entirely on his own, and that Asquith and Grey had approved in advance the Campbell-Bannerman statement. Even Rosebery was now convinced that his was indeed "a lonely furrow" and that his "separation" from the Liberal Party was complete. He soon disappeared from the political scene.

Would Balfour brave another parliamentary session, would he dissolve and appeal to the country, or would he merely resign, shifting responsibility to the Opposition before a general election? Those were his alternatives. On December 4 he resigned. The opposition press said it was merely another of his tricks. It is true that he was well aware of the fresh breach in the Liberal Party on Ireland; certainly he hoped that this might hamper the formation of a strong Cabinet and that in the process the Liberals would lose favor with the electorate. Tactically it was about as good a time as he could have hoped for. But there was also Balfour's defeat by the Chamberlainites within his own party. Necessity as much as tactics explains his resignation.

It was logical that Campbell-Bannerman should succeed, though many party politicians thought it unwise for him to take office before an election. Apparently Campbell-Bannerman did not hesitate. His biographer says that he accepted office out of consistency with his attacks on the Balfour Cabinet. But Campbell-Bannerman was a shrewd and experienced politician, and we may assume that he also considered it good politics. He took office on December 5 with the understanding that a general election would follow. The formation of his Cabinet posed one formidable problem: what of the Liberal Imperialists? Rosebery had eliminated himself, but there were still Asquith, Grey, and Haldane. Though they had come to respect Campbell-Bannerman, they did not have much confidence in him as a prospective prime minister. For one thing, he was suffering from a heart ailment; he had just returned, on November 12, from his annual visit—this time an extended rest cure—to Marienbad in Bohemia. His poor health forced him to miss more than one critical debate in the Commons. But the Liberal Imperialists also questioned his ability as a parliamentarian; in his long years in opposition he had frequently shown to disadvantage in duels with Balfour and Chamberlain.

In September 1905 the three Liberal Imperialists had met in Relugas House, Grey's fishing lodge in the Scottish Highlands, and had agreed that they would serve under Campbell-Bannerman only if he would accept a peerage and go to the Lords, permitting Asquith to become leader of the Commons. But they had hardly counted on the necessity of forming a Cabinet before an election. Now, in December, when Grey refused at first to enter the Cabinet save on the terms of the "Relugas Pact," Campbell-Bannerman, bolstered by his wife, stood firm. For the sake of unity in contesting the coming election, the Liberal Imperialists were soon persuaded to take office, Asquith to the Exchequer, Grey to the Foreign Office, and Haldane to the War Office. On December 11 the new ministers groped their way through thick black London fog to Buckingham Palace to receive the seals of office.

The Liberal Landslide

When Campbell-Bannerman became prime minister in December 1905 the state of the major parties in the Commons stood at 370 Liberals and 218 Conservatives. The election of 1906 more than reversed these numbers, with 377 Liberals and 157 Conservatives (including 25 Liberal Unionists). Counting the 83 Irish Nationists and 53 Labor (29 elected under the banner of the Labor Representation Committee and 24 Lib-Labs), the Government now controlled 513 seats. While a Liberal victory had been generally expected, its proportions, in these terms, was well beyond the most optimistic Liberal expectation. In popular vote the Conservatives polled 43 percent, indicating a far closer election than in the results in the Commons. The distribution of the popular vote greatly favored the Liberals.

The campaign was one of the most spirited in parliamentary history, with the polls recording an 83.7 percent turnout of the electorate. The question of free trade easily dominated. The tone was set at the Liberal Party rally in the Albert Hall, December 21, 1905; as the crowd of 9,000 assembled they sang, "Stamp, Stamp, Stamp, upon Protection" and "No More Joe." The Liberals exploited the divisions within the Conservative-Unionist ranks: the "whole-hoggers," who were the Chamberlainites, demanding a protective tariff; "the little piggers," that is, Balfour and his dwindling following, favoring a tariff of retaliation; "the free fooders," who were the Unionist free traders, particularly set against an import duty on food. And the Liberals also made the most of Nonconformist grievances. "The Churchman and the Brewer we will drive them from the land, for the Non-conformist children are marching hand in hand," they sang. Nonconformists regarded the Education Act as a limitation of religious freedom, the Licensing Act as a defeat for temperance, tariff reform as oppressive to the poor, and Chinese labor in South Africa as unchristian.

The Conservatives sought unsuccessfully to revive the issue of "pro-Boerism." Their argument in its more extreme form was stated by the *National Review* (January 1906): Sir Henry Campbell-Bannerman "has associated with himself in office, save for a handful of Liberal Imperialists, the most extraordinary collection of the enemies of their country ever assembled in a Cabinet." But, generally speaking, the South African War had become, in Morley's phrase, "dead meat," and the

Liberals generally avoided voicing strong anti-imperial statements. More successful was the Conservative attack on Liberal identification with Irish home rule; Liberals were the "apostles of imperial disintegration," declared Balfour. And Chamberlain asserted that the Liberal Cabinet was merely a Home Rule and Little Englander Government which could hope to survive only with Irish support. The Liberals, on their part, tried to put to one side the Irish issue, declaring that Home Rule constituted no immediate objective.

Polling was spread over a period of two weeks. But as the results began to trickle in (they were announced by magic lanterns along the Embankment and in Trafalgar Square) the outcome was not long in doubt. The first report was from Ipswich—two Liberals elected where there had been one Liberal and one Conservative. In the returns of the first two days, the Conservatives lost 21 out of 27 contests and did not register a single gain. As polling proceeded, Lancashire recorded a smashing victory for free trade, with 29 seats to the Liberals, 12 to Labor, and 14 to the Conservatives. In Manchester all 9 seats went Liberal, and Balfour himself was defeated in a constituency which he had represented for twenty years. In London and suburbia the results were almost as sensational; whereas 67 Conservative and 8 Liberals had been returned in 1900, now there were 46 Liberals, 26 Conservatives, and 3 Laborites. The Liberals and Labor carried every seat in Wales and 58 out of 70 seats in Scotland.

The Conservatives remained strong only in the universities and in North Ireland, Liverpool, Sheffield, and Birmingham. *The Times* declared: "Birmingham stands where it does because it possesses reasoned beliefs." The *Westminster Gazette* replied: "Rather it stands where Mr. Chamberlain stands; . . . it moves with great rapidity from one 'reasoned belief' to another 'reasoned belief,' from Old Liberalism to the Newest Toryism, from Free Trade to Protection."

On the tariff issue, the election was a vote for the status quo— obviously the country was not yet ready for a protective tariff; at the same time, it did not repudiate protection. Actually, the question ceased to be a major political issue after the election. The swing back of the Nonconformist vote to the Liberal Party in part explains the magnitude of its victory. Nonconformists in the new House numbered well over 150—probably the largest number in any Parliament since Oliver Cromwell. But, all the same, 1906 proved to be the last general election in which Nonconformity, as such, was a significant factor.

For the Liberals, naturally enough, it seemed a complete vindication. And Gladstone Liberals, Liberal Imperialists, and Radicals were back together again. Just how Campbell-Bannerman "arrived" in 1905–6 has puzzled a good many historians, for he did not provide strong leadership either before or during the election. Undoubtedly the result was more a reflection of a loss of confidence in Conservatism than conversion to Liberalism. And it is not that Campbell-Bannerman was so popular but that Balfour had lost status, even in his own party. We are told, for example, that Lord Curzon, a Conservative peer and viceroy of India (1898–1905), was contemptuous of Balfour's defeat.

The Rise of Labor

The election of 1906 was sensational in many ways. Not the least was the return to the Commons of a new voting power in the fifty-three representatives of the working class. The *Review of Reviews* gave over an entire issue to the new Labor M.Ps. For the Labor Representation Committee—that federation of socialist groups and trade unions in 1900—it was a great achievement to have increased its representation from four to twenty-nine, particularly when only fifty constituencies had been contested. In February 1906, in annual conference, 350 delegates representing nearly a million affiliated members changed the name officially to the Labor Party. A summary of its fortunes since 1900 is in order.

The history of the Labor Representation Committee had been largely that of internal organization and development of electoral techniques. Its membership grew steadily and its financial base was strengthened. Annual conferences repeatedly rejected the use of the term socialist and refused to sponsor a doctrinaire program. Trade unionism, on the other hand, gradually abandoned its prejudice that a candidate sponsored by Labor would only take votes from the Liberal candidate and "let the Tory in." A notable action was taken at the Newcastle Conference in February 1903 in the resolution requiring all officials and endorsed candidates "to abstain strictly from identifying themselves with or promoting the interests of any section of the Liberal or Conservative parties."

Further impetus to the Labor Representation Committee came from an unexpected source, the law courts. In 1901 the Taff Vale decision, reversed in the Court of Appeal but upheld in the Lords, held that a trade union was subject to an injunction and could be sued for the actions of its officers and members. The Amalgamated Railway Servants Society had very nearly refused to support the strike on the Taff Vale Railway in Wales, but now found itself with £42,000 in costs and damages to pay. While no similar suits followed outside Wales, it was taken for granted that this judgment would drastically limit strike activity. It was welcomed in some Conservative circles as a needed brake on growing trade union power. But it ran counter to the widely held legal opinion of the intent of the legislation of the 1870s—legislation considered the Magna

Carta of trade unionism. Many years later, when Stanley Baldwin said, "The Conservatives can't talk of class war; they started it," he had in mind the situation after Taff Vale when the Conservative Government did not modify by statute the effects of this judgment.

Until then working-class candidates had been faring very badly in by-elections. But within twelve months in 1902–3 they won three contests. In the Clitheroe division of Lancashire, D. J. Shackleton, a millworker who had become a trade union official but had remained a Liberal in politics, accepted the label of the Labor Representation Committee. He was also a Nonconformist and a temperance man. He had the support of the cotton unions, which had hitherto been neutral politically. The Liberals decided not to contest the seat and Shackleton was returned unopposed. In the contest for Woolwich, which the Conservatives had won by default in 1900, the Labor Representation Committee put up Will Crooks, a cooper by trade and one of the most representative of workingmen, an ardent pro-Boer who had been a member of the London County Council and mayor of the London borough of Poplar. He easily defeated his Tory opponent. Then, at Barnard Castle, Arthur Henderson, early in life apprenticed as a molder and, in turn, a trade union official and city councilor, was the first Labor Representation Committee candidate to defeat both the other parties.

Lib-Lab Collaboration. In the background of these victories in 1902–3 is a gradual working out of an electoral understanding between the Labor Representation Committee and the Liberal Party. Indeed, just as the L.R.C. conference in February 1903 was proclaiming political independence, its leaders, MacDonald and Hardie, were quietly and secretly negotiating an electoral agreement with Herbert Gladstone, the Liberal chief whip, and Jesse Herbert, his secretary and aide. It was an entente and not an alliance, and its best expression is in a memorandum which Gladstone wrote, March 13, for his chief, Campbell-Bannerman. Gladstone said he was prepared "to ascertain from qualified and responsible Labour leaders how far Labour candidates [could] be given an open field against a common enemy;" and he would try to persuade local Liberal associations "to abstain from nominating a Liberal candidate and to unite in support of any recognized and competent Labour candidate who [supported] the general objects of the Liberal Party." In August Gladstone drew up a list of thirty-five constituencies in which the Liberals might reasonably allow the L.R.C. a free hand. Campbell-Bannerman approved.

In 1903 Liberal leadership regarded this collaboration as almost essential for a return to office. The working-class vote constituted three-fourths of the electorate, and a very considerable proportion had voted Conservative in 1895 and 1900. Now Liberals hoped to wrest many urban seats from the Conservatives. But the first fruits of cooperation went to the L.R.C., in Henderson's victory in July 1903 at Barnard Castle. The local Liberal Association insisted on contesting the seat but its candidate received little support from the national organization. On the other hand, doctrinaire socialists were disturbed and even suspicious, but MacDonald and Hardie protested their steady adherence to independence. However, collaboration did, in fact, continue and almost assured an excellent showing for the L.R.C. in 1906. Of its thirty candidates unopposed by Liberals, twenty-four were victorious.

For voting strength the L.R.C., and its successor, the Labor Party, drew increasingly on the trade unions, now largely convinced by Taff Vale of the necessity for a working-class party. Trade unionism also provided an ever larger share of party leadership; of the twenty-nine M.P.s elected by the L.R.C. in 1906, twenty-three were from unions. A major recruitment came with the adherence of the Miners' Federation in 1909. Labor, in and out of unions, remained in the Edwardian years for the most part a provincial movement, one reason the London press was slow to recognize its importance. Electoral accommodation with the Liberals continued until 1914, and until 1911 the Labor Party generally supported Liberal policy in Parliament. Consequently, to many it appeared that Labor would eventually be absorbed by Liberalism.

Socialist Societies. Each of the socialist societies within the Labor Representation Committee had its own history. The Social Democratic Federation withdrew in 1901 when the Labor Representation Committee refused to go "socialist." The small Independent Labor Party suffered from a clash of personalities among its leaders. So did the Fabian Society, for Wells's earlier remark that it was "in urgent need of a searching psychoanalysis" still had point after 1900. The Fabians had few ideas in common. When the leadership, dominated by Webb and Shaw, refused to disavow the South African War, the Independent Labor Party element, including MacDonald, resigned. Graham Wallas left the Fabians in 1904 on the tariff issue. H. G. Wells, who joined the society in 1903 out of friendship for the Webbs, soon found himself in fierce dispute. He favored a more militant type of socialism. He read to the society a paper, "Faults of the Fabians"; "permeation," he said, would get them nowhere. Soon after he resigned.

As for the Webbs, they were absorbed in their own interests. One was the newly formed London School of Economics—Sidney Webb had managed to divert a goodly portion of a bequest for Fabian propaganda to the formation of a school for the scholarly study of economics. Another was secondary education, particularly technical education, in London. The Webbs did not take the Labor Representation Committee or the Independent Labor Party very seriously and were rather blind to the talent and sense of purpose in those organizations. They preferred to permeate the older parties. So there was a steady round of dinner parties at 41 Grosvenor Road, Westminster, conveniently located hard by the Houses of Parliament. Each dinner had its celebrities, each had its purpose. After 1900 the Webbs were particularly attached to the "Limps" (Liberal Imperalists). Through their intimate friend Haldane they became well acquainted with H. H. Asquith and his wife Margot. By 1903 they were cultivating the Conservative prime minister, Arthur Balfour, who was equally attracted to them. Sidney was appointed in 1903 to the Royal Commission on Trade Union Law, and Beatrice to the Poor Law Commission in 1905. The Webbs in these years likewise entertained a past prime minister (Rosebery) and other future ones (Bonar Law and Winston Churchill). Friendly relations were maintained with Joseph Chamberlain. Nearly everyone of note seems to have turned up at one time or another. "They all have a certain usefulness," wrote Beatrice. But there is no record of the appearance of the Liberal Party leader, Campbell-Bannerman, or of the secretary of the Labor Representation Committee, Ramsay MacDonald. Churchill received little attention until after 1908 and Lloyd George very little at all. The Webbs lacked "political-mindedness." It has even been suggested that their only interest in the working class was as a subject for study, but this is a very prejudiced view indeed. The contacts at the Webb *salon* were stimulating to all, or nearly all, who came. The twentieth century would not have been the same without it. Wells, in *The New Machiavelli* (1911) held the *salon* up to ridicule, but many others just as wise have testified to its atmosphere of good will and intelligent purpose.

Toward Social Democracy

The election of 1906 had implications much wider than as a stimulus to working-class politics. It ended, insofar as can be dated, the control of Parliament by the "landed interest." Nearly half of those returned in 1906 were new to the Commons and they represented new elements. The "country gentlemen" lingered on and were still frequently found in high places, but, generally speaking, the Commons after the election broadly reflected varied aspects of English life, with increasing strength from business, law, finance, journalism, and labor. Parliament was no longer "the first club in Europe"; frock coats and top hats were no longer *de rigueur*. Here are two striking illustrations. In 1906 a

Liberal barrister soundly defeated Arthur Balfour by a poll of 6,403 to 3,423; and J. R. Clynes, a trade union official and a candidate of the Labor Representation Committee, turned out a Conservative privy councilor, Sir James Fergusson, who had been an administrator in the colonies, by a vote of 5,386 to 2,954.

The changing character of the Commons is merely a delayed reflection of the change in the electorate. Though the suffrage had been greatly extended by the Reform Bills of 1867 and 1884, not until 1906 did the new voters demonstrate their power. Policies of *laissez-faire* and government retrenchment were popular when those who voted paid the bills. But now the bulk of the voters had no income tax to pay (only incomes in excess of £160 were subject to tax), and they were easily persuaded to approve much larger national budgets.

Elie Halévy, the French historian of modern Britain, has provided us with a convincing interpretation. Nineteenth-century liberalism, he says, did not win in 1906. In domestic affairs the real significance of the election is in its impetus to social democracy: the rising demand for better standards of living for the workingmen, for greater equality of opportunity, for limitations of economic privilege, and for security against sickness, unemployment, and old age. In 74 percent of the constituencies the vote went against the Conservatives, who had not given most of the voters what they wanted: legislation to meet their problems in the twentieth century. Though seldom articulated by the common man in these terms, it was a reflection of changing opinion toward existing society, a restive attitude toward tradition, a demand for organic change.

This was more in spite of than because of traditional parties' policies. Over the years the Conservatives had, on the whole, been more socially minded than the Liberals; but "Tory democracy," always dictated more by expediency than by principle, had been watered down under the Salisbury-Balfour leadership. Acceptance of responsibility for social legislation—to correct Taff Vale and deal with other problems of the workingman—was implied in the return of the Liberals to power. They had absorbed the radicalism of Cobden and Bright in the nineteenth century. Would they now embrace the radicalism of the twentieth?

An End to Isolation

Nor was the Liberal success in 1906 a victory for the Little Englandism of Gladstone. On the contrary, the abandonment of diplomatic isolation became a nonpartisan policy. Were the Liberals the party of peace? So they usually said. Yet in 1914 under their aegis Britain would embark on the first general European war since 1815. In 1906 the key to Liberal policy is found in the role of the Liberal Imperialists. The breach between them and the Little Englanders was finally closed in December 1905, and in the process the "Limps" captured three strategic positions in the new Government: the Exchequer, the Foreign Office, and the War Office. To one of these appointees, he does not say which, Halévy remarked how strange it was that the Liberal League, formed in 1902, should now fade away. The reply: "But the Liberal League did not vanish. What happened is simply that in 1905 it absorbed the Liberal Government. That is why we went to war in 1914."

4 The New Liberalism

Élie Halévy
*The Rule of
Democracy,
1905–1914,*
2d ed. (1952), p. v

During the years whose history I relate England was
hastening alike "towards social democracy" and "towards
war." It was hastening alike towards both with equal
rapidity. We must not be deceived by the noise of party
strife. Apparently the Unionists were the party of opposition to Socialism, the Liberals the party prepared to make
concessions to Socialism. In reality both parties, stripped of
their historic significance, were yielding with a unanimity
which was resigned rather than enthusiastic to the pressure
of the working masses. Apparently the Unionists were the
party of war, the Liberals the party of peace.... Neither
wanted war: both yielded inevitably to the pressure which
the increase in the German navy exerted upon the nation.

George
Dangerfield
*The Strange
Death of Liberal
England* (1935),
p. viii

It was in 1910 that fires long smoldering in the English
spirit suddenly flared up, so that by the end of 1913 Liberal
England was reduced to ashes.

George Bernard
Shaw
*The Matter with
Ireland* (1926),
p. 79

Political opinion in Ulster is not a matter of talk and bluff
as it is in England.

1906–1914

After 1906 our next point of vantage is 1910. In that year, on May 6, Edward VII died and the last great assemblage of European royalty in Britain gathered for the funeral. In domestic politics, 1906–10, we have first the leadership of the even-tempered Campbell-Bannerman and then the talents of Asquith and Balfour, to whom politics was something of a friendly game. Following a clash on the floor of the Commons, the two might be found arm in arm at the next gathering of society. In this period David Lloyd George and Winston Churchill leaped into prominence. Important questions came before Cabinet and Parliament. How would the new Liberal Government define its "mandate" of 1906? How was that mandate to be fulfilled with a House of Lords overwhelmingly Conservative? What was to be the answer to the demand "Votes for Women" from "suffragettes" who resorted to demonstration and violence? Would the Alliance System be able to preserve peace in Europe? How was the German challenge to British naval superiority to be met?

The Campbell-Bannerman Cabinet

Historians have generally recognized that in December 1905 Campbell-Bannerman formed one of the ablest Cabinets in British political history, certainly the strongest Government of the cen-

81

tury before World War II. It included Liberal Imperialists, party moderates, Little Englanders, and Radicals—all sections of the rejuvenated Liberal Party were represented. It included many names that were to be eminent in English public life for the next generation.

It is curious that Joseph Chamberlain never reached "the top of the greasy pole" and that Henry Campbell-Bannerman did. Of the former's grand manner, platform grace, or parliamentary skill, Campbell-Bannerman had almost nothing. But he was good-humored and he was direct. During the dark years of Opposition he had put aside his own advancement and had sought first and last the unity and success of the Liberal Party. He may often have spoken in platitudes, his political addresses uninspired, and he may indeed have been "a sufficiently dull man." But one always knew where he stood and could count on his loyalty. His strong character was manifest in 1905 as he formed his government. Others had sought to control the distribution of key Cabinet posts and, indeed, to dictate his own role. "It is I who am the head of this Government: it is I who have the King's command," he declared, clearing the atmosphere. There was more than rhetoric in the tribute passed some years later by H. W. Massingham of the *Nation*: "What was in him was an iron mould of character and a rare capacity, in which humorous observation was a chief part, for testing it or its absence in others."

Even so, it is not easy to assess his leadership. "C.B." had no defined program, he was not a social reformer, he gave little direction to the Cabinet and seldom interfered in the operations of departments of state—perhaps salutary since his was a Cabinet of diverse characters and outlooks. Probably "C.B's" most notable personal success was in the fulfillment of his South African policy—the granting of self-government to the Boer states in December 1906. The Balfour Government had moved very slowly toward making good the assurances given in the peace treaty in 1902. By 1905 status midway between colonialism and self-government, called "representative government," was about to be activated. But it was not "responsible government" (an executive responsible to the legislature)—a development which the colonial secretary, Lyttleton, said "no sensible" men would approve.

Immediately after the election of 1906, Campbell-Bannerman, supported by General Smuts, moved to scrap the Lyttelton constitution and to establish at once full and complete self-government for the Transvaal. At a crucial meeting on February 8, details of which, because of conflicting evidence, cannot with any certainty be reconstructed, the Cabinet decided to grant the Transvaal responsible government. Campbell-Bannerman's initiative and unqualified support were significant, though perhaps not as decisive as has been often asserted. In the Commons debate Balfour called the action "the most reckless experiment ever tried in the development of a great colonial policy." In a one-minute reply in the midst of Commons turmoil a confident "C.B." declared that he had never listened to "a more unworthy, provocative and mischievous" speech. The possibility of defeat in the Lords was circumvented by resort to an ancient but still legal procedure—letters patent issued by the Crown on the basis of an Order in Council. In 1907 similar provision was made for the Orange River Colony. These moves were a vindication of Gladstonian principles and constituted a significant modification in imperial policy from the jingoistic days of the war. Boer leaders, especially Botha and Smuts, proved to be entirely loyal to the Empire, an attitude fostered by their admiration and respect for Campbell-Bannerman. But before long Conservative policy was also vindicated. Its objective had been South African unity under the British crown, and this was achieved in 1910 in the Union of South Africa (Cape Colony, Natal, Transvaal, and Orange River Colony), a development in which the high commissioner, Lord Selborne, a holdover from the Balfour regime, had a major role.

In solving the problems of political disunity the British were left with less authority and direct influence than before the Boer War. On the second great problem, native policy, the British after 1902 abandoned responsibility. It was perhaps assumed that the English element would develop a constructive program through economic expansion. But for every white man there were five or six blacks; there were poor whites as well as poor blacks. Although the last Chinese coolie returned home in 1910, 100,000 Indians remained in Natal and a large Portuguese population was scattered throughout the area. This problem of a heterogeneous population was now a South African and not a British concern, save in the British protectorates. In general terms, this relationship reflects the new character of British imperialism in the early decades of the twentieth century. The bouyant and aggressive imperialism of the nineteenth century gave way to the atmosphere of dominion status—collaboration between Britain and the colonies—leading to self-government and eventually to independence.

Asquith, Grey, Haldane

Second in command was Herbert Asquith at the Exchequer. A Yorkshireman, a Nonconformist, no landed aristocrat but from a substantial middle-class background, he was fairly representative of the more dominant attitudes in the party. Debates over fiscal policy and his own budgets provided opportunity for his extraordinary political talent on the floor of the Commons; there he became a leading spokesman for the Government.

At the Foreign Office, not Lord Cromer who was C. B.'s first choice but who declined for reasons of health, not Sir Charles Dilke, another logical choice, had not a divorce scandal years before excluded him from consideration, and neither James Bryce nor John Morley, either of whom, no doubt, would have accepted with alacrity, but rather Sir Edward Grey, a leading Liberal Imperialist. Certainly his appointment won as much approval from Conservatives as from Liberals. He was an aristocrat, a country gentleman with an estate of 2,000 acres. Also he was not without some experience, for he had been parliamentary undersecretary in the Foreign Office, 1892–95. Yet in many ways his was a strange appointment. He had idled his way through Balliol College, Oxford, and had remained parochial in his outlook (Northumberland was the center of his world); and it was a paradox that in these years when Britain was increasingly committed to a continental policy, that her affairs should have been directed by one who seldom traveled outside the British Isles, who had little first-hand knowledge of Europe, and spoke no French. Apparently Campbell-Bannerman had no great confidence in Grey, yet before long he was conducting his office with infinite pains and conscientiousness, as even the Radicals in the party recognized.

Soon the general character of the Grey years at the Foreign Office was indicated. Within a few weeks the new foreign secretary was giving an encouraging if guarded reply to the French ambassador's inquiry concerning British policy in the event of a German attack upon France. Just at this time came the Algeciras Conference in which the Germans challenged the Anglo-French settlement in Morocco which had left France with a free hand. When tension was at its height Grey noted in a confidential memorandum (February 20, 1906):"If there is war between France and Germany it will still be very difficult for us to keep out of it." The atmosphere remained charged despite a settlement on the immediate issue, and very soon conversations between the French and British Military staffs were underway. While these did not bind Britain to any particular action, she was, at least from the French point of view, committed to giving France general support in a sensitive area such as Morocco. It so happened that in that same February of 1906 the British launched at Portsmouth the *Dreadnought*—a battleship of revolutionary design in speed and armament. Its consequence, within a few years, was a persistent and strident Anglo-German naval rivalry in dreadnoughts which became the chief obstacle in the way of any accord between the two nations.

The atmosphere of these developments is reflected in a lengthy memorandum on Anglo-German relations, distributed on January 1, 1907, throughout the Foreign Office and prepared by Eyre Crowe, its senior clerk. It called for strengthening the *Entente* with France to maintain the balance of power in Europe and insisted upon British naval supremacy as the best insurance against rising German ambitions. This memorandum was approved by Grey and is, indeed, a reflection of his own views. It was just at this time that Grey wrote President Roosevelt in the United States, insisting on maintaining the *Entente* with France in order to keep Germany in check.

As to the prime minister, he did not fully share these sentiments but did not interfere. As a matter of fact, he was not always kept fully informed. His distance from actual policy is illustrated by his article "The Hague Conference and Limitation of Armaments," which appeared in the first issue of the new Liberal Radical weekly, the *Nation* (March 2, 1907). Its point—that with general guarantees of peace, armaments could be safely reduced—was unrealistic and had no effect upon deliberations at the Hague Conference in the summer of 1907. More significant were the Anglo-Russian negotiations then in progress, resulting in the Convention signed in August. Like the understanding with France, it was a settlement of differences outside Europe (this time in Persia, Afghanistan, and Tibet). Within a year or two the Triple Entente had an identity of its own, as a foil to the Triple Alliance.

As to the War Office, Sir John Fortescue, the military historian, summarizes the period after 1902: "For four years there was unprofitable discussion; and then the task of setting the nation's military house in order was taken in hand by Richard Burton Haldane." Haldane, who sacrificed a £20,000-a-year practice at the bar to join the Cabinet, had hoped to be lord chancellor; he rejected the attorney-generalship and requested the War Office—by that time regarded with reason as the graveyard of reputations. The Boer War had revealed almost hopeless confusion, but the years 1902–6 were not quite as barren as Fortescue's comment would indicate. A good start toward bringing the war office up to date was made in the findings (1903) of a royal commission on the conduct of the South African War. The crucial recommendations in 1904 of the Esher War Office Reconstitution Committee strengthened the Committee of Imperial Defence, with the prime minister in control and with a permanent secretariat to bring together the action of responsible ministers and the knowledge of service experts. Also, an Army Council was to replace a single commander-in-chief. In these developments Balfour provided constructive leadership.

But even more imaginative was the contribution of Haldane. With his knowledge of German army practice and with his extraordinary facility for mastering detail, he had a plan of military reorganization ready for Parliament early in 1907. He had strong support from Grey, who well understood the relation between military strength and foreign policy, and from Campbell-Bannerman, held in thrall by repeated reference to Lord Cardwell, the war secretary responsible for celebrated reforms and under whom C. B. had served 1871–74. And with his use of traditional party language playing down the role of the military, his emphasis upon a voluntary system of recruitment, his professed concern for economy, and his unqualified support from the prime minister, Haldane disarmed Radical Liberal sentiment committed to retrenchment. His program was promptly adopted. The most important features were (1) the establishment of an Expeditionary Force of 160,000 (six divisions), fully equipped, ready for instant mobilization, and sufficient in size to strike on the Continent if necessary; and (2) the creation of a second-line or Territorial Reserve Army of militia and volunteers which by 1910 would number 276,000. Almost as significant were his provision of a General Staff for the Army Council and his establishment (1906) of an Officers' Training Corps. In effect, Haldane prepared Britain for World War I. Mobilization took place in 1914 according to plan. At the same time, the cost of maintaining the Army right down to 1914, even with a price rise, remained less than in the year before Haldane became war secretary.

Talent and Disappointment

David Lloyd George, the rising Liberal Radical had hoped for the Home Office, but when forced to be content with theBoard of Trade proceeded to make the most of it. His two years in that office (until his promotion to the Exchequer in 1908) produced solid achievement. Significant legislation was enacted concerning the merchant marine, copyrights, and patents. The Port of London Authority replaced a confusion of private dock organizations. The agitator Lloyd George proved to be a responsible minister and a brilliant administrator; but he was also revealed as something of an opportunist, for much of his legislation reflected protectionist philosophy.

One of the most interesting, but also one of the most unfortunate, appointments of 1905 was intended to conciliate labor—the designation of the Radical, John Burns, hero of the London Dock Strike and Hyde Park orator, as president of the Local Government Board. Campbell-Bannerman appointed him with more enthusiasm than he did Lloyd George. G. P. Gooch later noted that Burns's "tenure of office disappointed everyone but himself." This popular but decidedly vain man proved to have no administrative ability whatsoever. His class-consciousness had waned and he developed into a reactionary, doing more harm than good for the cause of labor. But for him there probably would have been basic change, bafore 1914, in the Poor Law, and also significant advance in town planning.

But Burns was the exception. Elsewhere was more talent: James Bryce as Irish Secretary, Herbert Gladstone in the Home Office, John Morley, a pacifist, whose return to Cabinet office as secretary for India was a personal triumph. These three continued the Gladstonian tradition. The scholar Augustine Birrell was at the Board of Education, and the political writer Sydney Buxton at the Post Office. A Radical pro-Boer, Sir Robert Reid, became lord chancellor. Outside of the Cabinet, in junior rank, were Herbert Samuel, as undersecretary for Home Affairs and Winston Churchill, now thirty-one, as undersecretary for the Colonies. The latter, since his superior was in the Lords, represented his department in Cabinet committees and presented Government policy in the Commons.

The Opposition

As for the Conservatives, though seriously reduced, they were in no chastened mood. They still had Balfour. He found a seat in the City of London and returned to the Commons in March 1906, in time to participate in a debate on a Government resolution to put the Commons on record as opposed to a protective tariff. He staged one of his brilliant exhibitions in an effort to debate the question to death. But Campbell-Bannerman refused to respond to his questions: "They are utterly futile, nonsensical and misleading. They were invented by the Right Honorable gentleman for the purpose of occupying time in the debate. I say, enough of this foolery. . . . The tone and temper of this Parliament will not permit it. Move your amendments and let us get to business." A Liberal Party demonstration followed.

Joseph Chamberlain had the support of two-thirds of the Conservatives returned in 1906 and he hoped that in Opposition his party would take up his crusade. But in July he suffered a stroke, and, though he lived on, partially paralyzed, until 1914, his public career was ended. He had led revolts which all but wrecked both major parties. Had he succeeded Gladstone instead of bolting the party, the Liberals might well have absorbed the working-class movement in politics and there might have been no Labor Party as such. Social security legislation might well have come twenty years before it actually did. Quite possibly, the career of Joseph Chamberlain made more difference to England than that of any prime minister between Gladstone and Lloyd George. The incapacity of Chamberlain left Balfour unchallenged as Conservative leader in the Commons.

Lords vs. Commons

The Liberals did not forget a Balfour remark of the election campaign. At Nottingham on January 15, while the polling was still in progress, but the Conservative defeat fairly clearly indicated, he said with his usual assurance that it was the duty of everyone to see that "the great Unionist Party should still control, whether in Power or in Opposition, the destinies of this great Empire." What did he have in mind, said the Liberals, if not the House of Lords? Thus the constitutional issue of the role of the Lords in a democratic society was thrust into politics. It was not an issue to stir the emotions of the people, and it must not be permitted to obscure the more significant theme of these years—the extension of social legislation. At the same time it was an issue which preoccupied the politicians, influenced their policies, and in part determined their careers.

The Position of the Lords

Now the precise function of the Lords in the English constitutional system was uncertain. Theoretically England was still governed by King, Lords, and Commons. But in the well-known phrase of Justice Holmes, the life of the English constitution "has not been logic, but experience." As a force in political practice the House of Lords had steadily declined since the seventeenth century. It had lost effective power over the king's ministers; an adverse vote did not upset a Cabinet. Precedent had sanctioned the general control of the Commons over money bills, a matter supposed to have been settled in the seventeenth century. In other legislative matters the Lords had remained active and was inclined to assert a role coordinate with that of the Commons, though some accepted the principle that the Lords should not obstruct proposals which had the demonstrated support of the electorate. The composition of the Lords had never been reformed and its largely hereditary character presented by 1900 something of an anomaly.

For the situation in 1906 there were several special considerations.

1. The House of Lords, despite its claim to be the "watchdog of the constitution," was no nonpartisan body. Because of the mass desertion of Gladstone by Liberal peers on Irish Home Rule, it was now overwhelmingly Conservative. Of the 602 members who might participate in its proceedings, only 88 considered themselves Liberal; others were either Conservative (355) or Liberal Unionist (124). (The remaining 35, including bishops and princes of the blood, cannot be classified politically.) There were no labor peers.

2. In the ten years prior to 1906 the Lords had been unusually cooperative with the Government of the day. But, of course, that Government had been Conservative. It was possibly this fact which enabled the Lords to approve such highly partisan measures as the Education Bill (1902) and the Licensing Bill (1904), both of which involved radically new procedures and for which the Cabinet had no electoral mandate.

How would this same House of Lords treat the program of a Liberal Cabinet?

3. On the other hand, and with considerable reason, the Conservatives held that the Liberals had unfairly exploited certain issues, notably education and Chinese labor, in the 1906 campaign and that their great preponderance in the Commons did not indicate anything like an equal preponderance of support in the country at large. The Conservatives thus maintained that if the Liberals were prepared to use their power in the Commons to destroy the legislation of the previous administration, they had every right to use their power in the Lords to save it.

4. If an actual impasse developed, there was always the "safety valve" of the constitution. The sovereign might, upon the advice of his ministers, exercise his prerogative and create a sufficient number of new peers to control the decisions in the House of Lords. Only once had this been actually invoked—in 1712 in the surprise creation of twelve new peers by Queen Anne to insure Tory control of the Lords and its acceptance of the Preliminaries to Peace to end the French war. In 1832 the threat to create some fifty new peers was sufficient to persuade the Lords to pass the Great Reform Bill. After 1906, if it became necessary to exercise this prerogative, as many as four hundred new peers might be required.

The Parliamentary Session of 1906

The issue of Lords vs. Commons dominated the politics of the first year of the new Government; during 1906 the Lords either destroyed or seriously modified an Education Bill, a Plural Voting Bill (limiting to one vote those who had property qualifications in several constituencies—a long-standing Liberal grievance, for plural voting generally favored the Conservatives), an Agricultural Holdings Bill, and an Irish Town Tenants Bill.

The controversy between the two houses is best illustrated in the fortunes of the Education Bill, the most important proposal of the session. The Liberal Cabinet held that it must right the wrong suffered by Nonconformists in the Education Act of 1902, which seemed to provide Anglican religious instruction at public expense. But to reconcile the conflicting claims of Anglican, Protestant Nonconformist, and Catholic was virtually impossible, and the bill introduced into the Commons in 1906 proved of significance only in underlining the issue with the Lords. It passed the Commons by a majority of 192. In a famous speech Balfour said, "The real discussion of this question is not now in this House ... ; the real discussion must be elsewhere; ... it is in the highest degree improbable that the Bill will come back in the shape in which it leaves us." Balfour virtually directed the course of the measure in the Lords, from which it returned to the Commons in effect an entirely different bill. The Lords' amendments were rejected *en bloc* (an unusual procedure) by the Commons, 416–107. When the Lords stood by its amendments the Cabinet dropped the measure.

Though the Liberals would have it that the House of Lords had destroyed their entire legislative program, the session of 1906 was actually one of considerable accomplishment. An important Workmen's Compensation Act, significantly regarded as a nonpartisan measure, amended existing legislation and extended the liability of the employer to six million additional workers. There was also the first of a series of acts providing free or cheap meals for school children, and this likewise met with little opposition from the Conservatives.

The most important act of the session was the Trade Disputes Act. It was a foregone conclusion that the Liberals would modify by legislation some of the effects of the Taff Vale decision—two-thirds of the Liberal candidates in the 1906 election had spoken out for reform. But just how far should such legislation go? The royal commission of 1903 had proposed that statute law should safeguard unions from actions like that of the Taff Vale suit (in other words, that peaceful picketing during a strike should be legalized) but that blanket immunity from lawsuits of whatever nature should not be accorded trade unions. This solution appealed to lawyers like Asquith and Haldane in the Cabinet, and, accordingly, a Government bill was so drafted. But trade union leaders in the Commons announced their incapacity to understand such legal technicalities and they introduced their own measure providing for complete legal immunity. To the discomfiture of many in the Cabinet, this substitute bill was accepted by the prime minister without warning, perhaps because he too could see no point to the "quibbling" in the original bill. Passage of the substitute bill was followed by a flurry of strikes, and the question in the public mind of what was proper and what improper in a strike was not settled.

The Trade Disputes Act was a victory only for the working class. To most Liberals in the Cabinet and in Parliament it was not the legislation desired. Acceptance by the Conservatives in the Lords was a matter of simple expediency. While rejecting the Education Bill and the Plural Voting Bill, they accepted the Trade Disputes Bill—a measure they liked even less—for they did not care to alienate the entire working-class world. In this instance both parties bowed to the more extreme demands of social democracy.

But in parliamentary politics that which overshadowed all else at the end of 1906 was the Lords' rejection of the Education Bill. The Government, as the Opposition frequently suggested, might have appealed to the country. But apparently the Cabinet felt uncertain of the outcome on this issue alone; and the party strategy, as it developed, was to postpone a general election until other grievances against the Lords accumulated—a policy which the Government called "filling up the cup" and which the Opposition called "ploughing the sands" (meaning a fruitless endeavor).

For Reform of the Lords

Yet the Liberals must take the initiative. In the speech from the throne which opened the 1907 session of Parliament, the Government announced a new legislative program, referred to "the unfortunate differences between the two Houses" which were impairing the parliamentary system, and added that "His Majesty's Ministers have this important subject under consideration with a view to a solution of the difficulty." This prompted a proposal in the Lords for reform of its membership—three-fourths to be "life peers" appointed by the Government. But the Liberal leader in the Lords, the very able Lord Crewe, said the Government would sponsor no change in the membership of the Lords until after its power had been determined. The vital matter was the relation of the Lords, no matter how constituted, to the Commons.

Campbell-Bannerman favored the simpler policy of maintaining the supremacy of the Commons, and proposed that the Lords have only a suspensive veto on Commons legislation. On June 24, 1907, a resolution was introduced into the Commons, "That, in order to give effect to the will of the people as expressed by their elected representatives, it is necessary that the power of the other House to alter or reject bills passed by this House should be so restricted by law as to secure that within the limits of a single Parliament the final decision of the Commons must prevail." The debate was memorable. Balfour charged that the Government was deliberately framing its measures in the hope of getting them defeated. The Conservative *Pall Mall Gazette* declared the purpose of the Government "is the reduction of the British Constitution to the autocracy of a single chamber." Lloyd George came up with his famous remark that the House of Lords was not the watchdog of the constitution; it was only "Mr. Balfour's poodle." Churchill referred to the Lords as "a one-sided, hereditary, unpurged, unrepresentative, irresponsible absentee." After the defeat of a Labor amendment calling for abolition of the House of Lords (it mustered 100 votes from Labor, the Irish and a few radicals), the original resolution was carried 432–147.

Save for Haldane's Army Bill, 1907 produced no important legislation. The Liberal Cabinet could not agree on education, and a new bill that was introduced into the Commons was shortly withdrawn. The proposed new Licensing Bill was not even introduced—this likewise was not a strong issue on which to force a showdown with the Lords. Of a series of land measures for England, Scotland, and Ireland, none were enacted in the form they left the Commons, two were rejected outright by the Lords, and two others were modified almost beyond recognition.

Asquith's Government and Social Reform

In April 1908, his health shattered, Campbell-Bannerman resigned (he died a few weeks later). He was succeeded by Asquith, now fifty-six and approaching the peak of his career; he was to be prime minister until 1916. His succession seemed inevitable, met no opposition, but also was greeted with no great enthusiasm. The explanation is in the quality of his leadership. His strengths were generally recognized: a keen mind, good judgment, even temper, loyalty to his associates—there was no resignation from his Cabinet because of conflict of opinion. And on the floor of the Commons he was impressive indeed. But as Lloyd George and many others repeatedly said, "He was a man of no initiative." Possibly this was because he had little if any political philosophy. He is often referred to as a "Whig," one to whom, in eighteenth-century terms, the chief object of politics was to get into office and stay there. His familiar answer to a difficult problem was: "Let's wait and see."

Though hardly a Radical, his Cabinet changes indicated no shift to the right. Most important were the promotions of Lloyd George to the Exchequer and Churchill to Cabinet rank as president of the Board of Trade. At this time these two were associated with "the radical opportunist wing of the Liberal Party." But just how radical and just how opportunist remained to be seen. Churchill contributed "The Untrodden Field in Politics" to the *Nation*, March 7, 1908, in which he laid out the social reforms to which Liberalism must give itself. He and Lloyd George were largely responsible for the sudden extension of "social legislation" in the early years of the Asquith administration. Under pressure from labor, legislation for the first time limited the hours of work for adult male workers in the coal mines on the general principle of an eight-hour day. In the budget proposals presented in 1908 by Asquith, the chief interest was in the provision for "old age pensions." This, however, was hardly a party matter; adoption sooner or later was certain; in the election of 1906 no candidate ventured to oppose the principle. The matter was now taken out of the ineffectual hands of John Burns (at the Local Government Board), and the Old Age Pensions Bill was sponsored by Lloyd George and speedily enacted. The House of Lords was not particularly enthusiastic but was outmaneuvered; it is doubtful that the Lords would have rejected the measure in any case. It provided for outright, noncontributory pensions (any contributory scheme, the Government argued, would have greatly delayed its operation). Every person (with a few exceptions) at age seventy was to receive a pension of five shillings per week unless his total income was over £21 per year. For incomes between £21 and £31 per year the pension was scaled down to one shilling per week. In a short time nearly one million persons were receiving this pension.

In another area, reform of the Poor Law, there was failure. In February 1909 the report of the royal commission appointed by Balfour in 1905 was published. A majority report was signed by fifteen members, most of them Conservatives; a minority report was signed by four, including Beatrice Webb—the report being written largely by her husband. Both reports advocated drastic change in Poor Law administration: abolition of the special Poor Law guardians, who had administered a grudging relief since 1834, and the concentration of authority in the county councils with administration in the hands of experts. Here again John Burns obstructed, and changes had to wait until 1929.

But the minority report went much further. It pointed out that since 1834 there had gradually developed various services (public education, public health regulations, workmen's compensation, unemployment legislation, and now old age pensions) which aimed not at alleviating poverty but at preventing it. It therefore proposed the complete abolition of the old Poor Law with its philosophy of punishing poverty, the abolition of "poor relief" as such, and the extension of welfare services which would provide to all a minimum standard of life regardless of earnings. Continuation of the old Poor Law, which aroused especial hostility in London, and failure of the Government to adopt the principles of the minority report began the breakup of the Lib-Lab alliance in Parliament.

Churchill's elevation to the Cabinet was a well-deserved promotion, for he had been the most active Liberal in the Commons outside of the Cabinet. Upon his appointment to the Board of Trade he is quoted as saying, "This cake has been given me too late. Lloyd George has pulled out all the plums." Nevertheless, in his brief tenure (he was advanced to the Home Office in 1910) Churchill made as distinguished a reputation as Lloyd George.

Both Poor Law reports had recommended the establishment of a system of labor exchanges as a means of dealing with unemployment. The Webbs, impressed with the work of young William H. Beveridge in demonstrating that unemployment was normally confined to the "casual worker," said to Churchill, "If you are going to deal with unemployment you must have the boy Beveridge." When John Burns showed his usual distaste for action, and demurred, Churchill made it the concern of the Board of Trade. The Labor Exchange Bill rapidly became law (September 20, 1909) and Beveridge became the first director of the exchanges which opened early in 1910. There was scarcely any objection to the idea; "almost as obvious a public institution as the Post Office," says Clapham. By 1914 the exchanges were annually filling over a million vacancies.

Churchill also acted in another direction. The problem of "sweated labor," particularly female labor at home, was arousing attention. But fixing of wages seemed a particularly shocking invasion of private rights; in 1908 a Select Committee on Home Work asked timidly whether wage boards in selected trades might not be attempted as an experiment. Herbert Gladstone at the Home Office was unwilling to assume responsibility, so Churchill sponsored an Act for the Establishment of Trade Boards for Certain Trades, which listed the tailoring, paper-box-making, chain-making, and lace industries as "sweated" industries for which trade boards might be established. The act was slowly implemented, with the first minimum rate schedules (for tailoring) coming only in 1912. But it established the revolutionary principle of fixing by law "a decent wage" in industries not protected by unions.

It is well to bear in mind that this legislation of 1908–9 (old age pensions, labor exchange boards, trade boards for sweated industries, the Children Act providing a system of juvenile courts) as well as the social legislation of 1906 was accepted by the Lords; in the long run this was of more significance than the rejection or modification of the more controversial proposals.

Education and Licensing

Nevertheless, in contemporary politics all else was overshadowed by the controversy of the Lords versus the Commons. The Liberal Party had not abandoned hope for its own Education Bill. In 1908 a serious effort was made to draft a compromise measure which would satisfy both Anglicans and Nonconformists. This endeavor failed, and again the Government dropped its measure. But it was now not so much the House of Lords as growing public indifference which defeated Nonconformist efforts to modify the statute of 1902. Religious instruction in the schools was no longer a vital issue with the electorate as a whole. Had it been otherwise, the Government would have persisted and would have forced a showdown with the Lords.

This does not mean that secular education made no progress. In 1902 education had become a public function. It so remained. The standards of elementary education steadily improved. Secondary education became increasingly democratic, for the Board of Education by various regulations began to close the gap between elementary education for all and secondary education only for those going into professions. Higher education expanded in the great municipal universities, with perhaps the most important development in these years coming in the reorganization of the University of London—comprising three university colleges, ten medical schools, six theological schools, the London School of Economics, and others.

Experiments in higher education for the working class had begun. In 1899 Ruskin Hall (later Ruskin College) for a working-class constituency was opened at Oxford. Though at first limited to forty or fifty resident students, correspondence work soon enrolled some six thousand others. In 1903 the Workers' Educational Association was established, with lectures and tutorial classes in industrial centers. Financed in various ways—by the Board of Education, local authorities, trade unions—by 1914 it had 179 branches and 11,430 members studying for the most part social problems, economics, and economic history.

Such developments were more important for education than the bickerings in Parliament. But Nonconformists still had their principles and frequently linked their ideas on education with their views on public houses. There was a good deal of talk about "the alliance of beer and the Bible," and Dr. Clifford had a way of referring to "the friends of the Drink Trade and advocates of state control of churches." In 1908 the Liberal *Daily Chronicle* printed a "Remarkable Black List" consisting of the names of sixty-two peers who were stockholders or trustees in brewing companies. But temperance was no more promising an issue than education on which to go to the country. So the Government proceeded slowly. By 1908 a measure on licensing had been carefully prepared and passed through the Commons. Its object was the gradual reduction in the number of public houses by one-third; for a period of fourteen years compensation was to be given for licenses withdrawn. Some Nonconformists did not like the fourteen-year period, and many Conservatives spoke of the proposal as confiscatory and contrary to the public interest. More moderate elements were anxious for a reasonable compromise. Edward VII urged Lansdowne, Conservative leader in the Lords, to accept the measure, and the bishops in the Lords generally favored acceptance. But the bulk of the Conservative peers, perhaps smarting under their tactical defeat over old age pensions, met at Lansdowne House in Berkeley Square and decided in the face of a small but distinguished minority to reject the bill. The vote in the Lords on November 27 was 272–96—at least "a first class funeral," remarked a Liberal peer, noting the extraordinarily large attendance.

The Lords' Last Stand and Surrender

In 1909, however, the Liberals seized the initiative through the Lloyd George budget. It has been often suggested that the

Liberals deliberately framed this budget to challenge the Lords and precipitate a crisis. Obviously Lloyd George and the Cabinet sought to
recapture parliamentary initiative for the Government; but the budget
was no trivial maneuver, for it was revolutionary in its practical purposes. The cournty was notified well in advance that it would have new
and controversial features. Lloyd George was confronted with the task of
finding £16,000,000 in new revenue for a proposed budget of
£164,000,000 in order to finance dreadnaughts for the expanding Navy
and to cover the old age pension program. Its unusual features were
these: (1) sharp increases in death duties (inheritance taxes); for example,
estates of £1,000,000 and over were to be taxed at about 25 percent; (2)
increases in income tax schedules, which continued the distinction between earned and unearned income first made in 1907; on incomes of
£5,000 or more there was to be an additional super-tax, an innovation;
(3) land taxes, of which the most significant was a 20 percent tax on the
unearned increment in value when land changed hands; (4) higher levies
on tobacco and spirits.

The People's Budget

The budget was introduced by Lloyd George on April
29, 1909, in a four-and-one-half-hour presentation. There was much
emphasis upon badly needed social legislation; it was a budget "for
raising money to wage implacable warfare against poverty and squalid-
ness." How would Liberals and Unionists respond—this one might anticipate, was the major question. After a few days of quiet came the
storm. The Liberal press acclaimed it as "the People's Budget;" the Conservative press condemned it as "revolutionary and socialist." The *Pall
Mall Gazette* referred to it as "a dead weight upon the limbs of industry
and an insuperable obstacle to its health and expression." Leading London financial houses petitioned the prime minister: "The increase of the
death duties . . . and of the income tax, coupled with the super-tax,
would injure commerce and industry." The Unionists, led by Walter
Long, organized a Budget Protest League. More important, many Liberals, in the well-to-do business class, were antagonized.

A Budget League carried the issue to the country, with Churchill as the
most active of its advocates. Lloyd George spoke less often in public (he
was constantly on the floor of the Commons), but in July in his famous
Limehouse speech to an audience of four thousand of East London's poor
he lashed out against profiteering landlords, waxing rich on unearned
increment in land values. No one else had his power with a large audience. In the Commons the budget had a tumultuous reception. From

June until November it was debated almost continuously, throwing into complete confusion other legislative proposals for the year. Session after session went on long past midnight, often lasting until the breakfast hour the next day. The attention of the Commons was thus occupied for seventy-three parliamentary days and there were 554 roll calls. On a strict party vote (the Irish abstaining, for they were opposed to the increase in tobacco and alcohol taxes) the measure passed the Commons on November 4 by 379–149.

Meanwhile, there was every indication that the Lords would reject it. The problem then developed: did the Lords, in spite of precedent to the contrary, have the constitutional right to reject a financial measure adopted by the Commons? Liberal leaders (particularly Lloyd George and Churchill) were now anxious for a showdown with the Lords and were quite prepared for rejection; the budget presented strong grounds for the assertion of the supremacy of the Commons. Churchill declared at Leicester early in September, "If the Lords win, they will have asserted their right not merely to reject legislation of the House of Commons, but to control the finance of the country," and in this event "we will smash to pieces their veto." Asquith at Birmingham (September 17) declared, "Rejection by the House of Lords is . . . out of the question . . . . Is this issue going to be raised? . . . That way Revolution lies." And Lloyd George (in October) at Newcastle said, "The Lords may decree a revolution which the people will direct."

The Conservatives were somewhat divided. Moderates warned against rejection as the course which in the end would prove the most disastrous for the House of Lords. There were extremists like Lord Milner with his remark, reject the budget and "damn the consequences." Tariff reform advocates favored rejection, for they felt that such budgets would destroy their contention that social reform could be financed only with the additional revenue which a protective tariff would provide. In the end Lansdowne rallied opposition in the Lords around his amendment, "that this House is not justified in giving its assent to the Bill until it has been submitted to the judgment of the country." On this basis, after a brief debate before packed galleries, the Lords on November 30 rejected the budget 350–75. Rarely had so many peers assembled at one time. The "backwoodsmen," as Lloyd George dubbed the Conservative backbenchers, had turned up to do their duty.

Two days later (December 2) the Government carried in the Commons, 349–134, a resolution, "that the action of the House of Lords in refusing to pass into law the financial provision of the year is a breach of the Constitution and a usurpation of the rights of the Commons." It sounded like the seventeenth century.

Shifts of Power and Issues

The Lords had not only rejected a budget, but they had also decreed a general election. This was held in January 1910. The constitutional issue—the proper sphere of the Lords—was rather too theoretical for the average voter. He was confronted with the issue of the budget versus a protective tariff. The budget was the more popular and the Government emerged with a slender victory: Liberals 274, Conservatives 273, Irish Nationalists 82, Labor 40. Thus the major parties returned to a state of equilibrium after the extraordinary imbalance of 1906. The Liberals were unhappy because they had lost their majority in the English constituencies and were now dependent upon the Irish and Labor; the Conservatives had hoped for a majority of perhaps a hundred; Labor had just held its own. Only the Irish were happy, for they now held the balance of power.

The election settled the question of the budget; in due course it was accepted by the Lords. But the issue had shifted. With a smaller majority the Asquith Government was now prepared (1) to destroy the Lords' veto and (2) to grant Irish home rule. (The two were inseparable, for the Irish in 1910 would support the budget, as reintroduced, only if they were assured that the bar of the Lords to home rule would be removed.) This took time. The hitch was over the role of the Crown. To curb the House of Lords, to force upon it drastic limitations of its legislative power, would require royal assurance that, if necessary, a sufficient number of new peers (perhaps three hundred, perhaps even four hundred) would be created to enable the Liberals to carry the measure through the Lords. Edward VII did not approve of coercing the Lords. He was disturbed and perplexed and anxious for a harmonious solution. In December he indicated that he would give guarantees for the creation of new peers only after a second general election on the specific issue of the Lords' legislative veto.

In March 1910 Asquith introduced into the Commons resolutions as the basis of an act of Parliament. The essentials were these: (1) financial measures—so defined by the speaker of the Commons—were to become law within one month after being sent from the Commons to the Lords; (2) other measures were to become law without the consent of the Lords, if passed by the Commons in three successive sessions, in effect limiting the Lords' veto to approximately two years; (3) the legal limit of the Parliament was to be reduced from seven years to five years. Asquith satisfied criticism within the Cabinet by adding a preamble which proposed, after the limitation of the powers of the Lords, to reconstitute its membership on a popular instead of a hereditary basis. In April these resolutions were adopted by the Commons with support of the Irish

Nationalists, for now Asquith had assured them that the issue with the Lords would be forced to a conclusion.

Succession of George V and Truce

At this point, on May 6, after a brief illness Edward VII died. It is not always easy to get at the truth about British sovereigns. Something of a legend promptly grew up around King Edward: he was made out to be a great liberal monarch, the friend of the people, the champion of peace, the statesman who changed the destiny of Britain. But, in fact, his actual influence on the course of events was slight. He was ill-prepared for a role of any great responsibility and he was lazy. He did take an interest in foreign policy and in defense but sought no important role. Domestic problems bored him, and so it was of no great moment that he disliked Campbell-Bannerman, was opposed to reform legislation and against women's suffrage. He had no conception of the dynamics of the twentieth century. Yet, it may be added, that as a constitutional monarch he was a success. He was not a troublemaker. He was rather skillful with people and he was without pretense and hypocrisy; he liked pomp and ceremony but did not take himself too seriously (he had a way of referring to "my fellow subjects").

In personal qualities his successor, George V, was to prove much the opposite. Conventional in outlook, he disliked high society and disapproved of clever people. He was a celebrated philatelist and was proud of his collection. He had no special intelligence, but was modest, possessed of good judgment and a high sense of duty. He and Queen Mary went through the coronation ceremony "with a shade too much of gravity" to suit some, but this was a trait which soon endeared them to their people. For the first time in modern history both king and queen spoke English without a heavy foreign accent. In an age critical of the trappings of royalty, yet which regarded the royal family as the one stable element in a changing world, George V was to prove an ideal sovereign for twentieth-century Britain. He and the queen were less successful as parents, but that is another story.

For a time party bitterness subsided. The party leaders decided upon a political truce and sought to resolve the problem of the Lords in a constitutional conference. From June until November four Liberals and four Conservatives deliberated in secret, but to no avail. Very likely the issue of home rule doomed the conference to failure from the start. Lloyd George, already the opportunist, made a spectacular proposal: a coalition cabinet with a nonpartisan program on all outstanding questions. The idea had its attraction, but produced pricks of conscience as well. One of the conferees, Austen Chamberlain, wrote: "What a world we live in, and how the public would stare if they could look into our minds and our letter-bags." And Balfour is reported as saying, "I cannot become another Robert Peel in my party"—a reference to Peel's abandonment of the principle on which he had come to power. In any case mutual distrust between the parties killed the proposal.

The Parliament Act of 1911

In the fall of 1910 the constitutional issue was again insistent. The role of George V is fully revealed in the magnificent life written by Sir Harold Nicolson, who had access to the king's personal and public papers. The king was much embarrassed; he was reluctant to give guarantees for the creation of new peers, but without them Asquith would have resigned. If Balfour had formed a Government, he could hardly have maintained it and an election would have followed in any case. And so on November 16 King George gave Asquith the necessary assurances.

In the second election of 1910, in December, the campaign was apathetic, the controversy was stale, and the poll fell off sharply from that of the previous January. The results were essentially the same: Liberals 272, Conservatives 271, Irish Nationalists 84, Labor 42. The Conservative popular vote was slightly more than the Liberal. But the Liberal Government was the first since 1832 to survive three elections in succession and politically was in a strong position. So far as the public was concerned the issue was resolved.

But it took time to close the matter. In February 1911 the Parliament Bill, essentially in the form of the resolutions of 1910, was introduced into the Commons. Asquith dominated the debate and firmly pushed the bill past nine hundred amendments. On May 15 Churchill in the final speech for the government declared, "The powers retained by the House of Lords ... will be formidable and even menacing.... I stand here not merely astonished at our own moderation, but upon occasion I am almost aghast." The bill passed with a majority of 121.

Meantime, the peers were debating their own measures—one providing for popular referendum on matters in dispute between the two houses, another for an elaborate reform in membership—either of which would have more drastically changed constitutional practice than the Commons measure. Such diversionary tactics came sharply to an end when Lord Morley stated that the Government bill would stand no matter what the composition of the Lords. The Lords subjected it to drastic amendments unacceptable to the Government. Asquith now made formal request of the king for the guarantees promised the previous November.

The guarantees were duly given; but as a concession to the king, the House of Lords was to have one more opportunity to pass on the original bill. Asquith had on hand a list of some two hundred fifty names as recommendations for new peerages. When he appeared in the Commons on July 24, the first session after public announcement of the royal guarantees, he was not permitted to speak. For some thirty or forty minutes he remained on his feet in the face of Opposition cries of "Sit down!" "Divide!" "Traitor!" "Let Redmond speak!" "American dollars!" "Leave out the King; who killed him?"

Such was the tension and the bitterness of the closing days of this controversy. The final stage was confined to the Conservative ranks in the House of Lords. Would they face the inevitable and accept the Parliament Bill? Or would they force the creation of new Liberal peers? Lord Lansdowne advised accepting defeat. But there came to life a "No Surrender Movement" of the "die-hards" or the "ditchers" (both from the phrase "dying in the last ditch") led by the former lord chancellor, Lord Halsbury, now eighty-seven years of age. Another group, called the "hedgers," proposed to abstain from voting and thus permit the measure to pass. But as the "No Surrender Movement" developed strength, it became evident that a goodly number of the "hedgers" must actually vote for the measure or it would fail. The final debate was held August 9–10 in the hottest weather in seventy years—on August 9 a reading of 100° was recorded at Greenwich. Lord Morley announced unequivocally that if the measure were defeated a sufficient number of new peers would be at once created to insure its acceptance. But until the very end, while the members were returning from the division lobbies, the issue was in doubt. The bill passed, 131–114, but only because it had the support of 13 out of 15 bishops and of 37 Conservative peers.

On August 10 George V recorded in his diary: "So the Halsburyites were thank God beaten. It is indeed a great relief to me and I am spared any further humiliation by a creation of peers."

The Parliament Act did not, in fact, constitute a revolution. The first clause, concerning the limitation of the Lords' veto over money bills to one month, has never been invoked. It has been generally recognized that the peers in refusing the 1909 budget had acted unwisely. But also there have been restrictive rulings of the speaker as to what constitutes money bills; curiously enough, the budget of 1909 itself, under the definition of money bills as hereafter applied, would have been refused certification. The second clause, limiting the Lords' veto on other legislation to two years, has been invoked only three times: in bills for the disestablishment of the Anglican Church in Wales and for Irish home rule, both during 1912–14, and in 1947–49 in the act in effect limiting the Lords' veto to a single year. The functions of the Lords have remained much as before. Nevertheless, in constitutional practice the act of 1911 is the most important legislative change since 1832. The relationship between Lords and Commons was regulated by statute. Thereafter it would be impossible for the Lords to challenge the supremacy of the Commons. This principle as constitutional law was a corollary to the democratization of the suffrage for the election of the Commons.

In accordance with the preamble to the Parliament Act of 1911, Asquith set up a Cabinet committee to consider proposals for reform of the Lords' membership. Nothing came of it. The Liberal Party's grievance against the Lords was that it was using its power in a partisan fashion. To reform its membership would merely provide argument for reestablishing its power—and this would mean a new constitution, which the major parties have generally shied away from. Not for over half a century was there a serious effort at reform.

1910–14 "Domestic Anarchy"

The designation of 1910–14 as years of "domestic anarchy" is more than a rhetorical flourish. The last ditch stand of the 114 "die-hards" in the House of Lords on August 10, 1911, is characteristic. The revolt of the Lords very nearly brought the English constitution to a standstill. The temper of politics does change. The Parliament Act of 1911 made inevitable a third home rule bill, and in its wake would come the threat of mutiny and civil war in Ireland. The first industrial strikes inspired by workmen themselves and unauthorized by trade union leadership came in 1910; ahead were syndicalism and the possibility of direct action through a general strike. On July 1, 1911, the German gunboat *The Panther* put in at Agadir to test the *Entente Cordiale*. From November 18, 1910 ("Black Friday"), dates the militancy in the suffragette story. We may even venture into the arts and remind ourselves of Virginia Woolf's exclamation, ' On or about December 1910 human character changed," concerning the post-impressionistic exhibition in London. And romanticism in poetry was finally left behind in the appearance of *Georgian Poetry 1911–12* in 1912. One may choose his own time and his own context, but in these years one moves suddenly into a quite different England.

Although, as one tries to relive English experience after 1910, he is overwhelmed by a sense of rushing downhill, with complete loss of control, toward some unknown disaster. This is, of course, partly induced by a sense of impending fate as one knowing the outcome retraces the immediate background of World War I. But it is not entirely an interpretation imposed after the event. Contemporaries were aware that their world was getting out of hand. Very many people began to put their own "principles" first, with a total disregard for the principles of others. It was a period to which remarks about the phlegmatic Englishman, his sense of fair play, his genius for compromise, and the "stability" of his institutions do not apply. It was a very un-English period.

Party Politics

The crisis over the Lords left the Conservatives bitterly divided—the central issue was Balfour, who had favored allowing the Parliament Bill to pass the Lords without opposition. A "Balfour Must Go" movement led to his resignation on November 8, 1911. The next day, Asquith, at the Lord Mayor's banquet at the Guildhall in the City, referred to Balfour "as the most distinguished member of the greatest deliberative assembly in the world." But Balfour's "finest hour" was ahead; as an elder statesman he was to render outstanding service under divers governments. His successor in 1911 was not, as might have been expected, either Austen Chamberlain or Walter Long (neither could gain sufficient party support), but a compromise selection, Andrew Bonar Law, and surprising indeed, since he had not held Cabinet office and at the outset of the selection process could not have been certain of more than 40 votes out of the 280 in the Parliamentary Conservative Party. By nature he was diffident and somber, rather narrow in point of view, deadly in earnest, relentless in opposition. His abilities as a party leader remained to be tested.

As for the Liberals, after their virtual destruction of the Lords' legislative veto, one might expect to find them opening the gates to further reform. As it happened, the Parliament Act of 1911 concluded the radical phase of the Liberal administration and also constituted the final stage in the unnatural Lib-Lab alliance. The coalition of interests which had made possible the decisive Liberal victory in 1906 was breaking up. By 1910 the Liberals had forfeited the confidence of middle-class Nonconformists. By 1911 they were losing the confidence of labor. They would soon be threatened with the loss of confidence of the Irish. At most any time in 1913 the Government would probably not have survived a general election. But we need not reach the conclusion, argued by some historians, that as early as 1910 or 1911 the Liberal Party confronted an inevitable decline and fall with a corresponding rise in the fortunes of Labor. One has only to be reminded that at this time the Labor Party was itself in desperate straits. And there are other historians who suggest that in these prewar years Asquith and Lloyd George were incompatible, foreshadowing the crisis in leadership in the party during the war. But of this there is little evidence.

The National Insurance Act

In 1911 there was one more piece of social legislation, and a very important one: the National Insurance Act. The general plan had been outlined by the Government in 1909. This act provided for insurance against sickness and disability for workers between the ages of sixteen and seventy, under formal contract of service, whose annual incomes were £160 or less, and for nearly all manual workers regardless of income. It was a contributory scheme (the chief variation from German practice which served as something of a model), with the employer to contribute threepence per week, the employee fourpence (female, threepence), and the government twopence. The most important benefits were ten shillings a week for sickness and five shillings a week for disability. Under this act, fourteen million were promptly insured, constituting practically the entire wage-earning class. It was to be administered by "approved societies" under state supervision. The act also provided unemployment insurance, but limited this to industries in which employment was considered most uncertain, particularly engineering and building trades. In its initial form, unemployment insurance applied to somewhat more than two million workers; it was a contributory scheme and provided variable benefits (six or seven shillings a week) for fifteen weeks in the year and was to operate through the labor exchanges. In introducing the measure (May 1911) Lloyd George said it was no complete remedy for social evils but would "relieve untold misery in myriads of homes."

The measure attracted far more public attention than the Parliament Bill, and stirred up protest in a variety of areas. The Medical Association called the "panel system" of doctors an unwarranted interference with a private profession. "Society" organized a crusade against "the licking of the stamp" (the law included household servants, and contributions of master and servant were registered in stamps affixed to a card). The more militant Labor M.P.s and the Fabian leadership attacked the contributory feature and argued that it would work against the lowest-paid individuals. To them the measure appeared merely an extension of "poor relief," and they proposed instead the principle in the minority report of the Poor Law Commission—that the State should assume full responsibility, in Beatrice Webb's words, for "a minimum standard of life" regardless of earnings. In meeting this criticism and in balancing the vested interests, Lloyd George, pushing the bill through the legislative procedure, was at this political best.

Lib-Lab Split

The Insurance Act of 1911 marks a fairly distinct break in Lib-Lab collaboration. The Labor Party had not made much independent progress since 1906. By-elections reflected little advance. Within the party, trade union objectives and socialist doctrine could not be reconciled. And the party suffered a major setback in the Osborne judgment in the House of Lords in 1909, which held that compulsory trade union dues could not be used for political purposes: election campaigns, political party expenses, payment of salaries to members of Parliament. Since 1867 trade unions had been using their official funds for just such purposes. This decision, in one sense, strengthened the party—the Miners Federation affiliated with Labor soon after. In the parliamentary elections of 1910 Labor just about held its own, thanks to support from the miners and continuation of general electoral cooperation with the Liberals. The effects of the Osborne judgment were partly offset by the provision by statute in 1911 for payment of £400 a year salary to members of Parliament. Outside the ranks of labor there had been no great enthusiasm for payment of members. The Osborne judgment itself was not modified by legislation until 1913, and then in no manner satisfactory to the unions. In sundry ways the Liberal government now seemed much less disposed than in 1906 to give Labor what it wanted.

There were other factors in the growing estrangement of Labor from Liberal politics: dissatisfaction with the policy of the Government toward women's suffrage; restlessness with the unaggressive leadership of MacDonald in the Parliamentary Labor Party; growing agitation for a truly independent labor party with a socialist program (for example, the socialist *Herald* was founded in 1912 and the weekly *New Statesman* in 1913).

Trade Unions: Triple Alliance

The incidence of industrial strikes in 1910–12 seemed to contemporaries unusually heavy; many were sporadic and spontaneous and developed without authorization from trade union officials. In 1910 a number of small strikes were fought on limited issues. Then 120,000 cotton workers struck in Lancashire; 30,000 miners walked out in Wales and troops were called in. A fourteen-week strike of boilermakers was directed as much against the union as against the employers. In 1911 there were comprehensive strikes of seamen and firemen, and of dock workers in London and Liverpool. Most important was a general railway strike; in two days it was over, but the public became aware for the first time of how paralyzing to the life of the nation such a strike could be. The climax came in March 1912 with a five-week strike of the Miners' Federation, involving 850,000 miners and affecting 1,250,000 workers in other industries. An act of Parliament only partially satisfied the miners' demand for a minimum wage. This was a nationwide strike; so was the transport workers' walkout of the same year.

Behind this unprecedented "epidemic" of strikes was the vague dissatisfaction of workers—particularly unskilled workers conscious of the decline in real wages—with political processes. Patience and orderly conduct seemed to be getting them nowhere. During the years 1910–13, some 1,500,000 were added to trade union rolls. Furthermore, into labor thinking now came the ideas of syndicalism, with emphasis upon economic organization as the core of society and the doctrine that labor should control political action through direct economic action—the sympathetic strike and the general strike. Times improved in 1913–14; strike activity tapered off. But the most militant of the unions—the miners, the railway men, and the transport workers—were quite dissatisfied with the outcome of their recent strikes. Late in 1913, upon the suggestion of Robert Smillie, the miners' leader, the three unions agreed to act together in what came to be called the Triple Alliance. They represented industries with a body of two million workers, two-thirds of whom were unionized. In June 1914 they created a Common Council. Labor agreements with employers would be synchronized; new demands would be made simultaneously. It has been suggested that the purpose was not a general strike but merely three separate strikes at the same time. The distinction is slight. It was well understood what stoppage of all transport would do to food distribution and what the cessation of the coal supply would do to industry. In spirit the Triple Alliance was syndicalist.

Precisely how far the Triple Alliance was prepared to go was unclear. It was not the child of the Trades Union Congress but the product of restlessness in member unions and in labor ranks generally, regarded as merely a means for improving bargaining power and not as an instrument for coercing the nation. Nevertheless, by the summer of 1914 the Scottish coal operators were announcing a cut in wages, the railway men were preparing new demands, and transport workers were inflamed by the failure of a strike in Ireland. Nationwide walkouts in these industries were imminent. If they acted in concert, the effect would approach that of a general strike. Lloyd George and Lord Morley among politicians and Frank Hodges and Ben Tillett among labor leaders expected another such outbreak of industrial unrest in the autumn of 1914.

The Suffragettes

The phrase "direct action" is also applicable to the extremes to which the "suffragettes" resorted in these years. In the climax of the feminine revolt we find similar tendencies to violence and irresponsible disregard for the law. The women's movement had become a serious national problem.

There had been in recent years a rapid development of women's role—in education, in the professions, in civil rights, and in local politics. But in national politics nothing had been accomplished. In the main concern, women's suffrage, no Government, Liberal or Conservative, would make the matter a party issue—each party was itself divided on the merits of the question. Bills for women's suffrage introduced into Parliament died for lack of Cabinet support.

From before 1900 the "suffragists" had worked patiently and calmly in the cause of women's suffrage. The atmosphere changed abruptly with the appearance in 1903 of the W.S.P.U. (Women's Social and Political Union), organized by Mrs. Emmeline Pankhurst. She and her followers, soon called "suffragettes," developed their own tactics: "Votes for Women" demonstrations in public places and at mass meetings in Hyde Park attracting crowds by the hundreds of thousands, public meetings, deputations to Downing Street, interruptions in the House of Commons—anything to attract attention and to create such a scandal that demands would be granted. After 1908 they resorted increasingly to disorder and violence: wholesale window breaking of Government offices in Whitehall and of business offices nearby; personal and physical attacks upon Government leaders. Suffragettes clamoring for attention chained themselves to the grille of the railing in the public gallery of the Commons. Trials and imprisonment for incitement to riot led to hunger strikes in prison and these to forcible feeding. During 1911–14 the suffragettes got almost completely out of control. Arson was resorted to, with fires set in railway carriages, restaurants, public buildings, even in churches. In April 1913 estimated value of property damage was £36,475 and in June £54,000. A bomb partially wrecked a house being built for Lloyd George. Pictures were slashed in the National Gallery, there was similar destruction in the British Museum, and anything else "a woman could think of." Perhaps the ultimate in suffragette activity was reached in the action of Emily Wilding Davison, who darted out in the path of the king's horse on Derby Day 1913 as the horses were sweeping around Tattenham Corner on Epsom Downs. Miss Davison died a few days later; more than 2,000 suffragettes marched in procession as the body was transferred from Victoria Station to St. George's Church in Bloomsbury and thence to King's Cross Station.

In Parliament, Conciliation Bills providing a degree of suffrage failed 1910–12, though their mere introduction testified to some results from militancy. In 1913 larger success seemed likely when Asquith announced that a non-party vote would be permitted on a women's suffrage amendment to the Franchise Reform Bill. But the speaker ruled such amendments out of order and the Government dropped the entire proposal. Throughout the protracted controversy it was evident that the militancy of the suffragettes further alienated those opposed to or uncertain about their cause and restricted the efforts of those favorably disposed. More intelligent and more responsible methods of propaganda might well have brought a measure of women's suffrage before 1914. As it was legislation did not come until 1918.

The Revolt of Ireland

In April 1912 the Liberal Government sought to make good a long-standing commitment—the third Home Rule Bill was introduced into the Commons. In the light of subsequent developments this bill seems a mere palliative. It incorporated the "federal idea:" Ireland through her own Parliament was to be autonomous in Irish affairs save for certain federal matters (the crown, foreign affairs and defense, post office, old age pensions, and national insurance) which were reserved for the British Parliament. John Redmond, the Irish Nationalist leader, was also, strangely enough, pro-English and one who would abide by parliamentary decisions at Westminster. It was hoped that he would prove to be an "Irish Botha" and, like the great Boer general, succeed in reconciling his land to Great Britain.

But the story of these years is quite otherwise; around this bill accumulated all the party bitterness engendered since the turn of the century. For one thing, the Liberals after the elections of 1910 might well have been more conciliatory—after all, they did not enjoy a majority from England proper. On the other hand, the Conservatives, smarting under defeat over the Lords issue, permitted their policy to be directed by the Irish wing. But the crucial factor was a divided Ireland: Ulster offered to the parliamentary Opposition the opportunity for almost complete intransigence. The unique history of Ulster by the twentieth century had produced a highly industrialized, overwhelmingly Protestant area, in contrast to rural and Catholic southern Ireland. And particularly since the days of Gladstone, the Ulster Orangemen had been growing in self-consciousness and in hatred of the Irish Catholics. By 1910 Ulster was solidly Unionist; home rule, it was feared, would destroy their way of life, ruin their industry, and impose a crushing burden of taxation.

After some fifteen years of quiescence Irish Home Rule became again the leading issue in British politics. The Ulstermen, led by the Unionist M.P., Sir Edward Carson, more combative than Redmond, no Ulsterman himself but an Irish Protestant from Dublin who had been solicitor general in the Salisbury-Balfour Government, proposed that in the event of home rule, a separate government should be established in Belfast for

Ulster, and this, if necessary, in defiance of anything the British Parliament might decree. On September 23, 1911, Carson shouted to a crowd of 50,000 near Belfast: "I now enter into a compact with you . . . and with the help of God you and I joined together . . . will yet defeat the most nefarious conspiracy that has ever been hatched against a free people." Many Liberal politicians thought this was mere bluff. But now to Carson's leadership the Conservative Party leader, Bonar Law, Canadian Presbyterian by birth and now a Scots-Ulsterman by sympathy, promptly added his support. A Volunteer Army for Ulster was soon in the process of formation; and in April 1912 both Carson and Bonar Law, with some seventy other M.P.s, attended a giant demonstration in a Belfast suburb with 100,000 "volunteers" in review. By September a "covenant" was in circulation, pledging signers to use "all means which may be found necessary to defeat the present conspiracy of a Home Rule Parliament for Ireland . . . and to refuse to recognize its authority." In a dramatic ceremony at City Hall, Belfast, Carson signed first, and half a million others followed—some in blood.

But Southern Ireland had also come alive. The Gaelic League, the Abbey Theatre, a syndicalist labor movement and Sinn Fein—these all had overtones implying that nothing but a united Ireland would suffice and perhaps suggesting revolutionary aims as well. An Irish Nationalist Volunteer Army was formally organized in 1913 to counter the Ulster Volunteers.

Thus, while the third Home Rule Bill was slowly making its first journey through the Commons, the issue was already drawn between Ulster and the rest of Ireland, and in Britain between the Government and the Opposition. The story in detail (1912–14) is tortuous, yet its general spirit may be conveyed briefly and accurately. At Belfast in July 1912 F. E. Smith, a young Conservative M.P. rising to prominence, declared that issues of conscience now set aside the normal bars against resistance to law. About the same time Bonar Law in a gigantic rally at Blenheim Palace was saying: "I can imagine no length of resistance to which Ulster can go in which I should not be prepared to support them, and in which, in my belief, they would not be supported by the overwhelming majority of the British people." Bonar Law informed one of the king's private secretaries that unless the Government submitted the Home Rule Bill to popular judgment in a general election, the alternative might be civil war. By such irresponsible talk constitutional processes seemed to be challenged. Carson was either fanatical or playing a dangerous game; Bonar Law was the victim of his own limitations of mind. As for Smith, we can borrow G. P. Gooch's phrase: "his authority was never equal to his fame."

But such intransigence in Conservative leadership was matched by the weakness of Asquith and the Cabinet. The prime minister was, in fact, at his worst—his failure to act was not so much the exercise of calculated caution and patience as it was the absence of any will to act. In 1912 Asquith seriously considered a general election to secure endorsement of home rule, but then the Marconi Scandal broke—Cabinet ministers were found speculating in the shares of a company with which the Government had contracts—unwise though hardly dishonest conduct. The Government lost face and Asquith would not risk a poll.

In March 1914 the home rule measure, twice passed by the Commons and twice rejected by the Lords, was introduced a third time. The central issue shifted to the Army and a matter of discipline. The bulk of the military was stoutly Unionist. Henry Wilson, the director of military operations in the War Office, now became, in effect, as his own diaries reveal, a Unionist agent advising the Ulster Volunteers. Many of the military began to echo the language of Conservative Party leaders that it would be unconstitutional to use the British Army in Ireland and, in the incident often called "Mutiny at the Curragh," declared they would not obey any orders to coerce Ulster. When the war secretary (J. E. B. Seely), the chief of the Imperial General Staff (Sir John French), and the adjutant-general (Sir Spencer Ewart) were found to be equivocating on this issue and circulating suggestions that the Government really had no intention of employing the Army to coerce Ulster, they were compelled by the circumstances to resign. The Times (March 25) ran a leader, "The Plot that Failed."

King George, who felt keenly his responsibility but also appreciated the delicacy of his constitutional position, finally succeeded in bringing party leaders together in conference at Buckingham Palace, July 21. "Today the cry of Civil War is on the lips of the most responsible and sober-minded of my people," he said, and pleaded for a settlement "in a spirit of generous compromise." But an impasse was soon reached on the boundaries of Ulster—especially the status of Fermanagh and Tyrone—and failure was reported to the Commons July 24. That day in the Cabinet, after lengthy consideration of the Irish crisis, Sir Edward Grey read a document just brought to him from the Foreign Office. It was the Austrian ultimatum to Serbia. Winston Churchill, in a celebrated passage in The World Crisis, records: "As the reading proceeded it seemed absolutely impossible that any State in the world could accept it. . . . The parishes of Fermanagh and Tyrone faded back into the mists and squalls of Ireland, and a strange light began immediately, but by perceptible gradations, to fall and grow upon the map of Europe."

Several days later the scheduled consideration of amendments to the Home Rule Bill was postponed—the European crisis took precedence. In September the original measure was passed the third time by the Commons. On approval of the king it became law, but its operation was suspended until the end of the war. It is the view of many historians that only the outbreak of World War I prevented civil war in Ulster in 1914. But with the threat from without, "domestic anarchy" became domestic unity.

On the Eve of War

No series of diplomatic crises foreshadowed war in 1914 as would be the case twenty-five years later in 1939. Indeed, in public thinking, a general conflict involving Britain seemed less likely in 1913 or 1914 than at most any other time since 1906. Respected voices such as that of Norman Angell in his bestseller *The Great Illusion* (1910) discounted the possibility of a European war. Intelligent readers of the press must have noted with reassurance that the issues of the Balkan Wars in 1912–13 had been settled not through a confrontation of alliance systems but through the concert of Europe. Subsequent problems in the Balkans seemed remote. Anglo-German naval rivalry had, of course, brought tension from time to time, but by 1913 Britain had abandoned the two-power standard and the situation seemed stabilized. Even the Moroccan crisis of July 1911—the Germans sent the gunboat, *The Panther,* to Agadir on the Atlantic coast to question French predominance in Morocco and perhaps to test the Anglo-French *Entente*— failed to alert the English people. Lloyd George's strong Mansion House speech, in which he made the incident a matter of "national honor," attracted little attention.

The key to Grey's policy in Europe and, thus, to Britain's role in 1914 is found in the *Entente* with France. Grey stopped short of a formal military alliance, sought by French diplomats, but after Agadir he and Asquith did encourage closer collaboration of British and French military and naval forces. In this they had the active support of the new first lord of the Admiralty, Winston Churchill, who only shortly before had been a strong critic of the government's big navy policy. Grey, it should be added, did seek earnestly to reduce tension between England and Germany, and, in fact, proposed a formal accord. Haldane, war secretary, was dispatched to Berlin in February 1912 to negotiate a naval agreement. But all such efforts were checked by the German insistence upon a nonaggression pact, or similar pledge of neutrality in the event of a European war. And this Britain would not give. Instead, ties with France were strengthened with a commitment to consult in case of crisis. On November 22, 1912, Grey sent to Cambon, still the French ambassador in London, the British version of this new phase:

From time to time in recent years the French and British naval and military experts have consulted together. It has always been understood that such consultation does not restrict the freedom of either Government to decide at any time whether or not to assist the other by armed force. . . . The disposition, for instance, of the French and British fleets respectively at the present moment is not based upon an engagement to cooperate in war.

You have, however, pointed out that, if either Government had grave reason to expect an unprovoked attack by a third power, it might become essential to know whether it could in that event depend upon the armed assistance of the other.

I agree that, if either Government had grave reason to expect an unprovoked attack by a third Power, or something that threatened the general peace, it should immediately discuss with the other, whether both Governments should act together to prevent aggression and to preserve peace, and if so what measures they would be prepared to take in common. If these measures involved action, the plans of the General Staffs would at once be taken into consideration, and the Governments would then decide what effect should be given to them.

Grey and Asquith intended merely to clarify the British interpretation of the agreement to "consult" and not to assume any obligations. But this statement was part of a process by which, in the words of Samuel R. Williamson (*The Politics of Grand Strategy: Britain and France Prepare for War, 1904–1914,* 1969), the *Entente* was being "shaped, nurtured and reinforced by strategic circumstances." Nearly all historians would now agree that in the last analysis it was the *Entente* which took Britain into World War I.

5 The Great War

Winston
Churchill
The World Crisis,
1916–1918
(1923), p. 827

Before the war it had seemed incredible that such terrors
and slaughters, even if they began, could last more than a
few months. After the first two years it was difficult to
believe that they would ever end. We seemed separated
from the old life by a measureless gulf.

George
Dangerfield
The Strange
Death of Liberal
England (1935),
p. viii

The war hastened everything—in politics, in economics, in
behavior—but it started nothing.

H. G. Wells
An Englishman
looks at the World
(1914), p. 33

What will hold such an Empire as the British together?

Derek Fraser
The Evolution of
the British
Welfare State
(1973), p. 164

The First World War had a profound influence upon
British society, for quite simply it swept away a whole
world and created a new one ... This war was in fact the
greatest watershed of modern British history. However, the
effects of total war in the twentieth century have been as
much concerned with accelerating as with diverting the
course of social policy.

1914–1918

Between 1914 and 1918 the attitudes and feelings of the British people were caught up in the demands and responsibilities of the immediate present, a present cut off from the past and leading into an uncertain future. Daily routine and normal expectations were uprooted; the exigencies of war administered a series of shocks to careers and ambitions, to family life, to industrial management and labor oganization, to politics and government, to religious belief and social custom, to morals and morale. In two considerations—the impact on society of war, and the relation of that war to forces already in motion—we have a basis for assessing, in terms of British experience, the first conflict of such magnitude since Napoleon. We must face the imponderable—to what extent was World War I a unique and decisive factor in promoting change?—an issue raised by the quotations at the head of this chapter. An answer will emerge as we proceed. In order to give this theme adequate treatment, a narrative of the military and naval history of the war will be omitted.

The Advent of War

The war came abruptly. The Liberals in office were by tradition "the peace party," not given to an aggressive foreign policy, still inclined to stand aside from continental quarrels, and, generally speaking, more favorably disposed toward Germany than toward France. It was rather to the Conservatives that war with Germany had seemed inevitable.

Since 1906 foreign policy had been the well-guarded province of the Foreign Office under Grey. Not until October 1912, when Lord Morley raised the question, was the Cabinet, as a group, informed of the military conversations long in progress with France which by then had authorized a significant division of responsibility on the high seas—Britain to be responsible for the Atlantic and the Channel, France for the Mediterranean. Even then the Foreign Office brushed aside any suggestion of commitment to France. But in May 1914 naval conversations were extended to Russia.

The Balkan crisis between Austria and Serbia (on June 28 a Serbian assassinated the Archduke Francis Ferdinand, heir to the Hapsburg throne of Austria-Hungary, while on a visit to Bosnia) caught the Foreign Office by surprise. And, as we have said, the matter did not come before the British Cabinet until July 24, the day after the Austrian ultimatum to Serbia. Thereafter events moved rapidly. Russia came promptly to Serbia's support and began mobilization July 25. The Alliance system came alive. Germany stood by Austria and declared war on Russia August 1. France, under the terms of the Franco-Russian Alliance was bound to support Russia and by August 3 was at war with Germany. In Britain there was a political crisis within the Cabinet—a story which gradually came to light after the war.

The effective element in a complex situation was the revival of the old antagonism between the Liberal Leaguers (especially Asquith, Grey, and Haldane) with Churchill now in their camp, and the rest of the Cabinet. A Government representing two quite different policies in foreign affairs had never defined Britain's obligations in the *Entente Cordiale*. In the present crisis, as long as the issue remained implementing "obligations" to France, that is, treating the *Entente* as an alliance, the clear majority of the Cabinet was against intervention. And so on the evening of August 3 the Cabinet seemed about to fall apart.

Instead, substantial unity developed from concern for traditional British interests in the Channel and in the Low Countries. When the Cabinet met Sunday morning, August 2, word had just been received of the German declaration of war against Russia and of the German entry into Luxembourg (which seemed to render invasion of Belgium inevitable). The Conservative Party leaders had already assured Grey of their unqualified support for intervention. Grey now secured, though with difficulty, Cabinet authorization for assurances to France and warning to Germany that German naval operations in the Channel would not be permitted. To the French ambassador this seemed to settle the matter.

Cabinet waverers (including Lloyd George, Morley, Lewis Harcourt, John Simon, and Herbert Samuel) lunched together, and their resistance seemed to be reforming. But in the evening the neutralist position collapsed. The Cabinet agreed on intervention in the event of "substantial violation" of Belgian neutrality as guaranteed by international treaty. Next morning came news of the German ultimatum to Belgium to permit passage of troops, and Cabinet support for intervention strengthened. Only two dissentients, Lord Morley and John Burns, resigned. C. P. Scott of the *Manchester Guardian* records Lloyd George as saying that "he had done his utmost for peace but events had been too strong for him."

Lloyd George himself tells us that on that Monday afternoon, August 3, he and the prime minister walked through dense crowds (it was August bank holiday) from Downing Street to the House of Commons, where Grey made his first public report on British policy. His dramatic announcement to a packed House (with the French and Russian ambassadors in the diplomatic gallery) enabled him to put the case for intervention in such persuasive terms that on the division he carried the House, save some forty—a sprinkling of Liberals and some Laborites. The day following, August 4, Grey demanded assurances on Belgium—the Germans had five hours in which to reply. In London there was confusion confounded, but the deadline (11 P.M. in London) came without answer. Big Ben tolled the hour. Crowds in or near Downing Street broke into "God save the King." Churchill wired the fleet: "Commence hostilities against Germany."

This outline of events leaves unanswered a difficult but important question. Were Asquith and Grey, even in July-August 1914, entirely candid with Cabinet, Parliament, and nation? It may be argued that violation of Belgian neutrality was not the essential cause of British intervention. In this view, the naval pledge to France on August 2 was used to mislead the isolationist element in the Cabinet. Not until later that day did the Belgian question assume importance—the Cabinet then reversed the position taken as recently as July 29, when there had been a consensus of opinion against recognizing any obligation either to France or Belgium. And Asquith then wrote to the king: "The cabinet consider that the matter if it arises will be rather one of policy than of legal obligation." Now, with the news August 4 that the Germans had entered Belgium, Asquith recorded, "This simplified matters." Soon after Lord Bryce wrote: "We did not drift, for it looks as though the Foreign Office has meant all along that we should go in to support France, no matter what Germany might do." Grey, a man of conscience, was perhaps not altogether clear just what impulse did motivate him. On August 9 he wrote that but for Belgium "we should have kept out of it." A little later he observed that the war was a great catastrophe, but once it came, for England to have remained neutral would have made it even worse. We may conclude, with some assurance, that Grey, backed by Asquith, was prepared to intervene on the simple issue of support to France; the Belgian issue merely made their task in the Cabinet easier. Grey has been held vulnerable by the Italian historian Albertini, and others, for failing to announce British intentions before mobilization on the Continent was beyond control. But it should be remembered that Grey could not act alone and until August 2 did not have sufficient Cabinet support. And the whole question of Britain's entrance into the war is put in entirely different perspective if we accept Fritz Fischer's well-documented *Germany's Aims in the First World War* (1967), in which he concludes that for Germany, controlled by a "military oligarchy,"· the war immediately became a part of her world policy. With victory she would dictate a peace, with a *Mitteleuropa* under German military and economic control, with adjacent territories annexed and satellite states surrounding her. Had not Britain intervened, so Fischer believes, the war might well have resulted in German hegemony over all of western and central Europe. Fischer's conclusions are now controversial, particularly among German historians, but are likely in time to receive wide acceptance.

Public Reaction

The British people had faced these developments uncertainly (thus encouraging aggressive action from Germany), yet paradoxically emerged with a generally united front. The Government white paper with its resumé of diplomatic exchanges, issued August 5, set uneasy minds at rest. The important segments of the Liberal press (the *Daily News,* the *Manchester Guardian,* the *Nation,* and the *Economist*) had pleaded for neutrality until the very outbreak of war. Then, recording the conviction that "a mistaken course of foreign policy pursued over ten years has led us to the terrible conflict in which we are now engaged" (*Daily News,* August 5), they settled down to wholehearted support of the war. Though Labor Party leaders (Hardie, Henderson, Lansbury) had denounced war to a huge crowd which jammed Trafalgar Square on Sunday, August 2, the labor movement proceeded, with few dissenting voices, to support Government policy. H. G. Wells wrote in the *Daily News* on August 14, "I find myself enthusiastic for this war against Prussian militarism . . . . Every sword that is drawn against Germany is a sword drawn for peace." In Parliament, only on the fringes of Liberalism and from a few members of the I.L.P. (including MacDonald, who resigned as chairman of the Labor Party in Parliament) did criticism continue. In November 1914, members of these groups formed the Union of Democratic Control, a propaganda organization for a moderate peace settlement and the democratization of foreign policy, which influenced President Wilson's ideas.

The coming of war broke into an atmosphere of domestic strain. Since 1909 there had been tension, threat of violence, renunciation of reason, a grim sense of impending catastrophe. Now conflict had come. Contemporary comment indicates that the reaction was direct, immediate, and uninhibited. In journalism the shift is represented by the sudden change in tone of Horatio Bottomley's *John Bull*, a sensational weekly catering to popular tastes. A pro-Austrian position was maintained as late as the issue of August 8 (an article headed "To Hell with Servia"); but in the issue of August 15 the cover displayed John Bull in a sailor's cap bearing the inscription "H.M.S. Victory," and the leading article proclaimed "The Dawn of Britain's Greatest Glory." If Bottomley had no convictions to change, the new *John Bull* changed those of its readers. On August 5 the Liberal elder statesman Lord Courtney wrote, "The difference between today and yesterday is infinite." A few months later Lloyd George declared that a poll on August 1 "would have shown 95 percent against... hostilities.... A poll on the following Tuesday (August 4) would have resulted in a vote of 99 percent in favor." Novelists caught the mood. Mary Agnes Hamilton in *Dead Yesterday* (1916) has one of the characters say, "After all these years of unreality and sham, a big thing like this gives one the sense of having escaped out of the tunnel into the air." And in the most significant of the war's novels, *Mr. Britling Sees It Through* (1916), H. G. Wells tells us that at Matching's Easy in rural Essex there soon developed a feeling "that we have to plunge through catastrophe to opportunity." Mr. Britling says:

> I am not sorry I have lived to see this war. It may be a tremendous catastrophe in one sense, but in another it is a huge step forward in human life. It is the end of forty years of evil suspense. It is crisis and a solution.... Now everything becomes fluid. We can redraw the map of the world. A week ago we were all quarrelling bitterly about things too little for human impatience. Now suddenly we face an epoch. This is an epoch. The world is plastic for men to do what they will with it. This is the end and the beginning of an age.

Such testimony could be multiplied. In August 1914 domestic troubles quickly faded. The war became a moral crusade. Englishmen were inhibited from using force to solve the problems of the British Isles, but it seemed to them proper and inevitable to employ it to save the world.

From Asquith to Lloyd George

Could a Government of amateurs wage successful war? Would the constitutional processes of a democracy prove sufficiently elastic to permit the quick, effective, and often arbitrary action the emergency would require? These were, in general terms, the political questions of the war. Parliament could, of course, enact any legislation it pleased, subject in practical terms to the exigencies of politics and the demands of public opinion. For example, a general election was by the Parliament Act of 1911 due in 1915, but the partisanship of a national poll was avoided by the simple expedient of a series of parliamentary resolutions postponing the election until the end of the war. The fundamental changes within the existing Government were (1) May 1915, the transformation of the Liberal Cabinet of Asquith into a Coalition Cabinet of all parties under his leadership; (2) December 1916, the reorganization of the Coalition and the transference of leadership from Asquith to Lloyd George. These drastic changes in the exercise of power were accomplished without benefit of electoral or even of parliamentary action.

Until May 1915 normal party lines were preserved in Parliament. Asquith sought to develop policy for the conduct of the war through a War Council, originally of eight persons, rather than through the full Cabinet of twenty-one. But the Opposition soon became dissatisfied with the course and conduct of the war. There was failure and frustration on the western front. Criticism was concentrated on Lord Kitchener, hero of Egypt, South Africa, and India, and, thus, already something of a legend. At the outset (August 1914) his appointment as war secretary seemed amply justified—even though this meant bypassing Haldane, who had prepared the army for this war. But Kitchener had the proper perspective—he was almost alone in prophesying a long exhaustive war; his appeal for 100,000 volunteers for "four years or the duration of the war" set everyone talking. His famous photograph with the piercing eye, the pointed finger, and the legend "Your Country Needs You" was everywhere. But his efforts to combine the role of commander-in-chief with that of secretary of war proved a failure, for he had no understanding of the civilian side of the Army, was incapable of discussing differences or sharing responsibility. The first great failure of the war—the shortage of ammunition ("the shell scandal")—was attributed to him. But outside official circles his prestige remained unimpaired. Was Kitchener a great man or was he "only a great poster?"—as Margot Asquith put it.

But a factor which led more directly to the political crisis of May 1915 was the Churchill-Fisher controversy. Churchill at the Admiralty had recalled Fisher as first sea lord soon after the outbreak of the war. Churchill wished to force the Dardanelles (to eliminate Turkey—now in the war against the Allies—and to open up a supply route to Russia and win over wavering neutrals in the Balkans). Fisher had a quite different scheme, that of a Baltic landing behind the German lines. But Fisher gave way and the Dardanelles campaign was approved by the War Council in January. From first to last this was a matter of improvisation—a complex of conjecture, decision, indecision, order, counterorder, as Sir Maurice Hankey, secretary of the War Council tells us. The relation of naval attack to army support constantly changed. In consequence, by May 1915, after heavy losses on land and at sea, the allied attack on Gallipoli had been completely checked. Fisher, unwilling to send the naval re-enforcement requested by Churchill, resigned. Churchill presumably was responsible. It was a situation made to order for the Unionists. On May 17, Bonar Law wrote Asquith that unless his party was permitted to share responsibility, it must become an active Opposition. And Law secured Lloyd George's support for a Coalition.

Coalition Cabinet

Asquith met the emergency by reshuffling his Cabinet to include the important Conservatives (Bonar Law, Balfour, Curzon, Carson, Austen Chamberlain) and one Laborite (Arthur Henderson, now chairman of the Parliamentary Labor Party). But Asquith retained more control than is sometimes accorded him—among the Conservatives only Balfour (Admiralty) was given a key post. In the long run, more important was the shift of Lloyd George from the Exchequer to the newly created Ministry of Munitions. And to satisfy the Conservatives, Churchill was demoted to a post of only nominal importance (Duchy of Lancaster) and Haldane, lord chancellor, was dropped altogether. The Conservatives had been out to get Churchill, but according to Churchill's official biographer, Asquith was set on pulling him down anyway. He soon left the Government and went to the front as a battalion commander. As to Haldane, he was sacrificed to wartime prejudices of public opinion which labeled him "pro-German."

In the interests of more efficient decision-making, Asquith replaced the War Council with a War Committee of the Cabinet—three to five members. But the new Government was hardly "national" and the quality of Asquith's leadership did not improve. Lloyd George not unfairly summed him up: Asquith "conceived his function as that of the Chairman of a Committee. He came to Cabinet meetings with no policy which he had decided to recommend, listened to what others said, summed up ably the discussion, and then as often as not postponed the decision."

As the prestige of Asquith declined, that of Lloyd George increased. Since August 1914, in his handling of war finances, in negotiating successfully with trade unions, and as the most persuasive representative of the Government at public meetings, his reputation had been on the rise. During his year of tenure as minister of Munitions ninety-five new factories opened, and certain types of production were now turned out in a matter of weeks, even of days. Lloyd George was widely hailed as "the one man who can win the war."

In June 1916 H.M.S. *Hampshire* struck a mine off the Orkneys, and Lord Kitchener, who was aboard, was killed. With support from the Conservatives in the Cabinet—though reluctant support from Asquith, who probably would have preferred Lord Derby, proposed by Generals Haig and Robertson—Lloyd George succeeded to the vacancy in the War Office. Margot Asquith thought the Lloyd George appointment a "Balaclava blunder" and added to her diary, "It is only a question of time until we shall have to leave Downing Street."

The year 1916 proceeded on its way with increasing frustration, disaster, and tragedy for the Allies: the German offensive nearly successful at Verdun; the indecisive naval encounter of Jutland—the British public could not then know that the German High Seas Fleet would not again venture in force from its base; the failure of the Allies to gain a decision along the Somme; the recovery of Germany from the Brusilov offensive; the vacillation of Romania. In a press interview on September 28, deliberately arranged, Lloyd George declared that Britain must challenge "the defeatist spirit which was working from foreign quarters to bring about an inconclusive peace and which appeared to find an echo even in some responsible quarters in England." And he concluded, "The fight must be to the finish—to a knockout." A few days later, with Asquith's approval, Lord Lansdowne, a member of the War Committee of the Cabinet presented a memorandum declaring that a "knockout blow" might be far distant and suggesting that Britain encourage the idea of a peace of "accommodation." A confidential document, it may well have stimulated Cabinet members already committed to a more vigorous conduct of the war.

The Fall of Asquith

The prime minister was now bowed in personal grief over the loss of his son in September on the Somme. Nevertheless, the personal attacks on his leadership heightened. Shortly after Lloyd George became war minister, Sir Max Aitken (later to become Lord Beaverbrook) said of Asquith, "A man who has been beaten once can be beaten twice." Aitken, along with Bonar Law, had urged upon Asquith the

Lloyd George appointment to the War Office. Asquith's final defeat came on December 6, 1916, with the reorganization of the Government under Lloyd George with effective power in a small War Cabinet. This change was long in preparation. The fundamental cause was widespread demand for more effective war leadership. An important manifestation was the frequent meeting since early in the year of the self-styled "Ginger Group" of Milner, Carson, L. S. Amery, F. S. Oliver, Geoffrey Robinson (editor of *The Times*), and later, Waldorf Astor.

It is impossible to reconstruct with any precision the immediate background of Asquith's departure from Downing Street—the chronology of events and the roles of individuals. "A more tangled situation can hardly be conceived," recorded the archbishop of Canterbury on December 4, in the midst of the crisis. So it has remained since for historians, among whom no consensus has formed. Yet the reader should delve into the matter for his own satisfaction. To a considerable degree, the conduct of the war was at stake, and possibly the outcome as well; it was a landmark in the history of the Liberal Party; it went far in determining the political fortunes thereafter of Asquith and Lloyd George. As an introduction to the problem, here are the main developments.

From the "Ginger Group" mentioned above we move to a series of conferences, after November 20, of the Liberal Lloyd George and the Conservatives Bonar Law and Sir Edward Carson. Brought together by Aitken, they concluded that there must be a small War Cabinet with Asquith himself shorn of effective power in the conduct of the war. Asquith was aware of these conferences—they were hardly conspiratorial, as sometimes suggested. On December 1 a memorandum was sent to Asquith proposing a War Committee to direct policy subject to the veto power of the prime minister who, however, was not to be the committee chairman, a vital point. Asquith, after some uncertainty, insisted upon being chairman, and not "relegated to the position of an arbiter in the background." Thus he wrote Lloyd George who, December 2, sent Bonar Law a celebrated note which has fascinated historians ever since its publication by Lord Beaverbrook in his *Politicians and the War* (1928). The complete text reads: "I enclose copy of the P.M.'s letter. The life of the country depends on resolute action by you now." The crux of the problem for historians is Lloyd George's attitude and position at just this time. But certainly he did not then enjoy to any degree the confidence of Conservatives in the Cabinet. Their reaction was to urge Asquith to resign with a view to reorganization of the Government. As it happened, Bonar Law only conveyed the general tenor of their resolution to Asquith, who apparently interpreted it as a move against his continued leadership. But these uncertainties might have been clarified had it not been for the leading article in *The Times*, December 4, written by its editor (after a briefing by Carson) which was hostile in tone to Asquith and which laid bare the vital issue—proposals of a war council with Asquith shorn of a decisive role. Asquith at once informed Lloyd George that he could not accept a war council unless he (Asquith) as chairman retained "supreme and effective control of war policy." Now Lloyd George and the Conservatives found themselves in alliance. Conferences followed which baffle reconstruction. Resignation from the Cabinet of Lloyd George and leading Conservatives brought Asquith's own resignation on December 6. A suggestion that Asquith might remain in a Cabinet headed by Bonar Law got nowhere, and on the evening of December 6 Lloyd Geroge was asked by the king to form a new Government. After several days of "herculean efforts" (as one historian aptly describes it), Lloyd George succeeded.

Lloyd George to Power

In the new administration Conservatives held most of the important posts and predominated in the War Cabinet of five: Lloyd George, Bonar Law, Curzon, Milner, and Henderson. As chancellor of the Exchequer, Bonar Law alone had departmental duties; the others might be assigned to various missions. The Cabinet took for granted parliamentary support, and Lloyd George seldom appeared in the Commons. The War Cabinet was sufficiently small to be summoned on brief notice; during 1917 it met more than three hundred times. In *The Times* the parliamentary correspondent referred to the new ministry as "without doubt the boldest political conception of our time." Certainly its formation was the most important political development of the war.

Public opinion was generally confident that more effective leadership would come from Lloyd George and was not concerned with niceties of political scruple. Historians have generally credited Aitken with the major role in pulling off the shift, but Aitken, in his own account, gives himself only a modest part. For him a peerage (as Lord Beaverbrook) was the substitute for the Cabinet post—the Board of Trade—he expected and the minor office he rejected. The central fact is that Asquith had found himself in an impossible situation. He wrote to a friend on December 10, "I saw that I could not go on, without dishonour or impotence or both; and nothing could have been worse for the country and the war." He also had little heart. On the ninth he said to the archbishop of Canterbury, "I have not had one single day ... since Whitsuntide 1914, without the burden pressing ceaselessly upon me, and I have found, especially since Raymond's death, a lack of resilience ... which makes everything terribly trying." His supporters declared that he acted in complete patriotism and was the victim of a conspiracy. For Asquith it proved, as we shall see, the point of no return—his subsequent efforts at reuniting and rejuvenating the Liberals falling well short of success.

To examine either Asquith or Lloyd George is to emphasize the striking difference between them, and perhaps also to recognize, as did their close associate for many years, Herbert Samuel, that each had a touch of genius. As to leadership in time of war, Lloyd George's own postwar comment is to the point:

> There are certain indispensable qualities essential to the Chief Minister of the Crown in a great war. . . . Such a minister must have courage, composure and judgment. All this Mr. Asquith possessed in a superlative degree. . . . But a War Minister must also have vision, imagination and initiative—he must show untiring assiduity, must exercise constant oversight and supervision of every sphere of war activity, must possess driving force to energize this activity, must be in continuous consultation with experts, official and unofficial, as to the best means of utilizing the resources of the country in conjunction with the Allies for the achievement of victory. If to this can be added a flair for conducting a great fight, then you have an ideal War Minister.

By implication, Asquith did not have these qualities—a view shared by Churchill and Balfour. Lloyd George now proceeded to demonstrate that he had them in abundance. The stated war aim of Britain was the defeat of the enemy. Lloyd George himself was never more specific, despite the implication of the "secret treaties" to which Britain had been a party. There was the agreement prior to Gallipoli that, if the Allies were victorious, Constantinople and the Straits should go to Russsia. By the Treaty of London (April 1915) Italy entered the war on the side of the Allies in return for the promise of the Austrian territories of Tyrol, Istria, and northern Dalmatia. And in the Sykes-Picot Agreement (May 1916) the English and the French decided on their respective zones of interest after the war in the Turkish territories of Mesopotamia and Syria. Proposals from President Wilson and from Germany for an exchange of war aims and for efforts at a negotiated peace were rejected by the British government.

The great man of World War I was not Herbert Henry Asquith, the Liberal Imperialist, but David Lloyd George, the pro-Boer of 1900 and the reluctant supporter of war in 1914, now "towering like a giant above every other figure in the war," in Maurice Hankey's words. Lloyd George weathered the many political storms of 1917 and 1918. His political judgment was shrewd, almost uncanny. He eliminated Carson from effective influence in the Government. He neutralized the role of Lord Northcliffe, proprietor of *The Times,* in the conflict between "the Frocks" and "the Brass Hats" over the fashioning of military strategy.

Above all, at home, throughout the Empire, with the Allies, he was the organizer of victory.

Of the Cabinet changes in December 1916, Lloyd Geroge later wrote in his *War Memoirs*, "I neither desired nor sought the premiership." Many in 1916 would have said otherwise. But perhaps the most satisfactory commentary came years later from Winston Churchill. After Lloyd George's death in March 1945, Churchill in recounting his career before the Commons said, "Presently Lloyd George seized the main power in the State and the leadership of the Government." And after an uneasy stir in the House, Churchill added, quoting Carlyle on Cromwell, "He coveted the place; perhaps the place was his." The "Welsh Wizard" was possessed of great personal charm, and also of great personal ambition. He was as well a man of tremendous capacity. Without him Great Britain could hardly have emerged so successfully from World War I. It would have been well for his reputation in history had his career ended then and there.

Wartime Controls

As an episode in economic history the war was a contest of endurance between rival economies. The story of Britain's own employment of resources for war purposes is one of trial and error, of improvisation without any guidance from past experience.

The nature of the impact of war on the national economy was only slowly realized. It is noteworthy that Sir Edward Grey in his crucial address to the Commons on August 3, 1914, should have minimized the task. "For us with a powerful fleet, which we believe able to protect our commerce, to protect our shores, and to protect our interests, if we are engaged in war, we shall suffer but little more than we shall suffer even if we stand aside." To most contemporaries the weakness of this extraordinary remark was not apparent. And many were quick to accept another Grey remark, that the war could not last more than three months. There would be "business as usual," and "just leave things to Kitchener."

Shortly after the first battle of the Marne (September 1914) the *Economist* referred to "the economic and financial impossibility of carrying on hostilities many months on the present scale." The daily expenditure was then only about one-fourth of what it eventually became. It is true that the serious monetary problems of Great Britain date from these years; but few in 1914, least of all those in financial circles, had any notion of the limits to which the national economy might be stretched. Lloyd George's first war budget (November 1914) doubled the income tax and the surtax; this was only a beginning. During the last complete fiscal year of the war the Government spent approximately

£2,700,000,000, in comparison with the £197,000,000 of the last pre-war fiscal year. The general price rise in the interim was approximately 100 percent.

The War Economy

As the war continued, the Government exerted increasing control over the economy. But this regulation was cautious and seldom deliberate, certainly never doctrinaire. Nothing should impede the war effort of course, but at the same time there should be a minimum of interference with private business and with individual liberty. As a foundation for broad exercise of governmental authority Parliament enacted the Defense of the Realm Acts (DORA). The initial act (August 8, 1914) authorized the Government to issue general regulations "for public safety and defence of the Realm." The second (August 28, 1914) provided for general control over armament plants. The third (March 1915) permitted the Government to requisition factories and control production. Through DORA, popularly depicted as a troublesome old lady who delighted in taking the fun out of life, the Government might interfere with daily routine in innumerable ways.

Actual controls over industry were at first limited to restrictions on production and on the use of raw materials, with priorities established for the needs of the armed forces. This authority was exercised through advisory commissions, usually consisting of operators, workers, and governmental officials. Where production was restricted, profits were guaranteed, by subsidies if necessary, at the prewar level. In the course of the war, control most nearly approached government ownership in the railroads, munitions, and coal. A committee of prewar managers operated the railroads for the Government. A Ministry of Munitions with broad power was established in May 1915. Reorganization of the Government under Lloyd George in December 1916 led immediately to the establishment of a Ministry of Labor and controllerships for shipping, food, and coal. The administrative results were uneven, for streamlined techniques produced under wartime pressure often collided with the more deliberate procedures of the civil service.

Maintenance of a substantial portion of British overseas trade was, of course, essential to the civilian as well as to the military economy. In 1914 Great Britain owned 42 percent of the world's steam shipping, and 87 percent of this British merchant marine operated in foreign trade. Though countless hulls and countless seamen went to the bottom of the North Sea and the Atlantic, overseas trade held up remarkably well through 1916, with control limited to the requisitioning of transports.

But unrestricted German submarine warfare produced a condition of emergency in 1917, and general authority over all tonnage was announced, to be exercised when necessary. Thus the import space for raw cotton was greatly reduced (wool and linen had priority for war needs), and this action led to the creation of the Cotton Control Board to allocate the supply of raw cotton actually imported.

Food became a serious wartime problem. Before the war Britain was producing just about one-third of her necessary food supply and only about one-fifth of her requirement in wheat. In 1905 a Royal Commission on Supply of Food and Raw Materials in Time of War had declared that food imports would be amply protected by the Navy. Until the autumn of 1916 this view proved correct; then the developing shortage in shipping began to affect seriously the food supply. Measures designed to increase home production were adopted. Local authorities were empowered to allot unoccupied lands for cultivation. Minimum prices were guaranteed in wheat, oats, and potatoes, and minimum farm wages were established. Restrictions were clamped on the brewing industry, and the quality of flour was regulated. In April 1917 the manufacture of flour became a government monopoly; white bread gave way to "war bread."

In spite of such measures, in the course of 1917 wheat, meat, tea, and sugar came into short supply. Prices soared and in some instances doubled those of prewar days (a four-pound loaf rose from about 5½ pence to a shilling), and long queues in front of food stores became a common sight. Even so, the Government persisted for some time in the view that "business as usual" would solve the problem, and when eventually a rationing system was reluctantly established the Government found itself far behind public opinion. The "heroic age" of food control (the phrase is that of Beveridge, then an official in the Food Ministry) came during the administration of Lord Rhondda as food controller, June 1917–July 1918. Rhondda was cited by Lord Curzon as "the only popular Food Controller in Europe." His department was given control over most food and most drink—to control imports, prices, and profits—though the degree of authority actually exercised varied widely from time to time.

Rationing itself did not come until the early months of 1918 and was limited to meat, sugar, and fats (butter and margarine). A national system operated by local authorities worked smoothly. The key to its success was the registry of each consumer with a particular retail dealer; this made possible the careful regulation of distribution in accordance with actual requirements. Ration books were normally honored; when stocks ran out the shop was closed. The system proved generally equitable and queues disappeared. It was never found necessary to ration bread, and fortunately so, for there was a wide variation in individual consumption.

Government subsidies maintained adequate flour supplies. "The success of rationing," concludes Beveridge in his history of food control, "is a supreme case of muddling through by brilliant improvisations, made necessary by shifting policy and division of counsels."

"Labor Unrest"

Lloyd George in his *War Memoirs* introduced his discussion of "Labor Unrest" with this observation: "Of all the problems which Governments had to handle during the Great War, the most delicate and probably the most perilous were those arising on the home front." Labor leadership was thoroughly patriotic and, generally speaking, union membership supported the war. An immediate labor truce was declared by responsible union officials; the strike would not be used as an instrument of policy. But, unhappily, the war came just at a peak of industrial tension. Though prewar issues became dormant, new sources of friction soon developed. Demands of the war economy seemed to threaten established wages, hours, and conditions of work. There was much shifting of labor, occasional unemployment, rising prices, and pressure of overtime and of production goals.

Munitions plants were brought completely under governmental contol in July 1915. Union rules were modified to permit "dilution" of skilled labor (dividing the task of skilled labor and assigning certain operations to the unskilled) and to provide for compulsory arbitration. Labor hardly realized that restrictions were also imposed upon management. Disorders and sporadic strikes soon became the rule in munitions plants. Similar tensions developed among engineers and miners. This unrest was not inspired by union officials, but stemmed rather from shop stewards, a new element in labor, and from the workers themselves.

During the course of the war, government control was never formally established over industrial labor generally. In 1917 Lloyd George proclaimed the necessity for industrial discipline, but he continued to improvise a policy short of compulsion. Stoppages and strikes were increasingly serious in 1917 and 1918; in August 1918 even the London police went out on strike. For most of the working class there was, relative to other classes, an improvement in the standard of living; but grievances accumulated nonetheless: prices, liquor control, pay disputes, "dilution," fatigue from overtime and from Sunday work, woefully inadequate housing. From 1914 to 1918 trade union membership doubled, from a little over four million to a little over eight million. Labor's growing militancy was also reflected, as we shall see, in the more aggressive policy of the Labor Party.

Enlistment and Conscription

Military conscription was delayed. At the outset resistance to the idea was profound and almost unanimous. Traditional prejudices came alive: conscription would inevitably lead to a strong standing army in peacetime, and a standing army was, of course, a symbol of tyranny. Voluntary enlistment was the English way. There was simple patriotic appeal; there was also music hall recruiting. *England Expects* was staged at the London Opera House with Phyllis Dare singing, "Oh, we don't want to lose you, but we think you ought to go," and with Horatio Bottomley in front of a huge Union Jack delivering his "Prince of Peace" speech in the intermission.

Until June 1915 enlistment remained adequate, but then on reaching the two million mark it began to sag. Yet national registration in August showed another two million as immediately available. Conservatives began to urge some measure of compulsion; Lloyd George was quickly won over, and by October Kitchener as well. Asquith, however, still resisted. But the Derby scheme of deferred enlistment, with unmarried men to be called up before married men, did not bring adequate enlistment, and some form of conscription was inevitable. The first measure (January 1916) conscripted bachelors. Asquith was "frightened to death over the bill" but accepted it, although his home secretary (Simon) resigned and nearly half of the Liberals in the Commons either voted against the bill or abstained from voting altogether. Additional manpower requirements submitted by the Army Council in April could be met in only one manner. And thus in May 1916 came the first general conscription in English history; the law applied to all males between eighteen and forty-one; eventually the age limit was extended to fifty-one. Bonar Law was probably correct in his observation that only a coalition Government could have pushed through this measure. In the end nearly every physically fit man in Britain, some six million out of ten million within the prescribed age limits, went into uniform.

Conscientious objectors numbered about sixteen thousand. For this small minority the war had its special meaning. They had advocates in Parliament (notably the Liberal member Philip Edward Morrell). Cases were handled not without sympathy but, as the war continued, under rather arbitrary rulings. By 1917, in order to be exempt from service, proof of Quaker membership was usually required. About thirteen hundred went to prison. They gave an astonishing variety of reasons, from matters of principle to mere matters of opinion, for refusing to serve. To each individual it was a personal experience; this is reflected in a series of essays written after the war and published in 1935 as *We Did Not Fight*.

The National Mind

Wells's novel *Mr. Britling Sees It Through* is as near a war journal of the nation in 1914–15 as one can hope to find. Only when the German armies encircled Paris in September 1914 did Mr. Britling realize that "doing our utmost does not mean standing about in pleasant gardens waiting for the newspaper." Britain was attempting "to readjust its government and particularly its military organization to the new scale of warfare that Germany had imposed on the world." The frustrations of the men at the front came to be appreciated by those at home. "My boy in Flanders," said Mr. Britling, "says our officers have never learnt to count beyond ten, and that they are scared at the sight of a map." The jolts came swiftly: this was a war of peoples, and not just the fiendish creation of a few evil men; war made humanity bitter and cruel, intolerant and insensitive—"to be at war is to hate"; Haldane, the former war secretary, was being condemned as "a German by choice"; the mentality of the German people was beyond comprehension; the "funk classes," or the "pasty-faces," at home who refused to fight or work constituted an affront to society. Eventually Mr. Britling comprehended the nature of modern war: it was in itself a crime. J. A. Spender has written: "The Great War arose out of a state of opinion which regarded war as a legitimate and normal method of promoting national interests.... The crime was not to make war, but to make it unsuccessfully.... As our neighbors pointed out, we had been more frequently at war than any of them."

From early 1916 Mr. Britling's story may be continued elsewhere. Caroline Playne, for example, provides it in *Society at War* (1931) and *Britain Holds On, 1917–1918* (1933). Her books were composed in the atmosphere of pacifism so strong in the 1930s, and her judgments take insufficient note of the actual demands of a war situation. One could not have been as detached during the war. Yet the data she marshals are carefully collected from contemporary sources. One follows the change in the national mind from the exaltation of 1914 to the bewilderment of 1915 and to the resignation and grim sense of purpose of 1916; the waning interest in war maps as the little flags remained stationary month after month; the psychological effect of atrocity stories; the complacency and sentimentality of much of religious and political propaganda; the tyranny of rumor with the spy mania and the hunt for "aliens"; the wishful thinking in reaction to the peace feelers of 1916; the stimulus of America's entrance into the war; and the emotions of an exhausted nation as the war drew to its close. It was a profound national experience touching all classes and all ages. The few who tried to stand aloof suffered just the same. War patriotism hardly permitted an individual point of view. Bertrand Russell spoke later of the difficulty in wartime "of resisting mass suggestions, of which the force becomes terrific when the whole nation is in a state of violent collective excitement."

The Cost of War

How does one describe the war's losses? "All over England now, where the livery of mourning had been a rare thing to see, women and children went about in the October sunshine in new black clothes. Everywhere one met those fresh griefs, mothers who had lost their sons, women who had lost their men, lives shattered and hopes destroyed." Thus Wells in 1915. Altogether 160,000 wives lost husbands and 300,000 children lost fathers.

"If all losses [in war] of the hundred years which lie between the Napoleonic Wars and the World War of 1914–1918 are counted, the result will prove a fraction only of the number of deaths during the World War," we read authoritatively. Of the approximately 6,000,000 Britons in uniform about 750,000 lost their lives (88 percent were killed in action) and 1,700,000 were wounded. If an Englishman remembers anything of this war, he recalls the appalling casualty lists during the battle of the Somme in 1916. In the first day of this offensive, total casualties numbered 57,000 (including 20,000 dead), just about one-half of the infantry forces engaged. In the course of four or five months along the Somme, British losses totaled more than 400,000 in killed, wounded and missing. Air raids on Britain, however, took an almost negligible toll, with only 1,413 killed during the entire war.

On the battle front, death by enemy action was no respecter of persons or of families. Among the war dead were five grandsons of Lord Salisbury (the prime minister), a son of Rosebery, two sons (killed only six months apart) of Bonar Law, a son of Lord Lansdowne, a son of Arthur Henderson, a son of Kipling. The young poet, Rupert Brooke, died of blood poisoning off the island of Skyros in the Aegean. Raymond Asquith, the eldest son of the prime minister, fell leading a charge along the Somme. John Buchan later referred to Raymond Asquith as "beyond doubt the most remarkable figure of his Oxford generation." His death is representative of Britain's war loss. Of all men between twenty and forty-five, one in eleven was killed and more often than not they were the strongest in physique and the most promising intellectually. Twenty years later England was to miss sadly the vigor and leadership of the young men who died in the Great War.

However, in economic terms, and everything considered, the war did not have a seriously depleting effect on the quantity of manpower. Nor was the loss to Britain's industrial plant serious in comparison with countries bombarded and invaded. The most significant loss, at least at the time, was that of more than seven million gross tons of shipping— calculated to be about 38 percent of the merchant fleet in 1914. Of capital assets abroad about 4 or 5 percent was lost by confiscation and 10 percent lost by sale. In the long run the chief inroad of the war economically was the effect on foreign trade. In 1918, imports by volume were 27 percent below those of 1913; exports had fallen off 63 percent. Of course, much of this change was merely representative of an abrupt drop in international trade generally. But expansion of production in the United States and in Japan was rather ominous.

A Question of Glory

In national psychology, as well as in most other phases of the war, the formation of the Lloyd George Government in December 1916 was both an end and a beginning. It terminated any serious prospect for a negotiated peace, for the new Cabinet was committed to "the knockout blow." Mrs. Humphry Ward, the popular novelist, had already in June 1916 published *England's Effort: Letters to an American Friend*. To her question, "Has England done her part?" she gave a vigorous and optimistic affirmative. Now, in 1917, she visited battlefields in France and wrote *Towards the Goal*. She avoided the unpleasant and wrote in platitudes of "this war for civilization and freedom," and again lifted the morale of the thousands who read her.

In wartime the military and civilian worlds do not readily communicate. To the combat soldier of 1917 and 1918 the war was a unique experience. To him the war came to mean exhaustion reaching almost to the breaking point; the war had but one simple goal—the end of the fighting. Yet his weariness of body and of spirit was partially comprehended and shared at home. There was difference only of degree in the dislocations which were the price of this war, in the tensions produced by relentless demands in the factory as well as in the trenches.

Those writers who were least in sympathy with the war were generally the most articulate in expressing its psychological effects: the delusive power of vague idealism, the dulling of thought and imagination and sympathy by grief and hardship. Bertrand Russell's pacifist views on conscription cost him his lectureship in Trinity College, Cambridge. He was tried in June 1916 before the lord mayor of London "for statements likely to prejudice recruiting and discipline of His Majesty's forces" and fined £100. His *Principles of Social Reconstruction* (1917), published in the United States as *Why Men Fight*, made his name generally known among the reading public. His unconventional approach to problems of war and peace, of property and education, of marriage and religion, had a mixed reception. In his contribution to *We Did Not Fight* (1935) he dealt more incisively with the effects of war on people's minds. "One of the most surprising things about the war to me was its power of producing intellectual degradation in previously intelligent people, and the way in which intellectual degradation clothed itself in the language of a lofty but primitive morality." If Bertrand Russell seems unrepresentative, we may turn to the autobiography of John Buchan, no iconoclast, and read, "I acquired a bitter detestation of war, less for its horrors than for its boredom and futility, and a contempt for its *panache*. To speak of glory seemed a horrid impiety."

Much of the formal literature of the period is documentary. Many of the younger writers, serving with the forces, came to be opposed to the war: Robert Graves, Osbert and Sacheverell Sitwell, Herbert Read, and Wilfred Owen. Others like Clive Bell, Lytton Strachey, and Aldous Huxley were conscientious objectors. Writing about the war was at first idealistic, celebrating its glories and the heroism of fighting men. John Masefield wrote in 1916 in celebration of the Gallipoli campaign (1915): "They had failed to take Gallipoli, and the mine fields still barred the Hellespont, but they had fought a battle such as has never been seen upon this earth. What they had done will become a glory forever, wherever the deeds of heroic unhelped men are honoured and pitied and understood." Rupert Brooke wrote a few war poems, including the 1914 sonnets:

Now, God be thanked Who has matched us with His hour,
And caught our youth, and wakened us from sleeping.

A Sense of Horror

Masefield, Brooke, and other "Georgian" poets popularized the reading of poetry and some of the more chauvinistic critics predicted a great renaissance of letters. But writing hardly took the course they expected. The mood of war poetry quickly changed; soon it was not of national achievement or of personal valor but of the horror of never-ending pain and death, of the filth and squalor of the trenches, of man's inhumanity to man. This mood is sometimes said to have found its deepest expression in Wilfred Owen, killed at the front in the final week of the war. In an unfinished preface he wrote, "The subject of it [his book of poems] is War, and the pity of War. The Poetry is in the pity."

But the transition is best summarized in the phrase "from Rupert Brooke to Siegfried Sassoon." In 1914 Sassoon was twenty-eight years of age; he had come to manhood in a land and in an era which he loved; his few prewar stanzas were written for his own pleasure to record his joy in living. Until 1916 he accepted the war as inevitable and justified; as an infantry officer he received the Military Cross for heroism in rescuing wounded under fire. But in *A Soldier's Declaration* his new position is clear: "This war, upon which I entered as a war of defence and liberation has now become a war of aggression and conquest." His words came to the attention of Parliament. His friend Robert Graves and others intervened and arranged to have him sent to a hospital. But he soon returned to active duty and the imminence of death. His name became well known to servicemen with the publication of *The Old Huntsman* (1917), which reflected his growing bitterness with the war, a mood which came to fullest expression in *Counter-Attack* (1918), poems written in 1917–18 and one of the best records we have of the impact of the war on a sensitive nature. There is no self-consciousness. He makes full use of his powers of satire; he is absorbed in the wastage, the vileness, and the futility of war. "To Any Dead Officer" has the awesome line "Good-bye, old lad! Remember me to God," and the relentless ending "I wish they'd killed you in a decent show." After a head wound in the summer of 1918 ended his active service, *Counter-Attack* led to a friendly interview with Winston Churchill, who offered to find him a post in the Ministry of Munitions. Churchill knew some of Sassoon's war poems by heart and admired his talent though hardly his point of view. But Sassoon's poems were not anti-English; they were anti-war.

Shaw, Galsworthy, Bennett, and Wells—each had his say. But now Shaw alienated with his constant criticism of British conduct of the war. "Common Sense About the War," published in the *New Statesman* in November 1914, was badly timed and brought him only abuse and disapproval. His play *Augustus Does His Bit* (1916) is a sharp assault on the British governing class. *Heartbreak House* (1917), with its magnificent preface, is Shaw's most penetrating comment on the emotional response in Britain to the war.

Galsworthy catches and expresses the agony and grief which the conflict brought to individual lives. This is particularly notable in *Saint's Progress* (1919). As an official in the Ministry of Information, Arnold Bennett became intimately acquainted with the civilian side of the war. And his sensitive nature broke under what he experienced. In *The Pretty Lady* (1918), we have Bennett's outcry against the hopelessness of war. He sees the war through his character, one G. J.:

> The sense of its measureless scope was growing. It had sprung . . . out of the secret invisible roots of humanity . . . . It transcended judgment. It defied conclusions and rendered equally impossible both hope and despair . . . . His faith in his country was not lessened . . . . [But] the supreme lesson of the war was its revelation of what human nature actually was. And the solace of the lesson, the hope for triumph, lay in the fact that human nature must be substantially the same throughout the world . . . . All that he knew was that he had a heavy

day's work before him on the morrow, and in relief from insoluble problems he turned to face that work, thankful.

Newman Flower, the publisher, tells us of a week end early in 1916 in the Essex home of H. G. Wells. Into Flower's hands was placed the manuscript of *Mr. Britling Sees It Through.* "I had one of the biggest thrills in my publishing life.... It was the War—the War as it was shaping the lives of any British family." The manuscript had been composed in almost daily installments for twelve months beginning early in 1915. When published in 1916 it at once enjoyed such widespread popularity that public speakers and clergymen came to assume the familiarity of their audiences with it. To Siegfried Sassoon it was "more of a revelation than anything I had met with." Sitting in an army hut in a camp near Liverpool on the eve of 1917, he copied these words of Mr. Britling into his notebook: "It is a war now like any other of the mobbing, many-aimed cataclysms that have shattered empires and devastated the world; it is a war without a point, a war that has lost its soul; it has become mere incoherent fighting and destruction, a demonstration in vast and tragic forms of the stupidity and ineffectiveness of our species."

The title of Wells's novel reflects the changing attitude of many middle-class Englishmen toward the war, an attitude in contrast to the mood of the Lloyd George War Cabinet. By 1917 Wells himself was active in the agitation for a negotiated peace. "The return to sanity," Wells tells us later, in his autobiography,

took the greater part of two years. My mind did not get an effective grip upon the war until 1916 ... Mr. Britling is not so much a representation of myself as of my type and class, and I think I have contrived in that book to give not only the astonishment and the sense of tragic disillusionment in a civilized mind, as the cruel facts of war rose steadily to dominate everything else in life, but also the passionate desire to find some immediate reassurance amidst that whirlwind of disaster.

Behind the 1920s is the psychology of the nation at war—a composite of idealism and dulled processes of thought, of self-sacrifice and bitterness, of loyalty and shattered nerves, of grief and resignation, of hope and despair.

The Balance Sheet

We must now face the question raised at the beginning of this chapter: in simplest terms, What was the impact of World War I on Britain? It would be easy to conclude from contemporary observation that an entirely new era in the history of Britain begins. And one frequently finds historians today who dwell on the transformation of social and economic life in the years 1914–18. An interesting example, which arrests attention, is Arthur Marwick's *The Deluge: British Society and the First World War* (1965). He emphasizes "the dissolving effect on class structure" of the war and adds "that while society had changed, the State had not." In this he found "the key to the tragic aspects of Britain's inter-war years."

Of course, to many thousands, even hundreds of thousands, of those who lived during World War I, the war made a difference beyond calculation. But it must be remembered that the vast majority of those now living in Britain were then not living, or have no clear memory of those years. For them the war has a different meaning. Viewed in larger context it may be argued that the *general course* of British history was little affected by the war which was rather a manifestation than a cause. The war was a very important episode but was rather a landmark than a catastrophe. The war did not in itself change British society and institutions. But if there was no great change in direction, there was considerable acceleration; and sometimes this was abrupt. All this we shall have in mind as we proceed.

Cabinet Government and Parties

Cabinet government gives some evidence of undergoing radical transformation. During the war the Cabinet was twice reorganized without action from Parliament or from the electorate. And the concentration of power in the War Cabinet under Lloyd George seems without precedent. The House of Commons had apparently gone into eclipse. Yet these developments do not run counter to the general trends in constitutional development in the twentieth century. The Cabinet has increasingly, in practice, controlled Parliament. As to the role of the prime minister, the war merely pointed up the extraordinary powers which had already developed in his person—as leader of the party in the Cabinet, in Parliament, and throughout the nation.

One permanent change was made in governmental machinery. In December 1916, with the advent of the Lloyd George Government, a Cabinet secretariat was created. Until then, there had been no minutes of Cabinet meetings, no record of discussions and decisions; frequently a minister had to write around to his colleagues after a Cabinet session to ascertain what actions had been taken. Now a permanent secretariat was established to record Cabinet meetings and to coordinate the activities of ministers. No longer could a minister ignore or evade a decision already reached in Cabinet session. And a vital source of information became available to the future historian.

Circumstances of war drastically weakened (some would say destroyed) the Liberal Party. Its traditional principles disintegrated. Military intervention in 1914 divided the party, and the modest tariffs of the McKenna budget in 1915 and military conscription which came in 1916 were more Conservative in principle than Liberal. Some Liberals soon supported the idea of a negotiated peace. In 1915 a Liberal Government was diluted with Conservatives. The Easter Rebellion in Ireland in 1916 seemed to open the way to Home Rule (with Ulster apart), but the opportunity was lost and with it the vote of 80 Irish Nationalists. After the shift from Asquith to Lloyd George in December 1916, the Liberals, so prominent since 1906, largely disappeared. Conservatives dominated the Cabinet and the Asquith Liberals took on the cast of an Opposition. The decisive break came in May 1918 with the Maurice debate. Sir Frederick Maurice, director of military operations, was dismissed, and in retaliation accused Lloyd George of falsehood before the Commons concerning the strength of British forces in France at the beginning of 1918. Asquith demanded a select committee to investigate; Lloyd George chose to regard the matter as a motion of censure. Though the debate hardly supported his case, Asquith persisted. His motion was defeated with only ninety-eight Liberals and a handful of others supporting it. With this split "the historic Liberal Party committed suicide," comments A. J. P. Taylor. But the decline and fall of the Liberal Party is more complicated than that. In broader terms the war years made increasingly clear that the essential cleavage in twentieth-century politics would be between conservative élitism and social democracy and reenforced prewar indications that Liberalism and Labor would go their separate ways.

The Labor Party

For the Labor Party itself the war brought new problems and a new stimulus. During the Edwardian years it had just managed to hold its own. It was a house divided and faced the handicap of a minor third party in a two-party system. The advent of war at first only intensified these difficulties. There was, of course, no serious "stop the war" movement, Marxist in character. But a right wing among the conservative trade unions was belligerent almost to the point of jingoism; center elements accepted the war as an evil forced upon Britain but were hopeful for a moderate peace acceptable to all nations; leftist elements, ardently socialist in outlook (strong in the Independent Labor Party and the Fabian Society), were distrustful of the motives of the Government, saw no justification for "a fight to the finish," promoted vigorous discus-

sion of war issues, and after 1916 urged a negotiated peace which would
end the holocaust as soon as possible.

This divided sentiment was found in the Parliamentary Labor Party,
which therefore gave little direction to party policy. When the Coalition
Government was formed in 1915, the pacifists, led by MacDonald,
crossed the floor and sat in "opposition" below the gangway. Other
Labor M.P.s generally supported the Lloyd George Government when it
was formed in December 1916, but the party Executive voted in his favor
only by 14–11. It was perhaps natural that the half-dozen well-paid posts
then allotted to Labor helped to smooth out some of the difficulties. Yet
at a restless party conference in January 1917, Henderson said in defense
of his role in the Cabinet, "I am not here to please myself or you: I am
here to see the war through." That the conference then overwhelmingly
endorsed participation in the Coalition is merely indicative of the ca-
pricious nature of Labor sentiment at this time.

But in the end the war did solidify Labor. There never was any formal
break in the ranks of the Parliamentary Party. Other elements became
increasingly influential, in particular the party Executive. Trade unionism
strengthened its hold on labor, including a strong minority socialist sentiment through the shop steward movement. All but the most conservative elements were sensitive to the threat the war posed to the "rights" of
labor. A working-class consciousness grew and spread.

But circumstances, rather than ideological purpose, determined the
outlook of the Labor Party at the end of the war. First there was the
Stockholm Congress proposed for the summer of 1917 and designed as
an international socialist conference, representing working classes from
all nations at war, to define war aims and propose the terms of "a
people's peace." Henderson, back from a mission to Russia early in
1917, felt that a strong democratic socialism was essential as an alternative to Bolshevism. He strongly supported the proposed Stockholm Congress; he had a stormy time with Lloyd George and others of the Cabinet
and resigned. He emerged triumphant from a Labor Party Conference,
though this was more a personal endorsement than approval of the idea
of the Congress, on which the Conference was about evenly divided. The
Congress itself never convened. Yet historians of the Labor Party consider this the decisive moment in party fortunes; out of Henderson's
resignation from the Cabinet (August 1917) came reorganization of the
party constitution.

Henderson, along with MacDonald and Sidney Webb, found common
ground in the insistence upon Labor Party independence in stating war
aims, particularly in challenging the doctrine of national self-interest
inherent in the "secret treaties." The terms of these wartime agreements
among the Allies for postwar territorial changes were released by the

Bolshevik Government in Russia following the revolution in November 1917. A Labor Party confernece in December 1917 endorsed various statements by President Wilson and stressed the need for a peace without territorial conquest, a limitation on arms, the elimination of colonial imperialism, and establishment of a system of international security. Lloyd George was persuaded to attend a trade union conference in London on January 5, 1918, and he called for a peace of reconciliation including "the creation of some international organization to limit the burden of armaments and diminish the probability of war." Three days later Wilson proclaimed his "Fourteen Points," which became the Allied basis for peace terms.

More fundamental was Labor's reorganization of party structure. A new constitution adopted in February 1918 supplemented membership through affiliated organizations with individual membership through local Labor associations. This opened the way for mass membership without previous affiliation with a trade union or a socialist society. This is of particular significance in view of the 1918 Representation of People Act—now for the first time the working class dominated the electorate. Equally as significant was the provision for the election of the national Executive (the chief governing agency next to the conference itself) by the party conference voting as a single constituency; the Fabian Society and the Independent Labor Party lost representation as such. The role of trade unionism in the party was enhanced—for example, at the party conference, unions voted by "Block," as an undivided whole.

In June 1918 another party conference adopted the controversial restatement of party purpose. Labor advocated "a new social order based not on fighting but on fraternity—not on the competitive struggle for the means of bare life, but on deliberately planned cooperation in production and distribution for the benefit of all who participate by hand or brain ... [Four pillars] we propose to erect: (a) the Universal Enforcement of the National Minimum, (b) Democratic Control of Industry, (c) the Revolution in National Finance, and (d) the Surplus Wealth for the Common Good." It is usually emphasized that here for the first time the word "socialism" appeared in a Labor Party statement. But, argues the most recent treatment (Ross McKibbin), the reason is not ideological. The left wing in the party had not gained strength during the war. In fact, quite the contrary—there was no forseeable future in the party for an ideological extremist. The language in the statement of purpose was chosen to make a distinction from the Liberal Party, and indicated a party doctrine different from that of the older parties. It was suitable language for the leading working-class party in the allied nations, also suitable for a party of diverse elements with no agreement on doctrine.

There remained one important step—the declaration of independence from other parties. The majority of Labor members in Parliament wished to support the Coalition at least through the period of peacemaking. But in September 1918 the Labor members of the Ministry, with a few exceptions, left the Government. In November a Labor Party Conference with Shaw as the most effective speaker adopted a resolution "that the Party shall resume its independence and withdraw its membership from the Government at the close of the present Parliament." The vote was 2,117,000 to 810,000. The party was now "socialist" in language, national in character, and independent in action.

Women's Rights and the Franchise

Women's suffrage and a further liberalization of the voting franchise for men would certainly have come in time. The war hastened them. The Representation of the People Act of February 1918 came out of the report of a nonpartisan Speaker's Conference on Electoral Reform, appointed in 1916. This statute abolished all property qualifications for men—only a residence requirement remained. The vote was given to women over thirty who occupied or owned land or premises with an annual value of £5 or whose husbands did so. The age limit was apparently prescribed out of consideration of the possible consequences of the control of parliamentary elections by women voters. This legislation considerably more than doubled the electorate—a more drastic effect than that of any of the electoral reform measures of the nineteenth century. And just before its dissolution Parliament passed a supplementary bill permitting women to sit in the House of Commons.

"The women are splendid" was a standard though banal statement during the war. Women's suffrage is only the most tangible evidence of their rapidly changing position. The war brought them out of the home. There were changes in occupation, in dress, in hairstyles, in legal status. It was gradually recognized that a place would have to be made in the postwar economy for over 500,000 women with no opportunity for marriage. But it was the contribution of women to the war which brought success in the campaign for "women's rights." At first quite slow, from late 1915 the push of women into industry and into government jobs was rapid. Once the social barriers to female employment gave way, women broke through at all points. In certain areas—clerical, commercial, administrative—employment of women about doubled during the war. On a June day in 1918 a procession of women swept down Constitution Hill to Buckingham Palace to present an address from the women of Britain to the king and queen on the occasion of their silver wedding anniversary. There were the V.A.D.'s (Voluntary Aid Detachment of Nurses); the Women's Legion; the WAAC (Women's Army

Auxiliary Corps); the WRENS (Women's Royal Naval Service); munitions workers with an anti-gas section in red and a T.N.T. section in yellow; women police; omnibus and railway women; nurses; ambulance drivers; General Post Office workers; gas, light, and coke women.

Reconstruction and Reform

Other transitions may be briefly noted. Stephen McKenna once observed that politics in England were dissocialized when Asquith became prime minister (1908) and were commercialized when Lloyd George took his place (1916). Mrs. Humphry Ward was more than poetic when she remarked that during the war for many "the door of the future had fallen mysteriously ajar." In village life there was a minor revolution. It was later recalled that villagers had been heard to say, "How happy this war has made many of us." They had in mind separation allowances (often in excess of what the housewife had available before the war), greatly improved agricultural wages, and higher prices for produce. The agricultural laborer, in fact, attained a position of respectability which his class had not known for two generations. On the other hand, country house life was disappearing. With rising taxation, particularly in death duties, the economic basis of aristocracy was crumbling. Haldane was understating when at the outbreak of the war he said, "We well-to-do will have in the future to live on half our incomes." The war produced no such group of aristocratic intellectuals as "the Souls" of a generation before. Everywhere—in the country and in the city, in the armed forces, in politics and in business—strict class lines were blurred. Perhaps for the first time in English history a person's station in life was not revealed in his dress. Marriages across class lines became common. Well-established standards of good conversation, correct etiquette, and good taste rapidly deteriorated. Social taboos which had governed education, the servant class, and the amusement world also gave way.

In "reconstruction" is another important link during the war between the past and the future. "Let us take what comfort we can from these facts—a new heat of intelligence, a new passion of sympathy and interest which, when the war is over, will burn out of itself the rotten things in our social structure and make reform easy which, but for the war, might have rent us asunder." Thus Mrs. Ward in 1918. The promise of "a better world" is a recurring note in war propaganda. The war would end one day, and some good must emerge from it. The word "reconstruction" itself began to be used in 1916; it was something of a tonic to flagging spirits. A new Cabinet department—Labor—was created in 1916. H. A. L. Fisher, appointed to the Board of Education by Lloyd

George, delivered his maiden speech in the Commons in April 1917. He dealt at length—for more than two hours—with his subject of educational reform, and was rewarded with unusually heavy applause, in part a testimony of the interest of the House in some subject other than the war.

Lloyd George had a special genius for sensing and capitalizing upon moods in public opinion. Upon becoming prime minister at the very moment of crisis in the military fortunes of the war, he was looking ahead, so he enthusiastically reiterated, to a great era of reform. In March 1917 he told a Labor delegation: "The present war ... presents an opportunity for reconstruction of industrial and economic conditions of this country such as has never been presented in the life of, probably, the world." A Ministry of Reconstruction, formalizing a previous committee, was created in 1917 and was soon busily engaged in investigating all phases of British industrial life, as well as housing, public health, and transport. But would such a ministry be able to define postwar problems and develop solutions? Would material standards of living be raised, as well as moral and intellectual ones? These questions were asked again and again—prophetic, perhaps, in the doubts repetition suggested. Yet the Education Act was encouragement to the reforming spirit. Fisher, a well-known historian and vice-chancellor of the University of Sheffield, set out to overhaul the educational system. His Act of 1918 enlarged the powers of the L.E.A.'s (Local Educational Authorities). The general purpose was to establish a national system of education available to all. While the school-leaving age was fourteen, a local authority could extend the school leaving age to fifteen. Further schooling was to be provided for all over fourteen who qualified. All in all it was the most comprehensive measure of tax supported education yet enacted; unfortunately, many of its provisions were not obligatory and, thus, its implementation was uneven.

In other areas, actual "reconstruction" and "reform" were necessarily put off until after the war. The important question raised during the war was the extent to which the State itself would be directly concerned. "Little by little and year by year the fabric of State expenditure and State responsibility is built up like a coral island, cell on cell," the *Economist* reported in 1895. During 1914-18 this process merely picked up speed, with the adoption of military conscription and with controls on industry, trade, food, and natural resources. Although these wartime controls were not long enough in operation to be accepted as social habit, apparently they had worked. Many would urge that they be continued. The average person was made well aware of his changing world.

Could Britain capitalize in peacetime on the patriotism, the high sense of national duty, and the grim courage which the great majority of its people manifested during four long years of war? When the armistice came on November 11, 1918, no one knew the answer. It was apparently on that day that Osbert Sitwell wrote:

> ... we were yet illusioned about the peace. During the passage of more than four years, the worse the present had shown itself, the more golden the future, unreal as the conventional heaven, had become to our eyes: an outlook common, perhaps, to those of all ages of war and revolution. And today ... that long present had suddenly become changed to the past, clearly to be seen as such. Hence both the joy and earnestness of dancers in street and square tonight; hence, too, the difficulty of finding a way in which to describe to the reader the movements that so precisely interpreted conflicting emotions: the long-drawn-out misery and monastic stultification of the trenches, and then the joy of a victory that in the end had rushed on us with the speed and impact of a comet.

6 Aftermath of War

T. E. Lawrence
Introduction to
*The Seven Pillars
of Wisdom*,
quoted in David
Garnett, ed.,
*Letters of T. E.
Lawrence* (1938),
p. 262

It felt like morning, and the freshness of the world-to-be intoxicated us. We were wrought up with ideas inexpressible and vaporous, but to be fought for. We lived many lives in those whirling campaigns, never sparing ourselves any good or evil: yet when we achieved and the new world dawned, the old men came out again and took from us our victory, and remade it in the likeness of the former world they knew. Youth could win, but had not learned to keep, and was pitiably weak against age. We stammered that we had worked for a new heaven and a new earth, and they thanked us kindly and made their peace.

Thomas Jones
Lloyd George
(1951), pp. 195–
96

Lloyd George, said Lord Gladstone, was not as Herbert Fisher called him, a genius thrown up by a cataclysm, but a genie let out of a bottle by a rash mistake of the Conservative Party which was now making desperate efforts to get him back into safe confinement.

1918–1924

At 11 A.M. on that rainy November day, the firing of maroons in London announced the war's end. A few minutes before, Lloyd George had thrown open the door of No. 10 Downing Street and impulsively shouted advance notice to those gathered in the roadway. Not far away, at the window of his room in the Ministry of Munitions, Winston Churchill saw the streets toward Trafalgar Square, which had been silent and empty, suddenly fill with a mass of hysterical and agitated humanity. Pigeons fluttered around Nelson's Column. Crowds milled through Charing Cross, Trafalgar Square, and Piccadilly Circus, and then those who could moved in the direction of Buckingham Palace to be greeted by the royal family. Big Ben, silent during the war, boomed again; and in the evening the street lights, dimmed for more than four years, blazed anew. Out near Garsington in Oxfordshire, Siegfried Sassoon, walking in the river meadows that morning, heard "a sudden peal of bells from the village church and saw little flags being fluttered out from the windows of the thatched houses on the hill." Herbert Morrison, a conscientious objector and a future Cabinet minister, was at work in a market garden at Letchworth when the sirens sounded and the church bells rang. "I stopped digging," he tells us, "put my foot on my spade and experienced a quiet and profound emotion." Throughout Britain vast crowds or small groups gathered in city street, in marketplace, in cathedral close, at cottage gate. Each individual had his own thoughts but scarcely anyone was unmoved. For all it was a solemn moment in history.

145

Of Armistice Day, in striking contrast to *Counter-Attack,* Sassoon wrote:

Everyone suddenly burst out singing;
. . . .
Everyone's voice was suddenly lifted;
And beauty came like the setting sun:
My heart was shaken with tears; and horror
Drifted away.

In these lines he captured the passing mood—a brief return to selfless unity and idealism; an absence of bitterness, revenge, and national pride.

This mood is worthy of some documentation. On Saturday, November 9, came the annual procession of the lord mayor of London. The archbishop of Canterbury tells us about the Guildhall banquet that evening:

[Lloyd George was greeted with a reception] without parallel in my experience. As he came up the Hall, and the whole company stood on chairs and shouted and waved, I was standing by Arthur Balfour . . . and I remarked with amusement on the demonstration to a man who, ten years before, was regarded in the City as unutterable, and Balfour's reply in the din was shouted into my ear, "Well, the little beggar deserves it all."

On Monday afternoon, the eleventh, Lloyd George reported to the Commons on the terms of the armistice. He concluded: "This is no time for words. Our hearts are too full of gratitude to which no tongue can give adequate expression." The House adjourned to St. Margaret's Church across the street and was there joined by the Lords for a service of prayer. "I do not suppose there has ever been in our history a more significant recognition of the Divine Presence and aid than in this sudden attendance of the Houses at Divine Service in lieu of a Commons debate," wrote the archbishop in his diary. He read the lesson from *Isaiah* including these lines:

The Spirit of the Lord God is upon me; . . . he hath sent me to bind up the broken-hearted, to proclaim liberty to the captives, and the opening of the prison to them that are bound. . . . For as the earth bringeth forth her bud, and as the garden causeth the things that are sown in it to spring forth; so the Lord God will cause righteousness and praise to spring forth before all the nations.

That evening the prime minister gave serious attention to the proposal that the blockade be lifted and that food ships be quickly dispatched to Germany. On five successive days the king and queen rode through the least favored streets of London. They attended a service of thanksgiving in St. Paul's while a vast throng massed outside, the men with heads uncovered. On November 18, in a ceremony held without precedent in the spacious Royal Gallery of the Palace of Westminster, George V received a congratulatory address from Lords and Commons who sat in joint assembly with representatives of the dominions and of India. In response the king said, "May good-will and concord at home strengthen our influence for concord abroad."

The Election of 1918

Now let us shift our attention. It is in the course of the parliamentary election (the polling was on December 14) that we see the mood change. Some months past Lloyd George had pretty well made up his mind to continue the Coalition Government into the postwar period; back in April he had sounded out the Webbs as to the possibility of cooperation from Labor. This failed; so did efforts to reconcile Asquith and his wing of the Liberal Party. He was more successful with Bonar Law and the Conservatives, with whom, by October, he had reached agreement on retention of the Coalition and an early appeal to the country in a general election. They both agreed to set aside differences of principle between Liberals and Conservatives on fiscal reform, Irish home rule, and disestablishment of the Church in Wales.

Lloyd George's public statements at this time were conciliatory, moderate, even idealistic. His campaign to perpetuate the Coalition was launched in September; in an address at Manchester he dwelt upon the theme of reform and reconstruction. On November 12 he declared to Coalition Liberals gathered at 10 Downing Street:

> We must not allow any sense of revenge, and spirit of greed, any grasping desire to override the fundamental principles of righteousness.... Now is the great opportunity of Liberalism!... If there are personal differences, in God's name what do they count in comparison with the vast issues and problems before us? Let us help to regenerate the people, the great people who have done more to save the world in this great crisis than any other nation.

Idealism, Bitterness, Apathy

The Coalition campaign opened formally on November 22 with a manifesto proposing an ambitious program of reconstruction: decontrol of industry, land reclamation, a national housing program, reform of the membership of the Lords, home rule for Ireland without Ulster, and responsible government (by gradual stages) in India.

"We appeal ... to every section of the electorate, without distinction of Party, to support the Coalition Government in the execution of a policy devised ... for the furtherance of the general good." On November 12 the prime minister had said, "I would quit this place tomorrow, if I could not obtain the support of Liberals." Coalition candidates received a letter of support from both Lloyd George and Bonar Law, who agreed that Lloyd George Liberals, to the number of about 150, were not to be opposed by the Conservatives. But some 229 Liberals were refused the "coupon," as Asquith dubbed it. Was Lloyd George's purpose to preserve as many Liberals seats as possible, or was it primarily to defeat those Liberals who had opposed his policies or had voted against him in the Maurice debate? There has been heated argument over this point— perhaps Roy Douglas's conclusion that Lloyd George did not care about either preserving or destroying the Liberal Party as long as he was in control is as reasonable as any.

The Liberals excluded from the Coalition were fighting a hopeless battle from the start; in more than 500 of the 707 constituencies Coalition Conservatives and Coalition Liberals pooled their resources. Labor was far more hopeful. Labor contested 361 constituencies, in comparison with a previous high of 78 (January 1910). "Labour's Call to the People" announced a "comprehensive and constructive" program for the rebuilding of the world..

As between Coalition, independent Liberal, and Labor, issues were quite undefined. But the language of the campaign soon became precise, bitter, and extravagant. The independent Liberal press denounced the "rush election" as "the plan for the extinction of all independent opinion" (*Westminster Gazette,* November 13). "The nation is in the presence not of an election but of a conspiracy" (*Daily News,* November 23). Just before polling day the *Daily Express* retorted with the headline "How would the Germans like you to vote? Think it over."

The campaign of the Coalition began with the accent on reconstruction; it ended with demands for revenge upon Germany. In .this sharp shift of emphasis Lloyd George did not, as sometimes charged, take the lead; nor was he as immoderate as some of his followers or as extreme as the Northcliffe press. It was not he who made the remark "We shall squeeze the orange until the pips squeak." Nevertheless, it is interesting to follow his actual words as the campaign progressed. At Wolverhampton on November 24 he said, "Don't let us waste this victory merely in ringing joy bells." This must be a land "fit for heroes to live in." On November 30 he declared to Lord Riddell that the Germans "must pay to the uttermost farthing. But the question is how they can be made to pay beyond a certain point." Shortly after, before an excited audience in Bristol, he departed from his prepared manuscript and minimized the difficulties. He suggested that German capacity "will go a pretty long way." We must have "the uttermost farthing," and "shall search their pockets for it." As the campaign closed, he summarized his program: (1) trial of the Kaiser, (2) punishment of those guilty of atrocities, (3) fullest indemnity from Germany, (4) Britain for the British, socially and industrially, (5) rehabilitation of those broken in the war and (6) a happier country for all. He was giving the country what it wanted. At a luncheon party "he talked of nothing but the election—of what cries went down with the electorate, and what did not"—so Duff Cooper, who was present, wrote in his diary.

While most of the press catered to the popular demand for revenge, some elements expressed disgust. Massingham of the *Nation,* normally Liberal, advised voting Labor. *The Times* declared (December 4), "Nobody, we imagine, has any doubts that Mr. Lloyd George would have been wiser if he had frankly gone to the country on his own great record and his own view of social reform without any attempt at securing pledges or making bargains over candidates." The *Economist* could find no grounds for enthusiasm anywhere.

Despite the efforts of the politicians, the campaign did not excite much public interest. Even the party labels were confusing. *Punch* for December 4 ran a full-page drawing labeled "The Voter's Nightmare" and in its issue of December 18 commented dryly, "The preliminary announcement that nearly nine hundred candidates must fail to be elected . . . has been received with a good deal of quiet satisfaction." Delay in arranging for the armed forces vote disfranchised most of it. Slightly more than 50 percent of the electorate voted—a small proportion for a twentieth-century election. But the voting public had been completely transformed—something like 75 percent of those who had the franchise in 1918 had not previously qualified.

The result was a victory beyond all expectation for Lloyd George and the Coalition: success in some 520 contests—of which 136 were won by couponed Liberals—out of a total of 707. Within the Coalition, Conservatives controlled more than two-thirds of the seats. The Asquith independent Liberals were crushed and emerged with only 33 seats. Asquith himself failed of reelection in the constituency which had returned him for thirty-two years. The 59 seats won by Labor made them the strongest party in opposition in the new Parliament—labor had polled 22 percent of the popular vote, a leap forward and indicative of things to come. However, their militants (Henderson, MacDonald, Snowden) were all defeated by "coupon" candidates; conservative trade unionists predominated among the winners; leadership in Parliament fell to William Adamson, limited in outlook and in ability. In Irish constituencies the old National Irish Party (the party of home rule) returned only 7; Sinn Fein (the party of revolution) almost swept the board with 73 seats, but these seats were not taken.

Peacetime Coalition and the New Commons

The policy of Lloyd George in this election constitutes one of the most controversial episodes in his career. Was he justified in going to the country at just this time? Should he not have accepted the advice of George V, who cited the unfortunate precedent of the khaki election of 1900? Did Lloyd George deliberately exploit the circumstances of 1918?

The answers depend on where one turns. But it is well to keep in mind certain facts. An election immediately after the war seems to have been almost inevitable. The Parliament elected in 1910 was, by 1918, no longer in any sense representative. Since then the electorate had been expanded, Labor had grown restless and more powerful, national problems had radically changed. No Cabinet could have hoped to succeed after the war without assurance of popular support. While the sheer necessity for an election can hardly be proved, the arguments for an early poll, quite apart from matters of partisanship, were very strong. Furthermore, there was nothing sinister in Lloyd George's decision to perpetuate the war Coalition. Churchill made a similar proposal after World War II. In 1918 the alternative for Lloyd George was reconciliation with Asquith, and that would have been difficult indeed. Lloyd George, of course, catered to the Conservatives, but times change: a political realignment might be in the making.

In 1918 the consequences of a continuation of the Coalition under Lloyd George could not be foreseen. The extent to which that Government was responsible for the terms of peace and for the crisis at home and abroad in postwar years cannot be established, though Asquith Liberals asserted the contrary. It is highly questionable whether an exclusively Tory Government—the only conceivable alternative to the Coalition—would have been any more successful. In the United States, President Wilson fought the congressional elections of November 1918 on a strictly partisan basis, and this brought upon him much the same kind of criticism as was heaped upon Lloyd George for *not* reverting to strictly partisan politics.

These points seem valid and relevant. Yet it was soon apparent that the election of 1918 was itself quite unfortunate. The operation of the constitutional process in England depends on party, and normally England "does not love coalitions," for they render effective criticism of governmental policy difficult. The very chamber of the House of Commons makes no provision for a multiplicity of parties. Now the existence of four distinct political alignments (Conservative, Coalition Liberal, Independent Liberal, and Laborite) confounded an essential feature of cabinet government, that of the establishment of party responsibility for policy. While the Coalition, Conservative-dominated, enjoyed a crushing superiority in the Commons, the popular vote for its candidates was only slightly in excess of the popular vote of the defeated parties.

In point of fact, it was not a representative House, some would say the least representative since 1832. Nearly all the effective leaders of Opposition parties had been defeated. And it was unfortunate for a land which needed unity that those who were elected were predominantly wealthy and predominantly commercially minded. Austen Chamberlain tells a story quoting Lloyd George as referring jocosely to the "Associated Chambers of Commerce" behind him. In bitterness the defeated exploited the celebrated remark by Baldwin to Keynes that the new House was "a group of hard-faced men who looked as if they had done well out of the war." The remark was perhaps uncalled for, but it does not stand alone. Harold Nicolson called it "the most unintelligent body of public-school boys which . . . the Mother of Parliaments has known." And a reputable historian (F. S. Northedge) refers to the 1918 Parliament as "certainly one of the most insular and ignorant in British history."

The election campaign left the country's leadership divided, not on principles but by personal grievances. Opposition forces felt that they had been victimized, and they were not inclined to be moderate or fair-minded toward those who had taken advantage of them. There was now much less chance that the peace conference could be approached in a reasonable manner and that a policy of domestic reform and reconstruction could be formulated on a basis of mutual good will and in the national interest. The unhappy consequences were soon apparent.

The National Temper

But this general election must not be judged out of context. It is merely an important episode in the war's aftermath. Any Parliament, no matter its composition, would have been on the defensive, for the Commons had lost prestige during the war, with debates ill-attended and little heeded. Any Cabinet and any Parliament after 1918 would have had difficulty in establishing sound policy acceptable to the nation in the face of baffling postwar problems and new party alignments. The politicians, Lloyd George included, conducted themselves at least as intelligently and at least as responsibly as the nation at large. The mood of Parliament reflects the general mood of the nation, which probably received the quality of leadership it deserved.

Divisions, Anxieties, and Frustrations

In this section we are concerned with the entire decade of the twenties. The morale of Britain in these years is something which could not have been predicted. Hers was more the psychology of a land which had lost confidence in its rulers than one now in gratitude dedicating its energies to the uses of peace. The national outlook reflected more the divisions of a land torn by defeat than a unity born of sacrifice to a great ideal. It was the mentality of a land affected with a malaise.

Some of the elements may be easily distinguished. In the eighteen months after the Armistice nearly four million men were returned to civilian life. Immediately evident was the antagonism between "the Fighting Forces" and "the Rest," as phrased by the authors of a very stimulating treatment of the 1920s, *The Long Week-End*. The veteran was very conscious of the gap between industrial wages during the war and his own meager service pay. He was not disposed to take very seriously the stories of suffering at home. A million veterans came home to find their old jobs in the hands of men who had never gone off to war or in the hands of women. Furthermore, combat troops had come to know "the enemy" as fellow soldiers in the trenches—human beings like themselves caught in a terrible predicament—and not as "the Huns" of the popular press. These veterans shared little in the popular cry for retribution and revenge. Richard Aldington describes these veterans further: "turbulent, impatient, full of strange oaths, contemptuous of anything that looked like humbug... always getting together in groups and talking in a strange jargon of their own about one topic—the war, which they refused to discuss with anyone who had not been in it."

"On the other hand," he continues, "was the civilian population, frayed in its nerves, crushed with taxation, anxious about its own future, with all its benevolence and emotional sympathy long since exhausted. ... Not until the flood of war books ten years later did they realize what the young men had endured."

It was partly a conflict of generations. To those returning from the trenches, the war had been the most important experience they had ever known. They came back restless and expectant, and with no desire to have restored the world of 1914 which had produced the war. They were ready "for a new heaven and a new earth." But they were quickly and perhaps too easily disillusioned. They found that their elders did not wish to make a place for them, in fact, pretty much ignored them.

The "lost generation" had many spokesmen. What seems abnormal in the pages of T. E. Lawrence (as in the bitter words quoted at the begin-

ning of this chapter) or in Vera Brittain's *Testament of Youth* (1933)—
especially the chapter "Survivors not wanted"—becomes normal and
more convincing elsewhere. C. E. Montague's *Disenchantment* (1922) is
"an essay on disillusion." And E. L. Woodward in his charming and
poignant autobiography, *Short Journey*, remarks:

> Most of the scholars who wrote our books had been prevented by age
> or health from going to war. It struck me that very few of them, or
> the civil servants who had been in London for the four evil years, had
> any idea of the immense moral destruction, the lowering of standards,
> the confusion and disorder of mind which modern war must produce
> over the area where the fighting has taken place, and among ordinary
> men within the battle zones.

In October 1919 Woodward "sat" for a fellowship at All Souls in Oxford. While waiting for his viva voce, which would conclude the examination, he listened to "the Oxford talk" of other candidates:

> While I was listening to the conversation in the Warden's lod-
> ging... I knew well enough that for my own generation, and particu-
> larly for those of us who had been in the army, the war was an ex-
> perience likely to dominate the rest of our lives. I thought also that
> the survivors of this generation would be able to use in peace their
> experiences learned in war. I thought that the future was in our
> hands; that we should get the support of those immediately younger
> than ourselves; that our elders would listen to us, and, for very
> shame, be ready to give us a directing control over the management
> of affairs. These hopes have been disappointed.

But hardly all of the lost generation were as eager to reconstruct the
world as T. E. Lawrence, Vera Brittain, or E. L. Woodward suggest. John
Buchan remembered that there was much indifference, much avoidance
of public duty and personal responsibility. Like its elders, H. G. Wells
tells us in *The World of William Clissold* (1926), youth was ready to
leave "the working out of the Millennium to anyone else who chose to
bother. Nobody chose to bother."

"Mass Civilization"

Not until a decade after 1918 did the war become the
subject of popular literature. Most people were "fed up" with the war;
this phrase was developed for the occasion. The reading public had
greatly increased during the war, but the literature of the masses was the
literature of escape, particularly "the thriller" and "the shocker." Edgar
Wallace (1875–1932) wrote and published at least 170 volumes—many
of his novels were delivered to a dictaphone.

For the masses the lowest standards set the tone. It was the era "of the exploitation of the cheap response" (F. R. Leavis). One observer, for a parallel, goes back to the Paris immediately after the fall of Robespierre's Republic of Virtue. The desire for amusement and for distraction clamored for satisfaction; the response is plain to be seen in *Bystander* and other popular magazines. Sport was commercialized—the focus of attention was Wembley, constructed originally for the British Empire Exhibition of 1924. The sport stadium (with a capacity of 125,000) was opened in 1923, when 160,000 jammed the field and stadium for the Football Cup final. In 1925 the Wembley buildings were taken over by the Wembley Stadium and Greyhound Racecourse, Ltd. Dog races became the great rage; the electric hare, added in 1926 to stimulate the dogs, was dispatched around the track at sixty miles per hour, and each race lasted about thirty seconds. The high quality of the music hall of Marie Lloyd and Harry Lauder gave way to the cheapness of the cinema, where most any picture was a success. Amusement became mere pastime.

"People are dancing as they have never danced before in a happy rebound from the austerities of war," reads the *Daily Mail,* February 1919. The word "ragtime," originally a term of derision, as in "ragtime regiment," became an accepted term for an accepted type of music. And it was also "this Jazz Age." There was dancing in the morning, there was dancing all night, there was dinner dancing between courses, there was a style of dancing which would have shocked Edwardians, and there were dances without chaperones. Vera Brittain later wrote of the dances night after night in the Grafton Galleries, where Canadian soldiers in the struggle of combat looked down from the walls on dancers below. "And shadows of dead men, watching 'em there" (Alfred Noyes).

In 1919 there was a complete London "season." A record Derby brought out extravagant betting; the papers were full of the favorite, "The Panther," and something like national panic developed when he came in fourth and the winner paid off 33 to 1. The Henley Regatta was renewed. Mlle. Suzanne Lenglen scored the first of many triumphs on the center court at Wimbledon. In August came a holiday rush without precedent; for many it was the first real holiday in five years. Some 300,000 went to Blackpool; other thousands went to Yarmouth and to Clacton. Only a small fraction found accommodations.

Other aspects of manners and morals took on the same character. Radical changes in women's styles—short skirts and bobbed hair—inspired many coarse jokes. Sexual standards, particularly among the working classes, became greatly relaxed. Among Oxford undergraduates there was a pronounced Bohemian tendency in extremes of dress, attitudes, and behavior. In these changes in manners we have one of the few developments of the postwar years which can be directly attributed to the war.

"Minority Culture"

"Low-brow" and "high-brow"—terms imported from America—gained currency in Britain and illustrate the widening gap in the twenties between the "gay world" and the "intellectual world," between "mass civilization" and "minority culture." Sensitive and inquiring minds were toughened by the war, which underscored the predicament of mankind in the twentieth century. Science had revealed an infinite complexity in nature and in mankind. Modern physics denied the inexorable relation of cause and effect in the physical world. Albert Einstein (1879–1955) eliminated the concept of absolute space (as a fixed system) and of absolute time (as a generic term connecting past, present, and future) and replaced them with a new concept, that of space-time, denoting relativity. The Scottish anthropologist Sir James Frazer (1854–1941) in *The Golden Bough,* a fundamental book in the twenties, eliminated most of the mystery and much of the authority from the realm of religious belief and social custom. Sigmund Freud (1856–1939) replaced old mysteries with new: the world of man's subconscious and unconscious behavior. The brilliant Dean Inge (1860–1954) of St. Paul's Cathedral, of whom it was said that he was sorry he was a Christian, became "the gloomy dean"; in 1922 he referred to the nineteenth century as "the most wonderful century in human history" and saw little hope for the future. The Webbs lost their buoyancy; in 1928 Beatrice was writing, "Are we perchance on the brink of a catastrophic subsidence in physical comfort and mental development?"

After the war the most active minds in literary circles were ready for a sharp break with the past. To reflect life as it is, to get at the real meaning of human experience and to clothe it in adequate language, now required wholly new techniques of analysis and new forms of expression. The best of the old writers—Moore, Hardy, Bennett, Galsworthy, Wells, even Shaw—seemed not only outmoded but even second-rate. In employing society as a framework for analyzing the individual they were missing the point. Plot, setting, and narrative are mere contrivances of the writer to satisfy his reader. Reality, so the new approach held, is found in the individual, and the world about him is significant only insofar as he is aware of it. His response is complex and must be explored at various levels of consciousness. Therefore, the first duty of the writer, in a phrase, is to get "inside the individual."

Of course "the old masters" continued writing and continued to be read. John Masefield, poet laureate in 1930, published his narrative poem *Reynard the Fox* in 1919. Shaw seemed to be at the height of his powers with *St. Joan* in 1923. Galsworthy was just completing *The Forsyte Saga* in the early twenties, and Bennett continued writing almost until his death in 1931.

But the powerful voices were now elsewhere. What is often considered the avant-garde was the "Bloomsbury Group" (already mentioned), a London circle focusing on Leonard and Virginia Woolf and the Hogarth Press, which was primarily interested in ideas—creative, unconventional, experimental ideas. Its members were intensely serious, very self-conscious (though the "Bloomsbury" label was more used of them than by them) and, though hardly consistent with their emphasis on the experimental, quite dogmatic. From one of them in 1918 came a work which made literary history. World War I ended not with a masterpiece in the form of a song of praise or hymn of gratitude, but with Lytton Strachey's *Eminent Victorians;* the adjective, one must emphasize, was satirical. In this repudiation of the Victorian achievement we have a significant introduction to postwar literary production. Freud's influence, particularly his explication of the conflict between the conscious and the unconscious, found special expression in the works of E. M. Forster and Virginia Woolf. The latter considered the conventional novel with comedy and tragedy, triumph and catastrophe, a false representation of life. In her essay on "Modern Fiction," originally written in 1919, she said: "Life is not a series of gig-lamps symmetrically arranged; but a luminous halo, a semi-transparent envelope surrounding us from the beginning of consciousness to the end. Is it not the task of the novelist to convey this varying, this unknown and uncircumscribed spirit, whatever aberration or complexity it may display, with as little mixture of the alien and external as possible?" It was a question that her own writing attempted to answer.

The "stream of consciousness" style was brought to perfection in James Joyce's *Ulysses,* first published in France in 1922 but banned in England until the thirties. Joyce presents through "internal monologue" all the sensations and experiences of three individuals in the course of one day. At a casual glance the work seems but a chaos of disconnected thought and feeling. Some reviewers found it "unreadable," some "unquotable," and others "unreviewable." Yet Joyce was so much of a virtuoso that Leopold Bloom emerges as one of the most distinct characters in modern literature.

Poetry was given a new direction by T. S. Eliot, whose *The Waste Land* (1922) came to symbolize for many the problem of life. Man and his environment no longer harmonize; the modern "waste land" is society uprooted and adrift. The poem employs Eliot's famous ironic contrast,

the fusing of "memory and desire"; the symbolism is learned and sometimes obscure. Some critics found him unintelligible; others found him
pretentious and arrogant.

The Human Problem

But within a decade that which had been considered
esoteric became commonplace. Eliot's poetic drama *Murder in the
Cathedral* (1935) was widely produced. The work of Aldous Huxley was
acclaimed. Students in provincial British universities and in midwestern
American colleges came soon to be absorbed with Eliot, Virginia Woolf,
and eventually Joyce as well. These writers were widely imitated, though
usually with indifferent success. Their techniques came into popular and
uncritical usage. And so the high-brow, the middle-brow, and even the
low-brow proved to have much in common. If the Edwardians had been
disenchanted with the past, the postwar generation was disenchanted
with the present. Life must be "debunked." The complexities of urban
civilization, the impact of new knowledge, the disillusion with the
idealism of the war, all underlined the human problem.

That intellectuals could not agree on the answer is another characteristic of the age. If there could only be "clarification of fundamental ideas,"
as Sir Herbert Samuel put it later in his *Memoirs*. Some felt that bare
recognition of the problem was its solution. "Not speechless with shock
but finding the right language for thirst and fear," said W. H. Auden in
tribute to Eliot on his sixtieth birthday. For others the only reality was
subjective, the way out in personal vanity and social anarchy. The answer
to the claims of society was disengagement; the problem could be profitably examined only in a spirit of irony and fantasy. But many looked for
salvation through politics and social reform. Members of the Bloomsbury
Group were generally "leftist." Sassoon became literary editor of the
Daily Herald, and Ezra Pound a Fascist. Some, particularly in the thirties,
turned to communism. H. G. Wells pinned his hopes on a "World State";
in 1920 he wrote *The Outline of History* to demonstrate the artificiality
of nationalism and the vitality of the common experience of mankind.
There were signs of a widespread religious revival. In the twenties a
strong "modernist" movement swept through the Church of England;
conferences considered the theme "the humanist Christ," and a commission analyzed divergent opinions of Christian belief. But the war experience stimulated concern within the Anglican Church for the social order
as well. In Birmingham in 1924, a Conference on Politics, Economics,
and Citizenship (COPEC), interdenominational in character, chaired by
William Temple, then the bishop of Manchester, undertook, in the words
of the secretary, to establish "a norm of Christian thought and action for

the further working out of a Christian order." "Capitalism," "Imperialism," "Industrialism" all came under attack. The ideas tested at this conference more than lingered on. In a broader context, many an individual went his own way seeking peace of mind. Julian Huxley in *Religion without Revelation* (1927) revived the conflict between science and religion and sought to secure the best of both worlds. C. S. Lewis, an Oxford scholar, found salvation in orthodox Anglicanism, T. S. Eliot became an Anglo-Catholic, and the novelist Evelyn Waugh was converted to Rome.

At all levels of literacy and sophistication new bearings were being sought. That English thought came to be charged with the ideas of the highbrows is testimony to their depth and validity. That Britain produced creative and experimental minds and then sifted and absorbed their contributions is indicative of her own vitality.

Abortive Reconstruction

Economic developments and politics lend themselves more readily to chronological treatment. Our first pause in their examination will be at the end of 1924. In the interim after 1918 Britain soon found herself, with some surprise, in economic straits which were to remain a fairly normal feature of her national life. A program of reconstruction had been envisaged—decontrol in industry and its modernization, a housing program, educational and social reform. But events proved otherwise, and an increase in economic distress widened the cleavage between left and right. Four administrations and three general elections provide a shifting pattern in which the most dramatic development was the replacement of the Liberals by the Laborites as a major party and the formation of the first Labor Government in 1924.

Boom and Depression

For most people the immediate problems were economic. And yet, save in very general terms (such as problems of "decontrol," concern over a national debt twelve times that of 1913, the process of the changeover from war production to peacetime enterprise), no one anticipated just what the demands of the postwar situation would be. It would have been more healthy for the economy, if grave difficulties were to appear, had they appeared promptly. Yet, as it happened, for eighteen months (until the spring of 1920) there was a postwar boom no less real, if artificial. In industry a demand for goods to replace depleted stocks and considerable need for capital to restore peacetime production provided stimulus. The Agricultural Act of 1920 encouraged production of wheat and oats with minimum prices guaranteed. Tenant farmers felt greater security and began to buy the land which they cultivated. Generally speaking, wages and prices rose along with full employment.

But the farmer, the policy makers in Westminster, and men of business and industry were thrown off guard. In the course of 1920, conditions radically changed. Agricultural prices collapsed and the Corn Production Repeal Act of 1921 recognized the reversal of the farmers' fortunes. For the economy generally, when supply caught up with demand, when foreign countries took steps to stimulate their own production, when financial interests took fright and curbed credit, when European markets were once more open to American and Asiatic production—all this reacted unfavorably against Britain.

Let us first take a general view. Economic analyses generally consider the period 1919–29 as a whole; but since in Britain the situation was stabilized from 1925 to the world depression of 1929, these findings will be relevant to our immediate period. For more than a century, Britain's economy had been geared to production for a world market, with heavy imports in food and raw materials. It was, indeed, in her view, "one economic world" controlled by herself. She seemed to have taken in stride the competitive challenge from the United States, Germany, and Japan in the prewar years. But the Great War had intensified economic nationalism—and each nation was learning to live on her own, with the United States in particular zealously competing for world markets held by Britain. In consequence, by 1924, Britain was maintaining her export position only in those commodities which were expanding the least. Britain's share of the world's exports, of whatever nature, fell from 13 percent in 1913 to 11 percent in 1929. And the proportion of her total production directed into foreign trade declined over these years. Total production did not reach prewar levels until 1924.

It is not easy to make an accurate and intelligent assessment of Britain's economy in the twenties. The ablest of the economic historians disagree on some of the fundamentals. Derek H. Aldcroft and Harry W. Richardson, in recent studies, while recognizing the general decline in Britain's relative position since the nineteenth century insist that the postwar period was not one of stagnation and that her record stands up well against that of other countries. In particular, they stress the structural changes in Britain's economy—the modernization of technology and the development of new industries—rayon, electrical engineering, chemicals, and especially motorcars. Other scholars, writing a few years earlier, in particular W. Arthur Lewis and A. J. Youngson, point out the limitations of the British achievement, the delays of industrial and political leadership in meeting changing conditions, and the ultimate failure of Britain to keep pace with her rivals. While recognizing that both these positions have merit and are hardly contradictory, we shall tend to emphasize the weaknesses in Britain's economy, which, in the long run, are the factors of most significance, factors social as well as economic, in our examination of Britain in transition.

The postwar boom ceased in the spring of 1920; a year later, hosts of the unemployed were parading with banners: "Wanted in 1914; not wanted now." In 1920 insurance applied to nearly all the unemployed, and thus the widely publicized figures were accurate and well known. By July 1921 unemployment reached 2,000,000 constituting 22.4 percent of all insured workers; in the shipbuilding and in the iron and steel trades the figure was 27 percent. The proper figure for comparison for the years 1901–13, would be about 6 percent as an average. To be sure, the July 1921 situation was abnormal because of the coal strike, but even at the end of 1923 (a year after the coal settlement) the figure was 13 percent. At no time during the period from 1922 to 1929 did the unemployment figure fall much below 10 percent of the insured workers, with the average about 12 percent.

Opportunities Missed

The twin problems were lagging production and rising unemployment. To have solved the first would have ameliorated the second. It was certainly not easy to determine precisely what steps to take, but business and government did not make sufficient attempt. Leadership was proud that Britain seemed to have weathered the war years better than any other nation and was still second only to the United States in economic strength. Business interests usually proposed nineteenth-century solutions for such problems as there were. Economic laws were fixed; the "system" would in time right itself. Away with DORA and all it stood for. World Trade would be recaptured by free trade abroad, *laissez-faire* at home. As for the British pound, the country must, of course, return to prewar parity of exchange. If this meant a price rise above that of her competitors, costs of production would have to be reduced.

In contrast, as we now see the situation, it would seem that Britain might well have profited by such steps as these: (1) restriction of imports and stimulation of home industry for home consumption; (2) the development of greater strength in producer goods (such as machinery, chemicals, implements, and automobiles) for export; (3) more prompt modernization of the coal, steel, and textile industries; (4) a more flexible foreign exchange, less commitment to the prewar gold standard; thus, a stimulus to export trades and a corresponding decline in imports, and, hopefully, rising levels of employment.

But, of course, much of this comment is hindsight; the results of the policies Britain did pursue cannot be fully seen until 1929. Until then, living on a somewhat reduced national income, she was able to pay her bills abroad and even have a little surplus to invest abroad. A slightly favorable balance of trade was maintained, but at the expense of a high rate of unemployment and a very low standard of living for many. The general strike of 1926 could not be foreseen nor the financial crisis of 1931 nor the staggering unemployment figures for the early thirties. But with a more flexible and more imaginative policy in the twenties Britain might well have weathered these difficulties more promptly and with less distress.

Versailles and Foreign Policy

Similarly, in international relations, Britain was unable to return to "normalcy," to prewar stability based on balance of power, to a climate favorable to world trade upon which her economic well-being so much depended. The initial problem was in part psychological; she could not decide just where her national interests lay in a changing world; idealism and self-interest conflicted. Only gradually did the outline of her postwar policy emerge: diplomacy by negotiation to reduce tension, disarmament to a degree to slow down the arms race, opposition to drastic change in national boundaries on the continent, a general rehabilitation of Germany and a strengthening of imperial and commonwealth ties.

But there was little orderly thinking along these lines in 1919. At first the loudest voices (including the Coalition parties in 1918) demanded a severe peace imposed upon Germany and her allies, and as Shaw remarked (in the preface to *Heartbreak House*), the Government "did not find it as easy to escape from this pledge as it had from nobler ones." But more often than not Lloyd George's own role as one of the "Big Three" at the Paris Conference (January-June 1919) was that of mediator between the realism of Premier Clemenceau of France and the idealism of President Wilson of the United States. During a crisis in negotiations in March 1919, Lloyd George went off to Fontainebleau for the weekend and returned with "Some Considerations for the Peace Conference Before They Finally Draft Their Terms." In this memorandum Lloyd George urged reasonable terms of peace which would not arouse a revengeful Germany and thus provoke future wars. Reparations should not be so heavy as to drive Germany into the hands of the Bolsheviks. He promptly received a telegram from his supporters in the Commons demanding that he keep to his election pledge "to present the bill in full, to make Germany acknowledge the debt, and then to discuss ways and means of obtaining payment." Lloyd George returned to London and in a brilliant reply in the Commons (April 16) maneuvered out of the difficulty. It was an "oratorical Austerlitz," said Garvin in the *Observer*.

Britain had a very considerable part in the drafting of the Covenant of the League of Nations, the first major action of the Conference. A postwar international organization had been accepted in principle by the Allies during the war; in Britain it was usually conceived of as an extension of the idea of the concert of Europe—little change in Britain's own position, political or military, was envisaged. The very term, "League of Nations" was coined by an Englishman—G. Lowes Dickinson, political scientist and historian. A draft statement by Lord Robert Cecil of the British Foreign Office, along with Wilson's proposals, provided the basis for the Covenant. And the League promptly provided a settlement of the thorny problem of German colonies, all surrendered at the end of the war. They became "mandates," exercised under authority of the League; Britain was given the mandate over German East Africa (Tanganyika); the Union of South Africa received the mandate over South West Africa; Australia over New Guinea; and New Zealand over Samoa. Thus, much the greater part of the German colonial empire came under British and Commonwealth control. As for the Turkish empire, the Treaty of Sèvres in 1920 gave Palestine, Mesopotamia, and Trans-Jordan as mandates to Britain.

In Britain public opinion played a very important role in the aftermath of the peace conference, and mistakes were made not so much at Versailles as at home. The treaty (signed at Versailles on June 28) was, to be sure, promptly ratified by the House of Commons with only four negative votes (three of them Irish outraged that the principle of self-determination at the peace conference had not been applied to Ireland). But this vote was misleading, and very soon large sections of public opinion moved against the treaty—partisanship led to inconsistency, and the treaty was debated in the spirit of the election of 1918. The Liberals, the Laborites, and the Union of Democratic Control were now as intemperate as Lloyd George had been during the election campaign. The weaknesses in the treaty and the excesses were blamed on Lloyd George, who had generally stood for moderation in the treaty-making process. Narrow politics and ill nature go far to explain the enthusiasm for John Maynard Keynes's *The Economic Consequences of the Peace* (1919), easily the most influential of the attacks on the Versailles Treaty. Had the resilience of a nation at war held over into the peace, it is not likely that Keynes would have written these lines: "In this autumn of 1919, in which I write, we are at the dead season of our fortunes. The reaction from the exertion, the fears, and the sufferings of the past five years is at its height. . . . We have been moved already beyond endurance and need rest. Never in the lifetime of men now living has the universal element in the soul of men burnt so dimly."

But indifference can be more dangerous than pessimism. As circles of opinion widened from Westminster they were increasingly sterile—without vitality, witout purpose, without maturity. The nation which had readily believed that it was a war to end wars and a war to secure peace with justice was not prepared to use British power to promote those objectives. Once the German threat seemed eliminated, peace was regarded as merely a habit of mind and not an object of foreign policy. France's problems were not understood. As one writer put it, "The North Sea is wider than the Rhine." Britain's spirit had brought victory but did not extend to a realistic appraisal of Britain's good fortune in the past in relation to a changing present nor to an understanding of the aspirations and needs of other peoples.

Clash of Interests and Ideologies

Before we trace the course of politics after 1918 we must take cognizance of a subtle change in British political parties. This is well introduced by a remark of Arthur Balfour early in the century: "Our alternating Cabinets, though belonging to different parties, have never differed about the fundamentals of society. . . . It is evident that our whole political machinery presupposes a people so fundamentally at one that they can safely afford to bicker; and so sure of their own moderation that they are not dangerously disturbed by the never ending din of political conflict."

Down to 1906 the natural distribution of mankind as either Liberal or Conservative, immortalized by Gilbert and Sullivan in *Iolanthe*, did not constitute a serious cleavage of the British people. And so the bitterness which characterized politics seems astonishing. For with few exceptions the leadership of the two major parties still shared the same social background. They dressed alike, were educated alike, even looked alike. Winston Churchill and F. E. Smith, though in opposite camps, were close personal friends. Geoffrey Robinson (later Dawson), who became editor of *The Times* in 1912, was a Unionist by conviction, but his friendships included most of the leading Liberals. These examples could be multiplied.

The Edwardian years, we may say, marked the end of this rather accidental distribution of voters between traditional parties and the essential harmony of society and politics. After 1918 the Liberals were so sharply divided between those in the Coalition and those in the Opposition that any reassembling seemed next to impossible. It was a conflict of loyalties rather than a conflict of ideas. The Liberal Party was ceasing to have any cohesion in leadership or in constituency. The Nonconformist vote, long identified with Liberalism, ceased to have any identity politically and was distributed among all parties. Furthermore, any notion that the Liberals were the party of the middle class was losing force. The very term "middle class" was losing its magic, as C. F. G. Masterman tells us in his brilliant *England After War* (1922). No longer was the working man, whose numbers in the electorate expanded in 1918, prepared to follow the Liberal lead. As for the Conservatives, they were for the moment comfortably situated, but dared not examine too closely the ties which bound them to Lloyd George. And as a matter of practical politics of the future, they had to capture some of the growing working-class vote.

To replace the traditional division between "Liberalism" and "Conservatism," an entirely new alignment seemed in the making—one based on economic class interests, on ideological attitudes toward social change, on conflicting views of the role of the State, on Britain's role in the world. After the war, the stimulus of fear—fear of the other side— accelerated the trend.

The Right

The right drew its strength from business, from the well-established professional classes, from members of the Church of England, and from what remained of the landed aristocracy. It adhered, in general, to the dominant philosophy and attitudes of the late nineteenth century: political democracy with effective leadership of the elite; governmental regulation of society kept to a minimum; distrust of the masses and, therefore, distrust of labor; confidence in the essential rightness of the British Empire; and reliance upon the sterling qualities of the "British character." More particularly: in fiscal policy they were committed to the maintenance of the gold standard but were tending in the direction of protection; in foreign policy they favored retreat to a position of semi-isolation, with cautious support of the League of Nations and the stabilizing of Europe (particularly of Germany) in the interests of British trade; they were fearful of Soviet Russia, to whom they were unreservedly opposed; they believed that imperial ties should be retained and strengthened. This is a general statement; there were, of course, exceptions, and differences in detail. But the strongest bond within the right was opposition to "socialism." This concern led them at times to regard the views of the extremists within the labor movement as representative of it generally and to be fearful of efforts to coerce the nation. One of their number referred in 1923 to the "division between constitutionalism and socialism."

The very existence of a Coalition Government inspired conjecture about possible political combinations. There was effort at formal merger of Liberal and Conservative, to strengthen the right. Churchill, by nature a centrist with no distinctive political philosophy, sought to capitalize on this mood. In July 1919 he declared that "the democratic forces in Conservatism and the patriotic forces in Liberalism cannot longer be kept apart," and he called for "a Central Combination, ending the old Party system and all its evils." In March 1920 Lloyd George discussed with Coalition Liberals the possibility of forming a National Democratic Party; a year later the label "Fusion" was suggested. Early in 1922 a Cecil-Asquith-Grey alliance seemed to have a new Liberal-Conservative Party in the making.

The Left

On the other hand, the possibility of a broadly based union of the left was briefly in the minds of Laborites and Opposition Liberals. Dissident Liberals, most of them Fabians in formal membership or in general social outlook, shifted over to Labor. Included were Leo Chiozza Money (of *Riches and Poverty* fame), who was a Liberal M.P. until 1918; C. P. Trevelyan and Noel Buxton, who finished out their long parliamentary careers as Laborites; Lord Haldane, the war secretary and lord chancellor of the Asquith Government; H. W. Massingham, editor of the *Nation,* who reluctantly abandoned his notions of bringing together Radical Liberalism and Labor, and was in a real sense converted to Labor; Arthur Posonby (whose father had been private secretary to Queen Victoria), a Liberal M.P. from 1910 to 1918 who returned to the House in 1922 as a Laborite; William Temple, a rising churchman who was to become archbishop of Canterbury.

Those associated with the Left were not united by ideology but did manage to achieve considerable agreement on an immediate program: nationalization of key industries, particularly those in which wage scales were unsatisfactory; opposition to the gold standard; a program for housing and other social services; general support of the League of Nations and the principle of collective security, together with repudiation of the principle of the balance of power; a hostile attitude toward imperialism with special sympathy for Indian nationalism. Immediately after the war, the Labor movement included some strong voices for "direct action" in industry and "socialism" in government. Two quite different publications of 1920 will illustrate. An American writer, Arthur Gleason, accurately presented the mood of a section of the British working class; "Britain is faced by universal unrest in the working class and by a demand that economic power shall be shifted from the owners of capital to the workers" is the opening sentence of his *What the Workers Want: A Study of British Labour*. From a quite different background there was R. H. Tawney's *The Sickness of an Acquisitive Society*, published by the Fabian Society. An economic historian at the London School of Economics, Tawney suggested that the nation "had stumbled upon one of the turning points of history." Society must be reorganized "on the basis of function," with abolition of "proprietary right" when not accompanied by "performance of service." Economic activity must assume its proper place "as the servant, not the master, of society."

Thus, there was evidence of the widening of the breach between the right and the left, perhaps extending to ideology. A dramatic moment came on March 20, 1923, in the socialist motion in Parliament by Snowden that "this House declares that legislative effort should be directed to the gradual supercession of the capitalist system by an industrial and social order based on public ownership and democratic control of the instruments of production and distribution." This resolution, he added, was intended "as a direct challenge to the holders and defenders of the capitalist system." The debate was widely publicized. With the Conservatives overwhelmingly in control, the resolution was, of course, defeated (368–121). In April 1923, a dispute in the Commons led to a disorderly scene and the lusty singing of "The Red Flag" by Labor back-benchers. In June there was still another socialist demonstration in the Commons. Two years later the Cambridge Union debated a motion that the "practical application" of the principles of socialism "will promote the happiness of the English people."

Certain members of the Independent Labor Party were intrigued with the possibilities of international cooperation among socialists. In February 1919 MacDonald, Henderson, J. H. Thomas, and other British Laborites forgathered with continental socialists at a world socialist conference at Berne. But actual flirting with international communism was limited to a few. The Communist Party of Great Britain, formed in 1920, was never more than a few thousand in number; its persistent efforts for affiliation with the Labor Party were overwhelmingly rejected year after year by the National Executive and by the annual party conference. MacDonald himself, after brief hesitation, led the fight against association of British Labor with the Third International. Short of allegiance with an alien movement, there was, however, serious agitation for militancy within the Labor Party itself. In the years 1919–21, party conferences several times endorsed the use of the general strike. Whether doctrinaire socialists such as F. W. Jowett of Bradford, George Lansbury of Poplar, or John Wheatley of Clydeside would ever get control of the party was for a time uncertain.

But as the historian Maurice Cowling (*The Impact of Labour 1920–*

24, 1970) has observed, at this time the labor movement was "a ragbag of attitudes, purposes, programs and intentions." That which provided unity of a sort was trade union leadership and trade union interests; they were not socialist in any militant sense. As a class, the workers and their families, were not moved by socialist propaganda—Cowling observes that they had a much greater passion for sports. The leaders were politically rather than socially minded, and that leadership gained power and prestige when the weak parliamentary committee was replaced in 1920 by the General Council of the Trades Union Congress. J. R. Clynes, long respected in the trade union world and created a privy councillor in recognition of services rendered during the war, became leader of the Parliamentary Labor Party in 1920. Success in by-elections called attention to Labor's expanding role, quite independent of Liberalism. Party strength in the Commons rose to 142 in the general election of 1922. James Ramsay MacDonald, chairman of the Independent Labor Party since 1921 and now (1922) back in Parliament, was elected to party leadership. His narrow victory (a margin of five over Clynes) was due to support from the I.L.P., particularly from the militant "Clyde Brigade" of eleven from Glasgow and vicinity, who then regarded MacDonald as sharing their ardently socialistic doctrines. It proved to be the most important vote in the Parliamentary Labor Party in the century, for it was this vote which placed MacDonald in line for the premiership, though perhaps few of his supporters had this in mind then.

Postwar Politics under Lloyd George

The Coalition Government, established in 1916 and confirmed in the election of 1918, came to an end on October 19, 1922, when the Conservatives in Parliament voted their party's independence. It now seems remarkable that the Lloyd George Government survived this long, so limited were its achievements and so wide were the differences of policy within the Cabinet itself.

On November 8, 1922, shortly after Lloyd George's resignation, the *Westminster Gazette* printed the following: "Lloyd George in 1918: 'What is our task? To make Britain a country fit for heroes to live in. . . .' Lloyd George in 1922: 'I am not against the working man, but I implore him not go down the wrong avenue seeking a paradise that is not there.'" Now the *Westminster Gazette* was a Liberal organ hostile to the Coalition. Nonetheless, these quotations are an accurate reflection of the gap between Lloyd George's easy promises of "a new society" and the actual accomplishments of his Government. The essence of "the condition of England question" in the postwar years was how to improve the living standard of the workingman and how to establish harmonious relations between employer and employee. The weakness of Lloyd George's record was not so much failure of achievement as the equivocal character of all his efforts in social reconstruction.

Labor Relations and Social Legislation

In the months immediately following the armistice, local strikes of engineers and shipyard workers on the Clyde and in Belfast aroused concern, and the Government summoned a National Industrial Conference of employers and trade union representatives in Central Hall, Westminster, late in February 1919. The delegates convened in high expectation that a new charter of labor relations would be drafted that would include machinery for arbitrating industrial problems. The conference unanimously passed recommendations for a minimum wage, for a maximum normal forty-eight-hour week, for policies which would stabilize employment, and for the creation of a permanent National Industrial Council to advise the Government. Sir Robert Horne, minister of labor and chairman of the conference, read a message from the prime minister promising immediate and sympathetic attention to any proposals made. But once the conference adjourned, its recommendations were apparently ignored. Quite naturally, therefore, Lloyd George's move in calling the conference was widely interpreted as nothing more than tactical.

Of the early strikes, that of the coal miners was most serious. Early in 1919 the Miners' Federation announced its postwar program: increased wages, a six-hour working shift, and nationalization of the industry. A strike was planned which, it was hoped, would have the support of its allies (railway and transport workers) in the reestablished Triple Alliance. Lloyd George persuaded the Miners' Federation to put off the strike and to participate in a royal commission to investigate the problems of the industry, including the question of nationalization. This commission, under the chairmanship of Justice Sankey, was equally divided between those acceptable to the miners and those acceptable to management. An interim report (March 20), recommending some though not all of the miners' demands on wages and hours, was accepted by the miners. In its final report (June 23) the commission unanimously supported nationalization of coal royalties. A bare majority (Sankey siding with the miners' representatives) recommended "either nationalization or a measure of unification by national purchase." Sankey, however, differed with the miners on the nature and method of national control, and the Government chose to interpret the recommendation as inconclusive and used a strike which broke out in Yorkshire as justification for rejecting nationalization altogether. Even the recommendation for nationalization of royalties got nowhere. The only tangible results of the Sankey Commission were the Coal Mines Act of 1919, establishing a seven-hour day—seven hours at the coal face—and temporary legislation in 1920 limiting profits and continuing governmental subsidy and control. The baiting of the owners' representatives by the miners' representatives during the deliberations of the Sankey Commission was not forgotten or forgiven and seems to have contributed to the uncompromising attitude of the operators in the following years. The Sankey Commission proved to be but the first of five such on the coal industry before 1925. Continuation of controls and subsidies maintained operation but left uncertain the destiny of the industry and evaded the central problem of the differences between operators and miners. While the seven-hour day for miners did not last, trade union power was reflected in the change, in 1919, in working hours throughout most of industry—the shift from a nine-hour day to an eight-hour one, and the shortening of the work week from about 54 hours to about 46–48, with no reduction in wages.

The Coalition Government did move positively in two directions, housing and unemployment insurance. Dr. Christopher Addison's wartime Ministry of Reconstruction had emphasized the dire need for new housing; at the end of the war the situation was more acute than at the beginning, with normal construction falling far behind and a great proportion of available dwellings unfit for habitation. Local authorities in 1919 declared that at least 400,000 new dwellings were required, an estimate soon stepped up to 800,000. The Housing and Town Planning Act of July 1919, sometimes called the Addison Act (Addison had become the first minister of Health), provided for government subsidies through local authorities. Though the initial grants were reduced, under this act some 200,000 houses were constructed by March 1923. This was hardly more than a beginning; the really important consequence was that the Ministry of Health, with housing as its chief concern, came to be taken for granted. This change in public policy was a necessary prelude to any larger program of construction.

The Addison Act of 1919 encountered little opposition. Nor did the Unemployment Insurance Act of 1920, for the principle involved had been established in 1911. During the war, application was extended to munitions workers and after the war temporarily to soldiers and industrial workers displaced by demobilization. The 1920 act provided for joint contribution from employer and employee; after twelve weeks' contribution the worker was entitled to benefits for fifteen weeks in a year (fifteen shillings for men, twelve shillings for women). Some eleven million workers, including eight million not previously insured, were brought within the scope of the act—all those earning less than £250 a year, save domestic servants, farm laborers, and civil servants. No one in

1920 could foresee that almost immediately the act would be invoked on a vast scale. The contributory system broke down, but the principle of state aid was now generally accepted. "Extended benefit" was created to provide grants for those who had exhausted their rights, and the insurance system soon became the unfortunate "dole." Very shortly the system became utter chaos, with a mass of piecemeal legislation concerning contributions and benefits.

Settlement of the Irish Question

More than any other single issue the Irish question dominated politics during 1918–22 and determined the fortunes of the Coalition. In 1918 the Irish voted for independence in electing under the banner of Sinn Fein seventy-three members of the British Parliament. On January 7, 1919, twenty-six of them gathered in the Mansion House in Dublin and formed an independent assembly, Dail Eireann. Most of the others, including Eamon de Valera, elected president of the new state, were in British jails. "The Troubles" ensued, with a state of undeclared war between Irish Volunteers, who had become the I.R.A. (Irish Republican Army), and the R.I.C. (Royal Irish Constabulary), the latter soon reinforced by special British police wearing Khaki uniforms and black helmets (the "Black and Tans"). While the ordinary pursuits of peace continued, guerrilla war in 1919–20—sudden death, ambush, roadblocks, terrorizing by day and sudden raids by night, hunger strikes, torture, arbitrary imprisonment, jail breaking—developed another bizarre and tragic chapter in Irish history. Sections of the British press, such as *The Times,* the *Manchester Guardian,* and the *Daily Mail,* were shocked to find the British Government meeting foul means with foul.

The prime minister, fumbling for a solution, first thought in terms of home rule and would go no further. A Bill for the Better Government of Ireland, introduced in 1919, provided for partition and home rule, with one Parliament for the South and another for Ulster. When this bill became law at the end of 1920, terrorism still was unbridled. Fortunately, a new and different note was soon introduced. On June 22, 1921, George V went to Belfast to inaugurate the new Parliament for Ulster. Guided by the counsel of General Smuts, prime minister of South Africa, the king used the occasion to appeal to all Irishmen "to forgive and forget, and to join in making the land they love a new era of peace, contentment and good will." His biographer, Harold Nicolson, declared that this address "inaugurated a new and wiser stage in the whole disordered story."

This comment appears justified. The next step was a truce drawn up in Dublin, effective July 11. A few days before, General Smuts, as "Mr.

Smith," made a secret visit to Dublin and urged De Valera to negotiate. De Valera headed an Irish delegation which arrived in London, July 12, for a ten-day stay. Lloyd George now took the long step of offering De Valera "dominion status" while insisting upon Irish allegiance to the British Crown, safeguards for British defense in Ireland, and recognition of the right of the Government of Northern Ireland to determine its own future. De Valera, in various and somewhat conflicting counterproposals, was willing to accept "external association with the British Commonwealth Group," but adhered tenaciously to the principle of Irish unity (including Ulster) and "essential independence" for all of Ireland. On this impasse the negotiations broke down.

In October they were renewed in London without De Valera, who remained in Ireland perhaps as a matter of strategy. The Irish delegation was headed by Arthur Griffith, the creator of Sinn Fein, and Michael Collins, who had been the very soul of I.R.A. activity. Though dedicated to the Irish cause, they were not extremists. The chief negotiators for the British Government were Lloyd George, Austen Chamberlain, Lord Birkenhead, and Winston Churchill. It was auspicious that each group promptly came to like and respect the other. But the discussions were dramatic in the extreme and repeatedly seemed about to collapse. The principals all played important and almost equally decisive roles. But it would appear that it was Lloyd George who saved the situation; his charm, his understanding of human nature, his resourcefulness, and even his capacity for effective bluff were used to consummate advantage. At one crucial point, on the all-important issue of the relation of northern Ireland to southern, he proposed a boundary commission to determine the boundary line on the basis of local sentiment. It was bait offered as a lure to the Irish delegation, and by no means an honest gesture on Lloyd George's part. After all expedients seemed exhaused, at 7:30 on the evening of December 5, 1921, he confronted the Irish delegation with a choice between accepting a treaty of agreement or a state of war. At 2:30 the following morning the Irish delegation, which had no power of plenipotentiary, affixed their signatures to an agreement providing for the Irish Free State with dominion status and a separate Parliament in Ulster if northern Ireland so decreed.

The Irish Dail endorsed the agreement, but by a narrow margin, 64 to 57. The Irish Nationalists were divided. De Valera and his followers repudiated any and all allegiance to the Crown and insisted on a republic with mere "external association" with Britain. The other element, led by Griffith and Collins, accepted independence and dominion status as an honorable settlement which would enable Ireland to realize her national destiny. Bloodshed was not over. In the summer of 1922 Sir Henry Wilson, retired chief of the Imperial General Staff and popularly thought of as behind Ulster's resistance to the Free State, was shot and killed at the entrance to his London house, and Michael Collins was slain in Ireland. But in December 1922 Saorstat Eireann, literally translated as the Irish Free State, was established, a settlement which continued without modification until 1937.

It was Lloyd George's one great postwar achievement. He had succeeded in his dual policy of preventing either section of Ireland from coercing the other and yet of keeping both within the Empire. George V, in extending congratulations, recalled that many years before, Lord Morley had said that the day would come when Conservatives would grant home rule. To this final solution, which went far beyond the original proposals of Gladstone and of Asquith, the Unionist Birkenhead, Austen Chamberlain, Curzon and Balfour all gave their support. But not Carson, now a law lord, who with Birkenhead and Bonar Law had led the fight against home rule in 1913–14. He and Birkenhead had a bitter exchange in the House of Lords. "Of all men in my experience that I think are the most loathsome it is those who will sell their friends to conciliate their enemies," said Carson.

A Tottering Coalition

The Irish settlement was the beginning of serious difficulty for the Coalition. It led to consideration in the Cabinet in January 1922 of the possibility of dissolution of Parliament in the thought that a general election would draw the elements of the center more closely together; if for no other reason, the Coalition would be supported for want of an alternative. Lloyd George soon repudiated the suggestion, but stronger opposition came from those Conservatives who wished to postpone the election until a suitable alternative to the Coalition was provided—namely, a Conservative Government.

The Geddes report added to controversy within the Conservative ranks. In August 1921 a committee had been set up under the chairmanship of Sir Eric Geddes to recommend to the Exchequer all possible reductions in national expenditure. Early in February 1922 Birkenhead (the lord chancellor) heralded the soon-to-be-issued report as a very remarkable document which would guide the Government in every case except where national security was at stake. The report (issued that month) included substantial reductions in expenditures for education and health services as well as for the armed services. The controversy over the merits of the "Geddes axe" once again split Conservatives, and Lloyd George might well have resigned had he not been bolstered by the support of Austen Chamberlain, since March 1921 the Conservative leader in the Commons. Before the Geddes report was adopted, the controversial economies were greatly reduced.

The Failure of Open Diplomacy. In the end, foreign policy, which had catapulted Lloyd George into the highest office, was the occasion of his downfall. Here, above all, one might well have expected him to succeed—"the Welsh Wizard," quick in thought and action, shrewd judge of men, adept at negotiation, and by March 1921 enjoying vast prestige as the only survivor in office of the Big Four at Versailles. And British power was then the strongest element in European politics. Lloyd George's general policy was constructive in that it was conciliatory, sought to perpetuate peace, establish mutual good will, and restore normal economic intercourse. And he was confident enough, for he proposed to bypass the devious methods of the "old diplomacy" and solve problems by direct discussion in open conference. During the years 1919–22 in some twenty-three full-dress diplomatic conferences, the political heads of the states of Europe came together.

Lloyd George's policy achieved partial success at the Washington Arms Conference of 1921–22; on capital ships the famous ratio of approximately $5 : 5 : 3 : 1.75 : 1.75$ was adopted for the United States, Great Britain, Japan, France, and Italy, respectively. Great Britain was to reduce her strength by 40 percent. This was the first step in Britain's surrender of naval supremacy. But this was in full accord with the Ten Year Rule set forth by the war cabinet back in 1919 that "it should be assumed for framing revised Estimates, that the British Empire will not be engaged in any great war during the next ten years." And the Anglo-Japanese Alliance of 1902, renewed in 1911, was not again renewed in 1922. Though Britain's role in the Far East deteriorated, her association with the United States was strengthened.

However, in European diplomacy—in the difficult questions of reparations, inter-Allied war debts (especially obligations to the United States), and general disarmament—one conference merely passed the problems on to the next. The central point at issue was French and British policy toward Germany. In the interests of her national security, France sought strict enforcement of the Versailles treaty, while Britain, with her economic well-being at stake, strove to implement the treaty, even revise it, with a view to stabilizing Germany politically and economically. The climax of failure came at Cannes and Genoa. At the Cannes Conference (January 1922) of Lloyd George, Premier Briand of France, and the premiers of Belgium and Italy, a satisfactory solution seemed within reach. Then suddenly Briand fell from power. It was impossible to deal with his successor, Raymond Poincaré, who turned from the Great Powers to the smaller states, particularly those in the Little Entente (Czechoslovakia, Yugoslavia, and Romania); and the ambitious Genoa Conference of April and May, so carefully arranged by Lloyd George, and representing thirty-four countries, including Germany and Russia, but without Poincaré, was sheer failure.

Crisis in the Near East. Then came the Turkish question. In 1918, with the total defeat of the Ottoman Empire, there seemed to be no issue in the Near East that the diplomats could not solve. But soon to the comparatively simple problem of partitioning the Ottoman Empire were added special claims submitted by the Greeks and uncertainties over the future of Constantinople, and confusion confounded in the successful Nationalist revolution within Turkey under Mustapha Kemal. The Treaty of Sèvres (1920), drawn up in the midst of this rapidly changing situation, was doomed as soon as it was signed. And the new problems posed soon gave to this latest phase of the "Eastern question" a quite disproportionate significance.

In British politics the basic difficulty was that while Lloyd George was pro-Greek to the point of romanticism, the Conservatives in his Government were pro-Turk. This conflict of attitude came to a head in the Chanak episode. The Treaty of Sèvres had provided a neutral zone on both the Asiatic and the European sides of the critical area of the Straits. In the summer of 1922 the Greek Government recalled from Anatolia some of its units confronting the Turkish army of Mustapha Kemal and sought permission to occupy Constantinople in the neutral area. Permission was refused, though Lloyd George in the Commons spoke words of encouragement to the Greeks. The partial withdrawal of Greek troops had inspired a Turkish offensive in Anatolia; the remaining Greek troops were routed and the Turks in September moved into the neutral zone on the Asiatic side of the Straits. In this area, near the Dardanelles, British units were stationed at Chanak, where Turkish troops were soon "grinning through the barbed wire." Lloyd George asked for support from Italian and French troops stationed in the neutral zone and on September 15 sent out an alarm to the dominions requesting them to be prepared to lend a hand if needed.

Lloyd George promptly found himself in trouble. France and Italy at once recalled their troops from the neutral zone. The dominion Governments, showing rather less than enthusiasm, requested consultation in the formulation of policy and declared that in the present emergency their own Parliaments must be consulted. At home Lloyd George had Cabinet support only from Churchill and Birkenhead. The prime minister indeed had bypassed his foreign secretary, Lord Curzon. At Chanak the restraint of the British commander, General Harington, and the good judgment of Mustapha Kemal (he could well afford a little patience, for he was steadily nearing his goal) prevented hostilities. By October an agreement ended the crisis and the Treaty of Lausanne (1923) soon replaced Sèvres. Matters were patched up with France. Very likely Lord George's policy had more to do with checking Mustapha Kemal in 1922 than his many detractors have recognized. Harold Nicolson, a biographer of Curzon, greatly admired "the daring displayed by Mr. Lloyd George and Mr. Winston Churchill in thus saving Great Britain from humiliation." Churchill himself wrote in *The World Crisis* that British policy "prevented the renewal of war in Europe."

The End of a Career?

Whatever its merits, Lloyd George's policy contributed to an untenable position at home. By the end of the summer of 1922 he was increasingly on the defensive. He had failed on the problem of reparations. The "honors scandal" was mounting. Since 1918 an increasing number of peerages, baronetcies, and knighthoods had gone to businessmen and newspaper men, a circumstance which aroused suspicions of connections with party funds. In the summer of 1922 this matter was sent to a parliamentary committee of inquiry. And now the policy in the Near East was opposed by a hostile public whose enthusiasm for Greece waned with the restoration of the pro-German King Constantine after the war.

The active revolt began in August 1922 when some of the younger Conservatives in the Ministry confronted their party superiors with profound misgivings about the wisdom of trying to maintain a party policy within the Coalition. In September the movement was stimulated by rumors that the Cabinet contemplated dissolution of Parliament before there would be opportunity for criticism of its policy at the annual conference of the Conservative Party scheduled for November. After the Chanak crisis, party veterans joined the revolt. On October 7 *The Times* printed a letter from Bonar Law, wherein he, in effect, dissociated himself from Lloyd George's policy in the Near East. Soon after, Lord Curzon and Lord Salisbury committed themselves against Lloyd George.

On the morning of October 19, some 275 Conservative members of the House of Commons met at the Carlton Club to decide their future. Austen Chamberlain, their parliamentary leader, without airing his own hostile views of Lloyd George, pleaded for maintenance of the Coalition, and in so doing sacrificed favorable prospects of becoming prime minister himself. His remarks brought only scattered applause. There was even less enthusiasm for Balfour's appeal for loyalty to the prime minister. Honors of the occasion went to Bonar Law and Stanley Baldwin. Bonar Law, apparently undecided until just the day before, but now ready to make a bid for leadership, spoke rather subtly of the disastrous effects on party organization which continued association with the Coalition would mean and announced that he would vote against it. More interesting was the sudden prominence of Baldwin. He had been in the cabinet (as president of the Board of Trade) only since March 1921. He had never been enthusiastic for the Coalition, born of "the infamous election" of 1918, as he termed it. Now, in straightforward language, he put the case against maintaining this connection. He agreed that Lloyd George was a "dynamic force." But "a dynamic force is a very terrible thing; it may crush you, but it is not necessarily right. It is owing to that dynamic force . . . that the Liberal Party, to which he formerly belonged, has been smashed to pieces; and it is my firm conviction that, in time, the same thing will happen to our party." But the outcome was fairly clear from the start; the Conservatives voted 185 to 88 to contest the next election as an independent party. At five o'clock that afternoon Lloyd George resigned, and a few days later Bonar Law was selected as Conservative leader; he kissed hands as the new prime minister.

Lloyd George's career as Cabinet member was over. He was but fifty-nine. His failures after 1918 were not solely of his own making. His very achievements were, ironically, unfortunate politically. But he was always one to claim credit when success came. And he promised much. Perhaps it was rough justice that now he should have to accept responsibility for failure. He was not the man to provide leadership for a coalition government in peacetime, for he had earned the loyalty of no one. Alistair Cooke in a television comment in 1975 declared that Lloyd George brought the downfall of the Liberal Party—for a simplified statement, about as good as any. There is general consensus in judgments about him. His methods nearly always aroused suspicions as to his aims. The variations on this theme are endless. "Nobody is bound by a speech," was his own response to questions about war aims. Viscount Samuel in his *Memoirs* remarks: Lloyd George was "a strange amalgam of opposite qualities. Quite sincere in his passion for social progress as an end, there was in him a strain of cynicism as to the means—and indeed towards life in general—which lessened the confidence he could command." To Beatrice Webb he was "a blatant intriguer," and a generally friendly Beaverbrook remarked: "He did not seem to care which way he travelled, providing he was in the driver's seat." His personal and family life was as stormy as his political life—the details became general knowledge only some years after his death. Frances Stevenson, Lloyd George's secretary since 1912, was also his mistress—she relates the story in her autobiography, *The Years that are Past* (1967). In 1942 she became his second wife. If you try to characterize him in a sentence, the words come tumbling out: a warm, ebullient, and resilient personality; friendly and accessible to all; a genius at the conference table (had he remained in office, he might have prevented the crisis in the Ruhr); a radical idealist in his humanity; a sheer opportunist in politics. In the end one must have admiration for the extraordinary career which carried him from a small Welsh village to world prominence. In the words of a leading historian of the period, Charles Loch Mowat: "Thus ended the reign of the great ones, the giants of the Edwardian era and of the war; and the rule of the pygmies, of the 'second-class brains' began, to continue until 1940."

Three Elections in Three Years

Bonar Law formed a Cabinet with what elements he could find (thirteen Conservative ministers in the Coalition refused to join) and promptly (November 15) went to the country. His election manifesto has become famous: "The crying need of the nation at this moment . . . is that we should have tranquility and stability both at home and abroad so that free scope should be given to the initiative and enterprise of our citizens, for it is in that way far more than by any action of the Government that we can hope to recover from the economic and social results of the war."

On this appeal for "tranquility" his party carried 347 seats, a clear majority of 87. But though 5,500,000 voted Conservative, 8,300,000 voted for candidates of other parties. Labor swelled its ranks in the House of Commons to 142 with over 4,000,000 popular votes; its victories included the reappearance of MacDonald and Snowden and the election for the first time of Clement Attlee. The rapidly rising constituency of Labor was now manifest, including the emergence of a strong socialist element, the Clydesiders from the Glasgow area, with 21 victories out of 28 contests. With good reason C. P. Scott said to Lloyd George the day of the election: "The Liberal Party if it is to count for anything will have to be in the full sense Radical with strong affinities with Labour." Though the Liberals polled a respectable popular vote (over 4,000,000), their 117 seats were about evenly divided between the Coalition Liberals (now known as the National Liberals) and the Independent Liberals, led by Asquith (he had returned to the Commons in 1920 in a by-election.) One of the Liberal candidates, Winston Churchill, convalescing from an appendectomy, ran a poor fourth at Dundee, where two were elected.

The Search for Conservative Leadership

Bonar Law remained in office only until May 1923, when a chronic throat condition, finally diagnosed as cancer, forced his resignation. He died in October and, rather surprisingly, his ashes were buried in the Abbey. Tributes in Parliament were a little forced, but he was genuinely praised as a man of great courage in the face of family tragedy. Few writers have been able to follow his career with much warmth. As the leader of the Commons after December 1916, he was more valuable to Lloyd George than is generally recognized; and he had real gifts as a parliamentarian. But even to many of his friends and supporters he was a person of narrow views and limited interests, distrustful of enthusiasm and idealism, uninterested in ideas. He was not a man to inspire others.

Lord Curzon, deputy prime minister and leader of the House of Lords, had every expectation to succeed. His Excellency the Marquess Curzon of Kedleston was a rather fabulous person—twenty-five years back, at the age of thirty-nine, he had been viceroy of India; now, as foreign secretary, he was again in the ascendant. He had just returned triumphant from Lausanne. Bonar Law resigned on Sunday, May 20, and had requested that the king not seek his advice as to his successor. However, a memorandum, unsigned but actually written by one of the private secretaries of Bonar Law and purporting to express his own views, reached the king's hands. This memorandum urged the claims of Stanley Baldwin, the chancellor of the Exchequer, and probably had some weight with the king, though Bonar Law's biographer argues persuasively that it was not an accurate representation of Bonar Law's views. Bonar Law, we are told, expected Curzon to be named.

Lord and Lady Curzon were spending the weekend at one of their several estates, Montacute in Somerset. They had no telephone. On Monday Curzon received a brief note from Bonar Law with word of his resignation. That evening a telegram arrived from the king's private secretary, Lord Stamfordham, summoning him to London. It could mean but one thing: the king would ask him to form a government. However, the next day when Lord Stamfordham called at Carlton Terrace, the Curzon town house, it was only to inform him that Stanley Baldwin had been selected. Curzon was stunned. "I was present," Lady Curzon writes, "and George could not restrain his tears." Baldwin was "a man of no experience . . . and of the utmost insignificance," cried Curzon. So, like Austen Chamberlain in Beaverbrook's phrase, he "stumbled on the threshold of 10 Downing Street." There were several reasons for passing him over. He had never really recovered stature after his resignation in 1905 as viceroy of India, brought on by his autocratic ways. He very much lacked the confidence of his Cabinet associates, many of whom heartily disliked him. Beaverbrook's chapter in *Men and Power* on "His Royal Pomp" is harsh but properly calls attention to Curzon's long record of disloyalty to his friends, notably in 1911, when he deserted Balfour; in 1916, when he deserted Asquith; and in 1922, when he deserted Lloyd George. In the king's mind, reinforced by advice from several quarters, apparently the chief consideration was that the prime minister should not be in the Lords. "The difficulty today would be insuperable," the king said to Lady Curzon. Curzon remained as foreign secretary.

G. M. Young says that Stanley Baldwin became prime minister because no one better was available. This is a fair statement. Though in Parliament since 1908, for years he made little impression—he was under ordinary circumstances not an effective speaker. Bonar Law had known his father and as chancellor of the Exchequer appointed Baldwin the financial secretary. As president of the Board of Trade in 1921 he became generally popular. "Patience, good humor and an unexpected readiness in answering questions are gifts to which the House of Commons always responds" (G. M. Young). Then in 1922 chancellor of the Exchequer under Bonar Law, Baldwin rapidly rose in Cabinet and public esteem. Soon after the completion of the American debt settlement, in a foreign policy debate (February 16, 1923), he made a characteristic speech, concluding with these words:

> It is no good trying to cure the world by repeating that penta-syllabic French derivative, "Proletariat". . . . The English language is the richest in the world in monosyllables. Four words of one syllable each are words which contain salvation for this country and the whole world. They are "Faith," "Hope," "Love" and "Work." No Government in this country today which has not faith in the people, hope in the future, love for its fellow men, and which will not work and work and work, will ever bring this country through into better days and better times, or will ever bring Europe through or the world through.

It is a speech which Baldwin's admirers often quote. Here, as his biographer said in another connection, was "a simple earnestness which brought the issue, whatever it might be, within the moral comprehension of the common listener." Curzon could not possibly have spoken in such a manner. The man in the street recognized in Baldwin one of his own kind.

But for some time his position politically was insecure. Within six months of taking office he dissolved Parliament and staged the surprise election of December 1923. In the interim months the Government moved uncertainly—a cartoon in October showed the prime minister "just gliding about." Curzon continued his brilliant management of British interests in Turkey, but the French occupation of the Ruhr (1923) in default of reparations deliveries brought the Anglo-French Entente almost to an end. A Housing Act led to a substantial building program with government subsidy but under conditions which put the new construction out of the reach of the working class. In 1923 unemployment still stood at 13 percent, with insurance and relief funds seriously depleted.

Baldwin concluded that the most urgent problem was political—the first requirement for effective Government policy was a stronger and more united Conservative Party, with such dissidents as Chamberlain, Birkenhead, and Balfour back in the fold. To this end he boldly proposed, as party policy, a return to a protective tariff. During the war a bare beginning in that direction had been made with the limited McKenna duties (33.3 percent ad valorem duties on cars, motorcycles, watches, musical instruments), and in 1921 the key industries duties had applied tariffs to precision instruments and chemicals. Otherwise, free trade still prevailed. Baldwin himself was protectionist by principle. At Plymouth on October 25, 1923, he proposed protection of the home market as a means of fighting unemployment. A week later in the Free Trade Hall in Manchester, he spelled out more explicitly a program of fiscal reform. Only a year before, Bonar Law had pledged "no fundamental change in the fiscal system"; and so to secure a fresh mandate Baldwin determined upon a general election. The decision was his alone. There is evidence that he acted quickly to forestall a tactical move by Lloyd George in favor of protection. Many of Baldwin's fellow Conservatives (notably Curzon, Birkenhead, and Lord Derby) were outraged at his casual manner. The king was also gravely concerned and told Baldwin that he thought it was a serious mistake to plunge the country into a domestic dispute over free trade when the European situation was so critical.

The First Labor Government, 1924

The polling came December 6. The results, compared to those of 1922, were as follows:

	1922	1923
Conservative	347	257
Labor	142	192
Liberal	117	158

Baldwin's majority in the Commons, which without the election he might have retained for four more years, had vanished. He had acted contrary to the advice of the Cabinet and apparently without regard for the consequences. The Conservatives now dropped the issue of protection, which was not to be revived for some eight years. But there were, even in December 1923, signs that Baldwin was achieving his larger goal—the closing of Conservative ranks and complete separation from Coalition Liberals. Even before the polling, Chamberlain and Birkenhead were negotiating for a return to the Cabinet.

On the face of it, however, the election had two quite different results. The transformation in political affiliations, and, in particular, the crystallization of attitudes of the vastly enlarged electorate after 1918, gave Labor its first opportunity "to govern." But at the same time, the revival of the issue of protection reunified those who still called themselves Liberal. The portrait of Lloyd George had been brought out of hiding and rehung in the National Liberal Club, and he and Asquith had issued a joint election manifesto for free trade. Second, no party emerged with a majority. The Liberals held the balance of power. In certain Conservative and Liberal circles it was widely proclaimed that a Labor Government would be a disaster. Balfour advised Baldwin to accommodate himself in some fashion to Asquith; and Churchill (again among the defeated Liberals) and Birkenhead were willing to go to considerable lengths to prevent Labor from coming to power. But this Baldwin never seriously considered; an agreement with Lloyd George was beyond the realm of possibility; moreover, Baldwin was quite prepared to let Labor make use of its opportunity. And George V, contrary to some Labor accusations, was insistent that if the Government lost control of Parliament he must send for the leader of the Opposition.

Asquith soon made his own position clear. He had no intention of forming a coalition with the Conservatives when the election had turned on the issue of free trade. The only alternative to a Conservative Government was a Labor Government, and this prospect caused him no alarm. On December 18 he told the Liberals of the newly elected House that it was a novel experience to be proclaimed as a potential "saviour of society." He added, "If a Labour Government is ever to be tried in this country, as it will be sooner or later, it could hardly be tried under safer conditions." As for MacDonald, as early as December 10 he declared that, if asked, he would try to form a Government.

When Parliament met in January 1924, Asquith supported the Labor amendment of "no confidence" to the address from the throne, and the Baldwin Government was out by seventy-two votes. MacDonald was summoned to the palace. The king recorded in his diary, "I had an hour's talk with him; he impressed me very much; he wishes to do the right thing. Today 23 years ago dear Grandmama died. I wonder what she would have thought of a Labour Government."

The Cabinet and Problems of a Minority. On January 8 Duff Cooper went to the Labor victory demonstration in the Albert Hall and found it "a very tame show with no note of revolution." There was little sign of radicalism in the Cabinet organized by MacDonald. The selections were mainly his, despite the clamor of other voices in the party. For some offices he was hard put to find suitable candidates, particularly for the law offices and for the military services. Trade unionism received only a few offices, though 136 of the 192 Labor members in the new Parliament had been associated with manual labor, 46 of them with coal mines. But Robert Smillie, the miners' president until 1921, refused office, and elsewhere among trade unionists talent was limited. Finding it difficult to dispose of the Foreign Office (the country was briefly astounded by the rumor that it might go to J. H. Thomas, a party stalwart but totally unfit for that office), MacDonald retained it for himself. Several ex-Liberals were included, notably Lord Haldane, who with mingled pleasure and misgiving became lord chancellor, and Charles Trevelyan, who became president of the Board of Education. Two were selected from the militant socialists, the very able John Wheatley from Clydeside in the Ministry of Health and the Bradford I.L.P. leader, F. W. Jowett, in the Ministry of Works. Arthur Henderson insisted on the Home Office and got it. Everything considered, it was about as good a Cabinet as could have been assembled. But only Henderson and Haldane and Lord Chelmsford at the Admiralty (he was a former viceroy of India) had had previous government experience. The swearing in at Buckingham Palace was an event unique of its kind, with "Wheatley—the revolutionary—going down on both knees and actually kissing the king's hand" (Beatrice Webb). Notwithstanding the limited character of Labor's electoral victory and the predominance of moderates in the new Cabinet, it was a historic occasion. Twenty-four years after the formation of the L.R.C. in 1900, the Labor Party had polled some 4,350,000 votes, had elected two-fifths of the House of Commons, and had formed a Government. Working-class people thought of MacDonald as the man of the hour and looked forward to great achievement.

Presumably Labor could count on support from the Liberals. But with the Liberals themselves so scattered in their sympathies it was problematical just what that support would mean in practice. Asquith himself was enjoying a renewed sense of power in holding the balance between the two major parties. And, taking the long view, MacDonald knew that any support from the Liberals was temporary; indeed, Labor was seeking to replace the Liberals in the body politic. But the immediate day-to-day problems of the new Government lay in the inexperience of the new ministers, in their inability to master the routine of their respective departments, and in their failure to agree on priorities in Government policy (for example, just when should unemployment be tackled?). The prime minister took office enjoying the respect and admiration of most of his colleagues, but there was no real esprit de corps in the Cabinet, some members of which had opposed MacDonald for party leadership after the election of 1922. But perhaps MacDonald's chief limitation as prime minister in 1924 was in his failure to establish good rapport with the members of his party in Parliament.

Policies, Domestic and Foreign. In domestic matters the Labor Government scored very limited success. The Cabinet seemed diffident about enunciating novel policies. For one thing, the general idea seemed to be that "we must not annoy the Civil Service." Another obstacle was the financial policy of Snowden, who produced a budget in 1924 which, it has been said, was more Cobdenite than socialist. He abolished the McKenna duties held over after the war, and he reduced taxes. The Liberals were lyrical in his praise. Snowden's financial caution, which henceforth dominated his attitudes and policies, was entirely unexpected. But the fact is he never would produce money to finance public works designed to fight unemployment. On unemployment, indeed, the Government did nothing save take refuge in such phrases as "socialism is the only cure." The Ministry of Labor was occupied with strikes as frequently under this regime as under the former.

A brighter aspect was the creative energy in the Ministry of Health, where John Wheatley and his chief aide, Arthur Greenwood, produced an Housing Act (August 1924) significant for its new scheme of subsidies to local authorities for housing to be rented to the working class at regulated rates. This legislation proved to be basic for council housing between the wars.

But it was in foreign affairs that this short-lived Government left its mark. David Marquand, in the latest and best biography of MacDonald, emphasizes his "virtuoso performance." At international conferences MacDonald's fine presence, his good mind and elegant manners, served him and his country well. Labor now dropped its talk about revising Versailles. With the assistance of financial experts and with a happy turn of affairs in France which replaced Poincaré with Herriot, MacDonald was able at the London Conference (July 1924) to set in operation the Dawes Plan (also known as the Experts Plan) for reparation payments and to make arrangements for the evacuation of the Ruhr. At the League of Nations Assembly in Geneva in September, Arthur Henderson and Lord Parmoor helped implement proposals of MacDonald and Herriot, in the formulation of the protocol to the League Covenant providing for compulsory arbitration of international disputes. (Labor was out of office before the protocol came up for ratification.) In these matters there was something like a bipartisan policy, with Baldwin kept thoroughly informed and with continuity of policy from his administration.

But Labor's attempt to restore normal relations with Soviet Russia ran into trouble and in the end brought the Government down. The Soviet Union was formally recognized a week after Labor took office. This set the stage for a mounting attack on Government policy toward Russia which paralleled the long, drawn-out negotiations, begun in mid-April, producing a commercial treaty and a general treaty setting prewar claims of British citizens in Russia. The latter was a complicated document which included a clause guaranteeing a British loan to Russia upon the formal signing of this treaty. The announcement, August 6, of the initialing of these agreements was the signal for a concerted attack by the Conservatives soon reinforced by Lloyd George and many of his fellow Liberals. The treaties were in some details vulnerable, but they represented a measure of achievement in the face of great difficulty in an area in which it was imperative that progress be made (the resumption of normal trade relations with Russia). The Labor Government in the autumn session could hardly have survived an attempt to get these agreements ratified by the Commons, but the immediate occasion of its fall was the "Campbell case." J. R. Campbell, Communist editor of the *Workers' Weekly,* published an article (now attributed by a Communist historian to the Communist leader in England, Harry Pollitt) which seemed to urge British factory workers to refuse to participate in wars against their fellow workers in other lands. Campbell was charged with incitement to mutiny, but the attorney-general shortly withdrew the charges with the explanation that the article in question was merely "a comment upon armed military force being used by the State to repress industrial disputes."

It was suggested that the withdrawal of charges was for political reasons. In answer to a question in Parliament, September 30, MacDonald denied that he had been consulted by the law officers. The Conservatives thereupon gave notice of a vote of censure and the Liberals of a demand for an investigation by a select committee of inquiry. MacDonald, rather surprisingly, announced that he would consider the matter one of a question of confidence in his Government. We now know that this was no devious move against his Cabinet on MacDonald's part, but rather that he was under great pressure both in the Cabinet and in the Parliamentary Labor Party to meet the challenge. Indeed, Labor was tired of being a minority Government. The Cabinet agreed that if it were defeated, Parliament would be dissolved. In the debate on October 8, MacDonald's explanation did his cause no good—he admitted that his previous statement had been inaccurate and that, in fact he had discussed the Campbell case with the law officers. Some of his own colleagues (Snowden and Wheatley) regarded his remarks as "evasive" and unconvincing. The roll call went against MacDonald, 368 to 198. He dissolved and called for a general election. It was the third in three years.

The Election of 1924

The chief issue of the campaign was the Russian policy of the Labor Government. And the chief incident was the appearance of the "Zinoviev Letter" in the press, October 25, just four days before polling, which promptly produced a confusion which has not been fully unraveled to this day. The headline in *The Times* read: "Soviet Plot. Red Propaganda in Britain. Revolution Urged by Zinoviev. Foreign Office Bombshell." The letter purported to be a communication dated September 15 from Zinoviev, president of the Comintern in Moscow, addressed to the British Communist Party, advising on tactics for obtaining control of the British Labor Party and launching the revolution. Apparently it was only a copy, not the original, which reached the Foreign Office in some mysterious fashion on October 10. Learning that the *Daily Mail* had also somehow secured a copy which it was about to publish, the Foreign Office handed the letter over to *The Times* with a protest, a statement which tacitly accepted the genuineness of the letter. This was not the act of MacDonald, who was on election tour, but of civil servants in his department. In response, the Russian chargé d'affaires in London and Zinoviev himself denied the letter's authenticity. When the prime minister finally commented (two days after public knowledge of the letter), it was by way of dissociating himself from the protest issued by his own department, thus playing into the hands of Conservatives and Liberals who took for granted the bona fide character of the letter and exploited the situation to the full. The "Red scare" was tailor-made for their general case of associating the Labor Party with Russian Communism. But excitement over the Zinoviev letter was no more than a manifestation, and that it was the essential cause of Labor's defeat cannot be seriously maintained. The campaign was also notable for the first election addresses by radio. MacDonald did not improve the opportunity by using for the occasion an address to a vast crowd in Edinburgh. Stanley Baldwin spoke quietly and effectively from the studio and, as L. S. Amery tells the story, with Mrs. Baldwin knitting at his side.

As a result of the poll, the Labor strength in the Commons dropped to 151, despite small gains in popular vote largely at Liberal expense. Labor unity at the top was shattered, with MacDonald held by some of the party's leaders as responsible for the defeat. On the other hand, it was manifest that Labor had firmly established itself as a major party. For the Liberals the results were disastrous, the campaign marking another stage in their disintegration. Their tactics against the Government had boomeranged, for they emerged with only 42 seats, with their popular vote dropping from 30 percent to 18 percent. Asquith lost to a Laborite in a straight fight at Paisley and on his return journey to London could only solace himself by reading the latest Wodehouse. Winston Churchill finally extricated himself from the Liberal fold and was returned as a "Constitutionalist" with strong Conservative support. For the Conservatives the result was overwhelming victory with 48 percent of the poll and 414 seats in the Commons—a gain of 161. The existence of a Labor government had caused more people to think of politics as either Conservative or Labor, while the emergence of the "Communist" issue led many who normally voted Liberal to vote Conservative to insure Labor's defeat. Baldwin had quietly regained control of his party and made a broad appeal to the electorate for a "new Conservatism." It is abundantly clear that the scale of the Conservative victory is to be explained by the collapse of the Liberals, from whom the Conservatives wrested more than a hundred seats. But it should be added that the Conservatives polled more working-class votes than did Labor. For the first time since 1918 a party was returned to power without a large majority having voted against it. The two-party system was operating once again. The new Government was to remain until 1929.

7

The Quest for Tranquility

P. J. Grigg
*Prejudice and
Judgment* (1948),
pp. 106–7

My own object will have been achieved if I can help dispose of the idea, wheresoever it may exist, that Mr. Baldwin was, as it were, a pygmy who found himself almost by accident in charge of great events, and who discovered that the events were beyond his capacity to direct or even to understand.

Mary Agnes
Hamilton
*Remembering My
Good Friends*
(1944), p. 99

1918–1931 ... was not, at the time, felt as charged with doom. We hoped, we worked, hard and faithfully. We even enjoyed ourselves. Good things were begun; worthy foundations laid.

Sir Ivor Jennings
Party Politics,
vol. 2: *The
Growth of Parties*
(1961), p. 289

What happened in 1931 is one of the parlour games of the Faculties of Economics and Politics.

1924–1931

Reputations of public figures have strange adventures—but few much stranger than that of Stanley Baldwin, with his recognized capacity, achievement, and prestige in the mid-twenties, and the very general disillusion concerning his will to action, his judgment, and his leadership ten years later. If one is inclined to place Baldwin among the "Guilty Men" and associate him closely with the failure of British policy before World War II, then it will not be easy to do justice to the earlier years when he dominated the Conservative Party so impressively.

Of one matter we may be quite sure, and that is his extraordinary success in unifying and strengthening his party after the collapse of the Lloyd George Coalition. The Conservatives in 1924 scored the first solid victory for any party since the war. Head-hunting ceased and place hunters were satisfied. During the brief tenure of the first Labor Government, elements in the Conservative Party which had remained loyal to Lloyd George in 1922 quietly made their peace. The new Conservative Cabinet in 1924 included Austen Chamberlain at the Foreign Office and Birkenhead at the India Office, and very soon Balfour as lord president of the Council. Baldwin's most surprising success was in the installation at the Exchequer of Winston Churchill, who only a year before had referred to the Baldwin Government as "brainless, spineless and dangerous." Churchill was himself startled—"the vicissitudes of politics are inexhaustible," he remarked, quoting Disraeli. Still a staunch free-trader, Churchill was no doubt under considerable suspicion in a Conservative Cabinet. But "he would be more under control inside than out," commented Baldwin to Neville Chamberlain. And Baldwin was happy to have Lloyd George isolated.

To get rid of Lloyd George—this, Maurice Cowling concludes, was one of three great decisions made by the Conservative Party. The others were to take up the fight against "socialism" and to make Labor its chief antagonist in politics. With each of these Baldwin was closely identified. But his approach was more complex than is usually recognized. His attitude toward Labor was both sympathetic and antagonistic. Like certain Tory leaders before him (particularly Disraeli and Joseph Chamberlain), Baldwin accepted many of the aims of the working-class movement, a concern, in his case, partly grounded in a religious, even evangelical, outlook. He was prepared to accept the Labor Party as a responsible element in British politics, an attitude not shared by many of his close associates. At the same time, Labor and Liberalism must be prevented from uniting.

"Baldwinism"

But even in the twenties one is brought up sharply by the question of Baldwin's quality as a national leader, particularly in the context of Britain's postwar problems. This is a question of his personality, his philosophy of life, his character, his capabilities. In broad terms it is a question of whether he was in the right profession. Many of his contemporaries, his friends included, noted his distaste for business, the long hours spent on the Treasury bench immune from his secretaries, and the magnetic attraction of the smoking room of the House. He admired F. S. Oliver's *Endless Adventure* (1930), a brilliant defense of Sir Robert Walpole's policy of inaction. Even his admirers feel compelled to deal with his "fatal inertia," his "laziness." They agree that Baldwin had no policy calculated to lead to a carefully defined objective. But these are long-range observations; limitations in leadership had not yet manifested themselves in 1924. The editor of *The Times* noted that Baldwin was "singularly free from self-advertisement." To his supporters he was a plain man, perhaps not specially gifted, but one who voiced in terms easily understood what was in the mind of the ordinary man. Lloyd George, though brilliant, had proved erratic, opportunistic, irresponsible. In contrast, Baldwin was patient, modest, trustworthy, conscientious. At the end of 1924 he was in a position to his liking, for his political judgment had been vindicated, he was committed to no particular policy, and circumstances would govern his decisions. Political life was being cleansed of bitterness. Baldwin sought only stability, peace, and good will; "tranquility" was his goal, and without apology. "Baldwinism" had arrived.

It is hardly surprising that direction and initiative were often found elsewhere. In foreign affairs they were provided by Austen Chamberlain. Circumstances were favorable for advancing British interests, since the Dawes Plan for stabilizing German currency had come into effect on September 1, 1924. The new Government also inherited the Geneva Protocol, as yet unapproved by Parliament. This "booby trap," as Lloyd George called it, involved a commitment too general to be acceptable to the Cabinet, which set it aside in preference to a "European protocol." This policy led to the Locarno pacts of October 1925, which received but passing notice in a Britain engrossed with the most serious postwar phase of the coal problem. Nevertheless, the details are fascinating. Stresemann and Luther representing Germany, Briand for France, and Chamberlain for Britain met together at Locarno on the Swiss shores of Lake Maggiore. With no formal organization and with the press barred, conferences were held in the Palais de Justice, at the bedside of Stresemann who was briefly ill, and during a lake excursion on *The Orange Blossom* arranged by Briand to celebrate Mrs. Chamberlain's birthday. Britain, France, Germany, Belgium, and Italy bound themselves to maintain the territorial provisions of Versailles with respect to Germany's western boundaries and the Rhineland; Germany's eastern frontier was to be stabilized by arbitration of disputes. And she was to be admitted to the League of Nations. On the evening of October 16, the treaties were initialed in the Palais de Justice, and then the statesmen moved toward the windows to watch the twilight gather on Maggiore. It was Austen Chamberlain's greatest hour and he savored it. He was rewarded with the Garter, and he told the Commons that Locarno was merely the beginning of general European reconciliation. He shared (with Charles G. Dawes of the United States) the Nobel Peace Prize for 1925. A splendid beginning, certainly.

A few swift statements must likewise suffice to reenforce for these years what has already been said about the twenties in economic terms. For much of the western world, 1925 marked the end of postwar economic crisis; now for the first time European production moved beyond the 1913 figures. Germany's economy had stabilized and the United States was moving into the boom years of Calvin Coolidge. At first it appeared that Britain would keep abreast. One essential, it seemed, was "to make the pound look the dollar in the face." Under Churchill's direction, but most likely on the initiative of Montagu Norman, the governor of the Bank of England, Britain returned in April 1925 to the prewar sterling parity of £1 equals $4.86. Production began to rise with a slight improvement in profits and real wages and some decline in unemployment. From 1927 British ship launchings reached 75 percent of the 1911–13 level and amounted to well over half of that throughout the world. But these favorable signs were illusory. While British production as a whole rose a modest 12 percent in the years 1925–29, she lagged behind her competitors. The restoration of the prewar gold standard proved a hindrance, especially when Belgium, Poland, and France all returned, in 1926–28, to gold at low sterling values. For the pound sterling was now overvalued externally about 10 percent; that is, prices for British goods sold overseas were about 10 percent higher than the level on which they could compete successfully. This was a severe handicap for the staple industries—coal, textiles, and shipbuilding—and was particularly injurious to newer industries struggling to get a footing in the foreign market and now even more vulnerable to foreign competition at home. By 1929 the annual *volume* of British exports was still below the figure for 1913 while the annual *value* of her exports had declined since the return to gold in 1925. The value of world exports, generally, since 1925 had increased.

The General Strike of 1926

The general strike of May 4–12, 1926, may appear to be a climax of the 1920s, as the culmination of ideological tension, as a natural and inevitable outcome of economic failure, as a watershed in postwar industrial history. A careful examination suggests that this view is not only superficial but wrong. The strike came as a surprise to the nation and it cannot be said to have been the deliberate act of the labor world. It came not at the crest of postwar industrial tension, but after the gap between the right and the left had been narrowed, when militant trade unionism was blunted and aggressive Labor Party tactics tamed, when industrial management was beginning to cooperate with organized labor, and when the Conservative Party was under moderate leadership. The strike is deserving of attention not so much as a phase of industrial relations as for what it reveals about England in broader terms—her leadership, her morale, her energy.

Unionism and the Coal Industry

Why was there a "general strike" in 1926? In the first place, there was the unhappy state of the coal industry. From solving many problems in the nineteenth century, coal had become, as Osbert Sitwell has said, the root of all evil in the twentieth. The wages of sin is death, and the nation now reaped the full harvest of a policy of prodigality and indifference to the future which had characterized the industry before 1914. Production dropped from 287 million tons in 1913 to 164 million tons in 1921. The multiplicity of operators contributed to inefficiency—there were in 1924 about 1,400 separate mining companies, though 323 produced over 84 percent of the coal; royalties for coal ownership were paid to some 4,000 persons and compensation for other rights (water and way leaves) to as many more. Rising cost of production in Britain contrasted with declining cost elsewhere. Competition from electricity and gasoline contributed to the decreased demand for and thus the falling price of coal. The final blow to Britain's onetime great export trade in coal came with the return to the gold standard in 1925. The significance of all this to the miner was that if government subsidies were withdrawn, the industry felt justified in paying wages only about 20 percent in advance of 1913 though the cost of living was nearly 100 percent higher. In coal the rate of unemployment was higher than in any other industry. From their position as one of the best-paid segments of labor, the miners had become one of the poorest. If government support were withdrawn, crisis would be inevitable.

A second factor was the character of trade unionism. During the war, "militancy" which demanded "direct action" had been held in check, but it gathered new strength with the end of hostilities and the weak showing of Labor in the election of 1918. Postwar developments—the feeling that the Government did not keep faith on the report of the Sankey Commission and the limited success of the railway strike of 1919 and of the coal strike of 1920—gave impetus to the Triple Alliance as an agency which might wrest from management the initiative in industrial relations. Trade union militants who had enthusiastically supported MacDonald in 1922 soon lost confidence in him. On the other hand, leadership of the unions of the Triple Alliance did not reflect this strain of militancy. Robert Smillie, broken in health and spirit, retired from the presidency of the Miners' Federation in 1921; the general secretary, Frank Hodges, was more the politician than the labor leader. J. H. Thomas, general secretary of the railway men, was no militant and was reportedly on good terms with Lloyd George. Ernest Bevin, from 1921 general secretary of the transport workers, was legalistically minded. Then also, the Triple Alliance had no policy-making body which could represent and commit all three unions. Who had the power to call and to end a strike embracing the three unions? What would happen if in a dispute the interests of the three unions conflicted?

These contradictions within trade unionism explain many of the developments in the coal industry after the war. Back in February 1921 it was announced that decontrol would come March 31. Management thereupon declared that wage agreements of 1920 would no longer be honored and new contracts would be negotiated by districts, with substantial reduction in wages. The Miners' Federation demanded a national wages board and a national wages pool to provide "equal pay for equal work." Negotiations failed and a coal strike began April 1. The issues enlisted Triple Alliance action, and in short order notices were posted calling for a general strike to begin Friday night, April 15. At the last moment Hodges was persuaded to accept negotiations for a temporary wage settlement, and the general strike was canceled despite repudiation of Hodges's decision by the miners' executive. The miners, still on strike until July, in the end were forced to drop their demand for a national wages pool and to accept a national wages agreement (administered by districts) in which wages with a minimum guarantee were geared to profits. Another government subsidy was to slow down the wage reductions. In the trade union world, April 15, 1921, went down as "Black Friday." The *Daily Herald* declared on April 16, "Yesterday was the heaviest defeat that has befallen the Labour movement within the memory of man."

For several years thereafter, the 1921 wages agreement governed the industry. In 1923 the industry's condition was improved by heavy coal exports during the French occupation of the Ruhr. But a supplementary agreement in 1924, more favorable to the miners, proved unworkable after the Ruhr settlement and subsequent losses in the coal market abroad. When the government subsidy ended, the coal operators announced on June 30, 1925, the abandonment of the minimal addition to the standard wage in effect since 1921; the alternative, said management, was a return to an eight-hour day underground. The new wage scale was promptly rejected by the miners with the support of the officials of the Trades Union Congress; the new scale, they said, guaranteed profits and not wages. At first the Government ruled another subsidy out of the question; but the whole trade union movement rallied to the support of the miners, and Baldwin soon gave way and announced an extension of the subsidy for nine months. In the interim still another royal commission would make inquiry. This settlement was announced on Friday, July 31—"Red Friday" in labor parlance. Labor had won this round. Why had the Government given way? Baldwin's answer a few years later: "We were not ready."

The Samuel Commission and the End of Negotiations

The chairman of the new commission was Sir Herbert Samuel, the Liberal statesman who had been high commissioner in Palestine, 1920–25. With him were appointed men of prominence and reputation who likewise had no connections with the coal industry: Sir William Beveridge (director of the London School of Economics), Sir Herbert

Lawrence (a banker), and Kenneth Lee (a cotton manufacturer). For six months they labored—one of the most strenuous periods in their lives, Samuel and Beveridge remarked. Their unanimous report, issued March 10, 1926, sold 100,000 copies in pamphlet form, Samuel tells us. The report was generally favorable to the miners in proposing nationalization of coal royalties, amalgamation of small collieries, and numerous reforms such as a national wages board, family allowances, and improved working conditions. But the commission also declared its conviction that government subsidy was unsound and should cease. For the time being, therefore, a wage cut was inevitable and much to be preferred to the return to an eight-hour day. The wage cuts should fall on the highest-paid categories and should not affect those whose wages were already at a subsistence level. However, it should remain with the miners to choose between reduced wages and a longer workday.

The ensuing controversy cannot be reconstructed with any completeness, for no detailed record was kept of many of the conferences. Misunderstanding developed among the miners and among the operators, as well as between them, as to what was proposed and what was acceptable. The Samuel Commission had made no specific legislative proposals for implementing the recommendations on reorganization of the industry. Consequently, discussion focused on elimination of the government subsidy and on reduction of wages. On these matters the Miners' Federation was adamant. "Not a penny off the pay, not a minute on the day" became the slogan. The president was now Herbert Smith, a man of few words. For all proposals counter to his he had a stock response, "Nowt doin." The new secretary was A. J. Cook, more emotional and more voluble but equally uncompromising, and a man of some Communist leanings besides. Smith and Cook were convinced that if they could force the continuation of the government subsidy, nationalization of the industry would inevitably follow. They were receptive to a proposal worked out by T.U.C. officials with Baldwin for coal industry reorganization, but they insisted that reorganization must be under way before any wage reductions could be accepted. Mine operators were equally stubborn and would offer but one concession—a return to the eight-hour day and a new national wages agreement on the 1921 model. This proposal, announced April 30, was rejected by the miners the same day. That night at midnight, lockout notices at the mines went into effect; existing wage agreements had expired.

The next day (May 1) some 828 executive officers of unions affiliated with the T.U.C. met in Memorial Hall and voted overwhelmingly (in terms of union membership the vote was 3,653,527 to 49,911) in favor of "coordinating action" in the interest of the miners (that is, a strike in certain trades) and for granting full power to the General Council of the

T.U.C. to settle the dispute. But these resolutions, without clarification, proved ambiguous. Exactly what power with reference to the miners' demands had been delegated to the General Council of the T.U.C.? This was a matter of some moment, if the General Council should prove more conciliatory than the miners' officials. But the first action of the General Council was to set midnight, May 3, as the hour for the strike to take effect.

But now it was the General Council of the T.U.C. and not the Miners' Federation which renewed negotiations with the Government. By the early hours of Sunday, May 2, agreement had been reached on a general formula calling for a cancellation of strike notices, continuation of the subsidy for two weeks, and settlement of the coal dispute within the framework of the Samuel report. Confusion now followed upon confusion. When approval of this formula was sought from miners' officials, it was discovered that they had all left London the evening before; they were recalled but it was Sunday evening before they returned. Throughout the day no further word reached the Cabinet from the General Council of the T.U.C. It has been suggested that Baldwin, now exhausted by the protracted discussions, gave way to the extremists in the Government. Late Sunday evening, just as the general formula was about to be set down in more precise terms, Baldwin suddenly summoned T.U.C. officials to the Cabinet room and handed them a memorandum which declared that since "overt acts have already taken place," the Government could not resume negotiations until after "repudiation of the actions referred to . . . and an immediate and unconditional withdrawal of instructions for a general strike." Baldwin presumably had in mind the refusal that evening of printers on the staff of the *Daily Mail* to print an editorial denouncing the looming strike as "a revolutionary movement" which could not be tolerated by "any civilised Government." It was a trivial incident in itself, but it was now close to midnight. T.U.C. officials in consultation with the miners' representatives drew up a statement denying any responsibility for the *Daily Mail* incident and, armed with this statement, returned to the Cabinet room only to find it empty and in darkness. Baldwin had retired for the night. A. W. Baldwin, the prime minister's son, in his account adds that the union leaders were apparently unaware that secretaries were available to receive any message.

The parliamentary debate the next afternoon (May 3) is surely unique in preliminaries to general strikes. Baldwin for the Government and J. H. Thomas for the T.U.C. spoke with moderation and pleaded for courage, restraint, and good will. Others continued a discussion which extended from four in the afternoon until eleven at night. While this debate was in progress, Thomas met with the attorney general and Baldwin met with representatives of the T.U.C.—to no avail. At midnight the strike went into effect. Both management and miners had rejected the Samuel Commission report. The lockout notices posted in the mines by management precipitated the orders of the T.U.C. for a general strike. The necessary condition for a renewal of negotiations on the coal dispute was a simultaneous withdrawal of both lockout and strike notices. Baldwin and the Cabinet made no effort to bring this to pass.

It was not literally a general strike but it did affect some 3,000,000 workers (the total membership in unions affiliated with the T.U.C. was about 4,300,000). Workers called out were the miners, all transport workers, all dockers, all printers, all in steel and chemical trades, all employed in power plants (save those furnishing light), and all engaged in building trades (save those constructing homes and hospitals). The response within these categories was almost unanimous—altogether, a response far greater than anticipated.

A Strike "Under Wraps"

As we now look at it, the general strike of 1926 seems a bizarre episode. There was, for example, no clarification as to the purpose of the strike. Trade union leaders repudiated any suggestion of revolutionary intent, referring to "a national strike" rather than "a General Strike", "It is merely a plain, economic, industrial dispute where the workers say, 'We want justice,'" said J. H. Thomas in the Commons. J. R. Clynes later referred to it as "a sympathetic strike on an extensive scale." Even *The Times* declared (May 11) that few of the strikers had revolution in mind. Yet, what *was* the point of the strike if not to coerce a duly constituted Government? And how could it have succeeded except as a revolutionary act? The Cabinet initially took the position that the intent was indeed coercive. In the debate on May 3, Winston Churchill said that "either the parliamentary institutions will emerge triumphant ... or ... the existing constitution will be fatally injured."

It is often said that the nine-day strike passed without violence or threat of violence. This is incorrect. The atmosphere of the early days was ominous, with rumor replacing news. In London the king's Life Guards donned khaki. The second day the air was thick with a dark fog. At the Elephant and Castle, an important junction of six thoroughfares on the south side of the Thames, food trucks were attacked and a strike-breaking bus was overturned. Thereafter disorders occurred each evening somewhere in London. Violence broke out elsewhere, notably in Glasgow. Police clashed with strikers. The intemperate official paper, edited by Winston Churchill, demanded "unconditional surrender" by the strikers. Yet it is true that no loss of life can be attributed to the strike, surely another fact almost unique in the history of general strikes. There was no shooting and there were no barricades. It was on the whole a strike conducted "under wraps." Strikers themselves alleviated distress. For thousands it was a lark. Strikers played football with the police, and heirs and heiresses and undergraduates from Oxford and Cambridge operated busses, lorries, and even railroad trains. The famous convoy (May 8) of one hundred lorries escorted by twenty armored cars manned with troops, dispatched from Hyde Park across London to the docks in order to load flour and meat, moved without incident. The *British Worker,* a strike sheet issued by the General Council of the T.U.C., remained moderate. The B.B.C. wireless reports were reliable so far as they went—some news was suppressed. George V counseled moderation, and his advice somewhat neutralized pressure on Baldwin from Churchill, Balfour, Neville Chamberlain, and Birkenhead for stronger measures.

Had the strike continued for long, its character might have changed. That it ended promptly may be explained by several factors. From the start the Government had a psychological advantage—ever since "Red Friday" it had assumed the eventuality of a general strike and had in readiness emergency measures, especially government lorries for moving food and transferring goods from the docks. Armed forces were made available, though used sparingly. On the other hand, labor had been caught unprepared. The General Council of the T.U.C. had moved from a position of support for the miners to one of challenge to the Government. Yet neither the Council nor the leaders of the Parliamentary Labor Party wished to use the general strike as a weapon.

Baldwin promptly declared the strike "unconstitutional." From a prominent Liberal came the independent support he needed. Sir John Simon, now a lawyer of immense prestige, on the evening of May 6 in the Commons, referred to "this utterly illegal proceeding" which "disregards all contracts of employment;" this strike, he declared, violated the Trade Disputes Act of 1906. A few days later his words were confirmed judicially in the High Court of Justice. The nation was prepared to accept this view, and on this mood Baldwin capitalized. On May 8 he broadcast an appeal for an end to the strike and a declaration that all effort would be renewed for dealing with the coal dispute. "Can you not trust me to ensure a square deal for the parties—to secure justice between man and man?"

By this time it was well known that T.U.C. officials also hoped for an early end. A suitable formula was provided by Sir Herbert Samuel: revision of wages should await "sufficient assurances that the measures of reorganization proposed by the Commission will be effectively adopted." But Samuel did not speak for the Government, and Baldwin never accepted this memorandum. The Miners' Federation, which had not been consulted, rejected it outright. Nevertheless, the General Council of the

T.U.C. found it satisfactory, and a deputation, including Arthur Pugh
(the chairman), J. H. Thomas, and Ernest Bevin appeared at 10 Downing
Street at noon on May 12 to declare the strike at an end. Bevin pressed
for assurances about resumption of negotiations with the miners but was
brushed aside by Baldwin's generalities. That afternoon Baldwin received
an ovation in the Commons. He spoke of "a victory of the common
sense . . . of the best part of the whole of the United Kingdom, and it is of
the utmost importance . . . that we should resume our work in a spirit of
co-operation, putting behind us all malice and all vindictiveness." The
king's message echoed this plea. Services of reconciliation were held in
churches and chapels throughout the land. Baldwin's broadcast to the
nation ended with Blake's lines:

> I will not cease from Mental Fight,
> Nor shall my Sword sleep in my Hand
> Till we have built Jerusalem
> In England's green and pleasant Land.

The General Strike of 1926 has become a familiar theme with commentators on the English scene, perhaps because of what seems to have
been its "un-English character." Fifty years later, I.T.V. commemorated
the event with a daily fifteen-minute program, from May 3 to May 12,
1976, a day by day account of what happened—without comment—a
half century before.

Unsolved Issues

For Stanley Baldwin the end of the strike was a great
personal triumph. He emerged with a prestige and moral authority exceeded in our own time only by that of Churchill during World War II.
The *Spectator*'s comment is representative: "The British people have
taken him upon their shoulders and lifted him into a position such as no
Prime Minister has occupied since the days of William Pitt." Only a few
weeks before, public sentiment had been overwhelmingly in favor of the
miners. However, the constitutional and legal issues raised by the Government swung public opinion, at least so far as the general strike was
concerned, to the government's side.

The government announced settlement of the strike in terms that
suggested unconditional surrender of labor; the T.U.C. spoke in terms
that suggested a labor victory. The workers responded with a sense of
relief, but many were bewildered and some were bitter. Relatively few of
the workers conceived of the strike as a revolutionary act, but they were
almost unanimous in believing in the moral rightness of the miners' cause
and the moral justification of labor's support for that cause. The return to

work was slow. There was something like "a second general strike," disordered and disorganized, inspired by indignation with trade union leadership and stimulated by instances of workmen suffering humiliation and reprisal on trying to return to the job. An interesting development came in the by-election in North Hammersmith at the end of the month, when a Conservative seat went Labor by a wide margin over the combined vote of Conservative and Liberal candidates. The sentimental view that all the British people accepted the outcome of the strike in a burst of patriotic feeling and general good will needs to be well qualified.

Inertia and Class Legislation

The outcome posed as serious a challenge to the Government as had the strike itself. For now Baldwin's Cabinet had its chance. Having made and won its point, it was up to the Government to demonstrate wisdom and deal in constructive fashion with the basic issues which led to the strike. What happened? In a word—nothing. D. C. Somervell in his critique of G. M. Young's *Stanley Baldwin* maintains that in doing absolutely nothing and letting the general strike teach its own lesson, Baldwin pursued the wisest possible course. It is a tenable view if one holds that the strike was a deliberate effort to overthrow constitutional procedures and to coerce the Government into submitting to the miners. But if one concludes that the strike was more the outcome of a chain of circumstances for which many elements shared a responsibility and might well have been prevented by a more imaginative policy of the Government as the intermediary between the parties to the coal dispute, then the Baldwin policy of inaction is open to serious criticism. In addition to driving home the "lesson" of the strike, which he did in season and out, Baldwin should have just as vigorously sought to implement the statesmanship of the Samuel Commission report.

In this situation Baldwin was at his worst—his efforts were brief, perfunctory, and unsuccessful. He did propose (May 14) reorganization of the industry and a temporary subsidy pending a new wages agreement to be worked out by a national wages board. Unfortunately, he was rebuffed by both sides, and so he distributed rebukes impartially, withdrew the offer, and relinquished the initiative. He then permitted himself to be outmaneuvered by the mine operators and introduced a bill (emphatically opposed by the Samuel Commission) for suspending the Seven-hour Day Act, thus permitting the return to an eight-hour day underground. It became law in July. An accompanying Mining Industry Act to facilitate amalgamation of coal companies was passed in the face of Labor opposition. Desultory efforts at negotiation continued into September, when the Government made further proposals which were repudiated with about equal intransigence by both Mining Association and Miners' Federation. The "coal stoppage" dragged on into December; when the men returned to work, it was on terms which varied from district to district but were in principle much like those offered by management prior to the general strike. The miners had lost out on all matters regarding hours and wages.

In 1925, Baldwin, in keeping with his policy of trusting Labor, had used his position to defeat a private member's bill which proposed that contributions of trade union members to the Labor Party be entirely voluntary. Now, in 1927, he changed his stance. He accepted (perhaps without fully approving) a Trades Disputes Bill demanded by the extreme right wing of his party, declaring illegal any strike (1) that had "any object other than or in addition to the furtherance of a trade dispute within the trade or industry in which the strikers are engaged" or (2) that was "a strike designed or calculated to coerce the government either directly or by inflicting hardship upon the Community." Further, it declared that no member of a trade union could be compelled to contribute to the political funds of his union unless he had first given written notice of his willingness to do so.

In the House of Commons the Labor Party fought the bill down the line. It was "a malignant endeavor on the part of the Government to back up organized capital in the struggles with organized labor . . . [a bill] totally opposed to the universally accepted principles of British justice," said Clynes. One of the most effective speeches was delivered by Snowden, who said that a general strike could not be prevented by making it illegal. Party leadership declared flatly that when it came to power the offensive statute would be repealed. In the end the Government, in order to speed up the legislative process, limited debate by use of the "guillotine," whereupon Labor memebers arose in a body and walked out of the House. In retrospect the bill hardly seems to have been justified, for it was class legislation and was not likely to affect trade union policy. Technically it was vulnerable by the vagueness of its language. It did not add to the stature of the Conservative Party and contributed to its defeat in 1929.

Toward Industrial Peace

In view of all this, that which transpired in the trade union world was rather surprising. At first the events of May 1926 hung like a dark cloud over its activities; the annual conferences of the T.U.C. in 1926 and 1927 convened in an atmosphere of gloom in direct contrast to the buoyant militancy of the gathering of 1925. But a new direction to its affairs soon emerged. Early in 1927 the executives of the affiliated unions accepted the report of the General Council of the T.U.C. on the general strike—the report maintained the consistency of the council's role. Though a considerable minority (mostly representative of the miners) sought to reject the report, thereafter the strike of 1926 was no longer an important divisive issue among trade unionists. At the 1927 conference a resolution condemning the adherence to industrial peace was overwhelmingly defeated, the chief speech against the resolution being delivered by Ben Turner, who became the chairman of the T.U.C. for 1928. Trade unionists generally recognized that if indeed the general strike had represented an effort to employ "direct action," that policy had failed and was now discredited. There must be no "general staff" to dominate British trade unionism. Labor must rely on seeking an improvement of the condition of the workingman through conciliation and negotiation and on changing governmental policy by political action. One result was a sharp drop in trade union membership. Even the use of the ordinary strike fell off rapidly; in the years 1926–39 it was a very small fraction (for a while one-tenth and later one-twentieth) of what it had been. A "minority movement," an organized effort to return to militancy, led by A. J. Cook, the miners' official who continued as a member of the General Council of the T.U.C., and by James Maxton, chairman of the Independent Labor Party, never constituted a serious threat to the policy of moderation now pursued by trade unionism.

Also, rather strangely, after the general strike we move into a period in which both management and labor manifested increasing readiness to seek and to accept a legitimate role the one for the other. In 1926 Walter Citrine became the general secretary of the T.U.C.; he remained until 1946 and proved the very soul of moderation and conciliation. The Mond-Turner conferences were another striking indication of a changing atmosphere. Sir Alfred Mond (created Lord Melchett in 1928) was the head of Imperial Chemical Industries, and Ben Turner, as already mentioned, became the chairman of the T.U.C. in 1928. Beginning late in 1927 they jointly sponsored conferences attended by leading industrialists and T.U.C. officials which eventually recommended the establishment of a national industrial council to inquire into industrial problems with a view to solving them by negotiation. While this particular recommendation was never formally implemented, its influence may be seen in the growing practice in some of the leading trades for regular negotiation between employer and employee.

The Conservative Record, 1927–29

R. K. Middlemas, a biographer of Baldwin, remarks, as he moves to the close of this period: "In many ways" it had proved "the most enlightened and effective administration for a generation." In contrast, we may listen to two members of that administration. Sir James Grigg, from 1921 to 1930 the principal secretary to the chancellor of the Exchequer, has written that it was Baldwin's policy "to take all the heat and a great deal of the light out of affairs. He definitely believed that happiness for a country consisted in having no history." L. S. Amery, the colonial secretary, tells us that the prime minister acted on the assumption that "the supreme duty of a Government is to stay in office." Thus, we introduce a discussion of the closing years of this Government, 1927–29.

For Want of Leadership

Middlemas observes that the Baldwin administration was a hard-working government genuinely concerned with Britain's problems. But the real issue is perhaps that of accomplishment. Let us look at several areas of endeavor. The immediate problem was unemployment, for which the figure remained in the neighborhood of 10 percent of the insured workers. At no time did Baldwin's Government come forward with "the comprehensive national policy" which the Opposition demanded. The prime minister, the president of the Board of Trade, the minister of labor, and, to a lesser extent, the chancellor of the Exchequer were content with optimistic platitudes. "I am happy to note encouraging signs of improvement in the state of trade and industry," reads the Speech from the Throne opening Parliament in February 1927. A year later the King's Speech included no reference whatsoever to the problem, and Baldwin, when challenged, insisted that the situation was improving and in time would right itself.

Closely associated with unemployment was the depressed state of basic industries—coal, iron and steel, textiles—revival of these trades would provide employment. Here also the Government refused to accept responsibility. In a parliamentary debate on coal (November 1927) even Conservatives noted with impatience that Baldwin did not participate. On another occasion (May 1928) a plea was made for assistance to depressed mining communities, now in a wretched state; the parliamentary secretary for Mines calmly replied that the Government was not responsible. The farmer's problem was completely ignored. Baldwin said that the Government could not consider imposing a tariff on imported food and advised farmers to leave politics alone.

Divergences of opinion within the Cabinet were almost as fatal to development of policy as Baldwin's lack of leadership. In fact, the editor of The Times frequently suggested that Baldwin reorganize the Cabinet. The divided counsels are best seen in the breach between Churchill at the Exchequer and Amery at the Colonial Office. In April 1927 Amery addressed a letter to his chief analyzing economic conditions and governmental policy. He pointed out that the country was being told that trade was reviving; if so, he said, it was "slow and painful," with industry working at little more than half capacity. He called attention to the growth of imports and advised their limitation by extension of tariffs with imperial preference. He associated Britain's economic plight with the policies of Churchill—his nineteenth-century ideas of direct taxation and free trade. Historians have reached much the same conclusion. It is not strange that Churchill, himself, has little to say, in his writings, concerning these years, and, that on the other hand they figure prominently in historical commentary, for example, Robert Rhodes James, *Churchill: A Study in Failure, 1900–1939* (1970).

Indeed, in fiscal policy we have one of the best examples of this Government's habit of drift. The gradual shift toward a policy of protection was too slow to have any noticeable effect. Under Baldwin there was cautious extension of "safeguarding"—application of duties to goods in certain industries to protect them from "unfair competition." But "safeguarding" was reserved for exceptions, and demands from Conservatives for its further extension embarrassed both Baldwin and Churchill. At the Conservative Party conference of 1927 Baldwin said that steel and wool were not really badly off; the next day other speakers declared that "safeguarding" was essential if those industries were to be saved. In a parliamentary debate (August 1928) the Opposition suggested that there seemed to be more than one Conservative policy on "safeguarding." Baldwin suavely replied that he was struck "not so much by the diversity of testiomony as by the many sidedness of truth."

In May of 1928 the Ministry of Labor published its annual report for 1927, a year in which, it said with a show of optimism, there was improvement in employment and a year "which has made the nearest approach to normal since the war." In June the Board of Trade presented figures on trade, saying that the country was making "jerky" progress. About the same time the prime minister told some seventy thousand persons swarming over the grounds of Welbeck Abbey at a party rally that the industrial policy of the Government had been fully justified. In July MacDonald moved a vote of censure on the Government for its failure to deal with unemployment. Now Baldwin took the problem seriously, but, as the usually impartial *Annual Register* put it, "his hesitating proposals evoked no enthusiasm in his own party and were treated with derision by the Labour Party."

Policy on education was uninspiring. A lead had been provided by the forward-looking report (1926) of the Hadow Committee, a consultative committee to the Board of Education. Its most important recommendation was the "break at eleven"—that is, at the age of eleven all children should leave the elementary school and be sorted out for the type of secondary or technical education best suited to their needs and abilities. To provide four years of continuous and purposeful secondary education it was further proposed that the school-leaving age be extended from fourteen to fifteen. (At this time only about one-fifth continued in school after fourteen.) While the idea of the "break at eleven" was not original with the Hadow Committee, its recommendation determined the future direction of educational policy. Now began the complicated procedure called "reorganization" of existing schools to carry out this proposal. But the Government did not implement the recommendation for raising the school-leaving age. There was little enthusiasm for an increase in funds to provide an extension of school facilities. In one debate the chief critic of the Government position was a Conservative, Lady Astor. "Sometimes I wonder whether I am in the right party, and I am sure that all right-minded people feel the same way."

One final example of Baldwin's posture in these years may be mentioned. Since 1911, reform of the House of Lords to strengthen its role as "a second chamber" had been part of long-range Conservative policy, with, however, little active discussion and no agreement as to the form the change should take. A Cabinet committee drew up a scheme presented in the Lords in June 1927. It proposed that the second chamber should have (in addition to royalty, the bishops and the law lords) about 350 members partly elected by the whole peerage and partly named by the Crown to sit for a term of years and be ineligible for reelection. As reconstituted, it was to have the power, when differing with the Commons, of forcing a general election.

Such reform would radically change the constitution, and accordingly the proposal met with severe criticism. J. L. Garvin, editor of the *Observer* and the most influential Conservative spokesman in the press, called the idea madness and a crime against the constitution. A newly elected Conservative M.P., John Buchan, delivered his maiden speech, a memorable performance, in opposition to the proposal. Laborites and Liberals were suspicious and inclined to interpret the scheme as merely a design to strengthen the Lords to Conservative advantage. But the really astonishing thing about the whole episode was the almost studied indifference of Baldwin when the proposal came to the Commons for debate. He said that the Government really had no official policy on the matter. After a brief airing the plan was dropped, but not without injury to the Conservatives.

Neville Chamberlain and Social Legislation

If this view of performance on domestic matters is accepted, what possible justification can be offered for the statement of

The Times during the election campaign of 1929: "In the Parliaments of the last fifty years only two or three will be found to rival in quality and quantity the output of the past four and a half years"? The writer quickly made clear that he had in mind, in the main, the social legislation sponsored by Neville Chamberlain, legislation which was generally noncontroversial. In 1924 this newest representative of the House of Chamberlain asked to return to the Ministry of Health (he had been there briefly in 1923) in the conviction that the new Government would stand or fall on its record in dealing with social problems. In a matter of weeks he had provided the Cabinet with his program—some twenty-five bills, all but four of which became law during his Ministry.

Chamberlain's guiding principle in social reform—which, he insisted, sharply distinguished his policy from that of Labor—was that the resources of the State should be used to assist those who were willing to help themselves. In 1925 he pushed through the Widows, Orphans and Old Age Pensions Act, which amended the 1908 legislation and required contributions for pensions before age sixty-five (sixty for women). It also provided additional benefits for those already covered by national health insurance. In 1926 came the creation of the Central Electricity Board under the Ministry of Transport to supervise privately owned power plants in order to unify and extend their services at reduced costs. Established with Labor Party support against considerable opposition from the industry, the board proved completely successful. In this same year the British Broadcasting Corporation (the B.B.C.) was chartered—a transition from a private company organized in 1922. It had been decided that wireless broadcasting should be a monopoly under control of the state. The B.B.C. was at once secure financially, depending not on advertising but on sale of receiving licenses. By 1930 there were almost 3,000,000 license holders in Britain, and by 1939, nearly 9,000,000. It became increasingly important in disseminating news, in providing entertainment, and in making the arts available to a wide section of the public. In unemployment insurance, benefit payments were now far exceeding contributions, and in 1927 a new act decreased both contributions and benefits and eliminated "extended benefit." At the same time, normal benefits were provided for an indefinite period. Thus, the effect of this measure was in line with the general tendency of the twenties, the transition from a system of social insurance by contract to a policy of relief according to need. By 1929 over 400,000 new dwellings were constructed with the aid of government subsidy under the Chamberlain Act of 1923, an impressive achievement despite the many complaints of ugly and poorly constructed "brick boxes." (Between 1919 and 1930, 1,500,000 new houses were built, a 20 percent increase in the country's housing.) Undoubtedly the most significant item in the Chamberlain program was the Local Government Act of 1929, the fruit of many royal commissions, which abolished the Poor Law unions and transferred care of the poor to county agencies. "Poor relief" became "public assistance." In general, the county councils and district councils were reorganized with wider authority. There was accompanying legislation, with the cooperation of Churchill's Exchequer, for "derating" (that is, lifting the burden of local taxation on industry and agriculture) with compensation to local authorities out of Treasury funds.

Such legislation increased the role of government in society and constituted another stage in the growth of the welfare state. The Labor Opposition gave general support, though it found much to criticize. The steps taken were held to be far too limited. Treasury economies stalled all but the most modest advances in the development of secondary education, and the new housing was out of the reach of the working class. Other legislation brought a sudden end in 1926 to "Poplarism"—a practice originating in George Lansbury's borough of Poplar—whereby relief payments had been considerably augmented by use of borrowed funds. Perhaps that which most seriously alienated Labor was the spirit in which the Chamberlain legislation was enacted. Its purpose was avowed to be "rationalization"—a general term for Conservative economic policy which sought to increase industrial production by partial monopoly, by wider use of machinery, and by reduction of labor, and which accepted unemployment as normal. Much of this seemed to Labor as nothing less than indifference to the rights and interests of the working class. Nevertheless, the fact remains that the Baldwin Government placed on the statute books far more social legislation than either the Labor Government which preceded or the one which followed.

Foreign and Imperial Policy

In foreign relations the Baldwin Government in these years made no important contribution. The treaties with Russia drafted by the previous Government were dropped and diplomatic relations severed. In 1925 the Locarno treaties had seemed vital and profoundly significant. Yet the enthusiasm and the optimism which they generated proved abortive. The spirit in which those treaties were conceived was a will to achieve collective international security, but Baldwin's Government did nothing to propagate that spirit. Germany's entrance into the League was delayed. Disarmament conferences foundered for want of courage in Britain and the United States; they could not agree on relative cruiser strength—Britain demanding "security" for her trade on the high seas, the United States demanding "mathematical parity." After failure of Anglo-American discussions at the Three-Power Naval Conference in

1927, Lord Robert Cecil resigned in bitter protest from the Cabinet and from the British delegation to the League. He announced his fundamental disagreement with a policy which refused to move toward collective security, arbitration, and disarmament. He told his fellow peers (he was now Viscount Chelwood) that the Cabinet's attitude was not so much opposition as indifference. In January 1929 the Government issued a memorandum outlining its view of its obligations under the League Covenant—a memorandum which the League of Nations Union (of which Chelwood was president) declared was no more than an endorsement of war as a means of settling disputes. On the other hand, it was easy enough for Britain to sign the Kellogg-Briand Pact (1928), renouncing war, but without any means of enforcement. It would seem that the normal gap between platitudes and action ·widened during this administration.

In imperial policy the Conservatives moved uncertainly toward new positions. The secretary of state for India, Lord Birkenhead, on one occasion wrote of "our expanding destiny as leaders of mankind . . . Our destiny is inevitable whether we look upon it as that which is woven on the loom of Time by a higher Power, or regard it as the reflection of a mighty past, the forecast of a still mightier future." Such language and thought mar the career of a very talented individual.

This outlook is not representative of the Colonial Office under Leopold Amery. While piously optimistic about the future of the Empire and though often pompous and self-important, he was a man of administrative capacity and a flexible mind, and took the lead in developing a new concept of colonialism. He brought about the creation of a separate Cabinet office for Dominion Affairs. The Imperial Conference of 1926 adopted the Arthur Balfour Report (drafted by the Inter-Imperial Relations Committee), which defined the status of Great Britain and the dominions in a surprisingly concise and unambiguous formula: "autonomous communities within the British Empire, equal in status, in no way subordinate one to another in any aspect of their domestic or external affairs, though united by a common allegiance to the Crown, and freely associated as members of the British Commonwealth of Nations." The clear import—abrogation of all British legislative control over the dominions—was not at first fully appreciated, but any uncertainty was removed by the Statute of Westminster (1931), which made this principle the law of the land. In foreign policy, in particular, this statute merely ratified an accomplished fact. At the Paris Peace Conference, the dominions had the appearance of independent states, and they had been consulted by Britain on every major policy decision thereafter.

In India, national aspirations, now led by "the Mahatma," Mohandas K. Gandhi, produced a series of crises. British policy since the war had been obscure—ultimate dominion status was repeatedly forecast, but always at some distant and uncertain date. The Act of 1919, introducing dyarchy (in the provincial governments authority was to be shared by legislative councils, in large part elective, and British agencies), had provided that after ten years a royal commission should review the situation. In 1927, Baldwin, with general approval, proposed that the commission be created at once. Under the chairmanship of Sir John Simon it soon began its labors.

The Swing of the Pendulum

In the minds of the English people the "condition of England" was the dominant concern in 1929, as the long-anticipated general election approached. Baldwin had stayed in office about as long as the law allowed. He was merely waiting for May 1, when the new electoral register provided by the Representation of the People Act of 1928 took effect. This statute gave the vote to women over twenty-one (the act of 1918 had limited it to those over thirty). The new register listed nine million new names, and women voters now outnumbered men in all but thirty-eight constituencies.

The election was fixed for May 30 and Baldwin apparently approached the poll with complacency. He seemed confident that the country was still behind him; in his campaign addresses he stood on his record without analyzing it, and he defined the election as between constitutionalism and individualism on the one hand and radicalism and socialist nationalization on the other. Unemployment was not really an issue, he declared, and, anyway, no easy solution was possible. Progress was being made in the export trade—in all seriousness he cited the export of broccoli to the Continent. *The Times* hinted at Baldwin's forthcoming defeat. *The Economist* was not impressed, and the *Annual Register* records: "The state of the country was not such as to make the bulk of the people enamoured of Mr. Baldwin's Government." Other observers had some fun. Baldwin was merely saying, commented J. M. Keynes, "We will not promise more than we can perform. We, therefore, promise nothing." The Conservative Party organization fell back on the Baldwin legend— the plain man upon whom all might rely. All over the country he smiled down from huge placards reading "Safety First" and "Trust Baldwin." In truth, it may be added that among Conservatives no one else shared his popularity.

Liberals' Last Try. The Liberal Party, now partially recovered from intraparty feuds, made its last great effort. When Lord

Oxford (Asquith had been raised to the peerage in 1924) formally retired from party leadership in 1926, Lloyd George became the chairman of the party in Parliament and Sir Herbert Samuel the chairman of the Liberal Organization Committee. Lloyd George labored under the handicap of his immediate past—his responsibility for the debacle of 1924 when his fund supported only three hundred candidates and the Liberals lost more than one hundred seats. But he worked hard, by choice and by default of others. He turned to publication to propagandize his ideas—a powerful plea for state action to create conditions more favorable to private enterprise. *Coal and Power* (1924) was a carefully written and widely read book, espousing ideas very much like those of the Sankey Commission—nationalization of royalties, consolidation of small companies, welfare funds for the miner—which he had ignored in 1919. Lloyd George also advocated the construction of gigantic power plants near sources of fuel and water to provide less expensive light and power. In 1925 he published *Land and the Nation* with suggestions for reviving agriculture. Restless, ambitious, full of vitality, Lloyd George explored every possible avenue of strategy and policy by which he might return to power, even to considering coalitions with Laborites or Conservatives.

Other Liberals caught something of his enthusiasm. Summer conferences were held at Oxford. Sir Herbert Samuel addressed more than 350 Liberal meetings in 1927–29. In 1928 the efforts of a special committee (Lloyd George, Samuel, Keynes, Rowntree, and others) produced the Liberal "Yellow Book," entitled *Britain's Industrial Future*, which advocated putting surplus capital to work to increase production and reduce unemployment. There would be a comprehensive public works program: housing, roads, power plants, drainage, and reclamation—proposals frankly admitting that Liberalism was changing. When Baldwin confessed that the Conservatives had no cure for unemployment, Lloyd George promptly declared that the Liberals did. *Britain's Industrial Future* was popularized in a pamphlet, "We Can Conquer Unemployment," issued in March 1929 and sold widely at sixpence. Keynes and H. D. Henderson produced another pamphlet, "Can Lloyd George Do It?" referred to by the *Economist* as "the most brilliant piece of election literature produced during the present controversy." Just before the poll more than one hundred well-known businessmen (by no means all Liberal) endorsed Lloyd George's ideas on unemployment.

Labor's Victory. For Labor the prospects were favorable. The Conservatives seemed to be played out, and by this time to very many people Labor might be the only alternative. Prestige lost in 1924 and 1926 seemed to have been recovered. By-election results had been favorable. Within the official party organization unity and morale seemed to have been restored in surprising fashion. Policy had been redefined. A basic statement appeared in *Labour and the Nation* (July 1928), which in broad terms proposed new trade union legislation, increase of unemployment benefits, a long-range policy of nationalization of basic industries (especially coal, agriculture, and transport), development of social services, reappraisal of imperial policies. The adoption of this statement over counterproposals from the Cook-Maxton faction constituted a great victory for the moderates. It provided the basis for an election manifesto drawn up by the party executive which muted references to "socialism" and emphasized proposals for reducing unemployment and for "national development." In broad outline the Labor program differed little from the Liberal.

Even the question of leadership in the Labor Party seemed to resolve itself without difficulty. To be sure, MacDonald's continued hold on the helm was something of a puzzle. "A fine facade, a platform performance, a substitute for a leader," wrote Beatrice Webb in April 1927. Mrs. Webb was prejudiced and hostile but she reflects the views of many others. By 1929 serious limitations to MacDonald's capacity for directing the party in Parliament were fairly clear—his tendency to blur issues, his waning enthusiasm for socialism, his preference for "society" over the company of his political associates. But these weaknesses were counterbalanced by his political assets—his charm, his self-control, his skill with people. And by 1929, under pressure from Arthur Henderson, his interest in a Labor Party program had been revived. He was still very popular out in the constituencies. In the last analysis, he stayed on as party leader because there was no suitable alternative. Henderson was without personal magnetism, Snowden had abandoned his reform ideas, Clynes was ineffectual, Thomas was distrusted, and Lansbury, though popular, was regarded as something of a wild man and not to be taken very seriously.

The poll for the new House of Commons gave Labor 287, the Conservatives 260, and the Liberals 59. The Conservatives suffered a serious defeat, polling a 10 percent smaller popular vote than in 1924. On the other hand, the election indicated no great swing to Labor, which polled a popular vote slightly lower than the Conservatives. But the Labor vote along with the Liberal produced a substantial majority (62 percent) of the electorate which had voted against the Conservatives, reflecting a restlessness, a want of confidence in Baldwin, a desire for a more vigorous attack on unemployment. For the first time, Labor emerged as the largest party in the Commons. For the Liberals this campaign was virtually the end. In spite of 512 candidacies supported by the "Lloyd George Fund," in spite of its most spirited campaign since 1918, in spite of apparent unity, in spite of Lloyd George's promise to cure unemployment in one year, in spite of the prestige of Samuel and Simon—in spite of everything, the party made a net gain of only 16 seats. The popular vote (25 percent) was respectable but was a poor third. Lloyd George's bid for a comeback had failed.

The Second Labor Government

The transition to Labor in 1929 was smoother than in 1924. It was now taken for granted that Labor would form a Government; Baldwin did not wait for Parliament to convene but resigned at once and the king sent for MacDonald. Offices were transferred to the new incumbents in good spirit. The new Cabinet was in some respects the counterpart of 1924, for twelve of the nineteen had served in the earlier Cabinet. But it was an even more moderate group, for the only left-winger included was George Lansbury in a minor post as commissioner of Works, in which he at once became popular by developing "the Lido" in the Serpentine in Hyde Park. John Wheatley, who left the Front Opposition Bench after the 1924 election, was not included. Arthur Henderson again pushed aside his natural modesty, insisted upon the Foreign Office and received it. Miss Margaret Bondfield as minister of Labor became the first woman member of a British Cabinet. The King's Speech promised a comprehensive legislative program on a multitude of topics; unemployment, foreign trade, coal, iron and steel, trade union status, housing and slums, national insurance and pensions. The second Labor Government seemed off to a good start and, indeed, won favor in its first six months.

Political fortunes, 1929–31, are interesting in two quite different respects. The first concerns the manner in which the Labor Government dealt with the nation's problems. The second is the more subtle and more complex story of political controversy within and between the three parties—a story of special significance in view of the formation of the "National" Government in 1931.

Foreign and Colonial Policy

The major achievements of the second MacDonald Government, as of the first, were recorded in foreign relations. The initial success was that of Snowden, the chancellor of the Exchequer, at the Hague Conference in August 1929, when the new Experts' Plan on German reparation payments, usually known as the Young Plan, came up for approval. Snowden, now called the "Iron Chancellor," refused to accept the plan, insofar as it cut Britain's share of reparations to the advantage of France and Italy. He termed French claims "grotesque and ridiculous" and returned home to receive a noisy acclaim as a national hero for having stood by "British interests."

However, the influence of the Labor Party outlook was in another direction. The foreign secretary, Henderson, had an excellent staff, including Hugh Dalton, his parliamentary undersecretary, and Viscount Chelwood, his advisor. Henderson had already contributed much to shaping Labor policy on international affairs, a policy which emphasized arbitration, reduction of armaments, and security through the League. This, he thought, was both the road to peace and the road to recovery for British overseas trade. His record warrants attention. At the same Hague Conference at which Snowden was so successful, Henderson presided effectively over the Political Commission which provided for the immediate evacuation of the Allies from the Rhineland. This was duly carried out. At the session of the League at Geneva in September 1929, Henderson and MacDonald were able to announce progress toward further naval reduction by agreement with the United States. Henderson signed the optional clause of the Statute of the Permanent Court of International Justice. Britain did lay down certain reservations to satisfy the dominions, but even so, this action constituted a reversal of policy since 1924. Parliamentary ratification followed in January.

The Government continued its efforts on arms reduction. In the autumn of 1929 MacDonald went to Washington for informal talks with President Hoover (the conversations on the bank of the Rapidan); these talks were a successful preliminary to the Five-Power Naval Conference at London in January 1930. If Dwight Morrow of the American delegation dominated that conference, he shared honors with MacDonald, who chaired the sessions with great skill. Agreement was reached by Britain, the United States, and Japan whereby every kind of naval construction had a ceiling. In general terms, the 5:5:3 ratio of 1922 on capital ships was now extended to cruisers, destroyers, and submarines. In capital ships there was to be a five year holiday. In sea power Britain accepted "parity" with the United States. Even though no serious problem of national security was involved, this agreement is a landmark—Britain was no longer "Mistress of the Seas." France and Italy were then unwilling to accept parity between themselves. In 1931 Henderson had direct talks with Briand in Paris and Mussolini in Rome and worked out with them the principles of an agreement. Unhappily, this understanding broke down through conflicting interpretations.

Policy toward Russia was painfully worked out, for all overtures by the Government were opposed by the Conservatives, who were inclined to overplay the dangers of Russian propaganda. Henderson seemed aware of this threat but felt that the problem of propaganda as well as questions of Anglo-Russian trade should be handled through normal diplomatic channels. However, MacDonald by reviving the issue of the Zinoviev letter aroused Russian suspicions and provided the Conservatives with an opportunity to embarrass the Government. Though the Cabinet decision to renew diplomatic relations received formal support in the Commons in November 1929, in a few weeks the Conservatives pushed through a resolution in the Lords, "that diplomatic recognition of the Soviet Union is at the moment undesirable." Shortly after, the new Soviet ambassador presented his credentials at St. James's Palace (where the prince of Wales acted for the king) and the British ambassador was received at the Kremlin. What might have been accomplished smoothly and quietly was brought about in an atmosphere of bitter party controversy.

Thus, even in foreign policy the results were uneven. But as far as Henderson was concerned, British policy was a consistent effort at implementing the principles he espoused. In May 1931, in recognition of his leadership at Geneva, Henderson was named president of the Disarmament Conference then in preparation. In August 1931, when the Government came to an end, the *Economist* spoke with enthusiasm of "the unusual distinction" with which Henderson graced his office and regretted his departure. His most important role and his most bitter disappointment were ahead—the Disarmament Conference of 1932.

In imperial affairs the second Labor Government confronted a variety of problems. In Egypt Lord Lloyd was removed as high commissioner, but Labor was no more successful than the Conservatives in working out mutually satisfactory treaty arrangements. In Palestine a considered attempt to reconcile Arab and Jewish claims broke down. In India, also, circumstances were a bar to efforts to solve the intricate problems of nationalism, there complicated by the rival efforts of Hindu and Moslem for control of the new India. An all-parties Indian conference attempted to frame its own solution, and the Nehru report (1928) recommended dominion status within the Commonwealth but failed to command general support. Meantime, as the British commission under Simon was completing its work, the Government called a round-table conference in London of British officials and Indian representatives to seek to reconcile differences before any parliamentary action was taken. But Indian sentiment stimulated by the Congress Party had been hostile to the Simon Commission from the outset, and the announcement of a round-table conference touched off a revival of the civil disobedience campaign. In May 1930 Gandhi was back in jail along with the Nehrus, father and son, and others. The next month the Simon report—an exhaustive inquiry—appeared, recommending responsible local government in the provinces and the creation of federal agencies whose exact nature should be worked out gradually on the basis of experience. In spite of the charged atmosphere, the First Round-Table Conference in November

1930 made progress in winning cooperation of the native princes in the plans for a federated India. MacDonald secured parliamentary approval for round-table discussions—he was at his best in presenting this matter. A favorable circumstance developed early in 1931 with the agreement between the viceroy, Lord Irwin (later Lord Halifax), and Gandhi for an end to civil disobedience, the release of Gandhi's supporters from prison, and the participation of the Congress Party in the Second Round-Table Conference scheduled for September 1931. By that time Labor was out of office.

The World Depression

Early in 1929, an economist, Sir Dennis Robertson, referred to England's economic situation as "a suppressed boom"—for industrial production was 53 percent above 1921, and 10 percent above 1913, with exports higher than at any time since the war, and with employment rising. But then came the world depression, and the context in which policy must develop changed abruptly. It was to be a world unfavorable to the ideas of Arthur Henderson in foreign affairs. Unemployment, instead of being a pesky problem, became a crisis. When MacDonald took office in 1929 it stood at 1,200,000; by March 1930 it was 1,600,000 (the highest in eight years); and by January 1931 at 2,600,000. It was this situation which ruined Labor at this time.

When Parliament convened after the Labor victory in 1929, Mac-Donald, in his speech on the Address from the Throne, called for a pool of ideas from all parties. This was unrealistic—the only possible cooperation could have come from the Liberals, and here Snowden was adamant against the Liberal proposal of borrowing and higher taxes, and the I.L.P. contingent was unalterably opposed to Lib-Lab collaboration. MacDonald himself had no source of sound economic advice. For an answer to unemployment he turned to the lord privy seal, J. H. Thomas, a man not without some ideas, but who proved unequal to his assignment. Thomas just about ignored a special Cabinet committee—George Lansbury, Sir Oswald Mosley, and Tom Johnston—assigned to him; according to Johnston the committee met exactly twice. Eventually Mosley submitted a formal recommendation, which was set aside for months and finally rejected. Thomas himself often said he had many things up his sleeve. If so, he never produced them. A debate (May 22, 1930) brought merciless attack from Mosley, lamely answered by Mac-Donald. Mosley resigned from the Ministry and Thomas was soon transferred to the Dominions office.

Sir Oswald Mosley himself was approaching a new stage in his career. In the Commons in 1918, at the age of 22, married in 1920 to Cynthia

Curzon (daughter of Lord Curzon), he was in turn a Conservative, an Independent, and a Labor M.P.; he had rapidly made his mark. He had extraordinary skill as a parliamentarian and in the 1920s was often "tipped" as a future prime minister. Failures of the MacDonald Government as much as his own ambition drove him from the Labor Party in 1930. Though he won considerable sympathy from Labor back-benchers and at the party conference (October 1930), he could not win much support for his attack on the policy of the Government. In February 1931, he set forth his views in A *National Policy* and announced the formation of the New Party. Four Labor M.P.s joined him (one of them, John Strachey, only temporarily). *Action,* edited by Harold Nicolson, lasted three months (October–December 1931). Aneurin Bevan, a coal miner who entered the Commons in 1929, was sympathetic with the original Mosley memorandum but would have no part in the bolt from Labor. Nicolson abandoned Mosley in May 1932. But in his novel *Public Faces,* published later in 1932, Nicolson forecast a Churchill-Mosley Government in 1936.

Though without a policy on unemployment, the Labor Government did undertake additional relief. In 1930, after legislative confusion confounded, an Unemployment Insurance Act abolished the requirement that the applicant must demonstrate that he was "genuinely seeking work." The number of those eligible for "transitional" benefits until eligible for regular benefits by virtue of contributions was increased, and the Exchequer was called upon to provide necessary funds. Conservatives attacked the measure as giving relief disguised as insurance, while left-wing Laborites found the benefits altogether inadequate. With rising unemployment and totally inadequate resources in insurance funds, real trouble was around the corner.

In attempting to redeem another pledge—repeal of the 1927 act permitting an eight-hour day in the coal mines—the Government found itself caught between the miners' demand for outright restoration of a mandatory seven-hour day and the insistence of the operators that such legislation would require wage reduction. Legislative progress was slow and painful. Tentatively, a compromise measure was introduced in November 1929 providing for a seven-and-a-half-hour day, nationalization of royalties, and authority to the Government to draft schemes of amalgamation. Serious modifications were proposed to win over the Liberals, more radical in this matter than Labor. Finally enacted in 1930, the Coal Mines Act proved to be the most important legislation affecting the industry between the wars. The seven-and-a-half-hour day survived, in Sidney Pollard's words, "symbolizing the end of the period in which the problems of the industry were to be solved at the expense of the miners." And the compulsory cartel system reduced production and maintained prices and profits. Reorganization of the industry was placed in the hands of a commission.

Real statesmanship, it would seem, might have secured an acceptable education act, raising the school-leaving age from fourteen to fifteen, thus implementing the Hadow report. In the face of all the problems—inadequate facilities, financial requirements, family maintenance allowances, aid to Catholic schools—the Government found it difficult to determine policy. There was no bill whatsoever until May 1930; this bill took nearly a year to pass through the Commons, and was defeated (and therefore hopelessly postponed) by the Lords. The bill's fortunes were curious. On one occasion, in January 1931, a significant amendment opposed by the Government was carried with support of 41 Labor votes. MacDonald blandly proceeded as though nothing untoward had occurred, and Churchill was moved to refer to the prime minister as "the greatest living master of falling without hurting himself." The president of the Board of Education, Sir Charles Trevelyan, was so disheartened by the bill's failure that he resigned in protest.

Labor had pledged modification of the Trade Disputes Act of 1927. The Government introduced a measure which sought to distinguish between the sympathetic strike and the general strike—a nice problem in language. In committee the Liberals amended the measure in terms the Government declared unacceptable. The whole matter was forthwith dropped. In housing the only advance was the Greenwood Act of 1930, which authorized government assistance for slum clearance.

A Divided Government

Such was the response of Labor to domestic problems. In August 1931 the *Economist* found the legislative record of the Government very "meagre" indeed. What is the explanation? Hugh Dalton, the undersecretary for foreign affairs in this administration, later referred to it as "a hard luck story"—a Government without majority control of the Commons confronting a world economic depression.

But another look at the Cabinet may suggest other explanations. There was James Ramsay MacDonald, pleased to find himself back at No. 10. The enigma of MacDonald grows. There are his obscure origin and his early socialist convictions. On the other hand, there are his fine presence, his aristocratic features, his Scottish burr, his literary allusions; he looked like "a prince among men," said a colleague. Now for the second time prime minister, he was enjoying his weekends at Chequers, had cultivated an interest in old furniture and in Dutch masters, and was a frequent visitor to the auction rooms at Christie's. He was now at ease with Baldwin and was much attracted by the Londonderrys, conservative of

Conservatives, who maintained one of the last of the great houses of London. He had lost interest in a "Labor program."

As for the chancellor of the Exchequer, Philip Snowden, he was busily engaged in orthodox policies of finance; he became a favorite in the City, which made him a "freeman." Some of his Labor associates found him warm-hearted, impulsive, and likable, while others dwelt on his excessive vanity, his antipathy for MacDonald, his wife's snobbishness. But of all Labor's leaders, J. H. Thomas most completely succumbed to "the aristocratic embrace." He was MacDonald's only personal friend in the Government—somehow Thomas was able to get through to the prime minister's remote personality. It was partly Thomas's gift as a storyteller, often of ribald tales, and this talent endeared him to the king as well. He had never been a socialist, at least not in any ideological sense. "I don't read any of those bloody books," Dalton once heard him say. Arnold Bennett called him "a card," but David Low said it more eloquently in his cartoon of "Lord Dress Shirt," showing Thomas in a starched front with a cigar hanging from a corner of his mouth, telling a story. He was perhaps the greatest disappointment of the administration, and his unhappy tale is not ended.

And there was Arthur Henderson. In the diaries, the autobiographies, and the letters, one finds nothing but respect for him. He was absolutely devoted to the cause of the Labor Party. Sir Robert Vansittart, the permanent undersecretary in the Foreign Office, liked him and admired him, though considered him merely "a respectable average" as a foreign secretary. He was often underrated at the time, but it would be common practice among historians looking back to regard him as the strongest and most effective member of the Cabinet.

These four constitute a fair cross-section of the MacDonald Government. It was not "a team." It is unimportant that there were few personal friendships in the Cabinet; it is exceedingly important that there was not much mutual respect, few convictions held in common, no corporate sense of responsibility, and no general will to succeed. The party leadership (exclusive of Henderson and Webb) used its minority position as an excuse for inaction. R. H. Tawney in his brilliant article in the *Political Quarterly* (1932) pronounced judgment: "The Labour Party is hesitant in action, because divided in mind. . . . It frets out of office and fumbles in it because it lacks the assurance either to wait or to strike."

MacDonald's control of the Parliamentary Labor Party was loosened. It was often remarked in these years that the prime minister was on better terms with the Opposition than with the rebels in his own ranks. For the most part these rebels were associated with the Independent Labor Party, an affiliate of the Labor Party, whose influence had some years before (1922) returned MacDonald to party leadership. There were now 147

Labor members of Parliament who also belonged to the I.L.P., though only 37 had been elected under its auspices.

The leaders of the I.L.P. (Maxton, Jowett, Brockway, Kirkwood, Wheatley, John Strachey) were suspicious of this Government from the start. *Labour and the Nation* had not satisfied them; the Speech from the Throne opening the new Parliament ("framed to avoid trouble," commented Jowett) made them uneasy. Their misgivings seemed to them more than confirmed by early legislative proposals, and they promptly concluded that the Government was making no serious effort to establish socialist policy. The answer that the Government must compromise to survive only increased their impatience. Why, they said, should Labor take responsibility for defeat of its own program? Why not make the Opposition responsible? In measure after measure the rebels attacked the government policy: they were critical of the failure to restore the Wheatley housing subsidy (which together with the Chamberlain subsidy had been reduced in 1927), indignant over the absence of an unemployment policy, disappointed with Snowden's budgets, dissatisfied with policy on social services, and so on. Early in 1930 MacDonald resigned from the I.L.P.—he had been a member since 1894. The I.L.P. conference in the spring instructed its parliamentary group to reorganize on the basis of acceptance of I.L.P. policy. Some eighteen responded and they became an independent "group" and sat apart on the two top benches below the gangway. Wheatley died soon after. The significant era of the I.L.P. was at an end.

And a Divided Opposition

The Conservatives were no better off. Baldwin's ineffectiveness in the closing years of his administration had produced restlessness. The differences between Churchill and Amery in the "shadow cabinet" revealed something of the dilemma of the party. Churchill was opposed to the London Naval Treaty, hostile to any significant change in the status of India, staunchly free trade, and given to issuing solemn warnings that a policy of protected imperial trade might unite the Laborites and the Liberals. Amery, on the other hand, was wholly committed to tariff reform and to the development of the concept and practice of the Commonwealth. As long as possible Baldwin was content to let the one cancel the other out.

Baldwin vs. the Press Lords. Another disruptive factor in the Conservative Party was provided by the "press lords," Beaverbrook (owner of the *Daily Express* and *Evening Standard*) and Rothermere (now in control of the *Daily Mail* and the *Daily Mirror*). Beaverbrook, alienated from Baldwin since 1924 and still inclined to underestimate him, after the Conservative defeat in 1929 started in the press his campaign for "Empire Protected Free Trade." "Beaverbrook is probably sincere in his Imperial aspirations," recorded Neville Chamberlain in his diary, "but mixes with them a desire to 'down' S.B." Beaverbrook and his disciples stumped the country in a strident campaign for free trade in the Empire walled off from the rest of the world. Early in 1930 Beaverbrook, with Rothermere's support, transformed his "crusade" into a new United Empire Party. (In the 1931 election, this party was to contest some fifty seats, held by Conservatives, in the south of England.) Baldwin had first countered by declaring "safeguarding" the party policy, but with no tariff on food; now he announced that the issue of a tariff on food would be submitted to the people.

This was only the first round. In May 1930 the Conservatives staged a "Home and Empire" campaign with a house-to-house canvass for pledges in support of safeguarding duties and imperial preference. But Baldwin would not come out for a food tax, and, bolstered by the loyal support of Neville Chamberlain, he was prepared for the next attack. Beaverbrook and Rothermere now threatened to oppose all Conservatives who would not accept a food tax. Further, Rothermere had written a Conservative M.P. that he would under no circumstances support Baldwin "unless I know exactly what his policy is to be ... and unless I am acquainted with the names of at least eight, or ten, of his prominent colleagues in the next Ministry." Baldwin read this letter as the climax of his defense before a gathering of Conservative M.P.s and candidates at the Caxton Hall in June. His comment: "A more preposterous and insolent demand was never made on the leader of any political party. I repudiate it with contempt, and I will fight this attempt at domination to the end." He received a vote of confidence and that afternoon in the Commons was greeted with an ovation from both sides.

The final test was in 1931. The issue was India. In March came word of the agreement between Gandhi and the viceroy, registering progress in the Government's program of round-table conferences. The Indian Committee of the Parliamentary Conservative Party, dominated by Lord Lloyd, whose anti-Egyptian policy had forced his resignation as high commissioner, and by Churchill, who had left the "shadow cabinet" the previous December, announced a boycott of further Indian negotiations. Churchill spoke of "the unimaginative incompetence and weak compromise" of British policy. So weak did Baldwin's hold now seem to be that he was advised by many of his associates to relinquish party leadership. Once again he was equal to the test. On March 12 he went into the Commons and completely dominated the debate, in effect a Conservative family argument. In one of the great speeches of his career he came out in support of the Labor Government's policy "for progressive realization of responsible government in India as an integral part of the Empire" (the words of the act of 1919). He concluded that if a majority in the party opposed this view, "in God's name let them choose a man to lead them." A week later came polling in a by-election (St. George's Westminster) where a candidate sponsored by the press lords made Baldwin's leadership in the party the sole issue. The Conservative organization put up Duff Cooper. Two days before the poll Baldwin went to the Queen's Hall and once again revealed the "tiger" in his character. He denounced the newspapers of the press lords as "engines of propaganda for the constantly changing policies, desires, personal wishes... of two men... What the proprietorship of those papers is aiming at is power, but power without responsibility—the prerogative of the harlot throughout the ages." Many years later, Diana Cooper (wife of Duff Cooper) wrote: "I saw the blasé reporters, scribbling semi-consciously, jump out of their skins to a man." Duff Cooper won the election and "the harlot speech" was long remembered.

These episodes point up several conclusions. When at bay, Baldwin had the courage and vitality to fight back. But his hold on the party was shaky. The press lords may have been associated with movements of questionable wisdom and doubtful political morality, but their activities reflected a wider restiveness with Baldwin's leadership. Another manifestation was the public appeal of a group of fourteen Conservative M.P.s in December 1930, over the heads of party officials, warning of dangers to democratic government. Churchill's alienation from Baldwin goes a long way in explaining Churchill's lone path in the 1930s. On the other hand, Churchill's break brought to the fore Neville Chamberlain, whose energy, capabilities, and self-confidence marked him for future party leadership.

Liberals and the State of Politics. The role of the Liberal Party, 1929–31, was determined by (1) its control of the balance of power in Parliament and (2) its polling of over five million votes in 1929, a strength which would be of great importance in the next election. Had Lloyd George enjoyed the confidence and support of the fifty-eight Liberals in the Commons, he might have used the situation to the party's and the country's advantage. But at least one-third of the Parliamentary Liberal Party were distrustful of him; Samuel tells us that the weekly gatherings were "not happy occasions." From early 1930 Lloyd George and MacDonald were in informal coalition. Joint party conferences were held, but without any agreement on electoral reform or on unemployment. Many Liberals found this collaboration offensive. In October 1930 the Liberal whip resigned and Sir John Simon suggested that every Liberal M.P. should vote independently of any official party policy.

This analysis forces one to the conclusion that British politics in 1930–31 were approaching a state of bankruptcy. This was a common topic of conversation and of writing at that time. The understanding we get from memoirs and autobiographies is now being reenforced by monographs based on less subjective material. We may conclude that leadership in the second Labor Government did fall short of demands made on it, and there was not much hope in other directions. Little save temperament divided Lloyd George and MacDonald, willing enough to join forces in the Commons for tactical purposes but unwilling to draft a legislative program on which their parties could agree. And Baldwin, the Opposition leader, displayed energy only when his own position was in jeopardy.

Financial Crisis or Tory Ramp?

In August of 1931 the MacDonald Labor Government was replaced by the MacDonald coalition or "National" Government. The occasion was a financial crisis in the City. The postwar slump in Britain had moved into the wider and deeper channels of a world depression. By 1931, even considering all invisible assets, Britain's balance of payments in relation to other countries was adverse, for exports by volume dropped 30 percent between 1929 and 1931. And in July 1931 unemployment stood at 2,800,000, or 23 percent of the insured workers.

Miss Margaret Bondfield, minister of Labor, periodically appealed to Parliament to extend the legal debt limits of the Unemployment Insurance Fund, otherwise totally inadequate to meet demands for benefits. By January 1931 the fund's deficit each week was almost £1 million, and by June the fund was in debt a total of £100 million. A truly "socialist" Government might have met the situation with heavier taxes (particularly on invested capital), perhaps with a capital levy or with nationalization of the Bank of England and of certain industries, perhaps with a program of government spending to increase consumer power. None of these solutions appealed to Snowden, whose proposals for tax increases were cautious and whose budgets were calculated to balance. When they did not balance and for 1929–30 left a deficit of £14.5 million and for 1930–31 a deficit of £23 million, a cry arose from banking circles for government economies and for a halt to borrowing for the Unemployment Insurance Fund.

In March 1931 Snowden appointed a committee, headed by Sir George May, until recently secretary of the Prudential Assurance Company to make recommendations. The report made public on July 31 was startling, predicting a deficit of £120 million in government expenditures for the current fiscal year. It recommended £24 million in new taxes immediately and reductions in expenditures totaling £96 million. The economies, it was suggested, might come in part from reduction of salaries of teachers, civil servants, and members of the armed forces. Two-thirds of the projected economies might come in the Unemployment Fund, where the committee recommended that contributions be increased and the individual benefit be cut from thirty shillings a week to twenty four—it was argued that there had been a corresponding drop in the cost of living since 1922. A Cabinet "Economy Committee"—MacDonald, Snowden, Henderson, Thomas, and Graham (president of the Board of Trade)—was to consider this report, with its first meeting set for August 25. But nothing was to interfere with holidays. MacDonald departed for Scotland and Baldwin set out for Aix-les-Bains in French Savoy.

But MacDonald was soon recalled. Bank failures in central Europe and the publicity given Britain's own difficulties brought a serious run on sterling. In a week's time the gold reserve of the Bank of England was drained by one-eighth. Emergency loans were secured from the United States and from France, but further credits, certain to be required, seemed to hinge on the prospects of a balanced budget. It was difficult to see how this could be achieved, save in some such manner as that recommended by the May Committee. On August 11 the officers of the Bank of England advised the prime minister and the leaders of the other parties that financial circles abroad had lost confidence in the existing British Government. Snowden now (August 12) informed the Cabinet Economy Committee that the estimated deficit by April 1932, under existing schedules, would be £170 million instead of the £120 million predicted by the May Committee. On August 19 the problem was passed on to the full Cabinet. On the twenty-first MacDonald and Snowden conferred with Conservative and Liberal leaders. Evidence from Chamberlain and Sir Samuel Hoare indicates that both MacDonald and Snowden agreed to reductions in unemployment benefits. Cabinet opposition to any such solution stiffened. Furthermore, the General Council of the Trades Union Congress at once flatly and angrily opposed any such action. Agreement between the full Labor Cabinet and the Opposition leaders seemed impossible. Tentative Cabinet proposals of economies, first of £56 million, including a 10 percent cut in unemployment benefits, and a bit later of £68 million seemed unlikely to get full Cabinet endorsement or parliamentary approval.

For a "National" Government

On Sunday morning, the twenty-third, the king, who
had hastily returned by special night train from Balmoral (he had arrived
there only the morning before), received MacDonald, who told him it
was doubtful that the latest proposal would receive the general approval
of leading members of the Cabinet, and in that event he must resign. The
king decided to consult the leaders of the other parties, whether on his
own initiative or at MacDonald's suggestion is not clear. Baldwin,
somewhat reluctantly back from Aix, could not be located promptly, and
Lloyd George was convalescing from an operation. So the first interview
was with Sir Herbert Samuel, who stated his opinion that adequate reductions in unemployment benefits could most easily be applied by the
existing Government. The next best arrangement, he said, would be a
"National" Government under MacDonald. The king's private secretary
recorded his conversation with the king and added: "It was after the
King's interview with Sir Herbert Samuel that His Majesty became convinced of the necessity for the National Government. It was quite by luck
that Mr. Baldwin did not come to see the King before Sir Herbert
Samuel." Shortly thereafter Baldwin reached the palace and agreed to
serve under MacDonald in a National Government, though he indicated
his preference for a continuation of the Labor Government. As a third
possibility Baldwin said he would attempt to form a Government with
Liberal support.

This was on Sunday afternoon, August 23. That evening, word came
from New York that further financial credits would probably be available if the latest budget proposals were acceptable to the City bankers
and received a favorable response from public opinion. So far as can be
ascertained, the Cabinet that evening stood eleven or twelve for the proposed cuts in unemployment benefits and eight or nine opposed. It was
fairly clear that the Government could not continue. Accordingly, the
Cabinet authorized MacDonald's resignation. He went at once to the
palace and said that he must resign. The king's private secretary recorded: "The King impressed on the Prime Minister that he was the only
man to lead the country through this crisis and hoped he would reconsider the situation. His Majesty told him that the Conservatives and the
Liberals would support him in restoring the confidence of foreigners in
the financial stability of the country." On MacDonald's advice, the king
agreed to consult the three party leaders. At this conference the following
morning (the twenty-fourth) the king urged the formation of a National
Government under MacDonald. It was so agreed.

When MacDonald broke the news that noon to the Labor Cabinet,
among the leaders only Snowden, Thomas, and Sankey (the lord chancel-

lor) were willing to remain in the new Government. That afternoon
MacDonald formally resigned as Labor prime minister and kissed hands
as the head of the new National Government. Announcement was then
made to the public. The major members of the new Government—four
Laborites, four Conservatives, and two Liberals—were sworn in on the
morning of the twenty-fifth.

Most of the labor world repudiated MacDonald's action. The Labor
Party Executive, the Consultative Committee of the Parliamentary Labor
Party, and the General Council of the T.U.C. met together on August 26
and adopted resolutions refusing support to the new Government. Two
days later the Parliamentary Labor Party elected Henderson as its new
leader. But the Conservatives and Liberals in Parliament formally voted
support for the National Government. The new government successfully
ended the financial crisis. The necessary credits were secured abroad.
When Parliament reconvened September 8, MacDonald, Snowden,
Baldwin, Chamberlain, and Samuel occupied the Treasury bench. Snowden's revised budget, providing new taxation and some retrenchment in
the current year and detailing economies of £70 million in the budget for
the following year, was passed by a vote of 309 (including 12 Laborites)
to 249 (including 241 Laborites). On September 21, by act of Parliament,
Britain went off the gold standard, a policy which Snowden had repudiated in August. The session was highlighted by bitter exchanges
between Labor and National Labor, as the MacDonald wing of the party
came to be called. On September 28 the National Executive of the Labor
Party formally expelled those M.P.s supporting the new Government.

Electoral Confirmation

Parliament was dissolved October 6 and a general
election announced for October 27. MacDonald asked that the National
Government be confirmed in office with "a doctor's mandate." Snowden's comment that Labor's program was "Bolshevism gone mad" is
some indication of the tone of this election. In the polling Labor was
routed, emerging with only 52 seats, and every ex-Cabinet minister save
Lansbury defeated. Labor's popular vote held up much better, with 31
percent, as against 36 percent in 1929. But most Liberals voted National,
and under that label, along with those who regularly voted Conservative
and a considerable number who had voted Labor previously, returned
556 members. Of these, 471 were Conservative. And 72 were Liberals
under Samuel.

Labor's two attempts in the 1920s to govern seem premature, for at no
time did its hold on the electorate approach majority control, not even of

working-class voters. To left-wing elements, the events of August and September 1931 merely constituted MacDonald's latest compromise. On any view, if Labor regarded its cause as a crusade it should never have assumed office with minority control of Parliament, save for the purpose of briefly dramatizing its stand. In the circumstances, as Sidney Webb pointed out in his article in the *Political Quarterly* early in 1932, the party had been "injuriously affected by what were only accidental successes."

More sobering is the inevitable conclusion that the British public was forced to pass judgment on a situation about which it knew next to nothing. The average voter knew only the rumors, the guesses, the forebodings, the charges and countercharges, the extravagant statements in the press. Even Lord Ponsonby, who had been in the Labor Ministry, could write:

> We outside, entirely ignorant of causes, only witnessed the outward symptoms which showed us that our political guides were losing their heads as anyone else would in such circumstances and under such pressure: return of ministers, the rush of the king from Scotland ... headlines, crowds, police, hectic movements, day and night meetings, the door of Downing Street loosened on its hinges by the constant passage of leading figures of all three parties as they hurried by the ever-present battery of photographers.

Of that which actually transpired, the historian now knows more than all but a handful of individuals knew at the time. Of tensions between individuals, within groups, within and between parties, he knows a good deal—but not enough. Very likely he never will. Nearly everything written then and since is highly prejudiced. It was that kind of crisis.

Problems of Interpretation

Was there a genuine financial emergency? The Labor Cabinet as well as the Treasury and the City bankers so declared. A question arose only after the formation of the National Government, when outraged Laborites declared it "a banker's scare," "a Tory ramp," while the leaders of the new Cabinet exploited the atmosphere of crisis. There *was* a financial emergency, but hardly a "crisis" demanding extraordinary political action. The fault of the Labor Government was in being caught unprepared, in being proved incompetent on large questions of policy, in not having made a serious assault on unemployment, in revealing an appalling ignorance of economics. The fault of the Conservatives and the Liberals and the City bankers was in not seeking alternatives to cuts in unemployment funds and in education grants, in holding

Labor responsible for the plight of sterling, in prolonging into the general election the sense of compelling urgency.

Around the principal figures the issues are almost too complex for brief analysis. In any case, statements must be tentative. We do not need to conclude with Snowden that it was "deliberately planned," or with Sir John Wheeler-Bennett that MacDonald and Baldwin were called "to the common duty of saving their country." However, it is unlikely that there would have been a National Government but for MacDonald. Did he act in a constitutional manner? His critics claimed that he should have consulted his Cabinet or the Parliamentary Labor Party before accepting, as their leader, the king's invitation to form a coalition Government. It was also asserted that the Cabinet, when authorizing MacDonald's resignation, assumed that the king would ask Baldwin to form a Conservative Government. The first charge raises a matter of constitutional practice on which opinions differ. The second is a question of fact on which the evidence is insufficient. There are more general problems: Had MacDonald for some time been paving the way for a coalition? Had he concealed his real intentions—was he not willing, even anxious, to bring the Labor Government to an end? Any such charges are unproved. A letter, written August 24, to Emanuel Shinwell, a member of the Labor ministry, indicates MacDonald's thinking just after he had announced to the Labor Cabinet the formation of the new Government. MacDonald writes that it was the best thing for Labor, which otherwise "should have been swept away in ignominy." Conditions have been created "under which the Party can continue as an Opposition." He emphasizes that the new Government is merely "a cooperation between individuals who are banded together to avoid a disaster. . . . As soon as the country gets on an even keel again, the Government will cease to exist." From all information now available it may be asserted that there was no "conspiracy," no advance "deal" with Baldwin. On the other hand, during the August days MacDonald did not conceal his lack of confidence in his Labor associates, with whom he was certainly less than frank. He did have a vanity for office. Though he declared repeatedly in August and September that the coalition was temporary (he was apparently at first reluctant to carry it into the election), he did accept its perpetuation.

For Baldwin much the same conclusion can be reached. It is true that in general he distrusted coalitions; after all, he had played a major role in the destruction of the Lloyd George Government in 1922. But now his position in his own party was precarious, and he found it easy enough to accommodate himself to MacDonald's leadership. As a sidelight, an interesting question is whether a poll of Conservative members of Parliament in August would have approved the adherence to a coalition under MacDonald.

In many ways the role of King George is the most interesting. Concerning the constitutionality of his action in asking MacDonald to form a National Government there has been much serious debate. It was charged then and afterwards by Leonard Woolf, Harold Laski, and others that MacDonald stayed on as prime minister as "the King's favorite," that the National Government was formed in "a palace revolution," and that the interference of the king in normal procedures of party government was dangerous to the future role of the Crown and the sanctity of constitutional practice. On the other hand, Sir John Wheeler-Bennett, in his *King George VI,* has referred to it as "an outstanding instance of constitutional wisdom." Sir Harold Nicolson, the biographer of George V, with learned support from Sir Ivor Jennings, has maintained that the king acted strictly within the bounds of constitutional principle and only in accord with the advice of his ministers. However, as one reads the precise account of proceedings recorded daily by the king's private secretary, which are the basis of Nicolson's narrative, the king seems considerably more than merely the sounding board of his ministers. Sir Robert Vansittart, the permanent undersecretary for foreign affairs, was of the opinion, as he later put it, that MacDonald "was talked into" heading the new Government. A more important testimonial comes from Baldwin; in an address in 1936 before the 1922 Committee he said, "In 1931 we conformed to the King's wish, and all my colleagues agreed with me in doing so." Nicolson's own account tells us that in September 1931, when it seemed that sharp differences within the National Government over fiscal policy (should it be free trade or protection?) might bring "the whole apparatus of National Government . . . crashing down," and when MacDonald was faltering and contemplating resignation, he was "galvanized" by the king, who urged MacDonald "'to brace himself up to realize that he was the only person to tackle the present chaotic state of affairs' and that even if Mr. MacDonald were to tender his resignation he, the King, would refuse to accept it." Very possibly George V intervened decisively in these events.

8

A Sea of Troubles

W. H. Auden
The Orators
(1932), p. 14

What do you think about England, this country of ours where nobody is well?

Charles Lamb
quoted in Drew
Middleton, *These
are the British*
(1957), p. 3

It was never good times in England since the poor began to speculate on their condition.

Stanley Baldwin
*House of
Commons,
Debates*, July 30,
1934

Let us never forget this. Since the day of the air, the old frontiers are gone. When you think of the defence of England you no longer think of the chalk cliffs of Dover; you think of the Rhine. That is where our frontier lies.

Gautier
quoted in Lord
Vansittart, *The
Mist Procession*
(1958), p. 533

One can pass through one's age without seeing it.

1931–1939

"The Annus Terribilis, 1931," to employ Arnold J. Toynbee's phrase, ushered in the 1930s. And Toynbee's opening sentences of the first chapter of *The Survey of International Affairs 1931* (1932) light up the stage. "The year 1931 was distinguished ... by one outstanding feature. In 1931 men and women all over the world were seriously contemplating and frankly discussing the possibility that the Western system of Society might break down and cease to work." Britain had been at the very heart of "the Western system of society" and her central endeavor after World War I had been to reconstruct, internationally, a political atmosphere of peace and security based on cooperation, moderation, and common sense which would support an economic structure still favorable to British production, trade, and financial leadership. Thus, in the "crisis," political and economic, international and domestic, in 1931, Britain had very much to gain and no less to lose.

And so the economy and politics, at home and abroad, will dominate our consideration of Britain in the thirties. These general themes will, of course, have many facets, some perhaps incidental, such as the Abdication Crisis of 1936, others generally grave in their import—the prolongation of the National Government, ideological debate and intellectual protest to an extent beyond any other period in the twentieth century, a very remarkable degree of economic recovery and with it an active call for a new social order, the failure of disarmament and the League of

229

Nations, and the coming to power on the continent of Fascism and Nazism, producing international tension leading to World War II.

In the Wilderness

It now appears that the events of August to October 1931 provide the key for understanding the politics of the thirties. Coincident with the general election came the opening performances at the Drury Lane Theatre, packed to capacity, of Noel Coward's *Cavalcade*. A work of sincere purpose, though not of much dramatic merit, this panorama of twentieth-century Britain owed its extraordinary success to its appeal to national pride and patriotism in critical times. It comes to final climax in the toast that "this country of ours will find dignity and greatness and peace again."

Cavalcade was no clarion call to action. But neither was the general election. When the National Government was formed on August 24, an official communique declared:

> The specific object for which the new Government is being formed is to deal with the national emergency that now exists. It will not be a Coalition Government in the usual sense of the term, but a Government of Co-operation for this one purpose. When that purpose is achieved the political parties will resume their respective positions.

That same evening Baldwin issued a statement:

> We Conservatives have consented for a limited period to enter a National Government . . . and there is no question of any permanent Coalition. The National Government has been allotted a definite task, and on its completion it is understood that Parliament should be dissolved as soon as circumstances permit, and that each of the parties should be left free to place its policy before the electors for their approval.

A Government without a Program

Nevertheless, when Parliament was dissolved six weeks later, the National Government sought an electoral mandate for its continuation. There were tactical difficulties, because of wide differences in professed party creeds, particularly on fiscal policy, which almost brought the Government down. But each party in the coalition was permitted to issue its own election manifesto. Each agreed to a general pronouncement of the prime minister asking for a vote of confidence in the National Government to insure "national unity." But "no one," he said, "can set out a programme of detail on which specific pledges can be given." In his opening broadcast MacDonald asked that party issues be subordinated to national interests.

What did it mean to say that party views were to be subordinated to the national good? Were MacDonald and Baldwin and Samuel expected to be wiser in a coalition than in a party Government? If they differed as party leaders on matters of principle, how were they to be expected to agree on a common policy under the National label? The voters in October 1931 were not asked to approve or disapprove of policy. The election was merely a referendum on the wisdom of forming the National Government.

A coalition Government without a program was in many ways a natural outcome of developments since 1918. Three-party division of the electorate had weakened confidence in party government. Within each party, feuds had sapped vitality and personalities counted for more than principles. And now, in 1931, the country accepted the disruption of normal political processes. It endorsed the view that party differences are incompatible with national interests. The Opposition, though polling 31 percent of the popular vote, was reduced to 9 percent of the Commons. Leadership in both groups was generally self-righteous, unrepentant, unimaginative.

As we now see it, 1931 held as little promise for solutions of international problems. On July 11 the three party leaders appeared before a gigantic mass meeting in the Albert Hall and hailed the forthcoming Disarmament Conference. "Let us proclaim that piety is not enough" (MacDonald). "We are bound by treaty and by promise to international disarmament.... Our hope in Europe is in the League of Nations" (Baldwin). "You will never effect real disarmament until you renounce war not merely on a scroll of paper but in the hearts of men" (Lloyd George). Unfortunately such platitudes were far removed from the realities of international politics.

Movements and Isms

In all these matters 1931 seems to be a focus and not a point of departure. Nevertheless, some new attitudes were forming. On election night a group in Bloomsbury was listening to the returns. John Lehmann writes later: "Faces grew longer and longer and prophecies of doom more and more despairing ... and the impenetrable, evil-tasting, olive-green fog that had blotted out London during the whole day seemed to me a symbol of the ominous obscurity of our future."

In the early thirties popular demands in literature were satisfied by such writers as James Hilton, A. J. Cronin, Edgar Wallace, and Noel Coward. They provided sentiment, excitement, sophistication. But a group of young writers, born in the best families and educated in "public" schools and at Oxford and Cambridge, were much more sensitive to the human problem. Among them W. H. Auden, Stephen Spender, C. Day Lewis, Louis MacNeice, were labeled a "movement" without themselves being aware of it, but did share, Spenders later tells us, "a kind of poetic conscience concealed within a social conscience, developing in several directions." They were involved in the social and political issues of their time. The growth of fascism provoked their answer, and they came out fighting. They were convinced that only drastic, revolutionary change would save England. In striving for a better England, some even seemed to find stimulating a Bohemian atmosphere of wretched living conditions and constant emotional entanglement.

Among intellectuals considerable enthusiasm developed for the idea of a "planned society." Marxist philosophy and Soviet experience should be examined. To Harold Laski, a political scientist at the London School of Economics, the lesson of 1931 was that a socialist society would come only through revolution. In 1933 he published *Democracy in Crisis*, "a philosophic-historic explanation of why capitalism and democracy are incompatible." G. D. H. Cole, an economist at Oxford, in *The Intelligent Man's Guide Through World Chaos* (1932) declared that the world must choose between capitalism and socialism. "My own choice is for Socialism; for I believe that the Capitalistic System has done its work and outlived its strength and usefulness." John Strachey, in his widely read book *The Coming Struggle for Power* (1932), appealed for outright revolution. In *The Necessity of Communism* (1932) John Middleton Murry, a literary critic, declared that "Russian Communism is impossible in this country," but "Communism in some form is inevitable." After a nine-day visit to the Soviet Union in July 1931, George Bernard Shaw declared that Russia was more successful in achieving responsible government in the interests of the governed than Britain, an enthusiasm shared by his friends Sidney and Beatrice Webb, whose *Soviet Communism: A new Civilization?* appeared in 1935. In the universities, socialist clubs, Marxist-oriented, grew in membership. Communist parties were organized, and Philip Toynbee, a Young Communist, became president of the Oxford Union. Soviet films became popular. *The Left Review*, established in 1934, was controlled by the British section of the Communist-dominated Writers International, and its most effective writers (Christopher Isherwood, Auden, Day Lewis) were held in thrall by Communist ideology and were committed in varying degree.

A similar impatience with the world drove others in an opposite direction. Some were attracted by Sir Oswald Mosley—tall, dark, handsome, arresting—as Lord Pakenham describes him. He set forth the program of his party (soon called the British Union of Fascists) in *Greater Britain*

(1932)—the title was a steal from Sir Charles Dilke. Action should replace debate, action under absolute authority to save the State from
chaos and communism. Fascism is "leadership of the people with their
willing consent along the path of action which they have long desired."
The first rally of the British Fascists was held in Trafalgar Square, October 15, 1932. Mosley's followers were never very numerous (by 1934
no more than twenty thousand), and he soon lost most of his original
Labor Party support. The historian of the movement (Robert Benewick)
assures us that "the effect of Fascism on British institutions and beliefs
was negligible." But Mosley represented a serious phase of the thirties—
the subordination of the individual to the "Movement," an irrational
appeal to the "Leader" concept, acquiescence to intimidation and violence. These same ideas are found in *Everyman,* in 1933 under the editorship of Francis Yeats-Brown. A very curious reflection is in the letters of
young Viscount Knebworth, in 1931 parliamentary undersecretary to
Duff Cooper in the War Department. "Antony" was fascinated by sport,
by socialism, by fascism, by Roman Catholicism, and was equally uncritical of them all. He wrote in one of his letters: "Forces, not people,
win elections . . . . Liberalism has produced neither order nor liberty, but
only a chaotic, faithless, unprincipled, dishonest muddle . . . . The world
appears to be shaking off the yoke of democracy . . . . The hour is so ripe
everywhere for a man, and a drive, and a policy."

In July 1936 Kingsley Martin, the editor of the *New Statesman and
Nation,* attended a mass meeting of the "Oxford Group." His immediate
reaction was that this movement had much in common with fascism. Its
origins are usually dated from Oxford in the early twenties, though most
Oxford men regarded the assumption of the Oxford label as grossly
presumptuous. "The Group" was in fact a curious blend of piety and
good living, humility and snobbery. Starting slowly, by 1932 it was
attracting considerable attention, particularly when "Bunny" Austin, a
tennis star, became associated. More properly called Buchmanism (after
its founder, Dr. Frank Buchman, an American) and later (after 1938)
called Moral Rearmament, it was a religious phenomenon which cut
across denominational lines and consisted in the main of special techniques for experiencing religion. It also had a specialized vocabulary, not
unrelated to its success. The object was "a changed life" through the
"guidance of God" during "the quiet time." There was public confession
of one's shortcomings and a sharing of one's religious experience with
others. Many individuals have spoken sincerely and convincingly of the
importance of "the Group" in their lives.

The wider significance of Buchmanism is that it reflected insecurity and
seemed to provide an easy way out of many personal problems. This may
also be said of the fashionable wave of pacifist thinking. In the decade

after 1918 writers were little attracted by the theme of war; now, in the early thirties, there was an avalanche of war books—by Sherriff, Sassoon, Aldington, Graves and others—with a common theme, the senselessness of war. Beverley Nichols's *Cry Havoc* (1933) probably had more influence than the speeches of any statesman. Vera Brittain's *Testament of Youth* (1933) articulated the experience of the lost generation and provided meaning for the shadowy memories of the Great War of those still younger.

Pacifism found other avenues of expression. David Low's popularity as a cartoonist began with his lampooning of war. In increasing numbers, men passed the Cenotaph, the war memorial in Whitehall, without removing their hats. The Oxford Union in February 1933 voted 275–153 in support of the motion "that this House will in no circumstance fight for its King and Country." On the face of it, this well-publicized episode was misleading. The issue had been sharpened to provide an avowed pacifist, C. E. M. Joad, with a position. The vote at the end of an Oxford Union debate was not on the merits of the question. What was more significant was the discussion in the press, which showed how confused and muddled was the thinking of the nation on war and peace, on preparedness and disarmament. Here, as elsewhere, there were both cynicism and sentimentality; but perhaps, as Chesterton said, they are not far apart, for both lack vitality, resilience, and depth.

National Government: "Safety and the Union Jack"

In the general election of 1931 the National Government made a virtue of divided opinion. To his own constituents at Seaham MacDonald declared, "I stand where I do with men who do not agree with me, men whose opinions I do not share . . . for the purpose of getting the nation over its temporary difficulties." The Conservative Party manifesto proclaimed that "it is imperative the Government should have a national mandate giving it freedom to use whatever means may be found necessary after careful examination to effect the end in view." The Liberals said they had responded to the prime minister's appeal for a continuation of stable government.

Protective Tariff and Imperial Preference

Whether such protestations of harmony would secure unity where there was actually divergence of opinion was soon put to the test in the most urgent of national problems, fiscal policy. Before the 1931 election Baldwin was of a mind that a tariff was "the quickest and most effective weapon" in meeting economic competition, but the Conservatives in the Government were not agreed on the form the tariff should take. Among the Liberals, Simon declared that an emergency tariff was needed, but the official Liberal manifesto declared that "freedom of trade is the only permanent basis for our economic prosperity and for the welfare of the Empire and the world," while Lloyd George held that tariffs would be of no value and denounced the election as a Tory trick. With Baldwin's support, MacDonald intervened to prevent the Conservatives from making a protective tariff the chief campaign issue and thus probably saved the National Government. On fiscal policy he merely asked for "a free hand."

"What will the voters make of this infinite variety of interpretations?" *The Economist* answered its own question—the voters had responded overwhelmingly to the twin appeal to crisis and patriotism and had voted for "Safety and the Union Jack." After the election, the Conservative majority in the Government set out to legislate a protective tariff. Neville Chamberlain, now chancellor of the Exchequer, promised an investigation which would be "careful, thorough, exhaustive, impartial;" but advocates of protection dominated the Cabinet committee, whose proceedings Sir Herbert Samuel, a Liberal, found "merely perfunctory." When this committee recommended (January 21, 1932) a general tariff, the free traders (Samuel, Sinclair, and Maclean among the Liberals; and Snowden, the National Laborite) prepared to resign, an action likely to have serious consequences. At the crucial moment Lord Hailsham (secretary for War) suggested that on the tariff question the minority of the Cabinet in disagreement should not resign but should be permitted to differ, even to the point of speaking against the measure in Parliament. Strangely enough, this satisfied the dissentients, and the king sent congratulations to the prime minister.

And so on February 4, 1932, nearly thirty years after Joseph Chamberlain had inaugurated his campaign for fiscal reform, one of his sons introduced a measure providing a general duty of 10 prcent on all imports except most raw matarials, food and imperial items. Samuel, rising from the Treasury bench, spoke vehemently against the bill. The debate was surprisingly brief and the vote overwhelmingly favorable. Liberal and Laborite free-traders in the Government went into the "no" lobby, but only seventy-eight in all. Thus the Government departed from "collective responsibility," a principle with *The Times* called merely one of the "niceties of constitutional procedure." But the *Economist* called the action "a farce . . . a betrayal of the electorate," while the *Manchester Guardian* declared: "Mr. MacDonald has in six months been the instrument for carrying through two constitutional revolutions. In the autumn he broke up the British Party system. Last week he broke up the Cabinet system." The feeble Opposition tried to make something out of it, but a vote of censure mustered only thirty-nine votes. During the debate Baldwin said, "Who can say what is constitutional in the conduct of a national Government? It is a precedent, an experiment ... and we have collective responsibility for the departure from collective action."

This "agreement to differ" did not survive. In April the duty on manufactured goods was raised to 20 percent, on certain articles more. The protectionists now proposed preferences within the Empire and the ground was well laid for the coming Ottawa Imperial Conference. It was arranged that MacDonald should not attend and that the British delegation should be headed not by the secretary for the Dominions (J. H. Thomas, a National Laborite) but by Baldwin. At the conference (July–August 1932), after much elbowing for position, Britain agreed to extend preferences on foodstuffs from the dominions, which in turn agreed to give increased preference to British goods. *The Times* spoke of the "firm foundation for future progress," and Neville Chamberlain, a member of the British delegation, declared that at Ottawa the Empire was "born afresh." But as to increasing British trade, the actual results were meager.

The chief effect was political, for after Ottawa the free traders could no longer be contained. When the Cabinet reconvened in September, Snowden, Samuel, Sinclair, and seven junior ministers resigned. Chamberlain privately noted that it was a step toward a "fused party under a national name which I regard as certain to come." MacDonald, however, issued this statement to the press: "The National Labor Ministers make the same appeal to the electors as we did twelve months ago—that the nation needs a non-Party Government, and that purely Party considerations would weaken our national influence in the world and would be a blow to the movements now at work towards world recovery."

Out of the Depression

To speak of economic matters in more general terms, the depression continued in Britain until 1933. Thereafter recovery was substantial and fairly rapid. Whereas in the years 1929–32 the drop in total production was 16 percent, by 1937 the volume of production was 50 percent above 1932 and 33 percent above 1929. Even with falling prices, profits were 10 percent higher in 1937 than in 1929, with income allotted to wages rising 7 percent. The extent to which this recovery was assisted by government action—the departure from gold and the depreciation of the currency, "cheaper money" through lower interest rates, the adoption of protection, and the extension of imperial preference—is controversial. The immediate effects were beneficial: prices of British goods in foreign currencies were lowered and the volume of trade temporarily increased. For two years the British exporter had an advantage, but then retaliation came, especially from the United States, which herself departed from the gold standard in 1933. Thereafter losses of the British to their competitors more than offset the increase of British trade with countries in bilateral agreements. The imperial agreements proved more helpful to the dominions than to the United Kingdom. In fact, Britain broke the links of international trade which had been in her interest. The World Economic Conference in London, June–July 1933, for all its high hopes (even the United States was to be represented), was doomed in advance. The stated purpose was to seek economic cooperation among nations and to ease quotas, tariffs, preferences, and prohibitions. This was a farce, for the world was now committed to economic nationalism.

The United Kingdom's share (that is, the share of her merchant marine) in world trade continued to decline. The export trades (textiles, coal, iron, shipbuilding) had no part in the recovery. The launching with fanfare in 1936 of the *Queen Mary*, "the stateliest ship now in being," was no more than a stunt. Throughout the thirties the balance of international payments remained unfavorable to Britain. Indeed, such recovery as she enjoyed was only in relation to conditions of the twenties, when she had not shared in the prosperity enjoyed by many nations.

But there *was* an industrial revolution in Britain during the 1930s, and this explains the form which economic recovery took. As its competitive power abroad declined, British industry turned increasingly to the home market where there was expanding consumer power—an increase estimated at 10 percent between 1929 and 1933 and a slower rise thereafter. Prices declined; real wages and real salaries rose. The losses fell on profits, on income from land, and on the unemployed. The average individual, in time of employment, had some cash left after necessities were paid for, and this extra went for housing, furniture, wireless sets, appliances, and automobiles. This was not generally recognized at the time; in 1934 the president of the Board of Trade said the home market was about saturated.

Including industries indirectly affected, the housing boom after 1933 accounted for one-third to one-half of the additional employment available. The middle and the lower-middle classes could now afford better housing. Average annual construction in the thirties was 270,000 houses, with a peak of 346,000 in 1936; altogether, twice as many dwellings were built as in the previous decade. Electoral engineering was the key to general industrial expansion and to growth in technological efficency. Next to housing construction, the new nonexport industries—especially motorcars, electrial appliances, industrial chemistry, and, in particular, the rayon industry—contributed most to recovery. In 1925 one out of every four automobiles sold in Britain was imported, by 1935 only one in fifty. By 1938 some three million motor cars were in operation—a dramatic rise, challenging the railways as a mode of transport. An accompanying phenomenon was a geographical shift—the new industries were located mainly in the midlands and in the south.

For agricultural revival, official action was more responsible. Britain could no longer afford to import the bulk of her food supply, and the Government, once committed to protecting the manufacturer, was equally willing to aid the farmer. By guaranteed prices through subsidies, quotas on imported food, acreage subsidies to encourage tillage, marketing boards, agricultural production was increased by 17 percent. While the amenities of life for the agricultural laborers improved much more slowly, their fortunes as well as those of the farm owners, after some sixty years of steady decline, only temporarily broken by the war years, 1914–18, began to improve.

The Unemployment Problem

The National Government could not deny the hard fact of continued high unemployment, still the most serious problem in Britain. The figures do show a marked decline but one not sufficient to change the nature of the problem. From a peak of about 3,000,000 at the beginning of 1933 (if the uninsured element were included the total would reach 3,750,000), unemployment had been cut by January 1937 to 1,700,000, a fairly constant figure until 1939.

The psychological impact of unemployment remained—the low morale of the skilled workers (particularly the miners and shipbuilders), the stark character of the "depressed areas," the consciousness of poverty. Even at its worst, unemployment in the United Kingdom never quite reached the proportions it did in Germany and in the United States; but in the United Kingdom it attracted much attention because of its persistent concentration in particular trades and in certain localities. The "depressed areas" were, as in the twenties, Clydeside in Scotland, Tyneside in northern England, South Wales, South Lancashire, and Ulster. Every month, year in and year out, the Ministry of Labor issued a report on unemployment—the statistics were well advertised. It was common knowledge in 1932 that nearly one out of every four insured workers was unemployed and that in some areas unemployment reached 50, even 70, percent. In Wales generally, unemployment reached 34 percent in 1933; by 1936 in the Rhondda district in South Wales over one-quarter of those without work had been unemployed for four or five years. Violet Markham, a member of the Unemployment Assistance Board, noticed one day in Jarrow (in Durham) what appeared to be a huge mass meeting; it turned out to be merely the daily gathering of the unemployed. In Jarrow the unemployed reached 75 percent of the insured workers. Stories of the jobless—their boredom and frustrations, their sufferings and worries, their dependence on others—were published in 1934 in *Memoirs of the Unemployed*. George Orwell vividly described the one-shilling lodging houses in his *Down and Out in Paris and London* (1933). Hunger marches, great and small, such as the march of two thousand from Scotland to London in February 1934 and the march of two hundred steel workers from Jarrow to London in October 1936, as well as the endless petitions to Parliament, the frequent mass meetings in London's Hyde Park, and the daily appearance of sidewalk artists and street musicians begging for a living—all this kept the public alive to the problem.

In the early thirties the Government, though profuse in pious hopes and vague assurances, initiated little action. The *New Statesman and Nation* was moved to say that "the Government has come to regard unemployment with public optimism and with private fatalism." Runciman, president of the Board of Trade, said that Jarrow "must work out its own salvation." In a debate in 1933 the prime minister admitted that unemployment could probably not be reduced to small figures within the next ten years. The "depressed areas" were soon rechristened "special areas."

More determined efforts were made by the Government to relieve distress. The depression vastly increased the problem of local authorities charged with administering unemployment benefits. In administration it was soon apparent that there were wide differences in practice, many anomalies, and some abuses. A royal commission recommended a clear distinction between unemployment insurance payments and unemployment relief; the Unemployment Statute of 1934 was enacted for administering relief; the Unemployment Assistance Board of six persons replaced approximately two hundred local authorities. This nonpartisan board discharged with competence its responsibility for about four million persons (workers and their dependents) ineligible for unemployment insurance. But for some time its problems were almost insurmountable. For one thing, the official agencies of labor would not cooperate. An effort to establish uniformity in practice led to the general application of the household "means test" by which the resources of an entire family were the measure for assessing the needs of any individual. In certain cases individuals received less than before; but a large family might be better off on relief than under employment. Violet Markham writes that "the course of events thrust family circumstances into unenviable prominence.... In industrial centres, home after home in the same street might be affected and grievances ran like wildfire from one to the other." When the Unemployment Statute went into effect, January 1935, an avalanche of protest forced postponement of the operation of the new scale of payments, and order was not reestablished until 1937.

Allowances for dependents varied according to age, but a family of four including two adults, one child eight to eleven, and another fourteen to sixteen, could collect up to thirty-four shillings a week in unemployment relief. Nearly 40 percent of the unemployed were soon receiving benefits entirely from relief. Relief payments were ameliorative but they could not overcome the effects of idleness, loss of self-respect, the presence of investigators, unfortunate terminology (the "dole" and the "means test"), interminable gossip about family circumstances. The curious fact is that these policies of a Government dominated by Conservatives, which aroused the bitterness of those on relief and which were treated scornfully by the Labor Party, were a step toward the establishment of the welfare state.

Diplomacy and Public Opinion

In world economic affairs statesmanship was unable to bridge the gap between pious hopes and the force of circumstances. And so it was in international diplomacy as well. The World Disarmament Conference was preceded by careful preparation. The pacification of Europe, already well along with Locarno, the Kellogg Pact, the evacuation of the Ruhr, and the suspension of reparation payments, was to be completed. All circles which believed in collective action seemed bouyant with hope and confidence. How much this optimism was shared by the National Government is uncertain, but apparently the Cabinet sincerely hoped the conference would succeed. With Arthur Henderson, the former Labor foreign minister, as president, the conference of more than sixty nations opened deliberations at Geneva in February 1932. At the end of five months no significant actions had been taken. In a parliamentary debate in November there was but a single effective speech. Winston Churchill declared that in the world as constituted disarmament conferences did more harm than good. At Geneva, French demands for security and German demands for equality canceled one another. The British delegates, led by Sir John Simon, foreign secretary, a man of great gifts and small conviction, took little initiative and assumed no responsibility. But it should be added that the Cabinet gave him little encouragement for adventures abroad. Was any cooperation to be expected from the United States? Had not Britain already reduced her air and land forces to a minimum? The National Government was unwilling to give France the unequivocal commitment of assistance which she demanded as compensation for her own disarmament.

Important decisions in international relations were not, as it happened, being made at Geneva. Force and threat of force were replacing negotiation. In September 1931, the Japanese intervened in Manchuria. Britain, in the midst of domestic crisis and frightened by a navy mutiny (in itself insignificant), seemed paralyzed and gave no lead. The League of Nations Council took no effective action. The United States, in economic straits, refused to support sanctions against the Japanese, who moved rapidly and by February 1932 had created the "independent" state of Manchukuo. The League had failed to prevent aggression, there was a serious break in Anglo-American cooperation, and France looked anew to her defensive alliances on the Continent.

In Germany, 1932 was the crucial year. Continued failure of the Weimar Republic to improve the economy at home and win concessions abroad gave the Nazis their chance. In January 1933 Hitler became chancellor and in a few months had destroyed the Republic. In October he made his first important diplomatic moves: he withdrew the German delegation from the Disarmament Conference and announced Germany's intention of resigning from the League.

It is often asserted that the National Government, had it been so minded, could have aroused the land in the early thirties to the Fascist threat and thus have prevented World War II. This would have been difficult to accomplish. If the Cabinet wavered between complacency and confusion on foreign policy, so did public opinion. Noel Coward's *Cavalcade* was shot through with vague pacifism. No matter how serious the international situation, war was not the solution. This position came more from timidity, even outright fear, and from lack of self-confidence than from pacifist views held by conviction. Aggression and force were abhorred, but why should they involve Britain? The League of Nations should be supported, of course, but League membership implied no special obligations for Britain. Also, British thinking remained more anti-French than anti-German; in the conflicting claims of France for security and Germany for equality, British sympathies were with Germany. As for the Nazis, their talk was too blunt and too bold, but there was much truth in what they said—and after all, the great danger in the world was from communism and not from fascism. This was the direction of much of the country's thinking.

Most Englishmen were opposed to rearmament. Was not the arms race in large part responsible for World War I? An important by-election in East Fulham (a London constituency) in October 1933 is instructive. In 1931 it had gone National by over 14,000. Now it went Labor by nearly 5,000 with the loser urging an increase in armed forces and the winner capitalizing on German intentions to withdraw from the League and referring to the "warmongering" activities of the Government. The Conservatives spoke of their loss of a "safe seat" in "a wild flood of pacifism." Labor hailed the vote as a vindication of its demands for disarmament and collective security under the League. One thing is sure:

it was not a vote for a strong foreign policy against aggression. Early in 1934 Thomas Jones, confidant of Stanley Baldwin, wrote, "One of the perplexities of those statesmen who think we shall have to rearm is how to bring the country to that point."

Ineffective Government, Ineffective Opposition

If British foreign policy between 1931 and 1935 was negative, this was a logical result of certain elements in the situation: the overriding importance of domestic problems, conflicting views in the Government, an impotent and confused Opposition, fear of communism and relative indifference to fascism, vague trust in the League of Nations and strong anti-war sentiment, lack of confidence in the United States. But the Government made no effort to develop a positive policy. Criticism was brushed aside. They seemed rather sure of themselves— MacDonald, Baldwin, Chamberlain, and Simon.

At the time, to any close observer, the tragic figure was the prime minister. Of MacDonald *The Times* declared fatuously in May 1933, "If anyone could ever be called indispensable to the State, he has won the title." He was invaluable, it is true, to the National Government, for his titular leadership preserved the fiction of a non-partisan Government. Baldwin, the real power, was content to work in second place. "It frees him from final decisions," wrote Thomas Jones. In Parliament MacDonald's effectiveness steadily declined. For one thing, his health deteriorated. His opponents made easy capital of his growing limitations. A speech in the Commons in November 1932 was full of "confusion, hesitation and bewilderment" (Lloyd George). "His sensitiveness sticks out six feet all around him, and one is afraid all the time of treading on his 'aura' " (R. H. Tawney). "The Prime Minister has the gift for compressing the largest number of words into the smallest amount of thought" (Churchill). His role in the National Government caused his critics in the labor world to forget his courage during the First World War and his unique services to the early Labor Party.

It would be difficult to substantiate the charge of the Opposition that the object of the "frame-up of 1931" was to prevent another Labor Government from taking office in the foreseeable future. But this view was widely held among industrial and political leaders of the labor world. Some were convinced that a general election would not come in 1936 at the end of the statutory period of the existing Parliament. The Labor Party after the debacle of 1931 was on the defensive. George Lansbury, the only Labor Cabinet minister to survive, became leader of the party in Parliament. He found it difficult to coordinate party policy in and out of Parliament since he was the only member of the National Executive in

Parliament and, though held in esteem and affection, did not hold views consistent with those of the majority of the party. But discussion and negotiation became easier when Arthur Greenwood and Arthur Henderson, both ex-ministers, were returned to the Commons in by-elections in 1932 and 1933. A positive political gain was recorded in 1934 when, under the leadership of Herbert Morrison, Labor for the first time won control of the London County Council.

The problem the party faced, in addition to the necessity for reestablishing morale, was that of clarifying its policy. In the twenties policy had been stated in terms so broad and so vague as to constitute no directive when in power. In 1932 the party conference resolved that in the next Labor Government "definite Socialist legislation must be immediately promulgated, and that the Party shall stand or fall ... on the principles in which it has faith." Nonetheless, the leadership remained moderate and gradualist. In 1932 the Independent Labor Party voted its formal disaffiliation. Its left-wing role was taken by the newly formed Socialist League, which, however, proved no more successful in luring the party from a policy which was legislative, parliamentary, and democratic. And year after year the Labor Party brushed aside overtures from the Communist Party of Great Britain for a United Front. A series of special reports led to the adoption in 1934 of a comprehensive program, *For Socialism and Peace*. The section on domestic affairs called for "great fundamental measures of economic reconstruction" and, supplemented by later reports, became the basis for the program of the Labor Government in 1945.

In foreign policy *For Socialism and Peace* seems ambiguous, for it supported collective security under the League and yet proclaimed a "peace crusade." It was in this area that Lansbury's position was most anomalous. He was by religious conviction a firm pacifist; yet the party, generally speaking, was moving hesitantly toward favoring strong resistance to acts of aggression. In 1934 Lansbury's offer of resignation was rejected, and it remained for the issue of sanctions in 1935 to bring these questions of policy and leadership to a head.

Baldwin and Foreign Policy, 1935

In May 1935 George V celebrated the Silver Jubilee of his accession. There was solemnity—four thousand persons, including the prime ministers of all the dominions, attended a service of thanksgiving in St. Paul's. There was pageantry—the king held his court in his Parliament in venerable Westminster Hall. There was emotion—in his broadcast to the nation the king declared: "I can only say to you, my very very dear people, that the Queen and I thank you from the depths of our hearts for all the loyalty—and may I say so?—the love with which ... you have surrounded us." Each evening for a week the king and queen stood on the balcony of Buckingham Palace and greeted the multitude below, and for several days running they drove through packed streets in the shabby areas of East and South London.

A month later Baldwin replaced MacDonald as prime minister. Walter Lippmann wrote in the *New York Herald Tribune*, "No other man in the United Kingdom could begin to command the confidence which Stanley Baldwin inspires at home and abroad." Since 1931 he had been lord president of the Council, a post without specified duties and without salary. From mid-1934, increasingly he filled in for MacDonald. Baldwin was indeed politically secure once again, and his prestige on the ascendancy, thanks to his successful sponsorship of the India Bill (the India Act of 1935)—providing for responsible government—in the face of Conservative opposition in the Commons led by Churchill and in the Lords by Salisbury. Many students consider the India Act Baldwin's greatest political achievement.

In his opening broadcast as prime minister, Baldwin said, "Let us continue ... to work in the future as we have done in the past as a National Government for the national good." He resisted pressure to include in the Cabinet Lloyd George, now an independent Liberal who was urging a "New Deal" type of program for combating unemployment, and Churchill, now an independent Conservative. Individually they would be difficult, he said, and "*together* would be impossbile." The only important change was the appointment to the Foreign Office of Sir Samuel Hoare, temporarily enjoying fame for his piloting of the India Bill through the Commons. He seemed some improvement over Sir John Simon.

Pacifism and International Tension

Foreign policy soon became the absorbing topic of the day. For its proper consideration, two developments in the opening months of 1935 must be noticed: anti-war sentiment in England was growing and Hitler was beginning to show his hand. Pacifist feelings were manifest in the rather startling success of the Peace Pledge Union started late in 1934 by the Reverend "Dick" Sheppard, who as vicar of St. Martin's-in-the-Fields ("the parish church of the British Empire") and as dean of Canterbury had become one of Britain's most influential clergymen. By the end of 1935, 100,000 had taken the pledge to renounce war and never again to sanction another. Among the peace publications that year was *We Did Not Fight, 1914–1918*, consisting of experiences of war resisters. But the most remarkable expression of pacifism is found in the results, announced June 25, of the much-heralded National Peace Ballot, conducted with the enthusiastic approval of the League of Nations Union. Ballots were marked by 11,500,000 persons, constituting 40 percent of the voters in Great Britain and Northern Ireland. All ballots were marked after November 12, 1934. The tabulation revealed a 90 to 95 percent affirmative vote for international disarmament, for maintaining British membership in the League, and for economic sanctions by the League against any aggressor nation. A particular question in clause 5 was crucial: "Do you consider that, if a nation insists on attacking another, the other nations should combine to compel it to stop by, if necessary, military measures? On this question 60 percent voted "yes," 20 percent voted "no" and 20 percent abstained.

The ballot was controversial even before the results were announced. The Government declared that the questions were misleading, Baldwin saying that any attempt at a "collective peace system" without the United States was useless. After the war Churchill wrote that implementation of clause 5 would have received overwhelming national support. But this does not necessarily follow. As D. C. Somervell has pointed out, the important question, that concerning *military action by Britain alone*, was never asked. The ballot posters read, "You shall decide War or Peace," but the exact meaning of the ballot remained obscure. It was a "peace ballot," yet the results endorsed not only disarmament but also collective security under the League, which the public apparently thought could be achieved without the risk of war. Vansittart later called the ballot "a free excursion into the inane."

In January 1935 the Saar, by plebiscite, returned to Germany. On March 16 Hitler repudiated the clauses on German disarmament in the Versailles Treaty and announced compulsory military service. "The chains have fallen," said the Nazis. Her industrial areas could now be defended. Let us parallel these actions with the course of British policy. In February Britain and France agreed that the armament clauses of Versailles must be revised. A white paper, March 4, announced Britain's decision to rearm. Late that month Hitler flatly told Simon (foreign secretary) and Anthony Eden (now, at thirty-seven, lord privy seal and coming into prominence) that the German Air Force was already on a par with the British. This statement rests on Simon himself, who adds that the British Air Ministry at once denied the correctness of Hitler's claim. In April MacDonald and Simon met with French and Italian representatives in the Borromeo Castle on Isola Bella off Stresa and created the "Stresa Front" condemning German rearmament in violation of the Versailles Treaty. They agreed to oppose "by all practicable means any unilateral repudiation of treaties which may endanger the peace of Europe." In May, Baldwin, about to return to No. 10 Downing Street, admitted that the previous November he had greatly underestimated the strength of the German Air Force. He announced an expanded schedule of construction

for the Royal Air Force but in the same announcement welcomed conciliatory statements just made by Hitler. In June, at a Conservative Party
rally, he insisted that the role of the League of Nations was cardinal in
British policy. In the same month, Britain was party to further changes in
Versailles in an Anglo-German naval agreement authorizing German
naval strength up to 35 percent of the British—construction was already
underway. There seemed to be something for everyone: formal protest,
no more, to German repudiation of the military provisions of Versailles,
and then further modification of Versailles by agreement; verbal adherence to a common front with France and Italy; protestations of faith in
the League; an increase in defense commitment.

Meantime the Abyssinian crisis developed. "Fate could hardly have
presented a worse ground for a test of principle," writes Keith Feiling,
Neville Chamberlain's biographer. To strengthen his regime, Mussolini
decided upon military conquest and colonial acquisition. For him the
time was propitious—with German rearmament, neither Britain nor
France wished to alienate Italy. Late in 1934 the venture began with an
"incident" on the border of Italian Somaliland and Abyssinia in East
Africa. Italy protested, Abyssinia referred the dispute to the League, the
League postponed action, the Stresa Front paid little attention, and Italian preparations for war continued.

Over the summer of 1935 British opinion took shape. Press and pulpit
became forums. The League of Nations should assert its authority—this
was the uniform demand: *The Times,* the *Telegraph,* the *Spectator,* the
New Statesman and Nation, the Church of England (notably William
Temple, archbishop of York), and the Free Churches. Government
spokesmen made more frequent references to the role of the League. And
on September 11 Sir Samuel Hoare addressed the League of Nations
Assembly at Geneva. "The League stands," he declared, "and my country stands with it, for the collective maintenance of the Covenant in its
entirety, and particularly for the steadfast and collective resistance to all
acts of unprovoked aggression." This address was greeted as an important change of position—it seemed like the voice of Pitt, of Castlereagh,
or of Palmerston. Churchill on the Riviera was "stirred." The Laborite
Herbert Morrison declared that Sir Samuel would have the support of the
nation. It was "a spark of genius" (*Spectator*). It made "clear at long last
where Great Britain stands" (*New Statesman and Nation*). On October 3
Italian forces invaded Abyssinia.

The Election of 1935

At home there was further complication—a general
election. This was not unexpected. On October 5 Baldwin addressed the

Conservative Party conference; in the words of a close friend, he "denounced the isolationists, reconciled the Party to the League by supporting rearmament, and reconciled the pacifists to rearmament by supporting the Covenant. Spoke strongly in favour of the trade unions. All with an eye to the Election." On October 23, in announcing the dissolution of Parliament, he declared it would be safe to have an election during the lull in the foreign crisis. The Government manifesto reads: "The League of Nations will remain ... the keystone of British policy .... In the present unhappy dispute between Italy and Abyssinia, there will be no wavering in the policy we have hitherto pursued. We shall take no action in isolation, but we shall be prepared faithfully to take our part in any collective action decided upon by the League and shared in by its members." Baldwin said the settlement must be fair to all parties but added that war was not contemplated. This was soothing; anyway, in the public eye, economic issues were more important. Baldwin again assessed correctly the mood of the voters and received a vote of confidence The polling on November 14 returned 428 pledged to support Baldwin, including 386 Conservatives. Opposition Liberals declined from 26 to 19, and Sir Archibald Sinclair replaced Samuel (who lost his seat) as their leader. Lloyd George failed in his final effort—through his Council of Action with its program of "Peace and Reconstruction" and an elaborate campaign to revive Nonconformity as a political force—to regain control of the Liberals and possibly return to power. £400,000 (most of it from the Lloyd George Fund) was expended and 362 candidates were endorsed by the Council. Only 67 were elected and these had no bond of unity.

Labor greatly strengthened its ranks, rising from 59 to 154. Its leadership in Parliament changed and became more effective. Morrison, Clynes, and Shinwell, all former Cabinet members, returned to the Commons. But serious differences in the Labor ranks had been brought forward by the Abyssinian war. Lansbury resigned his leadership in the Commons when a resolution to which he was opposed, endorsing League sanctions against Italy, was overwhelmingly adopted at a tumultuous party conference in October. The deputy leader, Clement Attlee, succeeded, but only after a contest with Arthur Greenwood, the most prominent individual in the party, and with Herbert Morrison, the organizer of party victory in London. Attlee won because his fellow Laborites in the Commons chose to reward his proven qualities as a parliamentarian. His task now was to make peace within the party, and he had to deal with new as well as old sources of discontent. Sir Stafford Cripps, brilliant lawyer and son of Lord Parmoor, advocated collaboration with British Communists; he and his associates (including Aneurin Bevan) were eventually expelled, in January 1939. The more significant division of opinion on national defense continued, for the party's "front bench" included Morrison, who had been a conscientious objector in World War I, Hugh Dalton, who was an ardent supporter of the League, and Cripps, who was a fanatical idealist. In these years Labor was hardly ready to return to office.

Ramsay MacDonald and his son Malcolm were the only members of Baldwin's Government to fail of reelection. Thomas Jones wrote, "It is not quite easy to preserve the 'National' facade and get rid of Ramsay." A seat was soon found for him and he remained in the Cabinet until its reorganization under Chamberlain in May 1937. He died in November 1937; "everybody" was at the service in the Abbey "except Labour members with few exceptions," commented Jones.

Examination of the general election of 1935 leaves difficult questions. Was the Conservative pledge of support for the League a fraud? For this position, when taken by the National Government, virtually eliminated the Abyssinian question as an election issue. Both the Labor party conference and the Trades Union Congress gave overwhelming support (close to 95 percent) for "all the necessary measures provided by the Covenant" against Italy. Another problem: Could Baldwin, either before the poll or after, have united Britain in opposition to Italy and in favor of rearmamant against aggression? It is doubtful at best. For one thing, his own party was not unified on foreign policy. And Baldwin himself had no instinct nor any liking for foreign affairs. In more general terms, G. M. Young, Baldwin's biographer, has written: "As in 1926, languor prevailed; the springs of action would not flow; the hand was put out to grasp the clue, but the fingers did not close." Is such a comment in order?

Whatever answers there are to these questions will be found in the policy actually pursued toward Abyssinia.

Abyssinia and the Question of Sanctions

After the announcement of the results of the Peace Ballot the Government greatly increased its verbal support of the League and the principle of collective security, but in statements which now appear ambiguous. At the Conservative Party conference, October 5, Baldwin said: "Fulfilling the obligations of the Covenant might have to be by force of arms." Neville Chamberlain in Glasgow, October 14: "We are not supporting the League because it is the League; we are supporting it because we expect it to prevent war by collective action." On October 22, Sir Samuel Hoare told the Commons that economic sanctions against Italy would be effective and that the Government would participate in such sanctions only in collective action under the League. On the twenty-third, Baldwin said the Government welcomed any "legitimate opportunity for settlement" which would be fair to Italy, to Abyssinia, and to the League. He added, "We have never had war in mind." And to the Peace Society on October 31: in Abyssinia "judgment may lead to action, at the extreme to coercive action. We mean nothing by the League, if we are not prepared, after trial, to take action to enforce its judgment. . . . You need not remind me of the solemn task of the League—to reduce armaments by agreement . . . . I give you my word that there will be no great armaments. Hoare told his constituency that the rumor that France and England might make "a deal" with Italy behind the back of the League was a "malicious suspicion" for which "there is no foundation whatever." The voter could make what he wished of such double-talk.

Let us now turn to private statements. In August, Hoare wrote Chamberlain that Baldwin, about to depart on his annual visit to Aix, "would think about nothing but his holiday, and the necessity of keeping out of the whole business almost at any cost." L. S. Amery talked with Hoare soon after the memorable address at Geneva in September and noted in his diary, "He refused to admit that ineffective economic sanctions must create the demand for effective ones, and that these would bring us to the verge of war." A few days later Amery found Chamberlain "frankly cynical" and of the opinion, in Amery's words, "that we were bound to try out the League of Nations . . . for political reasons at home, and that there was no question of going beyond the mildest of economic sanctions."

As a matter of fact, the possibility of a general war over Abyssinia had been ruled out by both Hoare and Pierre Laval (French foreign minister) as early as September 10, the day before Hoare's revivalist appeal to the League of Nations delegates. According to Laval's later statements, they agreed on "ruling out military sanctions . . . in a word ruling out everything that might lead to war." This is confirmed by Hoare's postwar account. Late in October Hoare advised Emperor Haile Selassie of Abyssinia to start negotiations with Italy for a compromise settlement. But early that month the League Assembly had ruled that Italy was making war on Abyssinia in violation of the Covenant. On November 1, at a meeting of the League committee established to implement this ruling, Hoare and Laval spoke of their efforts to find an honorable settlement acceptable to all. They were asked to continue these discussions and bring proposals to the League Council. Economic sanctions against Italy became effective November 18, but action was delayed. On December 5 Hoare reviewed his policy before the Commons and protested against "suspicions that the French and ourselves were attempting to sidetrack the League and to impose upon the World a settlement that could not be accepted by the three parties to the dispute." Two days later, tired out and all but ill, he departed for a Swiss skating holiday. At the last moment, at Laval's request and with Baldwin's approval, he agreed to stop off in Paris for further conversations.

The result was the Hoare-Laval proposal, drafted December 8, to be submitted to the League. As Hoare drove away from the Quai d'Orsay he was congratulated by his aides. The following morning, just as the official text reached London, the contents appeared in the French press to which they had been leaked, perhaps by Laval himself. About one-half of Abyssinia was to be handed over to Italy, which would transfer to Abyssinia a narrow corridor through Eritrea as an outlet to the sea.

For once, Baldwin and his Government had misjudged British opinion. The British response was, initially, stunned incredulity and then quickly a flood of protest, joined by all sections of the press except the papers controlled by Beaverbrook and Rothermere. There was but one theme: denunciation of the Hoare-Laval agreement as a betrayal of the League and a contradiction of the stated policy of the Government, so Austen Chamberlain declared before the Foreign Affairs Committee of the Conservative M.P.s. The archbishop of Canterbury, a confirmed Conservative, shook his head in bewilderment. Dawson in *The Times* dubbed the proposed outlet to the sea "a Corridor for Camels." An avalanche of mail from Conservative voters was delivered to members of the new House of Commons elected to uphold collective security against aggression. The Cabinet hesitated. "If we disowned Sam, the French would be angry and say we let them down," said Baldwin. But to save the Government from serious danger the Cabinet permitted Hoare to resign and then repudiated his agreement with Laval. The leading article in the *Economist* for December 21 was headed "The Triumph of Public Opinion." Anthony Eden, since June minister without portfolio for League of Nations affairs, became foreign secretary—further appeasement of public feeling, for he was associated with support for the League.

Sir Samuel Hoare never admitted his failure in tactics with Laval. Backed by the permanent undersecretary, Vansittart, he insisted that the only alternative was war with Italy, which would have driven Mussolini into Hitler's arms. It was better, they said, to retain Italy as a potential ally. Now this made considerable sense, for the one factor which makes intelligible the British and French concessions to Mussolini was their concern for the consequences of German rearmament. Should the Western powers find themselves at war with Italy, what sort of military coup might not Hitler bring off? Baldwin, in a speech in October 1935, had declared, "The whole perspective on the Continent has been altered in the past year or two by the rearming of Germany." It was a vital point, and the Government might well have made it the mainspring of a strong national policy. This would have required a great national effort, with the Government taking both Parliament and people into its confidence. The fact was the Government had no policy other than refusing to take effective measures unless British interests were directly involved. (For example, reinforcements had been sent to Egypt in the autumn of 1935.) The public was hopelessly confused and the Government did not clarify the situation and did not admit that sanctions against Italy, if effective, might lead to war. In April 1936, Thomas Jones wrote to a friend in Canada, "The country was wholly unprepared for the Hoare-Laval agreement—it was still on the heights of hope and endeavour where Hoare himself had placed it, whereas he had descended to the level of Paris politics." The Hoare-Laval proposals were, of course, dead, rejected by the British and by Mussolini and Haile Selassie as well. But so, in effect, were sanctions. The Italians completed the conquest of Abyssinia and in May announced the annexation of the entire country. And Britain had lost respect abroad.

A Year of Crisis, 1936

As 1936 opened, Baldwin looked forward to early retirement. His associates remarked his frequent reference to it, his lack of interest in day-to-day affairs (he seemed enthusiastic only about his private reading), his absence from important debates, his impatience with criticism. And it was perhaps the most critical year between 1931 and 1938—the difficult problems of rearmament and the "abdication crisis" at home, the Italian liquidation of Abyssinia, the unfolding of Nazi policy, the outbreak of the Spanish Civil War.

British world policy in 1936 was hesitant, indecisive, apologetic, content to drift—this is the language of the *Annual Register*. After the Hoare-Laval agreement the Government suffered many humiliations. In February Sir Austen Chamberlain, Conservative elder statesman, arose in the Commons and delivered a scolding. He demanded "evidence that everything is being done to prevent a continuance or a recurrence of such events as those for which the Prime Minister has twice stood at the Table of this House within the last two years, to ask the pardon of the House." In April, Churchill asked contemptuously, "What is the conviction of His Majesty's Government? . . . Are they waiting to see who pushes the hardest?" And on May 6, after the end of Abyssinian resistance, Churchill again: "This is a mournful occasion. We have encountered a great disaster. . . . I consider that the Prime Minister ought to have spoken in this Debate. . . . You cannot have all the power without having responsibility." The response was to restore Hoare to the Cabinet (in the Admiralty) and to abandon sanctions altogether (June 18). Then the Government had to face Lloyd George at his very best: "I have never before heard a

British Minister ... come down to the House of Commons and say that Britain was beaten. ... There is no evidence that the Government ever meant business over sanctions." Baldwin merely replied that sanctions had been abandoned because they had failed. It was his first participation in a foreign affairs debate in six months. In July a group of eighteen Conservative members of Parliament, led by Austen Chamberlain and Churchill, waited on Baldwin to express their concern about the very slow pace of British rearmament.

Hitler in the Rhineland

Meantime the structure of the international problem had been complicated by the most masterful of Hitler's moves—no accident that it came in the course of the failure to stop Italy in Abyssinia. On March 7, German troops moved into the Rhineland in violation of Versailles. At the same time, Hitler made comprehensive proposals for securing the peace of Europe for the coming twenty-five years. A new French Government was dubious of British support, and in any case was incapable of action to prevent this breach of Versailles and Locarno. When the League Council met, Litvinov (the Soviet representative) alone objected to the idea that "brutal infringement of international treaties and sabre rattling should confer upon a state the privilege of dictating to the whole of Europe its conditions for negotiations." Eden merely spoke of the necessity for reconstituting "the structure of security and confidence." The Council on March 19 formally declared that Germany had violated international treaties, but took no further action.

The British Government accepted the occupation of the Rhineland as a *fait accompli* and eagerly seized on Hitler's proposals for securing the peace, proposals, said Eden in the Commons (March 9), which must be approached "clearsightedly and objectively with a view to finding out to what extent they represent a means by which the shaken structure of peace can again be strengthened." Dawson of *The Times,* in these years his own foreign editor and a close friend of Baldwin, on March 9 ran an optimistic leader, "A Chance to Rebuild." Baldwin himself privately referred to Versailles as "iniquitous" and said he was determined in his final administration to "get alongside Germany." Eden did not condone the German action but was anxious for a friendly atmosphere in which to negotiate with Germany. "It is the appeasement of Europe as a whole that we have constantly before us," he said (March 26). Labor generally acquiesced. Hugh Dalton said in the Commons, "It is only right to say bluntly and flatly that public opinion in this country would not support and certainly the Labor Party would not support the taking of military sanctions or even economic sanctions against Germany at this time in order to put German troops out of the German Rhineland."

The common view was that Versailles had been unfair in disarming Germany. Was she to be condemned for occupying her own territory?—something quite different from Italian aggression in Abyssinia. There was little appreciation of the strategic importance of the Rhineland. At the time of Hitler's coup, a group was weekending at Lord Lothian's Elizabethan country house, Blickling Hall, in Norfolk. Those present included Lord and Lady Astor, Vincent Massey (Canadian high commissioner in the United Kingdom), Sir Thomas Inskip (soon to be appointed defense minister), Arnold Toynbee (the historian), Sir Walter Layton (editor of the *Economist*), and Thomas Jones. As Jones tells the story, on Sunday they telephoned their "shadow" conclusions to Baldwin: "Welcome Hitler's declaration wholeheartedly. . . . Condemn entry of German troops into forbidden zone . . . [but] not to be taken tragically in view of peace proposals which accompany it. . . . Versailles is now a corpse and should be buried. . . . Treat entrance to zone as assertion, demonstration, of recovered status of equality and not as act of aggression." Later in the month a Chatham House conference, conducted by the Royal Institute of International Affairs, considered "Germany and the Rhineland." Opinions were divided, but the dominant view was that Germany was justified, that Britain's problem was to determine how far Germany would go, that there was equal danger to peace from the Franco-Soviet mutual assistance pact of 1933, and that France should be assured of British aid only if she were directly attacked.

Just before the occupation of the Rhineland, Arnold Toynbee went to Germany, interviewed Hitler, and, as he reported to Thomas Jones, was convinced of Hitler's "sincerity in desiring peace in Europe." In September 1936 Lloyd George paid a friendly call on Hitler at Berchtesgaden, placed a wreath on the symbolic Nazi tomb in Munich, and returned quite enthusiastic about the whole thing. Lord Londonderry, who as secretary of state for air (1931–35) had sought to enlarge the Royal Air Force, was in Germany in 1936 and 1937; interviewed Hitler, Göring, and Ribbentrop; and returned hopeful over the possibilities of accommodating German and British policy. On the other hand, in June 1936, Duff Cooper, secretary of war, in an unofficial address in Paris emphasized the common interests of Britain and France with respect to Germany. The Government was embarrassed, the Labor Party outraged, and the press in an uproar over such "pro-French bias." In a leader July 6 *The Times* declared, "British opinion is determined . . . to come to grips with Herr Hitler's peace offer as representing the best immediate hope of the stabilization of Western Europe." This was a correct appraisal of

British feeling. Appeasement began in 1936 and it began in the minds and hearts of the English people.

Civil War in Spain

In July 1936 the Spanish Civil War broke out and added further difficulties to Britain's efforts to chart an effective foreign policy. The protagonists in Spain could not then be precisely delimited; there was as much division within the opposing forces as between. Only in the broadest terms can it be said that the "Loyalists" of the constitutional republic were supported by liberals, socialists, and Communists, and that the "National rebels" were supported by monarchists, property owners, the Church, and the Army. Yet public opinion had no trouble deciding: to those Englishmen who favored the rebellion the Loyalists were "Reds"; to those who opposed the rebellion the Nationalists were "Fascists." The Great Powers were immediately involved. Mussolini soon saw the potential advantage of an ideologically friendly government installed in Spain with his aid. Hitler saw the possibilities of weakening Italian ties with France and Britain. The new Popular Front government in France and the government of the Soviet Union favored the Loyalists. British opinion was divided, but the Government sought to prevent the Civil War from developing into an international conflict. So the Baldwin Cabinet became the chief sponsor of "nonintervention"—the Great Powers agreed not to intervene—which was established in August; it was the fortunes of this policy which concerned Britain until the formal end of the Civil War in February 1939.

The opening of the new session of Parliament in November 1936 provided opportunity for a general review of the international situation and of British policy in the light of the impact of Mussolini, Hitler, and Franco. The policy of disarmament had been abandoned, a minister for the coordination of defense named (though no ministry had been created), and modest increases voted for Army, Navy, and Air Force. But for what purpose? Under what circumstances might war come? These questions were never considered by the Baldwin Government. The address from the throne represented "complacency—to use no sharper word," commented the *Economist*. "We are not yet confident that His Majesty's Government have found a foreign policy," said Hugh Dalton. But what more could be said of Dalton's own Labor Party, which still rejected rearmament though advocating collective security? Eden was able to exploit the division in Britain to strengthen the authority of the League in negotiating an acceptable European settlement. But Eden was already isolated from prime minister and Cabinet. Peace has been our only aim, Baldwin iterated and reiterated. And in this debate he had the last word. But only after Winston Churchill spoke—he had been passed by in the search for a minister of Defense, and if this fact added a note of asperity to his remarks it was only natural. It was one of his most powerful speeches. He held Baldwin personally responsible for the delays in rearmament:

> The responsibility of Ministers for public safety is absolute and requires no mandate . . . The Government simply cannot make up their minds, or they cannot get the Prime Minister to make up his mind. So they go on in strange paradox, decided only to be undecided, resolved to be irresolute, adamant for drift, solid for fluidity, all-powerful to be impotent. So we go on preparing more months and years— precious, perhaps vital to the greatness of Britain—for the locusts to eat.

Baldwin as usual was courteous, reasonable, conciliatory. "I put before the whole House my own views with an appalling frankness." And he spoke of the tide of pacifist feeling in 1933 and 1934 and the loss of the Conservative seat at Fulham in 1933,

> on no issue but the pacifist. . . . I asked myself . . . what chance was there within the next year or two of that feeling being so changed that the country would give a mandate for rearmament? . . . Supposing I had gone to the country and said that Germany was rearming and that we must rearm, does anybody think that this pacific democracy would have rallied to that cry? . . . I cannot think of anything that would have made the loss of the election from my point of view more certain.

The meaning was obscure. Later, after the coming of war, the speech was misrepresented as saying that Baldwin admitted that he had won the 1935 election by concealing the need for rearmament. In *The Gathering Storm* (1948) Churchill made capital of this episode, with a nasty reference in the index: "Baldwin confesses putting party before country." What Baldwin actually said, but said ambiguously, was that had he called an election in *1933 or 1934* on the issue of rearmament he would have lost it. On either interpretation it was very damaging in 1936—"a mine beneath his own ranks," said the *Economist*.

Abdication of Edward VIII

Yet within a month came one of Baldwin's greatest triumphs, in his masterful handling of "the king's business." The "abdication crisis" actually lasted but eight days, from December 3 to December 10, 1936, but it was rather long in the making.

George V had never fully recovered from his severe attack of pneumonia in 1928. Early in 1935 his bronchial trouble returned, and though he stood well the grueling demands of the Silver Jubilee, it was clear by autumn that his health had seriously deteriorated. But his final illness was only of a few days' duration before death came at Sandringham just before midnight, January 20, 1936. His body lay in state in Westminster Hall for five days, the four sons of the dead king constituting the honor guard the final night. The funeral processions in London and Windsor and the burial in St. George's Chapel—simple, solemn, splendid—made a profound impression. There is evidence that the public was far more deeply moved than by either the death of Queen Victoria or that of Edward VII. George V, as Kingsley Martin has said, had become "the perfect father figure," and he and his family were thought of as sharing the tastes, the interests, the aspirations, the joys and sorrows of ordinary Englishmen. The archbishop of Canterbury in his broadcast sermon said simply: "Will not the historians be bound to ask, after all has Britain ever had a better King?"

The King and Mrs. Simpson. The prince of Wales moved into his new role of Edward VIII without enthusiasm, unwilling if not unable to assume the symbolic role which had characterized the monarchy since the closing years of Victoria. From the time of the accession the prime minister had little confidence in the new king and doubted that "he would stay the course" (so he remarked to Attlee). And he was well aware of the problems involved in the new king's friendship with an American-born lady already twice married and once divorced. As recorded by Thomas Jones, Baldwin said, "When I was a little boy in Worcestershire reading history books I never thought I should have to interfere between a King and his Mistress." Society knew all about the lady in question. But so rigid was the self-imposed press censorship that most people knew little or nothing of Mrs. Ernest Simpson, that the king was frequently in her company and that in the summer of 1936 she was one of a royal party on a Mediterranean cruise. Apparently Baldwin was able to ignore the matter until October, when divorce proceedings between Mrs. Simpson and her second husband were pending at Ipswich. Baldwin then suggested that this legal process be postponed and that Mrs. Simpson leave the country for six months. The king responded that this was the lady's own business.

From here on, details of the story are somewhat uncertain, but the main outlines are clear. In October the editor of *The Times* received an extensive account of the sensational coverage of Mrs. Simpson in the American press; he passed the report on to Baldwin and to Major Hardinge, the king's private secretary. On October 27 Mrs. Simpson was granted her divorce, with only routine announcement in the London press. The Government learned that it would have Labor support in opposing her marriage to the king. On November 13 Major Hardinge warned the king that the press could not maintain silence much longer and that a constitutional crisis was brewing which might lead to the dissolution of the Government and a general election over the issue of the king and Mrs. Simpson. He urged that the lady "go abroad *without further delay*." King Edward was "shocked and angry" and he responded by telling the prime minister on November 16, "I mean to marry her, and I am prepared to go." That evening he informed his mother, Queen Mary, and his brother, the duke of York, of his intentions. The duke of York, lacking in physical stamina, nervous, modest, and retiring, had never seriously considered the possibility of his own accession. He shrank from the prospect of the new role which fate seemed about to force upon him. His agonized feelings as the drama was played out were recorded in a diary commencing December 3.

It was on that day that the press, restive for some time, broke silence. The *Daily Mail* had been contrasting the concern of the king over the depressed areas of South Wales with the apparent indifference of the Cabinet, and *The Times* had denied any rift between king and Cabinet. On November 29 the papers carried an address of the bishop of Bradford, who wished that the king showed "more positive signs of his awareness that he stood in need of Divine Grace." Perhaps the bishop had in mind only the king's irregular attendance at Sunday services, but this loosened the bonds of silence and on December 3 *The Times'* leader, "King and Monarchy," referred directly to the problem of the king's marriage. The pro-king or "pro Simpson" view in the Beaverbrook and Rothermere press urged that Edward be permitted to marry the woman of his choice. But the Labor press, representing much Nonconformist sentiment, was solidly against the marriage. Harold Laski, in an important article in the *Daily Herald,* said that in a constitutional monarchy the king must always accept the advice of the Cabinet.

"Soft Words, Harsh Acts." In a week the crisis had passed. Baldwin brushed aside proposals for a morganatic marriage, Mrs. Simpson to be the wife of the king but not to be queen. This would require special legislation which, the prime minister said, the Government was not prepared to introduce and which the dominion Governments had said they would not uphold. It seemed possible that a "king's party" might form around a strange nucleus of Churchill, Rothermere, Beaverbrook, Mosley, and George Bernard Shaw. Sentiment outside London was overwhelmingly and decisively against the king, or at any

rate against Mrs. Simpson, as members of Parliament discovered while at home the weekend of December 4–6. And the king made clear his intention of abdicating if not permitted to marry Mrs. Simpson.

On Monday, December 7, as he faced the Commons, Baldwin found the king's support at the point of collapse. The remainder was routine. On December 10 the speaker read "a message from His Majesty." It began, "After long and anxious consideration, I have determined to renounce the Throne." Baldwin's report was one of his great parliamentary performances. As usual, he told the country little or nothing until the matter was settled. Now he apparently told all. In a simple, conversational tone of voice, and with apology for his few casual notes ("I want to ask the House . . . to remember that . . . I have had but little time to compose a speech"), he took the Commons step by step through the whole affair. He made his version seem the only possible version and received, says J. R. Clynes, "the most prolonged and moving cheering it has ever been my lot to hear in the House of Commons." The Abdication Bill was quickly passed, 403–5, and received royal assent December 11. That evening His Royal Highness Prince Edward addressed the country for the last time; he left the country to marry Mrs. Simpson the following year. The morning of December 12 an accession council proclaimed King George VI, whose first royal act was to constitute the abdicated king His Royal Highness the Duke of Windsor.

In reviewing the abdication crisis a critical student may discern a certain degree of humbug. The outcome was not as logical or as self-evident as Baldwin's report to Parliament made out. Nor were the principals uniformly and wholeheartedly high-minded. Baldwin's respectful remarks about Edward VIII in public were somewhat at variance with statements he made in private. Baldwin was charitable and sympathetic—after the issue was settled. Even then he never made public Mrs. Simpson's offer (December 8) to give up Edward and withdraw from the scene. One is reminded of A. J. P. Taylor's stricture: "This was always [Baldwin's] way: soft words, harsh acts." There is general agreement among students of this episode that Baldwin's approach to political problems—no plan of action in advance and his own attitude and policy determined by the course of events—here worked to perfection.

As to Edward VIII himself, Kingsley Martin came close to reality when he remarked that Edward "was not sure what he wanted to do." Though vaguely unhappy with his role, he did not design to be a "Radical King." He made no effort to build up a "king's party," but it is likely that he would have accepted support from any quarter. In his final broadcast he tried to assure the nation that he had been treated with full consideration; yet he was not permitted to present his case to the nation. The archbishop of Canterbury was much criticized for his broadcast, December 13 (one comment concluded, "how full of C-A-N-T-U-A-R"—a play on the Latin abbreviation in an archbishop's signature) but his words must have been representative. "Strange and sad it is," he said, "that [King Edward] should have sought his happiness in a manner inconsistent with the Christian principles of marriage, and within a social circle whose standards and ways of life are alien to all the best instincts and traditions of his people." Perhaps a cabman's remark to Kingsley Martin, "It wouldn't have done," sums it up.

For England at the time the matter of importance is that the episode was in no sense "a constitutional crisis." It was widely predicted outside the British Isles that the institution of monarchy would weaken. Of this there is no evidence. The country turned to the new king all the more easily because he was known to be very much like his father. Self-effacing and conscientious, his very nature made for conciliation. His reversion to the style of King George was happy.

George VI was crowned on May 12, 1937. Before the month was out, Neville Chamberlain, highly successful as chancellor of the Exchequer, had replaced Baldwin as his natural successor. Biographies of Baldwin are accumulating, but without much agreement as to his stature—this fascinating figure whose career explains so much of England's story between the wars because he is so typical of it. He seems to have been a more complicated individual than either his apologists or his detractors recognize. His will power, his resourcefulness, even his capacity for seizing the initiative, were underestimated. He was far more clever, much less modest, and much less candid than might appear. His wife called him "Tiger Baldwin"—a quality recognized by Lord Butler years later on the occasion of the marking of the centennial year of Baldwin's birth. Just precisely how honest he was, suggested Harry Boardman in the *Manchester Guardian* at the time of Baldwin's retirement, "might now be left to God." And so there are surprises as one follows his career. But he was given to saying that he sought only to achieve harmony, unity, and good will, and he probably meant it. "I shall always trust the instincts of our democratic people," he said in 1936. Thus he was inclined to accept situations. His words soothed but seldom inspired. In domestic affairs this was often helpful, sometimes essential. But in foreign affairs it proved disastrous. "He was not matched by gifts or temperament to this menacing hour," wrote Boardman after Baldwin's death.

Political Ideology and Social Thought

An examination of the closing years of the decade reveals several significant developments in English attitudes: the cleavage of opinion over the Spanish Civil War, striking modifications in thinking on social and economic questions, and the policy of appeasement toward Nazi Germany.

The Impact of the Spanish Civil War

Of the Spanish Civil War it has been written: "Never since the French Revolution has there been a foreign question that so divided intelligent British opinion as this." The Government stood officially for nonintervention, though its sympathies inclined toward Franco. The Labor Opposition, with some dissentients, also supported nonintervention (though complaining bitterly of inequities in its application), but its sympathies were pro-Loyalist. Active intervention by the Government on either side would probably have been impossible.

The public was little concerned with the technicalities of nonintervention but intensely interested in the ideological implications of the war. The press was openly either pro-Nationalist or pro-Republican, save for *The Times* and the *Telegraph,* which sought to report events of the war impartially. Some writers of distinction wrote in support of the rebels. Douglas Jerrold, editor of the *English Review,* 1930–36, arranged for Franco's dramatic flight from the Canary Islands to Morocco at the start of the war. Another prominent Roman Catholic, Arnold Lunn, motored through Nationalist Spain in March 1937. His *Communism and Socialism* (1938) dealt harshly with communism and by implication, approved of fascism. Wyndham Lewis in *Left Wings over Europe* (1936) defended the policies of Nazi Germany and of Fascist Italy and in 1937 came out wholeheartedly in support of Franco. Other writers with Fascist sympathies were Evelyn Waugh, who had reported the war in Abyssinia and returned enthusiastic about the Italian conquest, and Francis Yeats-Brown, whose *European Jungle* (1939) justified the use of force by Italy and Germany. The Right Book Club, the Friends of Nationalist Spain, and similar agencies organized sentiment for Franco.

Cleavage between Fascism and Communism. Pro-Republican sentiment in Britain was stimulated not so much by the troubles in Spain as by the cleavage between fascism and communism which liberals found symbolized in the Spanish Civil War, by violent opposition to Government policies alleged to be motivated by class interest, and by concern for Britain's weakness in international affairs. In December 1936, Churchill organized a gigantic mass meeting for "Arms and the Covenant" in the Albert Hall—a meeting whose import was somewhat reduced by the sudden eruption of the abdication crisis. A year later Clement Attlee led a group of Labor M.P.s on a visit to Republican

Spain; photographs taken in Madrid showed them giving the "clenched fist" salute; on their return they staged a mass meeting in demonstration for "arms, food and justice for democratic Spain."

Active support for the cause of Republican Spain came from left-wing Laborites as well as from Communists, who improved their position in these years. The literary world was one of the centers of activity. Much of the best poetry of the later thirties was inspired by the Republican cause. The Left Book Club, organized in 1936 with Victor Gollancz, Harold Laski, and John Strachey as the book selection committee, became a vehicle for Communist ideas since Communist writing constituted the bulk of the lively and intelligent writing of the left. In 1937 the *Left Review* sent out a questionnaire (signed by Auden, Spender, Louis Aragon, and Nancy Cunard) to 150 writers:

> Are you for or against the legal Government and People of Republican Spain?
> Are you for or against Franco and Fascism?

The answers appeared in *Authors Take Sides on the Spanish Civil War.* Though overwhelmingly in favor of Republican Spain, the responses showed more opposition to Franco than enthusiasm for the Republicans. There were, however, a considerable group of writers who found in the Civil War a vital testing ground of Communist ideology against Fascist, who felt that democratic processes had lost vitality and who supported with enthusiasm the Communist cause. These included Hewlett Johnson, styled the "Red Dean" of Canterbury, and Stephen Spender, who joined the Communist Party in 1936 and expounded the Communist position in his *Forward from Liberalism* (1937). Ernst Toller's *No More Peace* (1937), a satire on Nazism, was widely read in England. In 1937 a series of Marxist essays on the arts in Britain appeared under the title *The Mind in Chains*. The introduction written by C. Day Lewis concludes: "*The Mind in Chains* could never have been written were it not for the widespread belief of intellectual workers that the mind is really in chains today, that these chains have been forged by a dying social system that can and must be broken." Nearly five hundred of the two thousand British volunteers in the International Brigade of the Spanish Republican Army were killed, twelve hundred others wounded.

In the large, the Spanish Civil War may be said to have had two major effects on British thinking. In the first place, the minority voice opposed to the Government's foreign policy was greatly strengthened. The administrations of Baldwin and Chamberlain would not permit the issues of the Civil War to interfere with their efforts to conciliate Fascist Italy and Nazi Germany. R. G. Collingwood, philosopher and historian, wrote in 1938, "The British Government, behind all its disguises, had declared itself a partisan of Fascist dictatorship." Such criticism led to bitterness and bitterness to unreason. The Government was said to be the tool of class domination, with the "best people" supporting Franco. At the same time, a great reversal was beginning. Pacifism ceased to be fashionable; it was no longer the hallmark of liberalism, of opposition to Baldwinism and Chamberlainism. Many who had taken the "Peace Pledge" formally revoked their signatures. Of course, pacifism still had some articulate champions. "Embassies" were organized by the Fellowship of Reconciliation. In the interest of a world conference for "economic cooperation," George Lansbury interviewed President Roosevelt in 1936 and Hitler in 1937. John Middleton Murry in *The Necessity of Pacifism* (1937) presented an ardent and logical plea. But such individuals became isolated from general thought and were now more often associated with the right than with the left.

The Call for Social Action

To the gradual modification of public opinion on international questions the reorientation of attitudes toward social and economic problems at home bears little relation, for in this area the prominent figures were neither conventional nor revolutionary but imaginative and responsible. The affinity is with that outburst of social criticism before 1914 which was significant in modifying the traditional British way of life. If the pattern of thought in the late thirties may be summarized, it would be something like this: society did not always take care of itself for the better; the economic bases of modern civilization must be reappraised; and the ills of society would be corrected only through conscious and deliberate design and direction.

Historians now refer to the "Keynesian revolution" of the 1930s. The ideas and the influence of John Maynard Keynes, economist and Treasury official (1915–19), were cumulative—his influence outside his profession dates, as we have seen, from the controversy over Versailles after World War I. He was a member of the inner circle of the Liberal Party in the electoral campaign of 1929. It was then that he pointed out that since 1921 about £500 million had been paid out in unemployment benefits, sufficient to construct one million homes. In the same year he was appointed a member of the Macmillan Committee on Finance and Industry, whose report, strongly influenced by his ideas, was published in 1931. His articles in *The Times* in the early months of 1933, reprinted as *The Means to Prosperity*, advocated large government spending, increased loans, and remission of taxation, all to stimulate industry and create purchasing power. Eventually, in 1936, he presented his views in comprehensive form in *The General Theory of Employment, Interest and*

Money. Though Keynes was at first reviewed somewhat indifferently—he alienated the conservatives with his advocacy of the expansion of the role of government in business and offended the liberals with his defense of capitalism and the role of the individual—in time most economists came to respect his ideas and acknowledge his influence. The "revolution," in brief, was the denial of the inexorable nature of the laws of economics and the emphasis on intelligent experimentation in attacking depression, unemployment, and poverty. Accordingly, he proposed that society abandon the axiom that production should be directed where it will yield the largest return and, instead, turn to expanding consumption to stimulate production and wealth. Full employment, sharing of wealth, avoidance of excessive thrift, deficit spending—these were some of the means to an economy of abundance.

Social Research. Since 1900, society had become a vast laboratory for social research, and the economic depression after 1929 stimulated inquiry still further. In 1930 the London School of Economics published a *New Survey of London Life and Labour* and pointed out that since 1890 there had been a general increase in real wages of 20 percent, a general reduction of the workweek by 15 percent, and a lowering of the death rate from 20 per thousand to 13 per thousand. In 1889–90, 30.7 percent of the people of London were living in a state of "poverty;" by 1929 on the same standard this figure had been reduced to 9.6 percent. Seebohm Rowntree, who made the famous study of the city of York at the turn of the century, in 1936 made a new study of the same city, published in 1941 as *Poverty and Progress.* This time he included every working-class family. He concluded that by the standards of his earlier survey, 6.8 percent of the population now lived in "primary poverty" (below the line of bare necessities). In 1899 that figure had been 15.46 percent.

Table 4   Indices of Income in the United Kingdom at 1900 Prices, 1913–37 (1900=100)

Year	Index of National Income	Index of Income Per Head
1913	120.3	108.46
1923–24	115.3	106.0
1929	132	118.89
1931–32	129.3	115.25
1937	155.4	135.18

Source: A. J. Youngson, *The British Economy, 1920–1957* (1960), p. 135.

But now Rowntree redefined poverty by employing as a new standard a minimum diet for good health. The British Medical Association specified the diet. Rowntree found that 31.1 percent of the working-class population (or 19.1 percent of the entire population) were living below this minimum. The chief causes of this poverty were unemployment, insufficient wages when employed, and inadequate pensions in old age. Surveys of the same nature elsewhere—in Bristol, Southampton, Birmingham, for example—led to much the same general conclusion, though actual figures varied.

In 1936 an agricultural scientist, John Boyd Orr, issued for the Ministry of Health *Food, Health and Income: A Report on Adequacy of Diet in Relation to Income*. He pointed out that serious malnutrition among low-income families had often been denied. Now, in a widely publicized statement, he declared that the income of 50 percent of the people did not provide a diet completely adequate for health according to modern standards and that the average diet of the poorest group, comprising 4,500,000 people, "is, by the standard adopted, deficient in every constituent examined." Another authoritative study, *Poverty and Population: A Factual Study of Contemporary Waste* (1938), by R. M. Titmuss, led to the conclusion that for the previous ten years 50,000 deaths annually in the north of England and in Wales were caused by poverty. Other expressions, less academic in nature, dealt with the same theme. Lancelot Hogben, a biologist turned social scientist, in his *Science for the Citizen* (1938) insisted that there must be "Conquest of Power, Conquest of Hunger and Disease, Conquest of Behaviour." George Orwell, the novelist, was a good reporter, if not a good actor, in his endeavor to live the life of a "down and outer." His *Keep the Aspidistra Flying* (1936) has poverty in a large city as its chief theme. *The Road to Wigan Pier* (1937), often called his worst book, does present a convincing picture of poverty, overcrowding, and unemployment in the north of England.

Social research took other forms. One of the most prominent agencies was PEP (Political and Economic Planning), started in 1931 as a nonpartisan organization by a group of businessmen, civil servants, and educators interested in social and economic questions. From 1933 a series of reports came out year after year—on iron and steel, cotton, coal, international trade, public health, social service, housing, the press. A similar organization was the National Institute of Economic and Social Research, organized in 1938. One of its first publications was *Studies in the National Income, 1924–38* by A. L. Bowley of the University of London. He emphasized inequalities in distribution of national income. Tibor Barna in a study published in 1945 concluded that in 1937 from 5 to 6 percent of the national income (between £200 million and £250 million) was redistributed from rich to poor by progressive direct taxation. A royal commission headed by Sir Montague Barlow was appointed in 1937 to study the relation of industry and unemployment, essentially a study of the "depressed areas." A major interest of the Pilgrim Trust, a philanthropic organization founded by an American, Edward S. Harkness, was the problem of the unemployed. One of its investigations resulted in *Men Without Work*—the product of a remarkable committee headed by William Temple, archbishop of York—based on information gathered by unusually competent investigators. Many practical aids to the unemployed came out of this report. Lord Nuffield, who had made a fortune out of the motorcar industry, established in 1936 a trust fund of £2 million for stimulating new industry and for improving conditions in the "special" or "depressed" areas.

Planning: Programs and Beginnings. Economic and social planning must have special mention. Among the studies which appeared in the 1930s were *Plan or No Plan* (1934), a scholarly essay urging a planned economy, by Barbara Wootton, a social scientist of London University; *Reconstruction: A Plea for a National Policy* (1933); and *The Middle Way* (1938) by Harold Macmillan, a leading Conservative, urging minimum wages and industrial reorganization with partial nationalization; the various writings of G. D. H. Cole, a Fabian socialist, including *Economic Planning* (1935); *The Next Five Years: An Essay in Political Agreement* (1935), issued by a nonpartisan group (including Sir Arthur Salter, Geoffrey Crowther, Lord Allen of Hurtwood, Harold Macmillan—all Keynesian in outlook) representing miscellaneous vocations and recommending a "plan" for Britain; *Socialism Versus Capitalism* (1937) by A. C. Pigou, who was concerned about "the glaring inequalities of fortune and opportunity which deface our present civilization" and who found much merit in "planning" in dealing with unemployment.

Some years later, in 1954, the Conservative Party published a pamphlet incorporating "the Tory approach to industrial problems." In *Change Is Our Ally* we read:

> Up to 1914, the intervention of the State had been intended to protect the public or a section of it *against* industry.... After 1918, though the old forms of intervention continued, an entirely new one began. The motive of this was to assist industry in seeking its own advantage and efficiency more effectively than it was believed it could do unaided—to supplement or to counter economic forces by deliberate State action.

It is worthwhile summarizing what actually happened between the wars. Some one hundred twenty railroad companies, under government pressure, ceased to operate independently and amalgamated into four systems. In 1926 the Electricity (Supply) Act created the Central Electricity Board, which purchased current from private generating stations and distributed it through a "grid" to private or local authorities for retail. Stations which produced power at above the standard "grid" cost were forced out of business. The results were of incalculable importance, particularly when war came. The creation of the Exchange Equalization Fund in 1932 transferred to tne Government responsibility for the currency policy of the Bank of England and constituted, in effect, its nationalization. In 1930 and 1933 legislation provided for licensing companies for road passenger service and road haulage, creating a semi-monopoly. A measure of major importance was the act of 1938 nationalizing coal royalties; this statute, enacted by a Government dominated by Conservatives, brought actual nationalization of the industry much closer. Generally speaking, the Government in providing protection against competition was demanding greater efficiency. Thus, the duty placed on iron and steel importation in 1932 was dependent on the industry's reorganization. This resulted in a cartel for steel in which the British Iron and Steel Federation representing the industry and a committee representing the Government determined prices, controlled production, subsidized certain producers, and directed the planning of private firms. In agriculture, official policy reversed itself. Instead of *laissez-faire,* marketing boards were regulating domestic prices and production. Altogether, "nationalization" of industry under Labor after 1945 is much less abrupt than might first appear.

Prologue to War

Neville Chamberlain, so is the way with politics, alone of his family reached the top. He was industrious, thorough, methodical, humorless, and without sentiment. He seldom appeared in the Commons' smoking room. He thus makes a nice contrast with Baldwin. There was never any question of his right to succeed. In many ways he had been the most important member of the Government since 1931—Churchill called him "the pack horse" of the administration. Under normal circumstances he would have gone down in history as a competent and successful prime minister. But it was his fortune to lead the nation at one of the most crucial points in the twentieth century; he will always be held responsible for foreign policy before the Second World War.

And he will also be associated with the serious rift in English attitudes which that foreign policy created. Suspicion and rumor and hate went so far in 1938 and 1939 as to cause people to assert that policy (and pro-Nazi policy) was being made by "the Cliveden Set," that is, by Chamberlain and his "cronies," who came together weekends at the Astor country house, an hour from London. "The Cliveden Gang" was even referred to as a kind of "fifth column" influence in the Fascist cause. A famous cartoon by Low in the *Evening Standard* (January 3, 1938) depicted some of the "gang"—Garvin, Lady Astor, Dawson, and Lothian—doing "the Shiver Sisters Ballet" under Goebbels's direction. This is nonsense. Cliveden was, in fact, the scene of frequent lunches, dinners, and weekend house parties, but the attendance was miscellaneous—labor leaders and politicians, social workers, writers, educators, as well as members of the Government. Talk and discussion were informal and unplanned and represented a wide range of views. There was no conniving by a pro-Nazi "gang."

Chamberlain and his Advisers

But foreign policy actually was determined in rather narrow confines, immune from more catholic influences. The dominant voice was that of Chamberlain himself, for foreign policy was his primary concern from the day he became prime minister in May 1937. When, at the Exchequer, he prepared the first rearmament budget in 1936, he made his own appraisal of Fascist and Nazi designs, an appraisal which did not change until 1939. Nothing could shake his "self-sufficient obstinacy"—Lloyd George's phrase. With the overwhelming Conservative majority he could safely ignore the House of Commons. The Foreign Office itself played a subordinate role. "If only the Foreign Office will play up," he wrote at the beginning of his administration. As for Eden, the foreign secretary, he too was expected to follow the lead of his chief. For example, in July 1937, Chamberlain held conversations with the Italian ambassador in the absence of Eden. Chamberlain then dispatched a personal letter to Mussolini and noted in his diary that he did not show it to Eden, "for I had the feeling that he would object to it."

Chamberlain surrounded himself with advisers like-minded with himself. Sir John Simon was at the Exchequer and Sir Samuel Hoare at the Home Office. Lord Halifax was promptly given a major role and on Eden's resignation early in 1938 became foreign secretary. These formed an inner cabinet. The ambassador to Germany, Nevile Henderson, was well chosen. He wrote in 1939: "I think I may honestly say that to the last and bitter end I followed the general line which he [Chamberlain] set me, all the more easily and faithfully since it corresponded so closely with my private conceptions." Sir Horace Wilson, a Treasury official, was given an office at No. 10 and became the prime minister's daily companion on walks in nearby St. James' Park and his personal adviser on all questions. Another member of the inner circle was Geoffrey Dawson, editor of *The Times*, who had special sources of information and could be relied upon to express Government views. Dawson himself was by conviction pro-German and anti-French. Others close to Chamberlain were Lionel Curtis, who had had various contacts with imperial affairs, and Lord Lothian, secretary to the Rhodes Trust, Liberal member of the National Government in 1931–32, and subsequently ambassador to the United States in 1939. Lothian, as a Christian Scientist, tended to ignore the existence of evil. He interviewed Hitler in 1935 and in 1937 and was convinced that Germany "had a case" and that she was concerned "not with dominating other nations but with her own rights and her own place in the world." There were others, but these in the main were the men who determined British policy. They considered that they knew best, and their thinking was a curious combination of complacency and lack of nerve. They profoundly distrusted Russia. Their chief object was to avoid war—especially war with Nazi Germany, in which they refused to see anything seriously untoward and found much they professed to admire. They convinced themselves that Hitler was a reasonable man. Above all, he must be neither spurned nor offended.

Chamberlain's own point of view clearly emerged in 1937. Again and again he declared that the League of Nations had failed and the ideal of collective security must be abandoned. And it was not wise to depend upon the United States. He welcomed Roosevelt's Chicago "Quarantine" speech in October 1937, but wrote privately, "It is always best and safest to count on nothing from America but words." To build up a democratic bloc was merely to return to the alliance system and eventually to war. On the other hand, discussion and negotiation would dissipate issues and tensions likely to lead to war.

Getting on Terms with Hitler

"If only we could get on terms with the Germans, I would not care a rap for Musso." This was central to Chamberlain's thinking in 1937. He was aware that the status of central Europe, armaments and colonies were the areas of tension. Lord Halifax attended a hunting exhibition in Berlin in November 1937 and Chamberlain seized eagerly on the opportunity offered for an interview with Hitler. Halifax told Hitler that Britain would not oppose alterations in central Europe (Danzig, Austria, Czechoslovakia), but such changes must come by "peaceful evolution" and not by "methods which might cause far-reaching disturbances." This conversation convinced Hitler that Britain could be safely ignored in his plans for the Anschluss with Austria. Halifax himself attached little significance to the talks, but Chamberlain reported them to the Commons with some enthusiasm and recorded in his diary that they had created "an atmosphere in which it is possible to discuss with Germany the practicable questions involved in European settlement." What was a reasonable settlement? He tells us in a private letter. "I don't see why we shouldn't say to Germany, 'give us assurances that you won't use force to deal with the Austrians and Czechoslovakians, and we will give you similar assurances that we won't use force to prevent the changes you want, if you can get them by peaceful means.'" *The Times* (November 29) said that every effort must be made to amend by agreement the Versailles settlement on central Europe.

As the weeks passed, the Halifax-Hitler interview of November and what it revealed of British policy bulked large in the minds of the Nazis. A "secret" German Foreign Office memorandum, dated December 20 and supported by Weizsäcker, chief of the Political Department, spoke reassuringly of the "obvious progress in the British attitude" and declared that negotiations with Britain for peaceful change of the *status quo* would be to Germany's advantage even if they failed, for such an outcome would increase Germany's freedom of action. Ribbentrop, the German ambassador in London, in a "strictly confidential" memorandum for the Führer, dated January 2, 1938, reached somewhat different conclusions. He advocated:

1. Outwardly, continued understanding with England while simultaneously protecting the interests of our friends.
2. Quiet but determined establishment of alliances against England.

He advised:

We must . . . continue to foster England's belief that a settlement and an understanding between Germany and England are still possible eventually. . . . Today I no longer have faith in any understanding. England does not desire in close proximity a paramount Germany, which would be a constant menace to the British Isles. On this she will fight. . . . Every day that our political calculations are not actuated by the fundamental idea that England is our most dangerous enemy *would be a gain for our enemies.*

The few documents here cited are selected from a complete series of papers of the German Foreign Ministry for 1937–38 which was captured at the close of World War II. These papers indicate that while Chamberlain went on happily with his plans for negotiating away the tensions between Britain and Nazi Germany, the Nazis were grimly engaged in mapping diplomatic and military strategy for attaining their ends.

It has been charged, and with good reason, that from November 1937 Chamberlain gave "one impression to the House of Commons and a totally different one to Hitler and Mussolini." He certainly was not frank with the Commons; on December 21, for example, he dismissed inquiry about the Halifax visit with the remark that "no proposals were made, no pledges were given, no bargains were struck." Chamberlain's relations with the House generally deteriorated and his rapport with some of his advisers weakened. Lord Londonderry, who had generally been in sympathy with Government policy, wrote to his friend Ribbentrop, December 8, 1937:

> I feel in my own mind that if only Germany, in conference with Great Britain, France and Italy, could categorically state the limit of her ambitions and her desire to achieve as quickly as possible a real limitation of armaments, we should find that these terrible suspicions, ... that Germany is waiting until she is fully armed for a further development of her plans, can be removed. ... If we are just going on drifting ... waiting for German demands, then I am quite sure we must come up in opposition to some of these demands, and the catastrophe which we are one and all fearing will be upon us before we know where we are.

The Role of Italy

But Chamberlain had his own strategy: to strengthen his bargaining power with Hitler by settling all outstanding questions with Italy. Mussolini also was eager for a general understanding with Britain—a hope he voiced through Sir Austen Chamberlain's widow, now resident in Rome—for he wished to strengthen his position before being confronted with Austria's annexation by Germany. It was over Anglo-Italian policy that Chamberlain's differences with Eden reached the breaking point, leading to Eden's resignation on February 20, 1938. The immediate issue was the projected discussion with Italy, to which the foreign secretary would agree only if Italy gave assurances in advance of withdrawal from Spain. According to the colorful report of Count Grandi, the Italian ambassador in London, the differences between Chamberlain and Eden were on one occasion heatedly argued in his presence. There was also disagreement over a declaration proposed by France that the continued independence of Austria constituted a joint interest; to this Eden was agreeable, Chamberlain opposed. Lord Templewood (Sir Samuel Hoare), who has written in some ways the most illuminating commentary on the foreign policy of these years to come from an English participant, believed that the immediate cause of Eden's resignation was Chamberlain's unfavorable answer to a proposal from President Roosevelt (January 1938) for a world conference to draft general principles for the conduct of international affairs and provide for peaceful modification of international treaties. Chamberlain had replied that such a proposal might interfere with Britain's own efforts to come to terms with Italy and Germany—an answer made without consulting Eden and clearly at variance with his judgment. Eden resigned, in effect, because he was in favor of a stronger stand against Mussolini and because he refused to subordinate himself any longer to Chamberlain's personal diplomacy. His withdrawal produced some restlessness in Government ranks but received no overt support in the Cabinet. An Opposition motion of censure was easily defeated, though some twenty-five normal supporters of the government abstained from voting. Eden himself made no effort to lead a revolt. Halifax soon succeeded to the Foreign Office. In the outside world Eden's resignation was a sensation, for he had been an object of attack by Hitler and Mussolini, who now appeared to have Chamberlain and British policy under full control. The British proceeded to reach an agreement with Italy (April 16) by which each undertook not to add to her bases in the eastern Mediterranean or in the Red Sea without notifying the other. Britain gave some guarded intimation that she would recognize Italian sovereignty over Abyssinia, and the Italians agreed to the evacuation of foreign troops from Spain. The agreement proved of little value, for it did not come into force until late in the year and by that time the Spanish Civil War was all but over and Italy had developed new grievances.

Austrian Coup and Czech Crisis

The more immediate problem was in Austria, whose independence soon ended. In February Nazi pressure on Schuschnigg, the chancellor, forced reorganization of his Cabinet with the inclusion of the Austrian Nazi, Seyss-Inquart, as minister of the interior and of security. Of this deterioration of Austria's position Chamberlain showed no awareness in the debate (February 21) on Eden's resignation. He said, "The peace of Europe must depend upon the attitude of the four major Powers—Germany, Italy, France and ourselves.... If we can bring these four nations into friendly discussion, into a settling of their differences, we shall have saved the peace of Europe for a generation."

In Austria Nazi policy moved ahead inexorably. On March 9 Schuschnigg, fighting back, suddenly announced a plebiscite for the thirteenth to determine the future status of his country, but under pressure from Hitler he canceled the proclamation. His appeal to Britain for counsel brought a response from Halifax that Britain would not guarantee Austria protection. On the evening of March 11, German forces entered Austria; Hitler himself went to Vienna on the thirteenth and absorption of Austria into the Reich was proclaimed. Mussolini acquiesced. France was caught up in a Cabinet crisis; Russia was occupied with purge trials. "I am convinced," wrote Count Ciano in his diary March 12, "that

Great Britain will accept what has happened with indignant resignation."
As a matter of fact, Nevile Henderson in Berlin had already told the
Germans that his Government would not oppose the Anschluss, and he
was attending a party at Göring's house when word came of German
troop crossings into Austria. Chamberlain received the news as he was
giving a farewell luncheon to the German amabassador in London, Ribbentrop, newly appointed German foreign minister, who must have been
fully aware of what was happening. The British Government made a
formal protest to the Nazi coup (the protest was ignored) but Chamberlain in the Commons (March 14) quoted German assurances that the
integrity of Czechoslovakia would be respected.

Notwithstanding, a novel and important note now appeared in the
voice of the British Government. On March 10 Halifax told Ribbentrop
(the version is that of Halifax's memorandum, a text accepted by Ribbentrop):

> We recognized the reality of the problems from the German point of
> view connected with Austria and Czechoslovakia. [But there now
> seemed to be a spirit in Germany which threatened a peaceful settle-
> ment and this would be dangerous for all of Europe.] Experience of
> all history went to show that the pressure of facts was sometimes
> more powerful than the wills of men: and if once war should start in
> Central Europe, it was quite impossible to say where it might not end,
> or who might not become involved.

And Chamberlain himself, in commenting in the Commons (March 24)
on the situation in Czechoslovakia, went out of his way to say:

> Where peace and war are concerned, legal obligations are not alone
> involved, and, if war broke out, it would be unlikely to be confined to
> those who have assumed such obligations ... This is especially true in
> the case of two countries like Great Britain and France, with long
> associations of friendship, with interests closely interwoven, devoted
> to the same ideals of democratic liberty, and determined to uphold
> them.

Perhaps there was a limit to appeasement.

However, still strong in the Cabinet and in the Commons, Chamberlain gave no indication of any change in course; patience, negotiation,
and compromise would solve the problems of Europe just as they solved
difficulties in the business world. On March 13 he wrote his sister, "If we
can avoid another violent *coup* in Czechoslovakia, which ought to be
feasible, it may be possible for Europe to settle down again, and some day
for us to start peace talks again with the Germans."

It was more than clear that Czechoslovakia was the next problem.
There the *Sudetendeutsche Partei,* under Konrad Henlein, now claimed

for the German nationals full and equal rights with the Czechs as "a governing people." Such demands were a mere pretext, since Henlein had already given himself over to the Third Reich and Hitler had determined upon Czechoslovakia's destruction; even prior to the Anschluss Hitler was declaring in public broadcasts that the continuous "persecution" and "humiliation" of the Sudenten Germans might have to be resolved by war.

Chamberlain, for all his optimism, seemed prepared for the worst. On March 20 he told the Commons, "You have only to look at the map to see that nothing that France or we could do could possibly save Czechoslovakia from being overrun by the Germans." In his view, no matter what, the solution must be peaceful. He rejected a Soviet proposal for a European conference to organize action against further aggression and categorically refused to join France in a guarantee of military support to Czechoslovakia. His statement in the Commons (March 24) that no British interest in that area justified a prior guarantee of protection drew cheers from the Conservative benches.

But Halifax was now well ahead of his chief and it was he who issued a note of warning. In the war scare of May 19–21, when conflict between Germany and Czechoslovakia seemed imminent, he sent Ribbentrop a personal message through the British ambassador in Berlin: "I would beg him not to count upon this country being able to stand aside if any precipitate action there should start European conflagration." Both France and Russia affirmed their intentions of fulfilling treaty obligations of military support to the Czechs. However, war did not come at this time, mainly, it seems, because Hitler and his General Staff had previously decided against an immediate military solution of the Sudeten problem. Their new timetable for Operation Green set October 1, 1938, as the latest date.

Negotiations over Czechoslovakia

Negotiations between Henlein's party and the Czech Government made no headway despite Chamberlain's efforts. His "Runciman Mission" in August, designed to mediate, was a failure. Henlein was, indeed, only going through the motions of negotiation. Nazi propaganda reached its climax at the party congress at Nuremberg on September 12. In violent language Hitler demanded the right of self-determination for three and one-half million Germans in Czechoslovakia; this speech touched off revolt in the Sudeten land. On the fifteenth Henlein declared, "We want to return to the Reich."

Chamberlain then assumed full charge of British policy. He refused France assurances of support, shunned all overtures from Russia, and determined on direct talks with Hitler in an effort to prevent armed intervention in Czechoslovakia. On September 13 Chamberlain wrote George VI that the Government was still acting on the assumption that Hitler desired a peaceful solution. On the same day he wired the Führer, requesting an interview. Hitler was astounded (*"Ich bin vom Himmel gefallen!"*) and acquiesced. It was a forerunner of later "summit meetings." At Berchtesgaden on the fifteenth they agreed on cession of Sudeten territory to Germany on the basis of self-determination. Apparently Chamberlain's illusions were shaken, for on his return he told the king that Hitler had had every intention of settling the issue by force. Now he won support for the principle of self-determination from the Cabinet and from France, and after an initial refusal he secured the acceptance of the Czech Government. But back in Germany on September 22, Chamberlain was confronted with Hitler's new demands for stepping up the process of cession and providing for immediate German military occupation of German-speaking districts even before a plebiscite was held. This Godesberg memorandum was rejected in London, Paris, and Prague. Hitler responded in the Berlin Sportpalast, September 26, with his ultimatum in one of his most explosive speeches: Czech evacuation of the Sudeten areas by October 1, or war.

At this point George VI offered to make a personal appeal to Hitler. Chamberlain did not encourage this suggestion but instead, on September 27, delivered to the German Government, through Sir Horace Wilson, a personal message to this effect: If in pursuit of her treaty obligations France became actively engaged in hostilities against Germany, the United Kingdom would feel obliged to support her. Hitler's answer was defiance. War now seemed inevitable. Air Raid Precaution (A.R.P.) reguations had been ordered in effect on September 25. Some thirty-eight million gas masks were distributed, some one million feet of slit trenches dug as shelters; air raid wardens were alerted, police instructed, plans made for evacuating two million persons, including half a million school children, from London. On the evening of the twenty-seventh Chamberlain broadcast to the nation. His words were those of a provincial from Birmingham: "How horrible, fantastic, incredible, it is that we should be digging trenches and trying on gas-masks here because of a quarrel in a far-away country between people of whom we know nothing!" He had done all he could, he concluded; the country must wait on events.

But now Hitler left the door to peace open by offering to join in a guarantee of the integrity of the reduced Czechoslovakia. On the twenty-eighth Chamberlain replied in a direct personal message, "I feel certain that you can get all essentials without war, and without delay," and offered to return once more to discuss "arragnements" for the transfer of the Sudetenland. He also dispatched a personal message to Mussolini, asking him to urge Hitler to agree to one more conference.

That afternoon Chamberlain reported to a packed Commons, while silent crowds in Whitehall waited for news. He had been speaking for nearly an hour and a half when he paused to read a note handed to him by Sir John Simon. He turned back to the House: "I have now been informed by Herr Hitler that he invites me to meet him at Munich tomorrow morning. He has also invited Signor Mussolini and M. Daladier . . . . I need not say what my answer will be." Barrington-Ward, assistant editor of *The Times*, who was present, wrote that instantly "the whole place was on its feet. A huge prolonged cheer and a tempest of waving order-papers"—Attlee, Sinclair, and Maxton gave their blessing. Harold Nicholson called it "mass hysteria." The next day's leader in *The Times* was "On to Munich." At no time, it said, had Chamberlain's determination to avoid war "betrayed him into compromising that regard for justice and honour ... which alone can assure the confidence of the British people and of the world in British Foreign Policy." Before the Cenotaph in Whitehall, Londoners knelt to pray for his efforts to keep the peace.

Munich and Its Consequences

At Munich, September 29–30, 1938, was settled the fate of the Sudetenland, and, as it turned out, the fate of Czechoslovakia as well—without Czechoslovakia's being represented. The Big Four—Hitler, Chamberlain, Mussolini, and Daladier—drafted an agreement for the cession of the Sudetenland to Germany, on terms essentially the same as Hitler had demanded at Godesberg. The integrity of the rest of Czechoslovakia was to be guaranteed. Before departing from Munich, Chamberlain managed to see Hitler alone and secured his signature to a statement that the Munich agreement was "symbolic of the desire of our two peoples never to go to war with one another again," and "we are resolved that the method of consultation shall be the method adopted to deal with any other questions that may concern our two countries."

The immediate reaction throughout western Europe was profound relief. Daladier, as he returned to Paris from Munich, braced himself for a hostile reception. To his astonishment, he was met with delirious enthusiasm. Chamberlain's own return was triumphant. The king sent to the airport a letter of congratulation and summoned him at once to Buckingham Palace, where he stood on the balcony with the king and queen to receive a tremendous ovation. He told another crowd in Downing Street, "I believe it is peace in our time." He was overwhelmingly sustained in Parliament, and *The Times* called his report "An Impregnable Case." George VI, before returning to Balmoral to finish his interrupted holiday, addressed the nation and lauded "the magnificent efforts of the Prime Minister in the cause of peace."

But for Chamberlain, Hitler would have had his war despite the advice of his General Staff. As the Munich agreement was concluded, Hitler's face was "as black as thunder," recorded a member of the British delegation. Munich forced Hitler to reveal his objectives and his methods. He had also privately and publicly stated limits to his policy ("I have no further territorial ambitions in Europe"). Perhaps Chamberlain was not so naive as might appear. His biographer tells us that in the drive to London from Heston Airport (after Munich) Chamberlain told Halifax that he had prepared the peace pledge partly in hope and partly as a test of Hitler's good faith. It was for Hitler to demonstrate whether Munich had prevented or merely postponed war.

At the moment, Munich decided nothing, except for sealing the fate of Czechoslovakia and losing for the use of the Western powers some thirty Czech divisions. It neither vindicated nor repudiated appeasement. It did not greatly change Chamberlian's policy. It did not unify Britain. It was merely a lull in the pressures of Hitler's Reich. If one may try to summarize the policy of the Government and the feeling of the majority of the people after Munich, it would be something like this: Britain still hoped that peace might be maintained, was still committed to negotiation, was still unwilling to throw her lot in with that of France and Russia against Nazi Germany, and was still unwilling to make all-out preparations for war.

Yet here and there in governmental circles were marked exceptions. Thirty Conservatives abstained from voting on the motion to approve Munich, and they included several persons close to Chamberlain: L. S. Amery, Harold Macmillan, Lord Lloyd, and Duff Cooper, who resigned his post as first lord of the Admiralty. "I have ruined, perhaps, my political career," he told the Commons. "But that is a little matter . . . . I can still walk about the world with my head erect." In the debate Churchill declared that Munich was "a total and unmitigated defeat"; Harold Nicolson called it "one of the most disastrous episodes" in British history; Anthony Eden said the situation called for neither praise nor blame, but England should see that she did "not have to play so unpleasing a role again." Halifax had fewer illusions than his chief. He wrote the ambassador in Paris that "the greatest lesson of the crisis" was "the unwisdom of basing a foreign policy on insufficient armed strength."

But Chamberlain still clung to conciliation. He was "a tough man who sees very clearly between blinkers," wrote Kingsley Martin at this time. In the Commons debate Chamberlain reaffirmed his confidence in Hitler's good faith and he addressed the archbishop of Canterbury, "I am sure that someday the Czechs will see that what we did was to save them for a happier future." At the end of October he wrote his sister, "A lot of people seem to me to be losing their heads and talking and thinking as though Munich had made war more, instead of less imminent." He refused to broaden the Government, saying that he could not work with a divided Cabinet. In Hitler's word, he told the Commons (November 1), he had full confidence. Nonetheless, as the end of the year approached, his private correspondence shows him not very optimistic. It was certainly wishful thinking which led him to go with Halifax to Rome in January 1939 in a final effort to draw more closely to Italy. But while Mussolini seemed disposed to be friendly, relations between Italy and France had so deteriortated (Italy was laying claim, on grounds of nationality, to Corsica, Tunisia, Nice, and Savoy) that the visit accomplished nothing. In fact, it was merely a source of amusement to Mussolini, who said privately to Ciano, "These, after all, are the tired sons of a long line of rich men and they will lose their empire." In May Hitler and Mussolini joined in formal military alliance in the Pact of Steel.

Crisis Reborn

Munich did not moderate Hitler's policy. Hardly more than a week later he delivered at Saarbrücken a broadside against British criticism of his domestic policy. "It would be a good thing," he said, "if in Great Britain people would gradually drop certain airs they have inherited from the Versailles epoch. We cannot tolerate any longer the tutelage of governesses." He was furious at the British criticism of the Nazi pogrom against the Jews in November. Though he had given assurances of no further designs on Czechoslovakia, almost immediately, as the evidence of the Nuremberg trials shows, his actions were otherwise. On October 21 he issued a secret directive that the Wehrmacht be in readiness to crush the Czech state; in a supplementary directive on December 17 he declared that "outwardly it must be quite clear that this is only a peaceful action and not a warlike undertaking." Czechoslovakia was now breaking up into its nationalist components, and Hitler's method was to use the Slovaks as he had used the Sudeten Germans. When a sufficient breach had developed between the Slovaks and the Czech authorities in Prague, the Reich would intervene to maintain order.

When the new crisis came in March 1939, the Chamberlain Government seemed taken completely by surprise. On February 18 Nevile Henderson reported from Berlin his "definite impression...that Herr Hitler does not contemplate any adventure at the moment." It was probably this reassurance which led Chamberlain to write privately (February 19), "All information I get seems to point in the direction of peace." A few weeks later (March 10) the home secretary, Sir Samuel Hoare, in an address at Chelsea spoke of the prospects of a "Golden Age" in which

"Five Men in Europe, the three dictators and the Prime Ministers of England and France ... might in an incredibly short time transform the whole history of the world." And the day before, Chamberlain told a Commons press conference that the international situation was tranquil and the Government was therefore contemplating the possibility of a conference to consider general limitation of armament. An issue of *Punch* contained a cartoon, "The Ides of March," showing John Bull awakening from a nightmare. The nightmare, labeled "War Scare," is escaping from the window, while John Bull is saying, "Thank goodness that's over."

That issue was published March 15. The same day, at 6 A.M., seven German army corps moved into Bohemia and Moravia. This action came hard on the crowded events of the fourteenth, when the Slovaks had voted their independence and the elderly Czech president, Hácha, under threat of total destruction of Prague from the air, had capitulated and signed a document placing "the destiny of the Czech people and country with confidence in the hands of the Führer of the German Reich." Two days later the "independent" state of Slovakia also asked for German protection. Hitler announced that the non-Czech areas had revolted against "an intolerable terroristic regime" and "Czechoslovakia has thereupon ceased to exist." Bohemia and Moravia were proclaimed a protectorate and formally incorporated within the German Reich.

At first Chamberlain reacted normally. On March 14 he denied that any German aggression against the Czech state had taken place. On March 15 both he and Simon declared that since the state of Czechoslovakia had ceased to exist (after Slovakia's secession), there was no longer anything to guarantee. It was all very regrettable, but "let us not be deflected from our course—the search for peace."

Elsewhere the response was otherwise. The British press was outraged by Hitler's latest move. *The Times* led the way with a complete about-face. Its leader (March 16) declared, "The invasions, occupation and annexation of Bohemia and Moravia are notice to the world that German policy no longer seeks the protection of a moral case." The same day, a City gathering heard addresses from Harold Nicolson and Robert Boothby and adopted a resolution calling for action with other states "to sustain the rights and freedoms of small nations menaced by unprovoked aggression." And Chamberlain, himself, remarked: "I have decided that I cannot trust the Nazi leaders again." Prompted by Halifax, he rewrote the text of his next address (at Birmingham on the seventeenth). The revised version was a cry of anguish. He had been cheated. "How can these events this week be reconciled with those assurances [of Hitler]? ... Is this in fact a step in the direction of an attempt to dominate the world by force?" And he continued: "No greater mistake could be made than to suppose that, because it believes war to be a senseless and cruel thing, this nation has so lost its fibre that it will not take part to the utmost of its power in resisting such a challenge." And Halifax told the German ambassador in London that the German action against the Czech Republic was "in flat contradiction to the spirit of the Munich Agreement."

The End of Appeasement

This language heralded a revolution in British policy. There were immediate changes in the timetable of rearmament. Munich had brought about a thorough inventory of the services, but not until the spring of 1939 did preparation for war become the avowed intention of rearmament. Expansion of the Air Force was lagging behind the programs established. By February 1938, only 4,500 planes had been delivered, though the schedule of February 1936 called for more than 8,000 in three years. In April 1938, a new schedule called for the production of 12,000 aircraft in the ensuing two years and a war potential of 2,000 a month. The main development of the spring of 1939 was in steps to insure the attainment of this objective, and, indeed, to expand it. Comparatively speaking, among the services, the Navy was in by far the best shape. But only in 1939, after the Czech crisis, was the Admiralty authorized to plan for a "two-power standard," now defined as meeting requirements sufficient to protect British interests against Japan in the Far East and against Germany in the West simultaneously. As for the Army, "the Cinderella Service," until the spring of 1939, it remained reduced to five divisions and deficient in equipment under the doctrine of "limited liability:" that is, it was to be used for defense only. Even after Munich only two divisions were available for continental operations. In March and April of 1939 this was drastically changed—now a program for a field army of no less than thirty-two divisions was adopted.

The revolution in policy was a shift from limited commitment (thus retaining decision as to just when to go to war) to outright guarantee of military aid—a guarantee Britain had been unwilling to make to France before 1914 or to France on behalf of central and eastern Europe after 1918. The first stage was a British proposal (March 20) that the four powers (Britain, France, Russia, and Poland) agree to consult if the security or independence of any European state was threatened, but Poland refused to be associated with Russia. Britain then turned to Poland alone—her usefulness as an ally in a security system (to protect Romania, for example) was highly regarded. On March 31 Chamberlain made his momentous announcement in the Commons: "In the event of any action which clearly threatened Polish independence and which the Polish Government considered it vital to resist with their national forces, His Majesty's Government would feel themselves bound at once to lend the Polish Government all support in their power." He added that France had taken the same stand.

In the debate which followed, Chamberlain satisfied all his critics; even Sir John Simon (whom Sir Archibald Sinclair, the Liberal leader, referred to as "for more than seven years the evil genius of British foreign policy") fell into line. Chamberlain spoke of "a new epoch." This was understatement. Heretofore in the Baldwin-Chamberlain era, the National Government had made a practice of intervening on behalf of the strong against the weak, in defiance of the century-tried principle that Britain, in her own interests, must stand in the way of the preponderance of any one state on the Continent. The return to historic policy came not on issues arising in western or central Europe. Rather, guarantees were made in eastern Europe, where Britain had invariably shied away from commitment, and to Poland, a state difficult to assist militarily and whose Governments had no reputation for integrity. It is unlikely that six months before, anyone would have forecast such an outcome.

No formal agreement was reached between Britain and Poland until August 25. Perhaps Britain wished to leave open the possibility of the inclusion of the Soviet Union in a security system, though flat rejection by Britain of a Russian proposal (March 19) for a conference (Russia, Britain, France, Poland, Romania, and Turkey) to consider possible common action ended any hope for its early attainment. The issue of a Russian alliance stood in the way of complete British unity at this time. "If we are going in without the help of Russia, we are walking into a trap," a war of "a kind that would just suit Hitler," declared Lloyd George on April 3. Six weeks later Churchill asserted, "Without Russia there can be no effective Eastern Front."

Efforts at a Security System

As explanation for the failure of Britain and Russia to come together we may distinguish these factors: (1) persistent British suspicion of the good faith of Russia and doubts as to her value as an ally—these views were particularly strong in Chamberlain's own thinking; (2) a tendency to exaggerate the value of Poland as an ally; (3) the difficulties in persuading Russia and the small states of eastern Europe (particularly Poland) to act together; and (4) perhaps most important, as Arnold Toynbee suggests, the fact that mistrust between Britain and Russia was mutual—for the chief object of the policy of both was to avoid a break with Germany.

Within narrower limits Britain took action. On April 13 along with

France she gave guarantees of aid to Romania and Greece if their independence was threatened. On May 12 came an Anglo-Turkish declaration (followed by a Franco-Turkish declaration) of mutual aid in case of aggression leading to war in the Mediterranean. And on April 26 the Government proposed the first peacetime conscription in Britain's history—all twenty and twenty-one years olds were to be called up for six months of military training; an act was passed the month following.

But Chamberlain still had some illusions about Hitler. In his mind the purpose of the security agreements was not so much to prepare for war as to persuade Hitler to keep the peace. In this vein he wrote to his sisters. In this vein he spoke in public. On May 19 he spoke in the Commons of satisfying "the reasonable aspirations on the part of other nations even if this meant some adjustment of the existing state of things." Halifax vainly urged him to include both Churchill and Eden in the Cabinet—so we are told by R. A. Butler, who, as undersecretary at the Foreign Office, had good reason to know.

Hitler called the tune. As the spring progressed he determined to deal promptly with the Polish question in order to neutralize his eastern frontier in a war which he was now preparing against Britain and France. His specific demands—outright cession of Danzig and extraterritorial rights establishing communication across the Polish Corridor with East Prussia—would subordinate Poland completely to his policy. But these objectives, he was convinced, could only be achieved through war, and the destruction of Poland became settled policy. In April he prepared directives for Operation White, and in May he decided, after consultation with his high command, to "attack Poland at the first suitable opportunity." Soon after, this action was tentatively set for August 20.

In May, Chamberlain finally began to make serious overtures to Russia. But there, likewise, a profound change had occurred. Litvinov, commissar of foreign affairs since 1930, was replaced on May 3 by Molotov, "above all men fitted to be the agent and instrument of the policy of an incalculable machine" (Churchill). Molotov would enter into a tripartite pact with Britain and France only if the buffer states bordering on Russia were included in a security system. Russia would be given the right to intervene in those states and would thereby be strengthened as a power. This requirement proved the main obstacle to successful conclusion of any agreement. Eventually, on August 11, an Anglo-French mission arrived in Moscow hopeful of working out principles of military, naval, and air collaboration in advance of political settlement. All discussions were abruptly terminated with the announcement (August 22) that the Soviet Union had accepted German proposals and the completion (August 23) of a Russo-German nonaggression pact by which each party promised to abstain from aggressive acts against the other. The German offer to settle spheres of influence in the Baltic persuaded Stalin to give the nod to Germany rather than to Britain and France. The failure of British and French policy seems less inept than circumstantial. Stalin simply had more to gain from a pact with Germany, and Hitler wished to eliminate the possibility of large-scale conflict on two fronts.

Until the end Hitler strove for localization of his war with Poland. But after May, liquidation of Poland was his avowed intention regardless of consequences. A customs dispute between Danzig and Poland provided his excuse for intervention; the Nazi coup in Danzig (August 23–24) was soon followed by its formal incorporation in the Reich (September 1).

Mobilization and War

The course of events accelerated. Reports of a Russo-German agreement brought partial mobilization in Britain on August 22 and Parliament was summoned for a special session on August 24. In a packed House of Commons, an Emergency Powers (Defense) Bill was pushed through (the significant vote was 427–4) and at once accepted by the Lords, authorizing the Government to proceed by orders in council "for the securing of the public safety, the defences of the realm, the maintenance of public order." On the twenty-third, in answer to a strongly worded communique from Chamberlain, Hitler declared that the questions of Danzig and the Polish Corridor must be solved, blaming Britain for Poland's intransigence. However, he still had hope of detaching Britain and France from Poland; he postponed Operation White until the thirty-first and made his "final offer" to Britain. The Polish problem must be solved and German colonial demands met, but he would pledge his support of the British Empire, would accept the existing German frontier in the west, and would agree to an arms limitation. The British answer (August 28) declared that the Polish question must be settled by negotiation, that Poland's essential interests must be preserved, and that Britain would honor her pledges to Poland—these pledges had been formalized on the twenty-fifth with a binding mutual assistance pact. Hitler made some pretense of continuing negotiations with Poland and even proposed to Henderson a formal Anglo-German alliance. But early on the morning of September 1 the Wehrmacht moved across the Polish frontier. The Second World War had begun.

The immediate response in Britain was hesitation, partly through some uncertainty in the Cabinet as to the next move, partly to gain time to consider Mussolini's proposals of mediation, and partly because of delays in coordinating action with the French. A note to the German government on the evening of September 1 demanded cessation of hostilities against Poland. But this note was not an ultimatum. The following eve-

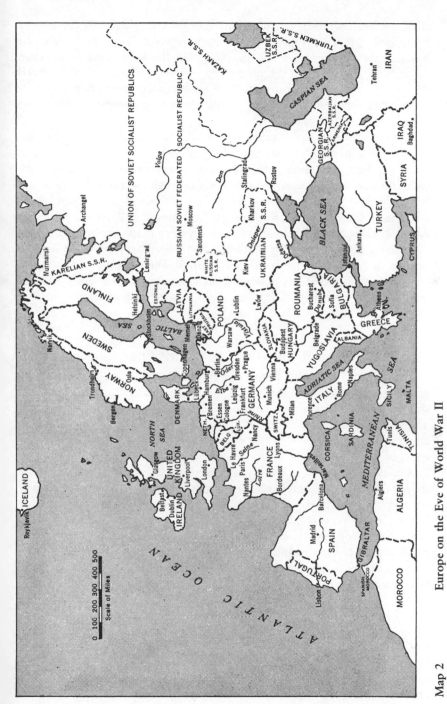

Map 2   Europe on the Eve of World War II

ning a silent but restless Commons greeted Chamberlain's halting announcement that no reply had yet been received. In Attlee's absence, amidst cries of "speak for England" from the Conservative benches, Labor's Arthur Greenwood voiced the general concern: "I am gravely disturbed . . . . I wonder how long we are prepared to vacillate at a time when Britain and all that Britain stands for, and human civilization are in peril."

The Cabinet met at 11 P.M. and took action. Accordingly, the next morning (Sunday, September 3) Halifax telegraphed instructions to Henderson in Berlin to present to the German government a two-hour ultimatum demanding cessation of operations against Poland. There was no reply, and at quarter past eleven, Chamberlain, from the Cabinet office in Downing Street, broadcast to the nation that Britain was at war. At noon he addressed Parliament: "Everything that I have worked for, everything that I have hoped for, everything that I have believed in during my public life, has crashed into ruins. There is only one thing left for me to do; that is, to devote what strength and powers I have to forwarding the victory of the cause for which we have to sacrifice so much."

The Question of Accountability

It soon became fashionable to hold the National Government accountable for the coming of war, but much the greater part of this kind of criticism represented wisdom after the event. Few people in 1936–37 foresaw the events of 1938–39. Even Churchill, with all his concern for rearmament, had no confidence in collective security and misread the character of Nazism and Fascism. His conclusion that the Second World War was "the unnecessary war" raises more questions than it answers. The public was less realistic than the Government. Even after Munich it is likely that a popular poll would have supported Chamberlain by a very comfortable margin. Such a statement cannot be documented, of course, but one has merely to read the press to find considerable corroboration. A striking example is found in the *Daily Express*, under the proprietorship of Lord Beaverbrook, who was a vocal adherent to appeasement. In frequent issues from September 19, 1938, to August 7, 1939, the *Daily Express* reiterated, "There will be no war this year or next year either." And the comment of Tom Johnston, a left-wing Laborite, must be taken seriously: "We all sensed the shame and humiliation of Munich, but most part of us hoped secretly that Chamberlain was right and that Hitler could be bought off at the expense of our acquiescence in his villainies towards the smaller nations." Not until war came did "appeasement" become an ugly word.

There is no evidence that a Labor Government would have done the job much better, not even that it would have done it much differently. The Laborites, as a group, were far behind the Conservatives on rearmament. They were hopelessly muddled in regarding pacifism and collective security as synonymous. Not until the summer of 1938 did Labor, in Parliament, challenge the Government's rearmament policy. As each difficulty came along, the nation accepted the easy way out, grasping at assurances, no matter how synthetic, that war could be avoided. "Were not the Conservatives in favour of armaments on the understanding that they were never to be used and the interventionists in favour of using them on the understanding that they were never to be provided?" is Arnold Toynbee's way of putting it.

This narrative of the background of World War II has been based on the research of leading scholars and includes frequent reference to the sources. Obviously it reflects, in the main, the English experience and is only a part of the story. No aspect of historical writing is more subject to changing "perspective" than is foreign policy. And already tricks are being played on Englishmen living before 1939. "Revisionism," that is, modification of accepted interpretations, particularly those operative at the time of the events under consideration, is developing apace. The orthodox view of the causes of the Second World War has come under attack. The word "appeasement" has almost disappeared from the vocabulary employed. One approach concerns Hitler's actions and his intentions. A. J. P. Taylor opened up this area in his *The Origins of the Second World War* (1961), arguing that Hitler had no designs on either England or France, that his policy in central and eastern Europe was merely an extension of Germany policy in the twenties, and that he bore no moral responsibility for the war. Characteristic of Taylor's approach is the question he raises of the authenticity and relevancy of the famous "Hossback Memorandum" of the conference Hitler held November 5, 1937, with the commanders of his armed forces, often referred to by others as a blueprint of Hitler's long-range plans for solving the problem of German living space (*Lebensraum*).

Then another interpretation insists that Chamberlain and his associates were not ideological in dealing with the Russian and the German problems and had no desire to set the one against the other. And it has been suggested that historians should examine more carefully Anglo-Italian, Anglo-Japanese, and Anglo-Soviet relations—particularly in 1939. Some of these questions and answers come together in one of the most recent reassessments, that of Maurice Cowling in his *The Impact of Hitler: British Politics and British Policy 1933–1940* (1975). He argues that foreign policy under Baldwin and Chamberlain, and the positions of Labor as well, were largely determined by the exigencies of party politics in Britain. Thus, he concludes that "Halifax was not the arch appeaser but the embodiment of Conservative wisdom who decided that Hitler must be obstructed because Labour could not otherwise be resisted." Then, even more recent is Simon Newman's *March 1939—The British Guarantee to Poland* (1976), which concludes that the guarantee to Poland was the climax of Britain's challenge to Germany for the control of Europe. Among these views there is as yet no consensus and the serious student must find his own answers.

One conclusion is fairly self-evident. It is put with studied restraint by F. S. Northedge (*The Troubled Giant*, 1966): "Few will deny that the twenty-three years of foreign policy [1916–39] were among the most unsatisfactory in the long record of the British government." British policy had failed to achieve its ends, which may be stated: international peace; avoidance of national commitments in advance; diplomacy by negotiation in the interests of stability; an international atmosphere favorable to British industry and trade and in which Britain and the Dominions would control events in their own interests and, as they saw it, for the good of the world. Not until the end of the thrities did her leaders spy either war or revolution on the horizon, and became aware of the significance of her growing estrangement from France, her loss of naval supremacy, her relative decline in economic power, and the consequences of devolution in Empire and Commonwealth. Toward Germany she had acted "diplomatically," certain that negotiation, sometimes called "appeasement," would straighten out difficulties.

In such an assessment we inevitably face the question of responsibility. No doubt the answer is in part in Britain's situation and in events and circumstances almost beyond control. But the narrative we have presented leads to other conclusions as well. W. N. Medlicott, often regarded as the dean of diplomatic historians, declares: "England was curiously deficient in leaders of commanding stature." And F. S. Northedge finds the answer in "a failure of ideas, or rather a failure to adjust ideas born in one age to the requirements of another." Chamberlain's weakness was not in want of industry or of devotion to duty, but in his lack of imagination and his failure of nerve. He stubbornly adhered to his own position and did not seek advice in the best quarters. His "equivocations," as Ian Colvin (*The Chamberlain Cabinet*, 1971) makes clear, were almost beyond conception. Public opinion was profoundly affected by the Hoare-Laval bargain and ready thereafter for instruction and guidance. This was not provided. What an American president did by way of educating the American people after war began in 1939, a British prime minister might have accomplished with the British people before it started. Baldwin, Simon, and Hoare, and Chamberlain and Halifax were all men of religion and men of peace. But this did not lead them to clarify issues (instead they obscured them) or to take Parliament and the nation into their confidence (instead they were less than candid). Conservative protests that Labor Party opposition hampered Government policy were and are absurd. A. J. P. Taylor has pointed out in another connection that with their great majority the National Government "could have done what they liked if only they had known what to do." The Government never seemed to realize that peace as well as war requires decision, policy, and power. World War II marks the end of Britain as a first-class power. Of this, Munich was the symbol. Could she under other leadership have more adequately discharged in the thirties the responsibilities which were then still hers as a great power? We can only say that as it was she did not.

9 World War II

C. P. Snow
*Two Cultures and
a Second Look*
(1964), p. 99

The worst doesn't always happen, as a friend said to me in the summer of 1940.

John Ehrman
Grand Strategy,
6 (1956): 350

When all is said and done, the Western Alliance [Great Britain and the United States] formed the closest and most far-reaching combination of sovereign states in war, on the basis of equality, that has yet been seen. It was an outstanding example of opportunities grasped and of difficulties subdued.

George Orwell
*The Lion and the
Unicorn* (1941),
pp. 87–88

The war and the revolution are inseparable. We cannot establish anything that a Western nation would regard as Socialism without defeating Hitler; on the other hand we cannot defeat Hitler while we remain economically and socially in the nineteenth century.

1939–1945

Soon after the prime minister completed his broadcast on September 3 announcing a state of war, the sirens sounded an air raid warning. London traffic halted; people in the street sought nearby shelters; officials in Whitehall took to their basements; members of Parliament went to the downstairs smoking room and some soon walked out on the terrace by the Thames to watch the balloon barrage rise quickly in the sunshine. It proved to be a false alarm; forty-five minutes later the "all clear" signal was heard. Before the day was out, a British passenger liner, the *Athenia*, was sunk by a German U-boat west of the Hebrides—one hundred twelve lives were lost. Thus, and quite properly, this conflict began as a civilian's war. But this distinction soon lost its meaning, for throughout the conflict the man in uniform and the civilian shared to a considerable degree the same experience. This common experience was shaped by the actual fortunes of war at home and abroad, from which no one was ever far removed. It is, therefore, the war itself—the planning in high echelons of command and the debates in Parliament; the problems of supply, shipping, and manpower; measures of defense both civil and military; and the operations on land and sea and in the air, culminating in final victory—which will be the central theme of our examination of this period. And since operations in western Europe, in the Mediterranean, and on the Atlantic determined the fate of Britain herself, our study of the war will be largely confined to these theaters. "Total war" is a term now so ominous that we need hardly pause to justify the military history of the most destructive conflict of all time as a central theme in our story.

"The Phony War"

If civilians were to engage in the war, civil defense was needed, and the British had made much preparation. In 1935 the Air Raid Precautions (A.R.P.) Committee issued its first circular to local authorities; thus began a program to educate the public, develop warning systems, and, in the event of war, plan for the preservation of vital services, repair of damage, and control of the population. A parliamentary act of 1937 imposed on city and county authorities the responsibility for drafting detailed plans for each area, and an overall regional control system was established. During the Munich crisis these measures were feverishly tested and, accordingly, improved. A Cabinet minister, Sir John Anderson, was made responsible for civilian defense. He promptly inaugurated a program of 2,500,000 shelters designed to protect 10,000,000 persons. The "Andersons" were outdoor household shelters made of steel—six feet high, six feet long, four feet six inches wide, sunk three feet in the ground with eighteen inches of dirt on top—providing protection for four persons (in an emergency for six) against blast, debris, and splinters but not against a direct hit; 1,500,000 were distributed free to low-income families. The Civilian Defense Act of July 1939 empowered the Government to appropriate buildings for public shelters, and obligated factories and shops to develop their own A.R.P. measures.

In September 1939, the immediate problem for many civilians was evacuation. The experience of Munich was not reassuring, for the premature flight of perhaps 150,000 to Wales and the West Country had all the symptons of general panic. Accordingly, the Government implemented a parliamentary report prepared in July 1938. The country had been zoned into evacuation areas, neutral areas, and reception areas. Evacuation was, generally speaking, to be voluntary, and this quite naturally complicated the job of planning. But it was estimated that if war came some 4,000,000 persons (1,400,000 from Greater London) must be relocated, the vast majority to be assigned to private homes. On September 1, 1939, the operation began. At the end of three days, 1,473,000 persons had been moved from evacuation areas and, so the official historian tells us, "without a single accident or casualty." But for some days and weeks there was demoralization in many reception areas as rural folk learned about city people. And criticism multiplied just because the expected attack on cities did not at once materialize. Also, as the war started, an elaborate scheme for redistributing hospital resources went into effect. Some 140,000 patients in hospitals in target areas were discharged or removed and some 200,000 hospital beds made available for air raid casualties. It was later discovered that evacuation under government auspices was only one part of the story, for during July and August of 1939, approximately 2,000,000 other persons had privately removed themselves from the danger areas, in many instances leaving England and moving to the dominions or to the United States.

The Chamberlain Government at War

Laborities and Liberals were invited to join the Government but declined to serve under Chamberlain. All parties did readily acquiesce in an electoral truce by which each party agreed not to contest a by-election against the candidate of the party holding the seat at the time of the vacancy. Chamberlain created a War Cabinet of nine, including Churchill in his old post at the Admiralty. Anthony Eden rejoined the administration. But Chamberlain refused to include Duff Cooper and Leo Amery—they had both opposed the Munich pact. The "War Book," prepared between the wars in the secretariat of the Committee of Imperial Defense, was opened and its carefully worked-out procedures put into effect. Prompt establishment of ministries of supply, of shipping, of food, of information, and of economic welfare; legislation authorizing the minister of labor to regulate employment (a national registration at once gathered information on manpower); an emergency budget with tax increases—such measures gave some notice of what this war would mean in terms of public policy.

Important operational decisions were reached. On September 9 the War Cabinet decided to plan for a three-year war (as a minimum), and on September 12 an Anglo-French Supreme War Council was established. Plans for the Royal Navy were based on the revised "two-power" standard, and programs were modified, giving priority to construction which could be completed by 1941. Prior to September 3, 1939, the air program called for 12,000 planes by spring 1940 and 5,500 more thereafter. On September 22, the Cabinet approved a new target of 2,550 planes a month by the third year of the war. As to land forces, four divisions (over 160,000 men) were dispatched to France in the first five weeks of the war. A target of fifty-five divisions from the Commonwealth was urged by some experts, and later (in February 1940) this figure was accepted by the Cabinet as a goal to be attained as early as possible. But except for provision of wartime scales of equipment, the Government did not attempt to go beyond the formal program of thirty-two divisions adopted the previous spring. Britain was committed to sending ten divisions to France by February 1940, with an additional twenty-two divisions to be ready for service on the Continent by September 1941.

The first operational phase of the war, the Polish campaign, was over in less than a month. Effective resistance ended September 17, and Poland was divided into German and Russian spheres of influence in an agreement signed September 28. Thereupon Hitler sent forth peace feelers, avowing that he had no war aims against either France or Britain. "Why should the war in the west be fought?" he asked. In Britain there was a flurry of letters to the Government appealing for peace, a surprising speech from Lloyd George, now "a defeatist," urging the serious consideration of any and all peace proposals, and some sentiment in the Cabinet that the German people could be set against their Nazi Government. After some delay, Chamberlain, in a speech before the Commons on October 12, declared that Hitler's assurances were worthless and that Britain would not recognize his conquests. In November, when the sovereigns of Belgium and Holland offered to mediate, George VI replied that Britain would consider only such proposals for ending the war as would achieve the purposes for which she had entered it.

Government Policy and National Morale. Chamberlain's own efforts as a war leader were uneven. Though publicly repudiating peace offers, he clung privately to the hope of a collapse of the German "home front" (a far greater possibility, in fact, was a revolt within the Army) and to a conviction that Hitler would not assume the offensive in the west. His weekly statements to the Commons were, to Harold Nicolson, "dull as ditchwater," also "glum and gloomy." Chamberlain was slow to adjust to the realities of war. At a Conservative Party gathering on November 22 he was partisan and complacent. On the floor of the Commons he brusquely pushed aside Labor suggestions on planning for postwar social reform. He seemed undisturbed by the slow increase in production and ignored appeals for a Ministry of Economic Planning.

The prime minister must, then, be associated with the temporary letdown in national morale over the winter of 1939–40. These were the months of "the phony war" (an American phrase) or "the Bore War" (an English phrase) or "the twilight war" (Churchill's phrase). Operations on land were at a standstill. While the Germans were occupied against Poland, the French might have attacked in the west. Instead they settled down in the magnificent Maginot Line—with its vast complex of tank traps, its subterranean railway, its garrisons stationed hundreds of feet below ground—and felt secure, apparently oblivious to the fact that these defenses stopped dead at the Belgian frontier. In early 1940, Attlee visited British headquarters in France and found a static defense line with no reserves and was told that the Germans "can't get through the Ardennes." But the longer the German offensive was delayed, the more time for British rearmament.

At home Britain relied, as usual, upon the protection of the seas and her naval power. Early disasters, such as the loss in September 1939 of the aircraft carrier *Courageous* by submarine attack and the destruction in October of the battleship *Royal Oak* by a U-boat which had penetrated the British base at Scapa Flow in the Orkneys, were a shock to public opinion. The fleet was temporarily based in the Clyde while the defenses at Scapa Flow were strengthened. But these blows seemed partly compensated for by German losses, notably that of the pocket battleship *Graf Spee*, scuttled off Montevideo (December 17) when trapped by British cruisers. Since October 1, the *Graf Spee* had destroyed nine British cargo ships. In February, her supply ship, the *Altmark*, known to have on board captured British crews, was followed into a Norwegian fjord by the British destroyer *Cossack*. The destroyer commander defied the Norwegians, boarded the *Altmark* by force, and freed some three hundred or more British prisoners.

But that which gave the British the most satisfaction was the apparent success of their blockade, which, it was confidently expected, would seal off Germany and eventually bring her to terms. Perhaps no direct assaults on land would be required. If it was to be an endurance contest, Britain would win. In this early stage of the war, overseas trade direct to Germany was assuredly greatly diminished. In order to keep out of range of enemy aircraft and to include Norwegain ports in the far north, the Navy controlled the North Sea by patrols between the Orkneys and Iceland and in the Denmark Strait, separating Iceland and Greenland. In the south, mine fields and destroyer patrols controlled the Straits of Dover. The British dominated Suez and Gibraltar, but could not limit traffic between the Black Sea and the Mediterranean. The most serious problem proved to be that of controlling German trade with European neutrals immediately adjacent. Efforts at agreements with these neutrals came to this: by the blockade Great Britain was able to check the flow of contraband goods from overseas through neutral countries into Germany, but she was unsuccessful in reducing the normal traffic in native products directly from those neutrals. Yet on the whole the Ministry of Economic Warfare at this stage was very optimistic. In his first report for the department since the beginning of the war, R. H. Cross told the Commons (January 17) that after four-and-a-half months of war Germany was in economic difficulties similar to those after two years of World War I. "We look forward to the day when we shall have so strangled Germany's economic life that it can no longer sustain her war efforts."

During the long months of winter (the coldest in Britain in forty-five years), the public sense of responsibility tended to give way to boredom. Petty criticism increased and absence of air raids led to impatience with blackout regulations. Evacuees streamed back home. Dance halls and cinemas reopened. Resorts were crowded during the four-day Easter holiday at the end of March. Rationing (in January) of ham, bacon, butter, and sugar was greeted as an annoyance.

The Fight for Norway. If the British people, as well as Chamberlain, thought they lived "on a magic island" (J. B. Priestley's phrase), they were soon jolted back to reality. In November 1939, Soviet demands on Finland led to her invasion, and a Russo-Finnish war ensued. The British fully sympathized with the Finns but at first did not seriously contemplate effective assistance, for that would likely have led to violation of Norwegian and Swedish neutrality. However, in February, Britain and France in the Supreme War Council agreed that a Finnish defeat must be prevented and accordingly began to organize an expeditionary force (100,000 men) for her aid. The *Altmark* incident (February) convinced Hitler that some such move was afoot, and he prepared Operation *Weseruebung* for the conquest of Denmark and Norway, in order, he said, to "prevent British encroachment in Scandinavia . . . guarantee our ore base in Sweden and give our navy and air force a wider start-line against Britain." The Russo-Finnish peace on March 12–13 seemed to reduce the possibility of British action against Norway, but Hitler decided to proceed promptly—all other naval operations had given way to this project, and after April 15 the nights would be too short to provide a cover of darkness for the naval units.

Prepared with meticulous care, this operation was executed not, as the story often has it, by fifth-column activity but through perfect coordination of German land, sea, and air forces—in Hitler's words, "one of the sauciest undertakings in the history of modern warfare." Shortly after 5 A.M. on April 9, assaults were made simultaneously on Copenhagen and on all major Norwegian ports as far north as Narvik. By nightfall Denmark had capitulated, and all Norwegian port targets were in German hands.

As this operation unfolded, the British were engaged in a maneuver of their own—the laying of mines in territorial waters off the western coast of Norway to check the flow of Swedish ore by rail through Norway to Narvik and thence by steamer through the "Leads" (the passage inside the islands parallel to the coast) to Germany. This was commerce vital to

Nazi war production. From the beginning of the war the British had their eyes on Norwegian coastal waters but hesitated to offend or alienate a country jealous for her neutral status and anxious to avoid giving either belligerent cause for intervention. Finally, however, French insistence and Churchill's will prevailed, and early on the morning of April 8 the Admiralty began laying mine fields off the coast near Narvik. Furthermore, a military support was to occupy key Norwegian ports on the North Sea when and if "the Germans set foot on the Norwegian coast, or there is clear evidence that they intend to do so" (so reads the official British account).

Thus it happened that on the morning of April 8 a group of British destroyers, led by the battle cruiser *Renown* and bent on laying mines in the Norwegian Leads off Trondheim, made contact with units of the German battle group proceeding along the coast and destined for Trondheim and Narvik. Both sides sustained serious damage. The British, now aware that a major German move was in progress, suspended mine laying and canceled the military expedition. German units were able to reach their targets at the appointed hour. Only in the Narvik fjords did they have difficulty. There, on the tenth, a group of British destroyers screened by bad weather surprised German naval units and merchantmen and inflicted heavy damage. Three days later the 33,500-ton battleship *Warspite* protected by nine destroyers, ventured daringly into the inland waters and with other British units destroyed the remaining German vessels. In these two encounters the Germans lost all ten destroyers which had transported troops to that area. The British lost but two destroyers.

But British naval prowess had not prevented Nazi invasion. The British, therfore, decided on counterinvasion. Prompt action might have taken Narvik, but delays in dispatching troops and conflicting views on the wisdom of an assault prolonged preparations. The strategists turned their attention to Trondheim, a natural target, for it had a protected harbor with extensive port facilities for large vessels and gave access to transportation routes south to Oslo, north to Narvik, and east to Sweden. Operation Hammer, a frontal attack from the sea, was mounted but soon abandoned in the face of opposition from the three chiefs of staff, fearful of the force of German air power concentrated on the Home Fleet in the narrow Trondheim waters. It was decided instead to exploit landings already made at Namsos and Aandalsnes, well above and well below Trondheim, and then to develop a pincers movement against the city.

But Trondheim was never reached. The official historian tells us that "the pincers movement as a strategic concept lasted one week, as a practical venture even less." The designs on Trondheim were too much of a gamble; the War Cabinet decided to limit the offensive to Narvik, and British troops were evacuated from central Norway May 1–3. At

Narvik delays in preparations continued. When the Germans were at last displaced on May 28, the Nazi "Blitz" on the Continent reduced this success to a mere incident. Allied forces, after limited operations, were withdrawn early in June. Though the Allies had sent to Norway land forces considerably larger than the Germans', the effective use of air operations by the Germans was in the last analysis the deciding factor. For German superiority in the air neutralized the influence of British sea power along the coast in the North Sea and eliminated it altogether from such limited areas as the Skagerrak and the Kattegat in the south. In Norway itself the overwhelming power of the Luftwaffe prevented the British from establishing effective anti-aircraft units and from providing air bases for fighter planes, and it enabled the Germans to move reinforcements, munitions, and supplies at will, especially to isolated areas in the north, and in turn to hinder Allied communications and troop movements.

At the time, *Weseruebung* appeared an enormous Nazi victory. The Allied blockade was seriously threatened and the Nazis were provided with additional U-boat and air bases. British strategy broke down because of indecision and because of failure to integrate effectively air, sea, and land power. Even Churchill at the Admiralty shows up poorly. However, Germany had thrown nearly her entire Navy into the operation and emerged with the loss of half her destroyer strength and three of her eight cruisers and the temporary loss of her two heavy battle cruisers and one of her two remaining pocket battleships. Any attempt at invasion of Britain would have scant naval support. In the long view, this fact proved to be the most important consequence of the campaign in Norway.

From Chamberlain to Churchill

In May 1940, the Norwegian operations led directly to the fall of the Chamberlain Government. On April 4, five days before the Nazi assault on Scandinavia, Chamberlain made the most unfortunate speech of his career. He told a gathering of Conservative Party leaders that he now felt "ten times as confident of victory as ... at the beginning." Hitler had failed to take advantage of his initial superiority "to overwhelm us and France before we had time to make good our deficiencies.... He missed the bus." As the Norwegian campaign progressed, adverse sentiment developed against Chamberlain. The British public, only vaguely aware of the details, sensed total failure. Parliament was restless and disturbed. Tory critics of Chamberlain were meeting privately.

On May 2 Chamberlain announced to Parliament the withdrawal of troops from central Norway. His comment was weak. "If we have not achieved our objective, neither have the Germans achieved theirs." He did not mention Narvik. On May 7–8, an angry Commons debated the conduct of the war, with the strongest attacks on the prime minister coming from Conservative back-benchers. L. S. Amery, an old friend and associate but a critic of appeasement, determined "to bring the Government down if he could." Sensing support in the mood of the House, Amery concluded his bitter attack with Cromwell's famous words to the Rump of the Long Parliament: "You have sat here too long for any good you have been doing. Depart, I say, and let us have done with you. In the name of God, go!" After some uncertainty over tactics, Labor members called for a vote of censure. Chamberlain decided to accept the challenge and appealed to his friends for support. This was a mistake, for many in the House were in no mood to vote in a partisan manner. Chamberlain survived the division, but only by a vote of 281–200 (his normal majority was about 200), with about 40 Conservatives voting against him and about 60 Conservatives abstaining. A public opinion poll May 9–10 showed only 22 percent in favor of retaining Chamberlain as prime minister. When he learned that Labor would not enter his Government, he resigned (May 10). It had become "apparent," he broadcast to the nation, that "essential unity could be secured under another prime minister, though not myself." (He remained in the Government, amid rather general complaint, but died the following November.)

May 10 was a momentous day. At dawn the Wehrmacht crossed the frontiers of Holland and Belgium. Parachutists and glider-borne troops descended on key objectives. The "march of conqeust" in the west had begun. Late in the afternoon Chamberlain tendered his resignation to the king, who wrote in his diary for that day that he "told him how grossly unfair I thought he had been treated." The king was inclined to name as prime minister Lord Halifax, as "the obvious man," in spite of the fact that he was not in the Commons; but on Chamberlain's advice he sent for Winston Churchill. What other man in the English-speaking world would have responded as he? He writes later:

> I cannot conceal from the reader of this truthful account that as I went to bed at about 3 A.M., I was conscious of a profound sense of relief. At last I had the authority to give directions over the whole scene. I felt as if I were walking with Destiny, and that all my past life had been but a preparation for this hour and for this trial.... I thought I knew a good deal about it all, and I was sure I should not fail.

When the Commons met (May 13), Chamberlain was generously greeted with a "terrific reception," recorded Harold Nicolson. Churchill was received with more restraint—applause was more uninhibited from the

Labor benches than from Conservatives, many as yet not fully trusting Churchill. But his first words set the tone of his leadership. He had, he said, "nothing to offer save blood, toil, tears, and sweat.... You ask, What is our policy? I will say: It is to wage war, by sea, land and air, with all our might and with all the strength that God can give us .... What is our aim? ... Victory—victory at all costs, victory in spite of all terror; victory, however long and hard the road may be."

The Battle of Britain

As Robert Rhodes James observes, if Churchill's story had ended in 1938 or 1939 "we should be in the presence of a great personal tragedy." Ever impatient with the discipline of party, no ordinary circumstance could ever have brought him to the highest office. During the thirties, going nowhere politically, he wrote a romanticized version of Marlborough and the Grand Alliance against Louis XIV in the early eighteenth century—this reflecting his faith in England's destiny and his contempt for the petty quarrels of politicians.

But now his hour had come. "In May 1940 ... the British people divined that this nadir of their fortunes was the zenith of a leader under whose auspices they could wring victory out of defeat" (Arnold Toynbee). Churchill emerged as the only important public figure who did not in some way share responsibility for a policy which had taken the country into another war. The collapse of the western front in May 1940 and the threat of invasion provided him with the supreme opportunity of his life and brought national unity at last. The membership of the Peace Pledge Union sharply declined. Many of the rebels of the 1930s found that they were British after all. John Strachey returned to the Labor Party and took his turn as an air raid warden. C. E. M. Joad and Bertrand Russell abandoned pacifism. George Orwell's *The Lion and the Unicorn: Socialism and the English Genius* (1941) was war propaganda. John Lehmann and Stephen Spender, leftist writers in the thirties, joined the fire-fighting services. Some confirmed pacifists remained (for example, John Middleton Murry, Vera Brittain, Maude Royden, Christopher Isherwood), but pacifism was more of a luxury in this war than in the last, and was less respected.

In the crowded weeks of May and June 1940, waves of patriotic emotion swept over the country. "Destiny has come to this island with the speed of a bomber diving from the clouds" (*New Statesman and Nation*). The Labor Party's demand for reconstruction of the Government, said the *Spectator,* "led a movement not partisan or sectional but national." The Labor leader, Clement Attlee, became a member of the small (five-member) War Cabinet and, in effect, leader of the Commons in a truly national Government. On a single day (June 22) was enacted one of the most drastic pieces of legislation in English history—placing all persons and all property at the disposal of the Government as thought "necessary or expedient for securing the public safety." Administration of this act fell entirely to the lot of the new minister of Labor and National Service, Ernest Bevin, general secretary of the Transport and General Workers' Union since 1922 and chairman of the Trades Union Congress in 1937. A seat was promptly found for him in the Commons, and on the Government front bench, alongside Churchill. Bevin seemed to stand for "the other half of the English people"—so said J. B. Priestley in a memorable broadcast.

Another crucial appointment was that of Lord Beaverbrook as minister of aircraft production. His "magic" (Churchill) or use of "direct action" (Professor M. M. Postan) was compounded of dynamics, improvisation, bullying, and effective public relations. It was not a matter of planning for a three-year war; the weeks ahead were all that counted. Before the month of May was out, there was a marked increase in the output of fighters and bombers. In the fall, at the end of the critical phase of the Battle of Britain, Fighter Command had more aircraft than at the beginning. The total of British production for 1940 was 50 percent higher than that of Germany.

With Churchill a new twist was given to cabinet government. The War Cabinet rendered decisions only in matters of major policy. Details were passed on to powerful committees—the Lord President's Committee (a coordinating body), the Production Council, and the committees of civil defense, economic policy, food policy, and home policy. Churchill, as minister of Defense, took over the direction of the Chiefs of Staff Committee, composed of the heads of the three armed services and General Ismay, the prime minister's personal representative, who rendered incalculable service as a mediator between the statesmen and the service experts. In Churchill's words, "Thus for the first time the Chiefs of Staff Committee assumed its due and proper place in direct daily contact with the executive Head of the Government, and in accord with him had full control over the conduct of the war and the armed forces." Soon after he became prime minister, Churchill installed at No. 10 Professor F. A. Lindemann, an Oxford physicist, as a special adviser. He and his staff of assistants were to make specific investigations at the request of Churchill. As Lord Cherwell, Lindemann became a member of the Cabinet in 1942. His support in 1942 of strategic bombing of both industrial and civilian targets in Germany was behind the decision to give Sir Arthur Harris, the chief of bomber command, the signal to proceed.

Dunkirk and the Fall of France

Dunkirk, May 29–June 3, was the first great achievement of the new order and the new spirit. Following May 10, fighting in the west soon reached a climax. On May 14, the Dutch army capitulated, and three days later the Germans entered Brussels. On May 13–14, the Nazi forces smashed through the Meuse front at Sedan, and the Battle of France had begun. By the twenty-third, German armored columns were at the Channel, and the British Expeditionary Force and some French units were cut off from the main Allied force (mostly French) to the south and were in danger of annihilation or capture as they retreated toward the sea. But the corridor to Dunkirk remained open, largely through the stand of the British II Corps under General Sir Alan Brooke which protected the long flank on the Ypres front, entirely exposed after the Belgian surrender on the twenty-eighth.

From Dunkirk, 338,226 Allied troops (including 139,000 French) were evacuated to Britain. Soon after, Churchill told the Commons that just before the evacuation he had hopes of bringing back perhaps 20,000 or 30,000 men. Port facilities at Dunkirk had been destroyed and the harbor seemed useless. But the "defense perimeter" extended twenty-two miles along the coast and from two to six miles inland. Weather was generally favorable. German naval units could not interfere. Under protection of the Royal Air Force, ranging far and wide, evacuation proceeded—from the partially cleared harbor, from a wooden jetty extending four thousand yards into the sea, and from beaches stretching to the east and to the west. The bulk of the troops were rescued from the harbor by transports, destroyers, and mine sweepers, but thousands were rescued by "the little ships"—ferry boats, tugs, fishing craft, motor boats, and yachts. Most accounts say that about 870 ships participated. John Masefield called it "the greatest thing this nation has ever done." Churchill, in one of his greatest addresses, paid tribute to the brilliance of the Royal Navy and the Royal Air Force. And he turned to the threat of invasion; he had complete confidence, he said, that the nation could "outlive the menace of tyranny, if necessary for years, if necessary alone .... We shall defend our Island, whatever the cost may be, we shall fight on the beaches, we shall fight on the landing-grounds, we shall fight in the fields and in the streets, we shall fight in the hills, we shall never surrender." And throughout the land in tens of thousands of homes British Tommies retold the miracle of Dunkirk.

On May 19, the British chiefs of staff studied a report entitled "British Strategy in a Certain Eventuality." The contingency was soon upon them. France collapsed and Paris fell June 14. One June 16, Churchill refused to authorize France to make a separate peace unless the French fleet went into British ports before negotiations began. Admiral Darlan would only give assurances that the fleet would not fall into German hands. Pétain, the new French premier, rejected a British offer of complete union. On the seventeenth he announced that an armistice would be sought, and General Charles de Gaulle, now without a command, flew without authorization to London and inaugurated the Free French Movement. France signed an armistice with the Nazis on June 21 and hostilities ceased on June 25. In the course of these crowded events Italy entered the war June 11; Mussolini had been emboldened by the defeat of France and was anxious to share in the spoils of victory.

Britain Alone

In a broadcast June 18, Churchill said, "The Battle of France is over. I expect that the Battle of Britain is about to begin ... Hitler knows that he will have to break us in this Island or lose the war." That same day the *Evening Standard* carried David Low's well-known cartoon: a lone soldier looks out from the Dover Cliffs and shouts defiantly, "Very well, alone!" The evacuation of Dunkirk had left behind just about all the heavy equipment (including guns and tanks) of the British Expeditionary Force; in Britain, there remained barely enough equipment for two divisions. But a Gallup Poll taken just after the fall of France showed that only 3 percent of the British people thought they might lose the war. Churchill tells us that the question of whether Britain would continue the fight never appeared on the agenda of the War Cabinet. Priestley in a broadcast June 5 said, "Soon, some of us may die, but nobody can say of us now that we are not alive, and it is a fact that while one disaster piles upon another many of us have told each other that never have we seen or enjoyed so lovely a Spring." The summer and autumn of 1940 was for Britain the most critical period of the war. Then the British people could only defend their island and hold Germany at bay. But when German military might had been depleted and assistance came, Britain's stand in 1940 would provide a solid base from which a massive attack could be mounted and released against Fortress Europe.

The Threat of Invasion. From early May the British chiefs of staff assumed that Hitler had long contemplated invasion of the British Isles and had a master plan in readiness against the day set. Such was not the case. The German high command had not looked much beyond the conquest of France, and Hitler himself had never seriously entertained notions of absorbing Great Britain. At the start of the war he hoped to contain her by blockade, by air and sea. Not until May did he consider invasion. Even then he came to the notion gradually; just as the British during the previous winter had nourished hopes of a German collapse from within, so Hitler, after the Battle of France, was somewhat confident that the British would voluntarily seek an end to the war on his "moderate" terms—return of German colonies and British acquiescence in German domination of the Continent. On July 19 he made a last bid for peace. Before a Reichstag session in the Kroll Opera House in Berlin he declared, "In this hour I feel it my duty before my conscience to launch once again an appeal for reason on England's part." Three days before, he had issued a directive, "Preparations for a Landing Operation against England." The text reads in part: "The aim of this operation is to eliminate Great Britain as a base from which the war against Germany can be continued, and, if it should be necessary, to occupy the country completely." In July, it would seem, the Germans determined their strategy for the immediate future. Britain must be eliminated, "if necessary" by occupation (Operation Sea Lion). And Russia was to be attacked either that year or the next. Churchill, in turn, defined British war aims—unconditional surrender of the enemy.

Also, in July, Churchill made "a hateful decision, the most unnatural and painful in which I have ever been concerned," to prevent the French fleet from falling to the enemy. French ships in English ports were seized, and naval units in the harbor at Oran in North Africa, after failing to heed an ultimatum, were fired on and disabled, save the battle cruiser *Strasbourg* which escaped to Toulon. In the engagement at Oran, nearly thirteen hundred French lives were lost. In the Atlantic at Dakar, the 35,000-ton *Richelieu*, "the most powerful battleship in the world" (Admiral Pound), was put out action. French vessels at Alexandria were disarmed. Professor J. R. M. Butler points out that the British had no way of knowing that, at least for the time being, the Germans, in the appearance of moderation, had no intention of demanding the French fleet. Nor did the British know that on June 24 Admiral Darlan, minister of marine in the Pétain Government, had signaled units of the French fleet that "under no circumstances are they to fall into enemy hands intact." But Mr. Butler concludes that fuller knowledge is unlikely to have made much difference. Justification of the attack at Oran was nowhere more ardently debated than among the British themselves. It is interesting to compare the caution toward Norway a few months before with this bold action against the French fleet. The British were now at a last stand. For the first time in 125 years an enemy could attack directly across the narrow seas. Naval supremacy, the only superiority Britain possessed, was threatened, and Churchill and his advisers concluded that war with Vichy France must be risked.

But in the summer of 1940 much more turned on air power. Before invasion the Nazis must attain air superiority over Britain. The Germans therefore set out to destroy the Royal Air Force (usually referred to as the R.A.F.) as an effective weapon and to disable the British aircraft industry; secondarily, they sought to weaken coastal defenses and to shatter British morale. In prospect it seemed an unequal battle. On August 10, it is reckoned, the Luftwaffe had in readiness for use against Britain just under 2,300 serviceable aircraft of all types, including about 1,000 long-range bombers whose attack could be brought to bear on Britain all the way from Norway south and west to Brittany. To meet the assault British Fighter Command could not hope to get airborne more than 600 to 700 aircraft at any one time.

Defense, Civil and Military. What form could the defense of the United Kingdom take? Prewar estimates had predicted up to 1,700 fatalities a night in London alone under heavy bombing. By June 1940, about 2,300,000 "Andersons" had been distributed thoughout the land, and shelters in factories, railway stations, and trenches had been enlarged; altogether, said Sir John Anderson, protection against blast and splinters was available for 20,000,000 persons. By September over 100,000 had been moved out of the coastal areas in the south and east.

In July, General Sir Alan Brooke, as one who had had experience against the Wehrmacht in France and Belgium, replaced General Sir Edmund Ironside as commander-in-chief, Home Forces. He determined upon a defense strategy of "mobile offensive action." He limited work on the "stoplines," which had been designed to provide linear defense, to road junctions and centers of communication; he moved his forces forward so as to meet the enemy before it was well established; and he made his field artillery and anti-tank guns mobile and in readiness to strike at the points of German landing. He also had operational control of the Local Defense Volunteers (soon renamed the Home Guard), formed in May and numbering 500,000 by the end of July. Coastal defenses from Sussex to the Wash and beyond were reinforced. Mine fields guarding the coast were extended seaward. Open stretches and broad highways were obstructed against aerial landing, and roads and bridges to ports and airfields were ready for destruction at a moment's notice. Blockships, mines, and demolition charges made access to harbors hazardous for the enemy. Air and naval units patrolled the coast. A network of radar now extended from the Orkneys to the Isle of Wight and protected all the eastern approaches to Britain. The fighter planes did not take to the air until the signal came of the approach of the enemy raiders. Radar, so many believe, made possible victory in the Battle of Britain.

The immediate danger seemed to be from parachutists. Official warnings were issued and guards stationed in the offices in Whitehall. Directional signposts were removed and shops were asked to remove or conceal all maps and guidebooks. In a contemporary *Punch* cartoon, a lad says to persons in uniform: "I'll tell nobody where anywhere is." Church bells were silenced save as an alarm against descending parachutists.

Operation Eagle

The first bombs fell near Canterbury on May 10, 1940; the first on London June 18. After June 17, nearly every night enemy aircraft appeared somewhere over Britain, but until August the raids were on a small scale, did comparatively little damage (seaports and shipping in the Channel were the main targets), and provided civilians with good experience for the heavy raids to come. In the month following mid-June, 150 civilians were killed in raids; in the succeeding thirty days the fatalities doubled. The word "incident" came into use, a word "wonderfully colorless, dry and remote," as John Strachey then said, and applicable to everything "from the destruction by enemy bombs of two foxes to the major disaster in March 1943 at the Bethnal Green Underground Station... when 178 were killed." Enemy raids increased in intensity so gradually that the designation of July 10 as the opening day of the Battle of Britain is entirely arbitrary.

On August 1, Hitler and Göring issued orders for Operation Eagle in an all-out effort against the Royal Air Force, air fields, radar stations, and London docks to cripple British defenses and gain air supremacy in preparation for invasion. Initially, D-day (the Germans called it S-day) was tentatively set for mid-August, but German Navy officials, dubious over the wisdom of Sea Lion, said they must have until September 15 to work out details of transport and must have ten days' anticipation of the invasion date to clear English mine fields and lay their own in protection of their route across the Channel. Hitler finally set the date for September 21 or soon after. Leading echelons of nine divisions were to make the initial landings and with two airborne formations establish beachheads on two short stretches in Kent and Sussex. In the first three days, 120,000 men would be landed, and ten divisions completely established in eleven days. Aerial reconnaissance kept the British somewhat informed, and early in September all England knew that invasion craft were creeping along the coasts of Holland, Belgium, and France to prepared points of embarkation from Ostend to Le Havre. We now know that on September 4, the German naval staff said that by the nineteenth they could have available 168 transports (totaling 704,000 tons), 1,910 landing barges, 419 tugs, and 1,600 motor boats.

The first massive assault of Eagle came on August 13 with heavy daylight attacks in several waves, 1,485 sorties in all, two-thirds of them by fighter planes. Airports were the chief targets. Only minor damage resulted; the score for the day in planes lost was the Luftwaffe 45 and the British Fighter Command 13. Two days later, 1,800 enemy aircraft, including 600 bombers, swept over Britain in five waves. That day the British lost 34 planes, the Germans 75. The raid demonstrated the ineffectiveness of daylight assaults based on Norway and Denmark without fighter escort, and the heavy attrition in German bombers. Their proportionate use in subsequent raids was reduced.

Beginning August 23-24 there was sustained attack for three weeks, with nearly 1,000 enemy planes, on the average, over Britain daily. These were the days, it is said, when Britain came closest to defeat, for her own crews and planes were being lost faster than they could be replaced. Between August 23 and September 6, the British lost 295 fighter planes and suffered serious damage to 171 more, as against a total German loss of 385 planes, including 138 bombers. In that fortnight 103 R.A.F. pilots were killed or missing. Liverpool-Birkenhead was the first industrial center attacked on a large scale; for four nights running, an average of 157 bombers raided that area. The Germans achieved considerable success against radar stations and sector command posts (which directed defense), and it was perhaps fortunate that major attention was soon turned to London.

        The Blitz. On September 7, Göring spoke of this "historic hour" when Germany was to deliver a stroke right into the enemy's heart. The "Blitz" had begun. The British chiefs of staff felt that the time of invasion might be upon them and one of the great moments in English history was at hand. The signal "Cromwell," a defense against invasion, went out to certain commands. That afternoon 320 German bombers were over East London, and the fires they started lit the way for 250 bombers that night. These attacks left 1,000 dead. Here are a few extracts from the account of the night of September 7–8, in perhaps the best of the books on the Blitz, William Sansom's *Westminster in War*:

> Towards six o'clock the fiction of unease became fact, the man on the street learned that something had been happening in the East End ... and Report Centres ... knew that at last the Luftwaffe had struck hard, there and then, that afternoon in London proper. The docks were ablaze. And as the sun set, those in the West End streets grew conscious of the unbelievable, for the sunset occurred not only in the accustomed West ... but also incredibly in the East over St. Paul's and where the City of London was held to lie .... When the

western skies had grown already dark the fierce glow in the East
stuck harshly fast and there was seen for the first time that black
London roofscape silhouetted against what was to become a mo-
notonously copper orange sky . . . .

Then, just after eleven o'clock, the first high explosives fell—a stick
of five bombs in the vicinity of Victoria Station. . . . People were killed.
People were wounded. The powdered smell of smashed plaster
and brick poisoned the air for the first time. Glass, illimitable, spread
itself across the pavements and out over the road—it seemed to lie two
or three inches thick.

The next night, that of Sunday, September 8, John Lehmann was in his
flat in Mecklenburgh Square when bombs struck, and he wrote about it
in his diary a few days later. After dining off "half a bottle of wine and an
apple and some chocolate biscuits," he lay down fully dressed on his bed.

Gunfire began to rumble in the distance, and now it seemed to get
nearer, with the persistent, maddening sound of aircraft overhead.
Then I could distinguish bombs dropping. Then suddenly three
whistling, ripping noises in the air, as if directly overhead, getting
closer, and each time violent concussions followed by the sound of
tinkling glass . . . . When the noise of the aeroplanes seemed to be getting fainter again, I went to the window and looked out on the
Square: . . . incendiary bombs were burning merrily in the garden. . . . A little later as I was standing by the stairs, there was another tremendous explosion. . . . I went to the door and peered out:
the sight that met my eye was an enormous bellying cloud of grey
dust advancing down the road towards me like a living thing I
opened the door and met the man from No. 46 . . . in a tin helmet,
who said there was an unexploded time-bomb in the garden and they
were evacuating the shelter there . . . . When I turned around I
thought part of Byron Square looked rather odd; it was only a few
seconds later that I realized I was looking at a tree beyond—Byron
Court had simply been blown to bits. As I passed it on the way to the
shelter, the presence of death and murder seemed very vivid to
me . . . .

And in the shelter: the hours passed by and one longed for dawn,
knowing the Nazis would retreat from it and our ascending daylight
fighters . . . . Someone produced a Dostoevsky novel, a group of
young women huddled in an angle of the stairs with what looked like
powdered hair—but they had just been rescued from the ruins of
Byron Court and it was rubble dust. Then more bombs whistled
by—and the banging of the lavatory door sounded like bombs too—
incendiaries were dropped outside . . . . At last, in the grey light of
morning, the all-clear went.

On the night of September 9–10, great fires and high explosives brought death to another 500. The massive assaults continued another week. On September 12, a single aircraft suddenly appeared through the clouds over Buckingham Palace and dropped six bombs, most of which fell in open spaces. By good fortune no one was killed. The king and queen were in the palace—their close call was not revealed to the public until after the war. On the fifteenth (a Sunday), later chosen as the day to commemorate the Battle of Britain, the British claimed 185 enemy aircraft destroyed. The number was actually about 60, but only 26 British fighters had been sacrificed. In a week the Germans had lost 200 aircraft; the Royal Air Force was still in being and henceforth had the better of it. British Bomber Command stepped up its attack on the German invasion fleet, and by September 21 over 10 percent of the transports and barges had been sunk or seriously damaged.

A *Defiant City*. During these days the daily routine in London never halted; the king remained and so did his ministers. Printing House Square was hit, but next morning *The Times* appeared with the same unchanging format for the front page—all advertisement and no news. Churchill remained at No. 10 until the latter part of September when he moved offices and living quarters to the "Annexe," a reinforced structure overlooking St. James' Park. During the Blitz Lord Halifax, foreign secretary, slept in the air raid shelter of the Dorchester Hotel. Of ordinary folk, one out of every seven in the metropolitan area slept in public shelters—basements, trenches, railway arches, and "tube" stations of the underground railway. For thousands the era of "tube dwelling" began, without planning or invitation. People merely moved in. Later, in November, a census revealed that 4 percent of London's population was regularly sleeping in the "underground," and 37 percent in some other form of public shelter. Only a master artist could paint the scenes. There was an extraordinary degree of order and discipline, leadership and direction coming spontaneously from the tube-dwellers themselves. Post-raid services—ambulance service, rest center accommodations for eating and sleeping, "kerbside" meals and provisions for restoration of gas, water, and power—rapidly improved in efficiency. In the second great population movement, between September 1940 and January 1941, a million and a quarter people throughout Britain relocated.

Churchill's broadcasts never minimized danger but always imparted confidence. On September 11, he likened the occasion to the days when Britain was threatened by the Armada and those when Napoleon's Grand Army contemplated invasion. While Churchill voiced and interpreted national pride and courage, J. B. Priestley interpreted the common man to himself. His Sunday evening broadcasts, "Postscripts," after the nine o'clock news, were eagerly awaited. One evening he advocated "hard work and high jinks" as a good wartime motto; on another occasion he spoke of "the decent, kindly, courageous, ordinary folk of Britain— namely the salt of the earth." He told of those at defense posts, those who came to long night watches after a long day's toil, and he spoke of the view from the rooftops of London, "the colossal panorama of a defiant city." The press echoed these moods. "We face the terrific threat of Nazi invasion together and in knowledge of our danger" (*New Statesman and Nation*, September 14). "The battle for the destruction of the soul as well as the substance of the Empire continues . . . It is the crucial hour, but the odds are not in Hitler's favor" (*Spectator*, September 20). "It may be a privilege to see history in the making, but we have a feeling that it is being overdone at the present." (*Warden's Bulletin* for Hampstead, August 1, 1940). Everything considered, the English people seemed to have been extraordinarily cheerful in the summer of 1940.

Though of course the British did not know it, Hitler never did ratify a final date for invasion. On September 14 he told his advisers that "in spite of all successes the prerequisite conditions for Operation Sea Lion have not yet been realized." On September 17 he postponed it "until further notice" and October 12 he canceled the whole operation for 1940. The effort to gain control of the air over Britain had failed. From the middle of September the losses of the Luftwaffe were about double those of the R.A.F., which was now building faster than it was being shot down. British intelligence was able to follow the dispersal of the invasion fleet after September 18, and by the end of the month the British high command felt confident that the Battle of Britain had been won. Hitler had in fact always been doubtful of the wisdom of invasion. A *Punch* cartoon of September 11 has a quiet scene in a park with an elderly woman confiding to a friend, "These air raids give me the feeling that Hitler appears to be a great deal more worried than he seems."

Economic Warfare. After October 5 daytime bombing of London almost ceased. Hitler turned to economic psychological warfare to bring England down. From September 7, when the great assault on London began, until November 2, about 160 bombers on the average were over the city each night. In these raids 9,500 Londoners lost their lives. The heaviest attack was on the night of October 15, when 410 bombers dumped 540 tons of high explosives on the city, killing 400 persons and temporarily demoralizing transportation and public services. But London was given a chance to recover when from November 2 the Luftwaffe turned its attention to other industrial targets. The massive assault by 450 aircraft on Coventry the night of November 14 continued until 6:30 the next morning and left 554 dead. The Germans used "Ruffians," a new "pathfinder" device for locating objectives and releasing bombs at precisely the right moment, but hardly necessary that moonlit night. A few nights later Birmingham was struck. In London heavy attacks were received December 8–9, when 400 bombers swept over the city. The Elizabethan Hall of the Middle Temple was badly damaged. On the night of December 29–30, a dramatic fire, quite out of control, spread over an area wider than even that of the Great Fire of 1666. The Guildhall was burned out and eight seventeenth-century churches gutted. In general, casualties were much lighter than anticipated, property damage much greater. Even so, throughout the land, from July 1940 to the end of the year, 23,002 civilians were killed in raids (the large majority in metropolitan London), heavier casualties than in the armed forces. Damage from incendiaries far exceeded that from high explosives, and in January 1941 the Government instituted an elaborate and compulsory system of fire watching.

In retaliation the War Cabinet decided that in Germany "the civilian population around the target areas must be made to feel the weight of the war," as well as the industrial areas. This attack began in October 1940; in December there was an experimental "crash concentration" of 134 bombers on Mannheim; early in 1941 Bremen, Hanover, and Cologne were struck. However, these efforts met with indifferent success—an official survey, with careful study of air photographs, revealed that this phase of strategic bombing in 1940–41 had almost no effect upon Germany's war economy. The British bombers could not locate their targets—even on moonlight nights, only one-sixth of the planes dispatched came within five miles of their designated targets. This air offensive was discontinued, for a time, in November 1941.

African Hostilities; American Sentiments

Though the Battle of Britain dominated the last half of 1940, important developments were taking place elsewhere. In September coastal guns and naval units of Vichy France prevented the Free French supported by the British Navy from seizing Dakar in West Africa. In Libya the Italians took the offensive, for Mussolini determined to invade Egypt in order to keep pace with any German landings in England, and eventually to make land connection through Egypt with East Africa. On September 13 the Italians moved across the border but soon came to a halt only fifty miles within Egypt. They had insufficient transport, tanks, and armored cars to maintain communication through their line of camps. In December General Wavell, British commander in the Middle East, directed a daring counteroffensive. The Western Desert Force, under General O'Connor, in a month's time moved across the desert, breaking the Italian defenses and capturing their camps one by one, destroying eight Italian divisions and pushing well across the border into Cyrenaica. This offensive provided a tremendous lift to British morale during this bleak winter at home.

Across the Atlantic "the attitude of the United States Congress was well behind the public sentiments of the American people, and the attitude of the President well ahead" (Wheeler-Bennett). But all three were moving toward extending aid and comfort to Britain. At the outset, sentiment against "getting involved in Europe" was overwhelming. In the autumn of 1939 only after a bitter debate did Congress restore legislation permitting the Allies to obtain arms and other matérial on "a cash-and-carry basis." In May and June of 1940, as Telford Taylor reminds us, the United States for the first time faced the possibility of a Nazi victory in Europe. In his first letter to President Roosevelt after becoming prime minister, Churchill wrote, "I trust you realize ... that the voice and force of the United States may count for nothing if they are withheld too long. You may have a completely subjugated, Nazified Europe established with astonishing swiftness, and the weight may be more than we can bear." On June 10 President Roosevelt, addressing the graduating class of the University of Virginia, committed the United States to extending "to the opponents of force the material resources of this nation." American aid "short of war" began. At the end of the summer the United States transferred to Britain fifty overage destroyers, badly needed for convoy duty, in return for the lease of air and naval bases in the Atlantic. While negotiations were in progress, Churchill told the Commons, August 20, that Britain and the United States "will have to be somewhat mixed up together.... I do not view the process with any misgivings. I could not stop it if I wished.... Like the Mississippi, it just keeps rolling along. Let it roll." The British regarded Roosevelt's reelection in November for an unprecedented third term as a solid blow struck at the Nazis.

The Spreading Conflict

The major events of the war in 1941 were the German counterattacks in Libya and the German invasion of Greece and Crete, the sustained bombardment of Britain until July, the war of production and the inauguration of lend-lease by the United States, the Nazi invasion of the Soviet Union, and the Japanese attack on Pearl Harbor bringing the United States into the war.

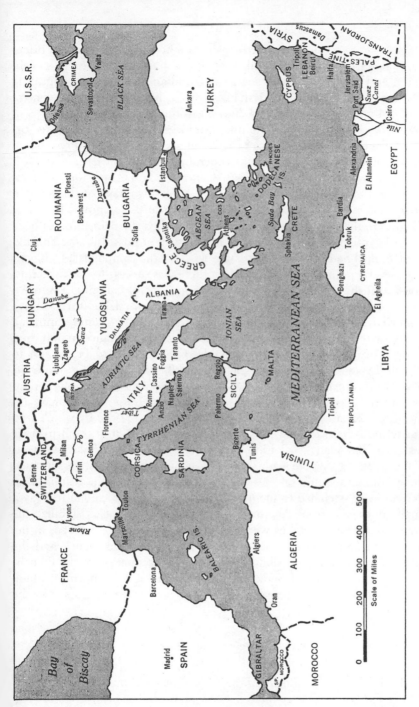

Map 3   Mediterranean Theater of Operations

Africa and the Middle East

In Libya the British straightway continued their offensive, taking Bardia and Tobruk in January and Benghazi early in February, and in the process seizing 25,000 Italian prisoners and capturing 120 tanks. To bolster the Italians Hitler quickly dispatched General Rommel and a light motorized division to the scene, as the first units of the Afrika Korps. At the same time, the British Defense Committee ordered General Wavell to check his advance, to establish a secure western flank in Egypt and to withdraw considerable forces to the delta of the Nile in readiness for transfer to Greece. General Rommel, without advance approval of the German high command, took advantage of the reduced British forces and, somewhat even to his own surprise, moved from one position to the next, until by April he had pushed the British forces back to the Egyptian border, save for a garrison still in possession of Tobruk. But Rommel had insufficient strength to carry the campaign into Egypt.

At several points in the Middle East there was success for British arms. To protect the Red Sea for Allied shipping, General Cunningham, in "a masterpiece of administrative planning and of economizing force," drove from Kenya into Italian Somaliland and struck into Abyssinia, capturing Addis Ababa (April 6) and ending serious Italian resistance in that area. In Iraq prompt action averted trouble. Oil pipelines to Haifa and to Tripoli (Lebanon) passed through Iraq, and Basra (near the Persian Gulf) now assumed great importance as a way station for receipt of air reinforcement from the United States. In 1941 an Iraqi Government unfriendly to Britain refused to honor an agreement of 1930 by which Iraq was to aid Britain in time of war. Hostilities broke out at the British air base near Baghdad. A division was sent from India to Basra. General Wavell, after a dispute with General Auchinleck, commander-in-chief, India, and with some reluctance (his slender forces of the Middle East were already stretched to the utmost), dispatched to Baghdad in May a small contingent from Palestine. This proved sufficient to stabilize the situation, for the Germans were not yet ready to interfere. Then, in the late spring and early summer, joint effort by the Free French and the British destroyed any possibility of a German occupation of the French-mandated territories of Syria and Lebanon. French authorities taking orders from Vichy were defeated, and the territories were occupied by the Allies.

Failure in Greece and Crete

But the actions in the Middle East were peripheral. The bitter conflict for control of the Aegean brought only frustration and failure. The war in Greece entered a new phase in the spring of 1941. The initial invasion by the Italians (beginning October 28, 1940) had been repulsed by the Greeks, who spurned offers of British aid until February 1941. By then the Germans decided that they must lend the Italians a hand in Greece as well as in North Africa. At this point the role of Yugoslavia was crucial, for if she could be persuaded to join the war against Italy before Germany intervened, her troop movements into Albania from the north would virtually end the Italian threat. When a coup in Belgrade ousted a pro-Axis Government on March 27, Britain hoped to induce the new regime to join the Allied side. Such overtures were unsuccessful. The Nazis forced the issue with their offensive in the Balkans, with upward of half a million troops launched April 6 against both Greece and Yugoslavia. The forces of the latter capitulated on April 17 after having slowed the advance of the Wehrmacht. During February and March a British Commonwealth expeditionary force of 58,000, including Australians and New Zealanders, arrived in Greece from Egypt. The Greek alliance committed the British to rendering aid; furthermore it had been hoped that the dispatch of reinforcements would bring in Yugoslavia, and Turkey as well, on the side of the Allies. The Greeks now contributed to the Allied military predicament by refusing to withdraw from Albania and Macedonia in time to stabilize a line which might have been held. The Germans took advantage of the scattered deployment of Greek and Commonwealth troops along a wide front and broke through with ease, forcing surrender of the Greek forces on April 21. The Commonwealth troops never did come into general contact with the enemy and withdrew by stages until evacuated, 21,000 of them to Crete, leaving behind quantities of artillery and transport.

The Battle of Crete (May 20–31) was profoundly important in demonstrating that superior naval forces were no match for superior air power. The few units of the Royal Air Force on the island were withdrawn before the main battle began. With German air bases close at hand (at Athens, at Cos, at Rhodes) and with British bases in Egypt too far distant for effective combat over Crete, it was a simple matter, as one historian has put it, that Crete could be attacked by air but could not be defended. Beginning May 20, German airborne troops descended on the island. The ensuing battle lasted twelve days. The Royal Navy, at great cost to itself, prevented German reinforcements from arriving by sea. But the Luftwaffe encountered little opposition in lifting supplies and men to strengthen the German position. The Commonwealth forces, ably and gallantly led by a New Zealander, General Freyberg, fought day after day without relief under relentless aerial attack "beside which," Admiral Cunningham (naval commander in the Mediterranean) reported to the British high command, "that in Norway was child's play." With the loss of control of coastal areas, particularly Suda Bay, the only anchorage suitable for the Navy, the conflict became hopeless. Eighteen thousand men were evacuated to Egypt; the greater part, after days of toiling through the hills, was lifted by the Navy from a tiny beach under frequent aerial attack at Sphakia on the south coast. Fourteen thousand, dead or captured, were left behind. The historian of the Mediterranean has written: "No soldier from . . . Crete is likely to forget it." Nor is any sailor. Three cruisers and six destroyers were sunk; one aircraft carrier, three battleships and many other elements were damaged; some eighteen hundred seamen lost their lives.

"Looking back upon the unceasing tumult of the war, I cannot recall any period when its stresses and the onset of so many problems all at once or in rapid succession bore more directly on me and my colleagues than the first half of 1941." The words are Churchill's. Following the evacuation from Greece, Parliament debated war policy at length. It was hardly a question of confidence, for on a formal motion only 5 out of 452 voted against the prime minister, who received one of the greatest ovations of his career. Then came Crete, the loss of which "is the focus for many anxieties," reads the *New Statesman and Nation* for June 14. Parliament showed concern over Suez lest Britain be outwitted there, as perhaps she had been in the Aegean. Churchill's reassurances proved sound; German losses in Crete were so heavy that Hitler never repeated that type of campaign. Considerations both military (the advantages of maintaining a Balkan front) and political (British obligations to Greece) required the British to make the effort they did.

After the loss of Crete had come the failure in mid-June of Operation Battle-axe, a British offensive in the Western Desert of North Africa designed to clear the Egyptian border of the enemy and to raise the siege of Tobruk. Churchill transferred Wavell from the Middle East command to the Indian Theater. The air commander-in-chief was also replaced. Military historians have pointed out the slender resources with which these commanders were forced to operate in the Mediterranean and the fact that, just as they were removed, the shortages in men and equipment began to be made good. Perhaps it would have been wiser to postpone Battle-axe a month or so.

The blow of the loss of Crete was somewhat softened by the news of the destruction four hundred miles off Brest of the 41,000-ton German battleship *Bismarck* on May 27 after a dramatic chase by British units. Several days before, the *Bismarck,* on a hunting expedition in the Atlantic, had sunk the British battle cruiser *Hood* off Greenland.

The End of the Blitz

It was also a grim spring at home. It is difficult to realize that not until the war was three years old were there as many soldiers killed on the field of battle as women and children killed at home. The German aerial attack had continued through the winter, with major targets shifting from week to week and from month to month. With improved spring weather the raids increased in intensity. Quentin Reynolds, the American correspondent, wrote, "Nothing I have seen prepared me for the sight of Plymouth after it had been bombed five nights" in one week (April 22–29). Six hundred were killed and 20,000 homes were destroyed. Early in May bombs fell on Liverpool seven nights in succession, with a death toll of about 1,900. London remained a major target. On April 16–17 raids by 450 bombers left a death list of 1,180, and 2,250 fires were recorded. Six churches were destroyed and the north transept of St. Paul's was wrecked. In another prolonged attack, May 10–11, 1,436 lives were lost, the chamber of the House of Commons was destroyed, and the famous churches of St. Clement Danes in the Strand and St. Mary-le-Bow ("Bow Church") in Cheapside were gutted.

During these spring weeks many living on the fringes of cities trekked into the countryside each evening. The London tubes filled again at nightfall. As Londoners groped their way through the darkness, powerful beacons criss-crossing in the sky searched out enemy planes as targets for anti-aircraft guns. We can read an unvarnished account, with touches of humor, of the activities of an air raid warden in John Strachey's *Post D* (1941)—the American edition bears the title *Digging for Mrs. Miller*. We catch something of the atmosphere when we read the words of an R.A.F. pilot (soon after lost on a mission) that "the war was practically never discussed except as a joke."

Most persons had worked out better arrangements for protection than in 1940, when, it was estimated, had all availed themselves of shelters provided, the death toll would have been reduced 50 percent. Experience had shown that many persons who sought refuge under stairways and heavy furniture had emerged safely from direct hits. The new "Morrison," ready late in March, provided shelter for two adults and one or two children, all lying down, and could carry the debris of two floors. It was a rectangular steel frame six feet six inches long, four feet wide and two feet nine inches high. The bottom was a sort of steel mattress and the top was steel plate one-eighth inch thick. Sides were of wire mesh, so no lateral protection was provided. During 1941 the Government placed orders for over one million of these shelters.

The Blitz is generally said to have ended with a great night raid on Birmingham on May 16. Thereafter regular night attacks ceased. Since July 1940 the German bomber force in the west had shrunk from 1,291 to 757 planes. Göring had now to husband German strength for Russia. The Ministry of Home Security declared that "effective damage has not been serious in relation to the national war effort" and that there had been no serious interference with industrial operation, transportation, or port facilities.

Problems of Manpower and Supply

In war production the significant problem was that of manpower. In 1936 it had been pointed out that British manpower could not be put to effective use without "a general recognition of the issue before the country, popular support of the government, and a government strong enough and decisive enough to make use of this popular support." That these conditions were achieved was a consequence of the revolution in national psychology in May and June of 1940. The measures taken provided the economic basis for victory: the Emergency Powers Act of May 22, 1940, which gave to the minister of labor and national service "the control and use of all labor"; the establishment of the Man Power Requirements Committee, June 1940; the Essential Work Order, March 1941, by which the minister of labor was able to place or retain labor in particular employment; and the Registration for Employment Order, March 1941, which empowered the minister of labor to register age groups of men and women for possible industrial service. Actual application of a policy of industrial conscription was cautious and restrained. Until the summer of 1941 migration of labor was largely voluntary. Then more effective measures became necessary. About eight million men and women (one-quarter of the population of working age) were in the armed services, civilian defense, or munitions plants. For these categories it was estimated that an additional two million would be required by June 1942. These would have to come from civilian industry and from those still at home. Cabinet decisions and acts of Parliament began to budget available man and woman power. In December 1941 new legislation, enacted with little opposition, subjected all persons eighteen to fifty years of age to some form of national service. By then 94 percent of all males between the ages of fourteen and sixty-four had been mobilized into the services or into industry. Also, the Government developed a satisfactory wage policy mainly through controlling the cost of living. Prices of essential food were kept down by subsidy, and unsettled disputes between union and management were sent to a new National Arbitration Tribunal whose decisions were final.

Lend-Lease from America. In 1941 the foundation was laid for another source of war supplies. In May 1940 Churchill wrote President Roosevelt of Britain's dire need of arms and other supplies: "We shall go on paying dollars for as long as we can, but I should like to feel reasonably sure that when we can pay no more, you will give us the stuff all the same." In December, a few weeks following Roosevelt's reelection, Churchill outlined Britain's requirements in aircraft, arms, and shipping. He added, "The moment approaches when we shall no longer be able to pay cash." Roosevelt now conceived of "lend-lease," which would "eliminate the dollar sign." This policy he put into words acceptable to the American people in one of the most important of his "fireside chats" (December 29). For her own "national security" the United States must "support the nations defending themselves against attack by the Axis.... We must be the great arsenal of democracy." While the congressional debate over the Lend-Lease Bill was in progress, Churchill broadcast, February 9, a message to Roosevelt. "Put your confidence in us.... Give us the tools and we will finish the job." On March 11, 1941, lend-lease became law. The bill provided for the manufacture, disposal by sale, exchange, lease, or loan of "any defence article for the government of any country whose defence the President deems vital for the defence of the United States." Now it was to be aid from the United States even at the risk of war. By July $4,000,000,000 had been assigned to agencies for aid to the British. Yet American aid hardly revolutionized the British war effort in 1941. With the best of intentions the United States could not deliver much at once.

The Battle of the Atlantic. On March 15 President Roosevelt declared that the United States must maintain "a vital bridge of ships across the ocean—the bridge of ships which carry the arms and the food for those who are fighting the good fight." Britain's plight in shipping was now acute. Between May 1940 and December 1941 her losses from enemy action amounted to 36 percent of her available tonnage at the outbreak of the war; about half of the crews involved were lost. The peak came in April 1941 when 195 ships, totaling nearly 700,000 tons of British, Allied, and neutral shipping, were destroyed. In 1942, 1,200 merchant ships, British or British-controlled, were lost. In general, until April 1943 British merchant shipping was being sunk faster than it was being replaced.

German submarine warfare had been extraordinarily successful, especially against unescorted merchantmen. Also, that which remained of the German surface navy eluded discovery and played havoc with convoys. The British Navy of necessity stretched its resources to the utmost, with oftentimes three or two destroyers or even one alone escorting a convoy, as compared with eight or ten in the First World War. British shipping itself was less efficient, what with the necessity of making longer journeys to evade pursuit and with delays in ports from crowded facilities. In

February 1941 Hitler issued special directives for an intensification of the war on the high seas and in the air against import harbors, shipyards, and ships afloat. In March Churchill declared that "we must assume that the Battle of the Atlantic has begun."

In 1941 Britain had to make up her shipping losses from her own yards, from captured enemy shipping, and from captured blockade-runners (the latter mostly belonging to Vichy France). In the spring President Roosevelt inaugurated naval patrols of the United States fleet in the western North Atlantic to broadcast warnings of movements of German ships and aircraft. The United States took over the protection of Greenland in April and began assisting in the defense of Iceland in July. And with the aid of the Canadian Navy, an escort base at St. John's, Newfoundland, was developed by the British, making possible "end-to-end" surface escorts for convoys.

The next phase of American participation came in September when her own Navy began to provide escort for British convoys in the North Atlantic. In November the Neutrality Act was further modified, permitting United States merchantmen to be armed, to enter combat zones, and to carry supplies direct to belligerent nations. The vast program of merchant ship building in America was now under way. Also, though the British hardly realized it, Germany was having difficulty building U-boats rapidly enough to cover her own losses. For Britain the future in the Atlantic, in the long run, was bright.

Attacks on Russia and the United States

On June 22, 1941, came one of the "climacterics" of the war. One hundred and twenty divisions of the Wehrmacht attacked Russia on a 1,500-mile front extending from the Baltic to the Black Sea. Hitler hoped for possession before winter of the Ukraine (wheat), of the Donets Basin (coal and manganese), and of the Caucasus (oil). Churchill was not taken by surprise. The very day of the invasion he broadcast a welcome to Russia in the common cause against Nazi Germany. He was unabashed by his long opposition to communism. "I will unsay no word.... But all this fades away before the spectacle which is now unfolding." On the twelfth of July Britain and Russia formally engaged to render each other mutual assistance and to make no separate armistice or peace. Britain was no longer "alone." Now photographs of Stalin appeared alongside those of Roosevelt and Churchill in factories and other public places.

Soon came the first of the Roosevelt-Churchill conferences—on August 9–12 in Placentia Bay, off Newfoundland. The prime minister arrived for the secret rendezvous in the battleship *Prince of Wales,* the president in the cruiser *Augusta*. For joint religious services Churchill chose the hymns—"For Those in Peril on the Sea" and "O God, Our Help in Ages Past." The Atlantic Charter, a statement of common ideals in world affairs (such as, no aggrandizement as a result of the war, political self-determination of all peoples, international collaboration in trade and raw materials, disarmament, and a system of international security), was issued and a variety of topics discussed—aid to Britain and to Russia, priority in supplies, policy toward Japan.

For the remainder of the year the historian fixes his attention on Russia and the United States. Churchill has remarked that though Russia's entrance was an important step toward winning the war, for the first year she was a positive obstacle. For one thing, vital supplies were diverted to her. And Stalin demanded an immediate second front in Europe against Hitler. Between September 28 and October 1 Lord Beaverbrook and Averell Harriman were in Moscow and arranged for supplies—aircraft, tanks, anti-aircraft guns, jeeps, and so on—to the value of roughly $1,000,000,000 to be supplied by the United States and Great Britain in the succeeding nine months. On October 29 Roosevelt notified Stalin that Russia was eligible for lend-lease up to $1,000,000,000.

Meanwhile, the German attack on Russia had proceeded pretty much according to plan except in the north, where the advance on Leningrad and Moscow had been stayed. In October the attack on Moscow was renewed; its fall was widely anticipated. During these weeks Stalin vainly importuned Churchill for an attack in the west. But neither Leningrad nor Moscow fell, and the Russian counteroffensive in December was the turning point in the war for the Soviet Union.

As for the United States, she did not have to linger much longer on the brink. The decision was made for her. On Sunday evening, December 7, Churchill was dining at Chequers with the Americans, Ambassador Winant and Averell Harriman, when news of the Japanese assault on Pearl Harbor came over the radio. Later that same evening came news of the Japanese attacks on Malaya and Hong Kong. On December 8 both Britain and the United States declared war on Japan. On December 11 German and Italy declared war on the United States. The attack on Pearl Harbor rendered a certainty what might otherwise have been well nigh impossible—the American people entered into the war united. The British were thrilled but generally restrained. Churchill before Parliament was sober and matter-of-fact. But he wrote later of his feelings on December 7.

> No American will think it wrong of me if I proclaim that to have the United States at our side was to me the greatest joy . . . . So we had won after all. . . . Britain would live. . . . How long the war would last or in what fashion it would end, no man could tell, nor did I at this

moment care. Once again in our long Island history we should emerge, however mauled or mutilated, safe and victorious . . . . Being saturated and satiated with emotion and sensation, I went to bed and slept the sleep of the saved and thankful.

Perhaps so, but there was nothing but defeat and frustration immediately ahead.

The End of the Beginning

After Pearl Harbor, Churchill arranged for another meeting with Roosevelt. The *Duke of York* zigzagged her way across the Atlantic and Churchill arrived in Washington on December 22 for a stay of three weeks. Addressing Congress, he gauged perfectly the mood of his audience. "It becomes still more difficult to reconcile Japanese action with prudence or even with sanity. What kind of a people do they think we are?" These remarks brought a roar of approval from the legislators, and the American people accepted Churchill as one of their own.

The United Nations was born of this visit. Roosevelt and Churchill drafted a pact in the name of twenty-six nations, reaffirming the Atlantic Charter and pledging against a separate peace. The idealistic tone had an important psychological effect in the United States. For the British, the pact meant that a Grand Alliance would now confront Hitler's Germany. During this conference Britain and the United States agreed on a unified high command, known as the Combined Chiefs of Staff. It had been in the making since January 1941, when secret Anglo-American staff talks started in Washington. A joint report presented in March 1941 outlined common strategy to be employed in case the United States was "compelled" to go to war. Now this union of purpose became a reality. It was agreed that Enemy No. 1 was Germany. General Wavell was selected as supreme Allied commander for the Southwest Pacific Command. Plans for a landing in French North Africa were discussed in secret and very tentatively set for the spring of 1942. Joint bodies for munitions, shipping, and raw materials were established. This conference was entirely harmonious, but it was clear that the United States had immediately assumed the leading role in the conduct of the war.

A Succession of Defeats

Of this high-level planning the average Britisher knew nothing. His reactions were induced by day-to-day events. To him the United States had entered the war in the midst of disaster. On December 10, 1941, the battleships *Prince of Wales* and *Repulse,* based at Singapore, while on mission to prevent Japanese landings in Malaya were sunk by Japanese aerial attack. Six hundred of the 2,600 aboard were lost. Hong Kong fell on Christmas Day. Before the new year the Japanese had captured Wake Island from the Americans, were in control of the Pacific between the Hawaiian Islands and the Philippines, and were in a position to attack Australia. And in North Africa, by mid-January, the Germans were again on the offensive. It was, therefore, a restless Parliament to which Churchill returned. He bluntly asked for a vote of confidence as an answer to the rumors that his Government might be dismissed. He said, "No one need be mealy mouthed in debate, and no one should be chicken hearted in voting.... Everyone in these times must do what he thinks is his duty." The debate, while frank, was not hostile, and Churchill was sustained 460 to 1.

But the bad news continued. On February 15 Singapore fell, "a heavy and far-reaching military defeat," Churchill admitted. To the people at home it was far more humiliating when three German warships slipped out of Brest harbor and made their way to Baltic ports. And, accordingly, criticism of Churchill in his dual capacity as prime minister and minister of defense continued. At their weekly luncheon, February 17, the king found Churchill "very angry about all this, and compares it to hunting the tiger with angry wasps about him." To meet the demands for change, Churchill did reconstruct his Government. Lord Beaverbrook was appointed to a new Ministry of Production, but his duties then brought him into close contact with Ernest Bevin in the Ministry of Labor and National Service, and they were personally antagonistic. Also Beaverbrook was in poor health. He was soon replaced by Oliver Lyttelton. Sir Stafford Cripps, who had been ambassador to the Soviet Union, was in the popular mind responsible for Russian entrance into the war, and thus the hero of the Left, entered the War Cabinet as lord privy seal and leader of the Commons. Churchill was glad to place him in the spotlight, but without great power, since the prime minister viewed him as a possible troublemaker.

On February 28 George VI wrote in his diary, "I cannot help feeling depressed at the future outlook. Anything can happen, and it will be wonderful if we can be lucky anywhere." He was right. The next few months brought only a succession of defeats. In early March the Dutch East Indies fell to the enemy. The Japanese invaded Burma, forcing the British (on March 7) to abandon Rangoon, the one port suitable for landing supplies en route to China. By May all of Burma, including the southern end of the China Road, was lost and China cut off from India save by air. In April the Philippines surrendered after a heroic defense by the Americans. First efforts at an Allied command—the A.B.D.A. (American, British, Dutch, Australian) area in Southeast Asia under General Wavell—failed. In North Africa a British offensive had been checked by Rommel. On the eastern front, the Russian push, so promising during the winter, slowed down, and in May the Germans launched a new offensive in the Crimea which brought the capture of Sevastopol on July 1. Over Germany and over Britain there was an exchange of nuisance raids until March 28, when 234 British aircraft set Lübeck ablaze and destroyed half the city. The Germans retaliated, on Hitler's orders, with the "Baedeker" raids on Bath, Bristol, Norwich, York, and Canterbury. That against Exeter, May 3, destroyed the shopping area and most of the medieval quarter. "Tip-and-run" raids then became the standard German attack. Defense was hardly possible; fighter bombers came in low and swift. But taken in the large, these raids were not serious. The R.A.F., under Harris, took some satisfaction in the first of its 1,000-bomber raids—on the Cologne area May 30–31 and on the Essen region June 1–2.

In London the wartime scene was now taken for granted—the gaping holes converted into reservoirs for fighting fires, the brick shields and sandbags before public buildings and subway entrances, the blackout, especially eerie on foggy nights, the dimly lighted railway stations. After long hours of work by day, men took their turns fire-watching at night— "lonely, uncomfortable, tiresome but not exacting," wrote Harold Nicolson. Public meetings, church services, theatrical performances, were abbreviated and confined to daylight hours. In the spring of 1942 the point system was extended to canned goods, cereals, dried fruits, sweets, and biscuits, and a five-shilling limit was imposed on food at restaurant meals. In April gray bread replaced white. When Mrs. Roosevelt visited the king and queen in October 1942 she found the rooms of Buckingham Palace damp and chilly, and the meals, as the minister of food (Lord Woolton) told her, such as "might have been served in any home in England and which would have shocked the king's grandfather." For over a year now, to save newsprint, the daily papers had been reduced to four pages (eight pages for those of periodical size).

Demands for a Second Front

In June the public was afforded a fleeting glimpse of war strategy. On the twelfth it was announced that during May, Molotov, the Russian foreign minister, had been in London and Washington. A treaty with Britain called for mutual aid, no separate peace, and a postwar agreement (to last twenty years) on economic cooperation and renunciation of territorial ambitions. This much the public was told. The treaty represented considerable reduction in Russian claims since the previous December; the British foreign secretary, Anthony Eden, had then been confronted in Moscow with demands for Russian annexation of the Baltic states along with parts of Finland, Poland, and Romania as compensation for Molotov's signature to a formal treaty of alliance.

That the Russians were willing to compromise may have been occasioned by hopes for a second front. The stalemate in Libya had halted plans for an Allied invasion of French North Africa. An alternative plan for direct cross-channel invasion had been proposed by the Americans Harry Hopkins and General Marshall in London in April. A limited version, designated Operation Sledgehammer, envisaged such landings before the end of the year in the event of an "imminent collapse" of Russia or a sudden breakdown of German opposition. To Churchill, Sledgehammer seemed precipitate, risky, and at best of narrow advantage. He avoided commitment on this limited phase and sent the Americans home only with his general approval of cross-channel invasion. In Washington, Molotov's persistence won inclusion in the official communique (accepted by Britain as well as the United States) of this statement: "In the course of the conversations full understanding was reached with regard to the urgent tasks of creating a Second Front in Europe in 1942." Churchill made clear to both Washington and Moscow his qualification that an invasion must be launched only when the situation was favorable, but Soviet news agencies now took it for granted that the second front would come in 1942.

Under these circumstances Churchill again conferred, in June, with Roosevelt in Washington. At once Churchill reverted to his earlier proposal for landings in French North Africa. The discussion abruptly ended with the news of the Rommel thrust in the Western Desert—the "Desert Fox" had captured Tobruk, advanced toward El Alamein, was threatening the entire delta. To help meet the serious danger developing in the Middle East, the Americans pledged three hundred new Sherman tanks and one hundred self-propelled anti-tank guns to make good the British losses in their tank battle with Rommel. Some aircraft were also sent. Back in London the prime minister faced the House of Commons in one of its most critical moods of the war years. It was moved "that this House has no confidence in the central direction of the war." The alternatives were not clear, but the debate revealed, in Sir Stafford Cripps's words, "a very grave disturbance in the House of Commons and in the country." Churchill was stung and fought back. He said (July 2): "If those who have assailed us are reduced to contemptible proportions and their Vote of Censure on the National Government is converted to a vote of censure upon its authors, make no mistake, a cheer will go up from every friend of Britain ... and the knell of disappointment will ring in the ears of the tyrants we are striving to overthrow." Only 25 voted for the motion, 476 against, with approximately 30 abstentions—a more substantial victory than the Government had expected.

Apprehension and Discontent. As the summer progressed, news from combat areas still aroused gloom. The entire British force in Egypt was in danger. The second great German offensive in eastern Europe began in the middle of June; Rostov fell July 27, almost without a fight. A vast conflict for Stalingrad and control of the Volga was in the making. The U-boat toll on Allied shipping was still ahead of new construction. Only from the Pacific came good tidings, with the strategic victory of the Americans over the Japanese in the Battle of the Coral Sea in May and the decisive victory off Midway in June. These were the first of the great battles in the Pacific which were essentially carrier vs. carrier, with aircraft responsible for all the striking and all the losses. Thereafter the danger of further Japanese conquest in the Pacific was slight.

Disturbing rumors appeared in the American and the British press. Production in defense plants fell off. The commando raid on Dieppe on August 19, "a reconnaissance in force" (Churchill's phrase), proved a useful experiment in the concerted use of air, land, and sea power. But it was repulsed with heavy losses: over half of the force of 6,100 (largely Canadian) were killed, wounded, or captured. The operation aroused public anticipation of landings in force, which proved without basis.

Apprehension and discontent were well founded, for the Allies had been slow to come to any agreement. On July 17 Stalin wired Churchill that "the Soviet Government cannot acquiesce in the postponement of a second front in Europe until 1943." But Churchill had already decided to bury Sledgehammer. Supported by his chiefs of staff, he came out, July 7, flatly against any landings in France in 1942. Accordingly, the American chiefs of staff recommended to the president that the main American attack be shifted to the Pacific. But Roosevelt was unwilling to abandon common action with the British, and he insisted that at some point an attack in 1942 must be directed by American ground forces against German ground forces. He dispatched Harry Hopkins, General Marshall (Army chief of staff), and Admiral King (chief of naval operations) on July 16 to London. In one week, agreement came—on Operation Gymnast (for security reasons renamed Torch), an invasion of French North Africa toward the end of October at the latest. Thus, in this conflict of strategies the British won, and they were content that Torch be an essentially American undertaking with General Eisenhower in charge.

There remained the problem of Stalin. In mid-August Churchill flew to Moscow. In his first interview he told Stalin that there was to be no landing in France in 1942. The next two hours were "bleak and sombre." Eventually Stalin warmed to Torch, at one point exclaiming, "May God prosper this undertaking!" The visit terminated with an informal evening in Stalin's private apartments in the Kremlin, lasting until 2:30 A.M.

Churchill broke his return journey at Cairo and conferred with a team just formed: General Sir Harold Alexander, the new commander in the Middle East, and General Bernard Montgomery, newly appointed to the command of the Eighth Army in the Western Desert.

But nearly three months passed before Torch was lit. In September the battle for Stalingrad raged in its streets. In answer to a question from an American reporter, Stalin said that aid to the Soviet Union required "the full and prompt fulfillment by the Allies of their obligations." Churchill labeled this period "Suspense and Strain." He wrote, "The inner circle who knew were anxious about what would happen. All those who did not know were disquieted that nothing was happening." When he reported to Parliament, September 8, on his visit to Moscow, a packed chamber began to empty before he concluded, and only a handful remained for the debate, which soon petered out. Such apparent apathy was difficult to explain; but the *Economist* (September 12) suggested that the Commons was getting tired of its job, a perceptive comment. The Trades Union Congress (in September) and the Transport and General Workers Union (in October) passed resolutions reflecting impatience with delays in taking the offensive in Europe.

Lord Moran, Churchill's physician, recorded in his diary that in 1942 Winston was convinced "that his life as Prime Minister could be saved only by a victory in the field." Cripps, who might have led a revolt, had lost prestige through the failure of his mission to India in March—in vain he had offered a guarantee of complete postwar independence in return for full support in the war. But his differences with Churchill over the conduct of the war continued. He decided to resign from the War Cabinet but delayed this action until Torch was well under way so as not to injure the Government.

North Africa: The Turn of the Tide

Torch was slowly mounted. On November 5 Eisenhower and his staff flew from London to Gibraltar and established headquarters in the tunnels of the fortress. Soon great convoys from the United Kingdom and from the United States began converging on the straits and on the coast of North Africa. On November 8 landings were made at Algiers (largely by British troops) and at Oran and Casablanca (largely by Americans). The French defense put up, in the main, only a token resistance, and in three days the initial phase was completed. Beachheads were created for building up forces which could then move eastward toward the British armies now only 1,200 miles distant in the Western Desert.

On November 13 Eisenhower flew to Algiers and made the "deal"

with Admiral Darlan, now commander-in-chief of all French forces
under Vichy, by which Darlan's administration of North Africa was to
remain undisturbed in return for his military cooperation with the
Allied Forces. Darlan was the legal representative of Vichy, and his orders
to French troops for "a cease fire" were carried out in French West
Africa (Dakar) as well as in North Africa. The Allies failed to get
the remnants of the French fleet at Toulon, but so did the
Germans; the fleet was scuttled in the harbor. Darlan had kept his
word. Nevertheless, the "Vichy deal" brought much criticism in Britain,
only partially allayed by Churchill in a secret session of Parliament,
December 10, during which he read a statement from Roosevelt and
reviewed the entire political problem in North Africa. De Gaulle and his
Free French were furious at this bargain with Darlan, the man of Vichy.
The problem of Darlan himself was eliminated with his assassination in
Algiers on Christmas Eve.

Elsewhere in these closing months of 1942, the military outlook was
transformed. The Germans were stopped in Egypt, and the Eighth Army
offensive under Montgomery, with its great superiority in both men and
tanks, in late October broke through the powerful German front, for-
tified in depth though it was, in the twelve-day epic battle of El Alamein,
marking, says Churchill, "the turning of the 'Hinge of Fate.' " The R.A.F.
made a magnificent contribution with attacks on Axis convoys and with
destruction of tankers at sea carrying badly needed fuel for German
transport and armor. In the battle itself Montgomery handled his tank
units with a skill and daring which more than matched the maneuvers of
the panzer divisions under Rommel. As the battle ended, Rommel was in
full retreat; the Eighth Army swept across the desert and across the
border, scattering Germans and capturing Italians. By Christmas the
British were well inside Tripolitania, more than 1,200 miles beyond their
starting point. The city of Tripoli was entered January 23. Ten days later
Churchill told Montgomery's headquarters, "In days to come when
people ask what you did in the Second World War, it will be enough to
say: 'I marched with the Eighth Army.' "

On November 19, 1942, the Russians launched their long-prepared
counterattack at Stalingrad. German forces tarrying too long were
enveloped, and eventually (February 1943) some 90,000 were captured.
By then the entire German front had been pushed back to Rostov and
Kharkov, and by March the Caucasus, the Don, and much of the Ukraine
had been cleared of the enemy.

On November 15, 1942, the long-silent church bells rang out in
Britain—in celebration of El Alamein. "These miraculous weeks" is
Harold Nicolson's happy phrase in "Marginal Comment" of the *Spectator;* the tide had turned. But it was, of course, Churchill who best
expressed the change in the fortunes of this war. At the lord mayor's

luncheon in the City of London on November 10 he said, "This is not the end. It is not even the beginning of the end. But it is, perhaps, the end of the beginning."

"A People's War" and "A People's Peace"

By 1943 another phase of the war had come into focus. On December 2, 1942, the Beveridge report on "Social Insurance and Allied Services" was published. Its appearance revealed the gulf between the thinking of the prime minister and of many of his country-men on the problems of postwar Britain. In a broadcast, March 21, 1943, Churchill, spoke of a "Four Year Plan" of reconstruction, but with no mention of the Beveridge plan and strongly warned against commit-ments for a future which no man could foresee. In the six volumes of *The Second World War,* Churchill never anticipates postwar domestic prob-lems.

On the other hand, most Englishmen took it for granted that this war would bring fundamental social and economic change. The antisocial behavior of a small minority—such as those engaged in the "black mar-ket" and those who moved into the country hotels "for the duration"—stimulated this attitude. But more important was the general atmosphere of the war. It was a leveling experience—leveling in the risks of war, in food, in shelter, in clothing, in amusement. Taxation provides a striking illustration. Income tax and surtax reached 97.5 percent on the highest incomes. A family of four on an annual income of £1,000 paid 40 percent in taxes instead of 19 percent. Furthermore, war conditions increased the need for social services, and this consideration, as well as the influence in the Treasury of J. M. Keynes and H. D. Henderson, made plans for postwar reconstruction a factor in budget projection. It was generally agreed that if shortages continued after the war, controls would remain.

It was a paradox of the war that it alone seemed able to end unem-ployment, that it brought sorely needed supplementary payments to old age pensioners, that it substituted a personal means test for the detested family test, and that it brought greatly improved wage scales. Despite the war "austerity," many members of the working class now enjoyed higher living standards. The official "Ploughing Up Campaign" increased the acreage under tillage by 40 percent and the increase in domestic produc-tion successfully met the reductions in food imports, eventually 55 per-cent of prewar levels.

For Reconstruction through Planning

The public was well aware of these adjustments in the economy as well as of the goals in war production achieved by cooperative enterprise under governmental direction. If problems of war could be solved in this fashion, why not the problems of peace? "Reconstruction" became the magic word; in the early years of the war it appeared everywhere, in all sections of the press, in sermons, in surveys and reports of official and unofficial committees, in speeches in Parliament. The idea of "reconstruction" seemed to justify such language as "a people's war" and "a people's peace." As early as the summer of 1940 J. B. Priestley was saying that the young were now asking, "What kind of a world will come out of this war?"

Reconstruction is the central idea in a series of war pamphlets published by the Macmillan Company and sold for threepence. One of the more widely circulated was R. H. Tawney's *Why Britain Fights,* which is shot through with the author's conception of the social implications of the war—the quest for "social justice" and the creation of opportunities through which all might participate in "the treasures of civilization." What now seems a remarkable article appeared in *The Times,* July 1, 1940, shortly after the evacuation from Dunkirk: "If we speak of democracy, we do not mean a democracy which maintains the right to vote but forgets the right to work and the right to live. If we speak of freedom, we do not mean a rugged individualism which excludes social organization and economic planning. If we speak of equality, we do not mean a political equality nullified by social and economic privilege." In November 1940, *Mass Observation* reported the widespread feeling that the war was in some sense revolutionary.

The Church of England blessed the idea of reconstruction. On January 7–10, 1941, a conference of 240 clergy and laity was held at Malvern on the invitation of Dr. Temple, archbishop of York, "to consider from the Anglican point of view what are the fundamental facts which are directly relevant to the ordering of the new society that is quite evidently emerging, and how Christian thought can be shaped to play a leading part in the reconstruction after the war is over." T. S. Eliot, Dorothy Sayers, and John Middleton Murry addressed the conference. A year later, Dr. Temple, now archbishop of Canterbury, wrote a "Penguin Special" on *Christianity and the Social Order* in which he outlined "a Christian social program" concerning family life, education, income, labor's role in industrial management, leisure, and liberty. In September 1942 a mass meeting organized by the Industrial Christian Fellowship filled the Albert Hall. Temple urged public control of land and money, the archbishop of York stressed the need for a national housing program, and Sir Stafford Cripps discussed the role of the Christian in public life.

These developments within the Church became somewhat controversial with the sudden death, in October 1944, of Archbishop Temple, and the succession not of George Bell, the bishop of Chichester and now recognized as the Church's outstanding leader—but of Geoffrey Fisher, bishop of London. There was much speculation then and since—Was Fisher considered "a safer man?"—Bell had spoken out in the Lords against "saturation bombing" by either side. But Fisher, it may be added, served the Church well for nearly twenty years.

The vogue for planning, so strong in the thirties, continued. A pamphlet issued by a government agency in 1943 lists more than a hundred "unofficial organizations working on postwar planning in Britain." They were concerned with industry and economics, land, town planning, housing and amenities, agriculture, education, medicine, and health. The well-known Royal Institute of International Affairs issued many reports, including that of a Chatham House Reconstruction Committee (1944) on *The Economic Lessons of the Nineteen-thirties*. One of the "lessons" was that the *laissez-faire* system is inadequate for the modern world. A leading economic historian, Ephraim Lipson, published in 1944 *A Planned Economy or Free Enterprise: The Lessons of History*, an academic discussion, moderate in tone. He said, "The alternative no longer rests between laissez-faire or an increasing measure of State interference. It rests between conscious and coordinated direction of national resources, or an opportunist policy producing a mass of contradictory expedients to cope with emergencies without due regard to their ultimate reactions." It is doubtless true, as Lord Woolton pointed out later, that these analyses came from those who believed in planning; those who had other views said little.

Governmental Investigations and Reports

During the early years of the war, special parliamentary committees on matters of town and country planning deliberated. The commission headed by Sir Montague Barlow, appointed in 1937 to study "The Location of Industry and the Distribution of Industrial Population," in its report, January 1940, recommended redevelopment of congested urban areas and dispersal of industries and population, with a view to balanced employment throughout the nation. The committee further recommended a central governmental authority to implement its suggestions. Another commission, appointed in October 1941 and headed by Lord Justice Scott of the Court of Appeal, reported in August 1942 on "Land Utilization in Rural Areas." The report stressed the importance of maintaining good agricultural land and of preserving the "natural amenities," and revitalization of certain decaying towns by industrial use of vacant and derelict sites. A third committee of experts, headed by Mr. Justice Uthwatt of the High Court, was appointed in January 1941 "to make an objective analysis of the subject of payment of compensation and recovery of betterment in respect to public control of the use of the land." Its report, *Compensation and Benefit*, rendered in September 1942, recommended the immediate vesting in the State of the rights of development of all lands outside built-up areas, on payment of fair compensation; a planning authority given power to purchase properties in built-up areas needing redevelopment; the appointment of an official, with no departmental responsibilities, to coordinate the work of existing departments concerned with national development.

The Beveridge Report. Another investigation, quite different in nature, had also been in progress. In June 1941 Sir William Beveridge (director of labor exchanges, 1909–16, and director of the London School of Economics, 1919–37) was made chairman of an interdepartmental committee (representing twelve departments) "to undertake, with special reference to the interrelation of the schemes, a survey of the existing national schemes of social insurance and allied services . . . and to make recommendations." In December 1941 a preliminary memorandum incorporated the reports of the several departments, outlined the heads of a general scheme, and proposed as a basic principle that each and every person should be guaranteed an income at the subsistence level. By that time, questions of policy had arisen on which only a "responsible" minister could speak, and in January 1942 the status of departmental representatives on the committee was changed to that of "advisers." Thus, only Beveridge himself signed the final report, for he alone of the committee was not a governmental official. The report was placed on the table of the House of Commons on December 1; that evening Beveridge introduced his "plan" to the public in a brief broadcast; the following morning it was announced in the press. The report set out certain principles: that social insurance should be a part of a general policy of social progress, that in the last analysis social security could be achieved only through cooperation between the individual and the State, and that the State "in organising security should not stifle incentive, opportunity, responsibility." It proposed a unified system of compulsory social insurance embracing all persons, but classified in its application according to security needs. There was to be flat rate of contribution, a flat system of benefit. It would establish a "national minimum" of income based on subsistence standards and guaranteed to every individual and every family even if earning power were interrupted or destroyed. Special benefits were provided for unusual expenses in connection with birth, marriage, or death. A Ministry of Social Security was to be established. Beveridge included a few words on his own philosophy of reconstruction: "The statement of a reconstruction policy by a nation at war is a statement of the uses to which that nation means to put victory, when victory is achieved."

The report was an immediate sensation. Many London newsstands were completely sold out early on the morning of December 2. With few exceptions the press received the report enthusiastically. *The Times* (December 2), indeed, was lyrical:

> [The report] has transformed this aspiration [freedom from want] into a plainly realizable project of national endeavour.... The central proposals must surely be accepted as the basis of Government action.... The Government has been presented wih an opportunity for marking this decisive epoch with a great social measure which will go far towards restoring the faith of ordinary men and women throughout the world in the power of democracy.

The *Economist* (December 5) referred to the report as "one of the most remarkable state documents ever drafted.... The true test of the Beveridge Plan is whether or not it will inspire, regardless of vested interests, a nation-wide determination to set right what is so plainly wrong and a series of prompt decisions by the Government to ensure that whatever else this war may bring, social security and economic progress shall march together."

A Gallup Poll in mid-December showed that nineteen out of every twenty persons interrogated had heard of the report. Sales figures were issued a year later: 256,000 copies of the full report, 369,000 copies of an abridged edition, 40,000 copies of an American edition. In the minds of many it heralded, as one historian has written, "a sort of Utopia."

Decision Postponed. Thus, by the end of 1942 four reports dealing with problems of reconstruction awaited action. An enthusiastic discussion in the House of Lords in October 1942 on town and country planning seemed a favorable preliminary. However, when the new Parliament convened in November, the king's speech did not mention any proposals for legislation concerning use of the land or concerning social insurance. To expressions of disappointment Sir William Jowitt, now in charge of planning for reconstruction, replied only in general terms. On December 17 the prime minister wrote a memorandum to several members of the Government: "I hope that in studying the various proposals for social reform, land development, etc., you are giving full consideration to our post-war financial situation.... Nothing would be more dangerous than for people to feel cheated because they had been led to expect attractive schemes which turn out to be economically impossible."

The Beveridge report came up for formal consideration in the Commons in an extended debate February 16–18, 1943. Though each speaker praised Beveridge and approved the general principles of his plan, the Commons, in a resolution presented by the Government, merely welcomed the report as "a comprehensive review" and "a valuable aid in determining developments and legislation which should be pursued as part of the Government's policy of post-war reconstruction." Churchill did not participate in the discussion, and Government spokesmen expressed little enthusiasm. An amendment seeking stronger endorsement of the report, as the basis for early legislation, failed 338–121. As the debate proceeded, it became acrimonious. With but two exceptions, all Labor members not in the Cabinet or Ministry voted with the minority, while the Labor members in the Government (including Attlee, Bevin, Cripps, and Morrison) voted with the majority. This was the one occasion in the course of the war in which the Parliamentary Labor Party revolted against its leadership. The Government later announced that the report had been referred to a committee of heads of certain departments assisted by a selected staff of civil servants.

What was the explanation of this turn of affairs? Much of the press was puzzled and angry. *The Times* (February 19) spoke of this week's "disappointment" and of "a crisis which need never have arisen." The *Economist* (February 20 and 27) referred to it as "a crisis of free government and democracy.... The question: 'Has the Government accepted the Beveridge Report?' remains unanswered." In the House of Lords, February 25, Lord Addison said that he could not "recall a Parliamentary issue that was worse bungled." He explained that the resolution endorsing the report in broad general terms was intended to provide the basis of "a discussion without prejudice ... so as to give an opportunity for views to be freely expressed and for the general sense of Parliament to be ascertained by the Government." But, Lord Addison continued, on the first day of the debate a Cabinet member "announced certain Government findings in regard to the Report," and debate then concentrated upon his statement "rather than initiating a wide unprejudiced discussion of the Report itself."

This is a reasonable explanation as far as it goes, but the matter was more complicated. It seems likely that the Conservatives and the Laborites found it embarrassing to deal on a nonpartisan basis with such an inflammable subject as social insurance. Lord Pakenham, in those days Beveridge's personal assistant, states that even before the report appeared, the attitude of some members of the Government was "unpleasant"; and he suggests that the Conservatives were unable then to deal effectively with social issues, were rather skeptical of phrases like "social security," and were not to be won over easily. The leading Labor members of the Government have never revealed the inside story. (Attlee later, in 1961, did say that there was no disagreement in the Cabinet concerning the merits of the report but a difference of opinion only on when it should be adopted. He added, rather surprisingly, that Churchill wished to put it into effect as an act of his postwar Government.) Press reports at the time made a good deal of the divisions within the Parliamentary Labor Party, particularly the hostile attitude of Ernest Bevin toward Beveridge. In the course of the debate Herbert Morrison spoke warmly of Beveridge and was obviously embarrassed. Beveridge himself was a factor. Neither Labor nor Conservative, he was incurably vain and had little political instinct. He should have been more sensitive to the problems of implementing a one-man report on so controversial a subject. He later referred to himself as the victim of "Boom and Boycott," for his report was never again considered in Parliament. Nonetheless, over the air and in the press it came to represent the tone of a new national outlook for postwar Britain, and became indelibly associated with the Labor Party.

It must be remembered that this was time when the fortunes of war seemed finally to favor the Allies. Churchill had just returned from the Casablanca Conference, following the landings of Torch and Montgomery's victory in North Africa. His mind was on impending military decisions and he was impatient of any considerations which distracted his attention. During the February debate he was ill. But there are on record two of his memoranda on the Beveridge report, dated January 12 and February 14, suggesting that Cabinet members not commit themselves to initiating legislation or supporting special appropriations, and cautioning against committing future Parliaments on social questions.

In the autumn there were further repercussions in Parliament. The King's Speech opening the new session, November 24, 1943, declared that the Government would make plans for the transition from war to peace. But no legislative proposals were mentioned, a disappointment to some. An amendment sponsored by Labor members, not put to a vote, regretted that the Government had not yet made up its mind on the Beveridge and Uthwatt reports: "We invite His Majesty's Government and Parliament to say definitely whether they intend to grapple with the aftermath of the war in a much more thorough, comprehensive and intelligent way than Parliament did after the 1914–1918 war." Strong support for this amendment came from a group of young Conservatives led by Lord Hinchingbrooke. But Lord Woolton, just appointed the first minister of Reconstruction, was not to be pushed around. He declared in the Lords (December 8) that people must not expect too much, that the basis of social security was full employment, which depended largely on the initiative and energy of the people, and that the Government had no intention of swallowing whole the reports of Beveridge, Barlow, Scott, and Uthwatt.

Social Reform during the War

Nevertheless, by the end of the war many steps in the direction of social reform had been taken. While there were no recommendations on the Beveridge report as such, the Government in 1944 issued a series of white papers in many of which Lord Woolton had a hand: (1) social insurance—proposals following those of Beveridge more closely than had been expected; (2) compensation for industrial injuries; (3) a national health service (there seemed to be general agreement among the parties in this respect); (4) full employment. The paper on "Employment Policy" was welcomed by the General Council of the Trades Union Congress, which proceeded to outline its own goals of direct state control of certain segments of industry by nationalization, and indirect regulation of private industry through price and licensing controls. In 1945 another white paper outlined plans for reform of local government. On these matters there was no legislation until after the war.

Early in 1943 a central planning authority was created in the new Ministry of Town and Country Planning. In June 1944 a white paper presented certain alternatives to the details of the Uthwatt report, the chief of which was that developmental rights were to be vested in owners of land but proposals for development had to be approved by the planning authority. More controversial were the provisions for compensation and betterment. Legislation in November 1944 facilitated purchase of land by local authorities and laid the foundation for the planning envisaged in the Barlow, Scott, and Uthwatt reports.

Without much doubt, the most significant piece of domestic legislation during the war was the Education Act of 1944, the most important legislation on that subject since 1902. Just as the important Fisher Act of 1918 was stimulated by war, so this war forced the British to resolve some of the complexities of their educational problems. On September 1, 1939, a provision of the act of 1936, raising the school-leaving age to fifteen, was to go into effect. Instead, on that day began the mass exodus from evacuation areas. This operation posed entirely new difficulties; evacuees when relocated often discovered there were no classrooms and no teachers. By January 1940 a million children had been four months without schooling or school medical service. The Board of Education estimated that even in London 92,000 children were not in school. Such conditions provided an opportunity for examining the more persistent deficiencies of the educational system.

A tremendous outpouring of books and pamphlets made the reading public conscious of the problems. Important publications included Francis Williams's *Democracy's Last Battle* (1941), attacking class distinctions in education; *The Future of Education* (1941) by Sir Richard Livingstone, president of Corpus Christi College, Oxford—it stressed adult education, proved an "explosive book" and became a bestseller; *Education for the People* (1941) by Dr. F. H. Spencer, a former school inspector in London; *A New Order in English Education* (1942) by H. C. Dent, editor of *The Times Educational Supplement*. During June and July of 1941, *The Times Educational Supplement* carried four leading articles on educational reform.

R. A. Butler, the president of the Board of Education, was himself a dedicated student of the problem—he had, for example, read what the French historian, Elie Halévy, had to say about the Act of 1902. His official report in October 1941 summarized the Board's "Green Book" which had outlined proposed educational reforms. Out of the ensuing discussions, surveys, and suggestions from local educational authorities, from political bodies and religious organizations, there emerged general agreement on broad principles: equality of educational opportunity, a uniform scheme of education at the primary level, a variety of educational opportunities at the secondary level and all guaranteed without fees, the raising of the school-leaving age to fifteen, extension of technical and commercial education, and availability of university education to those qualified, with financial need no bar.

The Board of Education produced a white paper in July 1943. Some experts felt that it did not fully implement the principles professed—the role of the "public" school, for example, remained a thorny problem—but even the critics regarded it as "progress" in the attack on "class education." *The Times* (July 24, 1943) said that it marked "the greatest and grandest educational advance since 1870." On the other hand, it must be recorded, Churchill gave it little interest or encouragement. But, all in all, the process by which this white paper became the parliamentary act of 1944 is a monument to the capacity of Britain's political system, to the energy and intelligence of her educational leaders, to the general restraint exercised on the religious issue, and to Butler's leadership. Butler, himself, commented and quite justifiably: "During the war no other Minister on the home front had been able to bring his plans to fruition."

The Address from the Throne, November 29, 1944, outlined the areas of legislation intended for the period between war and peace. It referred to a comprehensive health service, an enlarged and uniform system of national insurance, industrial injuries compensation, family allowances, housing, and maintenance of employment. Churchill said that while of necessity the legislation of the current Parliament would be limited, eventually the entire program would be implemented since all parties were committed. Eden pledged Conservative support for its completion even if a Labor Government came to power. When could such unanmity on social questions have been found before September 3, 1939? A considerable part of the legislative program of the Labor Government elected in 1945 had its basis in the thinking and planning, and even in the decisions, of the Government of the war years.

From Casablanca to Normandy

After Torch and El Alamein, what next? On January 26, 1943, the British public learned that from January 14 to 25 Roosevelt and Churchill had conferred at Casablanca (on the Atlantic in French Morocco), that "the entire field of war has been surveyed theatre by theatre throughout the world" and that "complete agreement has been reached upon war plans and enterprises to be undertaken during the campaign of 1943 against Germany, Italy, and Japan."

This communique bore little relation to reality. Even on political matters Casablanca was indecisive. After Darlan's assassination in December 1942, General Giraud assumed authority in French North Africa. He and De Gaulle were brought together at Casablanca. But they remained incompatible. De Gaulle had one star and Giraud had five; De Gaulle would accept no subordinate position for the Free French and distrusted Giraud as quasi-Vichy; yet it was Giraud who controlled the French Army. Not for another six months were they reconciled as joint presidents of the French Committee of National Liberation.

With some reluctance, at Casablanca Churchill accepted Roosevelt's uncompromising "unconditional surrender" (reminiscent of the American Civil War) as the only basis for peace. Both soon qualified this formula, leaving less basis for the criticism which developed in some quarters that, had "psychological warfare" dominated their thinking and had peace terms been enunciated in the spirit of the Atlantic Charter, elements inside the Reich opposing Hitler might have been strengthened and an early end to the war might have come through German collapse. Churchill was permitted, though with the misgivings of his own Cabinet and of the Americans, to confer with President Inönü with a view to bringing Turkey into the war to facilitate an invasion of Hitler's Europe through the Balkans. The Turks accepted military assistance but would make no commitment.

Supply Problems Solved

On the gravity of the shipping shortage—in Sir Alan Brooke's words, "a strangle hold on all offensive operations"— Casablanca brought agreement but no solution. The shipping demanded by operations already undertaken was as nothing compared with the great fleets required to meet the growing commitments to Russia and Turkey, to fill the civilian needs of the United Kingdom, and to transport the vast armies and the quantities of supplies needed for the massive offensives now contemplated. For some time there was no reconciling the requirements of Britain and of the United States—for example, it came out that shipping space required for a fully equipped American G.I. was about twice that required for a British Tommy. In the process of drafting "a combined shipping budget" more realistic figures were used on both sides; and at the subsequent conference, in May, it was found possible to reduce a combined deficit in shipping from between 2,250,000 and 3,250,000 dead-weight tons to a figure of from 750,000 to 1,250,000 tons, which was considered manageable. What was far more important, by the summer of 1943 the American shipbuilding program was in high gear, with new shipping sliding down the ways in fantastic numbers.

In the course of 1943, the fortunes of war on the high seas completely changed. Hitherto there had been a gap in the mid-Atlantic where no air patrol protected convoys. Now air support from Iceland and Newfoundland began to accompany convoys the entire journey. Radar was vastly improved. Thus, losses in merchant shipping in the North Atlantic declined sharply (March 1943, 477,000 tons; April, 245,000 tons; May, 165,000 tons; October, November, and December together, 146,000 tons). Allied toll on U-boats climbed just as quickly. Altogether, in the year following June 1943 there was little impediment to the gigantic movement of men and supplies from the United States to the United Kingdom. In the Mediterranean, with Allied control the U-boat menace ceased. Convoys to the Middle East now took the Suez route rather than the Cape route, cutting the journey an average of forty-five days.

The situation in northern waters was also transformed. Convoys to Russia via the North Cape to Archangel had been the prey of the remaining surface units of the German Navy based in Norwegian waters. Accordingly, those convoys had been halted in March 1943 as the hours of daylight increased. But in September the great German battleship *Tirpitz* was maimed (and put out of action for some months) in a Norwegian fjord by British midget submarines. The convoys to the Arctic were resumed for the dark months ahead. Then, the day after Christmas, the *Scharnhorst,* the one remaining German battle cruiser, was sunk off the North Cape by H.M.S. *Duke of York*—the *Scharnhorst's* superior speed had been reduced by torpedoes from British destroyers when she had attempted to attack a convoy. Thereafter, serious danger of surface attack on northern convoys was removed, for the British Home Fleet was in complete control.

First Assaults on Fortress Europe

In contrast to the dramatic successes at sea, Allied air power was built up quite slowly during 1943, and strategic bombing operations were hesitant and even experimental. The Casablanca Conference authorized a great Allied strategic offensive based on the United Kingdom and directed against German industry. But the Combined Bomber Offensive, under Air Chief Marshall Sir Arthur Harris, did not receive its formal directive until June 1943, when it was instructed to destroy German military and economic power as a preliminary to invasion. *Pointblank,* as this operation came to be called, did not achieve any decisive results in 1943. There were a few major attacks in July, such as the British assaults on Essen in the Ruhr. At about the same time, the so-called Battle of Hamburg constituted one of the most destructive assaults of the war; with British night raids alternating with American daylight attacks, six thousand acres were left in ruins and the known dead ran to above 40,000. But in general the Luftwaffe defense was so effective that daylight missions were checked by the fighter force of the enemy. Long-range support was needed for the American missions. When they ventured deep into German territory, losses were heavy; in an attack against the Regensburg-Schweinfurt area on August 17, sixty bombers, constituting 19 percent of the attacking force, were shot down.

On matters of military strategy the Casablanca Conference brought to light deep-seated differences between Britain and America which plagued their relationship almost to the end of the war. The "complete agreement" of the Casablanca communique was then only a pious hope. The Americans made clear their recommendation: the next major blow in Europe (the second front) should be an all-out cross-channel invasion of northwest France at the earliest possible date. On the other hand, the British discouraged such operations in 1943 in the interest of more limited operations in the Mediterranean which would clear the Germans out of North Africa and permit the Allies to establish naval and air bases for striking, in concert with Russia and, hopefully, Turkey, in Churchill's words, "at the underbelly of the Axis in effective strength and in the shortest time." The Americans finally agreed that an attack on Sicily should be made, with the favorable July moon as the target date. And it was tentatively agreed that preparations should be made for limited landings on the Cotentin Peninsula in northwest France in August or September.

But the high command had to weigh the demands of other theaters of action. The Americans wished to have sufficient landing craft available for amphibious operations in the Far East—in the Solomons, and particularly in Burma, where they hoped to reopen the road to China and Chungking and thus bolster the Chinese forces. It was agreed at Casablanca that the assault on Burma should be made by British, American, and Chinese forces in concert, with a tentative target date of November 15, 1943. But first the British were to undertake a limited offensive from India along the Bay of Bengal to the port of Akyab, before the monsoon came in May, in order to improve the air route to China, while the Chinese, in the course of the spring, were to move through northern Burma and beyond to Yünnan.

The pattern of decision making which now developed between Great Britain and the United States was that tentative plans were made through compromise, with final decisions postponed as long as possible and ultimately dictated by the circumstances of the moment. Russian policy—as long as Stalin could not be drawn to any of the conferences—remained pretty much an enigma but was usually very sensitive to the immediate fortunes of the war. Thus, Stalin was quite impatient with Churchill's report following Casablanca that no cross-channel attack was contemplated before August or September, and he declared in his order of the day, February 23, 1943: "In view of the absence of a Second Front in Europe, the Red Army alone bears the whole brunt of the war." But with the failure of the German counteroffensive in Russia in March and with the final clearing of Tunisia (and thus of all North Africa) of the enemy in May, his tone became more cordial. He sent the film of the Battle of Stalingrad to Churchill, who reciprocated with the film of El Alamein, "Desert Victory."

But the delays of final victory in North Africa made it impossible to mount an Allied cross-channel attack in 1943. This was recognized at the Trident Conference in Washington and at Roosevelt's secret mountain retreat, "Shangri-La," in May. It was agreed by the president, the prime minister, and their advisers that the invasion of Sicily should be exploited in such fashion "as might be calculated to eliminate Italy from the war"—this evasive language was used to encompass American refusal to authorize further offensives in the Mediterranean. The Americans, led by General Marshall, insisted on absolute commitment to the operation soon to be called Overlord—the cross-channel invasion of France—target date May 1, 1944, "to secure a lodgment from which further offensive operations can be carried out." The British were compelled to recognize that this undertaking had priority over any additional Mediterranean offensive. But they sought to abandon another project close to Marshall's heart, the Burma campaign. Its preliminaries, agreed on at Casablanca, had failed. The British had little confidence in the Chinese and wished to concentrate on the defense of India.

Invasion of Sicily and Italy. Churchill persuaded Marshall to accompany him from the Trident Conference to Algiers. There the Allied commanders were found agreeable to a campaign in Italy if Sicily succumbed quickly. This proved to be the case. The night of July 9–10, landings were made by American, British, and Canadian units. The only serious resistance came from German troops, which were gradually withdrawn from the island; the operation was completed August 17. Meanwhile, a Government under Marshal Badoglio replaced Mussolini, whose regime had disintegrated under military defeat. Here Anglo-American differences took another turn, for Churchill wished to conciliate the Italians in the hope of winning their support, even active military support, for his projects in the eastern Mediterranean, while Roosevelt demanded "unconditional surrender." But the latter soon abandoned this position and accepted negotiations which led to an armistice with the Badoglio Government on September 3. But Badoglio's intentions were uncertain and his actions difficult to interpret. He insisted on keeping the terms of the armistice secret until he announced them himself in Rome September 8. The Germans acted promptly, and the Italian land and air forces soon found themselves surrendering to the Germans rather than to the Allies. By the time Allied landings were made on the beaches at Salerno, September 9, the Germans were able to confront them undisturbed by the Italians. Badoglio himself soon escaped from Rome; his Government declared war on Germay and was recognized by the Allies as a "co-belligerent."

The British also made landings at Reggio, across the Strait of Messina from Sicily. From there the British Eighth Army moved north, capturing Foggia with its important airfields, while the Fifth Army (British and American), after being checked some time at Salerno, entered Naples. The Germans gradually withdrew into the Apennines, constructing a series of defensive positions in depth. There were also the October rains, and by November the Allied advance was halted in central Italy south of Rome with the Eighth Army holding the front along the Sangro River east of the Apennines and the Fifth Army in the west established along the southern banks of the Garigliano River as far as Cassino.

Grand Strategy for War and Peace

Meantime, Churchill in August had again crossed the Atlantic for the Quadrant Conference held in Quebec, in Washington, and at Hyde Park. Though the direct clash between cross-channel and Mediterranean operations remained, a grand design for the European war was drafted, a design which was to be implemented in all important particulars. Overlord, the invasion of France, was to take priority. Land-

ings in southern France were authorized as "a diversion." In Italy "un-
remitting pressure" was to be maintained on the Germans. The collapse
of Italian forces revived in Churchill notions of pushing the Germans out
of the southern Balkans back to the Sava-Danube line. He succeeded only
in obtaining authorization for a limited attack on the Dodecanese Islands. In his report on the Quadrant Conference to the House of Commons, September 21, Churchill referred hopefully to the situation arising
from the Italian armistice: "With the control of Southern Italy, to which
we confidently look forward in the near future ... our entry and perhaps
command of the Adriatic should become possible. All this opens far-
reaching vistas of action ... in the Balkans." But he was loyal to the
decisions at Quadrant and rejected suggestions from General Smuts
(prime minister of South Africa) and from George VI that the whole
matter be reopened in the interests of developing the Mediterranean
Theater as the main base of operations from which to attack Nazi-held
Europe.

John Ehrman in *Grand Strategy, August 1943–September 1944* contends
that Churchill in 1943 may have had "dreams" of a Balkan campaign but that he never intended that a major operation in the Mediterranean should develop at the expense of Overlord. Churchill's persistent
interest in the Mediterranean was, Ehrman says, merely a part of traditional British strategy—to retain flexibility against stronger forces on the
Continent, to have several targets available for exploitation, to keep the
forces of the enemy scattered. On the other hand, the United States, more
confident in its abundance of strength, wished to concentrate on "one
massive project." As between these two positions, the distribution of
landing craft for assault forces was the crucial problem.

At Quebec there was also a significant agreement on atomic
research—full collaboration between Britain and the United States in the
effort to construct atomic weapons and agreement that such weapons
would be employed for military purposes only with the consent of both
parties. Heretofore the significant advances in the knowledge of atomic
energy had been made in Britain, culminating with the report in July
1941 of the MAUD Committee, headed by Professor George Thomson of
Imperial College, London, that in their opinion an atomic bomb could be
produced. Thereafter, however, the initiative shifted to the Americans.

"A General International Organization." The Quadrant Conference had also considered postwar problems, and Roosevelt
and Churchill decided that the time had come for a tripartite meeting
with the Russians. Stalin was not then prepared to participate, but he
suggested that a meeting of a "military-political commission" in Moscow

be preliminary to a later gathering of heads of governments. As a result, a conference of foreign ministers was held in Moscow October 18–30. The Americans took the lead. Secretary of State Cordell Hull persuaded Molotov to include China in a Four-Power Declaration of General Security, recognizing, once the war was ended, "the necessity of establishing at the earliest practicable moment a general international organization." The four powers declared that after the war they would "not employ their military forces within the territories of other states except for the purposes envisaged in this declaration and after joint consultation." Another declaration called for the elimination of Fascism from Italy; a statement on German war atrocities said that the fate of major war criminals would be decided by Allied governments; an independent Austria was to be reestablished; and a newly created European Advisory Council in London was to study problems associated with the surrender of the enemy (such problems as occupation and reparations) and to present recommendations.

The United States and the U.S.S.R. had agreed to participate in a postwar international organization—this was the chief import. Secretary Hull reported to Congress that the conference had "laid the foundation for cooperative effort... towards enabling all peace-loving nations ... to live in peace and security." Eden was more restrained but told the Commons that the results of the conference exceeded his hopes. Stalin declared that as final victory came nearer, "the relations among the Allies ... have, contrary to the expectations of their enemies, grown stronger and more enduring." No one mentioned that the Russians had flatly refused to resume relations with the Polish Government in London, or that Molotov had plainly asserted that the U.S.S.R. had, in eastern and southeastern Europe, a sphere of special and exclusive interest.

Cairo and Tehran Conferences. Within a month (November 28) the Big Three came together at Tehran—another of the "climacterics" of the war. Churchill writes of the dinner at which he was host: "On my right sat the President of the United States, on my left the Master of Russia. Together we controlled practically all the naval and three-quarters of all the air forces in the world, and could direct armies of nearly twenty millions of men, engaged in the most terrible of wars that had yet occurred in human history."

A preliminary Anglo-American-Chinese conference was held at Cairo, November 22–26, Stalin refusing to confer with Chiang Kai-shek. Roosevelt hoped to get Chiang's support for the attack on Burma. Lord Mountbatten, supreme Allied commander in the new Southeast Asia Command, attended to get approval for operations his command wished to undertake. One of these, a sea-borne operation, had as its objective the capture of the Andaman Islands southwest of Rangoon in the Bay of Bengal. At British insistence the Combined (Anglo-American) Chiefs of Staff agreed to postpone decision on this operation until other enterprises had been discussed. But this position was compromised when Roosevelt privately promised Chiang an amphibious attack across the Bay of Bengal within a few months. In addition, the cleavage between British and American strategy in Europe persisted, the Americans insistent on no further delay on Overlord, the British still hopeful of the modification of Overlord to permit campaigns in the eastern Mediterranean.

The resolution of this deadlock—if deadlock it still was—constituted the most important strategic decision at Tehran. Stalin said flatly that all other operations in Europe should be subordinate to Overlord, which "should be some time in May and no later." It should be supported, he said, by a landing in southern France; the capture of Rome and other Mediterranean undertakings could be nothing more than "diversions." When Churchill persisted in one final plea for an Aegean campaign, Stalin said he "wished to pose a very direct question . . . . Did the Prime Minister and the British staffs really believe in *Overlord?*" According to the official British account, Churchill answered, "Provided conditions previously stated for *Overlord* were to obtain . . . it would be our stern duty to hurl across the Channel against the Germans every sinew of our strength." During an informal luncheon conference, Roosevelt told Stalin that D-day for Overlord had been fixed for sometime in May. Once the military issues were settled, the strain vanished. Elaborate toasts were exchanged at a dinner on Churchill's sixty-ninth birthday. Roosevelt gave Churchill a Kashan porcelain bowl, said to have been purchased that day at a U.S. Army post exchange. At the conclusion of the conference, a communique was prepared for the press on a note of "brevity, mystery, and a foretaste of impending doom for Germany" (Churchill). It declared that the military staffs of the three powers had concerted their plans for the final destruction of the German forces.

Back in Cairo, Churchill redoubled his efforts to get Turkey into the war, and the British staff was absorbed in tentative plans for operations in the Aegean in case of Turkish belligerency. Roosevelt broke a deadlock in Anglo-American differences on Southeast Asia by overruling his own chiefs of staff and agreeing to abandon the attack on the Andaman Islands, thus breaking the promise he had made to Chiang. In the war against Japan, American operations now assumed paramount importance as combined air, sea, and land operations began to reduce rapidly the perimeter of Japanese control in the Pacific. At Cairo Roosevelt decided on Eisenhower, and not Marshall, as supreme Allied commander for Overlord. He informed Churchill December 6, broke his journey back to Washington at Tunis to tell Eisenhower himself, and told the world in his Christmas Eve broadcast. And General Montgomery was to command the invasion forces of the 21st Army Group assigned to Overlord.

Build-up for Overlord

In December 1943 final victory over Germany was expected in 1944. But in the timetable each operation hinged on the successful completion of another—in terms of troops, munitions, shipping, landing craft. And so setbacks in some areas brought uncertainties about the wisdom of decisions taken elsewhere. Here were the important developments in the first five months of 1944. Hopes of Turkish belligerency did not materialize, and plans for an attack on Rhodes were soon abandoned. In December General Eisenhower had urged additional landing craft for Operation Anvil, the landings in southern France, to meet "the necessity for an initial broad and deep beach-head" by assault of three divisions instead of one. In January Montgomery insisted on five divisions instead of three for Overlord. The crucial problem remained the shortage of landing craft, especially the LST's (the tank landing ships), for sea-borne assault troops. Rome did not fall at once as anticipated. The stalemate north of Naples was not broken by the surprise landings in January at Anzio, one hundred miles north of the German lines. Hitler determined to hold the Gustav Line at all costs. Its key was Monte Cassino, crowned at 1,700 feet by the medieval monastery of St. Benedict. Even Allied aerial destruction of the monastery, February 15, did not break the line. At the same time, in the north, German reinforcements had contained the Anzio invasion at the beachhead. On February 22 General Wilson, now the Allied commander in the Mediterranean, said that no resources in Italy could be spared for Anvil, which he recommended be abandoned. The Allied high command decided to postpone Overlord from May 1 to May 31, giving more time for the assembling of landing craft and at the same time retaining the advantage of moon and tide. In the late spring a final breakthrough came at Cassino and at Anzio, and American troops entered Rome on June 4.

The British public was conscious only of the delays. In March and April of 1944 industrial absenteeism and unrest attained serious proportions. The new crisis could be met only by reallocation. New "budgets," with the armed forces and essential industries having priority, were drawn up by a special committee under Sir John Anderson and were to be implemented by thousands of employment exchanges in the Ministry of Labor. By March 1944 the British armed forces numbered 4,900,000. The number of working civilians since June 1939 had declined from

18,270,000 to 16,559,000. Of this latter figure, by mid 1944, 43 percent were engaged in war industry.

The "little Blitz" from mid-January to mid-April added to the strain. Fifteen major attacks were made, thirteen of them on London, with an emphasis on incendiaries. The night population of the "underground" increased from about three thousand to about fifty thousand, though most people remained only during the raids. The early raids were a complete failure, the later ones only moderately successful. In February, the month of the heaviest attacks, 901 civilians were killed, most of them in London. Generally speaking, only ten to twenty bombers reached the London area in any one raid. Defenses were effective; for example, three-fourths of the fires were extinguished by fire wardens. And Germany was wasting away her Air Force.

In the spring of 1944 the Combined Bomber Offensive of the R.A.F. and the American Eighth and Fifteenth Air Forces was striving to complete the execution of the undertaking phrased at Casablanca in these words: "the progressive destruction and dislocation of the German military, industrial and economic system, and the undermining of the morale of the German people to a point where their capacity for armed resistance is fatally weakened." Available aircraft had grown in numbers, as if by magic: whereas but 8,000 planes were produced in 1939, in 1941 it was 20,000, and in 1943 it was 26,000. Since the spring of 1943, the Combined Bomber Offensive had been mounting massive assaults, but with somewhat uncertain results. During the winter months of 1943–44, the British raided Berlin by night on sixteen occasions; in March 1944 came American attacks by day—for the first time Berliners saw solid formations of American Flying Fortresses overhead. The Americans undertook daylight precision bombing on priority targets (aircraft and oil industry, transportation centers). There were some targets of the R.A.F. in western Europe which brought the loss of French and Belgian lives. By D-day some forty-three German cities had been bombed. Nevertheless, the end sought by the Casablanca directive had not been achieved. It was the morale of the British Bomber Command which was destroyed—so great had been its losses. In a raid on Nuremberg, March 30, out of 795 bombers in action, 94 were lost and 71 damaged. And German military production had not yet been seriously affected. However, in April, 1944 came an important shift—long-range fighters accompanied the bombers as they swept in low to bomb predetermined targets. Aerial attacks in May on French railways rendered them of little value for movements of German reserves after D-day. And the Luftwaffe was rendered almost helpless. The Allies, it became evident, had won command of the air. And the success of Overlord was now far more likely.

Final Preparations. The British public knew little of these details, and nothing of the elaborately deceptive measures of Operation Bodyguard (false assembly of materials, misleading troop movements), designed to convince the enemy that landings would occur in the Pas de Calais and, after the actual landings of Overlord, to lead them to believe that the main attack was still to come elsewhere. This attempt at deception was successful.

Of one phenomenon in the spring of 1944 the British were acutely aware: the massing of American troops—1,526,965 is the official figure just before D-day—in the United Kingdom. Vast encampments mushroomed on the Salisbury Plain. London was perpetually crowded with G.I.s on leave; harsh accents controlled Piccadilly Circus and Trafalgar Square; American servicemen played baseball to silent but absorbed onlookers in Hyde Park; and queues for newspapers, for busses, for railroad tickets, lengthened. The Great Room of the Grosvenor House, "the largest ballroom in Europe," had become "Willow Run," as the Americans called it, an officers' mess for U.S. forces. After January 14, headquarters for Overlord were in Norfolk House, St. James' Square. Eisenhower's formal directive in February from the Combined Chiefs of Staff was brief and to the point: "You will enter the continent of Europe and, in conjunction with other United Nations, undertake operations aimed at the heart of Germany and the destruction of her armed forces." Eisenhower's initial task was to mount this operation, to reassure the British still dubious over its wisdom, and to adjudicate disputes among his subordinates. The marvel is not that there were disagreements, but that the disagreements were surmounted and that extraordinary energy and vast good will enabled the project to succeed.

On May 8 the final decision was made. D-day was to be June 5, when tide and moon were still favorable. On May 15 at St. Paul's School in London, the headquarters of the 21st Army Group, was held the most famous "briefing" of the war. Against the backdrop of a huge map of the invasion area, Overlord was explained by Eisenhower and his immediate subordinates to a distinguished company of His Majesty the King, Churchill and the War Cabinet, General Smuts, the British chiefs of staff, and scores of other high officers of various services. On June 1, British naval units left their bases bound for the assault area. Invasion forces were assembled in tented areas in the southern counties, each unit studying charts and maps of its particular assignment. Insurance policies and family allotments were checked. The troops received K and D rations, rounds of ammunition, French phrase books, invasion money. On June 3 the forces began to embark from channel ports: Portland, Plymouth, Portsmouth, Southampton, the Isle of Wight. Churchill boarded ship after ship to speed on the undertaking.

On June 3 the skies thickened with rain and a gale from the west; it was predicted that the bad weather would last a fortnight. Delay beyond June 7 would mean postponement at least until the nineteenth, when tides would again be favorable. For June 5 the prediction was high winds and clouds which would make landing hazardous and air support impossible. On June 4 Eisenhower postponed the invasion orders twenty-four hours and then early on the morning of the fifth issued the orders for the assault to be made the sixth—for an improvement in the weather lasting thirty-six hours was predicted. The German high command, on the other hand, received a forecast that bad weather would absolutely prevent any landings on the fifth or sixth. In indelible sentences Churchill sketches the culminating scene:

All day on June 5, the convoys bearing the spearhead of the invasion converged on the rendezvous south of the Isle of Wight. Thence, in an endless stream, led by the minesweepers on a wide front and protected on all sides by the might of the Allied Navies and Air Forces, the greatest armada that ever left our shores set out for the coast of France.

Triumph and Tragedy

At 9:33 A.M., June 6, Eisenhower's headquarters broke the news with the first communique on the invasion: "Under command of General Eisenhower, Allied naval forces, supported by strong air forces, have landed Allied armies this morning on the northern coast of France." British papers that morning contained this and little more, but were snapped up as fast as they appeared on the streets. At noon Churchill told the Commons that more than 4,000 ships had crossed the Channel and that invasion troops were being supported by about 11,000 first-line aircraft. "Everything is proceeding according to plan. And what a plan! This vast operation is undoubtedly the most complicated and difficult that has ever occurred." That evening the king broadcast an appeal for "a nation-wide, a world-wide vigil of prayer as the great crusade sets forth."

The headlines the British public received in the days that followed read like this: June 7—"Heavy beach fighting—Fifty mile long train of gliders—Reenforced positions seized in Cherbourg peninsula." June 8—"Everything is going excellently—Monty. We capture Bayeux." June 9—"Whole line holds—8th Army is there." June 10—"Great tank battle raging ... near Caen," with pictures of German prisoners and liberated French villages. The initial assault was a "soldier's battle" and no member of the high command set foot on French soil on D-day. But with the withdrawal of the Germans inland, Churchill on the tenth visited

Montgomery on the beachhead, and on the sixteenth the king crossed the Channel on a cruiser flying the royal standard to spend a day on the beaches where British and Canadian troops had landed.

A New Danger from the Skies

Just a week after D-day the first of the "flying bombs"—the V-1's—fell on England, and six people were killed. To the Government this was no surprise, for since 1943 intelligence agencies had been following the development of this new weapon and the preparation of launching platforms in the Pas de Calais. Allied bombardment of production areas and of launching sites delayed the attacks. On the night of June 12, 1944, set for the opening salvo, fifty-four launching sites were ready on both sides of the Somme, though two-thirds had not yet been tested. Something like 500 missiles were to be sent in the first "harassing fire." But there was delay in the arrival of safety equipment, and that night only 10 bombs were actually launched. Four reached southern England, the only casualties occurring at Bethnal Green. However, a few days later, on the night of June 15–16, 244 bombs were aimed at London, of which 73 reached the target. That morning, the sixteenth, the home secretary announced that the "pilotless aircraft" attack had started. Soon officially described as "flying bombs," they were popularly called "fly bombs," "doodlebugs," "buzz bombs," and "robots." They flew at about 2,000 to 3,000 feet, 300 to 400 miles per hour, and carried a ton of explosive. Their range was controlled by a propeller; after revolving a prescribed number of times, it stopped and the bomb dove toward the earth. Their penetrative power was slight and they set few fires, but the blast was enormous and a single bomb could produce widespread havoc. Their path was marked by the red flame of their exhausts, easily observable on a clear night.

Alerts now came night and day; clouds were no protection and daylight brought no relief. News reports were guarded, but on June 19 the *Daily Herald* reported that a church had been struck—this was the Guards' Chapel at Wellington Barracks near Buckingham Palace, struck at 11:20 A.M. during the singing of the Te Deum of a Sunday service. The bomb fell almost vertically onto the roof, which collapsed instantly along with heavy concrete girders; 120 were killed, about half of them civilians. In the period June 19–July 3 an average of 100 flying bombs every twenty-four hours was reported. Somewhat more than half reached London; the others were brought down by anti-aircraft guns, fighter planes, or the balloon barrage. Sixteen hundred persons were killed and 200,000 homes damaged. Total casualties were as high as in September 1940, though the proportion killed was much less. By mid-August the Govern-

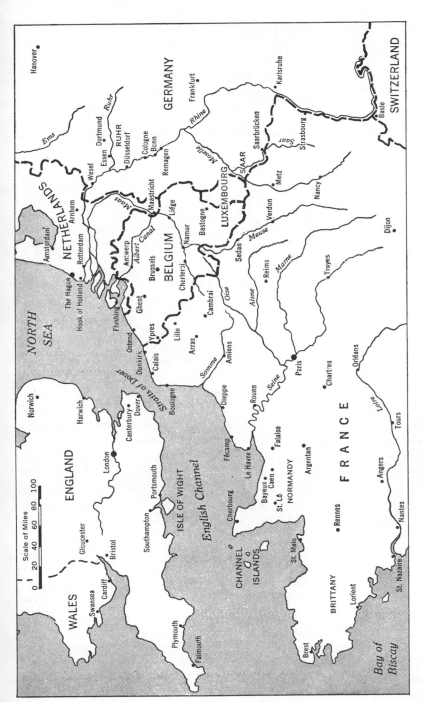

Map 4   Western Theater of Operations

ment had evacuated about 275,000 persons, mostly children and their mothers, from the London area, and it was estimated that well over 1,000,000 others left privately. German radio reported that London life was demoralized; actually no essential services were curtailed. Countermeasures, after a slow start, became effective with changes in the deployment of anti-aircraft guns and new radar devices. Of bombs sighted, the rate of their destruction rose from about 40 percent to about 80 percent by August. Altogether less than a quarter of the bombs directed at London ever reached the city. By September 5 the launching sites in northeastern France were in Allied hands, ending the important phase of the V-1s. By then the casualties were 5,475 killed and 15,918 seriously injured. Every London borough was hit, but the area south of the Thames suffered the brunt of the attack.

The War in France

The Allied invasion of Normandy was having its own vicissitudes. The initial phases of Overlord went well. On D-day, from west to east along the shores of the Bay of the Seine, the American forces landed at "Utah" and "Omaha" beaches and the British at "Gold," "Juno," and "Sword" beaches. By nightfall of the second day 250,000 troops were ashore, and a week later they had connected their beachheads and had moved inland on a sixty-mile front. Then there were setbacks. On the nineteenth "the worst June gale in forty years" struck the Channel. Two artificial harbors (the "Mulberries"), one at Arromanches and the other ten miles to the west, installed to assist landing of supplies, were rendered temporarily all but useless. Reinforcements and supplies fell far behind schedule and operations came to a standstill. Caen, a pivotal area blocking the way to Paris, was buttressed by the Germans. Cherbourg was finally taken by the Americans on June 26, but the port and quays could not be used for some days. The "*bocage* country" of Normandy—small fields separated by ditches, banks, and hedges—proved extremely difficult for artillery and tanks.

There were still differences in high-level planning. After Rome was taken (June 4) the British commander, General Alexander, said the Po Valley would be occupied by August. It was proposed to extend the Italian campaign into Istria and then penetrate the Ljubljana Gap toward the Danube as an alternative to Anvil, the invasion of southern France which had been reinstated as a late summer operation. Since resources would not permit both enterprises, General Wilson, the Allied commander in the Mediterranean, recommended that Anvil be dropped. Churchill promptly reopened the question in London, only to have Eisenhower, with the backing of the Joint (American) Chiefs of Staff, intervene in favor of Anvil, if resources permitted, as providing support in the decisive theater—France. But Churchill persisted in a telegram to Roosevelt on July 1. The president replied the next day. Anvil, he said, could not be abandoned without consulting Stalin: "At Teheran we agreed upon a definite plan of attack. That plan has gone well so far. Nothing has occurred to require any change.... My dear friend, I beg you let us go ahead with our plan." The British gave way but Churchill continued to sputter at home. He wrote, July 6: "Let us at least have a chance to launch a decisive strategic stroke with what is entirely British and under British command. I am not going to give way about this for anybody. Alexander is to have his campaign." But in good time he went to the Mediterranean to watch the assault that he had opposed. It came off on the scheduled day, August 15. After bypassing Toulon and Marseilles (taken later), the Allied forces swept up the Rhone Valley. By September 11 they were close to Dijon and on the fringe of territory held by the U.S. Third Army.

In the meantime, in July, a "breakout" had been achieved in Normandy. The supply crisis ended, at least for the time being. A series of operations was set in motion when the American forces broke out at St. Lô on July 25 and a strong tank attack under General Patton pushed south into Brittany. German armor still held the British and Canadians at Caen. But in August failure of a German counterthrust to the west, with a view to reaching the sea, thus cutting Patton's communications and splitting his forces, was followed by elaborate flanking movements by American and British-Canadian forces resulting in the partial envelopment of the German Seventh Army in the "Falaise Pocket," and Anglo-American forces destroyed or captured a host of the enemy in the closing weeks of the Battle of Normandy. It had been decided to bypass Paris—the city had no strategic value—and to force its surrender without a battle, but word reached Eisenhower's headquarters that it would not be defended. And so General Leclerc and the 2nd French Armored Division led the Allied march into the city on the morning of August 25. De Gaulle, whose Committee of National Liberation had been recognized in July by the Allies as the *de facto* civil authority in France, set up headquarters in the War Ministry. By September 6 Eisenhower's line (with British units in the north, American in Lorraine) extended from Antwerp to Namur, then south to Metz, and then west to Orléans and Nantes. Everywhere the Germans seemed to be on the run. The end of the war in Europe was "within sight, almost within reach," says the Intelligence Summary of Eisenhower's headquarters dated August 26.

Political and Strategic Problems

Diplomats and statesmen were striving to reach political decisions in pace with these fast-moving military events. In August

and September representatives of the Big Four Powers met at Dumbarton
Oaks, an estate near Washington, D.C., to implement the Moscow declaration of October 1943 concerning a permanent international organization. Some decisions were fairly easy. In the Security Council of the new
organization each of the Great Powers was to have the power to veto, but
in the General Assembly of all member nations unanimity was not to be
required. A Social and Economic Council, responsible to the General
Assembly, was to be created. However, when the United States suggested
that all nations be invited to join, Gromyko (the Russian delegate) asked
for separate representation for each of the sixteen republics of the Soviet
Union. Nor would Russia accept a British proposal that no Great Power
should exercise the power of veto in a dispute in which she was a party.
The Russians quite naturally feared the consequences "of their isolation
in a capitalist and potentially hostile world."

On September 11 Churchill and Roosevelt with their advisers, all fairly
sanguine of an early German collapse, gathered in Quebec. For the first
time a plan of campaign reconciled the American desire to get control of
roads and airfields in northern Burma in order to aid China with the
British concern for the reconquest of central Burma and Malaya. The
United States accepted the offer of the British fleet for Pacific campaigns
after the German war. British and American zones of occupation in
Germany were established. Lend-lease was to continue after Germany's
defeat to assist rebuilding of British industry. But the Americans rejected
the suggestion that assault craft be allocated for possible landings in the
Adriatic, and Roosevelt refused to discuss policy in eastern Europe until
after the presidential election.

Again Churchill was frustrated. He had not yet abandoned designs of
extending the Italian campaign toward Vienna, and he hoped to find a
way out of the political morass in eastern Europe, where the Russian
forces, larger than the combined Anglo-American armies in Europe, were
moving steadily west—by September they were well into Latvia and
Lithuania, were into Poland to the Vistula and beyond, and had overrun
Romania. Churchill told the Commons (August 2) that "it is the Russian
armies who have done the main work in tearing the guts out of the
German Army." And after the Quebec Conference he said to the Commons (September 28):

> Territorial changes on the frontiers of Poland there will have to be.
> Russia has the right to our support in this matter . . .; they are entitled
> to safe frontiers . . . . All the more do I trust that the Soviet Govern-
> ment will make it possible for us to act unitedly with them in the
> solution of the Polish problem, and that we shall not witness the un-
> happy spectacle of rival Governments in Poland, one recognized by
> the Soviet Union and the other firmly adhered to by the Western
> Powers.

For in August outlines of the Polish question were revealed. As the Russian forces approached the Vistula, the underground Polish Resistance in Warsaw rose August 1 against the Germans in control of the city. Despite urgent pleas from Churchill and Roosevelt, Stalin refused his assistance and turned his armies south to Romania—for military reasons, he said. But it was self-evident that he had no desire to support the cause of the pro-western Polish Government in exile, established in London, to which the Polish Resistance owed allegiance. Rather he had already set up in Lublin on July 23, the day the Russians took that city, a Communist-controlled Committee of National Liberation. To that group the crushing of the Resistance in Warsaw by the Germans, with enormous loss of life, was not disagreeable.

And so Churchill now "felt acutely the need to see Stalin, with whom I always considered one could talk as one human being to another." With the foreign secretary, Eden, he went to Moscow in October. Stalin seemed sympathetic to proposals of British landings in Istria, and he was ready to make a "deal" on the Balkans. It was informally agreed that Russian influence was to predominate in Romania and Bulgaria, and British influence to predominate in Greece, while the two nations were to share evenly in the affairs of Yugoslavia and Hungary. (Churchill in his report to the War Cabinet added that this was only an "interim guide" for the immediate future and was no attempt "to set up a rigid system of spheres of interests.") But on Poland Stalin would give no satisfaction either as to frontiers or as to the nature of its new Government. He also insisted that the "political aspects" of Russian participation in the far eastern war would have to be clarified and that Russian claims in Manchuria and Sakhalin must be recognized. He went into no detail. But on the whole, Churchill found the conference encouraging. He told the Commons, October 27, "Our relations with Soviet Russia were never more close, intimate and cordial than they are at the present time."

But Germany did not collapse and the autumn and winter brought some of the most serious problems of the war. In Greece quite unforeseen complications arose in the course of "liberation." When the Germans withdrew in October, a small British force landed and the Greek Government returned to Athens from Cairo. Churchill sought to strengthen the non-Communist forces, but his efforts to disband the guerrilla armies which included Communist elements failed, and fighting broke out between the British and the Greeks. In a short time sixty thousand British troops were on hand. Eventually, at the end of December, Churchill and Eden flew to Athens and, perhaps because Stalin left them a free hand, were able to bring about a temporary settlement. Archbishop Damaskinos of Athens was established as regent for the exiled King George II. This episode brought much criticism on Churchill and lowered his prestige. It seemed to many in both Britain and America that in Greece, as in Italy (where the British Government disapproved of Count Sforza as foreign minister) and in Belgium (where British troops prevented Communists from demonstrating), Churchill had supported the conservative, even the reactionary, groups against "the people." He easily survived a vote of confidence in Parliament, but only 23 of 172 Labor members supported his policy and some Conservatives abstained from voting.

German Counterattacks

On the evening of September 8, 1944, Londoners heard "a sharp report like a clap of thunder." The first rocket had struck at Cheswick, killing three persons. The ballistic missile known as the V-2 traveled at an enormous speed (4,000 miles an hour), moved in a parabola through the stratosphere, and struck without warning with tremendous penetrating power. The immediate area of a hit was devastated but the total area of damage was much more restricted than with the V-1. The British high command had followed the construction of the rocket, and the R.A.F. in August 1943 had successfully struck at the experimental station at Peenemünde on an island in the Baltic and later damaged storage and launching areas in northern France, delaying the use of the weapon. When the Allies overran northern France during the summer of 1944, the Germans were forced to move launching sites to Holland, twice the distance from London. Nevertheless, the attack was severe; until the end of November an average of six rockets reached London daily. All told, out of 1,403 rockets launched, about 1,100 reached the United Kingdom, about half in the London area. Approximately 2,700 civilians were killed.

On the military fronts proper in the early autumn of 1944 there was no occasion for elation. In northern Italy the Allies did not have a sufficient preponderance to break through the mountain barrier into the Lombard Plain; any immediate prospect of driving through Istria to Vienna was dim. In western Europe the Allied forces by September had far outrun their supplies and were unable to capitalize on their rapid advance across France and carry the war promptly into Germany. The Germans were afforded sufficient time to organize a new line of defense based on the Siegfried Line. The German success in repelling the British attack across the Lower Rhine at Arnhem in mid-September, the long delays in opening the approaches from the sea to Antwerp and thus solving the Allied supply problem, and the failure of American forces to make any significant advance toward the Rhine, either above or below the Ardennes, dispelled any illusion that the war would be over by Christmas.

Even so, no initiative was expected from the Germans. On December 15, Mongomery sent this message to his subordinates in the 21st Army Group: "The enemy is at present fighting a defensive campaign on all fronts; his situation is such that he cannot stage major offensive operations." General Bradley in Verdun had the same notion. But allied intelligence had failed. On December 16 the Germans struck with twenty-eight divisions (including panzer and parachute divisions) through the Ardennes, thinly held along a seventy-five-mile front by four divisions of the American Third Army. Hitler hoped for a psychological coup which would demoralize and perhaps divide the Allies. If it were successful they might be driven back to the Meuse, and Brussels and Antwerp would be threatened. Hitler did achieve complete surprise, and in the "Battle of the Bulge" German forces created a huge salient in the Allied line north of Luxembourg. By the nineteenth, their leading columns were approaching Liége and Namur. As a precautionary measure Eisenhower ordered a coordinated defense along the line of the Meuse to be prepared by the various Allied armies under Bradley and Montgomery. However, the German advance was contained. Along the southern flank American units, though isolated, held out against great odds at Bastogne until Patton's Third U.S. Army was able to stage a counterattack. At the same time, Montgomery, temporarily in command of all Allied troops north of the Bulge, held firm against the threat toward Liége and Namur and prepared a counterattack. By December 24 the German advance had been stayed in all sectors, the weather improved, and the Allied air forces were again in action; by Christmas Day the crisis was past. Ten days later the Germans were falling back steadily under Montgomery's counterattack; it was estimated that they suffered casualties of 120,000 and left 600 tanks in Allied hands. Also, Stalin had given assurance of a Russian offensive along the entire central front by the latter part of January; it actually began on January 12.

Following the liberation of Paris, Montgomery had strongly recommended a sharp thrust on a narrow sector directed toward the Ruhr, but Eisenhower ordered instead a more methodical advance toward the Rhine on a broad front from the North Sea to the Saar. (He had, of course, approved Montgomery's thrust to the north at Arnhem in September.) On December 12, according to Field Marshal Sir Alan Brooke, the British chief of staff, Eisenhower jolted the British with the remark that he did not hope to cross the Rhine before June. The German attack through the Ardennes, though repulsed, left the British high command pessimistic. Victory had been expected in 1944; now with depleted resources Britain faced the prospect of a war that might continue through 1945. The Bulge offered Montgomery yet another opportunity to stress his own ideas and to cast some doubts on the wisdom of Eisenhower's decisions, doubts shared by Brooke. One of the problems, according to a British version, was the obscurity with which Eisenhower in January outlined his plans for the Combined (British and American) Chiefs of

Staff. On closer examination it proved possible, though only after some show of temper on both sides, to reconcile the strategic aims of the British and the Americans. At Malta (January 30–February 2) the Combined Chiefs of Staff found that Eisenhower's report, when clarified and reworded, was acceptable. Eisenhower declared that he was prepared to "seize the Rhine crossings in the north just as soon as this is a feasible operation and without waiting to close the Rhine throughout its length." The British considered they had finally achieved their aim—concentration of the attack in the north—though an American account is that the Americans at the time considered it a victory for Eisenhower.

The Big Three at Yalta

Malta was preliminary to the Big Three Conference of heads of state, foreign ministers, chiefs of staff, and a host of supporting personnel (about seven hundred altogether in the British and American delegations) at Yalta in the Crimea, February 4–11, 1945. The plenary meetings were held in the Livadia Palace of the Tsars. The important issues were political, but the atmosphere was charged with military imperatives. Western leaders felt that a continuation of the Russian offensive was essential to an early end of the war in Europe. As the conference opened, the Red Army was occupying industrial Poland, as Stalin took pains to point out. In the Far East, Japan was far from defeated. The bitter fighting for the Philippines—six months of it—was still ahead. No landing had yet been made on the Japanese archipelago. It was calculated that even with Russian help the Japanese war would extend eighteen months beyond the European war.

Political decisions on the Far East came, almost incidentally, out of military discussions and out of some informal discussions between Roosevelt and Stalin. In return for entrance into the Japanese war, Russia was to recover rights and territories lost in 1905, was to acquire the Kurile Islands, and was to be assured of the continued autonomy of Outer Mongolia. This agreement was kept strictly secret, for termination of an existing Russo-Japanese neutrality treaty required three months' notice. Because of the notorious lack of security at Chungking, Chiang Kai-shek was not even consulted.

Churchill argued the case of the western Allies for a strong independent Poland. British interest, he said, "is only one of honor." Stalin moved from strength—the Russo-German boundary of September 1939 and Russian military occupation. "For Russia," he said, "it is not only a question of honor but also of security." For Poland's eastern boundary he was prepared to accept the Curzon Line, drawn up in 1919—a line somewhat less favorable than that of September 1939, though it left Lwów and the Galician oil lands in Russian hands. This boundary with slight modification was accepted without much difficulty by Churchill. Indeed, there was little alternative short of breaking up the alliance. The western boundary was left undetermined.

Poland's boundaries were in the last analysis less important than her form of government. Here the complication was that a "Government" in Lublin had been formally recognized (January 5, 1945) by Russia even though there was still in London the Government in exile. As we now see it, the formula agreed upon at Yalta was a masterpiece of ambiguity, declaring that the Lublin Committee of National Liberation should be reorganized to include "democratic" leaders from Poland itself and from Poles living abroad. The new "Provisional Government of National Unity" should be "pledged to the holding of free and unfettered elections as soon as possible on the basis of universal suffrage and secret ballot." If the formula left misgivings, Churchill and Roosevelt may have taken comfort from the "Declaration on Liberated Europe" in which the three powers agreed that "the establishment of order in Europe and re-building of national economic life must be achieved by processes which will enable the liberated peoples to destroy the last vestiges of Nazism and Fascism and to create democratic institutions of their own choice."

At Yalta the problem of the future of Germany was again pushed to one side, for military unity against Enemy No. 1 must not be jeopardized. Only immediate issues were settled. Occupation zones were confirmed, with France to have a zone. An Allied Control Council of commanders-in-chief of the occupying forces would operate from Berlin, which would be a special zone under collective administration. The thorny question of reparations, vital to Stalin, was passed on to a reparations commission; and any definitive action on plans for "partitioning" Germany, which Stalin had been advocating since 1941, was postponed, though at Yalta both Churchill and Roosevelt accepted partition as a possibility.

Hope Mingled with Misgiving. At Yalta some of the difficulties encountered at Dumbarton Oaks were resolved. It was to insure Russian cooperation in the organization of the United Nations that Roosevelt had been willing to give way on the more immediate problems of peace terms. On voting in the Security Council, Stalin accepted a compromise proposal distinguishing between (1) resolutions concerning breaches of the peace or threats to peace, or United Nations action to suppress such threats, which would require a unanimous vote of the permanent members of the Council, and (2) resolutions for peaceful settlement of disputes, on which no member of the Council which was a party in the dispute should vote. And Stalin abandoned his earlier demand for separate membership of all sixteen of the republics of the Soviet Union.

American and British delegations returned home confident and even exuberant in the prospect of victory over Germany and a continuation, even in peace, of the Grand Alliance. It is impossible for us to blot out the intervening years. But Churchill does effectively parry criticism when he writes, "What would have happened if we had quarrelled with Russia while the Germans still had three or four hundred divisions on the fighting front? Our hopeful assumptions were soon to be falsified. Still, they were the only ones possible at the time." According to his correspondence with Roosevelt, Churchill went to Yalta with misgivings. To what extent its proceedings restored his confidence in Russia is difficult to say; it is likely that any such confidence was qualified. He reported to the Commons, February 27, that the decision on the Russo-Polish frontier was in complete accord with British Government views. He had supported the Russian claim to the Curzon Line because that claim "is just and right." But he seemed deliberately to avoid looking into the future. He had returned, he said, with the impression "that Marshal Stalin and the Soviet leaders wish to live in honorable friendship and equality with the western democracies.... I decline absolutely to embark here on a discussion about Russian good faith.... Sombre indeed would be the fortunes of mankind if some awful schism arose between the western democracies and the Russian Soviet Union."

Churchill's report received general approval. Harold Nicolson declared that Russia had made real concessions and that Yalta was "without question the most important political agreement that we have gained in the war." However, a minority group strongly criticized the Polish settlement, and twenty-five members, mostly Conservatives, voted against the Government on the formal motion to approve Yalta. The issue, dimly realized, was the continuation of British influence in eastern Europe. Captain Thorneycroft approached this question when he said, "The real difficulty is in the apparent conflict between documents like the Atlantic Charter and the facts of the European situation."

The "facts" soon asserted themselves. Churchill's "fifty-fifty" understanding with Stalin on Yugoslavia came to naught. After Tehran the British had abandoned Mikhailovitch and his Chetniks and supported Tito and the Partisans. But with the advance of the Red armies into the Balkans in the autumn of 1944, Tito drew closer to Russia. He would not permit British landings on the Dalmatian coast, nor did he make any real effort to reach an agreement with the Yugoslav Government in London over the future of the monarchy. He emerged as master and signed a treaty of alliance with Russia in April 1945. In Romania, King Michael, who had collaborated with Russia since the invasion of August 1944, was forced by direct pressure from Moscow to reorganize his Government under Communist leadership in March 1945. And in Poland the Russians made no effort to harmonize the Lublin Government with the Government in exile, which soon repudiated the whole Yalta settlement. On the other hand, Russian suspicions were aroused that her allies, in order to gain advantage in the Balkans, were negotiating a separate military surrender in Italy (March and April). Similarly, suspicions of a separate arrangement with the Nazis developed in the final weeks of the European war when the Russian forces met with much greater resistance than did the western Allies. It was hardly strange, therefore, that delegates came to the San Francisco Conference, April 25–June 26, in a strained mood. The Charter of the United Nations was drafted and adopted amid prolonged argument over problems of membership, interpretations of the Yalta decision on the "veto power" in the Security Council, and international trusteeship of dependent territories. Anthony Eden, as foreign secretary, led the British delegation. He tells us later that during the conference he and Churchill "exchanged telegrams of foreboding as the Russian mood and methods became increasingly disquieting."

Victory in Europe

The atmosphere of gloom in military circles after the Battle of the Bulge and the attitude of caution in which western leaders went to Yalta are eloquent testimony that scarcely anyone in January 1945 anticipated that the end of the European war was close at hand. Pessimism was particularly strong among English and American air commanders, who concluded that their vast superiority was not bringing decisive results.

But the London Blitz was a trifle compared to the terrific punishment meted out to German cities toward the end of the war. For the allied high command had decided that, in the interest of an early end to hostilities and total victory, civilian areas must suffer as much as industrial. "Blind bombing" devices had now been perfected for use on the high percentage of days when visible bombing was impossible. In spite of poor flying conditions, February witnessed the greatest concentration of strategic bombing since the month before D-day. Raids of over 1,000 bombers were directed at Berlin (in one attack at least 25,000 were killed). During February and March, attacks were deliberately made on Dresden's civilian population. The R.A.F. attacked at night, and when American aircraft arrived the next day to continue the job, smoke was still rising to a height of 15,000 feet. No one really knows the death toll in these raids on Dresden—one authority places it at 135,000. Similar assaults were made on Magdeburg, Chemnitz, Regensburg, and Augsburg. In weight of bombs, the heaviest raids of the war came on successive nights in March, when 1,100 R.A.F. bombers deposited nearly 5,000 tons of explosive on Essen and Dortmund. The heaviest daylight attack was directed at Berlin, March 18, when 1,250 American bombers escorted by fighters dropped 3,000 tons of explosive. Strategic bombing ended April 16. The aims of the Casablanca directive had finally been achieved. Throughout the Reich, oil production had ceased, and airplanes, tanks, and trucks could scarcely move. Railway transportation was slowing to a halt. Allied armies moving across the Rhine found that industrial Germany had been destroyed.

Meanwhile, Montgomery's offensive on the northern flank had opened February 8 with a view to crushing German resistance west of the Rhine. Floods slowed the advance. In the center, units of Bradley's 12th Army Group reached the Rhine March 7 and, using the Remagen bridge, which the Germans had not destroyed, quickly established themselves on the east bank. Before the end of the month, other American forces had crossed the Rhine down to Switzerland. In the north, a crossing was eventually made March 23 at Wesel, where the river is 500 yards wide, "in the largest and most difficult operation undertaken since the Normandy landings," says Eisenhower's official report. It "sealed the fate of Germany." Now, in a week's time, the final phase of the master plan took form; a pincers movement surrounded the Ruhr. When the final garrison surrendered on April 18, about 325,000 German prisoners were in Allied hands. By then the battle front had moved to the line of Bremen-Magdeburg-Leipzig-Czechoslovakian border.

The Russians captured Vienna on April 13 and driving across Germany met American forces at Torgau, on the Elbe north of Dresden, on April 25. Berlin was encircled. On April 30 Hitler presumably committed suicide in the bunker of the Chancellery; the city fell to the Russians two days later. On April 29 the German commander in Italy surrendered to General Alexander; on May 5 German units directly to the north capitulated to the American commander, General Devers. That same day a German delegation at Lüneberg, Montgomery's headquarters, signed an agreement for the surrender of all German forces in the northwest. On the seventh, at 2:41 A.M., General Jodl, representing the German high command, signed at Reims (Eisenhower's headquarters) an unconditional surrender of all German forces. The next day at Russian insistence this ceremony was repeated in Berlin.

In the midst of these events President Roosevelt died at Warm Springs, Georgia, on April 12. Churchill in his eulogy told the Commons that during the war he and the president had met nine times in 120 days of close contact and had exchanged more than 1,700 messages. Churchill, a personification of courage himself, dwelt on Roosevelt's physical fortitude and referred to him as "the greatest American friend we have ever known, and the greatest champion of freedom who has ever brought help and comfort from the new world to the old."

Britain celebrated May 8 as Victory-in-Europe Day. After his customary Tuesday lunch with the king, Churchill at a brief session of the House of Commons formally announced the victory, and then, just as Lloyd George had done in 1918, he led his fellow members across the road to the parish church of Westminster for "a service of thanksgiving." At its conclusion, the official parliamentary account reads, "the bells of St. Margaret's Church were rung, in celebration of Victory." That day the royal family made eight appearances on the balcony of Buckingham Palace to greet the crowds assembled below. In the evening the "dim-out" of the last few months was replaced by floodlights, as the crowds, with the royal princesses among them, swarmed through the Mall, Whitehall, Trafalgar, and Piccadilly. On the thirteenth the king and queen attended a service of thanksgiving in St. Paul's, and on the sixteenth a similar service in St. Giles' Cathedral in Edinburgh.

Potsdam: A Crumbling Alliance

The final wartime conference of the Allies, and easily the least satisfactory, was held at Potsdam, July 17–August 2. Hitler, "the principal architect of the Grand Alliance," was gone. Military necessities gave way to political realities. Churchill's worst fears were realized: the United States wished to get out of Europe. At Yalta Roosevelt had said plainly to Stalin that the United States would not undertake to maintain occupation troops in Europe more than two years beyond Germany's defeat. American policy counted on the solution of postwar problems through the new United Nations Organization. Relief to war-torn areas would be provided by UNRRA (United Nations Relief and Rehabilitation Administration), established in 1943. At the same time, all notion of a peace of vengeance calculated to destroy German industrial potential had now departed, for both President Truman and the new secretary of state (James Byrnes) sought a reconstructed Germany and at the same time were inclined to be less conciliatory toward Russia than Roosevelt had been.

As for Britain, Churchill still hoped to recover some of her fast-waning prestige in eastern Europe, but the country as a whole was now primarily concerned with the problems of her postwar economy. The Labor electoral victory, announced in July, with a transfer of power from Churchill to Attlee at Potsdam, did not alter British policy, but it is a measure of Britain's changing perspective. Russia, that is to say Stalin, wished to continue the wartime alliance solely to exploit the victory over Germany—to strengthen her own national security, to reconstruct her industry and agriculture by drawing heavily on German resources and to secure western recognition of the Soviet-sponsored "peoples democracies" in eastern Europe.

There is considerable controversy over the meaning of Yalta; there is little over the meaning of Potsdam. Its code name, Terminal, is mocking. It was, in effect, the beginning of the "cold war." Such accomplishments as there were, were ambiguous. In accordance with recommendations from the European Advisory Council, a statement of policy on the occupation of Germany was issued, but in language permitting each of the occupying powers to act upon its own interpretation. A compromise agreement was reached on reparations—but again in uncertain language. Each occupying power was to exact reparations from its own zone, saving a minimum of resources and equipment necessary for maintaining a standard of life equivalent to that of other countries in western Europe. And Russia was to be given one-quarter of the industrial reparations exacted in the western zones of occupation.

Poland's western boundary was a subject of prolonged argument. Stalin wished to include large portions of German Pomerania and German Silesia (since their military occupation by the Russians these territories had been administered by the Polish Provisional Government in Lublin and Warsaw). Finally it was agreed that, pending settlement of frontiers at a peace conference, the disputed territory in the west would be placed under the interim administration of Poland. Subsequently, both Russia and Poland acted on the assumption that the powers at Potsdam had agreed in principle on establishing Poland's western frontier on the Oder and Western Neisse rivers, with the Stettin area to the west of the Oder included in Poland. On the other matters at Potsdam—the nature of Tito's Government in Yugoslavia, the character of the new regimes in other Balkan states and in Finland, the distribution of German merchant and naval vessels and the fate of Italian colonies—there was nothing but embittered controversy.

In Britain few illusions survived Potsdam. Churchill found no alternative to accepting, at least for the time being, the arrangements of Yalta and Potsdam on eastern and middle Europe: "We British have had very early and increasingly to recognize the limitations of our own power and influence, great though it be, in the gaunt world arising from the ruins of this hideous war." The new foreign secretary, Ernest Bevin, was no more optimistic. Concerning the chunk of German territory (one-quarter of her arable land) to be transferred to Poland, he said, "There was a kind of vacuum from which the Germans had been driven."

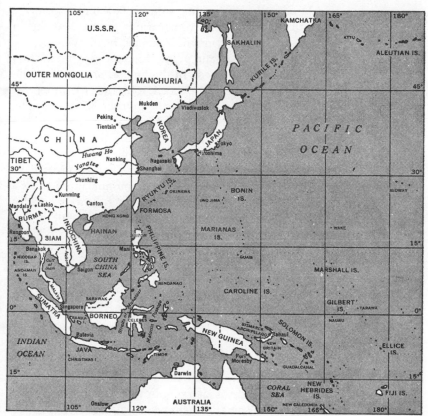

Map 5   Far Eastern Theater of Operations

Victory in Asia

In the Far East, the war's end came with even greater speed. In the China-Burma-India area victory seemed, in 1943–44, quite remote. But behind the Japanese lines in Burma, General Wingate's raiders, or "Chindits," maintained exclusively by air, played havoc with the enemy rear and very likely forestalled a Japanese drive into India. The new Ledo Road from India to North Burma (where it connected with the Burma Road to China) while under construction was covered by Allied armies, especially by Chinese forces under General Stilwell. Japanese offensives from central Burma towards India, designed to cut off Allied forces in North Burma, failed. These events were in 1944. In the spring of 1945 came the climax, with the plans outlined at Quebec the previous September bearing fruit. In February Mountbatten received a new directive, with liberation of Burma as his immediate assignment. The reconquest was a colossal undertaking involving some 500,000 men in several armies moving toward central Burma from various points near the Indian frontier, grappling with problems of distance, heat, swamps, and disease. The Irrawaddy River (at certain points several times the width of the Rhine at Wesel), had to be crossed. In the final phase, as the Allies were closing in on Rangoon, a sea-borne attack took the city unopposed on May 3, only a matter of hours ahead of the monsoon. Mountbatten then directed his attention to Singapore and Malaya.

At the same time American operations in the Pacific were being crowned with success. The critical naval battle of Leyte Gulf, October 29, 1944, in the center of the Philippine archipelago—the last great naval engagement in which naval guns were of paramount importance—eliminated the Japanese Navy as a threat. Landings followed on Mindanao in December and on Luzon in January, with Manila falling February 23. In the direction of the Japanese homeland, island hopping carried American forces to Iwo Jima, in February, and to Okinawa, in April, where a British carrier task force participated. After Okinawa was finally subdued, June 21, a target date of November 1 was set for the next objective, Kyushu, the most southerly of the main Japanese islands, only 450 miles distant. But scarcely anyone expected final victory over Japan until well into 1946.

With the end of the European war the Allied high command turned its attention exclusively to the Far East. The British recognized that the Americans should determine strategy in the Pacific. The British themselves were to continue in control of operations of a Southeast Asia Command, now enlarged. This arrangement was harmonious, in contrast to conflicts over operations in Southeast Asia earlier in the war. Russia committed herself to an offensive in Manchuria in the latter part of August. China was to all practical purposes ignored. In effect, each of the Great Powers was to act independently. Even in military matters the Grand Alliance was breaking up.

The arrangements among the Allies for an offensive against Japan never came off. On July 26 Truman, Churchill, and Chiang Kai-shek issued an ultimatum to Japan for unconditional surrender of all armed forces. "The alternative for Japan is complete and utter destruction." After consultation with the British, the Americans, on August 6, dropped an atomic bomb on Hiroshima, killing 77,000; on August 9 another bomb fell on Nagasaki. That same day Russian forces moved into Manchuria. On August 14 the Japanese agreed to unconditional surrender. On September 12 in the Council chamber at Singapore Lord Mountbatten received the surrender of Japanese forces (738,000 in all) in Southeast Asia. A formal capitulation of all Japanese forces had taken place on the U.S.S. *Missouri* in Tokyo Bay on September 2. This may be considered as officially ending the war.

For Britain the conflict lasted one day short of six years. In its course about 300,000 members of the armed forces of the United Kingdom lost their lives. Civilian casualties at home numbered 61,000 killed and 86,000 seriously injured, about half of these casualties occurring in the London area. The merchant marine lost 35,000 seamen and half of its tonnage. Of Britain's 13,000,000 homes nearly 500,000 were destroyed or rendered uninhabitable by enemy action, and about 4,000,000 others were severely damaged.

Such statistics are realistic—consequences of the war which bore on all Britishers to a degree. But as one draws further and further away in time, one's mind turns to less transient considerations. The war, we feel, should be put in perspective, in English history and, indeed, in the history of Western civilization. One approach, "inspired by an American's affection for England," is represented by Herbert Agar's *Britain Alone* (1972). He writes: "From June 22, 1940 when the Germans accepted the French petition for an armistice, until June 22, 1941 when Hitler invaded Russia, there was only Britain to save the West." Without being unduly partisan or nationalistic or ideological, the student in the Western world, still in the role of historian, may soberly ponder the consequences for the English-speaking world of a German victory. Surely the overriding consequence of World War II, as we now view it, was the defeat of Nazism and Fascism.

Inevitably historians compare the impact of World War I on Britain with the impact of World War II and not always with the same conclusions. We encounter sweeping generalizations: "The first world war caused a social and economic upheaval . . .Great though these changes were, the results of the second world war altered British society even more profoundly." (Francis Boyd, *British Politics in Transition 1945–63*, 1964). But there would seem to be more support for Henry Pelling's view (*Britain and the Second World War*, 1970) that the second war had much less impact on the British mind than did the first. The second war was taken in stride, for it was in a very real sense a "people's war"—the British people did, in fact, win this war. As to the effect of World War II on the economy, on society, on political structure, the answers are not self-evident. Pelling thinks that in their essentials, British society and economy were not much affected. Angus Calder (*The People's War: Britain 1939–45*, 1969) concludes that "the grooves of change" had long since been determined, with the war years merely accelerating the rate of change. A more challenging interpretation comes from Arthur Marwick (*Britain in the Century of Total War*, 1968) whose theme of "War, peace and social change 1900–1967" becomes something of a crusade. A representative declaration is

> The development of British society in the five years after the Second
> World War was primarily determined by the cost, economic and
> political, of victory, by the immense range of internal influences and
> cross currents set off by the war, and by the advent to power of a
> political party committed by origin to the interests of the working
> class and by philosophy to a belief in the power of the State to guide
> and control social and economic forces.

In such discussions we find the English once again preoccupied with the Emerald Isle, slow to comprehend that the world outside was being transformed, with results decisive for Britain's future. In the chapters ahead we shall, of course, be interested in Britain's fortunes at home, but we shall be increasingly aware that she has to a very considerable degree ceased to be the master of her own fate. So we shall return again and again to Britain's status as a national power in a changing world, to her role in Western Europe, to the meaning and relevance of any "special relationship" with the United States, to her efforts to replace Empire with Commonwealth, and to the strength of her economy in an ever more competitive world. These are essential to an understanding of the nature of the "transition" in Britain's fortunes in the twentieth century.

Socialist Britain and Welfare State

A. A. Rogow
The Labour Government and British Industry, 1945–1951 (1955), pp. 2–3

In point of fact, the policy of neither of the major parties is characterized by purity of doctrine. Thus, in 1945 the policies and programme of the Labour Government were, to a large extent, inherited from the war-time, Conservative-dominated Coalition Government, and similarly, the present Conservative Government has retained intact most of the legislative changes wrought by its predecessor.

Ernest Bevin presenting the text of the North Atlantic Pact to the Commons, March 18, 1949. Hansard, *Parl. Debates*, House of Commons, 5th ser., vol. 462, cols. 2535–36

The object and purpose of this pact is to make a real beginning, on the widest possible basis, of collective security in its true sense, and we hope that political conditions may become such that this collective security system may, if understanding can be arrived at, be expanded to cover the whole world.... This is the first time that the United States have ever felt able to contemplate entering into commitments in peace-time for joint defence with Europe, and it is a most famous, historical undertaking into which they are now entering with the rest of us.

1945–1951

The surrender of Germany and Japan in 1945 introduced one of the most crowded and perhaps one of the most significant periods in English history, a short span of six years in which the course of events and the decisions reached would determine the character of British society and the role of Britain in the world for the foreseeable future. Both intensive and extensive coverage are, therefore, justified. In certain respects it was a dynamic period: a legislative drive made nationalization, within limits, a policy of state; the "welfare state" emerged as the consensus of the British people; the British Raj in India ground to its end; and the mandate in Palestine abruptly ceased. In other areas—in the economy, in foreign relations and in Commonwealth policy—change was more halting, more tentative, and often more reluctant.

The "Revolution" of 1945

On July 25, 1945, in the midst of the Potsdam Conference, Churchill and Attlee returned to London for the counting of the ballots cast in the general election on July 5—the counting had been delayed to permit time for assembling the service vote. On July 28, Attlee, but not Churchill, went back to Potsdam, for Attlee was now prime minister. His party had won the election by a landslide, electing 393 members of Parliament, against 189 for the Conservatives. A week later, the *Eco-*

nomist commented, "The country has hardly yet recovered from its astonishment at what it did on July 5." Churchill, it would seem, never did fully recover. He later wrote of the power he exercised "for five years and three months of world war, at the end of which time, all our enemies having surrendered unconditionally or being about to do so, I was immediately dismissed by the British electorate from all further conduct of their affairs."

This transfer of power, so overwhelmingly endorsed, came abruptly, inasmuch as the war coalition at the very moment of its dissolution appeared to be at the height of its prestige. But Labor's victory in 1945 is not to be associated with the spontaneous joy and relief which greeted V-E day; it is, rather, to be understood only by probing political and social attitudes during the war years.

A significant indicator is the character of the parliamentary by-elections, which clearly reveal a substantial swing of voters to the left, and this despite the fact that the electoral register of March 1939 was still used. During the war there were 141 by-elections; of these, 66 were filled by the incumbent party without opposition, in accordance with the electoral truce among the three major parties. But in the other 75 polls there was opposition to the official candidate from some 104 other candidates running as Independents or as representatives of the new Commonwealth Party, founded in June 1942 by Sir Richard Acland, a member of a well-known Liberal family, now converted to evangelical Christianity and socialism. To this new party, political and social reform were essential to winning the war. Impetus came after the Government sidetracked the Beveridge report in 1942, and the seats of incumbents lost thereafter (16 of them) were largely a defeat of Conservatism. In general terms, the Independents and the Commonwealth Party represented a Labor or Liberal outlook. In these by-elections the swing away from the Conservatives varies but broadly upholds the polls of the British Institute of Public Opinion between June 1943 and June 1945 on voting intentions in the next general election which showed Labor leading by 7 to 18 percent. And *Mass Observation* repeatedly forecast that the next election would bring a Labor victory. That these signs of the times were little noticed merely indicates that professional study of voting behavior was then in its infancy.

An associated factor was the growing power and authority of radio broadcasting. During the war this medium had given currency to ideas of social and political change to a degree scarcely appreciated in any quarter. Reference has been made to Priestley's hold on the public through his broadcasts. By the end of 1943 "Brains Trust" had an audience of 29 percent of all over age sixteen—this remarkable program developed by Howard Thomas out of "Any Questions" and "Information Please" was "serious in intention, light in character" and made listeners "sit up and think." Those who were of a mind to ponder further found stimulus in E. H. Carr's remarkable articles on "Reconstruction" in *The Times*.

As for major party politics during the war, Labor kept a sharper eye on the future than did the Conservatives. Annually after October 1940, Prolongation Acts extended the Parliament elected in 1935, year after year. But Labor never contemplated continuing the coalition government beyond the emergency. In May 1941, Transport Office issued "Labor in Government: A Record of Social Legislation in Wartime." Labor was also looking ahead: "The Old World and a New Society" (1942) was a general statement of policy (though not a program of legislation) on postwar reconstruction. Thereafter a series of detailed reports set forth the Labor view on health, housing, land, transport, coal, employment, local government, and so on. In the debate in the autumn of 1944 over the bill extending the life of the existing Parliament still another year, it became fairly evident that with victory in Europe a new Parliament would be elected. In December the Labor Party Conference endorsed a statement of the National Executive of the party that "Labour's participation [in the Coalition] should continue just so long as ... it is necessary in the national interest and for fulfilling the purpose for which the Government was called into being."

On the other hand, the Conservative Party—perhaps in part because of its dominant position in the Government—made no effort prior to 1945 to redefine its policy or propagandize its views for the future. In March of 1945 a party conference adopted an electoral program stressing decontrol and a return to private enterprise. But Churchill, always more a national than a party figure, told the conference that if the Conservatives should win the approaching election and he should continue as leader of the party, he would seek an extension of non-party government. Shortly after V-E Day, addressing all parties in the Coalition, he suggested postponement of the election until after the end of the Japanese war. The alternative, he said, was immediate dissolution with the election in July. Clement Attlee, speaking with the overwhelming support of the Labor Party Conference then in session, rejected the idea of postponement, but along with Sinclair, Liberal Party leader, expressed a preference for an autumn election to permit time for servicemen to participate as candidates and as electors, and also to have available an up-to-date register of voters. In turn, Churchill rejected these counterproposals and, accordingly, resigned on May 23, with parliamentary dissolution announced for June 15. Polling was set for July 5, with the counting of the ballots to be delayed until July 26. The historians of this election tell of an Italian journalist who observed that there were few countries in Europe which would trust the Government to hold uncounted for twenty days ballots which might bring that Government to an end. During the interim period, the two months between May 23 and July 26, Churchill, by general agreement, presided over a "caretaker" Government.

The Election Campaign

We have in *The British General Election of 1945* (1947), written by R. B. McCallum and Alison Readman and sponsored by Nuffield College, Oxford, the first of a series of studies which we will use in analyzing postwar elections. A new science, "psephology," is around the corner.

The campaign really began in the House of Commons during the interim session. Attlee accused the Government of acting in self-interest in reducing the time customarily allowed before obtaining certain financial grants known as votes of supply. Arthur Greenwood, in attacking the Government for not dealing promptly and effectively with the land and the housing problems, found it not displeasing to return to the realm of controversy. He referred to Lord Woolton as "the Pooh Bah of the circus of ministers" concerned with reconstruction. But the strongest blast was from Emanuel Shinwell on a Labor request for an inquiry "into the ramifications and operations" of cartels and monopolies. He declared that "the principal monopolists of this country, directly or indirectly, are in His Majesty's Government," and designated Lord Beaverbrook, Oliver Lyttelton (president of the Board of Trade), and Lord Leathers (minister of war transport). A happier memory of this interim period is afforded by Hugh Dalton in his account of Churchill's "at home" at No. 10 on May 28. With tears streaming down his cheeks, the prime minister received the ministers (Tory, Labor, Liberal) of the war Coalition. "The light of history," he told them, "will shine on all your helmets."

The heart of the election campaign was a series of evening broadcasts, ten by the Conservatives, ten by Labor, and four by the Liberals. The B.B.C. estimated that the average listening audience was about 45 percent of the entire adult population, with Churchill's addresses attracting only slightly larger audiences than the others. Churchill's opening broadcast and Attlee's rejoinder were "pivotal events" which "exercised a profound influence," according to the election historians. Churchill, angry with the Opposition for insisting on breaking up the Coalition, was in a bellicose mood. After reproaching Labor as derelict in its patriotic duty, he launched into a diatribe against socialism:

> There can be no doubt that Socialism is inseparably interwoven with totalitarianism and the abject worship of the State . . . . Socialism is in its essence an attack not only upon British enterprise, but upon the right of an ordinary man or woman to breathe freely without having

a harsh, clumsy, tyrannical hand clapped across their mouth and nos-
trils. A free Parliament—look at that—a free Parliament is odious to
the Socialist doctrinaire.

And he dwelt on the horrible prospect of life under a totalitarian state
using "some sort of Gestapo."

The next evening, in a masterful reply, Attlee made the most of the
popular mood of amused skepticism left by this denunciation by Churchill of trusted colleagues in his war Government. The prime minister,
Attlee said, "wanted the electors to understand how great was the difference between Winston Churchill the great leader in war of a united
nation, and Mr. Churchill the party leader of the Conservatives," Herbert Morrison said, "Winston was having a night out."

On ideology Labor spokesmen proved the abler tacticians. They refused to take seriously the association of British socialism with Hitler and
Mussolini, and said flatly that Churchill did not mean what he said. And
when, in the second week of the campaign, the Conservatives raised the
"Laski issue"—they endeavored to exploit a remark attributed to Harold
Laski, Labor Party chairman, that if general consent did not bring Labor
what it sought, the party must turn to violence—Labor rather successfully brushed it aside as merely another Conservative effort to
frighten the country.

Clearly the outcome of the election did not hinge on the character and
success of the war coalition, a point on which so much of the Conservative campaign was focused. The ubiquitous photograph of Churchill carried the caption "Vote Nationalist—Help Him Finish the Job." It was a
somewhat irrelevant admonition, for the war effort was not a party
achievement. Churchill's prestige, great as it was, was limited to his role
as a war leader. Otherwise he was still distrusted, by many Conservatives
as well as by Laborites. And the Conservative Party as a whole was
finally held accountable for Britain's record at home and abroad in the
thirties.

But Laborite leadership no more than Conservative divined the mind
of the electorate. This was not directed at such little understood concerns
as foreign policy during and after the war, but rather at the manner of life
at home. What would the new government do—for employment, for
food and housing, for health and education, for social security? Housing,
for example—41 percent of those questioned in a public opinion poll on
June 11 listed it as the single most important issue of the campaign—
seems to have been of more concern than ideology, more important even
than personalities. On this same poll, full employment and social security
followed housing as important issues. On such matters the Conservatives
had no defined solutions. They spoke vaguely of full employment and a

prosperous land and denounced "planning" and "nationalization" as inconsistent with a free Britain. On the other hand, Labor's manifesto *Let Us face the Future* declared that "the People deserve and must be assured a happier future than faced so many of them after the last war." Legislation was proposed, designed to achieve an improved economic and social order through conscious planning and public control. But it may well be that the party campaigns did not seriously affect the outcome. A *News Chronicle* poll just before the campaign revealed that 84 percent of those questioned said they had already decided how they would vote.

Labor Landslide

The interval of three weeks between polling and the counting of the ballots was given over to cautious speculation. The great unknown was the vote to be cast for 307 Liberal condidates; this vote and that for Labor would divide the opposition to the Conservatives; the effect of the Liberal vote on the distribution of seats was impossible to forecast. The day before the ballots were counted, Churchill told the king that he expected a majority of thirty to eighty. Attlee, on the other hand, was apparently not at all confident. But the result—with almost 73 percent of the electorate voting, remarkable considering the unsettled state of voting registers and a limited service vote—was a tremendous victory for Labor. Returning 393 members to Parliament, Labor had a clear majority of 146 over all other parties and groups. Conservatives were reduced to 189, Liberals to 12, with 22 for Independents and minor groups. A factor in the Labor victory, worth noting, was the armed forces service vote. Discontent during the later years of the war is now registered in an estimated 90 percent of the service vote being recorded for Labor, with about 60 percent of those still in uniform included in the poll. It should also be noted that in one respect the "electoral system" magnified the Labor victory far beyond reality, for Labor in polling about 50 percent of the popular vote elected 61 percent of the new Commons. However, a more significant statistic is that the total popular vote for continuing the Churchill Government was about ten million, the total vote against about fifteen million. The national "swing" to Labor in relation to the previous general election (1935) was 12 percent. The Liberals were the real victims of this swing, since so much of the potential Liberal vote went Labor in order that the vote "not be wasted." Its defeated candidates included the party leader, Sir Archibald Sinclair, and Sir William Beveridge. Clement Davies now became leader of the Liberal Parliamentary Party.

By mid-afternoon on July 26, the broad results of the election were clear. Churchill acted with unprecedented speed. At 7 P.M. he was at

Buckingham Palace to tender his resignation; a half hour later Attlee drove into the Palace Yard in his small family car and kissed hands as the new prime minister. On July 27 the Parliamentary Labor Party confirmed Attlee as leader. Since 1935 there had been general agreement that he was the man most able to preserve harmony among various factions in the party. To be sure, he was without dramatic qualities but he was moderate in policy and even in temper; he was hard-working and entirely above reproach in personal integrity and party loyalty.

The Attlee Cabinet

Cabinet appointments brought some surprises. Hugh Dalton, undersecretary of foreign affairs in the last Labor Government and minister of economic warfare under Churchill, left his first interview with Attlee with the impression that he was to be foreign secretary. Ernest Bevin anticipated being chancellor of the Exchequer. But Attlee reversed these roles, and apparently for reasons of his own, not disclosed in his autobiography or elsewhere. According to Dalton, whose memoirs are enlightening, Attlee decided that Bevin and Morrison (as leader of the House of Commons) would be incompatible in handling domestic problems. The king, we know, urged Bevin rather than Dalton for the Foreign Office. The Bevin appointment was popular in the party, for Dalton's political manners had not won high marks. Also, events had proved Dalton nearer right in the thirties than his party associates. For such independence, as Mary Agnes Hamilton has wryly pointed out, his party never forgave him. For the Exchequer he had had training—during the thirties he taught public finance at the London School of Economics.

But Ernest Bevin became the number-two man in the Cabinet. His career reflects the social changes in politics in the twentieth century. Brought up in extreme poverty, orphaned at the age of eight, he made his own way in life from the age of thirteen; a ginger beer cart driver in Bristol, then an investigator for the Dockers' Union, in time he became secretary of his union (after 1921 this was the Transport and General Workers Union) and eventually chairman of the T.U.C. First and last he was a trade unionist; he had scarcely a trace of the socialist doctrinaire. His political career dates from 1941.

Herbert Morrison's cockney background was equally humble. The son of a policeman and a housemaid, he acquired formally nothing beyond an elementary education. He made his mark politically in London municipal politics and in time became a prominent contender for party and for national leadership. During the war he was home secretary. Now, as lord president of the Council and leader of the House of Commons, he was situated, as he no doubt wished, so as to dominate the legislative program of the new Government. Sir Stafford Cripps became president of the Board of Trade—he was to prove more moderate in office than in opposition. A. V. Alexander returned to the Admiralty, a veteran of seven years at the post. The most startling appointment was that of Aneurin Bevan to the Ministry of Health. Until then a Labor back-bencher, closely associated in the thirties with the "lunatic fringe" on the extreme left, his appointment was greeted in some circles with apprehension, and even in Labor quarters was regarded as a gamble. Generally speaking, youth was not well served in Attlee's appointments; all important posts went to veterans. Of the ministry of thirty-seven, eight had at one time been coal miners, and eleven had been active trade unionists.

The Pattern of Reconstruction

Now, for the first time in English history, the Labor Party was in power with a majority over all other parties. On the opening day of the new Parliament, August 1, 1945, an observer from the press gallery in the Commons looked down upon an interesting scene. As the newly elected House crowded into the elegant chamber (with the Commons' chamber destroyed, the Lords' chamber had been appropriated), over half were there for the first time; in the ranks of Labor, two-thirds were new. The story is told that one Conservative observed, "Gracious, they look just like our constituents." The Tory minority greeted Churchill with "For He's a Jolly Good Fellow." Behind the Treasury bench Labor rose in force and responded with "The Red Flag."

Nationalization

The King's Speech opening this session reads in part: "My Government will take up with energy the tasks of reconverting industry from the purposes of war to those of peace, of expanding our export trade and of securing by suitable control or by an extension of public ownership that our industries and services shall make their maximum contribution to the national well-being." With this statement and amplifying clauses, the Labor Government served notice of a program which it proceeded to implement with astonishing speed. The first phase was completed in about two years' time. All action was based upon parliamentary enactment. No private interest was confiscated without compensation. The guiding principle in "nationalization" was that of operation of industry through "public corporations" and not directly by government departments. In practice, management remained for the most part in the hands of those who had directed the industry when privately owned, and managerial procedure remained little changed. The role of labor was unchanged; collective bargaining remained the basis of negotiation with management, and the right to strike was unaffected. Such was the general character of "nationalization" in these years.

First came nationalization of the Bank of England; the bill was introduced in the autumn of 1945, was passed through legislative channels with little challenge, and became law on March 1, 1946. Perhaps the best comment was that of Quintin Hogg, a Conservative M.P., who in 1947 wrote that the measure could only be described "as an elaborate game of make-believe." When introducing the bill, Hugh Dalton admitted that the relationship between the Bank and the Treasury Department of the Government would be little changed. One clause, the only one to provide for any kind of Government interference, did seem to give the Treasury some control of credit, but this clause was eventually softened by a provision that the initiative should come from the Bank. The Bank of England, it has been said, was placed in a position very much like that of a Federal Reserve Bank of the United States. Lord Catto was immediately reappointed governor and was to be assisted by sixteen directors chosen by the Government from finance and industry; previously the directorate had been self-perpetuating. Former stockholders received government stock, bearing the same yield as the old stock.

On the future of the coal industry, the *Economist* in April 1945 made a celebrated statement: "Support for the principle of public ownership of the mines is now very wide, extending probably to two and a half of the three parties." The Reid Committee, composed of mining engineers, mine managers, and company directors, was constitued in 1944 by the Coalition Government with a mandate to propose "technical changes." It recommended very drastic measures of centralization. In accepting the report, the Government intimated that its recommendations would be legislated. Other committees of experts appointed by the new Government in 1945 pointed to the depletion of coal reserves, the low level of productivity, unstable conditions of the market and of employment in the industry, the unhealthy state of labor-management relations, and the miserable living conditions in colliery towns. The Coal Industry Nationalization Act, introduced in December 1945, was enacted in July 1946, with transfer to public ownership scheduled for January 1, 1947. The measure, in the course of its parliamentary journey, generated more controversy than the differences between the two parties warranted. The Tories tended to attack details of the measure rather than the principle of naitonalization.

The act provided for a National Coal Board, appointed by the minister of fuel and power and consisting of nine representatives of various functions within the industry (such as finance, technology, labor, marketing), who were to operate all coal mines subject to the general supervision of the ministry. This public corporation replaced more than eight hundred private companies, which surrendered their assets for a compensation of £164,600,000, a generous figure. The first chairman of the new board was Lord Hyndley, who since 1931 had been a managing director of Powell-Duffryn Ltd., the largest of the companies. His new salary was set at £8,500. Sir Charles Reid, the mining engineer who had headed the committee bearing his name, became production manager.

A white paper on civil aviation, September 1945, indicated that three corporations (British Overseas Airways, British European Airways, and British South American Airways) operating under the Ministry of Civil Aviation would determine general airlines policy; legislation introduced in April 1946 became effective in August. The Cable and Wireless Act, enacted in 1946 and effective January 1, 1947, created a public corporation out of Cable and Wireless Ltd. for overseas communication; a board responsible to the postmaster-general replaced the directors. Electricity was nationalized in August 1947 and placed in the hands of a board subject to the oversight of the Ministry of Fuel and Power. In effect, the legislation merely extended to all operatives the authority of the Central Electricity Board created in 1926. Though opposed by the Conservatives, this act aroused little public interest.

Private and corporate capital, especially schemes for raising new capital, was brought under public control in the Borrowing (Control and Guarantees) Act of 1946, passed in the face of heated opposition. Proposals drafted during the war for the more beneficial use of land now bore fruit. The Distribution of Industry Act (1945) passed by the Coalition Government required official permission for location of industrial buildings and empowered government agencies to attract industry to certain areas. The Town and Country Planning Act of 1947 (effective July 1, 1948) laid down the principle that all development of property was to proceed according to the requirements of planning, but planning under county and county-borough authorities. The number of agencies with power dropped from 1,441 to 145. The act dealt boldly with the problem of "compensation and betterment." All changes in the use of land must be approved by the local planning authority. The State alone was to benefit financially from the development of the land or changes in its use.

As to agriculture, Labor had no party policy. Eventually, in August 1947, the Government enacted a measure "to make further provision for agriculture"—a measure which the minister of agriculture said was "a product of the combined wisdom of the different sections of the industry and of the advertised views of the three major political parties in the House." All agreed that prices and markets should be guaranteed, and wartime legislation was made permanent. There was never any talk of nationalization. The Tories waived the division on the second reading; during the debate all sides approved the measure and praised its sponsor. Eventually, under this legislation 75 percent of the produce of the average farm was sold at a guaranteed price and in a guaranteed market. And so the happy revival of agriculture, begun in the 1930s and stimulated by the necessities of the war, continued, now spurred on by the need for home production to reduce imports. The increase in farm income was phenomenal. In 1949 the average farmer with two hundred acres could maintain himself and his family and have a clear profit of £500 a year. Twenty years earlier he would have been in the red.

More central to Labor's program was the Inland Transport Act introduced November 1946, enacted August 1947, and effective January 1, 1948. But here also, past developments eased the process. In 1922 some 121 railroad companies had been consolidated in four companies, and in London passenger transport had been brought under public ownership in 1933. A Road Traffic Act of 1930 established some public control over passenger service; a licensing system was extended to trucking in 1933. Road transport of passengers and goods grew apace. By 1939 rails and roads were in bitter competition, and after the war Labor took the position that only strong measures would insure equitable distribution of capital resources for reconstruction and reestablishment of normal services. The measure enacted was drastic; it reached all railway and road transport, and also inland waterways, docks, and harbors, thus affecting the employment of nearly one million, or 6 percent of the working class. Opposition extended from superficial complaints that all railway cars would now be of the same color to serious queries about handling the complex financial structure of the companies, some with various subsidiary equities, such as hotel properties. Some simplification was provided in the decision to exclude all enterprises operating routes within a radius of twenty-five miles. A central British Transport Commission was created to operate through five boards: railways, docks, and inland waterways, road transport, London transport, and hotel executives. In the execution of the measure, the turnover of railways was relatively easy, for they had not been in competition; but the transfer of road freight, bus and coach service was another matter. One of the most thorny problems was in dealing with transport operatives carrying their own goods.

These were the measures of nationalization, 1945–47. For private enterprise, in 1948 still employing 80 percent of the working class, Labor continued techniques previously introduced. Government loans aided the motion picture industry, and a grant assisted cotton manufacturers in securing new equipment. The only novelty of importance was the estab-

lishment of the "development councils" in various industries to extend
the prewar policy of "rationalization" by which waste, duplication, and
disastrous competition might be reduced.

The Welfare State

"You will be asked to approve measures to provide a
comprehensive scheme of insurance against industrial injuries, to extend
and improve the existing scheme of social insurance and to establish a
national health service." In accordance with this statement of the king's
speech in August 1945, a series of statutes enacted in 1946–48 consolidated and extended a group of social services, constituting the "welfare
state," to provide protection against the normal contingencies the citizen
might experience. Income would be available in the event of unemployment, sickness, or industrial injury; pensions would ease one's old age;
supplementary grants would be available for additions to the family, for
pregnancy and for maternity care, for widowhood and for burial. Free
medical service would be available to all citizens. Lord Beveridge, a
proud man, can be pardoned for his words in 1948: parliamentary acts
since 1945 "amount substantially to an adoption of the [Beveridge]
Report.

Social Insurance. The National Insurance Bill (enacted
1946) was presented to Parliament as "to a large extent ... con-
solidating existing measures" of insurance resting on contributions
of the individual, his employer and the State. The catalyst to action
was, indeed, the Beveridge report of 1942, which laid bare the existing
situation:

> The first task ... has been ... a comprehensive survey of the whole
> field of social insurance and allied services .... The picture presented
> is impressive in two ways. First it shows that provision for most of
> the many varieties of need ... has already been made in Britain on a
> scale not surpassed and hardly rivalled in any other country in the
> world .... Second, social insurance and the allied services, as they
> exist today, are conducted by a complex of disconnected administra-
> tive organs, proceeding on different principles, doing invaluable serv-
> ice but at a cost in money and trouble and anomalous treatment of
> identical problems for which there is no justification .... There are
> serious deficiencies which call for remedy.

A Fabian Society investigation undertaken in 1943 by W. A. Robson of
the London School of Economics reached much the same conclusion: "If

persons with qualified and trained minds will apply themselves in a disinterested manner to a great social problem of this kind, the proper principles will emerge so unmistakably that the right solution will cease to be a matter of mere opinion and become a question of scientific knowledge." To a considerable degree this is what happened. The principles in the Beveridge report were endorsed by the white paper on social insurance presented to the Commons in 1944 and welcomed without a division. That white paper stressed the comprehensiveness of a new scheme of social insurance; it was to "embrace, not certain occupations and income groups, but the entire population." The organization of approved insurance societies originally established in 1911 was abolished; benefits would now be paid by the Government from the National Insurance Fund. In accepting these proposals, R. A. Butler for the Conservatives said:

> We regard this plan as part of a, mosaic or the pattern of a new society.... This Bill forms part of a series of Bills, starting with the Education Bill, which, I may say, foresaw the pattern of the new society long before this Parliament was ever thought of. The whole philosophy behind these measures, in which... we have played our part and shall play our part, is that the good things of life shall be more widely shared.

Associated legislation passed easily through Parliament and attracted little attention. The National Insurance (Industrial Injuries) Act of 1946 replaced earlier workmen's compensation laws and comprehended all injuries suffered in the course of employment. Previous legislation, while establishing the *right* to compensation, provided no machinery for prompt and satisfactory meeting of claims. With this act, benefits would be determined not by litigation but by administrative action. Compensation ceased to be the responsibility of the employer, and claims were paid from an insurance fund. Two acts provided assistance not derived from insurance funds. The Family Allowances Act (1945) authorized financial allowances to families under special circumstances. The National Assistance Act of 1948 provided any applicant with a weekly benefit sufficient for the minimum needs of food and shelter. With this act the famous Poor Laws, dating back to 1601, which had treated paupers as a class apart, came to an end.

> *The National Health Service.* National health insurance must have a longer story. It was the consequence of sustained effort over many years of the medical profession, of the public, and of Governments of various complexions to improve Britain's medical service and

extend its availability. The mandate of the act of 1946 was very simple, to provide "a comprehensive health service designed to secure improvement in the physical and mental health of the people." Its most radical feature, the subject of little controversy, was that it should apply to *all persons equally*, regardless of ability to pay.

This legislation was the outcome of thirty-five years of history. Though medical assistance from public authorities goes back to the Elizabethan Poor Law, modern legislation begins with the National Health Insurance Act of 1911, which applied to the lowest-paid groups and which, from contributions by employee, employer, and the State, provided medical service and benefits in case of loss of employment through illness. By 1939 this act, as supplemented, comprehended about seventeen million in a system of compulsory health insurance which was by then taken for granted. But in the interim, what had been "progressive" became "obsolete." By 1939 the system operated in the face of manifold limitations. (1) A cumbersome machinery of many "approved societies" and "insurance committees" duplicated effort and provided uneven service. (2) Coverage did not include many whose circumstances called for it: the self-employed, the unemployed, and dependent members of the family (it was estimated in 1938 that thirty-five million belonged to families whose chief wage earner received no more than £250 a year) and the slightly better-paid workers. (3) The range of benefits was not comprehensive— for example, dental care and optical care were not included. (4) The services of the medical profession were unevenly distributed—for most, high quality service and specialist service were not available.

World War II underlined the defects of a haphazard medical service and the advantages accruing from unified control and direction. It also produced its own crisis—"the medical history of the war reads like an administrator's nightmare," says one writer—with general practitioners reduced 50 percent, with medical service drastically cut in evacuation areas, with hospitals crowded beyond all previous experience. The strongest voices for reform during the war were doctors harassed by shortages and inadequate facilities, whose rewards varied widely depending on the nature of the clientele, and who were restless under restrictions imposed by "single-handed" practice. "The British have a socialized medical service simply because of the deplorable state of the old medical system," concludes an authoritative writer.

That the problem, in the course of the twenties and thirties, became an issue was in considerable measure due to the medical profession. The Dawson report (1920) represented the views of the Consultative Council on Future Provision of Medical and Allied Services, established by the newly created Ministry of Health. The report recommended a unified medical authority to provide the organization required by professional and public interest alike; this authority would make medical service available to the entire population, would distribute the services according to need, and would keep step with advancing medical knowledge and skill. In 1926 a Royal Commission on National Health Insurance suggested that the solution might be found in a service entirely divorced from insurance schemes and supported from general public funds.

The British Medical Association in 1930 published *Proposals for a General Medical Service for the Nation*, which was accepted by the representative body of the association and revised and reissued in 1938. These proposals urged an extension of health insurance and the reorganization of hospitals on a regional basis. Finally, in 1942, came the report of the Planning Commission of the British Medical Association and the Royal Colleges, an authoritative report which seems to have been representative of the views of the profession at the time. Some crucial questions were unanswered—the extent to which the service should comprehend the entire population, the financing of the program, the remuneration of doctors and surgeons—and the larger opinion seemed to favor extension of existing insurance schemes.

So it may be said that down to 1943 the idea of medical reform seemed to have the blessing of the profession, and proposals for implementing that idea were developing outside of politics. Drawing on the report of the Planning Commission of the Medical Association, on the Beveridge report, and on the experience of the wartime Emergency Medical Service, the Government in February 1944 issued a white paper ("A National Health Service") presenting a tentative plan for replacing "a complicated patch work of health services, a mass of particular and individual services evolved at intervals over a century or more." It laid down certain principles: (1) a comprehensive but noncompulsory medical service free of charge to those who wished to use it; (2) preservation of the existing doctor-patient relationship, with freedom of choice on both sides; (3) direction of the service by an agency which must be responsible, according to democratic processes, for its actions; (4) the enlistment of the best professional and vocational guidance in establishing the service. The Commons approval of this white paper was accorded without a division.

Yet it was this white paper which first made the idea of a national health service controversial and involved the Governments (this one and the one to follow) in a conflict with the medical profession which continued four years. For now the profession began to retreat, all its hitherto unexpressed reservations coming to the fore. A questionnaire revealed something like a state of panic. The profession was opposed to lay control of medicine through a governmental authority. They would accept a public agency nominally in control only if it were clear that the profession would make all major decisions. To them the idea of medical service actually controlled by the House of Commons was repugnant. Above all, the practitioners had no respect for civil service at the local level and feared the consequences of a hospital service controlled by boards representing county and town authorities. Under any Government a difficult problem would have emerged—that of enacting a measure by normal parliamentary processes in which the medical profession could not directly participate and yet winning the active support of the profession.

And so the National Health Service Act was legislated in an atmosphere of controversy and suspicion—and drama as well. The personality and energy of the minister of Health, Aneurin Bevan, "both a bard and a warrior," in turn charmed and infuriated the medical profession. His speech, April 30, 1946, introducing the measure for its second reading, was masterly. He was "a real Parliamentarian acting on the House through living speech," wrote the *Manchester Guardian*'s parliamentary correspondent. On the other hand, the initial response of the Opposition was "disastrous." Richard Law began with biting words and, soon on the defensive, was pushed to the declaration: "I am anxious to make clear our position on these Benches in regard to the principles of a national, comprehensive, 100 percent health service. Of course, we accept that principle today, as we accepted it in 1944, when the Coalition white paper was published."

He had conceded the main point. Much of the ensuing debate turned on Bevan's legislative methods and the character of his consultation with the British Medical Association. Bevan invited personal criticism and received it. There was, however, genuine concern from the critics for the fate of voluntary hospitals, for the future of the doctor-patient relationship, of the possibility of a salaried medical profession. On the other hand, as the *Economist* said (May 4), the critics would have had a difficult time producing a more satisfactory bill, one which would have more successfully reconciled divergent views and interests. There was unanimity to this extent—some kind of national health service was required. In the final debate Mr. Heathcoat Amory, Conservative, said, "By any test, this is a tremendous measure; . . . with all its faults it must go down in history as one of the outstanding ventures of this generation." It became law in November 1946 but was not to be effective until July 5, 1948.

An Ideological Revolution?

Economic historians, particularly those somewhat conservative in outlook, have suggested that nationalization, in the manner achieved in 1945–47, had behind it political rather than economic motives. This assertion contains a good deal of truth. It was not a new program born of radical fervor. For some years "nationalization" had been a catchword for Labor politics. Much of that which was now legislated had been put on paper back in 1934 in a statement, *For Socialism and Peace*, adopted at a Party Conference. And the 1945 election manifesto was hardly a challenge to capitalism.

Several additional observations are in order. In the first place, this legislation was of a piece, ideologically, with the general direction of national policy in the twentieth century. Public ownership is not far from public control, which in 1945 was nothing new. Between the wars, as has already been pointed out, government controls had encroached on privately operated electric power, coal, railroads, and road transport. By 1945 there was no such thing as "perfect competition" in any important industry. After 1931 "rationalization" frequently took the form of cartelization—in steel, shipbuilding, flour milling, cotton manufacture; cartels bought up and eliminated surplus productive capacity. Some cartels were provided for by statute; the Coal Act of 1930 provided for control of production through just such a cartel. Trade associations (about twenty-five hundred of them by 1944) often brought employers or producers together to limit output or to establish minimum prices—and thus "to protect the interests of the trade," as their constitutions usually phrased it. At the top stood the vigorous and powerful Federation of British Industries, whose general function was to encourage and assist these trade associations. And, in exercising its own controls, the Government often dealt with the associations directly. Elsewhere, *laissez-faire* continued to fade—in public controls on exchange, in the return to a protective tariff, in development of bilateral trade agreements and imperial preference, and in international agreements for guaranteeing markets, encouraging production, and insuring a steady flow of goods. Since 1931 the agricultural life of Britain had been revitalized by marketing boards of producers as provided for by the Agricultural Marketing Acts of 1931 and 1933.

In the second place, the idea of a "planned society" was made respectable by the Second World War. The war, it could be argued, was won by "planning." Through careful analysis of the present and mortgaging of the future, shortages were made good, raw materials allocated, and effective use made of manpower. Where necessary, powers of government were enlarged and used, and with scarcely any ideological justification or apology. As Rogow has said, there seems to be a "historical relationship between planning and war."

Probably any Government would have continued certain wartime restrictions and would have extended operation of the principle of public control. As it was, the Conservative Opposition challenged few bills—the Inland Transport Bill was an exception—on the merits of the changes proposed. In the House of Lords the Opposition majority sought to improve rather than to oppose measures submitted. We are told that on the ten major pieces of legislation in the 1946 and 1947 sessions, 1,222 amendments were presented by the Lords, and the Government accepted all but 57.

The Usefulness of Politics

What then, one may ask, produced the violent debates in the Commons, especially in the 1945–46 sessions? In part it was that the permanent civil service, the country's business interests, and the leaders of the Opposition were all annoyed by the Government's speed, a departure from the traditional English manner of gradual, piecemeal legislation. In eighteen months the major measures of nationalization, the important social security legislation, and the National Health Service Act had been enacted. The *Economist*, December 28, 1946, cried out in protest: "Let the Cabinet give Parliament time to think. Let Parliament give the Civil Service time to catch up with its duties."

The debate in Parliament was largely political. On November 19 Herbert Morrison outlined the program of nationalization to be presented. On December 6 the Conservatives put down a motion of censure: "That this House regrets that His Majesty's Government are neglecting their first duty"—reestablishment of peacetime production, housing, demobilization, budget economy."

During the debate, Churchill declared: "I believe profoundly that the attempt to turn Great Britain into a Socialist State will, as it develops, produce widespread political strife, misery and ruin at home." Attlee's response was that the motion of censure seemed to be directed against the voters for returning a Labor Government. From an unexpected source came support. Morrison was able to quote from a speech a few days before by the president of the Federation of British Industries: "We realize that industry ... must operate within the framework of government policies.... Whatever political views it may hold, industry will not be obstructive; ... whilst we will not abandon our principles or pull our punches we will seek a broad area of agreement on which the reconstruction of our national life can proceed."

Political sparring frequently returned. During the economic crisis of early 1947, Churchill and Attlee exchanged words over the doctrinaire nature of the Government's proposals. Attlee declared that Labor did not desire nationalization for its own sake. "It is simply a means to an end." That the line between Government and Opposition on occasion was very fine is seen in the remarks of R. A. Butler in the same debate. He did not, he said, attack the policy of "economic planning" because it was "socialistic." He attacked it because it had not worked. A few months later a group of leading Conservatives (Butler, Harold Macmillan, Sir David Maxwell-Fyfe, David Eccles, Oliver Stanley, Oliver Lyttelton) drew up an "Industrial Charter" accepting the general idea of government control and, within limits, measures of nationalization. The charter was endorsed, almost unanimously, by the party conference in October 1947.

The Labor Government legislated a program of reconstruction. Doubtless the Conservatives, likewise, had they won in 1945, would have legislated a program of reconstruction, though with differences. But it is exceedingly doubtful that a nonpartisan Coalition Government of Labor, Conservatives, and Liberals would have been able to do so. The programs, the ideologies, and the philosophies of the parties *did* differ. Even when there was essential agreement on principle, there were rivalries, jealousies, suspicions, bequeathed by history. In 1946 the Government repealed the obnoxious Trade Disputes Act of 1927, and, largely for personal reasons, it was admitted.

In a party guise one can often be more objective, one can certainly be more forthright in disagreement, than in a nonpartisan pose. It is to the everlasting credit of the British that in the most terrible crisis of modern Britain—the Nazi threat of 1939–45—personal differences and rivalries were submerged in the common interest of survival. But even then Conservatives and Laborites found it embarrassing to discuss postwar social and economic reconstruction. Just as it proved disastrous for reconstruction after World War I that the Lloyd George wartime Coalition continued in power, so with reason we may assert that it was fortunate after World War II that Britain reverted to party government. The usefulness of politics was rediscovered.

British Power at Home and Abroad, 1945–47

Hugh Dalton, the new chancellor of the Exchequer, suggested that he was too fully occupied with international finance to be concerned with international politics. The obvious comment is that now the two were in almost constant interdependence. It is significant that the new foreign secretary, Ernest Bevin, had been the wartime minister of labor.

Problems of the Postwar Economy

Britain's economic problems at the end of the war may be summarized as follows:

1. There was an urgency for restoring and if possible improving upon her prewar standard of living. It is estimated that real consumption by

the British people declined 15 percent during the war. Yet, even so, Britain had lived beyond her means, on capital and on borrowing. In the last year of the war she spent £2,000,000,000 abroad, while earning only £800,000,000.

2. A peacetime industry had to be reconstructed. Britain had sacrificed much of her economic power in winning the war. Her foreign capital assets were reduced one-third. The value of her remaining foreign assets in areas controlled by unfriendly powers was uncertain. Invisible income—from capital invested abroad, from shipping, from financial and insurance services rendered other countries—had in 1938 paid for 37 percent of Britain's imports. For 1946 these accounts taken together were on the debit side.

3. Demands for reparation of war damage and for new construction were far beyond Britain's capacity to meet. Normal maintenance had fallen behind, and outright destruction to industrial plant from enemy action was estimated at £1,500 million. The most urgent demands were for restoring railway rights of way, restoring to full efficiency plant facilities for generating electricity, and restoring plant facilities in the chemical and the iron and steel industries. Next in priority would probably be the requirements in labor and material for housing.

4. Sterling had to be bolstered as a sound currency. Britain's national debt at the beginning of the war was £7,000 million and at the end of the war £23,000 million. The immediate problem was to keep international payments in balance—receive as much from outside the country as was paid out. If the balance was adverse in the United States, Canada, the Argentine, and some European countries, it must be made good in dollars or in gold.

5. It came down to a matter of production which would satisfy consumer demands at home and provide a surplus for export. Only an expansion of exports would give Britain the credits, particularly in dollars, which she needed for the importation of foodstuffs and of raw materials for her own industry.

Government Controls. The Labor Government's approach to production and foreign trade was pragmatic. It took the natural course: controls had won the war of production against the Axis powers; the same kind of controls would revive peacetime industry and provide a surplus for foreign trade. Production was now controlled by restrictions on raw materials imported. For example, the Government imported all raw cotton and controlled its distribution. "Utility" production was encouraged; luxury production was limited. Licenses were requried to export raw materials and any manufactured articles (especially machinery and machine tools) needed at home. Domestic consumption was regulated by rationing, subsidies, and price controls, particularly on foodstuffs, and by building licenses. Demand for luxury goods was diminished by the simple operation of tacking on a very substantial purchase tax—from 33.3 percent to 100 percent of the original sale price. Any considerable factory restoration required a permit. New industrial enterprises seeking capital had to be approved by a Government committee of industrialists and bankers held over from the war.

Results were not impressive. There was, it is true, full employment, for the demand for labor far exceeded its supply, and this contributed to an illusion of prosperity. But in terms of goods produced and consumed, and in terms of foreign trade and foreign credits, the economy made only modest gains in 1945–46. Even at the end of 1946, the level of exports was only 10 to 15 percent over 1938, far short of the 75 percent increase declared necessary to maintain Britain's standard of living.

In applying wartime methods to peacetime problems, one important factor was missing: the imperatives of war. In 1946, at the annual conference of the Trades Union Congress, the chairman declared that with the advent of a Labor Government the trade union movement must recognize that in socialist Britain labor now shared responsibilities with industrial management for making industry more efficient, more productive. The goal of industry was now "the public interest" and labor must subordinate its own interests. But it did not so work out. More men at work did not necessarily mean more goods produced. Slackness set in. Stoppages, though not individually serious, were more frequent than in the thirties. Labor unions regularly sought higher wage scales, in nationalized industries as well as in private, even though the real-wage scale was already much above the prewar level. "The wage," said the *Economist* later (1949) in an interesting statement, "is coming to be regarded not as *quid pro quo* for a contribution to the economy, but as a species of welfare payment."

Treasury budgets were drafted with a view to controlling investment, encouraging export industries, controlling domestic consumption, and redistributing the national income. For foreign travel, limitations, changed from time to time, were placed on the amount of cash which could be taken from the United Kingdom. The cheap-money policy so successfully followed during the war was intensified. "Suppressed inflation" resulted. Excess purchasing power was created but did not raise prices in desirable consumer goods where price controls and rationing operated. There was thus no incentive to expand production in those goods. Increased purchasing, from rising wages and low interest rates, could develop only in consumer goods of second-rate importance. The overall result, however, was to raise the general level of costs of production and, thus, to raise the price of British exports abroad. In foreign exchange the British account for 1946 ended with an adverse balance of payments in the amount of £295 million, a deficit entirely accounted for in the dollar areas. In truth, Britain in 1945 and 1946 remained solvent only by continuing to borrow abroad, notably in the loans negotiated with the United States and Canada at the end of 1945. And here economic policy merged with diplomatic.

"British Interests" and Foreign Policy

The postwar pattern of British foreign policy was slow in taking shape and even slower in being accepted by the British people. After all, she had emerged from the war a victor—one of the Big Three. There was reluctance to face the hard fact that the war itself demonstrated that Britain no longer possessed the military potential for primacy in world affairs. Also, just what direction a Labor foreign policy would take was in the summer of 1945 conjectural. To many it seemed reasonable to expect that Labor would pursue a "socialist" rather than a "nationalist" foreign policy, that she would place "world interests" ahead of "British interests," and that she would find it relatively easy to establish rapport with other "peoples' " governments in Europe, even including that at Moscow.

Such did not prove to be the case. It was made clear from the outset that the new Government would adhere to traditional interests. The new foreign secretary, Ernest Bevin, gave the lead in the initial debate on foreign policy in the Commons on August 20. He accepted the remark from Anthony Eden (foreign secretary under Churchill) that in the war coalition the two had never disagreed on a fundamental issue of foreign policy. Commitments inherited from the war were honored—occupation forces in Europe, reoccupation of British territory temporarily held by the enemy, a facing up to the situation in the Middle East, the garrisoning of English bases in Gibraltar, Malta, Suez, Aden. While Britain now readily accepted the fact of life that the United States and Soviet Russia had emerged from the war as the two super powers, she was quick to show by her actions that she took seriously her role, in second place, where she stood without rivals. But unfortunately she defined this role in traditional terms: standing apart from Europe where she intervened only if her own interests were at stake, a world power enjoying a special relationship with the United States, and a unique association with the members of the Commonwealth of which she was the center. Her decision, January 1947, to make an atomic bomb arose not out of any crisis in foreign affairs but as a natural development from her role in the war. For one thing, the MacMahon Act of Congress in August 1947 ended Anglo-

American cooperation in this field. What was more important, as the third strongest power in the world, of course she must have nuclear weapons.

Such was Britain's outlook as the war ended. But the hard facts of life were soon upon her. Even by the end of 1945 it was evident (1) that Britain was dependent on the United States, in one way or another, for the restoration of her own economy and for her own national security; (2) that Britain and Russian interests in Europe were incompatible.

American Economic Aid. In August 1945 President Truman announced that with Japan's formal surrender lend-lease would cease. This statement merely implemented congressional action in April 1945 in expressly prohibiting the use of lend-lease for postwar purposes. The American view was that with the end of the war, peace treaties should be promptly drafted, all international economic controls should cease, and the world's economy should as promptly as possible return to its normal peacetime structure and the world market be decontrolled. It seemed fitting and proper to the United States that lend-lease was to serve the common war effort and not to restore Britain's economy and give her exports the advantage in the world market. Most Americans were oblivious to the fact, which seemed so patent to the British, that Britain's postwar economic problem stemmed from the sacrifices she had made during the war. Was the United States now to exploit British losses sustained in the Allied effort?

One matter, that of the wartime lend-lease account, was settled to general satisfaction. During the war British imports from the United States increased four times, with a balance of credits in favor of the United States of about $21,000 million. This item was settled in the spirit of the original agreement. In December 1945, a British commission, headed by Lord Keynes, concluded an agreement in Washington whereby over a period of fifty years the United Kingdom should pay to the United States a total of $650 million to cover "goods in the pipe lines" on V-J Day, surplus American stocks of goods and petroleum in Britain, and lend-lease goods held by Britain for civilian use. The principle was that Britain should incur no financial obligation for American aid consumed in the war effort.

It was another problem to arrange for some kind of aid to assist rehabilitation of Britain's industrial plant and its reconversion to peacetime use. British and American attitudes toward restrictions on trade conflicted. After prolonged negotiations, delegates drafted a proposal for an American loan to be accompanied by a "Financial and Trade Agreement." The United States would grant the United Kingdom a credit of $3,750 million which could be drawn on until 1951, to bear interest at 2 percent and to be repaid in fifty annual installments commencing December 31, 1951. By the more technical "Financial and Trade Agreement" Britain undertook, within a year after the loan was in operation, to make sterling available for currency transactions in any currency area and to consider seriously abandonment of trade preferences within the Commonwealth.

The British Parliament approved these agreements, but only after a frank debate in which many suggested that the United States was unfairly exploiting her advantage. Before an assemblage in the House of Lords, said to have been larger than at any time since 1911, Lord Keynes delivered a brilliant speech. He had hoped, he said, for aid from the United States "that approximated to a grant . . . . I shall never so long as I live cease to regret that this is not an interest-free loan." But he explained that the nominal rate of interest was necessary to give the proposal standing when it came before Congress. And he added, "These proposals on top of Lend-Lease . . . [are] an act of unprecedented liberality . . . . Has any country ever treated any other country like this in time of peace for the purpose of rebuilding the other's strength and restoring its competitive position?" Canada's loan of $1,250 million was more generous, for Canadian national income was one-twentieth that of the United States.

The Descent of the Iron Curtain. On Russian relations the Potsdam Conference of 1945 left both Churchill and Bevin pessimistic about the future. The attempt of the Council of Foreign Ministers in London in September and October to draft peace treaties with Italy, Romania, Bulgaria, Hungary, and Finland broke down over Russia's policy in Iran and in the Mediterranean (she sought a trusteeship of a former Italian colony, preferably Tripolitania), her demands for Italian reparations, and her insistence upon Allied recognition of Soviet satellite Governments in eastern Europe. British official reaction was in line with the comment in the *Observer* that this meeting "strongly, perhaps decisively consolidated the division of Europe and the world into zones of influence." In his remarks in the Commons, November 7, Bevin declared that one would have thought that much had been conceded to Russia. Now, one could not help being a little suspicious if she "wants to come right across, shall I say, the throat of the British Commonwealth, which has done no harm to anybody, but fought this war." In December, Bevin sought vainly to extend the Anglo-Soviet Treaty of 1942 against German aggression.

While Britain was being steadily disabused of reliance upon an extension into peace of the Grand Alliance, the United States clung to the hope that through the United Nations international cooperation could be achieved. And it was Russian policy to encourage the natural inclination of the United States to return to happy isolation. Most Americans were therfore shocked and dismayed by Churchill's utterance at Fulton, Missouri, on March 5, 1946.

> Nobody knows what Soviet Russia and its Communist international organization intends to do in the near future, or what are the limits, if any, to their expansive and proselytizing tendencies.... From Stettin in the Baltic to Trieste in the Adriatic an iron curtain has descended across the Continent.... I do not believe that Soviet Russia desires war. What they desire is the fruits of war and the indefinite expansion of their power and doctrines.

Stalin answered through *Pravda* on March 13:

> To all intents and purposes, Mr. Churchill now takes his stand among the warmongers.... I do not know whether Mr. Churchill and his friends will succeed in organizing ... a new military expedition against Eastern Europe. But if they succeed in this, which is not very probable ... then one can confidently say that they will be beaten just as they were beaten 26 years ago.

In effect, Anglo-Russian cooperation terminated in the summer of 1945. A comparable deterioration of Russo-American relations developed more slowly. The United States remained hopeful of results in the several meetings of foreign ministers summoned to draft peace proposals for Italy, Finland, and the Balkan states. Results finally came, and treaties were signed in February 1947, but along the way Molotov's uncompromising policy in eastern Europe—which resulted in Russian control of the Balkan states—alienated the United States. Nor were the first sessions of the Security Council at the United Nations promising. The German problem took shape in the disputes within the Allied Control Council; Russia was taking reparations from current production from her zone, while Great Britain and the United States exported food to their zones. A short-lived agreement in April 1946 permitted modest German production and provided for reparation payments. But difficulties soon returned, the major consequence of which was the establishment, May 1, 1947, of BIZONIA, an economic union of the British and American zones. After some months the French zone was included.

Bevin's situation was complicated by division in his own party. A minority element, leftist in ideology, held that a "truly Socialist" policy would find agreement with Russia, and this, rather than any special relation with the United States, should govern British actions. In November 1946 a resolution presented to the Commons by R. H. S. Crossman called on the Government "to provide a democratic and constructive Socialist alternative to an otherwise inevitable conflict between American capitalism and Soviet Communism in which all hope of World Government would be destroyed." The purpose of this resolution was only propagandistic, and the motion was defeated 353 to 0, with about 100 dissident Laborites abstaining. But this was just the beginning of Labor's trials within its own ranks.

Commonwealth and Empire

In Britain's rapidly changing position, internationally, after the war, to many the idea and reality of the Commonwealth seemed to offer the most promising future. The alternatives—just another European state or a satellite of the United States—were hardly attractive. For comprehensive and incisive treatment with insight, one turns to the work of Professor Nicholas Mansergh. He suggests that developments after 1945 confirmed a new ideal. "Equality of status," formalized for the dominions in the Statute of Westminster in 1930, was now replaced by "equality of function." The term "British Commonwealth," which had signified self-governing states, gave way to "Commonwealth," to include both dependencies and self-governing countries, the latter distinguished as "members of the Commonwealth."

The immediate background is uneven. Much is sometimes made of the fact that, among the dominions, all but Eire were committed to war against Germany by September 6, 1939—and these decisions were reached independently of the United Kingdom. But had Britain gone to war in 1938 it is not likely that any such unity would have resulted. And in 1939, in South Africa the Parliament voted for war by a small margin. Since his party was defeated on the issue, General Hertzog resigned as prime minister, to be succeeded by General Smuts. But, in view of that which has transpired since, one can only read, with nostalgia, Smuts's address to Parliament in Westminster in which he referred to the Commonwealth as "the greatest experiment in political organization, the proudest political structure of time, this precedent and anticipation of what one hopes may be in store for human society in the years to come." In Dublin there was an interesting state of affairs. To the surprise of no one, Ireland remained neutral and continued to be represented in Berlin by a *chargé d'affaires*. However Irish sentiment was strongly pro-British.

Equality of Function

The conduct of the war served to reinforce the notion of equality of function. Dominion Governments were kept well informed and were usually consulted about matters of major war strategy; an exception was in the projected operations for Greece and Syria in 1941, where tardiness in consultation led to friction with Australia, whose troops were much involved. The dominions retained complete control over employment of their forces. The prime ministers' meeting in London in 1944 was unlike the formal imperial conferences before 1939 in which the United Kingdom took the initiative, and was rather an informal meeting of equals in the Cabinet room at No. 10. Dominion leaderwhip was aware of the silent changes of the war in the power structure of the world—the partial eclipse of Europe and the relative decline of the United Kingdom. As the United Nations came into being, the dominions prepared to take their place as equals with the United Kingdom. The member nations of the Commonwealth left far behind that area of discussion concerned with the right of the dominions to accept or reject the leadership of the United Kingdom, and they concerned themselves with strengthening the Commonwealth in a world which otherwise would be dominated by the United States and the Soviet Union.

But this maturing of dominion status widened the gulf between the dominions on the one hand and India, Burma, and the colonial empire—still a sprawling assortment of some forty territories—on the other. On their behalf, the United Kingdom in 1939 declared war against Germany. In India, Burma, and Ceylon, where initial steps toward dominion status had been taken, this distinction rankled, particularly when it became evident that for them defense began at home. After the staggering losses to Japan in 1941–42, the British Raj never fully regained face in Southeast Asia. Loss of Singapore and loss of control of the Indian Ocean demonstrated that the Royal Navy was no longer Mistress of the Seas, that Britain could no longer, unaided, provide peace and security for her realm. Southeast Asia gained significance as a theater of the war—and in particular India, which Britain hoped to establish as a stronghold from which to send forth men and supplies to renew the conflict with Japan and to stand off the enemy in the Middle East.

Churchill and many of his Conservative associates had been consistently unfriendly toward the national aspirations of native peoples. And the notion that the people of Southeast Asia would readily agree that considerations of war took precedence over their own freedom was unimaginative as well as ungenerous. Smugness and complacency persisted. At an Anglo-American gathering in London, May 6, 1943, the secretary of state for India, L. S. Amery, spoke of the Indian Empire as "an indigenous system of government which spread over India from within in response to India's need for peace and unity." And Lord Hailey, who had spent many years in administrative posts in India, said, "It is not a question of whether Britain has any right to stay in India; it is a question whether, in present circumstances, she has a right to leave India."

Britain found the attitude of her powerful ally, the United States, embarrassing, not to say annoying. On colonialism there was considerable naiveté on both sides of the Atlantic. So readily did many Americans interpret the Atlantic Charter ("the right of all people to live under a government of their own choosing") as applying to all colonial peoples, that for a time the British spoke of "the liquidation of the British Empire" as one of America's war aims. In this area Churchill and Roosevelt could not communicate. It was Churchill's blind spot. He ignored the course of history. In the House of Commons in September 1942 he remarked that the Atlantic Charter had no relevance to Indian affairs, and two months later he spoke more bluntly to his American critics: "I have not become the King's First Minister in order to preside over the liquidation of the British Empire."

The End of the Indian Empire

During the war, attention to imperial questions usually focused on India. Her status must be viewed in the light of the policy of Conservative-controlled Governments since 1918. Each action taken—the Government of India Act of 1919, the recommendations of the Simon Commission (1930), and the Government of India Act of 1935—reflected exhaustive study and protracted deliberation. But each time, circumstances had outdistanced the concessions finally made. In 1939 the act of 1935 was nominally in force—"an Act to make further provision for the government of India" was its unpromising beginning. Once more the British Parliament chose to treat India as a special case, in this instance providing that each of the provinces should have responsible parliamentary government in local affairs and that a federation should unite India, including, with their consent, the native princely states. India accepted and put into effect with excellent results the reforms of provincial administration, but she ignored the plan of federation. For the confidence and cooperation of the Indian peoples were not to be won in this manner. Now her leaders looked on every British proposal with suspicion.

Hindu, Moslem, and British. By 1939 additional complications had developed; there was grave doubt whether peace and unity could be achieved even in the event of British departure. One difficulty was the division between British India and the native states, the latter still ruling more than one-third of the land and one-quarter of the people; but this difficulty was political and therefore likely to be fairly easy of solution. The fundamental change in the character of the Indian problem came with the rapid rise of Moslem nationalism in the 1930s and its culmination in 1945 as Moslem separatism. The development of provincial administrations largely controlled by Hindus struck hard at the autonomy of the Moslem communities, and the Moslem League, led by Mohammed Ali Jinnah, came into violent conflict with the Hindu National Congress, led by Jawaharlal Nehru. Now, as an alternative to British power the Moslems were confronted with Hindu power. By 1939 the issue was all but joined. In September the League declared that it was "irrevocably opposed to federation in any form." The Congress looked upon this problem as "purely a domestic one" which could be solved once the foreigners withdrew, and adhered to its demand for an Indian Assembly to draft the future constitution of a united India.

Then came the war. "England's difficulty is not India's opportunity," said Nehru, but India would "not come to the rescue of a tottering imperialism." When disaster after disaster threatened the loss of all Southeast Asia, and even Australia and New Zealand beyond, the British sought to win over the Indian leaders to active support of the war. These efforts culminated in the Cripps Mission in the spring of 1942. Sir Stafford offered freedom—Indians would determine their own future through an Indian Constituent Assembly representing the various states. The British Government solemnly declared that it would "not impose any restriction upon the power of the Indian Union to decide in the future its relationship to the other Member States of the British Commonwealth." There was one qualification: all this was to come after the war. "During the critical period which now faces India and until the new Constitution can be framed His Majesty's Government must inevitably bear the responsibility for and retain control and direction of the defence of India as part of their world war effort."

India rejected this proposal. The League feared for the independence of the "Moslem nation," and the Congress spurned proposals which delayed independence until after the war and which opened the way to partition. Nehru said that "India can only be defended effectively as a free country by the people themselves acting through their national government," and the Congress organized a "Quit India" campaign. Jinnah and the League then confounded the situation by supporting the war. In providing for a voluntary federation of Indian states the Cripps proposals tacitly accepted partition as a possibility and by widening the breach between Hindu and Moslem made ultimate solution more difficult. India insisted on solving her own problems, but she was now confronted with indisputable evidence that some of these problems were her own doing.

It was chiefly this rift between Hindu and Moslem which hindered the postwar Labor Government in fulfilling Labor's pledge to India, dating back to 1919, of unqualified self-determination. After proposals for an Indian Constituent Assembly came to nothing, Attlee, early in 1946, announced a Cabinet mission to India to establish machinery by which India would determine her future. "My colleagues are going to India with the intention of using their utmost endeavour to help her attain her freedom as speedily and fully as possible." The problem was plain: the Moselm League and the Hindu Congress must agree on the future of India. Would it be unity or partition? The Cabinet mission sought to establish an interim Government and a Constituent Assembly but met delaying tactics from the Congress and intransigence from the League, which eventually called for "direct action" in a Holy War. In the "Great Killing" in Calcutta, beginning in August 1946, about four thousand were slain in Hindu-Moslem clashes. Hindus fled in terror from East Bengal, and in adjoining Bihar Moslems were slaughtered. Only the appearance of Gandhi from village to village restored order in Bengal.

Independence for India and Pakistan. The British Government now determined to set a time limit within which Indian independence must be consummated and on February 20, 1947, declared that not later than June 1948 British authority in India would cease. Churchill called this pronouncement a cruel mistake which "put an end to all prospect of Indian unity." But Lord Halifax, in one of the great moments of his career, confessed to his fellow lords that it was no easier for him than for the Government to determine on a policy that was "right" for India. "I am not prepared to condemn what His Majesty's Government are doing unless I can honestly and confidently find a better solution."

This drastic move of the Government proved, in considerable measure, successful. The story largely revolves around the new viceroy (March 1947), Lord Mountbatten. The prestige of his royal blood (he was a cousin of George VI) and his success as Allied commander in Southeast Asia in the closing stages of the war proved important in his dealings with the native princes, but happily these were reinforced by his remarkable personality, intelligence, and tact. "His gift for friendship has triumphed over everything," one Indian put it.

Lord Mountbatten decided that the only solution was partition, and he won over both the Congress and the League. For the League it meant division of Bengal and the Punjab on a communal basis. Mountbatten also concluded that the time limit must be shortened or general civil war would develop. On June 3, 1947, proposals were announced simultaneously in London and in New Delhi. Lord Mountbatten in New Delhi declared:

The solution ... I put forward is that His Majesty's Government should transfer power to one or two Governments of British India, each having Dominion status, as soon as the necessary arrangements can be made.... I wish to emphasize that this legislation will not impose any restriction on the power of India as a whole or of the two new states if there is partition, to decide in the future their relationship to each other and to the other member states of the British Commonwealth.

The next day he held a press conference, attended by three hundred members of the Indian and world press, in which he finally put to rest fears still lurking in Indian minds that membership in the Commonwealth was not equivalent to independence. Nehru, in accepting the proposals for the Congress Party, said the idea of partition was painful. "Nevertheless I am convinced our present decision is right.... The united India we labored for was not one of compulsion and coercion.... Let us bury the past, insofar as it is bad, and forget all bitterness and recriminations." Mohammed Ali Jinnah appealed to Moslems to keep the peace and paid tribute to Mountbatten's impartiality: "It is up to us now to make his task less difficult and help him in so far as it lies in our power in order that he may fulfill his mission of the transfer of power to the peoples of India in a peaceful and orderly manner." In London Churchill warmly congratualated Attlee and Mountbatten for their success in getting the major Indian communities to agree on a procedure which would keep India in the Commonwealth.

The bill for Indian independence, only twenty clauses long, quickly went through Parliament. The measure had unanimous support. In moving the third and final reading, Sir Stafford Cripps said this would be "the last debate in the House on Indian Affairs." The act established two independent dominions, India and Pakistan, and by August 15, 1947, Independence Day, only three of the princely states had failed to join one or the other.

At half past seven on the evening of August 14, radio listeners in Britain heard the clock of the Council chamber at New Delhi strike midnight. At that moment Britain relinquished all authority in India. That day Mountbatten, in a shining white naval uniform, delivered his last message as viceroy in Karachi, which was to be the new capital of Pakistan. Jinnah responded with assurance of good will and friendship for the British nation. On the fifteenth he was installed as governor-general of the new dominion.

Nehru, scheduled to be the first prime minister of the new state of India, on the fourteenth told the Assembly at New Delhi: "Long years ago we made a tryst with destiny, and now the time comes when we shall redeem our pledge.... At the stroke of the midnight hour, when the world sleeps, India will awake to life and freedom." The next day Mountbatten and Lady Mountbatten drove in state to the Government House, and Mountbatten was installed as governor-general. The multitude without hailed him. In the ceremonies which followed before the Assembly at Council House, Dr Rajendra Prasad, president of the Assembly, made a moving statement. "Let us gratefully acknowledge, while our achievement is in no small measure due to our own sufferings and sacrifices, it is also the result of world forces and events, and last though not least it is the consummation and fulfillment of the historic tradition and democratic ideals of the British race."

Sor far, a happy ending, but this is not the whole story. A unified India was at an end. Partition was accompanied by chaos: mass migrations, property rights in confusion, the homeless by the millions. In the autumn of 1947 there was killing and arson, especially in the Punjab. On January 30, 1948, Gandhi was assassinated.

New Patterns in Southeast Asia. Elsewhere in Southeast Asia the nature of settlement varied. During the war the Burmese nationalists in opposing Japanese occupation were thinking of their own future. After the war, negotiations with the British over the transition to dominion status in Burma broke down. In December 1946 the British Government declared that it was for the people of Burma to decide their own future. "We do not desire to retain within the Commonwealth and Empire any unwilling peoples," said Attlee. A Burmese Constituent Assembly unanimously declared for an "independent sovereign republic" without Commonwealth ties. The British Parliament enacted Burmese independence; January 4, 1948, was the day of the transference of power. But the form of her government and the nature of her commercial connections remained British. The leaders of Ceylon chose to extend their representative government, accorded in 1931, to dominion status; and Ceylon was accordingly, on February 4, 1948, proclaimed a dominion "with the same sovereign independent status as the other self-governing countries of the Commonwealth."

In April 1949 the Commonwealth prime ministers met in London and issued a declaration which culminates British imperial history in the first half of the twentieth century. Their problem was to reconcile India's desire to be a republic, having no allegiance to the British Crown, with her desire to remain in the Commonwealth. Constitutional ideas and constitutional language again were flexible and ingenious. The prime ministers took note of India's desire to become "a sovereign independent republic." "The Government of India have however declared and affirmed India's desire to continue her full membership of the Commonwealth of Nations and her acceptance of The King as the symbol of the free association of its independent member nations and as such the Head of the Commonwealth." The other Governments then declared their acceptance of this declaration. "Accordingly the United Kingdom, Canada, Australia, New Zealand, South Africa, India, Pakistan and Ceylon hereby declare that they remain united as free and equal members of the Commonwealth of Nations, freely cooperating in the pursuit of peace, liberty and progress." On January 26, 1950, India became a republic.

The Republic of Ireland

Ireland, of course, had a story all her own. When the Irish Free State, under De Valera, in 1937 proclaimed itself an independent and sovereign state, it became in form though not in name a republic. In 1936 the External Relations Act, which recognized the final authority of Dail Eireann in all matters declared that the king might still give effect to policies in external affairs which had been decreed by the Irish Government. "External association," De Valera's solution for the Commonwealth tie, was supposed to replace dominion status. After the war, uncertainties over Eire's relation to the Commonwealth were settled, at least to a degree. In 1948 the Republic of Ireland Act repealed the External Relations Act of 1936 in order, declared the prime minister (John A. Costello), to eliminate friction between Ireland and Britain. Reciprocal citizenship with Commonwealth nations was retained. On Easter Day 1949, the anniversary of the 1916 rising, Ireland formally became a republic and left the Commonwealth.

It all seemed harmonious—but one deeply rooted source of ill will once more reared its head. This was the partition of Ireland. The Ireland Act of 1949 affirmed "the constitutional position and territorial integrity of Northern Ireland" and asserted that it would never cease to be a part of the United Kingdom without the consent of its own Parliament. This stirred the Dail to pledge "the determination of the Irish people to continue the struggle against the unjust and unnatural partition of our country" and to record "an indignant protest against the introduction in the British Parliament of legislation purporting to endorse and continue the existing partition of Ireland." But this was an expression of emotion, not of active policy. From 1949 Eire ceased to be a part of British politics.

British Failure in Palestine

In Palestine and in Egypt, Labor policy was guided by experience and seems to have been molded by somewhat conflicting impulses: the desire to protect British interests and the necessity for reducing British commitments abroad. In Palestine this required almost a *volte-face* in Labor attitudes. Since 1918 Labor, except when in power in 1929–31, had consistently supported, mainly on humanitarian grounds, the aspiration of Zionism. Even as late as May 1939, when the Chamberlain Government, trying to find a middle ground between Jewish and Arab pressures, issued a white paper restricting further Jewish imigration and projecting an eventual binational state in Palestine, Labor solidly supported a motion of censure. In 1944 the Labor National Executive urged Jewish immigration into Palestine "in such numbers as to become a majority. Let the Arabs be encouraged to move out as the Jews move in." And in the campaign of 1945 Labor proposed to rescind the white paper of 1939. With Labor's victory it was thus understandable that Zionists hoped for strong support for an independent Jewish state in Palestine.

The war had sharpened the differences between Arab and Jew. In Palestine the one million Arabs now outnumbered the Jews about two to one. But Zionist leaders stepped up their program, by illegal means as well as legal, to promote immigration to Palestine of Jews who had suffered from Axis terror in Europe. They hoped soon to outnumber the Arabs.

The new Labor Government, of course, soon found itself with a responsibility. It was caught between the pull of natural sympathy and traditional policy, and the necessity for retaining Arab good will in the Middle East to counter Soviet moves in that area. In 1946 Britain terminated her mandate over Transjordan and proclaimed the sovereign independent state of Jordan. In a close military alliance Britain agreed to maintain by subsidy the Arab Legion under its British commander, John Bagot Glubb, and in turn was permitted to keep her own troops in Jordan. For Palestine, policy making was more painful. In the fall of 1945 Bevin and Cripps, as a Cabinet subcommittee, recommended that Britain should not try unaided to establish a Jewish state. In November Bevin announced an Anglo-American inquiry into the problem of the mass of Jews in exile from lands formerly controlled by the Axis powers. Endeavoring to balance conflicting claims, the joint committee recommended the immediate opening of Palestine to 100,000 Jewish victims of persecution in Europe and endorsed the proposal of an eventual binational state based on equal representation of Arabs and Jews. The British mandate should be converted into a United Nations trusteeship. This proposal was generally unacceptable. The British were outraged by the attitude of an American Government, with Zionist sympathies, unwilling to share responsibility. Jewish terrorist organizations on July 22, 1946, blew up the King David Hotel in Jerusalem—British headquarters—killing about ninety persons. A further British proposal for provincial autonomy for separate Jewish and Arab areas, but under central administration, was presented to a conference in London late in 1946. To this conference the Palestine Jews refused to send representatives.

By 1947 British opinion leaned heavily toward outright withdrawal from Palestine. As Churchill said, Zionist demands had become an "unfair burden." The Government referred the whole question to the United Nations, which voted, November 1947, for partition, with an internationalized Jerusalem. But Britain, knowing that neither the Arabs nor the Jews would accept this settlement, did not support it. Instead, Britain announced that the mandate would end May 15, 1948. When Russia proposed enforcement of partition, the United States rejected partition altogether. Israel, a new state, was proclaimed on May 15 with prompt recognition by the United States. British forces withdrew and guerrilla warfare between Jew and Arab became open conflict.

The British had been victims of a situation compounded of their own good impulses, the realities of power politics, and the age-old conflict of Arab and Jew. For Labor it was a lesson in the responsibilities of office. Just before the mandate terminated, the Conservatives scored heavily. Kenneth Pickthorn told the Commons: "For a long time before they were in office ... [Labor] did everything that men not in office could do to prepare the situation with which we are now confronted. And the situation with which we are now confronted is such that nothing can be done that will not be wrong."

Egyptian Nationalism

In Egypt as well, native nationalism was victorious over British policy. Though Britain had protected Egypt from Fascist and Nazi threats and had spent great sums maintaining Allied forces there to Egypt's economic benefit, perspective in Egypt was limited. At the end of the war, Egypt insisted unreservedly that Britain withdraw all her military forces and permit absorption of the Sudan by Egypt. British interest after the war lay mainly in providing an adequate defense of the Suez Canal Zone and in insuring joint Anglo-Egyptian operations in case of an international conflict affecting the Middle East. All these matters had been "settled" by the treaty of 1936, in which Britain acknowledged Egypt's full independence and in which a military alliance permitted Britain to use Egyptian airports, to retain a naval base at Alexandria, and to occupy the Canal Zone. It was this treaty which the Egyptians now sought to revise.

The Labor Government decided that a satisfactory solution of the strategic problem hinged on a harmonious political relationship. Therefore, in May 1946, it proposed the withdrawal, in several stages, of all British troops from Egypt, in the hope that this gesture would induce the

Egyptians to continue the military alliance. In Britain this policy was opposed by the Conservatives, who declared that the Suez must be safeguarded by retaining British troops somewhere in Egypt. A second obstacle was in Egypt, where frequently shifting regimes (with one Government repudiating commitments of its predecessor) prevented any firm agreements. From 1947 relations deteriorated steadily. On March 31, 1947, the final British units were withdrawn from Cairo and from the delta, but not from the Suez area. A British proposal for an international force was rejected. Further complications came with the outbreak of war between Egypt and the new state of Israel. In 1951 a new element, dominated by the Wafd Party, the most ardently nationalist element in Egypt, came to power and abrogated the 1936 treaty. The British refused to recognize this act. Labor's tenure ended with the Egyptian problem still unsettled. Then came "Black Saturday," January 26, 1952, when mobs of students and workers burned about seven hundred business premises, most of them European-owned, in the heart of Cairo. Shepheard's Hotel, a symbol of the veneer of European civilization, was destroyed. Six months later the Army revolt brought the monarchy and the control of the Wafd to an end. Egypt's revolution was under way.

Economics and Diplomacy, 1947–49

In economics and diplomacy 1947 marked, as Kingsley Martin said in the *New Statesman and Nation*, the end of "the phoney war." Illusions lingering since 1945 were finally dispelled and realistic approaches to the perplexities bequeathed by the war were advanced.

In 1946 one could hardly have forecast the special character of the economy of the year ahead. Britain was at least stronger than in 1945. The volume of exports, while still quite disappointing, was climbing month by month and by the end of 1946 was above the 1938 level, while the volume of imports was one-third lower. The American loan, which reduced the deficit in international transactions by 50 percent over the previous year, obscured the fact that Britain's imports from dollar areas remained about three times her exports to those areas. Even the cautious *Economist* in July 1946 thought it might be possible "to keep the aggregate deficit over the next three years within the totals of the American and Canadian credits."

The Economic Crisis of 1947

The first source of trouble was beyond man's control. The winter of 1946–47 was "the most severe since 1880–81," reads the

Annual Register. Bitter cold, heavy snow, and solid ice interfered with industrial production and transportation from Scotland to the Channel. On January 5 a blizzard blocked tracks and highways. At Windsor snowplows, it is said, were used for the first time in fifteen years. London had eight days, late in January, with continuous frost. Big Ben froze up. More snow came early in February. In the Cotswolds hay was carried out to feed the sheep.

Dwindling fuel supplies were the first sign of serious economic difficulties—it was unfortunate for coal nationalization that the new Coal Board took control on January 1, 1947. In its first month of operation 300,000 more tons of coal were consumed than produced. Delays in transport made it difficult to replenish stocks of coal at factories and power plants. On January 13 it was announced that coal supplies for industry would be reduced 50 percent, with power plants given priority. Several weeks later (February 7), the quiet of a sparsely attended Friday afternoon session of the Commons was broken by an announcement from Emanuel Shinwell, minister fo fuel and power, of general limitations on the use of power. Industrial use was to be restricted, the weekly press was to be suspended for two weeks, power for domestic use was to be cut off from 9 to 12 in the morning and from 2 to 4 in the afternoon. An explosive debate followed—Shinwell was charged with failing to give adequate warning, and he argued that the crisis was caused by the weather—and the Government's prestige was considerably damaged.

Weather certainly continued a factor, with normal transport not available until the end of March. The Central Electricity Board, in heavy overcoats, met by candlelight in London to take stock. On February 10 the general restrictions on power went into effect, and power was not fully restored for five weeks. Four and one-half million workers were temporarily idle. Cripps was later to estimate that the stoppages cost Britain £200 million in exports. Nature aggravated the problem but did not create it. No economy was sound which could not withstand a few months of bad weather. The trouble was the lagging production, the slowdowns in mines and factories, the low stocks of fuel.

The Economic Survey. The challenge for new policies and new methods brought forward Sir Stafford Cripps, who now, in addition to his duties at the Board of Trade, was undertaking in Morrison's absence (he was recovering from a thrombosis) general economic coordination. For some months he and others had pleaded for increased production. Cripps was chiefly responsible for the first of the famous Economic Surveys, which, though it did not appear until February 1947, had been put together several months earlier and, therefore, reflects the thinking of the Cabinet well before the winter fuel crisis.

The survey states: "The object of economic planning is to use the national resources in the best interests of the nation as a whole. How this is done must depend upon the economic circumstances of the country, its stage of political development, its social structure and its methods of government." On March 10 Cripps announced "a joint planning staff, somewhat on the lines of the ... joint war production staff. . . . They will be specially concerned with the more immediate task of reviewing the programme for the rest of 1947 in the light of developing conditions."

An academic discussion over the merits of a planned economy—just about the last flurry of such debate—ensued. Was governmental action an improvement over the operation of price in the market in the distribution of goods and services? Oliver Franks, then a temporary civil servant in the Ministry of Supply, in lectures delivered during the spring of 1947 at the London School of Economics and published as *Central Planning and Control in War and Peace*, favored continuation of broad powers to the Government to determine "the ends of the national economy" and to develop measures to achieve those ends. But Lionel Robbins in *The Economic Problem in Peace and War* (1947), first presented as lectures at Cambridge University, while favoring "financial planning" to stabilize demand and to avoid both inflation and deflation, felt that public controls on expenditures would be unlikely to prevent or cure unemployment.

The Economic Survey of 1947—in popular form it circulated as *The Battle for Output*—focused attention on the industrial crisis, on the extended debates in Parliament, and on the prolonged discussion in the press. *The Times* called the survey "the most disturbing statement ever made by a British Government." The *Economist* spoke of the threat of "a national calamity" and placed no special blame on the Government. "The truth is that both political parties are bewildered; neither of them knows what can be done, or even what it wants to do." For a time politics took second place to national anxiety.

The survey called for production in 1947 of 200 million tons of deep-mined coal (an increase of 10 percent over 1946) and an increase in industrial production which would achieve a target in exports of 140 percent of the 1946 level. Cripps now developed techniques calculated to achieve these goals. He set out to increase production by regulation and by stimulating incentive, and to shift imports away from dollar areas. To increase man-hour production the National Coal Board, by agreement with the Miners' Federation, in May inaugurated a five-day week; overtime pay was increased. The federation promised the efficient employment of labor in the interest of increased production. Priorities in coal allocation continued, with the steel industry (which had maintained an excellent rate of production) promised enough coal to work at capacity. In the new budget (presented April 15) income tax relief was offset by increased duties designed to restrict the consumption of imports. The tobacco duty, for example, increased from 35 shillings 6 pence per pound to 54 shillings 10 pence. In June the Exchequer announced sharp cuts in the importation of tobacco, newsprint, and gasoline.

The Government organized a vast program of publicity; the country was plastered with posters: "We're Up Against It. We Work or Want." Political in-fighting was soon renewed, and the public was not permitted to feel that it was no one's fault. The Conservatives exploited the weaknesses of Government policy. Labor had lost the confidence of the country, the Conservatives said. Labor rebels took advantage also. "Keep Left," a pamphlet written by R. H. S. Crossman, Michael Foot, and Ian Mikardo and supported by twelve other Labor M.P.s, opposed British defense commitments, advocated a sharp reduction in the armed forces and attacked the close ties with the United States. This insurgent group was defeated in a meeting of the Parliamentary Labor Party on July 30; Attlee was given a vote of confidence.

Attlee and Austerity. By midsummer, events were moving faster than policy. American and Canadian loans were running out sooner than anticipated, for prices had risen steadily in America. British exports fell off sharply in the first half of 1947. The last push toward disaster came on July 15 when, in accordance with the original terms of the American loan, sterling became convertible; holders of sterling rather frantically changed to dollars and Britain's dollar deficit soared.

The Government took swift action. On August 6 Attlee presented to the Commons the Cabinet's "austerity" plan, which included (a) new targets for coal, steel, agriculture, exports; (b) reductions in the armed forces; (c) reduction in imports from dollar countries; (d) reallocation of raw materials; (e) "control of engagements" for labor. But these measures, he emphasized, were not to interfere with full employment, social security, the National Health Service, or the housing program. Much of the wartime direction of manpower was revived, in principle at least, and with the approval of the Trades Union Congress when assurance was given that it would be applied with care. Under the Control of Engagements Order, which went into effect in October, new employment could be secured only through the exchanges. Applicants would be advised to go into priority industries and under some circumstances could be directed to do so. But there was much talk about "the spivs and the drones," especially those in luxury trades who were as elusive as "eels and butterflies." In November an order required registration of all the unemployed and those in trades considered nonessential—football pools, amusement arcades, night clubs, and the like. By these measures it was hoped to draw into industry a million additional workers. Actually, these "frightening" measures, as the *Manchester Guardian* termed them, were not seriously enforced; their chief effect was psychological.

In August sterling convertibility was suspended. Now imports from dollar areas had to be paid for in dollars. "Siege economy" regulations went into effect, reducing the meat ration from one shilling twopence per week to a shilling. Meat and cheese in restaurant meals were reduced. Tourist allowances outside sterling areas were cut to £35 per year and then in October stopped altogether. Use of gasoline for pleasure driving was suspended. The bacon ration was halved.

The economic crisis of 1947, as might be expected, stimulated agitation for changes in national leadership, even from sources generally neutral and often friendly to Labor. The *Economist*, for example, called it "a political crisis, a matter of confidence." and declared that what was needed was not "petty tinkering" but a bold monetary policy to bring purchasing power in England down to the level of the stock of available goods. There was considerable criticism of Labor's insistence upon completing the enactment of the party's legislative program.

However, Attlee's party leadership was not seriously threatened. The only likely replacement was Ernest Bevin, and Bevin himself killed such rumors. Cripps's standing steadily improved; by the end of the year he was the one member of the Government whom the *Economist* treated with respect. In September he transferred from the Board of Trade to a newly created post, that of minister of Economic Affairs, where he was to have charge of all economic planning. In November this role was absorbed in his new appointment as chancellor of the Exchequer. Cripps's Treasury policy sought to strengthen the sterling area and reduce its dependence on the dollar area (thus he made agreements with countries with large sterling balances, such as Egypt, India, and Pakistan, to limit their policies of convertibility to dollars). All this, together with his general policy of retrenchment, at once won him friends in the City and alienated him from his one-time leftist associates in his party.

Marshall Aid

In 1947 the economic crisis was uppermost, in 1948 the international problem. But the two were never far apart. For British foreign policy the commanding circumstances, 1947–48, were the development of American economic aid through the Marshall plan, the rejection by Russia of American aid, the four-power disagreement over

Germany and Berlin, the formation of the Cominform, and the Communist coup in Czechoslovakia. Of these, the failure of agreement with Russia over Germany was most crucial. A series of conferences in 1947 brought no results and ended with the stormy and fruitless session of the Council of Foreign Ministers in November-December in London. Molotov of the Soviet Union rejected Bevin's proposal of a federal constitution for the whole of Germany. As four-power action deteriorated, Britain steadily committed herself to joint action with western Europe and to reliance for economic and military aid upon the United States.

On June 5, 1947, General George C. Marshall, United States secretary of state, in a commencement address at Harvard University, proposed in very general terms a plan for American economic aid to Europe. But, he said, "The initiative, I think, must come from Europe. The role of this country should consist of friendly aid in the drafting of a European program, and of later support of such a program so far as it may be practical for us to do so."

Marshall's statement was made almost casually. Bevin was one of the first to grasp its significance. Hardly more than a week later, in a speech before the Foreign Press Association in London, he said that Marshall's speech "will rank, I think, as one of the greatest speeches made in world history." It was, in fact, the beginning of the European Recovery Program.

American opinion and policy had been moving from semi-isolation and sentimental reliance on the United Nations to a position of active leadership of "the free world" against Russia. This reversal, comparable with that great swing of 1939–41, prior to Pearl Harbor, began with the ratification of the American loan negotiated in December 1945. President Truman pressed it; nevertheless, seven long months of debate in Washington and in the American press preceded ratification. In explanation of favorable congressional action, an authority has concluded: "The loan was negotiated and first presented to the American Congress and public as a means of assuring the early establishment of freer international trade; it was finally passed by the House of Representatives as a means of stopping Russia."

Russian policy also led to America's next step. Early in 1947 the British Government informed the State Department in Washington that Britain could no longer maintain her financial and military responsibilities in Greece. On March 12 the president of the United States asked Congress to approve credits of $400 million for Greece and Turkey and to authorize military and civilian missions. At the same time he promulgated the "Truman Doctrine": "I believe it must be the policy of the United States to support free peoples who are resisting attempted subjugation by armed minorities or by outside pressures . . . . I believe that our help should be primarily through economic and financial aid."

And then in June came Marshall's proposal. It proved both unifying and divisive. Molotov referred to the proposal as a threat to the sovereignty of European nations, and Russia and her satellites refused to participate. Of the twenty-two nations invited, sixteen sent representatives to Paris in July; and by September a report on the requirements of Europe for the years 1948–51 was drafted. Thus, while the British economy was deteriorating in 1947, Marshall aid was shaping the future. On December 12 Bevin told the Society of Pilgrims in London, with Marshall present, that "Britain has been reborn." Bevin's efforts to get American support for the defense of non-Communist Europe had succeeded. In April 1948 the United States Economic Cooperation Act was effective, and aid in the amount of $4,875 million was made available for the first year. Of that sum Britain was to receive $980 million after allowing for her own grants to Europe.

Achievement in 1948

We may now compare the British economy of 1947 with that of 1948. The Economic Survey had predicted for 1947 a deficit in balance of payments of £350 million. It turned out to be £630 million. Britain bought from dollar areas about three times what she sold, and while planning to spend £350 million abroad she actually spent nearly £1,000 million. But 1948 was a different story. The *Economist* for December 25, 1948, declared that the country had finally got on the right road with "the almost magical change that has occurred in the sensitive barometer of national standing, the prestige and position of the pound sterling" in the previous twelve months. And a few months later (March 19, 1949): "1948 will stand as an example of what can be achieved by economic planning which is based on clarity of thought and backed by political courage."

Here are some of 1948's achievements: in production an increase of 30 percent over 1946; in volume of exports an increase of 35 percent over 1938; a 10 percent increase in national income (only to a small degree accounted for by higher prices) and a 7 percent increase in consumption, both as compared with 1947; a surplus of £352 million in the budget, though Cripps had planned on but £300 million; a reduction of the national debt by £453 million; and most spectacular of all, as against a deficit in the international currency account in 1947 of £630 million, a deficit in 1948 of only £120 million, with a surplus of £30 million during the second six months of the year. If coal production fell just short of the goal, the coal export target had been more than achieved, and the output per man-shift showed distinct improvement.

The Economic Survey for 1949 declared that 1948 had as much exceeded expectations as 1947 had fallen short. How to account for the 1948 achievement? It was in part through American aid and through the Intra-European Payments Scheme (liberalizing international credit), both effective the last half of the year, and in part through more freedom for industry (in 1948 a vast number of licenses and permits were abolished). But to a considerable extent the explanation was in a greater national effort, in an improved spirit in management and labor, in greater industrial efficiency. There was general acceptance of the decision to curtail imports. Management and labor were behind the Government's aim to increase the output per man and to restrict rises in wages and prices. Trade unions agreed to more flexibility in jobs, with unskilled men doing semi-skilled work and with machinery replacing manpower where possible.

A white paper of December 22, 1948, argued that international payments could be fully balanced by 1952, when American aid would cease. A four-year production program was announced, with rather ambitious goals for coal, oil, steel, agriculture, export of cotton goods. And the year which followed, 1949, seemed to be moving along auspiciously by budget day, April 6. Cripps was masterful in presenting the new budget and the Economic Survey for 1949. Despite the achievements of 1948, he was extremely cautious, budgeting for a surplus of only £14 million and calling for a reduction in cost-of-living subsidies of 20 percent. Anthony Eden at once paid Cripps the highest of compliments and called his address "condensed and brilliant oratory," and another Tory spokesman referred to the address as "the end of an era of Socialist policy and Socialist propaganda." The only serious criticism came from the Labor rebels.

Disappointment in 1949

The year 1949 did not fulfill its promise. Production was satisfactory, retail price increases were slight, demands for wage increases were restrained. Yet the dollar deficit rose in the second quarter of the year to a figure twice that of the first quarter, a development somewhat anticipated in May by the revised estimate submitted by Britain to the Organization for European Economic Cooperation. Nevertheless, the United States reduced her appropriation about 20 percent, and defended the act partly on the ground of falling prices. As it worked out, American aid covered only slightly more than one-half of Britain's dollar deficit of $632 million in the second quarter. The explanation of the greatly increased deficit was the mild recession in the United States—the American demand for British imports declined and the British were pushed into a position of greater competition for the more limited markets in the remaining dollar areas. Of course, it came to this, that British exports were not sufficient to pay for her imports. Only by lend-lease, by American loan, or by American aid did it seem possible to keep the British foreign trade account in balance.

By September 1949 a financial crisis was imminent. No solutions came from a three-power talk (Britain, the United States, and Canada) in Washington. On September 18, sterling was devaluated 30.5 percent; the pound dropped in value from $4.03 to $2.80. The initial effect, by strengthening the competitive power of British exports in dollar areas, was to improve the British account in dollars and in gold. But devaluation also brought reductions in government expenditures (including subsidies) and pressures against wage demands. Its political effect was to lower Labor prestige and the reputation of Cripps, who had said in the House of Commons in July that the Government had no intention to devaluate. The ensuing controversy marked, in reality, the beginning of the campaign for the general election of February 1950. Even the *New Statesman and Nation* said that devaluation was no policy. In the Commons debate Winston Churchill reviewed the entire record of the Government. He concluded: "I grieve that in these perilous years we should be so harshly and needlessly divided. Only an appeal to the people and a new Parliament can relieve the increasing tension." Labor rebels got busy. The Government, said Aneurin Bevan, were "ordinary chaps" who found themselves in an "extraordinary set of circumstances." The Government survived the division, 353–222, but the negative vote was the largest yet mustered.

Into Western Europe?

In 1947, with the heightening of the "cold war," maneuver and countermaneuver replaced diplomacy in the relations of Russia and the West. Each side sparred for tactical advantage in the war of words. Britain had to reconsider both her position in Europe and her position in the world. Should she seek economic recovery and national security through European cooperation or through the Dominions, her colonies, and the sterling areas generally? Were her European and her Commonwealth ties incompatible?

At first Britain moved unilaterally in Europe, for she was wary of political federation. A treaty of alliance with France signed at Dunkirk in March 1947 and to continue for fifty years guaranteed mutual support in case of a war with Germany. Thus, French fears were allayed, but in reality this treaty looked only to the past and not to postwar problems. Bevin seemed to be considering a series of such treaties. But in the same year, the Marshall Plan accented general cooperation in current problems in western Europe. In Germany, Russian policy again called the turn. The economic union of the British, American, and French zones led to the cold-war battle in Berlin, June 1948 to May 1949. The Russian blockade of Berlin against access to its western sectors by rail, road, and canal was broken by the Anglo-American airlift to the city, in which, incidentally, the United States played the major role. Concurrent with the threat of a Russian unilateral control of a central German government, Bevin had been moving toward a West European unity. In a major address to the Commons, January 22, 1948, he declared: "The conception of the unity of Europe and the preservation of Europe as the heart of Western Civilization is accepted by most people . . . . The issue is whether European unity cannot be achieved without the domination and control of one great power." And after outlining the breakdown of four-power rule in Germany, he added: "Now we have to face a new situation . . . . Surely all these developments which I have been describing point to the conclusion that the free nations of Western Europe must draw closely together . . . . I believe the time is ripe for a consolidation of Western Europe." He never made a more important speech; his words won the immediate support of Churchill and Eden.

The Brussels treaty, March 17, 1948, brought together the countries of the Dunkirk treaty, and Belgium, Holland, and Luxembourg, which were already linked economically in Benelux. The signatories promised mutual aid to any which became "the object of an armed attack in Europe." Economic policies among the signatory countries were to be coordinated where possible, and a common effort was to be made to raise the standard of living in western Europe. A consultative Council of Foreign Ministers was to meet as circumstances required, and a permanent commission was to meet in London at least once a month.

Britain's position in the Commonwealth was accommodated to these commitments. The prime ministers in October 1948 formally approved, though cautiously, the idea of western European union "in accordance with the interests of the other members of the United Nations and the promotion of world peace." The major consideration would seem to have been that, with the relative decline of the United Kingdom as a power, the national interests of the other Commonwealth nations came to be associated with the success of Western union. In Britain itself, Churchill enthusiastically organized the United Europe Movement and attended the great demonstration for European unity at The Hague in May 1948. Once again Labor met trouble only from rebels in its own ranks, who interpreted Churchill's efforts as merely supporting a Western bloc organized to check the Soviet Union. Churchill was "not seeking a United Europe, but a Divided Europe," said the *Daily Herald*.

The next step was not long in coming. In March 1949 Bevin released a draft of the North Atlantic Pact; NATO was to include the signatories at Brussels along with Canada and the United States, with still other states invited to join. It was a military alliance, with the pious hope that the parties would encourage economic cooperation. The parties were bound to take all action necessary to establish the security of the North Atlantic area and its territory in Europe and North America, including forces in Germany and Algeria. The pact was approved by the Commons 333 to 6 and, so far as Britain was concerned, became effective with formal signatures of twelve states in Washington, D.C., on April 4.

British policy looked to Western Europe, the Commonwealth, and the United States to safeguard national security in "the free world" and to contain Communist ambitions. She called this an adaptation to the new international situation, not loss of power. But toward notions of European union in any political sense she was still very cautious indeed. Great Britain, alone of European lands, had emerged from the war with her institutions unscathed and with national unity and pride strengthened. As has often been suggested, the vital need for some rallying cry, other than nationalism, so apparent to most Europeans, was not shared or even understood in Britain. She participated, but without enthusiasm, in the formation of the Council of Europe in May 1949 (the framework included a Committee of Ministers and a Consultative Assembly). But she avoided official association with the European Coal and Steel Community (April 1951) in which production was to be controlled by a supranational body. Britain did arrange to be represented by a permanent delegation which would be empowered to reach agreements with E.C.S.C. But Britain's refusal to relinquish her right to arrive at independent decisions was widely noted. And the Conservatives when they came to power soon after did not change Britain's position.

"How Have They Done?"

In the course of the debate, September 1949, on devaluation of the pound sterling, Churchill spoke of the Labor Government which came to power in 1945: "Under the unchallenged working of our Constitution a new Parliament was brought into being by the free choice of our people.... The present Government were the result. The question now is, how have they done?" It was a pertinent question, for the general election was due by law not later than July 1950.

An interesting development in these years was the change in the Government's tone. The economic crisis of 1947, and to a lesser extent the crisis of 1949, caught the Government by surprise and left it on the defensive. Control softened into regulation and a more flexible policy was developed to meet a fluid situation. A tendency toward the doctrinaire disappeared; the Economic Survey for 1950 made no reference whatsoever to economic planning. But if we may conclude that Labor dealt indifferently or even unsuccessfully with sudden crisis, the party scored impressively in its program of legislation for achieving the general goals of "reconstruction" which most sections of English society welcomed after the war.

An Assessment of Nationalization

As we have seen, the legislation of nationalization did not constitute a revolution in economic thought. Most of the acts of Parliament (the Gas Act and some sections of the Transport Act were exceptions) were received with little fuss by private management and generally greeted by the public as "a good thing." In some instances, especially in utilities, one form of public control merely replaced another. Workers did not participate in management in any of the nationalized industries. Creation of a "public corporation" made it possible to retain the same type of leadership as before; now management was responsible not to stockholders but to the Government. But this was not like the responsibility of a foreign secretary or of a chancellor of the Exchequer to Parliament. The personnel of the public authority was not considered a part of the political machine; it had no relation even to the permanent civil service. A nationalized industry was responsible to a ministry only for general policy; the minister did supervise programs of training and research, and his approval was necessary for major reorganization requiring considerable new capital. But in an interesting Commons debate in March 1948, all parties agreed that parliamentary inquiry into nationalized industries was to be permitted only on matters of general policy affecting the public interest and not on details of operation.

Coal, Transport, and Gas. What had happened to "King Coal, the paramount lord of industry," as Lloyd George had called it during the First World War? The first four years of coal nationalization, 1947 through 1950, proved disappointing to its supporters and to its detractors alike. Overall production of coal increased about 10 percent, enough to constitute a modest talking point but quite insufficient for British domestic and export needs. Year by year reasonable increases in production goals were set, but in only one year, 1949, was the goal actually reached, and then barely so. Production never climbed much higher than 215 million tons and in deep-mined coal fell nearly 40 million tons short of prewar figures. It was thus a far cry from those halcyon days of 1913 when Britain produced 287 million tons, of which nearly 100 million tons went into foreign trade.

Production is closely associated with manpower. After 1945 the number of workers employed in the mines declined and by 1950 stood at the lowest point in the century. Production per man-shift now improved, but the increased use of machinery did not fully compensate for the shorter week and for absenteeism; the annual output per man remained, down through 1950, less than it had been in 1937.

It had been fondly hoped by the champions of nationalization that the miners as a class would be rejuvenated and would participate enthusiastically in bringing to pass "the new world." But while there had been striking improvement in their working conditions and in their wages—with fringe benefits they became the highest-paid workers in Britain—the morale of the miners was not much affected. If labor-management relations were not as stormy as in the twenties, they were not as quiet as in the thirties. Labor disputes in the first few years of nationalization accounted for annual loss of about 1,500,000 tons, a not insignificant item. Absenteeism remained higher than in other industries.

The Coal Board did not produce miracles. Reorganization of pits and introduction of machinery were limited. To avoid falling into debt, the Board raised prices. And in November 1950 it issued a plan calling for extensive capital improvement, and for eventual targets, by 1961–65, of 230 to 250 million tons. On the whole, the industry probably fared somewhat better after 1945 under nationalization than it would have under private ownership. In private hands, it is likely that stoppages from strikes would have been greater, that wages of miners and prices of coal would have gone higher, that overall production would have been somewhat lower.

On January 1, 1948 the British Transport Commission began to exercise its managerial functions. Each of its five boards was at once concerned with complicated transfers of property. For example, the property taken over from the private railway companies, we are told, consisted of "52,000 miles of track, 13,500 stations, 20,000 locomotives, 45,000 passenger carriages, 1,235,000 freight wagons, 100 steamships, 70 hotels, 50,000 houses, 9,000 horses, 25,000 horse-drawn vehicles, and 11,000 motor vehicles." The new transport stock issued in exchange for the securities of the private railway and canal companies and the London Passenger Transport was valued at £1,065 million. The controversy aroused over the details of enactment carried over into problems of operation, especially costs of operation. The main purpose of the act, to integrate rail and road, was not achieved.

The gas industry was not nationalized until 1948, and then only after a bitter fight in Parliament. With public control established over coal and electric power, Labor declared that gas must be nationalized to "achieve coordination in the sphere of fuel and power." The measure, as it happened, followed closely the recommendations of the committee established during the war under Geoffrey Heyworth, chairman of Unilever Ltd. In order to group producers of gas in larger units and thus provide more economical service, twelve regional boards were established with responsibility for the production and distribution of gas and coke. Above these boards was the Gas Council, which was to advise the minister of fuel and power, to negotiate with labor unions, to encourage research, and to control long-term borrowing in the industry.

Iron and Steel. "Most of the members of the Government are now heartily sorry that the word 'steel' ever crept into the pages of 'Let Us Face the Future,' " declared the *Economist* on August 16, 1947. This was an acute observation, for "steel" became the constant refuge of the forces opposed to nationalization and also a source of deep differences within the Labor Party itself. Steel was not a "public utility" and had not been under public control as had electricity, gas, and the railroads for years. As a matter of fact, the steel industry had "rationalized itself" and by 1939 had become "the most completely self-cartellized and controlled of any major British industry." The wartime agencies under the Ministry of Supply were replaced in 1946 by the Iron and Steel Board, which, so the industry claimed, exercised sufficient control over prices and over capital expansion in accordance with a plan for "modernization and new construction" recommended by the Iron and Steel Federation late in 1945. The record of iron and steel was, relatively speaking, excellent; the industry prospered before the war, and between 1946 and 1951 its production figures rose 48 percent, with the annual targets set in the Economic Surveys exceeded year after year. On the other hand, the success which the industry enjoyed seemed to come from just that element of quasi-monopoly in the industry which made it vulnerable to socialist attack. And Labor maintained that the industry's success was cautiously and narrowly conceived. Protected by tariffs, the industry advanced its prices in the thirties, and even in the best of those years never sought full employment.

And so there was promise of a serious and significant debate on how the industry might most nearly achieve its potential and, thus, best serve the nation. Instead, however, the industry and its proposed nationalization became the symbol of conflict between private enterprise and public control. In this battle over principle, iron and steel were often forgotten. In part this was because the case of each side had an essential weakness. No one could successfully argue that the iron and steel industry had failed, nor could one maintain that iron and steel was "a public utility" and for that reason should be publicly owned. Yet, management could hardly argue that the industry was altogether sound, that it fully met Britain's need for steel and labor's need for employment. Both sides could and did argue about the principle of the thing.

To Labor, steel nationalization came to assume the importance of a test case; failure to implement this proposal might bring an abrupt end to Labor's entire program and, perhaps, to its power. But for Labor, in office, there was added embarrassment in the difference in approach between socialist doctrinaires like Dalton, Bevan, Shinwell, and Strachey, and the more practical politicians such as Attlee, Morrison, and Bevin. By 1947 further complications loomed; steel nationalization, abhorred by American business, might jeopardize congressional approval of the American economic aid program. And so for one reason or another the Government delayed action.

By 1948, when Labor did "mean business," there was every indication that the House of Lords, under Conservative control, would use its power to deny final action for two years. Thus, it was doubtful that the measure could be enacted within the limits of the existing Parliament, scheduled to be dissolved not later than 1950. In anticipation, Labor had already introduced a bill to reduce the Lords' veto power to one year. This proposal led to an all-parties conference to consider once again reform of the House of Lords; but the problem of the relation of the two houses still could not be resolved. Labor insisted that even though "reformed," the Lords would not be democratic and, therefore, should not be empowered to check the will of the Commons for as long as two years. Labor persisted with the bill to amend the Parliament Act of 1911, and after a bitter debate in which all the standard arguments were resurrected, the bill became law in 1949.

In 1948 the Steel Nationalization Bill was introduced and received final Commons approval in May 1949, but the Lords insisted that operation await another election; so many Lords amendments had appeared in the course of the legislative process that Labor concluded that their consideration would postpone enactment well into 1950 and complicate the selection of a date for the election. Therefore, the two parties agreed that the Lords should approve the measure but that it should not become effective until January 1951. In the meantime, the election should have decided its actual fate.

Fortunes of the National Health Service

The National Health Service Act was enacted November 6, 1946, but the "appointed day" was not until July 5, 1948.

In the "tooling up" process in the interim, new extremes of prophecy were achieved in the ranks both of those who approved the new legislation and of those who were opposed.

The controversy within the medical profession culminated in two well-publicized plebiscites conducted by the British Medical Association in the months preceding vesting day. The first of these, in February 1948, indicated that about 90 percent of the profession disapproved of the act. But much criticism was stimulated by personal animosity toward Bevan, who remained unperturbed throughout the turmoil and predicted that the act would become effective as scheduled. When he gave assurances that there would be no salaried medical service and that general practitioners would not be moved arbitrarily around the country, much of the opposition evaporated; in the second plebiscite, in April, only 65 percent of the profession expressed disapproval of the act. And only about half of the general practitioners said they would be reluctant to enter the service. Then special committees, composed of medical men and laymen, recommended a scheme, generally found acceptable, by which doctors would have a choice between remuneration solely by "capitation fee" (based on the total number of patients) or a combination of fixed annual salary plus a capitation fee. Both doctor and patient would enjoy a voluntary relationship. The principle of competition was thus preserved. Further, it became clear that any practitioner who entered the service would be free to conduct his own private practice concurrently. Thus, by vesting day, many objections to the service had lost their force. The council of the Association therefore recommended acceptance by all members of the profession.

In its first years the Health Service operated somewhat shakily. Many problems were unavoidable. Thousands of individuals had received little medical attention since 1939, and with so much service now available without charge the demand was overwhelming. The Health Service was unable to increase at once the number of available doctors, and the hospitals were suddenly overwhelmed—hundreds and thousands of persons became hospital patients for the first time in their lives. In spite of the effort to work out a reasonable schedule of fees and payments, abuses and anomalies crept in. Previously hundreds of thousands of persons had purchased eyeglasses from self-test counters. Now, in the first year, something like seven million pairs of spectacles were prescribed by examination. The English have had a reputation abroad for ignoring their teeth; the dentists now faced a staggering demand for dentures. In a land of forty-seven million people there were but ten thousand dentists. Total cost of the Health Service to taxpayers proved to be far in advance of original estimates; the estimate for the fiscal year 1949–50 was £260 million; the actual cost was £359 million.

But problems were gradually solved or at least controlled, and by 1950 it was clear that the National Health Service was to stay. By then 97 percent of the population were enrolled on doctors' lists, and about 88 percent of all medical doctors and about 95 percent of all dentists were in the service. Politically the issue was settled. This was evident in 1949 when the Government presented its supplemental budgetary estimates with an item for the National Health Service. The Conservative Opposition was critical in debate but did not dare go on record as in favor of paring down the service. Thus, on the voice vote an absolute silence greeted the call for the negative. The country accepted the Health Service as an improvement over the chaos it replaced. The service did not immediately even approach the degree of success its enthusiasts predicted. It was too much to expect that the quality of medical service would at once improve. But medical attention was now available to all, and this was the matter of immediate significance to most Englishmen.

The Housing Program

As the year 1950 opened, the *Economist* remarked that Aneurin Bevan's housing program since 1945 had been "erratic, expensive and in some respects unjust. But judged by the paramount test, that of number of buildings completed, it has succeeded." The postwar situation required strong measures. One-third of England's homes were destroyed or damaged by enemy action during the war. In the decade 1939-49 the population of the United Kingdom increased by two and one-quarter million.

The basic statute, the Housing Act of 1946, established the principle that housing was a public and not a private problem, and was placed under the administration of the minister of Health. Bevan concluded that most people in Britain must rent housing and that, since private enterprise did not find such undertakings profitable, local authorities must assume responsibility, with national resources providing most of the financing.

Control of construction was exercised by about 1,470 local councils. It was established that for every four dwellings built by public authority only one could be built for private sale. Private construction was permitted on order only, not for speculation. Rentals of the new housing units were controlled and subsidized. Originally, the normal subsidy provided per house was £22 a year for sixty years, by which it was calculated that the rental of a "council house" would be only ten shillings a week. But with increasing costs of construction these figures were revised. By 1949 the deficits in the housing accounts of the London County Council meant an actual subsidy of about £36 a year. Even though rents rose considerably above the ten-shilling level, the demand for new housing remained far ahead of supply.

Altogether it was a fast-moving program after 1946, and it is not surprising that "council housing" remained a volatile subject with charges of inefficiency and waste, with concern for the effect of such public construction on the building industry, with the heavy burdens on the public treasury, and with charges of inequities in the fixing of rentals. Were the results satisfactory? The *Economist* pointed out that in the period 1945–50, about 806,000 permanent new homes and apartments were constructed; repair and conversion of existing buildings provided an additional 333,000 permanent units; 157,000 temporary houses were provided. This seems a considerable achievement. But it does compare somewhat unfavorably with results achieved in the thirties.

Education in Transition

The momentum of reform during the war produced the Education Act of 1944—in the words of an authority, "a deliberate attempt . . . to make . . . a coherent, coordinated and all-inclusive structure capable of providing for the total educational needs of the nation, up to the point at which the universities took over." The new Government in August 1945 recognized its obligation to activate this legislation "at the earliest possible date."

First of all, it was necessary to postpone the raising of the school-leaving age until more teachers and more adequate facilities could be provided. It was estimated that seventy thousand new teachers would be required to care for the additional pupils; yet by 1939 only about seven thousand new teachers were becoming available each year. This problem had been anticipated, and at the end of 1943 a special committee within the Board of Education produced what was "probably the most daring large-scale experiment ever made in the history of English education," an experiment which worked and without which the Education Act of 1944 would have failed. This was the Emergency Scheme for Training Teachers. All those between the ages of twenty-one and thirty-five who had engaged in some form of wartime national service were invited to apply for a one-year teacher-training course to be followed by two years of part-time study while teaching. Upon the successful completion of this course, they would be recognized as qualified teachers. Academic qualifications for admission to the program were somewhat flexible, personal characteristics being heavily weighted. Training was free and maintenance grants were included.

A small "pilot" class, in September 1944, demonstrated the soundness and popularity of the idea. With the end of the war apparently in sight, applications began to pour in. By July 1945 some twenty-five thousand were on the waiting list. By December 1946 thirty-one training colleges were in operation; they grew in number to fifty-five, including some housed in industrial hostels, some in "hutted" hospitals and some in army camps. The prospective teachers came from a broad range of previous occupations; more than 75 percent had attended secondary or technical school. To staff the training colleges the ministry daringly drew on "serving teachers," taken directly from the classroom and the administrative office. When the Emergency Training Scheme ended in October 1951, it had produced thirty-five thousand teachers, about one-sixth of all the teachers in active service.

The problem of physical facilities was also met by emergency measures. The HORSA were standardized huts and the SFORSA standardized furniture. Within three years' time 6,328 newschool rooms were provided and equipped.

In accordance with the general provisions of the 1944 act, the Further Education and Training Scheme was established to aid those whose education had been interrupted by war service. Some eighty-five thousand grants of necessary expense for full-time study had been made by 1949. Approximately half of these grants were for study in the universities. Of those receiving aid, 80 percent completed their courses.

But these measures were all temporary, and the act of 1944 had envisaged a new educational system on a permanent basis. The problems at first seemed almost insurmountable. The first regulations called for a certain standard to be maintained in all school buildings, and the Education Committee of the London County Council responded that not a single building within its jurisdiction met the specified standard. New school construction took second place to housing. Demands suddenly increased in April 1947, when the regulation raising the school-leaving age to fifteen became effective. However, by the middle of 1952 more than one thousand new schools had been constructed, teacher training had been overhauled, and the number of new teachers available each year was steadily increasing. The economic position of the teacher was strengthened with a uniform salary scale enforced by the Ministry of Education.

Probably the most important single reform in the act of 1944 was the provision for secondary education for all children, a provision which destroyed the remnants of the English tradition that democratic education meant only elementary education. The problems here were mostly of the long-range variety—new school buildings, suitable courses of instruction, and the types of schools necessary for the varieties of secondary education which would be offered. The alternatives open posed difficult choices for parents and for school authorities. Should it be the old grammar school whose training was nonvocational and prepared for universities and the professions, or the technical school which was strictly vocational, or the newest institution, the secondary modern school, designed to provide "a good all-round" education neither strictly academic nor strictly technical? Now the examination at "eleven plus" became even more significant.

In higher education the most obvious problem was admissions. There was a backlog of students whose attendance at university had been suspended or postponed by the war. And there was also the principle now espoused that university education should be available to anyone who could profit by it, regardless of his financial means. Some permanent procedures were now developed: government scholarships were extended and supplemented; scholarship holders from a university recieved supplemental aid from the Ministry of Education, up to full expenses, according to need. The report of the University Grants Committee for the period 1935 to 1947 showed that annual parliamentary grants in aid of higher education rose from £2,000,000 to almost £7,000,000. By 1951, 73 percent of the students in universities were receiving state aid, and 64 percent of the universities' budgets was underwritten by the government.

The war had underlined the inadequacies of technological education. The report of a special committee headed by Lord Eustace Percy led to the appointment in 1948 of the National Advisory Council on Education for Industry and Commerce. A program was inaugurated which would enable some thirty of the technical colleges to become advanced regional colleges granting technical degrees. In turn this proved to be a stimulus to university training—in two years the number of advanced students in science and technology had doubled.

An entirely different kind of intellectual inspiration created the University College of North Staffordshire, near Stoke on Trent, opened in 1950. Its mission was conceived as that of counteracting the heavy specialization which was traditional in English universities. A four-year course rather than the customary three provided a curriculum not dissimilar from the pattern of American colleges; a year entirely in general education (history of civilization, present-day problems, experimental science) preceded intensive study of the area of specialization.

At the same time, some interesting questions were being raised. Since class distinctions in education were supposedly eliminated, the old public school became more difficult to defend. Many such schools were now having difficulty maintaining standards; by 1948 it was said that the average government grammar school was as good as or better than the average public school. There was uncertainty about the role of higher education in a democratic society. Can culture be disseminated to the masses? What is the relation of scientific to technical training? And what is the relation of the traditional "grey stone" universities at Oxford and Cambridge to the new "red brick" universities?

A Balance Sheet

At the end of its survey of foreign and domestic affairs the *Annual Register* for 1949 attempted to draw up a kind of balance sheet for the year. This analysis was hardly more than a series of question marks. It appeared that Britain's position in the world, because of her close alliance with western Europe and the United States, was stronger at the end of 1949 than it had been in 1946.

At home the evolution of the welfare state and not the measures of nationalization constituted the permanent contribution of the Labor Government and the chief source of its political strength for the future. But the welfare legislation had weakened Labor's appeal as a socialist party, for it had not come about through class conflict, but rather in response to an overwhelming demand that the lot of the common man be improved.

To reformers whose concern was for social amelioration, many gains had been registered. Unemployment had virtually disappeared. The highest postwar unemployment until 1966 was 2.5 percent in 1946; by 1949 it was down to 1.2 percent and remained there—that figure is completely accounted for by the normal shifts in occupation. The share of national income which went to wages increased from 39 percent in 1938 to 48 percent in 1948, and through subsidies and controlled prices the purchasing power of real wages had increased. Even when the rise in prices is accounted for, public expenditures for social services nearly doubled between 1938 and 1950. The burden of taxation naturally fell most heavily on the well-to-do. By 1951 the rate was nineteen shillings sixpence on the pound on income above £20,000. It was thus rendered difficult to have left from earned income, after taxation, more than £6,000. For a married man this required gross income of £85,000. In 1949 only 86 persons in the United Kingdom were in this category, compared with 6,560 ten years before.

But the question was quite properly raised: "In attempting to 'maximize welfare' is the Government not in danger of preventing the maximization of the national income?" Increase in spendable income did not necessarily mean an increase in consumption. The Government white paper of February 1948 recognized this fact: "Until more goods and services are available for the home market there is no justification for any general increase of individual money incomes." The Labor Government had changed the nature of England's problem. It was no longer a question of poverty or of equality but rather the challenge to achieve for all her people a satisfactory standard of living. The extent to which Labor leadership was meeting this challenge was controversial.

The Path of Politics, 1949–50

In the fall of 1949 a general election was near at hand. But well before that, it was evident that Labor had lost the hold on the electorate which had made possible its great victory in 1945. By mid-1947, probably because of the economic crisis of that year and the austerity program instituted by the Government, Gallup Polls were showing the two major parties fairly evenly divided in the allegiance of voters. In November 1947 the Conservatives made sweeping gains in municipal elections. But not until January 1948 did Labor lose in a by-election a parliamentary seat won in 1945 (twenty-two other seats had been retained). This result at Camlachie constituency in Glasgow, together with a greatly reduced Labor majority at Gravesend two months earlier, led impartial observers to the opinion that had a general election been held then, Labor would have remained in power, but only by a much smaller margin.

Labor: Disaffection and Discipline

By 1948 Labor Party unity was threatened by disaffection in its ranks, a movement not strong enough to challenge the existing leadership but embarrassing enough to weaken the party in the eyes of the nation. The rebels were not all of the same mind in domestic affairs, but they shared views hostile to the Cabinet's foreign policy. On the extreme left, Konni Zilliacus was a constant source of trouble and so was a kindred spirit, L. D. Solley. But more dangerous was a wider front which from 1945 to 1947 called itself the "Third Force," independent of both Russia and the United States. As a separate power group in Parliament this movement had possibilities—Aneurin Bevan, for example, toyed with it briefly. Support came from the old I.L.P. pacifist element as well as from such left-wing intellectuals as R. H. S. Crossman, Michael Foot, and Ian Mikardo in the Commons and G. D. H. Cole outside. But the Third Force soon declined as an idea, perhaps because of its very compromise character.

The rebels turned rather to periodic harassment of their party leaders. Each foreign policy debate brought sharp questions from the Government benches; each annual party conference found Ernest Bevin on the defensive. The Bevin policy was "crypto-Fulton-Winston," said Zilliacus at the Margate conference in the spring of 1947. (The year before, Kingsley Martin had written in the *New Statesman and Nation* that the Labor rebels in the Commons included a few "crypto-Communists.") By autumn Zilliacus and his associates were attacking the American capitalists and the Marshall Plan. In May 1948 they said that Bevin's policy meant a drift toward war.

This criticism led to uproar, and uproar to expulsion. In April 1948 one Labor member was expelled from the Parliamentary Labor Party for supporting Communists in the Italian election; two others were expelled for opposing nationalization of steel. Bevin's Palestine policy damaged his standing in his party—it was undoubtedly the weakest phase of his policy—and in the debate of January 1949 a large-scale absentee vote brought the Labor majority down to ninety. In May 1949 Zilliacus and Solley were expelled from the Parliamentary Labor Party for opposing ratification of NATO, and the parliamentary private secretaries of four ministers were discharged for voting against the Ireland Bill. Some sixty-six other Labor M.P.s also voted against the Government on the Ireland Bill. They were admonished that it was proper to abstain from voting for conscience sake but not proper to vote against the Government on a party measure. Refusal of party endorsement at the next election might follow. In June the expelled Labor members formed the "Labor Independent Group" in Parliament. It is therefore not surprising that the party conferences of 1948 and 1949 met in a sober and chastened mood. The way to win the next election, said one Laborite, "is not to tear the party apart beforehand."

Conservatives: Frustration and Reorganization

But Labor so completely dominated the Commons that the Conservative story in this Parliament is largely one of frustration. In the autumn of 1945, the Conservatives, spurred on by their central council, made a head-on attack against the nationalization program of the Government. The vote of censure was defeated 381 to 197, altogether "a shadow-boxing display," as Cripps termed it. Ten months later, at the party conference of 1946, the Conservatives were still in search of a policy. They were able to probe the weaknesses of the Government in the economic crisis of 1947 but had no clear alternatives themselves. Finally, in October 1947, the party conference endorsed the "Industrial Charter." General support for nationalization of certain industries and the directing role of the state was qualified by a demand for decentralization of authority and reaffirmation of confidence in free enterprise. But in effect this document accepted the "revolution" of 1945. Other important Conservative Party statements followed in the next eighteen months: *The Agricultural Policy* supporting guaranteed prices in the Statute of 1947; *Imperial Policy* emphasizing "Empire economic partnership"; and *Scot-*

tish Control of Scottish Affairs. Such was "the New Conservatism," as it was coming to be called.

In national politics the Conservatives had to wait for the next general election. But they made considerable gains in the municipal elections of November 1947 and scored an even more impressive victory eighteen months later in the elections for the London County Council, which Labor had controlled since 1934. With a Conservative gain of thirty-six seats and a Labor loss of twenty-six, the two parties emerged with an exact tie, sixty-four seats each. These gains reflected a vast improvement in party organization. The contribution of the party chairman, Lord Woolton, probably falls a little short of what he himself later claimed for it. But certainly his energetic leadership was in important factor. A satisfactory party chest, the Central Fund, developed when Woolton disdained the goal of £250,000 suggested by others, boldly demanded £1,000,000 and got it. It was decided that election campaign expenses were to be paid by the constituency and not by the candidate, as heretofore, thus broadening the base from which the local associations could choose their own candidates. The role of the "party agent" was effectively developed. By 1950 in England and Wales, 527 out of 542 parliamentary constituencies had full-time Conservative agents, most of them highly trained and sensitive to the needs of the national organization. In the revival of the party the "Young Conservatives" (those under thirty) became increasingly active. And in terms of issues and policy the "intellectual powerhouse" of party recovery was R. A. Butler and his revitalized Research Department.

Questions of Party Policy

By 1949 Labor's problem was clear enough. In domestic policy its main objectives had been achieved. "The plain fact," said the *New Statesman and Nation* for May 15, 1949, "is that the Labour Party is reaching the end of the road which it first set itself to traverse in 1918 . . . . What next?" In foreign affairs the party's problem was that of reconciling the Bevin emphasis on safeguarding British national interests with the views of the left-wing section of the party, which was still insistent upon "a socialist policy" in world affairs.

Labor's predicament is apparent in *Labour Believes in Britain*, released by party leaders in April 1949. This statement was cautious even to the extent of recognizing the continuing role of private enterprise while affirming continued faith in nationalization. The domestic program was to be geared with a foreign policy whose precise nature it was impossible to blueprint. Labor was clearly trying to dig in.

But the Conservatives had their own problem, that of squaring a strong attack on Labor's record with endorsement of those elements in the program which the country had accepted and which no party hopeful of victory could reject. One answer was the bold one of the Young Conservatives. Their spokesman, Robert Boothby, at the party Conference in the spring of 1949 declared:

> Britain has undergone one of the greatest social revolutions in her history. The strength of the Tory Party in Britain and its continuance as a major force in British politics lie in its empirical approach to current problems and its readiness to accept facts, not as we would like them to be, but as they are. We accepted the revolution of 1832 and governed England for a considerable part of the nineteenth century in consequence. I am glad to tell you that we have accepted the revolution of 1945 and are looking forward to governing England again for a good part of the rest of this century.

Officially the Conservative response was propounded in *The Right Road for Britain*, issued in July 1949. The welfare state was approved, but administration was to be tightened and costs reduced. Existing nationalization, save the measure for iron and steel, was accepted, but the nationalized industries were to be overhauled and no further nationalization was advocated. To describe its tone the *Manchester Guardian* revived the phrase "Tory Socialism." This document, like *Labour Believes in Britain*, was frankly vote-catching.

A "snap election" called by Attlee to catch the Conservatives off balance was widely expected. But any such designs Attlee may have harbored in the summer of 1949 were affected by (1) the fortunes of the Steel Nationalization Bill and (2) the sterling crisis leading to devaluation of September 18. Eventually, on October 13, Attlee reduced the political tension by his announcement that the general election would not come before the new year. But when the Government in November reached a compromise with the Lords over the steel measure, speculation was renewed and continued until January 11, when Attlee announced the dissolution of Parliament for February 3, with the polling of February 23. The formal campaign would last a scant three weeks.

The General Election of 1950

Since 1945 parliamentary legislation had made several important changes in the electoral laws. Some strongholds of prestige were destroyed. The twelve university seats (those for Oxford and Cambridge dated back to 1603) were abolished, eliminating an "extra vote" for 228,769 persons. This measure evoked in opposition much the same arguments used to defend the rotten boroughs in 1831 and 1832—the argument of historic tradition and the claim that these seats were usually held by men of distinction. Since 1945 these seats had usually been held by Conservatives or independents and their elimination was politically to Labor's advantage. Also eliminated was the business premises franchise, which gave a second vote (though not in the same constituency) to a maximum of 70,000 voters. However, this extra vote had been of significant consequence only in the City of London. Now the last vestige of plural voting was gone.

"One vote, one value" was another Labor shibboleth; therefore, a redistribution of members sought to equalize the constituencies in terms of population—the previous redistribution had been in 1918. The total number of seats was reduced from 640 to 625, only 80 of which emerged with their old boundaries untouched. Redistribution actually favored the Conservatives. Another bastion of tradition was swept away when the City of London was deprived of separate representation. Since its resident population was small, as a constituency it was joined with the City of Westminster.

Two Roads to Welfare. The campaign in February 1950 had some interesting features, as well described by H. G. Nicholas in his account of this election. A record number of candidates took to the hustings, 1,868 for 625 seats. Labor and Conservatives contested nearly all; the Liberals fought 475 (50 percent more than in 1945) and the Communists 100. An intriguing episode was the exchange between Churchill and the *Manchester Guardian*, carried on with dignity and affection but also with verve and sting. Churchill was seeking the Liberal vote, and the *Guardian*, traditionally Liberal, could not but wonder what might happen to the fortunes of the party should Churchill return to his allegiance of earlier days. During the campaign the Conservatives did not tire of talking about the fortunes of the Groundnut (peanut) Scheme of 1949. This was part of a program for the development of East Africa; by 1950 it was seen as a huge fiasco; in 1949 there was an outlay of £23 million and nothing to show for it. Eventually, in January 1951, the whole project was abandoned save for a very limited experimental venture.

But the campaign, so long anticipated and so well prepared for, brought few surprises. The Labor and Conservative manifestoes were, allowing for some changes in emphasis, condensed versions of the longer party statements of 1949, already described. The chief differences between them were in methods proposed for implementing the social services, in the Labor stand for modest extension of nationalization as against a firm Conservative position against further nationalization, and in the attack of the one on the other's past record. The Liberal Party manifesto called for a halt to nationalization and dwelt on the importance of solving the dollar problem. The Communist manifesto held Labor responsible for betraying working-class interests. These party statements probably swayed even fewer voters than usual.

The radio campaign had moments of special interest. Well before dissolution of Parliament, J. B. Priestley launched the Labor campaign with a "non-party," "reasonable" appeal to the middle-class voter, disgruntled with high taxes and irked by restrictions, to think twice, remember the blessings of the Labor Government, and vote for its continuance. A week later, still before the opening of the formal campaign, Churchill spoke for the Conservatives. His design, like Priestley's, was to strengthen the morale of good party members. "As I see it, the choice before us is whether we should take another plunge into Socialist regimentation or, by a strong effort, regain the freedom, initiative and opportunity of British life." In the first of the formal election broadcasts, Herbert Morrison, like the astute politician he was, set out to woo the marginal voter. Thus Labor's policy was presented as moderate; its achievement, especially as dealing with unemployment, extraordinary; and the Tory past, lean and unworthy of the confidence of the electorate. Lord Woolton, the chairman of the Conservative Party, promised more housing, full employment, and in due time elimination of rationing and price control. Then came the Conservative retort to Priestley, a response to the Labor "myth" about the Tory failures of the 1930s. This was in the broadcast of Dr. Charles Hill, the "Radio Doctor" of the B.B.C. As secretary of the British Medical Association, he had engaged Aneurin Bevan in the conflict over the Health Service. He now set out to deflate Labor claims of achievement, to associate "planning" with racketeering, and to raise the ghost of the superstate.

The interest in Hill's broadcast was topped only by that in Churchill's address in Edinburgh the same evening. The announcement of America's decision to produce a hydrogen bomb had led to a statement from Attlee that a conference of heads of state of the Great Powers, as suggested and urged by some leading Quakers, might only "raise hopes unduly." Churchill in reply spoke of "a supreme effort to bridge the gulf" between Soviet Russia and the West. "It is not easy to see how things could be worsened by a parley at the summit if such a thing were possible." This speech brought foreign policy, for the first time, into the campaign. It is interesting that Churchill should have made such a proposal—that of a "summit" meeting—and that Labor should have minimized it. But for the campaign it might have been the reverse.

The final broadcast was made by Attlee. He and Mrs. Attlee had just returned from a 1,300-mile campaign trip which the election historian calls a *tour de force* of unassuming advertisement. The family car, pre-war and far from *de luxe*, Mrs. Attlee at the wheel ... the road side stops when, ahead of schedule, Mrs. Attlee would catch up on her knitting and Mr. Attlee would do a crossword puzzle—this was the very stuff of honest, uninvidious, unpretentious, non-queue-jumping, post-war Britain .... However worked upon by hostile critics, it could not be presented as part of a picture of Socialist folly and extravagance, nor as the curtain-raiser to class war.

Attlee told his audience that he had seen a "puissant nation" and he reviewed the record of his Government. He concluded with an appeal to the voters to continue in the path Labor had set. "I ask you to go forward along the road with us. We shall not fail you. Let us win through together."

Beneath all the campaign oratory one conclusion emerges: there was fundamental agreement by both parties, their leaders, and the rank and file, on essentials. The welfare state with its various social services was now taken for granted; nationalization and private enterprise seemed to exist fairly happily side by side and the British people wished it that way; the problems of the economy could be solved only by greatly increased national production; the future of Britain in the world was uncertain and, therefore, her role should be worked out with prudence and with forethought.

A Majority of Six. There was also general agreement in 1950 that February, with its short, dark days, its cold and fog, its rain and snow, was a miserable month in which to wage a general election. The twenty-third began with bright periods, but rain soon spread eastward and by evening enveloped most of the country in a downpour. Even so, about 84 percent of the electorate went to the polls. At Coventry, with 87.7 percent voting, the ballot papers gave out. But the national increase from 73.5 percent in 1945 is not so striking as it seems, since at least 5 percent of that increase is accounted for by a more accurate register and by the introduction of postal voting.

That evening, crowds streamed to Piccadilly and Trafalgar to see the early returns flashed on gigantic screens. The "battle of the gap" (there was a large initial lead for Labor with its early victories in urban areas) continued until the evening of the next day before Labor was assured of being still the largest single party. It was narrowly so: Labor had 315 seats, the Conservatives had 298, the Liberals 9, and the Irish Nationalists 2. The overall Labor majority had been reduced to 6. In popular vote Labor polled 46.1 percent and the Conservatives 43.4 percent. The Liberals' 9.2 percent, a figure which undoubtedly would have been higher had there been any possibility of national success, brought them only 9 representatives in Parliament. The swing of voters which brought almost even the Conservative and Labor ranks in Parliament was a mere 3.3 percent in the United Kingdom (3.4 percent in Great Britain), one in every thirty-three voters. Labor losses were chiefly in suburban areas of the big cities, where office workers and the professional classes lived. Their taxes had increased but their incomes had not.

Stalemate and the Election of 1951

The 1950 election was generally interpreted as a stalemate, in which no party received a mandate and by which no strong Government would be possible. In most quarters another election was predicted in short order, though on second thought it was generally agreed that another poll was unlikely to produce a much different result.

But that the new Parliament might keep alive for a while was apparent soon after it met March 6. In the king's speech the Government was cautious, saying that "only a limited programme of legislation" was proposed, though "other measures" would be introduced if necessary for national well-being, even though "likely to prove contentious." In the debate which followed, Churchill said the king's speech might have read: "My Government will not introduce legislation in fulfillment of their election programme because the only mandate they have received from the country is not to do it." He was unhappy about the absence of a strong Government but said both sides must act in the best interests of the nation. Sir Anthony Eden said that on foreign-policy matters the Opposition would not exploit the weakness of the small governmental majority. As it worked out, the Government easily weathered the early storms and came to the end of the first session in July at least as strong as at the beginning. While such a consequence would have been almost impossible on the Continent, English politics this time reflected restraint, common sense, and patriotism. The King's Government must go on.

The Battle of the Benches

The opening session of the new Parliament proved strenuous, for both Government and Opposition had to be prepared to muster their full voting power on short notice. The first test of strength was over steel. The Conservatives contended that the election had demonstrated the nation's disapproval of iron and steel nationalization and with Liberal support proposed, March 9, that the act of 1949 should not become effective until nine months following the next election. On this issue the Government could hardly have survived a defeat. The Labor whips exercised their full authority and detained Cabinet members until the division, forcing some of them to arrive quite late for a ballet in honor of President and Mme. Auriol of France. The Government survived, 310 to 296. Eventually the Steel Act went into effect, in February 1951, and a holding company, the Iron and Steel Federation, took over the stock of the private companies. However, the individual companies remained in being, continuing with their day-to-day operations, and the general impression was that any serious degree of nationalization would, in fact, await another election.

On March 13, 1950, the Government, this time with Liberal assistance, defeated an Opposition motion on housing by a majority of twenty-five. The debate was dominated by the "verbal pyrotechnics" of Aneurin Bevan. "It happens to be a fact," he said, "that since 1945, the housing record of Great Britain is better than that of any other nation in the world." There was a flurry of excitement on March 28 when seven Labor rebels (including Michael Foot, Tom Driberg, Ian Mikardo, Jennie Lee, and R. H. S. Crossman) voted against the Government on the issue of Seretse Khama, who was the chief of the Bamangwato tribe in Bechuanaland, had attended Oxford, and had married a white Englishwoman. His tribe was sharply divided over receiving him and his bride, and the British Government decided to exclude him from his homeland for five years. But on March 29, when the Labor whips were careless, the Government was defeated 283–257 on a fuel issue, a defeat which the Government brushed aside as unimportant. However, for that division twenty-one Labor M.P.s were absent without visible cause. The Government survived all divisions on items in the budget.

With the public the Government seemed to lose no ground. The elimination, for whatever reason, of most of the remaining controls probably was appeasing. The Control of Engagements Order of 1947 was canceled. The control of fish prices, the five-shilling ceiling on restaurant meals, gasoline rationing, were all discontinued, and the point rationing system for many foods, such as cereals, cookies, and canned goods, was also abolished.

The year 1950 proved a good one for Britain's economy. By April, Sir Stafford Cripps at the Exchequer was able to show a considerable improvement in the dollar foreign exchange account. The deficit for the final quarter of 1949 was only $31 million, as compared with $539 million for the third quarter of that year. There was actually a small surplus in the combined sterling and dollar account for the first quarter of 1950. The favorable terms of trade continued to the end of the year, and it was decided to terminate Marshall aid on January 1, 1951, fifteen months ahead of schedule. Britain had received a total of $2,400 million. For the future, aid would be granted only for arms.

The Korean War and Rearmament

Rearmament, which began in 1948 with the Berlin crisis, was doubled in expenditure with the advent of the Korean War in June 1950. The action of the United States, in providing land, sea, and air support for South Korea in accordance with the resolution of the Security Council of the United Nations, was at once supported by Britain. Royal naval units were placed at the disposal of the American command. A few days later the Commons gave unanimous approval. On July 7 the Security Council, on an Anglo-French motion, voted in Russia's absence in favor of a unified command in Korea to be chosen by the United States and to operate under the flag of the United Nations. By November General MacArthur's forces had cleared South Korea and had advanced in North Korea to the Chinese frontier. At this juncture Communist China intervened in force and United Nations units were gradually withdrawn from North Korea.

Chinese intervention raised new problems for Great Britain, particularly in her relations with the United States. Britain had refused to accept the notion, so common in the United States, that China was lost to the free world and was now but a satellite of Russia. Indeed, Britain had accorded China *de facto* recognition the previous January. She now hoped for a negotiated peace in Korea. Attlee was fearful of unilateral action on the part of the United States, was particularly concerned lest MacArthur's urge to bombard Manchuria and to use Nationalist Chinese troops in Formosa for raids on the Chinese mainland might prevail and general war with China ensue, and was even possessed of the notion that the United States might use atomic weapons. He therefore went to Washington early in December to represent both Britain and France and insure their consultation on any serious changes in American policy in the Far East. He was able to report that the United States, like Britain, wished to avoid a general war with China, and he thus relieved the tension in the House of Commons.

Differences, however, still remained. Britain wished to reestablish good relations with China and preserve a mutually profitable trade. British imports from China included some important items, especially egg products and animal foods. Any restrictions on Chinese trade would also be disastrous for Hong Kong. Consequently, Britain opposed imposition of any economic sanctions on Communist China, and she supported an American resolution in the General Assembly of the United Nations branding China as guilty of aggression in Korea only when that resolution was so amended as to rule out sanctions, pending further efforts at peace through a good-offices committee. President Truman's dismissal of General MacArthur in April 1951 relieved Britain's worst fears. At home

Britain's trade with China was well aired, and concern was voiced over reports of the export of strategic goods. The Government gave assurances that since the outbreak of the Korean War all goods of military importance had been excluded save rubber, on which restrictions had now been placed.

In August 1950 the Government had announced a program of defense totaling £3,400 million over the ensuing three years. In February 1951 this figure was revised to £4,700 million. By then Sir Stafford Cripps, broken in health, had given way at the Exchequer to Hugh Gaitskell, relatively unknown in politics. There were changes elsewhere in the Labor high command. Ernest Bevin was a sick man, as his photographs showed. Against his will he resigned in March 1951; he died a month later. It was Bevin more than anyone else in the Cabinet who committed the Labor Government to a foreign policy which adhered to concern for traditional British national interests. His dream was of Atlantic–West European unity with American military support. Bevin was buried in Westminster Abbey with the simple marker "The Right Honourable Ernest Bevin, M.P., Trade Unionist and Statesman, 1881–1951." He was replaced at the Foreign Office by Herbert Morrison—not, as it proved, a fortunate appointment, either for the Government or for Morrison.

More Problems for Labor

At this juncture, the Government's problems were exacerbated by the full rebellion of the most recalcitrant element in its ranks. The Korean War had widened the breach between the Bevin policy and that of the socialist left. At the outset, on July 14, 1950, a group of twenty-three Labor M.P.s put down a motion asking for mediation in Korea, the withdrawal of the United States from Formosa, and the entrance of Communist China into the United Nations. Attlee responded that there would be no deal linking Korea with China's entrance into the United Nations. Again in November the rebels sought to embarrass the Government with their motion calling for the establishment of a line in Korea beyond which United Nations forces were not to go. The revision upward in 1951 of the defense estimates was the occasion of a final breach. In an attempt to ease domestic expenditures, Gaitskell's budget proposed that citizens be charged for spectacles and for dentures. Now the issue was arms or social services. On April 21, 1951, Aneurin Bevan, unusually restless, resigned from the Cabinet. Other resignations followed: Harold Wilson as president of the Board of Trade and John Freeman as parliamentary secretary to the minister of Supply. During this crisis the prime minister himself was in the hospital with a duodenal ucler—under the circumstances hardly surprising. The Labor team was breaking up.

Britain's economy weathered well the first six months of the Korean War; it fared badly during the second. Defense estimates for the fiscal year 1950–51 were £741 million; actual expenditures were £981 million. In the budget presented in April 1951 the estimates called for increased expenditures over the previous year of £940 million, of which nearly £700 million was for defense. Higher taxes were offset by higher wages, which maintained a high consumer demand at home. Exports, which had shot up dramatically in 1950 from 1949, were stationary in volume in 1951 and sagged significantly in 1952. Once again, said the *Economist,* the land was living beyond its income. Measures instituted by the Government—renewal of price controls and dividend restrictions, higher income taxes, much higher purchase taxes on motorcars, television sets, and radios, reduction of butter and cheese ration—proved for the most part neither economically sound nor politically wise.

In the summer of 1951 the British people were briefly diverted by the Festival of Britain, a centennial anniversary of the Great Exhibition of 1851. It had rained in London on sixty-three of the first eighty-eight days of the year, but the summer was generally fine, and great throngs were drawn to the south bank of the Thames, where the main exhibitions were housed. The design was to present "British contributions to world civilization in the arts of peace." At separate pavilions one found such exhibits as the Land of Britain, the Natural Scene, Minerals of the Land, and the Sea and Ships. The Dome of Discovery was a striking and dominating pavilion of eight sections presenting British discovery and exploration on land and sea and in air and space. A third group of pavilions was concerned with the People, with exhibits on the Lion and the Unicorn, Homes and Gardens, the New Schools, Health, and Sport. Throughout the country the festival inspired special concerts, special exhibitions of the arts, special sporting events. Yet the realities of the mid-twentieth century could not be forgotten; the Festival of Britain came as postwar optimism was ebbing; sophisticated Englishmen did not take it very seriously.

Back to the Hustings

On September 19, 1951, the prime minister announced the general election for October 25; no one was surprised. The longer the Government put off its appeal, the less promising seemed its chances. The defection of Bevan and others in April 1951 was outward manifestation of a breach within the party ranks which did not close. In July the rebels were at it once again with their pamphlet "One Way Out," advocating a sharp cutback in the armament program and heavier taxation of the wealthy. Public opinion polls from February 1951 showed Labor trailing the Conservatives by gradually rising margins, and parliamentary by-elections showed a swing-over of proportions that indicated a substantial Conservative victory in a general election.

The Conservatives, for their part, were itching for another chance—in Churchill's words, for "one more heave"—which they were sure would overturn the Government. In a broadcast in March 1951 he declared that the Conservatives would employ their full "parliamentary and constitutional rights" to bring an early appeal to the country.

The prime minister himself was aware of a widespread demand for an election and a hope for the return of a strong Government. It is very likely that he agreed—scarcely anyone has questioned Attlee's paramount concern for the nation's interests. In asking for a dissolution and a new Parliament, he said in his broadcast, September 19, "I consider that the time has now come to ask the electors for a renewal of confidence in the Government, and to give it adequate Parliamentary support in order to deal with important issues with which the country is faced at home and abroad."

D. E. Butler has provided a dependable analysis of this election. The candidacies fell sharply, for the Liberals chose to contest only 109 seats (as against 475 in 1950) and the Communists contested about 10 (as against 100 in 1950). In 497 constituencies there were straight Labor-Conservative contests.

Policies and Platitudes. Though an October poll had been anticipated, neither major party made an effort to issue manifestoes in advance. They now appeared as a personal statement from Churchill, the Conservative leader, and in a statement drafted by a committee of Labor. These documents were not widely read, but they do provide a summary of much that was said during the campaign. The Conservative statement held Labor responsible for weakening Britain's position in the world since 1945. "Safety, progress and cohesion" were the Conservative watchwords in Commonwealth and imperial affairs. Imperial preference should be retained. The Government's rearmament program should be continued but must be more efficiently and more economically administered, and all means should be exerted toward achieving a united Europe, including Russia and her satellites. The Conservative Party pledged itself to the repeal of the Iron and Steel Act and to the serious revision of the Coal and Transport Acts in the direction of greater efficiency. Next to national security, the most vital concern of a Conservative Government would be housing, with a target of 300,000 new homes built per year. A Conservative Government would better administer education, health, and other social services. The Conservatives would see to it that the proper role of individual initiative was restored and that local governmental authorities would have returned to them their proper sphere in public affairs.

Labor, quite naturally, stood on its record and promised an extension of its policy of peace, full employment, stable prices, and social justice. Armament for collective security would circumvent war. But the development of backward areas in the world was equally important. In domestic affairs, Labor pointed proudly to a production record which stood at 50 percent over 1938. To solve the recurrent problem of the dollar gap, new sources of raw materials in the Commonwealth must be tapped, and any exclusive and restrictive business practices in England not in the general welfare must be eliminated. The successful policy in agriculture must be continued. The wage earner was in a far better position, comparatively, than he had ever been, but Labor would "press forward towards greater social equality and the establishment of equal opportunities for all." A minimum of 200,000 houses would be built each year. "Welfare at home, peace abroad" was the prospect of those who chose to go "Forward with Labour" rather than "Backward with the Tories."

These pronouncements reached the public mainly through the party broadcasts, which, as in 1950, were probably the most important aspect of the campaign. For major addresses, audiences ranged from 22 percent to 43 percent of the voters. Hugh Gaitskell for Labor dwelt on the necessity of heavier government spending, required by the rearmament program, and of maintaining food subsidies and social services. Probably the most effective broadcast of the entire campaign was that by Churchill—this time he spoke not only eloquently but moderately. He declared that full employment and the welfare state were a Tory achievement as much as a Labor one. The essential difference between the parties was in the attitude toward nationalization and extreme controls. Here again one of his phrases entered into the common language; the choice, he said, between Conservative and Labor was the choice between the ladder (on which everyone could rise) and the queue (in which everyone merely took his turn).

A Welshman, James Griffiths, boldly defended Labor's policy in coal nationalization and in the colonies (including the groundnuts experiment) and made a rather convincing case on these unpromising subjects. Richard Stokes spoke for Labor from the point of view of a businessman, but his effectiveness was somewhat compromised by his suggestion that Laborites rather than Conservatives were associated with Christian principles. Herbert Morrison, in his usual straightforward, matter-of-fact manner, made a good case for Labor's foreign policy and taunted the

Tories as having a nineteenth-century policy in a twentieth-century world. Anthony Eden answered, saying that Labor had no monopoly on collective security and the rule of law in the world; he was indignant that peace had been made a partisan issue. He insisted that Britain's prestige, particularly in the Middle East, had declined. In the final broadcast of the election series, Attlee spoke in a comprehensive fashion of Labor's stewardship since 1945; Labor, he said, had not sought to implement any doctrinaire program but, rather, sought to minister to the national welfare. And he defended Labor's policy in the Middle East.

There was the usual irresponsible talk, this time about Churchill and the Conservatives as "warmongers," from which Labor leaders did not entirely dissociate themselves; indeed, Labor was probably as guilty of "scare tactics" in 1951 as the Tories had been in 1924 or 1931. On the other hand, the Conservatives kept the "war mongering" issue alive by continually denying it. And though legitimately exploiting the division within the Labor Party over rearmament and foreign policy, the Conservatives often overstepped the bounds of scruple in suggesting the dangers to the country if one such as Bevan, with his "Communist" affinities, ever got to power.

The Swing to the Conservatives. On polling day, October 25, about 82.5 percent of the electorate cast ballots. By the early hours of October 26, the results of 319 contests were known. It was clear that no great change had occurred; the early Labor lead from urban victories was steadily cut away as rural constituencies reported. The Conservatives then took the lead, and by 5 P.M. their majority was assured. Attlee went at once to Buckingham Palace to resign and was soon followed by Churchill, who agreed to form a Conservative Government. He was seventy-seven.

The Conservatives emerged with 321 seats, Labor with 295, Liberals with 6, Irish Nationalists with 3. However, in total popular votes Labor was slightly in the lead (Labor had 13,948,605 and the Conservatives had 13,717,358), a circumstance which caused much less concern in England than it probably would have in the United States. For the entire United Kingdom the average swing to the Conservatives since 1950 was 1.1 percent and in Great Britain alone 1.3 percent (this was the average of the Conservative gain with the Labor loss). On the whole, the campaign itself went favorably for Labor; six weeks before polling, the British Institute of Public Opinion had given a 10 percent lead to the Conservatives. Polls during the campaign showed Labor steadily whittling away at the Conservative lead. The Liberals, contesting 109 seats, polled only three percent of the popular vote. Some voters, not many in the aggregate but representing enough votes to tighten the race, changed their minds during the campaign, and very likely on the peace issue. The vast majority voted as they always had done, at least since the war. It was a small number of voters—Liberals who without candidates of their own voted Conservative, and some disgruntled individuals, normally Labor, who switched—who made the difference. And so, even with the total popular vote slightly in Labor's favor, the 1951 poll provided a substantial Conservative victory in Parliament and in ending the rule of Labor may be considered a decisive election.

11

An Age of Affluence?
An Age of Illusion?
Thirteen Wasted Years?

Vernon Bogdanor and Robert Skidelsky eds., *The Age of Affluence, 1951– 1964* (1970), p. 7

Ten years ago it was possible, and indeed usual, to look back on the 1950's as an age of prosperity and achievement.... Today [1970] we are more likely to remember the whole period as an age of illusion, of missed opportunities, with Macmillan as the magician whose wonderful act kept us too long distracted from reality.

Kenneth Younger *Changing Perspectives in British Foreign Policy* (1964), p. 13

As a heavily populated, industrialized nation, dependent for her existence upon international trade and for her security upon the support of other powers, Britian cannot simply retreat into her shell. In the past she has influenced world events by methods which are now becoming obsolete. She now has to find new means for achieving similar ends. For her, international interdependence is not so much an aim which she can choose as a condition of her existence.

Mark Abrams quoted in E. A. Johns, *The Social Structure of Modern Britain* (1965), p. 51

During a pre-election survey I found that all working class families I approached were not concerned with a summit meeting or Nyasaland but only with making their homes warmer, snugger, tighter, more secluded and private.

1951–1964

As we move into the third quarter of the twentieth century we find our perspective shifting, the character of our material modified, our conclusions more tentative. The present thirty year rule bars from inspection official records (parliamentary debates are of course the major exception) and private papers are for the most part not available. In consequence, reputable biographies and scholarly monographs are still few. Much of the available material is "public knowledge," that is, journalistic in origin or nature. The historian uses much the same sources of information as do the editorial writer and the radio and television commentators. What all this comes down to is that while a narrative of events can be provided it is another matter to determine their significance and relative importance.

On the other hand, the historian of contemporary England, if we may so refer to these years, is much better served than was the historian writing at the end of the first quarter or the second quarter of the century. For one thing, the replacement in 1967 of the old fifty year rule with the present thirty year rule has opened nearly all the archives through the World War II years and beyond. Thus we are on solid ground, as historians, in the immediate background of the third quarter of the century. And the political scientist and the sociologist and the economist are now much better informed on current developments than were their predecessors. And so it is not so much that we lack knowledge of the events of this the third quarter of the century but rather that there is little consensus as to answers and conclusions. The excellent analyses that we have are often polemical in character, and also contradictory, and invite response rather than agreement.

With these caveats we now proceed to examine the course of British history 1951–64, variously described as "an age of affluence," "an age of illusion," or "thirteen wasted years." In this language there is a challenge. The much touted "welfare state," constructed under the aegis of Labor—will it persist and provide a "welfare society"? Britain—the strongest power in western Europe after World War II—what is her future in industrial production and world trade and military power? Can she keep abreast of her erstwhile enemies—Germany, Japan, Italy? In 1948 Churchill seemed to be voicing the sentiment of the British people when (in an address, October 9, before the National Union of Conservative and Unionist Associations) he set forth "the three circles" theory— that Britain's leadership in the future was assured by her association with three overlapping circles: the British Commonwealth, the United States and the English-speaking world, and a united Europe. It was a remark to be picked up repeatedly in the years that followed.

From Churchill to Eden, 1951–55

The fifties produced many surprises. The very first was the Conservative victory at the polls in 1951. Even as late as 1948 and 1949, when all indices indicated a decline in public support, Labor leaders still regarded the 1945 election as a revolution which had given them a permanent advantage. The fact was emphatically the contrary. Commencing in 1951, the Conservatives won three general elections in succession, an achievement without precedent since the Liberal victories before World War I. Furthermore, the election of 1959 was the fourth in a row in which the Conservatives had grown in strength in the Commons, defying the century-old experience that once in office a party steadily loses popular support.

But in 1951 such success was beyond the imagination of even the most optimistic Conservatives. A majority of seventeen in the Commons, garnered from a popular vote slightly less than that of Labor, was obviously a shaky foundation on which to build a bold and innovative policy. The new Churchill Government sought first of all to win the nation's confidence. It courted support from the working man; certainly it did not wish to alienate him. So no controversial legislation was introduced into the first session of the new parliament and very little thereafter. The welfare state was accepted and promoted. Denationalization was limited to steel (with considerable governmental control retained) and road trucking.

And the Conservatives took special pride in exceeding, during 1953 and 1954, their own goal of 300,000 new houses a year. Later, in 1955, as an indication of their open-mindedness, they established, amid great popular interest and after some controversy in their own ranks, commercial television under the Independent Television Authority.

Stabilization of the Economy

My Government views with grave concern the economic situation of the United Kingdom about which a full disclosure must be made to the Nation. The recent deterioration in the balance of payments causes increased anxiety and must be urgently remedied in order to restore the fullest confidence in the purchasing power of the pound, so that we may continue to be able to obtain from overseas the supplies necessary to maintain employment and an increasingly high level of production.

So reads the King's Address to the new Parliament, November 6, 1951. The *Economist*, in commenting on the Conservative victory, declared that "the magnitude of the task they have inherited is also a measure of their opportunity. If they demonstrate the vision that has been lacking in Labour they can revive their country and destroy forever the identification of Conservatism with the evils of the thirties."

Table 5   Indices of Industrial Production and of Volume of Exports, United Kingdom, 1947–54

	1947=100	
	Industrial Production	Volume of Exports
1947	100	100
1948	112	127
1949	119	139
1950	127	162
1951	131	164
1952	127	154
1953	136	159
1954	146	168

Source: *Annual Register of World Events*

The chancellor of the Exchequer, R. A. Butler, seemed to face up to the situation, declaring that the British people confronted the possibility of being "bankrupt, idle and hungry." The new Government did not hesitate to impose at once controls in some ways more restrictive than those earlier applied by Labor. Imports from all areas, sterling as well as dollar, were to be curtailed. Tourist allowances were reduced by 50 percent. The bank rate for borrowing was raised from 2 to 2.5 percent, and in March 1952 raised again to 4 percent to combat inflation. Capital development was thus discouraged, buying became cautious, inventory stocks were replaced conservatively. By mid 1952, these measures had brought results. Imports dropped 8 percent. At just this stage, a favorable condition developed, with the market for British goods shipped abroad on the rise and the prices for essential British imports on the decline. Thus, though between 1952 and 1954 Britain's percentage share of world trade in manufactured goods barely held its own, her overall payments showed a favorable balance which gradually increased. Sterling made an extraordinary recovery; by 1953 the dollar account in foreign trade of the U.K. was on even terms, for the first time since the war. The volume of exports was steady, with noticeable increase by 1954. A modest advance in domestic production meant proportionately more goods available for home consumption; the increase in domestic consumption between 1951 and 1954 was 12 percent. Other indices were equally favorable. Retail prices held steady, the supply of goods just about kept pace with purchasing power, investment was rising cautiously, modest income tax reduction was granted. Unemployment never rose above 2 percent. And to the delight of all, food rationing ended completely on July 3, 1954, when the final restrictions were lifted, and the housewives, at Churchill's bidding, threw the ration books into the fire.

In February 1952 the cares of this world were put aside in ten days of mourning for the loss of the sovereign; King George VI, in precarious health for some time, died on February 6, 1952, at Sandringham, of a coronary thrombosis. National grief for his passing was spontaneous and from the heart, for though not greatly endowed he brought to his unwanted and unexpected duties a deep sense of duty and responsibility, great physical courage, absolute candor, and a dignified simplicity. It was, of course, Churchill who struck just the right note in his memorial broadcast: "During these last months the King walked with death, as if death was a companion, an acquaintance, whom he recognized and did not fear. In the end death came as a friend." But, in accord with the nature of monarchy, attention quickly turned to his successor, in Churchill's words, "the fair and youthful figure, Princess, wife and mother." Princess Elizabeth had married Lt. Philip Mountbatten, R.N., created the Duke of Edinburgh, in November 1947. Any doubt as to the popularity and value of the royal family was dispelled with Elizabeth's coronation in June 1953. Seven thousand persons massed in the Abbey for ceremonies little changed in a thousand years, which were broadcast and televised for the rest of the world. The second Elizabeth, like the first, ascended the throne at the age of twenty-five and in a revolutionary era. Some ventured to predict another Elizabethan Age. But what sprang to many minds was the thought that of those alive in 1953 most would probably not live to see another coronation.

Churchill's resignation. Churchill in these years led his party perhaps more successfully than anyone else could have done. He himself went from one recognition to another. Just before the coronation of Elizabeth II, he was created a Knight of the Garter and the shift to "Sir Winston" was easier than anyone, himself included, had anticipated. Though he suffered still another stroke in July 1953 (less serious strokes in 1949 and 1950 had been kept a secret), he recovered, and on November 30, 1954, the occasion of his eightieth birthday, he received the nation's tribute. As always, he was equal to the occasion: "I have never accepted what many . . . have kindly said, namely that I inspired the nation. . . . It was the nation and the race dwelling all round the globe that had the lion's heart. I had the luck to be called on to give the roar." On April 6, 1955, he resigned (though staying in the Commons), and Sir Anthony Eden, the foreign secretary, became prime minister. It was a foregone conclusion. Back during the war, Churchill had formally submitted to the king his recommendation of Eden as prime minister in the event of his incapacitation. When Churchill returned to Downing Street in 1951, Eden again became the "crown prince."

One of Eden's first official acts was to call a general election for May 26, 1955. The Government had not lost a by-election since 1951. By 1953 the improvement in the economy was reflected in both opinion polls and local elections. The Conservatives had not returned the country to the thirties. But, oddly enough, in the campaign of 1955 the Conservatives returned to ideology. Their manifesto, "United for Peace and Progress," said the choice for the electorate was between "the years of Socialism or the years of Conservatism that have followed." Labor policy of further nationalization, the manifesto added, would lead to bureaucratic domination, and the revival of controls would mean a return of austerity. The Labor manifesto somewhat more cogently and persuasively proposed measures of action: high-level talks to achieve relaxation of world tension; stabilization of prices by agreements with Commonwealth lands, by elimination of monopolies, and by price controls if necessary; a health service with no charges whatsoever; educational reform with elimination of the "eleven plus" examination and the development of comprehensive secondary schools; a planned economy for industrial growth; and renationalization of steel and road haulage. But the standard account of the election declares that the choice for most electors was between men and not between measures or principles. Despite the use of television, extensively for the first time, the campaign was rather dull, with audience participation falling off in comparison with 1951 and the poll dropping to 76.7 percent. The outcome hinged on 150 seats, about evenly split in the previous election between the two major parties. Results generally followed predictions, and the Conservatives emerged with enlarged strength in the Commons—an overall majority of fifty-eight. Popular vote was 49.7 percent Conservative and 46.4 percent Labor. While the great majority must have voted as they did in 1951 (the new election map revealed little change, with Labor retaining the same areas of strength), there was an overall swing of 1.6 percent to the Conservatives. The outcome was a reflection of the improved condition of the economy. Since 1951, TV sets had increased threefold and automobiles by 50 percent.The budget, presented just before polling, reduced taxes still further and thereby dropped some 2,400,000 from the income tax rolls.

The Conservatives had been slow to realize the possibilities. To many the prospect had been hardly more than alternating periods of calm and crisis in an era still dominated by the dynamics of Labor. Only here and there were more imaginative voices to be found. Early in 1951 a handful of young men, formerly members of Conservative associations at Oxford and Cambridge, organized the Bow Conservative Club, a kind of counterpart to the Fabian Society. Independent of official Conservative organization, its purpose was political education and research. In 1953 Robert Boothby, Conservative M.P. and journalist, wrote in the *Political Quarterly* that "the problems of the balance of payments and of productivity are more important than those of full employment and social justice." In 1954 some young Conservatives, styling themselves the "One Nation Group," issued the pamphlet "Change Is Our Ally," which carried the message that radical economic change was essential if Britain were to increase her national wealth. Gradually, Conservative discussion, while taking for granted the continuance of the welfare state, shifted attention from the idea of fair shares to the notion of a national standard much higher than before the war.

Labor's Predicament

If the Conservatives were slow to seize the initiative, the Laborites only gradually realized their predicament. As early as 1949 and 1950 there was much evidence that factory workers were tired of restrictions on small pleasures, that the middle-income groups resented the increasing burden of taxation, that housewives were "fed up" with rationing, and that businessmen were impatient of controls. Yet Labor spokesmen still said it was not necessary to "rethink" Labor principles but only to "reapply" them. Party workers were surprised to find that tried and true shibboleths such as "full employment" and "nationalization" ceased to move even the faithful. In 1955 the Labor vote fell off 1,500,000 from 1951, the Conservative vote only 430,000. Unemployment did not exist; openings at Labor exchanges outnumbered those reported unemployed. Industries concerned with national resources had been nationalized and the welfare state established. "Fair shares" had been won. What next?—as the *New Statesman and Nation* had asked in 1949.

A policy statement, *Challenge to Britain,* issued in 1953, sought to find the answers to the problems of economic growth in further nationalization—the return to Government control of iron and steel and the partial nationalization of such industries as engineering, machine tools, chemicals, manufacture of aircraft—all vital to foreign trade and defense. And these ideas, along with proposed extensions of the welfare state, were incorporated in the party manifesto for the election of 1955.

But this manifesto, "Forward with Labour," did not make it at all clear just what the admonition "Forward" signified. Labor, as always, was a federation of various elements. Which group was in control? Was it the leadership in local constituencies who had little knowledge of practical politics? Or was it the more politically experienced members of the Parliamentary Labor Party who were prepared to modify policy in the interests of action? The balance of power lay with trade union leadership, who had behind them the huge trade union membership. Generally speaking, trade unions had cooperated with the parliamentary party. But in the fifties, some very significant changes were in progress. Trade union spokesmen, though possessed of little understanding of the complexities of the national economy and of international power, now became increasingly conscious of the immediate interests of their membership.

In sum, far more difference of opinion developed within the Labor Party over the role of "socialism" and the further extension of nationalization, over extending the operations of the welfare state, over redistribution of national wealth, than developed between the Parliamentary Labor Party and the Parliamentary Conservative Party. The cleavage within Labor was so persistent in matters of foreign policy and national defense that it came to be known as "Bevanism." Aneurin Bevan and his supporters wished to draw away from the capitalist nations of Western Europe and the United States and to develop closer associations with Russia and the states in Eastern Europe under her control. In March 1952 Bevan and fifty-six followers in the Commons voted against rearmament. The defense policy of the Government called for priority in the production of certain fighter aircraft, guided missiles, and other innovations in military equipment—a proposal the Labor Front Bench had decided not to oppose. Disciplinary action was mild and the episode was regarded as something of a victory for the Bevanites, who proceeded to capture six of the seven seats on the National Executive up for election at the party conference in October. Hugh Dalton and Herbert Morrison, elder statesmen in the party, were defeated by R. H. S. Crossman and Harold Wilson. However, in the Parliamentary Labor Party, itself, Bevanism remained much in the minority. Only Bevan was elected to the Shadow Cabinet, and his was the twelfth and last place. He was twice (in 1952 and 1953) defeated by Morrison for deputy party leadership in the Commons, and even in the balloting of a party conference, in 1954, he was defeated by Hugh Gaitskell in a contest over the party treasurership. But just prior to the election of 1955 he challenged in the Commons official support by Labor of the Government's decision to manufacture the hydrogen bomb. When votes were registered, sixty-two other rebels joined him in abstaining. After this, by a narrow vote, the Party Whip was temporarily denied him. It was not strange that in 1955 he conducted his own electoral compaign quite independent of Transport House (Labor headquarters), a fact exploited with glee by Conservatives. Bevan, alone of Labor spokesmen, could fill an assembly hall. Soon after the poll he was reelected to the Shadow Cabinet.

External Affairs, 1951–56

But all these matters have a much wider context. As late as 1929 Churchill could write: "The conclusion of the Great War raised Britain to the highest position she has yet attained." If so, her prestige plummeted in the thirties. Britain fought World War II in order to destroy Hitler's Germany, of course, but on the assumption that victory would restore Britain to a position of power and prestige in the world. And it was on this matter, which seemed somewhat less important to the Americans than to the British, that conflict over strategy between Britain and the United States often turned. The issue was political, and the British were forced to give way not so much because their ideas were less sound operationally as because the United States had the larger guns.

It was plain to see by 1945 that the power structure of the world was in upheaval brought on by war and revolution, technology and nationalism. But the preoccupation of Russia with Eastern Europe and the temporary return of the United States to isolationism gave Britain a few years to adjust to the new order before great decisions were thrust upon her. Only slowly did she realize that the means by which ends might be achieved had to be considered before policy could be formulated.

From the vantage point of the early fifties, the transformation of Empire into Commonwealth after World War II seems an impressive and durable achievement. The Asian lands, save Burma, upon attaining independence chose to remain in the Commonwealth. Kenneth Younger, director of the Royal Institute of International Affairs, in his remarkable book, *The Changing Perspectives in British Foreign Policy* (1964), more accurately catches the atmosphere of the fifties than do subsequent treatments of British policy. Younger declares that this liquidation of empire "represented the biggest contribution to world stability that Britain could have made in these years."

But this priority to the Commonwealth reenforced Britain's own sense of difference from the continent of Europe, so profoundly illustrated in the events of 1939–45. It was difficult for the British to comprehend then and in the years following that the Channel might soon lose its historic significance. A defense paper in February 1956 declared that Britain must remain a world power, and since 1952 defense had absorbed ten percent of the gross national product. This defense posture was based on "an effective nuclear capability"—back on October 3, 1952, the first British-made atomic bomb had been exploded off the Monte Bello Islands near the coast of Australia. At that time Britain alone of western European countries was developing nuclear weapons. All this left in the English mind little sense of the urgency for a new Europe that was found in Paris, Berlin, Rome, and Vienna—where the old order had been destroyed. In contrast, the British way of life had not only survived but seemed to have triumphed.

Collective Defense

Of course, British leadership was quite aware that interests of national security required cooperation not only with the United States but also with continental allies. By the fifties economic growth and living standards in some countries of western Europe were outdistancing those in Britain. The possibilities, both political and economic, of close association—indeed, even of some kind of union—now repeatedly forced Britain to reexamine her attitudes toward the Continent. But she would go so far and no further. The failure of the powers to unify Germany and the stabilization of the "cold war" between the Soviet Union and the West, led her in 1948 and 1949, in the Brussels Treaty and the NATO alliance, to abandon a century-long policy of temporary agreements for immediate purposes and to cast her lot for national survival in permanent military association with those with whom she shared common dangers. In May 1952, she would not join a supranational body to be called the European Defense Community—formed by France, Italy, the Federal Republic of Germany, and the Benelux countries—but she was willing, along with the United States, to give assurance of close political and military collaboration. The E.D.C, as it turned out in August 1954, was rejected by the French National Assembly, and thereby came to an end. But W.E.U. (West European Union), an elaboration of the Brussels Treaty, soon took its place. To the signatories of that treaty (Great Britain, France, Belgium, Luxembourg, the Netherlands) were now added West Germany and Italy. The general purpose of W.E.U. was to stabilize international relations "by promoting the unity ... and encouraging the progressive integration of Europe."

At the London Conference, September 1954, Britain made a move that was decisive—comprising one of those rare moments after 1945 in which British policy determined the result. In order to satisfy French fears over the reappearance in Europe of West Germany as a sovereign state, one which would certainly in time rearm, she formalized her obligations in Europe. The British foreign secretary, Sir Anthony Eden, declared: "The United Kingdom will continue to maintain on the mainland of Europe, including Germany, the effective strength of the United Kingdom forces now assigned to SACEUR [Supreme Allied Commander, Europe—under NATO]—four divisions and the tactical air force—or whatever SACEUR regards as equivalent fighting capacity." The conclusions of the London Conference were embodied in a series of agreements signed at Paris in October. Allied occupation of the Federal Republic of Germany was to cease and the Federal Republic was to be admitted to NATO and to be permitted to rearm, but only with unilateral assurances that she would not produce atomic weapons, long-range and guided missiles, or bomber craft. The West European Union, whose general purpose was to stabilize international relations "by promoting the unity ... and encouraging the progressive integration of Europe" came into existence upon the formal admission of West Germany (that is, the Federal Republic) and Italy to the Brussels treaty Organization (already comprising Great Britain, France, Belgium, Luxembourg, and The Netherlands). The Anglo-American aim of transforming West Germany from an enemy into an ally had been achieved.

The bond of common interest between Great Britain and the United States was the necessity of maintaining in the North Atlantic and in Western Europe a power matching that of the Soviet Union. In the Far East there was another strong tie in SEATO, committing Great Britain and the United States, along with France, New Zealand, Australia, the Philippines, Thailand, and Pakistan, to act in concert in resisting aggression in the Southwest Pacific. But frictions had developed nonetheless. Pervading nearly all problems was a basic difference toward Communism. In the American view, particularly under secretary of State John Foster Dulles, Communism presented essentially an ideological problem, a conflict without compromise which must be won at all costs. To the British, on the other hand, it was essentially a political and diplomatic problem; differences with Communist statesmen could be discussed and, hopefully, settled in the normal manner. This position often became "neutralism" as between "Communism" and the "West," particularly in many of the newly independent countries in the Commonwealth, an attitude regarded in the United States as politically unsound and morally untenable. American trade embargoes on goods of strategic value consigned to Communist lands bore particularly hard on Britain, which, desirous of Chinese trade, encouraged the notion of admitting Red China to the United Nations—all of which outraged policymakers in the United States. The Americans were also irritated by what seemed to them vestiges of "colonialism" in British policy in Cyprus, in the Suez Canal Zone, and in the Sudan in the early fifties. Even the Commonwealth was a source of trouble, for "preference" often stood in the way of harmonizing British and American commercial policies. And not without its effect was the inability of either the Truman or the Eisenhower administrations to appreciate or even understand the "welfare state" that had developed in Britain since the war.

In all matters of defense, British attitudes and policies were undergoing important change in the mid-fifties. The Defense white paper of February 1956 asserting a continuance of Britain's major role as a world power was abruptly followed a year later by a Government announcement of "the biggest change in military policy ever made in normal times." The defense budget was to be scaled down about 14 percent, forces in Europe to be reduced 10 percent, "air defense" was considered no longer practical, and from 1960 there was to be no more calling up for national service. "Collective defense" within the alliances, later called "interdependence," replaced the effort of the country "to protect itself in isolation." The explanation, at least in considerable part, arises from the Suez Crisis which occurred in the interim. To that we now turn.

Withdrawal from the Middle East

In Europe and in the Far East after 1945 Britain was the captive of circumstance. This she early recognized. In the Middle East her attitude was quite otherwise. There she sought to control events and to mold a power structure favorable to her interests, and there she was in for a series of surprises and humiliations. One approach is to suggest that after World War II Britain reaped the harvest of her seed of contradictions between the wars—support of Arab national movements, encouragement of Zionist aspirations for a Jewish national home in Palestine, maintenance of British spheres of influence. But failures since 1945 are to be explained not so much by the ineptness of British policy as by the want of power to see a policy through to conclusion. The British were slow to digest this fact. During World War II, with American assistance, she controlled the Arab world and encouraged the formation of the Arab League in 1945, the chief bond of which, be it noted, was hostility to Zionism. Postwar governments, Labor and Conservative, clung to the myth of British power. Her overall object in the Middle East was stability, to insure a steady flow of oil from Kuwait and Iraq (together accounting for nearly half the oil Britain used), to keep the approaches to Africa from falling to hostile states, and to retain influence in Jordan and Egypt as symbols of British power.

Suez. But what happened? As we have seen, British policy in Palestine was an unqualified failure. And now we come to the Suez episode of 1956. Quite unexpectedly Egypt had become the leader of the Arabs when army leaders in 1954 brought to power Colonel Nasser, who soon stabilized the local situation. He also assumed the leadership of the Arab League, which now repelled all overtures from NATO.

In the face of resurgent Egyptian nationalism, Britain's position in the Suez Canal Zone—which she still "occupied"—became untenable. In the Anglo-Egyptian treaty of 1954 she agreed to evacuate her troops by stages, in return for recognition of the Suez Canal Company (controlled financially by Britain) to operate the canal until 1968, an arrangement which at the time appeared to many as the prelude to a more harmonious relation between the Arab countries and the West. Eden, British foreign secretary, declared that the treaty would provide the basis for close military cooperation from Egypt. By June 1956 only British civilian personnel remained in the Canal Zone.

However, by then, any gains in good will accruing from military withdrawal were more than offset by frictions elsewhere. In April 1955 Britain joined the Turko-Iraqi Pact (in part, to secure renewal of rights to air bases in Iraq) which now became the Baghdad Pact; Pakistan joined before the year was out and Iran soon after. Britain tried to induce Jordan, as well, to join. Nasser regarded the Baghdad Pact as directly hostile to Arab unity as represented in the Arab League. According to his own account, in March 1956 he peremptorily requested of Selwyn Lloyd (British foreign secretary) that "no more Arabs" be invited to join the Baghdad Pact. And he told a London journalist that Britain knew "in advance" that the Pact "was in our opinion a threat to our vital interests ... I believe that by attempting to keep this area as a sphere of influence Britain will lose her real interests."

Now it was immediately after British adherence to the Turko-Iraqi Pact that Nasser attended the conference of Afro-Asian nations at Bandung. There, very likely, he decided on a policy of non-alignment toward both the Communist bloc and the Western bloc. The Chinese premier, Chou En-Lai, suggested that Egypt purchase arms from Czechoslovakia as well as from Britain and the United States. Such a deal, in effect with the Soviet Union itself, was made in September, 1955, an action resented by the western powers, and, indeed, feared—for it was evidence of a new Communist initiative in the Middle East.

Britain and the United States hoped to strengthen their position by providing loans—the United States 56 million dollars and Britain 10 million—for the construction of the Aswan High Dam, designed to assist Egyptian production to meet the needs of a rapidly expanding population. And it was proposed that the World Bank provide a loan of 200 million dollars. Negotiations between Egypt and the western powers, and between Egypt and the World Bank were well under way early in 1956. But disagreement over the Sudan halted the World Bank negotiations. And Nasser's recognition (in May) of Red China and his revival of a Soviet offer to finance construction of the dam were regarded by John Foster Dulles as an affront. Dulles and American opinion, generally assumed that any and all anti-western pronouncements or actions in the Middle East were Communist inspired.

On July 19 the United States formally withdrew her offer; this action was decisive, and Britain withdrew hers a day later; the World Bank offer ended as well, for it was dependent on western support. Nasser's answer, in less than a week (on July 26), came in a public ceremony in Liberation Square, Alexandria, commemorating the fourth anniversary of the ousting of King Farouk. Nasser announced the nationalization of the Suez Canal Company, with compensation for stockholders, whose revenues would finance the dam. The next morning Egyptians were operating the canal.

Nasser's action brought an abrupt end to Anglo-American hopes for an Egypt friendly to the West. Prime Minister Eden promptly (July 27) telegraphed President Eisenhower:

> We [Cabinet colleagues and Chiefs of Staff] are all agreed that we cannot afford to allow Nasser to seize control of the canal in this way.... We ought in the first instance to bring the maximum political pressure to bear on Egypt. For this ... we should invoke the support of all the interested powers. My colleagues and I are convinced that we must be ready, in the last resort, to use force to bring Nasser to his senses. For our part we are prepared to do so.... However, the first step must be for you and us and France to exchange views, align our policies and concert together how we can best bring the maximum pressure to bear upon the Egyptian Government.

But Washington was much more cautious. For one thing, the American government was nervous about Panama. But more important, the American view of Nasser's Egypt was quite different from that of the British. The United States saw the problem as essentially one of Egyptian nationalism which must not and could not be frustrated and one which, in Nasser's capable hands, might produce a progressive and stable land friendly to the West. But British leaders, like the French, viewed the matter as one of national interest and prestige: Eden, in his own words, regarded Nasser as a "megalomaniacal dictator" whose "stature" it was important "to reduce . . . at an early stage."

Representatives of 22 maritime countries met in London in August; 18 of these states agreed that the canal should be nationalized. But nothing came of it. Britain and France regarded the conference as a means of getting an immediate decision which would be forced on Egypt, which was not represented at the conference. The United States and other participants considered the conference as merely an instrument for negotiation. In fact, there was no basis for questioning Egypt's sovereign rights—Nasser himself rejected all proposals which would remove operation of the canal from Egyptian hands. (Such is a reliable summary by G. Barraclough in the *Survey of International Affairs 1956–58*.) American efforts to form a "Canal Users' Association" to operate in case the canal machinery broke down likewise failed. The French and British now took the matter to the Security Council of the United Nations with the result that on October 13 the Soviet Union vetoed a resolution calling upon the Canal Users' Association and the Egyptian authorities to cooperate to insure the satisfactory operation of the canal (thus implying international control). In actuality, the Egyptians proved quite capable of operating the canal by themselves.

Thereupon Eden turned to France. Another factor—the Egyptian-Israeli—had entered. Ever since the successful Israeli attack on the Egyptian border post in the Gaza strip in February 1955, the relationship had been incendiary. In the spring of 1956 open war was narrowly averted. Now on October 29 Israel launched a full-scale attack across the Egyptian border into the Sinai peninsula. (Ben-Gurion, the Israeli prime minister, later cited a military agreement between Egypt, Jordan, and Syria, which, he said, placed Israel "in direct and immediate danger" and rendered preventive action imperative.) The precise relation of Anglo-French policy to this Israeli attack cannot be determined; it probably depends on deliberations in Paris on October 16 between Eden and Selwyn Lloyd and their French counterparts, Mollet and Pineau. Apparently, the conversations were not recorded; absolute secrecy was maintained at the time, and since then the participants themselves have disclosed little. Eden's own account is incomplete, though he steadfastly maintained that Britain had no previous knowledge of Israel's plan to attack Egypt.

Our most reliable analysis of British policy, drawing on Lord Strang's *Britain in World Affairs*, declares:

> circumstantial evidence provides a strong presumption that decisions were taken which led directly to the Israeli attack on Egypt on 29 October and the subsequent Anglo-French intervention at Port Said.... Subsequent leakages of information and a number of significant indiscretions point with considerable force to the conclusion that there was collusion between France and Israel, while the British, though 'they may be cleared of collusion', 'pretty clearly had an inkling of what was afoot.'

Anthony Nutting, minister of state in the Foreign Office, who resigned over the issue a few weeks later, in his account (*No End of a Lesson; the Story of Suez*, 1967) seems to reenforce this conclusion. We do know for a certainty, from Eden's own account, that on October 25 the British Cabinet discussed the possibility of an Israeli-Egyptian conflict and agreed that in this event the British and French governments would call on both parties to stop hostilities; "if one or both failed to comply within a definite period, the British and French forces would intervene." And Eden frankly adds that they were merely "at last" taking "the action which we had long forecast."

The Anglo-French ultimatum was directed to Israel and Egypt on October 30, calling for withdrawal of forces on each side of the Suez Canal and a further demand on the Egyptians that Anglo-French troops be permitted to move "temporarily" into certain key positions. In his statement that day to the Commons, announcing this action, Eden implied that the United States had been consulted. He and Selwyn Lloyd and Harold Macmillan (foreign secretary and chancellor of the Exchequer, in turn, under Eden) seemed to take American support for granted. However, Eisenhower subsequently stated that his government had been neither consulted nor informed and that he himself had first learned of the action from press reports. Nor did Eden confer with Commonwealth governments. Later he declared that there was no time to consult the United States and the Commonwealth, but Mollet, the French premier, has said that the United States was not informed for fear that she would stop them.

The scene shifted to New York, where the Security Council of the United Nations was discussing the Israeli-Egyptian situation, when a dispatch announcing the Anglo-French ultimatum was received. In the face of strong opposition from the British and French delegates, Henry Cabot Lodge, Jr., the American representative, introduced a resolution calling upon Israel to withdraw its forces and on all members "to refrain from force or threat of force in the area" and "to refrain from giving any military, economic or financial assistance to Israel." This resolution was passed 7 votes to 2, but was defeated by the vetoes of France and Britain. Israel offered to stop hostilities if Egypt did likewise, but Egypt refused. Thereupon British aircraft bombarded Egypt from Cyprus, and six days later a force of troops and armor based on Malta arrived and made landings near Port Said.

World opinion quickly mounted against Anglo-French intervention. This weight of opinion was brought to bear in the General Assembly, to which action shifted after the Anglo-French vetoes blocked the Security Council. The Anglo-French position was consistently supported only by Australia and Belgium and occasionally by New Zealand. The bulk of American opinion was hostile, angry, and resentful. At home British attitudes were sharply divided, more so than at any time since Munich. In Parliament the division was generally along partisan lines, but it was reported (and Eden mentions these reports) that some dissident Conservatives (perhaps as many as thirty) were prepared to vote against the Government if the intervention continued. To compound Eden's difficulties, a dangerous run on sterling began, with gold and dollar reserves falling alarmingly.

On the evening of November 6, Eden announced in the Commons that since both Egypt and Israel had accepted a cease-fire, Britain would halt her operations. (France followed suit the next day.) His tone suggested satisfaction with the course of events as vindicating British policy. "I believe," he said, "that as we emerge from this crisis ... both the Commonwealth ... and our American friends, will understand the reasons which motivated us." The threatened Conservative revolt did not materialize; those Conservatives who had been critical of the Suez intervention, once the adventure was past, generally rallied to the support of the Government. In the crucial debate on November 8, only two Conservative speeches were hostile and only eight Conservatives abstained from the division. Appearances were saved, for the time being, by the substitution of a United Nations force for the Anglo-French. But Egypt refused to clear the canal (which she had closed by sinking blockships) until Anglo-French forces were completely withdrawn. When British ships next passed through the canal, it was not only owned but operated by Egyptians—the Anglo-French effort to put the canal under international control had failed. The episode revealed the uncertain character of Commonwealth ties; it alienated France; it weakened British bonds with the United States. As to the last, Macmillan's account in his autobiography is shot through with reproaches of American policy—her "series of blunders" and "Dulles indecision" and the American refusal "to understand" the British position. The United States, he says, seemed to regard the Anglo-French intervention as "a personal affront."

Most commentators conclude that the Suez venture, if not a mistake in policy, was certainly a blunder in operation. We may add that it accomplished less than nothing, for now any hope of reestablishing influence in the Middle East proved to be irretrievably gone. The Arab world lost all confidence in Britain, to whom it owed so much. Nasser himself might have vanished with an Israeli victory; instead he became an Egyptian hero, an Arab hero, the mouthpiece of Arab defiance to the West. Even in Jordan the British had lost out; in March 1956 young King Hussein suddenly dismissed Glubb Pasha, the British general in command of the Arab Legion. Eden associated this with what he considered to be a general Arab conspiracy led by Nasser. Hussein, in fact, acted for a very simple reason; he had to placate the army, the strongest force in his land. Iraq remained Britain's friend, but only until 1958, when violent revolution ended the days of King Feisal II, Nuri Pasha (the prime minister), and the British Alliance. The Baghdad Pact, renamed the Central Treaty Organization (CENTO), became a military alliance limited to Great Britain, Iran, Turkey, and Pakistan, supported by bilateral defense agreements with the United States. In subsequent developments among Egypt, Syria, and Iraq, Britain had no part whatsoever. Elsewhere in the Middle East the story was much the same. In an independent Kuwait (1961), forces of the Arab League replaced the British. British sovereignty did remain in Aden for a time, but Aden in 1963 took the first step toward independence, joining the British-protected Federation of South Arabia on a provisional basis. For all practical purposes, British "spheres of influence" in the Middle East were coming to an end.

New Leadership: Gaitskell and Macmillan

Just before Suez came reorganization of Labor Party leadership under Hugh Gaitskell, and just after, a shift in Conservative leadership to Harold Macmillan. These two men would dominate the political scene for most of the remainder of our period. Labor, in particular, was due for change. The 1955 poll revealed serious weakness in Labor Party organization and electoral machinery. Failure of some one and a-half million normal Labor voters to go to the polls had caused defeat in twenty-one constituencies. The report of the committee on party reorganization, under chairmanship of Harold Wilson, was so candid and revealing in its strictures that it was discussed in a private (unreported) session of the party conference. But even more important, party leadership was failing. In December 1955, Clement Attlee resigned as party leader—a post he had held for twenty years—to be succeeded by Gaitskell, forty-nine years of age, member of Parliament since 1945, and briefly chancellor of the Exchequer. He was chosen by the Parliamentary Labor Party and overwhelmingly defeated his opponents (Gaitskell, 157; Bevan, 70; Morrison, 40). Morrison, though deputy leader, was passed over because of his sixty-seven years; he was bitterly disappointed and at once resigned his deputy leadership, where he might have continued to render good service and have preserved some continuity in policy. But it was the conviction of the great majority, and with good reason, that a younger man was needed. Gaitskell, an Oxford graduate who had achieved first class honors and whose special topic had been "The Labour Movement," was a trained economist and a moderate in social philosophy, and was generally regarded as a man of intellect and integrity. His greatest support, an interesting and significant matter, was from the trade unions. But in one important respect he failed where Attlee had succeeded—in handling party rebels. In fact, with Gaitskell, the breach within Labor widened and lengthened, for the issues soon included nuclear defense, further nationalization of industry, complete disestablishment of the Church of England, withdrawal from all imperial commitments, reduction of defense to little more than a police force, and departure from the close alliance with the United States.

There was, however, an important difference: Aneurin Bevan himself became more moderate. As shadow foreign minister, he went along with Labor approval of the hydrogen bomb (1957–58) and supported Gaitskell's effort to rescue the party from a pledge of further nationalization. They stood together at the party conference at Brighton in 1957. Bevan's prestige took a big jump with the Suez crisis in 1956. In the censure debate he spoke moderately but with deadly effect; here he was unhampered by his obsession with class interests. "The Government resorted to epic weapons for squalid and trivial ends, and this is why all through this unhappy period Ministers—all of them—have spoken and argued and debated well below their proper form—because they have been synthetic villains. They are not really villains. They have only set off on a villainous course and they cannot even use the language of villainy." It was thereafter assumed that in the next Labor Cabinet he would be foreign secretary, a prospect which aroused much less trepidation than it would have a few years before. But late in 1959 he contracted cancer and he died in July 1960. From a laborer in the mines he had risen to a political career in the Commons, continuing for thirty years. After his death, expressions of respect and admiration for his intelligence, his warm heart, and his gift of speech extended even to the suggestion that he had been the only person in the Labor Party capable of harmonizing its various elements.

Highly significant changes were also taking place in Conservative Party leadership. It has been generally concluded that Sir Anthony Eden was not very successful as prime minister. His great day in history was his firmness against Hitler and Mussolini before World War II or perhaps his diplomacy in 1954 which helped to produce the Western European Union; but certainly not his brief period, less than two years (April 1955–January 1957), as head of Her Majesty's Government. Eden was at a disadvantage in succeeding Churchill, but while the comparison accentuates his limitations, it does not account for them. His party accepted him without enthusiasm. By 1955 he had unusual qualities only in manner and appearance and, thus, inevitably has been paired with Ramsay MacDonald. Certainly both had a way of evading the responsibility which goes with authority and of muddying up rather than clarifying issues. Neither, in his later years, had the sense of commitment necessary for successful leadership. On the Suez crisis of 1956, it is a matter of conjecture whether British intervention with France in the Israeli-Egyptian war or the withdrawal a week later did the Government the greater harm. The Government survived, but Eden, in ill health as well as ill at ease, resigned on January 9, 1957.

R. A. Butler was generally considered the logical man to succeed. He was greatly respected and contributed perhaps more than did any other individual to reconstruction of party policy after 1945. But his was not a personality which naturally attracted support. And his lack of enthusiasm for Government policy in the Suez crisis may have been a factor. All this came to light when Eden's Cabinet, the other Conservative M.P.s, and some Conservative Lords were canvassed. It was abundantly clear that Harold Macmillan was the man, and the queen was so advised by Churchill and the Marquess of Salisbury. Macmillan, now 62, was well prepared. Save for a brief interval, 1929–31, he had been in the Commons since 1924, and a member of the Cabinet since 1951. As minister of Housing under Churchill, his had been a brilliant achievement; under Eden he had served as foreign secretary and as chancellor of the Exchequer. He was regarded as progressive—since the thirties he had advocated planning to meet unemployment and other social problems. In the new Cabinet he retained Selwyn Lloyd as foreign secretary, an indication that the reorganized Government had no intention of apologizing for Suez. Butler would have liked the Foreign Office, but he gracefully accepted the Home Office and leadership of the Commons. Peter Thorneycroft was promoted from the Board of Trade to the Exchequer. Macmillan, himself, settled into No. 10 as though he belonged there. His general style and manner appealed to the British people. In short, his administration was off to a propitious start.

The Economy, 1955–61: A Delicate Balance

It is not easy to generalize about England's economy in the fifties. As early as June 1954, R. A. Butler, then chancellor of the Exchequer, felt sufficiently confident to issue a call to an abundant economy: "Why should we not aim to double our standard of living in the next twenty-five years, and still have our money as valuable then as now." But this statement was very premature. The favorable situation in May 1955 for the general election soured almost at once. A deficit in international payments developed, and gold and sterling reserves fell alarmingly. Macmillan replaced Butler at the Exchequer—Butler becoming leader of the Commons, presumably to coordinate the domestic program there.

British economy still operated in a delicate balance, and the slight advantage which had tipped the scales favorably in 1952–54 was more than offset in 1955–56. A deficit in international payments developed, and gold and sterling reserves fell alarmingly. The Suez crisis in 1956 required extraordinary dollar expenditures to make good the temporary losses in oil from the Middle East; the Government had been too prompt in encouraging a return to capital expenditure with a corresponding rise in imports. Again there was more money available than there was merchandise to buy, and retail prices moved back to an increase of 4 or 5 percent each year, with corresponding wage demands from industry. Wage restraints proposed by the Government failed.

Accordingly, in 1957 the Government again turned to monetary and fiscal control. The bank rate was steadily raised, purchase taxes were increased, installment buying was restricted, food subsidies were reduced, capital expansion in nationalized industries was checked. Further devaluation of the pound was widely expected. Instead, at the end of 1957, the bank rate was raised to 7 percent, the highest level in thirty-seven years. "The Bank," said the *Economist* in admiration, "has reclaimed the initiative with a thrust of unexpected boldness." This move saved the pound.

From 1957 to 1960 the economic situation was moderately favorable, though with mild fluctuations. In 1957, despite Suez, the value of British overseas trade was greater than in 1956. Measures to safeguard the pound brought a slight decline in foreign trade in 1958, which was more than wiped out in 1959, an impressive year. At the end of 1958, sterling was made freely convertible to dollars. And the bank rate was gradually lowered to 4 percent. Now there came a growth in bank advances, an extension of installment purchase credit, an increase in the travel allowance, and relaxation of restrictions on imports from dollar areas. In 1959 exports were 5 percent greater in value than in 1958, and by volume double those of 1938. Industrial production was 60 percent higher than in 1938 and 13 percent higher than in 1954. Production was increasing at a rate slightly in advance of employment, signifying an increase in productivity. At the end of the decade the rate of economic growth was about 3 percent annually.

Changing Patterns of Industry

Several additional comments should be made on Britain's economy in the fifties. We should first note that the advances did not come in nationalized industries. Had these industries continued under private ownership, production would probably have been somewhat lower, wages (except in coal) somewhat lower, and industrial relations somewhat more difficult. But performance in coal and transport fell far below the predictions of enthusiasts for nationalization. Production of coal, though on the rise, nearly always fell short of the goals. The average of production from 1951 to 1956 was only 211 million tons, and thereupon the Coal Board postponed until 1960 attempts to reach a target of 240 million tons. And in 1959 this estimate was drastically reduced. Not until 1965 would production meet estimated demand. Indeed, in the mid-fifties, some coal had to be imported. During the late fifties the output per manshift slightly improved, and the export of coal was resumed on a modest scale. Coal did pay its way after a time—this was deliberate on the part of the Coal Board. Rationalization of the industry began with widespread shutting down of collieries. The number of miners steadily declined.

Responsibility for the plight of the railroads can hardly be placed on nationalization. The railroads had not been a part of the boom of other kinds of transport, and soon they could not compete profitably with highway and air travel. Within the industry the difficulties were numerous: the problem of unification with road transport, the condition of equipment (especially rolling stock), and the low morale of workers no longer enjoying relatively high pay. A thorough overhauling of the railroads would mean increased charges, reduction in service, and even the termination of some lines. In 1960 both the Government and the Transport Commission appeared willing to undertake this task if the public was prepared to take the consequences. A white paper was published in December 1960, proposing a decentralization of transport, and this, as we shall see, became law in 1962.

The Central Electricity Authority increased productivity 160 per cent from 1942 to 1959, and was uncanny in forecasting power requirements. Rates remained low. The gas industry did not prosper under public ownership, but this was likely due to the declining use of gas as a fuel. But for all nationalized industries a new chapter was envisaged in a white paper (April 1961) on *The Financial and Economic Objectives of the Nationalized Industries* which set forth guidelines for the proper use of resources, for pricing, for determining the proper rate of return on assets—in short, a basis for testing the efficiency of the industry.

As to iron and steel, the Labor Government had not tampered with organizations of firms, and the Churchill Government of 1951 easily provided for a resale of the industry to private hands but under "an adequate measure of public supervision." This took the form of a new Iron and Steel Board (1953) created to determine domestic prices and supervise capital expansion. Throughout the fifties, Labor insisted that once back in power they would renationalize the industry. But the industry seemed to proceed in its operations little affected by change and talk of further change in ownership. Its problem, year in and year out, was to produce enough steel to meet the demand. Plans called for reaching a target of 29 million tons by 1963, as compared with a production of 12¾ million tons in 1946 and 15½ million tons in 1949. Production rose steadily, reaching 24½ million tons in 1960.

But significant changes in the pattern of British industrial production are found elsewhere. The sensational story is that of motor vehicles. The bare figures are impressive: production of pleasure vehicles rose from 219,000 in 1946 to 898,000 in 1955, and commercial vehicles from 148,000 to 341,000. In 1946 there were about 3 million motor vehicles of one kind or another in operation; in 1955 there were 6.6 million, by 1965 over 12 million. Motor vehicles became a major article in foreign trade, with Britain and Germany as the chief exporters. Startling advance was made in aircraft production as well—civil aviation was the fastest growing sector of transport after 1945. The greatest success was with the Vickers' *Viscount,* which by 1953 had proved itself. By 1960, 418 deliveries had been made. There was also greatly increased production in oil refining, in chemicals, in scientific instruments, in electrical equipment, and in nonelectric machinery of all kinds, including tractors. These items now figured prominently on the list of exports, with cotton, one of the traditional leaders, dropping far down the list.

Optimism or Pessimism? By the indices intelligible and meaningful to the average person at the end of the fifties, the times had been "good." A high level of employment had been maintained. Real wages rose nearly 40 percent in less than a decade, and by 1960 a family in ordinary circumstances could afford a television set (three-quarters of all the families had them), a refrigerator, and a motor car. One-sixth of the families had moved into new and better housing, taxes had been reduced and most economic controls relaxed. To say this is not to forget the achievement of the period 1945–51 in which prewar standards of living were restored, even in the face of priorities for reconstruction of devastated areas and a target (achieved) of exports 75 percent above prewar levels. But the times were much better in the fifties than in the late forties—that is the point.

Table 6   Indices of Industrial Production and of Volume of Exports
                 United Kingdom, 1954–64

| | 1954=100 | |
	Industrial Production	Volume of Exports
1954	100	100
1955	105	107
1956	106	113
1957	108	116
1958	106	111
1959	113	116
1960	120	122
1961	121	125
1962	122	128
1963	126	134
1964	135	137

Source: *Annual Register of World Events*

And so in 1960 the politicians (in all parties) were generally optimistic about the future of Britain's economy. The economists, on the other hand, were generally cautious or skeptical. G. D. N. Worswick, writing in 1962, concludes his chapter on "The British Economy 1950–1959" with his sobering remark: "The fifties ended on the note of record Christmas sales, but one could just hear voices saying that the sixties might bring the need for a new approach to economic policy." If Britain's record in the fifties and sixties "compared well with the record of the past," writes Sidney Pollard, *The Development of the British Economy 1914–1967* (1969), "it compared extremely badly with that of other contemporary advanced economies. The difference, the striking gap between the sluggish growth in output in Britain and the very much faster growth elsewhere, was so wide that the leading Continental countries, which for centuries had had much lower incomes and products *per capita*, began to catch up with and overtake Britain in absolute levels by the early 1960s." A striking example is West Germany, where in 1951 the gross national product was about 65 percent of that of the United

Kingdom. By 1962 West Germany had moved ahead. In Britain the relative rise in real costs of production placed her at a disadvantage in the competitive world market. A "Stop-Go" monetary policy made for a fluctuating economy and was no more than a temporary answer. The report in 1959 of the Radcliffe Committee on "The Working of the Monetary System" was intelligent and thorough but was preoccupied with inflation and largely ignored the problem of production. The British economy needed long-term planning: a tax structure which would divert a larger portion of the gross national product into capital investment for modernization of industrial technology; an extension of technological education; a realistic price structure especially in the nationalized industries; a national incomes policy to control inflation and industrial strikes and stoppages. Such measures were suggested in an important PEP report, *Growth in the British Economy,* issued in 1960.

The General Election, 1959

A more united Labor Party with imaginative leadership might well have capitalized on the weaknesses in Britain's economy. This and other matters—Suez and its aftermath, the rise in industrial strikes, unemployment, the Conservative long tenure in office—seemed made to order as political issues for Labor in the general election of October 1959. But Labor failed to take advantage of its opportunities. Gaitskell himself blundered in his rash pledge when he declared "there will be no increase in the standard or other rates of income tax so long as normal peacetime conditions continue," and this was followed with the report from Transport House that the purchase tax would be removed from essential goods—another declaration which could not be taken seriously.

On the other hand, Macmillan seemed, even to many critical of him, entirely in command. An economic policy, more than satisfactory for the moment—and that was what counted politically—seemed to have finally brought to actuality the "Butler Boom," a Conservative boast of 1954. The quantity of goods in the domestic market had increased, with retail prices holding steady. In April 1959 taxes had been cut substantially. All this was given a political cast in such campaign keynote slogans as, "You're Having It Good—Have It Better—Vote Conservative." In comparison with 1955, it was an exciting campaign, particularly in the Conservative camp, where professional direction made use of the growing understanding of opinion polls and of voting habits. As Butler and Rose tell us in the Nuffield volume, the Conservatives concentrated on "the party image" as more important than this issue or that. A gigantic public relations program, launched in 1957, came to a climax in the 1959 campaign itself. About £468,000, it is estimated, was spent on advertising alone, to establish a favorable "image" of Macmillan, to emancipate the party from the unpopular symbol of "privilege," and to associate it with the popular symbols of "peace," "prosperity," and "progress."

The poll revealed an additional swing (since 1955) of 1.2 percent to the Conservatives, who raised their overall majority in the Commons to 100 and scored a decisive popular victory, 49.4 percent to 43.7 percent over Labor. The Liberals, who had registered dramatic gains in by-elections since 1955, notably in the victory of Mark Bonham-Carter at Torrington in March 1958, were unable to maintain this momentum when a change in government was at stake. Though in 1958 the number of their candidacies was doubled, in 1955 they polled only 5.9 percent of the popular vote and their seats in the Commons remained at six. Even so they had fought a vigorous campaign and in some constituencies made marked advance; now under the new leadership of Jo Grimond, they were striving not just for survival but for recognition.

Labor's Search for Identity

If the Conservative "image" was bright and clear, that of Labor was blurred. The diverse elements within the party were plain to be seen; its controversies were open to the public. In 1959 Labor suffered its third defeat in succession. Thirty percent of the wage earners had voted against Labor; a majority of the new voters had not been attracted. Nor had the solid support of professional and white-collar groups won over in 1945 been retained.

Gaitskell's antidote was an attempt to rid the party of its old-fashioned doctrinaire socialist approach, particularly that associated with Point IV of the 1918 constitution: "to secure for the producers by hand or by brain the full fruits of their industry ... upon the basis of the common ownership of the means of production." And the party was pledged to the "eventual nationalization of all the means of production, distribution and exchange." But debate at the annual conference of 1959 revealed astonishing support for doctrinaire socialism and ended with the retention of Point IV in somewhat clouded form, thus perhaps satisfying both sides. *The Times,* perhaps forgetful of the nature of party constitutions, declared that the Labor Party had sacrificed an opportunity for a fresh start.

Campaign for Nuclear Disarmament. This controversy, however, did not enlist the emotions to anything like the degree of the issue over "unilateralism," whether Britain should decide of herself alone to renounce production and use of nuclear arms, or whether any such decision should be made only multilaterally. It began as a stirring of conscience. In its most aggressive form, unilateralism was found in the Campaign for Nuclear Disarmament (and associated movements) which at one time had the support of some fifty leftist members of the Parliamentary Labor Party in defiance of its policy statements. Organized early in 1958 with Julian Huxley, Dame Rose Macaulay, J. B. Priestley, and Sir Richard Acland included in its executive committee, the CND's inaugural meeting in the Central Hall, Westminster, February 17, 1958, drew some 5,000 to the hall and to nearby overflow meetings, for addresses by Bertrand Russell, J. B. Priestley, Michael Foot (an M.P. now representing Bevan's old Welsh constituency of Ebbw Vale), and A. J. P. Taylor, an historian and Oxford don. And soon was held the first of several annual marches at Eastertime to the nuclear research station at Aldermaston, near Reading—these had powerful force as propaganda. On Easter Sunday, 1960, the march culminated in a huge demonstration in Trafalgar Square with a crowd estimated variously from 60,000 to 100,000. The movement had an estimated support of 300,000 or more and published a paper, *Sanity*, which claimed a circulation of 40,000. The CND at first won the respect of many who did not support it, but it was weakened by extremists and by internal discord over methods to be pursued, particularly concerning resort to civil disobedience. An offshoot, the "Committee of 100," with Bertrand Russell as its president, staged a "Ban the Bomb" sit-down strike in Trafalgar Square on September 17–18, 1961. Perhaps as many as 12,000 assembled; after midnight the gathering got out of hand and the police arrested 1,314. A few weeks before, Lord Russell himself had been jailed for failing to keep the peace in his refusal to call off the demonstration. The "Committee of 100" absorbed another militant group, the "Direct Action Committee," in efforts to build up pressure within the CND.

The issues were carried to a stormy party conference of the Labor Party at Scarborough in October 1960. There the left wing, led by Frank Cousins of the powerful Transport and General Workers' Union, succeeded in carrying several resolutions, by small margins, for unilateral renunciation of nuclear weapons. Against the efforts of trade union leaders to dominate Labor M.P.s elected by popular vote and to swing the annual conference over to unilateralism, Gaitskell announced his determination to "fight and fight and fight again." On both counts he was successful, as confirmed at the party conference at Blackpool the year following. His prestige in the party and in the country was tremendously enhanced.

Thereafter Gaitskell's hold on the Parliamentary Labor Party was never seriously threatened. In November 1960 he was retained as party leader, 166 to 81, over Harold Wilson, not himself an extremist but one around whom leftists gathered. George Brown, a rightist, and staunch Gaitskell supporter at Scarborough, was elected deputy leader. Gaitskell's own views dominated *Signposts for the Sixties,* a Labor policy statement issued in the summer of 1961 and generally regarded as the most convincing enunciation of Labor policy since 1945. It proposed: an industrial planning board to establish priorities in capital expansion; revival of the National Research Development Corporation to stimulate production, encourage research, and revive sluggish industries; taxation of capital gains in wealth; nationalization of land required for housing and public use to prevent private exploitation; reorganization of education including development of comprehensive secondary schools and integration of public schools.

A Political Reorientation?

Just before the poll of 1959 Gaitskell declared: "There are signs of the breaking up of traditional loyalties." And after the poll the *Daily Mail* ventured to say that that election would be remembered as "a major upheaval, a turning point, a political watershed." Several years later D. E. Butler, senior tutor at Nuffield College, Oxford, in a radio talk on the Third Programme considered "the possibilities of realignment," something that happens "every forty years or so." Every age tends to indulge the notion of its own uniqueness. But there were certain factors in the years 1959–62 that indicated that a reorientation of British political life might well be in process.

By this time it was widely recognized that a kind of equilibrium had been established between the two major parties, despite the efforts of politicians to confront the voters with a choice between two contrasting ways of life. The essence of this equilibrium was an essential consensus, best illustrated in the term "Butskellism," a combination of the names of successive chancellors of the Exchequer—Gaitskell (1950–51) and Butler (1951–55)—invented by the *Economist* to emphasize the essential agreement in the economic policies of leadership in both parties. There was common acceptance of Keynesian doctrine—especially his general ideas of planning and freedom from orthodoxy. Furthermore, ever since their "Industrial Charter" the Conservatives had put it on the line that they accepted the new role of the state in the economy as well as the welfare state, as legislated by the postwar Labor Government. Indeed, Labor was faced with more dissent within its ranks in the fifties than there was difference between the official views of party leadership. In

1959 a Gallup Poll showed that 38 percent of those canvassed thought it made little difference which party was in office. In 1950, in a similar poll, the figure had been 20 percent. It was a decade of slogans rather than issues. Consensus never brings as much change as does controversy.

Then again, trade unionism, which had been so largely responsible for identifying the interests of the working class with Labor and which had provided most of the machinery by which Labor operated, was much less politically conscious in the fifties. Interest in nationalization as a socialist principle declined (though perhaps ready to flare up occasionally as in the party conference of 1959.) The average worker had no contact whatsoever with management, and so to participate in a "nationalized industry" carried no special meaning. When the railways became "British," railwaymen scrawled "These are now ours" on freight cars (waggons), but soon found this an empty sentiment. Full employment, social security, full legal status for unionism had been achieved. What more could politics do for the workingman? Stoppages were numerous but not serious, and agreements were promptly reached. Much industrial cooperation between management and labor was taken for granted, with industry-wide negotiation and arbitration increasingly successful. Political apathy among working-class voters was one of the reasons for the decline of Labor's voting strength. Indeed, many working-class people were attracted by the success of the economic policies of the Tories. Three-eighths of the members of trade unions did not pay the political levy to the Labor Party and probably one-quarter voted Conservative or Liberal. The General Council of the Trades Union Congress appeared at times to be almost nonpartisan—in 1951 it formally declared that it would cooperate with the new Conservative Government.

The Nature of Socialism. The decline of popular interest in nationalization and the failure of employees in nationalized industries to be loyal to the social character of this new form of industrial organization led Enoch Powell to write in the *Political Quarterly* in 1959 that the Labor Party was haunted by the fear that the majority of the electorate did not favor something labeled "socialism." But the ideologists answered that socialism as a doctrine seeking the transformation of society by subordinating all interests of the individual to the interests of society had not yet been tried in England, that the socialist ethic had never replaced the capitalist, and that the "revolution" of 1945 merely climaxed a half century of social reform and firmly established "welfare capitalism." Thus Ralph Miliband in *Parliamentary Socialism* (1961) speaks of a "basic question, namely whether the Labour Party is to be concerned with attempts at a more efficient and more humane administration of a capitalist society; or whether it is to adapt itself to the task of creating a socialist one."

On this question, a prolonged debate extended through the fifties and beyond. The *New Fabian Essays* (1952) emphasized the dignity of the individual which public ownership might not necessarily achieve. A group of Labor Party members organized the Socialist Union in 1951 "to think out afresh the foundations of a socialist faith." Their ideas appeared in a "Penguin Special." The conflict between capitalism and socialism, they said, was a matter of values. Socialism stands for equality, freedom, and fellowship, and the means for achieving these goals are economic security, fair shares, an expanding economy, and industrial democracy. They conceded that there is no assurance that a public enterprise will be operated in the general interest. The answer, they said, is in a mixed economy in which all economic power is subject to effective control, a control best secured by a balance of opposing forces—in a word, by competition.

A similar modification of classical socialism is found in *Industry and Society* (1957), a statement of policy prepared by a Labor Party committee. It emphasized the virtues of nationalization, but pointed out that ownership in private enterprise did not necessarily mean control. Following a suggestion put forward by Gaitskell in the 1955 campaign, it advocated an investment corporation set up by the government which would accept land and securities in payment of income taxes and in which pension funds and budget surpluses would be placed and in which the Government would exercise control and share in dividends and capital gains. Several veteran Labor Party leaders fought against this "shareholder state," but the report was overwhelmingly approved in party conferences of 1957 and 1958. Such views were not far from those expressed by C. A. R. Crosland, a young economist whose *The Future of Socialism* (1956) was treated with respect. He did not believe that further nationalization would foster socialism, no matter how defined, and favored the continuation of a mixed economy. In another connection he said "Labour must modernize itself or fail." In essays written between 1958 and 1962 published in *The Conservative Enemy: A Programme of Radical Reform for the 1960s* (1962) he asserted that "ownership is outdated" as an approach to society. The issues that will dominate politics in the future will be economic growth, mass media, incomes policy, education, and town and city "amenity" planning. Radical reform, he said, must leave behind the conservatism of both right and left. John Strachey retreated some distance from his position of the thirties. Writing in 1956 in *Contemporary Capitalism*, he declared that experience had proven Marx wrong and that democratic institutions tempered by Keynesian economics were producing an economy of abundance.

Aneurin Bevan wished to get on with the job of transferring economic power to the working classes, but his methods moderated as the decade progressed.

The New Left. In 1957, after the Hungarian revolt and the Suez crisis, a new tone—an insistent tone, one of protest—appeared in the New Left, composed largely of intellectuals (teachers, writers, scholars, journalists). At the start nearly all its adherents were under forty and most of them were under thirty. Politically, they belonged, if anywhere, to Labor, but they were critical of Labor leadership and unable to find in its activities any stimulus to creative thought and action. They had no interest in or understanding of trade unionism. They were less interested in politics than in "culture." The *New Left Review* was their chief mouthpiece. In 1960 *Out of Apathy* appeared as the first of the New Left books.

This writing insisted upon the ethical and aesthetic qualities in socialism. It was both morally and intellectually outraged at the quality of English civilization in mid-century, with its preoccupation with material values, with its "private affluence" and "public squalor," with its "new Barbarism of the Welfare State and Commercial Television" (in the words of Kingsley Amis). Society, said the New Left, must be subjected to a revolutionary kind of analysis in order to adjust the life of the people to the altered role of Britain in the world. Many members of the New Left expressed themselves through the Campaign for Nuclear Disarmament. The Labor Party was considered worthy of support only if it sought to make a new society.

The nature of this new society was best delineated in the writings of Raymond Williams, a product of the postwar world, an intellectual from a working-class background, whose sense of values clashed with that of the traditional. He said: "Only in projecting a new kind of community, a new kind of social consciousness can the Labour Party offer anything distinctive and positive." In *The Long Revolution* (1961) he recapitulated what he had been saying for a decade. He was prepared to abandon capitalistic notions of the consumer and the organized market in order to leave behind the irrelevancies of class and achieve a "common culture" in an industrial society in which only differences among people as individuals will count.

The torrent of words from the New Left was intelligent and creative, but emotional and often tortuous as well. In politics, it was essentially a movement of protest, but even here its only visible success was its campaign against commercial television.

Political reorientation is no doubt unpredictable, for when it comes it is the outcome of many factors, some of them small and accidental. The thought that a realignment of politics might be just around the corner in the sixties was in part inspired by the reflection that the Labor Party, as then in being, could hardly survive a fourth successive defeat at a general election. This, of course, did not happen. Furthermore, the economic context changed. But before we examine economics and politics during the last years of this long Conservative rule, we must turn our attention to Britain's external relations during the Macmillan era.

The Commonwealth: Winds of Change, 1956-64

In world policy, the Churchillian concept of British association with three overlapping circles (Commonwealth, United States and the Atlantic Community, and Europe) which we have mentioned earlier, is increasingly less realistic as the fifties progress, and by the sixties, as F. S. Northedge suggests, the circles no longer overlap; indeed, each is now pulling away from Britain.

Independence within the Commonwealth

Quite significant to the historian is the transformation of the role of the British Empire and the Commonwealth in the British scheme of things. But contemporaries, even the politicians, only slowly became aware of that which was transpiring. Withdrawal from India in 1947 seemed to have closed a chapter in British history. The new chapter, for the next decade, represented an endeavor to harmonize in a community of nations the traditions and interests of peoples of Asia and Africa with those of peoples of European origin. Reciprocal advantages in trade cemented these ties. Half of Britain's exports went to Commonwealth lands which, in turn, supplied more than half of Britain's imports. All member states, save Canada, belonged to the sterling area, with Britain as the banker providing loans for capital expansion and a basis for international exchange. That it was now the "Commonwealth" and not "the British Commonwealth" signified an equal status for all; the concept had been purged of "imperialism" and stood for a collection of communities—some sovereign states, some "self governing," and others still "crown colonies." The term "dominion" fell into disuse—in 1947 the Cabinet office of "Dominion Affairs" became "Commonwealth Relations." Since now there were republics as well as monarchies in the Commonwealth, a new form of royal title was required. At the Commonwealth Conference of 1952 it was agreed that each member state "should use for its own purposes a form of title which suits its own particular circumstances." Britain was seeking some middle ground between the old imperial ties to the British crown, on the one hand, and complete separation on the other; perhaps in the concept and reality of "Commonwealth" she could control the future and render successful a noble experiment. Thus went much of the thinking of the English people in the early fifties. But such reflection would soon undergo change.

In June 1955, the Queen's Address opening the new Parliament reads: "My Government will maintain and strengthen consultation within the Commonwealth for the fulfillment of our common aims and purposes." It is worthy of note that such a statement, which had appeared in the Address for some years, was never repeated after 1955—the era of "consultation" and "common aims" within the Commonwealth was over. In 1956 came Suez—if hardly the cause of that which followed, surely an anticipation. At the end of World War II there were six member states in the Commonwealth; in 1955 there were eight. But a dozen years later, by 1967, there were twenty-eight. To put it even more dramatically: in January 1957 the British colonial empire was still intact in Africa, with only the Union of South Africa in the Commonwealth; at the end of 1967 twelve other territories in Africa were independent states within the Commonwealth. This story of rapid change will take us also to the West Indies, to Southeast Asia, and to the Mediterranean. The simple fact is that after Suez the Conservative Government and then the Labor Government which followed in 1964 proceeded to liquidate the colonial empire.

Briefly summarized, this is what happened. In 1956 the Anglo-Egyptian Sudan became a sovereign state, and in 1960 British Somaliland was given independence, making possible its union with Italian Somaliland and, hence, the Somali Republic. These two states did not become associated with the Commonwealth, but they were exceptions to the general practice. Independence was granted to the Federation of Malaya in 1957, expanded in 1963 to include Singapore, Sabah (formerly North Borneo), and Sarawak—under the name of the Federation of Malaysia. Commonwealth ties were invoked when the United Kingdom troops fought in Sarawak against raids from Indonesia. Singapore seceded in 1965 but stayed in the Commonwealth. The tempo of disengagement from the British Crown picked up decidedly in the early sixties. Independence within the Commonwealth came to Cyprus and Nigeria in 1960, to Sierra Leone and Tanganyika in 1961, to Uganda and Western Samoa (which had been administered by New Zealand) in 1962, to Kenya and Zanzibar in 1963. A proposed East African Federation (Kenya, Uganda, Tanganyika, and Zanzibar) failed to materialize, but the Republics of Tanganyika and Zanzibar, after a stormy period, united in the Republic of Tanzania in 1964. In that year also came Nyasaland (renamed Malawi), Northern Rhodesia (renamed Zambia), as well as independence to Malta; in 1965 there was The Gambia. In 1966 came more new

Sovereign Member States of the Commonwealth, 1976
(with the year in which Dominion status or, later, Commonwealth status was granted)

United Kingdom of Great Britain and Northern Ireland
Canada: dominion, 1867
Australia: "commonwealth" with dominion status, 1901
New Zealand: dominion, 1907
India: dominion, 1947; republic, 1950
Ceylon: dominion, 1948; republic, 1970; became Republic of Sri
    Lanka, 1972
Ghana (formerly Gold Coast): 1957; republic, 1960
Cyprus: republic, 1960; approved as a Commonwealth state, 1961
Nigeria: 1960; republic, 1963
Sierra Leone: 1961; republic, 1971
Jamaica: 1962
Trinidad and Tobago: 1962
Uganda: 1962; republic, 1963
Western Samoa: 1970
Federation of Malaysia: 1963; territories in Malaya independent
    since 1957.
Kenya; 1963; republic, 1964
Tanzania: republic, 1964 (union of Tanganyika, independent,
    1961, and Zanzibar, independent, 1963).
Malta: 1964
Zambia (formerly Northern Rhodesia): 1964
Malawi (formerly Nyasaland): 1964; republic, 1966
The Gambia: 1965; republic, 1970
Singapore: 1965 (republic, seceded from Federation of Malaysia)
Barbados: 1966
Guyana (formerly British Guiana): 1966; republic, 1970
Botswana (formerly Bechuanaland): 1966
Lesotho (formerly Basutoland): 1966
Mauritius: 1968
Nauru: 1968 (special membership)
Swaziland: 1968
Fiji: 1970
Tonga: 1970
Bangladesh (formerly East Pakistan): republic, 1972
Bahamas: 1973
Grenada: 1974
Papua New Guinea: 1975
Seychelles: 1976

Former Members

Newfoundland: dominion, 1867; crown colony again in 1934;
    Canadian province in 1949
Burma: independent outside the Commonwealth, 1948
Irish Free State: 1921; left Commonwealth in 1949
Sudan: independent, 1956
Union of South Africa: 1910; republic and left Commonwealth,
    1961
Maldives: independent, 1963
Yemen P. D. R. (formerly Aden): republic in 1967
Pakistan: 1947; republic, 1956; left Commonwealth, 1972
British Somaliland: independent, 1960; joined with Italian Samali
    to form the Samali Republic

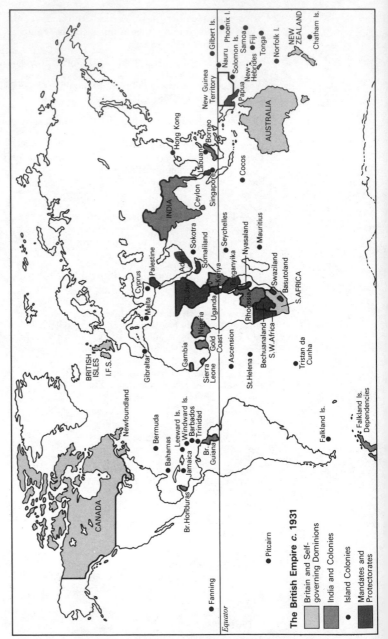

Map 6   **The British Empire, c. 1931**
Source: Nicholas Mansergh, *The Commonwealth Experience* (London: George Weidenfeld and Nicolson, 1969), p. 415.

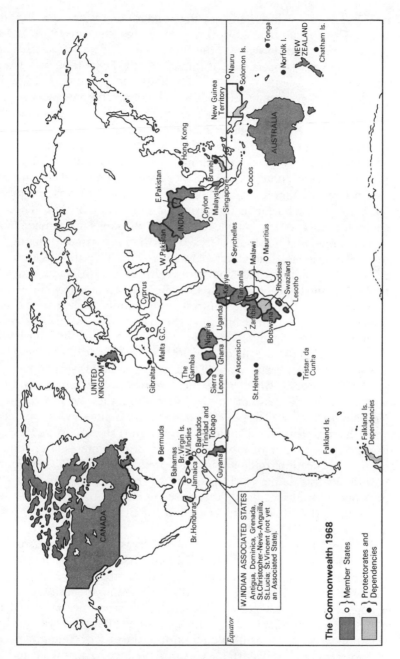

Map 7   The Commonwealth, 1968
Source: Nicholas Mansergh, *The Commonwealth Experience*, p. 414.

names: Lesotho (which had been Basutoland) and Botswana (Bechuanaland). The Barbados also became a sovereign state in 1966. Independence seemed to be in sight for the West Indies Federation (established in
1957), but with Jamaica's secession in 1961 the Federation was dissolved
and the larger islands—Jamaica, Trinidad and Tobago—became independent as separate states in1962. British Guiana became independent as
Guyana in 1966. (See Sovereign Member States of the Commonwealth.)

Mansergh's brilliant generalization that the transformation of the
Commonwealth after 1945 was "the product partly of conviction, partly
of experience, most of all, of circumstances" is pregnant with significance
for the fifties and sixties. A blunter way of making much the same point is
that the rise of aggressive nationalism in the colonies was accompanied
by a steady decline in enthusiasm for empire in Britain. These two
generalizations cover a complex of factors: Britain's mounting problems
as to national and imperial defense; growth of disharmony among Commonwealth states themselves; disunity in SEATO; the declining role,
relatively, of Empire and Commonwealth in British trade (after 1955
trade remained stationary with Commonwealth lands, while doubling
with Europe and the United States); anti-colonial feeling in the United
States and in the United Nations; the rise of the problem of colonial
immigration to England. There was also the role of the Third World.
Macmillan frankly recognized this problem in his address in 1960 before
the South African Parliament: "The great issue in this second half of the
twentieth century is whether the uncommitted peoples of Asia and Africa
will swing to the East or to the West. Will they be drawn into the
Communist camp?" The possible value of the Commonwealth in dealing
with this problem was emphasized in a report drawn up in 1963, by a
group representative of a wide range of British interests: government,
business, education, trade unions, the press, and so on. "The Commonwealth sits astride the world problem of the developed and the under-
developed nations ... [and] therefore represents one means by which
this huge problem can be tackled, and for Britain it represents perhaps
the best means."

It cannot be overemphasized that the British Empire came to an end
largely on Britain's own initiative. To a remarkable degree she was aware
of circumstance and in command of solution, often announcing the decision well in advance and occasionally voicing impatience with the tardy
acquiescence of the colony concerned. This procedure appeared to be
merely another example of continuity through change in the best British
tradition. In 1958 Macmillan did honor to the idea of Commonwealth in
his tour of India, Pakistan, Ceylon, Malaya, Australia, and New
Zealand—the first such journey by a prime minister while in office. The
issue of colonialism—particularly Labor's attack on Conservative policy

in Kenya and Nyasaland—attracted attention in the election campaign of 1959. And after the Conservative victory, the appointment as secretary for the Colonies of Iain Macleod (who had already shown brilliance as minister of Health and minister of Labor) brought into prominence the official policy of independence in Africa.

This phase of British policy reached something of a climax in Macmillan's celebrated address in 1960 at Cape Town, already mentioned. This passage of his remarks has been cited time and time again:

> In the twentieth century . . . we have seen the awakening of national consciousness in peoples who for centuries lived in dependence upon some other power . . . . Today the same thing is happening in Africa, and the most striking of all the impressions I have formed since I left London a month ago is of the strength of this African national consciousness. The wind of change is blowing through this continent, and whether we like it or not, this growth of national consciousness is a political fact. We must all accept it as a fact, and our national policies must take account of it.

One may comment that the course of events thereafter speeded up.

The South African prime minister, Dr. Verwoerd, in response to Macmillan's words at Cape Town referred frankly to his country's differences with Britain over racial issues. Back in 1948, General Smuts, a leading advocate of Commonwealth ties, was succeeded as prime minister by Dr. Malan of the Nationalist Party, which was committed to *apartheid* (segregation) and to absolute supremacy in Africa of the European element. At once Dr. Malan's policy and British attitudes collided in South West Africa, which was dependent on the Union. In 1958 the Nationalist Party strengthened its control of Parliament and emphasized its adherence to *apartheid* and republicanism. In March 1961 Dr. Verwoerd, at the prime ministers' conference in London, announced that in view of the attitude of Commonwealth countries toward racial policy in South Africa, his country, upon becoming a republic, would sever relations with the Commonwealth. It is significant that he requested a maintenance of trade ties within the sterling area. Otherwise, Dr. Verwoerd's statement was merely recognition of a breach that already existed. On May 31, 1961, South Africa became a republic. The long story ended in favor of the Boers.

British leaders, early in the fifties, had hopes that federation would be a useful and successful vehicle for promoting unity and partnership within the Commonwealth. This idea, as we have seen, was to have mixed results. Economic considerations led to federation in 1953 of the self-governing colony of Southern Rhodesia and the protectorates of Northern Rhodesia and Nyasaland, but it seemed impossible of success; Southern Rhodesia, completely in the control of whites, could not get along with the others, both of which were overwhelmingly African in population. Indeed, the Africans in all three lands had been opposed to federation from the start. In Nyasaland racial disturbances in 1959 and the findings of British commissions of inquiry in 1959 and 1960 led to the decision in London to break up the Federation. British policy was skillfully directed by R. A. Butler, first secretary of state; in July 1963, at the Victoria Falls Conference, he secured agreement for the formal dissolution of the Federation at the end of the year. Northern Rhodesia (renamed Zambia) and Nyasaland (now Malawi) quickly became independent, with Commonwealth status. Southern Rhodesia (renamed Rhodesia in October 1964) also demanded independence, but Great Britain refused to transfer sovereign power so long as the franchise remained restricted and some 3,970,000 Africans were in the control of 217,000 whites. In November 1964 the prime minister, Ian Smith, conducted a referendum which went 8 to 1 for independence (with a small vote and the Africans boycotting the vote). But the British Government warned that political and economic sanctions would be imposed if Rhodesia unilaterally voted herself independent.

"The Special Relation"

If one argues that by the sixties the Commonwealth no longer provided a unified community with common traditions and mutual interests, what can be said about "the special relation" of Britain with the United States and the Atlantic Community? Anglo-American solidarity could hardly be taken for granted and its operation at any time depended on circumstance. Mutual interests were essential. In point of fact, in the fifties there were many differences, some of them sharp: over trade, over atomic weapons, over Palestine, toward Red China, and toward Russia. Though allies in the Korean War, there was constant irritation. When Britain pulled out of the Middle East, the United States remained, though hardly by prior arrangement. Strangely enough, after the Suez crisis, the two countries did draw closer together, with Macmillan making a strong personal effort; a notable result was the amendment of the MacMahon Act in America to permit Anglo-American collaboration in atomic energy once again.

Macmillan pressed repeatedly for "a summit talk." Finally, the four leaders—Macmillan, Eisenhower, Krushchev, and de Gaulle—gathered in Paris in May 1960 to discuss problems between East and West, including the German question. But the meeting collapsed with the report that an American U2 reconnaissance plane had been shot down over Russia on May 1. Kruschev refused to continue discussions In his autobiographical volume, *Pointing the Way*, Macmillan records his "disappointment amounting almost to despair—so much attempted, so little achieved" and "the inept American handling" of the U2 incident, "with all its denials, contradictions, reassessments and excuses." The American secretary of state, John Foster Dulles, had been "a disaster." In April 1961 the Bay of Pigs episode, in which the United States Central Intelligence Agency supported an abortive attempt of Cuban exiles to oust Fidel Castro from Cuban dictatorship and failed, brought a torrent of criticism from England.

It is in this context that the remarks of Dean Acheson, formerly the American secretary of state, on December 5, 1962, at West Point, must be understood: "Great Britain has lost an empire and has not yet found a rôle. The attempt to play a separate power rôle apart from Europe, a rôle on being the head of a "Commonwealth" ... this rôle is about played out.... Her Majesty's Government is now attempting—wisely in my opinion—to reenter Europe." Macmillan responded vigorously: "In so far as he appeared to denigrate the resolution and will of Britain and the British people, Mr. Acheson has fallen into an error which has been made by quite a lot of people in the course of the last 400 years."

But the actions of Macmillan and those of the British government were in harmony with Acheson's pronouncement. As we shall see, Britain was indeed staking her future on membership in the European Common Market, the first step, other than defense, toward unity with Western Europe. A frequent verdict on British foreign policy, particularly from American observers (for example, George Ball's *Discipline of Power,* 1968), is that between 1945 and 1960 Britain lost a great opportunity. Distracted by the idea of the Commonwealth and her "special relation" with the United States, she failed to capitalize on her opportunity in Western Europe, where, as the strongest power at the end of World War II, she could have established leadership. But Britain in our time has not been accustomed to act in haste. She opted for the principle of balance of power on the continent, apparently oblivious to the lessons of the twentieth century in this regard. By the end of the fifties, her rivals on the continent, particularly France and West Germany, had forged ahead, politically and economically. Now in the sixties, belatedly some would say, she sought to "return to Europe." This development we shall examine in the context of the last years, 1961–64, of the Macmillan Government.

"Supermac" and Conservative Fadeout, 1961–64

Political fortunes of individuals and parties can change abruptly. Macmillan, after his great victory at the polls in 1959 became, in the cartoons, "Supermac" and "Macwonder." For the next two years he was at the height of his career—as spokesman for the nation, as leader of his party, and in confidence in himself. Suez had been put safely behind. Planning ahead became a central theme, and royal commissions were established to examine the economy, industry, education, traffic in the cities, radio and television broadcasting. And Macmillan continued to profit from internal conflict within Labor. But his own policies—in the economy generally, in colonial affairs (especially in Rhodesia), and eventually in his turn to the Common Market—were sowing seeds of trouble in his own party. Perhaps more important, the Macmillan Government ceased to be a "team"; repeated cabinet shakeups, while difficult of analysis, suggest not only differences in policy but Macmillan's lack of confidence in his subordinates and their fading loyalty toward him. Indeed, his subordinates became rivals. In Butler's somewhat cryptic phrase, Macmillan became "the best Prime Minister we have."

The Economy in Trouble

The dramatic upsurge of the economy in 1959, so helpful to the electoral fortunes of the Conservatives, proved short-lived. In 1960–62, three chancellors of the Exchequer in quick succession sought to deal with the country's financial and economic problems, an indication in itself that policies and measures were experimental and uncertain. By October 1960 the economy was at a standstill and the balance of international payments, an ever-sensitive barometer, was adverse again. Britain in 1960 spent abroad £344 million more than she earned. The situation soon brought criticism within as well as without Government circles. In a debate on economic policy in February 1961, Mr. Selwyn Lloyd, now chancellor of the Exchequer, proved ineffective, and from the Conservative back benches, the prime minister's son, Maurice Macmillan, M.P. from Halifax, joined in the attack. It was recalled that in his younger days the prime minister himself had often been impatient of party leadership. The National Health Service posed special problems, with costs exceeding estimates. The Government responded by increasing some small charges, such as for prescriptions and dentures—a measure which, though courageous on the part of the minister of Health, Enoch Powell, was, of course, unpopular.

The "Pay Pause." To bolster the economy, measures —familiar and unfamiliar—were invoked, culminating in the "little budget" of July 1961, in which the bank rate was raised to 7 percent and indirect taxes, including customs and excise, were raised 10 percent. And Mr. Lloyd called for "a pause" in all wage and salary increases "until productivity has caught up." The Government, he said, would at once apply the principle to civil service and nationalized industries; private industry, he hoped, would exercise similar restraint. Agencies that would plan for a proper incomes policy in an expanding economy would soon be announced. It was unorthodox, not to say surprising, for a Conservative chancellor of the Exchequer to call for artificial restraints on incomes and to talk about a planned economy. The *Economist* was lyrical about "the pay pause," as it was promptly called, and supported Lloyd's statement that a 6 percent increase in exports would justify no more than a 3 percent increase in personal incomes.

Self-discipline did not work, with much of the opposition coming, not unnaturally, from those whose wages and salaries might be affected. There was, indeed, "a pause in the pause." When Selwyn Lloyd reduced the bank rate one-half percent in October, the *Economist* declared impatiently, "No, Mr. Lloyd, No, No, No!" The Government sought to ease wage restraints by applying the policy in several phases, which operated unevenly in the economy, thereby merely bringing charges of inconsistency and unscrupulousness. In particular, trade union leaders were alienated by this interference with the processes of collective bargaining. The *Economist* remarked caustically that the General Council of the Trades Union Congress "continues to turn a blind eye to all major problems it does not like." Protests in civil service, unprotected by militant trade union leaders, took various forms—a "work to rule" slowdown in the post offices and a threat among women typists to produce no more than thirty words a minute (no one dared contemplate what this would do to Government business and the bureaucracy). Wage increases, of 4 or 5 or 6 percent and sometimes more, were granted to busmen, railwaymen, postal workers, engineers, and other civil servants, despite the "guiding light" of no more than 2 percent per person per year which Government urged early in 1962. The "pay pause" came to an end in mid-1962, with a return to a "free for all" in higher wages and salaries, leaving many sectors of the society grieved that during the pause their incomes had fallen behind. In a Gallup Poll, 65 percent believed the "pay pause" had operated unfairly. Meantime, the economy showed no improvement. Exports, while improving, were well below the general advance in world trade. Domestic production remained about stationary, with rising wages and salaries.

The condition of the economy was not reflected in electoral results until 1962. To be sure, the Liberals had registered small gains, but the possibilities were not appreciated until the by-election in the Kent suburb of Orpington, in March 1962, produced a Liberal victory, A Conservative majority of 15,000 was changed to a Liberal majority of 8,000 with the Conservative proportion of the poll dropping nearly 22 percent and the Labor 10 percent. The Liberal leader in the Commons, Jo Grimond, pronounced it "an incredible result." The party nearly wrested Blackpool North as well (the Conservative proportion of the poll dropping nearly 20 percent), and some of the more enthusiastic Liberals began drawing up a "shadow cabinet." Labor took what satisfaction it could from the fact that the Liberals made heavier inroads on Conservative strength than on Labor. In April, Stockton-on-Tees was narrowly retained by the Conservatives, but again the Liberals cut into the Conservative vote twice as much as into Labor. George Brown, deputy Labor leader, said bravely to his party, "Brothers, what are we worrying about?"

Cabinet Shake-up, July, 1962. The first parliamentary victory for Labor over the Conservatives since 1959 came in the by-election in Middlesbrough West in June 1962. Despite the intervention—this time, of a Liberal—Labor raised its share of the poll by over 4 percent. And when at Leicester in July, Labor easily held the seat, with the Conservative candidate coming in a poor third and polling 24 percent less than its share of the poll for 1959, the Liberal victory at Orpington was discounted as a freak and Labor's confidence was restored. As for the Tories, after the Middlesbrough West result, Reginald Maudling, colonial secretary, in a much publicized newsletter to his own constituents declared: "There is a general feeling we are not giving the dynamic leadership this country needs at this moment." Macmillan agreed, (as he tells us at some length in *At the End of the Day, 1961–1963*), and the very next day he acted with decision. Rumors of pending Cabinet changes had circulated, but no rumors approached the actuality on July 13. Out of office went one-third (seven members) of the Cabinet, soon joined by nine other ministers not of Cabinet rank. The leading casualty was the hapless Selwyn Lloyd at the Exchequer. His interview with the prime minister was, in Macmillan's words at the time, "a terribly difficult and emotional scene . . . . Naturally I tried to persuade him of the need for a radical reconstruction on political grounds." Lloyd's failure seems to have been in public relations. His very considerable contribution at the Exchequer was to associate the Conservatives with an incomes policy and with economic planning in the creation of the National Economic Development Council, an advisory agency.

Lloyd was replaced by Reginald Maudling, who had entered the Commons in 1950, and since 1959 had served as president of the Board of Trade and as colonial secretary. Now he rose to prominence for the first time. At the Ministry of Defense, Watkinson was replaced by Peter Thorneycroft, now fully rehabilitated. As chancellor of the Exchequer he had resigned in 1958 in protest against increased governmental expenditures in circumstances he deemed inflationary. About the only leading Cabinet position which remained unchanged was the Foreign Office; the Earl of Home, appointed in July 1960, remained. Most surprising of the departures was that of Lord Kilmuir, the lord chancellor who, as Sir David Maxwell-Fyfe, had been one of the chief architects of Tory recovery after 1945. In his memoirs, *Political Adventure* (1964), Kilmuir wrote bitterly of his dismissal "at seven hours notice" by a prime minister who had lost "both nerve and judgment." R. A. Butler, moved from the Home Office to the new post of first secretary of state (no departmental duties), was designated deputy prime minister and was thus perhaps ahead of such rivals for party leadership as Iain Macleod (still leader of the Commons), Edward Heath (lord privy seal), and the Earl of Home. The reaction of the Conservative members of the Commons to this drastic shakeup ("Night of the Long Knives," it came to be called) was mixed, with some seventy back-benchers gathering in angry conference. But solidarity returned when Labor moved a vote of no confidence.

Macmillan was still very much in control. This was evident in the Cuban crisis soon after (October 1962) when he stood firmly behind President Kennedy's action. Indeed, in Britain, as in America, during the crucial days when the world seemed on the brink of a nuclear war, opinion was divided. *The Times* came out in favor of a bargain: the United States to give up her bases in Turkey, and Russia her bases in Cuba. Mollie Painter-Downs wrote soon after in *The New Yorker* that the "principal emotion" in Britain appeared to be "continuing disbelief that the unbelievable was coming off."

The Cuban episode naturally directed attention in Britain to her own defense. The situation was not one to gratify those nationalists concerned for a British force dependent neither on NATO nor on the United States. British defense policy seemed in a constant state of change. Thorneycroft announced on August 1 that the Thor intermediate-range missiles had become outmoded; by agreement with the United States, 60 such missiles had been placed in Britain. At the same time, the short-range missile Blue Water produced by an English company was also scrapped, as NATO allies had decided to purchase a similar American-made missile. As a British nuclear force, Blue Streak had been abandoned two years before because it could only be launched from fixed pads, which were vulnerable. It was replaced by Skybolt, an air-to-ground missile that could be dispatched from bombers. Toward the end of 1962, the United States decided to abandon Skybolt in favor of Polaris missiles fired from submarines, and another difference developed with the United States. To discuss the new situation, Macmillan met President Kennedy at Nassau, in the Bahamas, in December. Macmillan had already received a statement from 120 Conservative back-benchers calling for retention of an independent British nuclear deterrent. In the Nassau agreement, the United States undertook to supply British submarines with Polaris missiles as a part of a new NATO nuclear force. Britain seemed to be in control, for in an emergency affecting Britain alone, the submarines would be under British operation. Technically it constituted an independent nuclear deterrent, but acutally it committed Britain to action with Europe in NATO. And the British began to move away from the position that they must be prepared to use nuclear weapons in the event of a massive Soviet attack with conventional weapons.

The Common Market

Indeed, whatever the problem, at home or abroad, in late 1962 attention seemed to be directed toward Europe. At the end of July 1961, as a phase of the fresh look at economic problems, Macmillan announced in Parliament the decision of the Government to make a bid for membership in the European Economic Community, popularly known in Britain as the Common Market, on condition that Britain's existing undertakings with other members of the Commonwealth be protected. On October 10, 1961, Edward Heath, lord privy seal, formally presented in Paris Britain's application for membership. The European Economic Community was organized by France, West Germany, Italy, and the Benelux countries in the Treaty of Rome (March 25, 1957), which became operative on January 1, 1958. Tariff reduction in an economic community was intended, as the preamble of the treaty stated, as preliminary to some form of political union. For some years after 1945, Britain had assumed that in seeking favorable conditions for her trade she would have to choose between the Commonwealth and Europe. However, from about 1955, her leadership showed increasing interest in the possibility of a free trade area in Europe, but without the implication of supranationalism found in the Treaty of Rome. Efforts to form a comprehensive European Free Trade Area failed because it proved impossible to reconcile the interests of the Six in the "Common Market" with the interests of others, because of American opposition, and because of persistent suspicions and fears of Britain and France about each other's intentions. And so a more limited association, EFTA (the European Free Trade Association of Britain, Sweden, Norway, Denmark, Austria, Switzerland, and Portugal), was formed in 1959. Tariffs were soon lowered within its ranks. A Conservative Government was now moving in the direction of freer trade.

By 1961 it was prepared to move even further. For although association with the "Outer Seven" was beneficial, it became apparent that for its members the E.E.C. had been even more useful, as a general reduction of 50 percent in tariffs, greater production, rising employment, and increased trade both within and without the area, and considerable attraction to American investment had demonstrated. And, after all, the E.E.C. now represented 169,000,000 people, and its member nations had accounted for one-sixth of Britain's foreign trade before 1957. In a major address in April at the Massachusetts Institute of Technology, Macmillan declared that economic division in Europe might well lead to political division, as "a canker gnawing at the very core of the Western Alliance."

As a Political Issue. Interest of the English people in the E.E.C. had grown slowly. But once the Macmillan Government had committed itself to probing the possibilities of membership, the issue of the Common Market promptly became in 1961 and 1962 not only a matter of overriding significance in economic and foreign policy but a decisive factor in domestic politics as well. One might have expected a division along established party lines, with Labor, in accordance with its traditional sympathy for international causes, providing hearty endorsement and with the Conservatives, with their concern for national and Commonwealth interests, opposed. But it proved quite otherwise. There was, indeed, every evidence that the issue might split both parties and lead to some kind of political realignment. In the debate following the Macmillan announcement of application for membership in July 1961, a Conservative back-bencher referred to the prime minister as a "national disaster," and some twenty Conservatives abstained from the division. It was concern for British sovereignty and fears for Commonwealth unity which produced this opposition from the Conservative right. And they were soon joined by the Labor left, for quite different reasons; that group was concerned lest Britain would have to accept policies and measures sponsored by Catholic leaders on the Continent which, in the view of British socialists, were often reactionary. And so while Heath busily engaged himself in negotiations at Brussels, party positions at home were somewhat agonizingly being established.

In the end Macmillan was able to count on either the support or the acquiescence of the bulk of Conservative opinion. He had strong backing from leading newspapers and journals which agreed with his assessment that the E.E.C. provided the way to economic recovery, the bolstering of national morale and the resolution of many international problems.

In Britain the chief obstacles to membership were the interests of agriculture and of the Commonwealth. Sometimes they were one and the same, for stated in ordinary language it was a matter of access to Commonwealth suppliers of agricultural products (particularly Canada, Australia, and New Zealand). Would the flow of these products be impeded by pricing policies within the community? In general terms, Commonwealth lands still accounted for one-third of British foreign trade. By August 1962, except for agreement on special treatment for New Zealand and a statement that "reasonable opportunities" would be provided for exports outside the Community, nothing was accomplished. The matter of conflict of interest within the Commonwealth was eventually faced in London, September 10–19, at the conference of Commonwealth prime ministers. Undoubtedly it was an "uncomfortable meeting," in the *Economist*'s phrase, for it was abundantly clear the Commonwealth support for British membership in the Common Market was lukewarm. But, as Macmillan pointed out, Britain was just as independent of the others as they were of her, and the Conference finally adopted a resolution acquiescing in British application for membership, but at the same time expressing anxiety for the future of economic ties within the Commonwealth and assuming that the British Government would keep in close consultation with her sister nations during the remainder of the negotiations at Brussels.

Macmillan placed a rather favorable construction on all this in his broadcast September 20. He declared that the Commonwealth prime ministers understood why Britain felt she should join the Common Market "and why it would be, in the long run, better—both for us and for them." He denied the validity of the argument that Britain must choose between the Commonwealth and the European Economic Community. The latter was "a work of Peace and Progress" which, given the right terms, Britain should join. He summarized his views in a pamphlet, "Britain, the Commonwealth and Europe," and received from his party conference in October general endorsement of his policy. "Britain is inevitably bound up with Europe," declared Heath, and he returned to Brussels determined to reconcile British and Commonwealth interests with commitments which would be made to the Common Market. The future did seem to rest on the outcome of negotiations with the Common Market, which appeared all the more vital for Britain's welfare after the Cuban crisis in October 1962. Macmillan made it clear that Britain had played no part in the episode, and it reinforced his notion that Britain's future was in Europe.

It proved even more difficult for Labor, in Opposition, to establish an official party stance. Gaitskell found himself in a position in which a combination of the left, fearful for the future of socialism, now joined by the right, which was concerned for Commonwealth interests, was pitted against a group of moderates in the center who strongly favored Britain's entrance into the Common Market. Gaitskell's private view was probably somewhat anti from the start, a matter of some personal embarrassment, since his most loyal supporters in the party were ardently in favor. At the party conference at Brighton in October 1962, it was essential that he establish an official position. In a powerful address, it became clear what his own opinion was—he was against entrance. For British interests, he declared, the economic arguments were about equally balanced with benefits to England coming at the expense of an independent British agricultural policy and Commonwealth trade. Politically, he said, it would mean the end of the Commonwealth; and, if it led to some kind of European federation, it would bring an end to "a thousand years of history."

                 Collapse of Negotiations. In July 1962 the *Economist* said: "to the French Government British membership of the Common Market now seems inevitable." At the time this was an entirely reasonable remark. In Britain, among those who favored entrance, it was generally assumed that the matter rested in her hands and that it was but a matter of time—in the end, other Commonwealth lands would be reconciled, British agricultural interests safeguarded, and the arguments of Gaitskell brushed aside.

But these considerations proved almost irrelevant. Negotiations ended abruptly with a pronouncement from de Gaulle. On January 14, 1963, he addressed a press conference in Paris:

> England is insular, maritime, linked by trade, markets, and food supply to very different and often very distant lands. She is essentially an industrial and commercial nation, and her agriculture is relatively unimportant ... In short, the nature, the structure, the very situation that are England's differ profoundly from those of the continentals. ... The question arises as to how far it is possible for Great Britain at the present time to accept a truly common tariff, as the Continent does, for this would involve giving up all Commonwealth preferences, renouncing all claims for privileges for her agriculture, and treating as null and void obligations entered into with countries forming part of the Free Trade Area. Can she do this? That is the question. It cannot be claimed that this question has been answered. Whether it will be answered one day is a matter which only England can decide.

A few days later, in Brussels, the French foreign minister asked for an indefinite "suspension" of negotiations. While it can be argued that de Gaulle exaggerated the extent of the gulf between Britain and the others and minimized the differences among the Six themselves, British entrance into the Common Market would have been effected, at this time, only with great difficulty. Gaitskell's reservations, arbitrary as they were, seemed more reasonable in January 1963 than in October 1962. And there were basic differences with France and West Germany as to the essential nature and future development of the E.E.C.

As it was, the collapse of negotiations altered the political outlook in Britain. Commitment to a policy of Britain in Europe seemed to provide the Macmillan Government with an opportunity to recoup its sagging fortunes. Had this policy succeeded, Labor would have been on the defensive. Now there would be no general election on the issue of the Common Market.

1963—Year of Surprises and Tragedies

And so the year 1963 began, a year of many surprises and tragedies—the failure at Brussels, the death of Gaitskell, a long freeze-up extending into March 1963 (one of the most severe winters on record, with repair bills for outside plumbing reaching enormous figures), the Profumo scandal, the nuclear test-ban treaty in July, the great train robbery in Buckinghamshire in August with a loss of £2½ million, the replacement of Macmillan by Lord Home, the assassination of President Kennedy of the United States, and no general election.

Labor–Gaitskell to Wilson. The month of January was marked out in memory not only by the collapse of the Common Market negotiations but also by the sudden and untimely death of Hugh Gaitskell, leader of the Labor Party, at the age of fifty-six. Taken ill with influenza in December, a virus infection brought on pleurisy and complications. On January 17 his condition suddenly became grave and he died on the 18th. In death he was hailed not only by all sections of his party as a great leader and statesman but by the nation, at large, as a person eminently worthy and fully qualified to be prime minister. His views on the Common Market disappointed some, but his death brought almost universal sadness and dismay. There was cut short, said the *Economist,* the life of a man

> who had in front of him, perhaps very close, all that a high, fair and unenvious mind, a precise, even punctilious intelligence, a real warmth and gaiety of companionship, stubborn application to the task, equally stubborn loyalty to his comrades, an unselfish vanity and honesty of always patriotic purpose had earned for him.

At first his logical successor seemed to be George Brown, deputy leader since 1960. The son of a lorry driver, Brown became a trade union official and entered the Commons in 1945. A man of rightest or moderate views, he was rather extravagant in his methods—for example, in 1947 he had led the movement to replace Prime Minister Attlee with Ernest Bevin. Brown was now the choice of the *Economist* as party leader, some indication of his standing. But while he had just defeated Harold Wilson once again, the previous November, for the deptuy leadership, it was widely thought that when leadership itself was at stake, the party preference would be for Wilson. In the balloting of the Labor M.P.s, Brown had the support of most of the party leaders in the "shadow cabinet" but not of the rank and file. Wilson was an easy victor on the second ballot, 144 to 103, after a third candidate, James Callaghan, the shadow chancellor of the Exchequer, had dropped out.

Wilson, now forty-six, was known as an intellectual with a brilliant record at Oxford, where he won first class honors in PPE (Philosophy, Politics, and Economics) and where he stayed on as a lecturer in Economics. He entered the House of Commons in 1945 and two years later at the age of thirty-one became president of the Board of Trade and the youngest Cabinet member since William Pitt. He promptly developed a reputation as a skilled debater and was soon associated with the left wing of the party. After Gaitskell succeeded to the party leadership Wilson was often found opposing, even sabotaging him. At the party conference at Scarborough in 1961, Gaitskell sorely needed support against trade union leaders, but it was George Brown who came to his aid, not Wilson, who, in fact, noticeably refrained from applause at the conclusion of Gaitskell's address. That Wilson as party leader had something to learn was made apparent by the trap into which he allowed himself to fall in a debate on the steel industry on February 18; when baited, he asserted that Clause 4 of the Labor Party Constitution was gospel for the whole party. He had frequently left himself open to charges of opportunism, for his views were not as leftist as his associations might indicate. On assuming party leadership, he gave every indication of wishing to achieve party harmony by promptly appointing to most positions in the "shadow cabinet" men who had voted against him as leader. He declared he would work for unity on the basis of *Signposts for the Sixties*, the moderate statement of Labor views, representative of Gaitskell, issued in 1961. He was at once vigorous in debate. On Heath's return from Brussels, Wilson told the Commons: "No British minister must ever again be put in the position of waiting outside in the cold while others decide our fate." And by visiting both President Kennedy in Washington and Krushchev in Moscow in the spring he began both to look like and act like a prime minister.

NEDDY and Dr. Beeching. Not unnaturally, after the collapse at Brussels, attention in Britain turned to domestic problems. Of major importance to the business world was the first report of the National Economic Development Council, which had been established in 1961, as part of Selwyn Lloyd's policy, to advise the Government in efforts for a planned economy. Promptly dubbed NED or NEDDY, the council made its first pronouncement in March 1962—a target of 4 percent annually in economic growth between 1961 and 1966. In July of 1962 Macmillan announced an associated commission, the National Incomes Commission (NICKY), whose duty was to inquire into and express views, in the national interest, on claims for wage and salary increases. In the spring of 1963 NED sought to spur on the country to achieve its target. In its report, "Conditions Favorable to Faster Growth," the council set forth the main requirement: the creation of "a high level of demand with a control on incomes and costs." Some wage agreements were exceeding the 3 percent increase indicated as the "guiding light" by the chancellor of the Exchequer, Reginald Maudling. He was referred to in the Annual Register "as the most knowledgeable minister to enter the Treasury for over a decade"; his policies in 1963 were on the whole effective. His annual budget (in April) provided for income tax relief in lower brackets, where the money released would be spent. He was conservative in his general objective, that of achieving "our growth target of four per cent a year without inflation." During 1963, production did increase almost 4 percent, exports were satisfactory (by volume increasing 5 percent), and unemployment dropped from a peak of 3.9 percent during the freeze-up to 2 percent. But all this was insufficient to meet the target of NED of 4 percent each year, 1961–66, since the actual growth in 1961–62 was only slightly over 1 percent each year. In 1963 there was a green-light economy, but there were indications that inflationary tendencies might require a red-light economy in 1964. Respect for Maudling and recognition of some improvement were not enough for the *Economist*. Its cover for an issue in April carried the caption: "Time for Change: Expand or Decay" and a leading article said, "Undoubtedly, Britain needs a new sense of direction and a new Government." In the months which followed, the *Economist* was to repeat this admonition many times over.

Less popular attention was given to NED than to the report "The Reshaping of British Railways," by Dr. Richard Beeching, the first general attempt by the Conservatives to modernize the industry. Since 1953, when road haulage was returned to private hands, British Railways had been going into the red, ever deeper, year after year. In 1961 Dr. Beeching, head of Imperial Chemical Industries, was made Chairman of the British Transport Commission. His instruction was to rationalize the industry and he carried out this assignment as the *Spectator* said: "without regard to political and social consequences." His proposals followed from two premises: the railways should do only the work they are best suited to do, and services which were not being used should be eliminated. Thirty-five pages of the report set forth the services (5,000 route miles—one-third of the total and accounting for only one percent of the total rail passenger miles) and stations (2,363 out of a total of 4,293— one-half of the stations had produced only 2 percent of the total passenger revenue and only 3 percent of freight receipts) which should be closed. Depots handling coal, about 500 in number, were to be gradually reduced to 100. Some 70,000 jobs were to be eliminated by 1966. To care for patrons thus denied railway service, adequate bus transport, which cost far less, should be provided. In answer to this report the cry of anguish was widespread, and the phrase "thanks to Dr. Beeching" became a familiar complaint and explanation as railway service was reduced in the years following in conformity with his recommendations. In 1962 the British Transport Commission was dissolved by a statute which set up independent boards for railways, docks, waterways, and London transport.

Neither NED nor the Beeching report were considered vote-catchers. In any case, local council elections in the spring of 1961 went heavily against the Conservatives. Labor elected more borough councillors than ever in the past. The Liberals, by this index, seemed to have returned to normalcy and comparative unimportance. Labor maintained its impressive lead in public opinion polls throughout the spring and summer, which indicated that had a general election been held Labor would have emerged with a majority of about one hundred in the Commons.

"Scandal '63"—The Profumo Affair. Current events were, indeed, not kind to the Conservatives in 1963. There was first in point of time the case of William Vassall, a clerk at the Admiralty, who had been sentenced in October 1962 to eighteen years imprisonment for passing secrets to the Russians. The prime minister established a judicial tribunal under Lord Radcliffe, an expert in security matters, to make inquiry. In a report issued in April 1963, the tribunal cleared of suspicion other officials whom report and rumor in the press had associated with Vassall, by his own testimony a homosexual blackmailed by the Russians into giving information. Two journalists had been sent to jail by the tribunal for refusing to divulge their sources of information. The tribunal added that although there was no security failure, the appointment of Vassall indicated that the selection system was "ill-adapted for assessing strength of character and freedom from those defects which the Russians might exploit."

The case of John Profumo, secretary of state for War since 1960, with its side issues, dominated the news for months and provided a peep show for all who cared to look. Miss Christine Keeler appeared three times on the cover of the *Economist,* and within months two versions and a novel were in print. Macmillan and his Government were shaken.

On March 21 several Labor M.P.s rose in the Commons and mentioned rumors in the press associating a member of the Government front bench with one Christine Keeler, described variously as "a model" and "a call girl," who, on being summoned as a prosecution witness in the trial of a West Indian in connection with a shooting incident, had disappeared. It was suggested that people in high places knew her whereabouts and had not informed the police. It was commonly known in the City and in Westminster that the minister in question was Profumo. The next day, flanked by the prime minister and the leader of the Commons, he appeared in the Commons and spoke briefly of his social acquaintance with Miss Keeler, but denied any knowledge of or responsibility for her disappearance, And he added: "There was no impropriety whatsoever in my acquaintance with Miss Keeler."

But information brought to Macmillan's attention by Wilson contradicted these statements and raised the question of national security. It seemed that one Captain Ivanov, naval attaché at the Russian Embassy, had also been associating with Miss Keeler, who allegedly had been asked to obtain nuclear secret information from the secretary of state for War. Her own statement on January 26 that she had been instructed: "Ask Jack when the Germans are going to get the bomb," finally reached Macmillan on May 29. He requested that the lord chancellor, Lord Dilhorne, make inquiry. The upshot was that on June 4 Profumo wrote the prime minister, resigning from the Government. He declared that there was no truth in the charges of a breach of security, but added that as to his statement in the Commons that there was no impropriety in his association with Miss Keeler, "I have to admit that this was not true, and that I misled you, and my colleagues, and the House."

All comment in the press was dominated by the pronouncement on June 11 by *The Times*—"It *is* a moral issue"—which went on to say that a policy of material affluence under the Tories had brought the nation "spiritually and psychologically to a low ebb." The *Spectator* responded that it was a moral issue only for Mr. Profumo but that it was a "political issue" and "an issue of national morale" of the first magnitude. Lord Hailsham on a B.B.C. television program declared: "*The Times* is an anti-Conservative newspaper led by an anti-Conservative editor.... A great party is not to be brought down because of a scandal by a woman of easy virtue and a proved liar."

When the Commons reconvened June 17, Macmillan faced his stiffest test as prime minister. Harold Wilson charged him not with duplicity but with inefficiency and even gullibility. Macmillan responded with a plea for personal vindication. The Opposition listened in absolute silence, providing him no opportunity to capitalize on interruptions at which he was a past master. The rest of the session was not so quiet. George Wigg, one of the Labor M.P.s who had first reported the rumors on March 21, launched a blast at Hailsham: "Whether I am in order or not, I call Lord Hailsham a lying humbug." But the remarks which made headlines came from Macmillan's own back benches—from Nigel Birch. He acquitted the prime minister of any charges of dishonor. "On the other hand on the question of competence and good sense I cannot think the verdict can be favorable." And he quoted Browning in "The Lost Leader"—". . . let him never come back to us!" In the division which followed, the Government majority was reduced to sixty-nine with twenty-seven Conservative abstentions—a few more and the Government would have been in danger.

But Macmillan's position was shaken, nonetheless, and had there been a prospective successor on whom various groups in the party could have at once agreed he might well have departed. But time was on his side, and as usual he made a good recovery from adversity. On June 28 he felt strong enough to say: "I hope to lead the party into the election." And on July 25, just an hour before he was to face a party gathering of back-benchers, the nuclear test-ban treaty, suspending all tests in the atmosphere, in outer space and under water, was initialed in Moscow by representatives of the U.S.S.R., the United States, and Great Britain. It was a triumph for Macmillan, the advocate of summit conferences. He was able to say at the party gathering: "My sole motive is to serve the party and the country—and when I go it will be after consultation with those people whose views I hold in the highest regard." And later the same evening in the House of Commons, a Macmillan with renewed self-confidence declared: "The House will, I know, understand my own feelings on seeing at last the result of efforts made over many years and of hopes long deferred."

On June 21, when his future was still in doubt, Macmillan had appointed Lord Denning, master of the rolls, to conduct a judicial inquiry into the Profumo case. By the time (September 26) the report was made, political repercussions had died away. But the report furnished perhaps the best summary and commentary on the episode. Lord Denning found no breach of security and found no truth in rumors that other individuals in high position had been involved in promiscuous gatherings. He indicted the press for giving easy currency to "scandalous information about well-known people." As to Profumo, Denning concluded that his conduct was such as to create a reasonable belief that his word might be doubted. "It was the responsibility of the Prime Minister and his colleagues, and of them only, to deal with this situation and they did not succeed in doing so."

During these months of 1963, Labor Party leaders appeared to be readying themselves for office, considering not only the transition in status from shadow cabinet to Government bench but also the reorganization of ministries with special consideration to economic planning and an incomes policy. Problems at this stage were not found within the party hierarchy but in the relation with trade union officials. While George Woodcock, general secretary of the T.U.C., was ready to concede the point that incomes should not rise as rapidly as in the past, such militants as Frank Cousins of the Transport and General Workers' Union and Ted Hill of the Boilermakers' Union were determined to maintain collective bargaining rights. At the T.U.C. gathering at Brighton in September, an overwhelming majority voted for economic planning and a small majority voted against any form of wage restraint—a curious inconsistency.

Harold Wilson had emerged as perhaps more shrewd politically, if less attractive personally, than Gaitskell. Wilson's prestige was enhanced by his address to the party conference at Scarborough in late September, considered his best public address to date. He sought to turn attention away from the old slogans about nationalization and welfare. "We are redefining and restating our socialism in terms of the scientific revolution," he said. Ten million new jobs would have to be created in the next dozen years to take up the slack from automation. And "because we care deeply about the future of Britain we must increase the resources of democratic planning." A Labor Government would establish a ministry of science and a ministry of higher education to set out a "crash" program for new universities. This last reference was particularly timely, since later in the month appeared the Robbins Report on Higher Education, proposing the expansion by 1973–74 of places in institutions of university status from 110,000 to 218,000. (These ideas were somewhat expanded by Wilson in his *The Relevance of British Socialism*, 1964.) On the platform at Scarborough he clasped hands with his erstwhile rival for party leadership, George Brown, amidst a thundering ovation.

From Macmillan to Home. The Conservative leadership crisis avoided in June and July came in October at the party conference at Blackpool. It was generally expected that Macmillan would inform the conference that he proposed to carry on and that he would receive full endorsement. However, on the eve of the session it was suddenly announced that the prime minister had been taken to a London hospital for a prostate operation. Two days later, on October 10, he notified the conference that he was relinquishing leadership. "I hope it will soon be possible for the customary processes of consultation to be carried on within the party about its future leadership," he added.

Two leading candidates at once emerged. One was R. A. Butler, now sixty, the runner-up in the selection of prime minister in 1957, who had held most of the major offices in the Government and since 1962 had been considered the "deputy prime minister." He had the reputation of having done everything well. The other was Lord Hailsham, fifty-five, member of Parliament since 1938, who had held various posts under Macmillan and was now minister for Science and Technology. He promptly declared that he would renounce his peerage, under the Peerage Act enacted the previous July, and would seek a seat in the Commons. Hailsham was first choice of Macmillan, who commented to Butler that fresh leadership was needed and that a Butler Government would differ little from his own. Reginald Maudling and Iain Macleod, long considered likely candidates to succeed Macmillan, now were clearly out of the running. As to Butler and Hailsham, while each had solid support, both confronted strong opposition; to some Butler seemed uninspiring and to others Halisham seemed too emotional. On October 14, Macmillan requested that the chief whip consult the Conservative M.P.s and that Conservative peers and party constituencies also be approached. Developments revealed surprising support for the foreign secretary, Lord Home, particularly as a second choice. A "Stop Home" movement, led by Macleod, Maudling, and Enoch Powell, minister of Health, took shape in the Cabinet. And Hailsham, whose own support declined, agreed to serve under Butler. But these moves were too late.

On October 18 Macmillan resigned and advised the queen to send for Home; he proved able to form a Cabinet. Butler, after a brief delay and presumably in the interests of party unity, agreed to serve as foreign secretary, the one major post he had not yet held; then Maudling and Hailsham went along. Only Macleod and Powell refused to remain in office. Butler's political career was approaching its end; early in 1965 he was created a baron as life peer, retired from politics, and became master of Trinity College, Cambridge. The *Economist* commented: " . . . in the last twenty years, he (Butler) has affected the course of domestic politics perhaps more profoundly than any other man and for the better."

But the shift from Macmillan to Home deserves further thought; we now have the accounts of all the principals. Macmillan's own version is best represented in Randolph Churchill's *The Fight for the Tory Leadership,* which was rushed into print early in 1964. Of Macmillan's efforts to gather party opinion, Churchill declared: "Never in the history of the Tory Party, or indeed of any other British political party, have such full and dilligent enquiries been made in the selection of a new leader." The result, according to his account, was that when neither Butler nor Hailsham could win commanding support, a small majority of all those consulted declared for Home. And he adds, if "second preferences were made effective, it is clear that Home would have walked with it."

But the other participants sharply disagreed and are more persuasive; it was their view that Macmillan controlled, if not dictated, the choice of his successor. Macleod in the *Spectator* (of which he became editor) quotes Churchill: "It can be argued that Macmillan did all he could during his seven years as Prime Minister to advance the fortunes of Butler." And Macleod responds: "The truth is that at all times, from the first day of his premiership to the last, Macmillan was determined that Butler, although incomparably the best qualified of the contenders, should not succeed him." According to Macleod only Hailsham could stop Butler. And when Hailsham failed to gather enough support, then Macmillan still refused to accept Butler. He turned to Home.

However, the new Government acted with more vigor than Home, "an amiable chap," had often been credited with. Macleod was replaced as leader of the Commons by Selwyn Lloyd, now rehabilitated, and Powell as minister of Health by Anthony Barber. Wilson's efforts to belittle the new prime minister fell flat. In an address at Manchester, Wilson said: "After half a century of democratic advance, of social revolution, of rising expectation, the whole process has ground to a halt with a 14th Earl." Two days later, on television, Home responded, "As far as the 14th Earl is concerned, I suppose Mr. Wilson, when you come to think of it, is the 14th Mr. Wilson." Home promptly accepted the proposals on higher education in the Robbins Report, prorogued Parliament, gave up his peerage, and, as Sir Alec Douglas-Home, easily won election to the Commons from a vacant seat in Scotland.

Macmillan's parliamentary career ended with dignity, as was his due. In a brief debate on the Denning Report on the Profumo Case, December 16, he spoke with assurance but in a conciliatory manner: "Of course I was deceived—we were deceived—and that, I admit is perhaps a serious fault." Macmillan left the House accompanied by Wilson. The following February he announced he would not seek reelection. Politically his record was very impressive. In the art of negotiation he had few equals. He performed something of a miracle in holding his party together after Suez and extending its years of power. Over the years his grand manner (his "Edwardian style," it is often termed) won both admiration and bitter animosity. He could not abide rivals, and this weakness contributed to his ill fortune at the end of his career. His supporters say that he struck just the right note for the fifties: his flexibility, his concern for national interests, his patience with the African problem. He seems to have prolonged "the Age of Affluence" and put off the evil day when crisis, both political and economic, would catch up. Everything considered, his leadership of party and country was of very high quality, and there seems little doubt that history will rank him high among Conservative prime ministers in the twentieth century.

Before we leave 1963, we must briefly record the assassination of President Kennedy of the United States on November 22, an event almost as much a part of the English scene as of the American. Kennedy's death was for the British a shock and a tragedy, the murder of this "first modern man to reach world leadership" (in the words of the *Economist*)—a foreign statesman whose popularity and stature in Britain have been matched only by that of Franklin Delano Roosevelt. In an extraordinary gesture, Parliament adjourned its session, after brief eulogies, on the day of the funeral in Washington, which was attended by the three party leaders. Eighteen months later Queen Elizabeth gave to the American people a portion of the meadowland of Runnymede on the south bank of the Thames between Windsor and Staines, close by the place where King John sealed the Magna Carta in 1215, as a memorial to President Kennedy "whom in death my people still mourn and whom in life they loved."

Pre-Election Campaign, 1964

In September 1963 Macleod, the party chairman, said: "The General Election will be in 1964; I am sure of that." He of course had in mind that the previous election had been held in 1959, and by statute only five years could elapse between elections. As 1964 opened, the best guess was that polling would come in the spring, and this notion was not dispelled until April, when the prime minister announced that it would not come before autumn. Even then the exact date was not disclosed until September.

Thus during much of 1964 the election seemed imminent, and every opinion poll, every by-election, and every political speech was scrutinized with a view to electoral implications. Sir Alec Douglas-Home had to establish himself with his colleagues and with the country. He had been of Cabinet rank only since 1957 and had never been concerned officially with domestic affairs. Even as foreign secretary, though considerably more effective than to some he promised to be, he did not become a public figure. As a public speaker he was effective in small gatherings. It was soon evident from opinion polls that his popularity was rising. Various Government papers, including a white paper on Defense, that the Government would "maintain the independent British deterrent" and close observation of the conflict between Turks and Greeks in Cyprus were evidence that the Government could govern.

Maudling's budget in the spring presented the familiar aim of "expansion without inflation." More controversial at this stage was Edward Heath, who pushed through legislation abolishing Resale (Retail) Price Maintenance. A storm of protest from small shopkeepers received backbench Conservative support. On the crucial vote the Government's majority fell to one, with 21 Conservatives in opposition and an uncertain number (between 17 and 25) abstaining. Many Conservatives, it seemed, could not face the implications of free competition. Heath went further and in a white paper on "Monopolies, Mergers, and Restrictive Practices" sought power to enforce recommendations of the Monopolies Commission. NED issued in March *The Growth of the Economy* with a favorable report on the record since 1962 and an expressed belief that the 4 percent growth target could now be achieved. But, it added, an expansion of exports of 5.1 percent per annum would now be required; otherwise, consumer expenditure, which was increasing at the rate of about 3 percent per annum since 1961, would have to be curbed. At it worked out, economic growth during 1964 was something better than 4 percent. At the same time, the terms of international trade turned against Britain; imports far exceeded exports and the balance of payments deteriorated.

Harold Wilson's problem was that it was generally taken for granted that Labor would win the next election. As frequently pointed out, he was in a position similar to that of Governor Dewey of the United States in 1948, and everyone knew what had happened to Dewey. Furthermore, until April, Wilson had no way of knowing when the Conservatives would dissolve Parliament and go to the country. At first Labor leaders were convinced that this would come not later than June, and from January to April Wilson toured the land, talking about the problems of government in an age of science and advanced technology, and party organization, generally, stepped up its activity.

Until June nearly all indices—opinion polls, by-elections generally, local elections—showed a continuation of Labor's commanding lead. The high point was undoubtedly the first elections, in April, to the Greater London Council (uniting the London County and Middlesex County Councils, including many Tory-dominated suburbs). Labor won 64 seats out of 100 with swings in the voting since 1959 of 6 to 10 percent in its favor. Other county council elections demonstrated decisive swings to Labor and in borough elections, Labor, already enjoying a commanding lead, more than held its own. Polls based on the sampling process indicated that Labor led the Conservatives, on a national basis, by 6.5 percent. All this indicated that a Labor majority of between one hundred and a hundred and fifty in the Commons might be expected.

The first indication of a reversal of the trend came in May with the by-election at Devizes (in Wiltshire) which Labor held, but with a swing in its favor of but 2.8 percent, the smallest in a by-election since 1961. From June onwards, local by-elections indicated a Labor decline. By July public opinion polls were showing decided shifts back to the Conservative position. By September Labor's lead seemed about wiped out, with some polls indicating a Conservative victory ahead. The students of this election, D. E. Butler and Anthony King, offer various suggestions for this shift of opinion—the preponderance of foreign affairs in the news at this time, the parliamentary recess, the decision of Labor to relax pressure, considerable economic recovery, and even "the glorious summer weather."

12 Labor and the Burdens of Power

Robert Rhodes
James
*Ambitions and
Realities: British
Politics 1964–70*
(1972), p. 293

This nation, with its formidable potentialities, its remarkable assets of intelligence and character, and its still-substantial wealth and influence, passed through the 1960s with few catastrophies but with few achievements.

Lord Boyle
quoted in David
McKie and Chris
Cook, eds., *The
Decade of Disillusion: British
Politics in the
Sixties* (1972),
p. 37

Successive British governments in the 1960s had one thing in common; they both found it much less difficult to beat off the parliamentary challenges of their opponents, than to keep the confidence of their own supporters, and the assurance of their continual support.

Wilfred
Beckerman, ed.
*The Labour
Government's
Economic
Record: 1964–
1970* (1972),
pp. 73–74

In the past the basic problem of the socialist movement in Britain has been the relationship between the Labour Party and its trade union allies, on the one hand, and the rest of society and the economy, on the other. The problem now is one of the relationship between the Labour Party, on the one hand, and the trade union movement on the other.

1964–1970

I beg leave to use Robert Rhodes James's phrase for the heading of this chapter. Nothing else seems quite so apposite. These years were almost uniquely critical, with tension mounting as Britain confronted problems few had anticipated. The historian of the future, with endless material from public and private papers to supplement the sources now available, will find himself absorbed in the conflict of ideas and personalities, with repeated crisis in the economy, with the estrangement of trade unionism from political party leadership, with the changing character of Britain's role in the world, and with the transformation of society. Here, we must content ourselves with telling in outline as best we can the story of what happened. It seems best to follow the course of events chronologically, even though with the same problems recurring again and again the narrative may appear somewhat repetitious. When we do venture an analysis it will be by way of presenting the response of the British people to their own condition.

We begin with an examination of the general election of October 15, 1964, which returned Labor to office after thirteen long years in opposition.

The Labor Government, 1964–66

On September 15, 1964, came the long-awaited announcement: dissolution of Parliament on September 25 with polling on

October 15—the exact date widely forecast since the previous spring. For a land already campaign-weary, formal electioneering was something of an anticlimax, which, so say the experts, probably did not much affect the result. Nonetheless, the campaign is worthy of attention, for it revealed the personalities and capacities of political leaders, as well as the interests of the people, and anticipated some of the problems ahead.

General Election, October 1964

With one or two exceptions Conservatives and Labor contested all 630 constituencies; the Liberals entered 365. (For the record, the Communist Party placed 36 candidates in the field.)

The issues may be readily examined in the party manifestoes—about 7,000 words long for each of the two major parties—whose appearance in mid September launched the campaign. The Labor statement, *The New Britain,* anticipated the announcement of the dissolution by several days; the Labor campaign was kicked off with a huge party rally at Wembley Park on September 12. Wilson declared:

> The choice we offer ... is between standing still, clinging to a tired philosophy of a day that is gone, or moving forward in partnership and unity to a just society, to a dynamic, expanding, confident, and above all, purposive new Britain.

A week later came the Conservative *Prosperity with a Purpose,* long in preparation and presenting few surprises. The party in power at election time is always on the defensive; it cannot advocate much change lest it be critical of its own record. So the Conservative manifesto praised its party's past achievements and pledged their continuance. A shorter Liberal statement was entitled *Think for Yourself—Vote Liberal;* the Liberals proceeded to stage a well-organized campaign designed to secure an impressive vote that would give them "a decisive position" in the Commons.

In a National Opinion Poll, about a week before the election, on the issues considered particularly important, by far the greatest number (72 percent) listed "Cost of living"; "Education," "Housing," "Pensions" followed in that order. At the bottom of the list were "Independent Deterrent," "Defence," and "Foreign Affairs," with 13 percent, 12 percent, and 10 percent, respectively. While such information does not bear close interpretation, it does tally with such other evidence as we have that domestic issues, particularly "prosperity," were uppermost in the minds of the electorate. Certainly prosperity was the subject of most of the advertising and campaign oratory. A Conservative banner read: "Conservatives Give You a Better Standard of Living—Keep It!" Party spokesmen maintained that only with a Conservative Government could an annual economic growth of 4 percent with effective price and wage controls be achieved. Labor argued that such a program, in fact, was not being achieved and could be realized only under the dynamic leadership of Labor. Only Labor, it was said, could coordinate state action with trade union goals. Wilson derided the economic policies of Sir Alec and Selwyn Lloyd, dubbing them "Stop-Go and Son," an allusion to a popular television show, *Steptoe and Son.*

The campaign was not greatly affected by current events; an exception is perhaps the publication of statistics in mid September showing exports disappointingly low and at the end of the month a sharp falling-off in the balance of payment figures. This state of affairs was rather successfully exploited by Labor with the Conservatives somewhat embarrassed. But it is not likely that a significant number of votes was swayed. A Gallup Poll early in October indicated that only a small number had fears of an economic crisis; the larger number, indeed, believed that the Conservatives rather than Labor would be the more successful in maintaining prosperity.

As usual, conflicting ideologies appear in the discussion of nationalization. The only significant issue was iron and steel, whose denationalization the Conservatives proposed to complete and Labor pledged to reverse.

For social services Labor put forward an ambitious program including the expansion of education, the removal of the two-shilling charge for medical prescriptions, the increase in national insurance benefits with an ultimate goal of benefits the equivalent of half-average pay. The Conservatives treated this as an idle dream. The price, said Maudling, is "too high"; it was a "menu without prices," one of Sir Alec's few election phrases. Labor responded that their program would be financed from greater national productivity. On housing the Conservatives boasted of their achievement and set an even higher target, 400,000 houses, for 1965. Labor proposed elaborate schemes for assisting and protecting owner-occupiers. Immigration from Commonwealth lands was discussed at length without a direct clash between the parties—both favoring some controls.

Foreign affairs seemed to have little voter appeal and were relatively little discussed. Very little reference was made by the two major parties to the Common Market, which, two years earlier, was considered likely to be the basic issue of an election; the Liberals alone enthusiastically welcomed the possibility of British membership. The Conservatives claimed partial credit for the nuclear test-ban treaty and emphasized the importance of Britain's defense effort. Their manifesto reads: "Britain must in the ultimate resort have independently controlled nuclear power to deter an aggressor. We possess this power today. Only under a Conservative Government will we possess it in the future." The Labor manifesto declared that under the Conservatives, British defenses were now "weaker than at almost any other time in our history." The Nassau agreement would not give Britain an independent deterrent. "It will not be independent and it will not be British and it will not deter." On this theme Sir Alec was at his best and he iterated and reiterated the importance of Britain's independent deterrent. In his final television address he declared:

> It is just at this moment, when France and China are becoming nuclear powers, that the socialist would propose to discard all control by a British Government over Britain's nuclear arm ... such a socialist decision ... would mean that we should surrender all our authority in world affairs and hand over the decision about the life and future of Britain to another country. This I am quite sure you cannot allow.

But the most important issue—even though least mentioned—was in the opinion of the students of this election "the feeling that it was time for a change."

A few additional comments should be made. Sir Alec Douglas-Home did not, in any real sense of the word, lead his party in the campaign. He was ineffective on television and in a large hall. He was much more comfortable on his "whistle stop" tours on which he was well received, particularly in rural areas. Even so, his words seldom made news. On the other hand, Wilson dominated the Labor campaign from start to finish. The contrast was apparent from the beginning—in the BBC program "Election Forum" on television and radio on three successive evenings shortly before the dissolution of Parliament. Each party leader was interrogated for thirty minutes (Jo Grimond, the Liberal leader, for twenty minutes) with questions selected from those sent in by 18,000 persons. Slightly over 8 million viewed the Wilson appearance, slightly under 8 million that of Sir Alec, and 5½ million that of Grimond. This program was the closest they came to direct debate.

"Hooliganism"—organized heckling and rowdyism—marred the campaign, though it was not representative and was confined to a few urban centers. Even so, the ugly and boorish behavior exercised thoughtful people and the incidents are not easily forgotten: Sir Alec at the Bull Ring in Birmingham proceeded with his set speech, unheard in the din by anyone; Lord Hailsham was virtually shouted down in Friends' House, Euston. It was a travesty of the democratic process, and the heckling rather than the speaking always made the news. As for the polls, inevitably they seem to attract more attention than the issues. But the opinion polls were of unusual interest in indicating the narrowing margin between the two major parties. On September 23, the Gallup Poll, for the first time in three years, had the Conservatives ahead, if only slightly. But in October, in most polls, a slight advantage returned to Labor, and a survey a week before polling date indicated that 46 percent would vote Labor, 45 percent Conservative, and 9 percent Liberal. In 62 marginal seats, which Labor must wrest from the Tories, Labor held the edge throughout by about 2 percent. But to win decisively required an overall swing to Labor since 1959 of about 4 or 5 percent.

A Labor Majority of Four. From August to mid-October Britain enjoyed the longest spell of fine weather in over half a century. But polling day, October 15, was, in most of the land, damp and dark and dreary, and the weather may have affected the size of the poll; at 77.1 percent of the electorate it was down slightly from 1959. But if the campaign seemed a bit dull and never-ending, the count was one of the most exciting in recent history. The urbanity of the announcers, really masters of ceremony, particularly that of the inimitable Richard Dimbleby of the BBC, and the learning of the psephologists held the close attention of audiences of high and low estate throughout the night and on into the next morning and afternoon. Early returns had Labor well in front and the computers were forecasting a Labor victory of at least 30 seats. But then Labor began to falter in the marginals and by 4 A.M. a victory of 10 to 20 seemed more likely. But the outcome was uncertain almost to the last, and it was not until 2:47 on the afternoon of the 16th that Labor had won its 315th seat.

Labor emerged in the end with 317 seats, the Conservatives with 304 and the Liberals with 9, providing Labor with an overall majority of 4. The popular vote was labor 44.1 percent (12,205,814), the Conservatives 43.4 percent (12,001,396), the Liberals 11.2 percent (3,092,878), and others 1.3 percent (348,914). The Liberals more than made their target of 3 million votes; had they contested all constituencies, their proportion of the total vote, on an estimate, would have been about 16.5 percent. Three more seats, and they would have held the balance in the Commons. Though Labor's margin of victory was small, the Conservative proportion of the vote dropped 6 percent since 1959, much of it resulting from abstention from voting in 1964. A direct swing of 3.5 percent (the average of the individual constituency swings) from Conservatives to Labor provided the greatest change in any general election since 1945.

Harold Wilson had a brief audience with the queen at Buckingham Palace shortly after 4 P.M. on October 16 and departed as prime minister, at forty-eight, the youngest man to head a Government in the twentieth century. He put together a Government of 101 persons, including junior ministers, with a Cabinet of 23, representative of the varied outlook in the party leadership. Only Wilson, himself, had had previous Cabinet experience. To George Brown, fifty, who had challenged him for the party leadership in 1963, he gave both position and prestige: as first secretary of state and minister of Economic Affairs (a new office), Brown's task was that of coordinating the operations of several related departments. He was, in effect, deputy prime minister, and his role in the next few years is one to keep in mind. James Callaghan, fifty-two, who had gone directly from secondary school into the civil service as a tax collector, and thence into trade union affairs on the way to the House of Commons, became chancellor of the Exchequer; Patrick Gordon Walker, fifty-seven, one-time history don, Commonwealth Relations secretary in the previous Labor Government, and associated with the right wing of the party, went to the Foreign Office. Lord Gardiner was made lord chancellor with an eye to law reform; Herbert Bowden became lord president of the Council and leader of the Commons; Lord Pakenham was created lord privy seal and leader of the Lords; Denis Healey became Defense minister.

"The Hundred Days"

On July 15, 1964, Wilson spoke of the serious problems which would confront the Government after the coming election: Britain's alliances and her role in the world, Commonwealth defense, the economy, and social services. "We are going to have to tackle all these problems at once; what we are going to need is something like what President Kennedy had after years of stagnation—a programme of 100 days of dynamic action." The phrase, "100 days of dynamic action" was, after the formation of the new Government, promptly revived by the press and set against the widespread feeling that a Government with a majority of four could not implement a strong program and, indeed, might not long survive. But Wilson, himself, set the tone of his administration, in his broadcast the night of his victory: "The Government have only a small majority in the House of Commons but I want to make it quite clear that this will not affect our ability to govern." And the enthusiastic optimism with which he entered office was shared by many throughout the land.

The new administration at once sought to reverse the unfavorable balance of payments—the very day of the election came word of the deficit for 1964 of about £800 million, even larger than anticipated. Devaluation was ruled out, perhaps because considered politically unsound. On October 26 a temporary 15 percent surcharge was imposed on all imports (save foodstuffs and raw materials for industry—books were soon added) and exporters were given tax relief. The new Parliament opened on November 3. The Queen's Speech referred to the "seven hundredth anniversary" of Parliament "recorded in this session" (Simon de Montfort's Parliament of 1265 is sometimes arbitrarily regarded as the "beginning" of the institution); on the Government's program it contained no surprises, following faithfully the party manifesto. A censure motion on November 9 from the Opposition regretting proposals for steel nationalization promptly put the Government to test on the touchiest of issues. The Labor Whip used all means possible to get the Labor M.P.s on hand for the division, and in spite of an attack of appendicitis and a heavy fog, succeeded. Liberals voted with the Opposition, but the motion was defeated by six votes. An emergency budget increased the tax on petrol (bringing the price to about 75 cents a gallon), and raised national insurance contributions with pensions increased. When a sterling "crisis" developed in November (at one point the commercial rate touched $2.79), the bank rate was raised from 5 percent to 7 (to the consternation of those about to negotiate mortgages); with the announcement of an international credit of three billion dollars, sterling strengthened.

Five weeks after the election Wilson was in Washington to discuss his notions of replacing the mixed-manned multilateral force under NATO with an Atlantic Nuclear Force to which Britain would contribute V-bombers and Polaris submarines. In a heated Commons debate on December 16–17, Wilson said a portion of the V-bomber force would be kept exclusively in British hands for peace-keeping purposes, but he did not disclose whether or not they would be equipped with nuclear warheads. The Polaris submarine program, he pointed out, would operate only on an interdependent basis, since all components were not available from British sources. He declared that the complaint of the Opposition that his proposal meant dropping the independent nuclear deterrent was meaningless, since there had been no such deterrent under the previous Government. The Government emerged from the division with a majority of 20. However it was fairly clear that the differences between nuclear policies of the new Government and the old were not great.

The chief embarrassment to the Government came from an unexpected source. It was necessary to find seats in the Commons for two members of the Cabinet—one for Frank Cousins, who had never been an M.P., the other for the foreign secretary, Patrick Gordon Walker, who had sat for nineteen years for Smethwick (Staffordshire) only to be defeated (quite surprisingly) in the October poll. Vacancies in two presumably safe Labor seats were created by elevating the M.P.s elected in October to the Lords as life peers. This maneuver was something of a boomerang. At the by-election in January Cousins did manage to win at Nuneaton, but with a considerable drop in the Labor majority. But Gordon Walker was defeated once again, this time at Leyton, which had gone Labor in October by nearly 8,000 votes. The explanation was probably Labor voters, irritated by having a candidate imposed on them, who stayed away from the poll. Gordon Walker, therefore, had no alternative but to resign as foreign secretary—to widespread regret, for he was widely respected in and out of his party—and Wilson had no alternative but to accept the resignation. Michael Stewart, another intellectual, well thought of but relatively inexperienced in the realm of foreign policy, became foreign secretary. Thus ended Wilson's hundred days, and it was time, according to the Opposition, to have an accounting. On a censure motion in the Commons in February—"if the Government have a shred of political integrity they ought to resign," said Sir Alec—the Government survived by 17. However, in five by-elections since October the results, though varying widely, showed an average swing back to the Conservatives of nearly 4 percent.

Churchill's Death. January 1965 marked the passing of Sir Winston Churchill, the last survivor of the wartime triumvirate (Churchill, Roosevelt, and Stalin), "the greatest Englishman of his time." Since his hip fracture in June 1962 he had been seen only occasionally in public. In 1963 he was made an honorary citizen of the United States. When he made his final appearance in Parliament on July 27, 1964, the Commons paid him a rare tribute—an official vote of thanks, to express "its unbounded admiration and gratitude for his services to Parliament, to the nation and to the world; remembering above all his inspiration of the British people when they stood alone and his leadership until victory was won." On November 30 he celebrated his 90th birthday. On January 15, 1965, it was announced that he had suffered a "cerebral thrombosis" (a stroke); he died on the 24th. As frequently said, he made history until the end. The body lay in state in venerable Westminster Hall for three days and three nights while a never-ending queue, sometimes several miles in length, moved past in honor and remembrance. On Saturday, January 30, the casket was placed on a gun carriage and drawn in funeral procession by one hundred sailors of the Royal Navy to the sound of muffled drums and slow music between lines of thousands of silent onlookers along England's most historic route—up Whitehall to Trafalgar, thence into the Strand and Fleet Street, and up Ludgate Hill to St. Paul's Cathedral. There the service was conducted by the dean and by the archbishop of Canterbury in the presence of royalty of Britain and of other lands, and heads of state and representatives from well over one hundred nations. Sir Winston's favorite hymns, including, "Who would true valour see, Let him come hither," and the American Battle Hymn of the Republic ("Mine eyes have seen the glory of the coming of the Lord") were sung. From St. Paul's, in accordance with Sir Winston's stated wishes, the coffin was drawn to the foot of Tower Hill, placed aboard a launch for a brief journey up and across the Thames to Festival Pier and Waterloo Station. By special train the body was borne to Bladon in Oxfordshire for burial in the family plot in the small churchyard, close by Blenheim Palace where Sir Winston was born. It was a ceremony and pageant in which much of the world participated—the television audience was estimated at 350,000,000. Four years later, at Fulton, Missouri, an American memorial was dedicated—the reconstructed Church of St. Mary, Aldermanbury, London, which had been gutted by German incendiary bombs during World War II.

Incomes Policy, Planning, and Steel

"To the end that all may share the benefits of rising productivity, My ministers will work for more stable prices and a closer relationship between the increase in productivity and the growth of incomes in all their forms." Thus reads the Queen's Address, November 3, opening the new Parliament after the Labor victory, on the much-heralded incomes policy of Labor. Action had been pledged. It was to this end and to the general modernization of British industry that several new departments of state were created in 1964. There was, as we have seen, the D.E.A. (the Department of Economic Affairs) under George Brown. Of almost equal importance was the selection of Frank Cousins as minister of Technology, an appointment warmly received in the trade union world, where he had been the secretary of the Transport and General Workers' Union. Sir Charles Snow, scientist as well as novelist, became Lord Snow and the parliamentary secretary to the Ministry of Technology. And Mrs. Barbara Castle, former Labor Party chairman, long-time supporter of left-wing causes, became minister of Overseas Development.

In presenting the new economic policy, it was hoped to disarm suspicion and criticism and to win general support. On December 16, 1964, in a formal ceremony at Lancaster House arranged by Brown, was signed *The Declaration of Intent on Productivity, Prices and Incomes* by representatives of the Government, of the Trades Union Congress, and of the Federation of British Industry. They all agreed "to take urgent and vigorous action to raise productivity throughout industry and commerce, to keep increases in money incomes in line with increases in real national output, and to maintain a stable general price level." Brown, for the Government, declared that the document "heralded the end of the class war";

fifty thousand copies were distributed for display in factories and trade union offices. Perhaps this was the high point of general enthusiasm for a prices and incomes policy—this before its implications for the future of collective bargaining were realized.

For six months discussion of policy ensued. White papers on *The Machinery of Prices and Incomes Policy* (January 1965) and then *Prices and Incomes Policy* (April 1965), which explained the criteria to be employed, were the outcome of these talks among representatives of the Government, of the Trades Union Congress, and of employers' associations. At this stage the Trades Union Congress through its General Council lent support (perhaps the prospect looked brighter than when the Conservatives were searching for an incomes policy) as did the Conference of Trades Union Executives affiliated with the T.U.C. But rather ominously the powerful Transport and General Workers' Union upheld collective bargaining as the chief function of trade unionism and voted No. In accordance with the white papers, a National Board for Prices and Incomes was established. The norm of annual wage increases was set at 3–3.5 percent. The Board was to pass judgment on proposals of price and incomes increases referred to it—acceptance of the Board's recommendations was voluntary. But the possibility of legislative sanctions on such recommendations in the future was made clear. The first chairman of the Board was Aubrey Jones, a Conservative M.P. from Birmingham, a member of the 1955 Government, and a leading industrialist. Initial reports from the Board were at least a modest victory for the D.E.A.; some proposals of price increases were cut back. It remained to be seen whether the atmosphere was favorable for a voluntary incomes and prices policy. Even though price increases had been restrained, the cost of living had risen 4 percent in 1964 and the retail prices advance continued in 1965. And existing agreements calling for rises in wages took effect automatically. In 1965 this included the postmen and the miners, and for engineering workers activation of a three-year agreement which itself would add 4 percent to the total wages bill.

The "socialist" budget in April 1965 was one of the toughest in years, designed to resist the inflationary trend. The chief aim, Callaghan said at once, was to reduce domestic consumer spending by £250 million— to be achieved by an additional sixpence on the standard income tax, by raising the motor vehicle tax from 15 pounds to 17 pounds ten shillings, by higher taxes on tabacco (a pack of twenty cigarettes would now cost seventy-five cents) and on wines, beer, and spirits. Business entertainment expense was disallowed (except for overseas buyers) as a deduction on income tax, controls were tightened on the use of the pound in foreign exchange, and for the first time a tax was imposed on capital gains—a 30 percent tax on all gains in value of property and securities held for twelve months (with owner-occupied homes exempt). New corporation taxes were announced as just ahead. The chancellor of the Exchequer pledged no devaluation of the pound. The TSR-2, a tactical-strike-reconnaisance jet bomber was abandoned, according to the minister of Defense, to save resources for more productive purposes—a courageous move, for this action would produce unemployment in the aircraft industry.

"My Government will initiate early action to re-establish the necessary public ownership and control of the iron and steel industry." The Government had been in no hurry to implement this item in its program, perhaps because it would be difficult in the face of a combined Conservative-Liberal vote and some doubtful Labor votes, and perhaps because interest on the Labor front bench was lagging. The industry had, in fact, remained semipublic under the Conservatives; prices and output and proposals for expansion were controlled by the Iron and Steel Board. And even Labor had no notion of "nationalizing" the industry entirely. The Government passed its first crucial test in May on the presentation of a white paper as a basis for legislation. Labor carried the day with a majority of four, but twenty-three M.P.s had to fly home from a meeting of the Council of Europe at Strasbourg and five others, though ill, were prevailed upon to get to the division. Even so, two Labor M.P.s who might have abstained from voting entered the lobby with their party only after George Brown gave some assurances of a willingness to compromise. The Government seemed loathe to force the issue. Further action was postponed until autumn: the legislative schedule was crowded; local election results were running against Labor; it was recognized that "nationalization of steel" aroused great opposition and did not inspire much ardent support. The issue was not mentioned in the Queen's Speech to Parliament in November 1965.

Patrick Gordon Walker's defeat in the by-election in January and his resignation as foreign secretary was at the time regarded as something close to a disaster for Labor. But attention quickly shifted to his successor, Michael Stewart, whose performances in the Commons at once won respect and admiration. His remarks and those of the prime minister in the opening months of 1965 reflected a genuine interest in "a return to Europe." In February, at the Geneva meeting of the ministers in the European Free Trade Association, the British Government announced an early reduction of the surcharge on imports, from 15 percent to 10 percent. In Rome, Stewart told the Western European Council that if her interests were protected, Britain would "ultimately want to join the Common Market." In June the Assembly of the Western European Union, composed of delegates from the Common Market countries and Great Britain, recommended the creation of a permanent conference of advisers from their respective countries to harmonize and coordinate foreign policies. And arrangements were made for a meeting of the Six with the Outer Seven before the end of the year. Whether all this was more than perfunctory is difficult to say, but Britain did seem back on the road to Europe.

At the same time, both Wilson and Stewart strongly supported American policy in Vietnam and in Santo Domingo, despite protests from left-wingers in the party and adverse sentiment from a considerable segment of the public in the country at large. Grave concern was also manifest in the meeting of Commonwealth prime ministers in June at which it was decided that Wilson and the leaders of four other states (Ghana, Nigeria, Trinidad and Tobago, and Ceylon) should undertake a mission to the countries concerned, with a view to establishing the basis for a peace conference. And in July, the Government despatched a special envoy, Harold Davies, to Hanoi in North Vietnam, to attempt to establish a framework for peace talks. Neither endeavor achieved anything of consequence.

Since October 1964 speculation had circulated freely as to when the prime minister would appeal to the country in an effort to strengthen his slender hold on the Commons. Such talk ended, at least for the time being, with Wilson's statement to a party rally in Glasgow on June 26. He reaffirmed the right of his Government to govern and stated that barring unforeseen circumstances there would be no general election in 1965: "Provided we are able to get our essential legislation through Parliament we intend to stay and see the job through."

Edward Heath. Public opinion was almost evenly divided between the two major parties, a situation that stimulated each to seek some advantage at the expense of the other. The political outlook, therefore, could change quite abruptly. Within a few weeks after the Wilson statement in Glasgow, the prospect seemed much less favorable for Labor. For one thing, the Conservatives secured a new leader. The likelihood of Sir Alec Douglas-Home relinquishing his post in favor of a younger and perhaps more vigorous man was commonly discussed. But there was no advanced notice of Sir Alec's resignation, which came on July 22. He was quite candid: "A considerable number of people felt another leader might be better able to win a general election."

The transition was smooth, in contrast to the dissension, and even bitterness, which attended the emergence of Lord Home in 1963. This was in part a consequence of a more formalized procedure, as established by Sir Alec himself the previous February. Effective decision was to be made by ballot among the Conservative M.P.s. Furthermore, two able men, each of whom had demonstrated great capacity, were already at the fore—Reginald Maudling, shadow foreign secretary, and Edward Heath, shadow chancellor of the Exchequer. Maudling, as an individual the more popular of the two, was thought to have the edge, but on the first ballot Heath polled 150 votes to 133 for Maudling. Under the rules, further balloting was in order, but Maudling withdrew, pledging support to Heath, whose selection was insured without further contest. The new leader, 49 years of age and a bachelor, was hardly in the traditional Conservative mold, for his family had neither wealth nor social position. But he had distinguished himself as a scholarship student at Balliol College, Oxford, where he was president both of the Oxford Union and of the Oxford University Conservative Association. He was first returned to the Parliament in 1950 and after 1960 was in the Cabinet as lord privy seal and as president of the Board of Trade. For the next ten years he and Wilson were to dominate English politics.

No doubt Health's prestige had been strengthened by the leadership he provided in opposition to the Finance Bill. Well into June that debate continued, with repeated defeat for the Government on matters of detail. Heath's own attack on increased taxes on corporations was particularly telling. As the debate proceeded, the presure on the pound sterling mounted. But Callaghan would not entertain the thought of devaluation, merely saying that he must resist the temptation to restrain the economy still further. But at the end of July he did just that; he announced additional austerity measures designed to deflate the economy; there was to be a further slowdown in public spending, a tightening of controls on installment purchases, delays in the operation of new welfare programs, and a cutback on mortgage assistance to local housing authorities.

"The National Plan"

It did appear that the Wilson Government was all but finished. Polls had opinion shifting over to the Conservatives. But this was somewhat dramatically reversed with the Government's adventuresome stand on prices and income in "The National Plan" (sometimes called "The Master Plan") which had been some months in preparation. Before it was published Brown persuaded the Trades Union Congress in its annual session (in early September) to accept a tightening of policy on wages, but on condition that a voluntary system should be tried before any compulsion was authorized. Even then there was a 37 percent vote in opposition, revealing a growing breach between the T.U.C. leadership and its membership. And the general secretary, George Woodcock, declared that if any controls on wages were to be established, it should be by the T.U.C. itself. The Confederation of British Industry (a merger of four employers' organizations) accepted the "National Plan," but also with reluctance.

Table 7   Indices of Industrial Production and of Volume of Exports, United Kingdom, 1965–76

1963=100	Industrial Production 1970=100
1965 – 112	1971 – 101
1966 – 113	1972 – 103
1967 – 114	1973 – 110
1968 – 120	1974 – 107
1969 – 123	1975 – 101
1970 – 124	1976 – 102

1961=100	Volume of Exports 1970=100
1965 – 116	1971 – 109
1966 – 121	1972 – 111
1967 – 119	1973 – 127
1968 – 136	1974 – 133
1969 – 150	1975 – 130
1970 – 154	1976 – 139

Source: *Annual Abstract of Statistics* and *Annual Register of World Events*

Thus, on September 16 "The National Plan," prepared by Brown's department of the D.E.A. in consultation with the National Economic Development Council (representative of both management and labor), was published in a white paper, 475 pages in length. In the not too distant background there was the record of the previous Government (of Macmillan and Home); through its National Economic Development Council, a goal of 4 percent per year growth in the gross national product had been set; the actual result had been 1 to 2.5 percent. The National Plan had the same general purpose—the building up of the economy to reverse the heavy deficits in payments in foreign trade. The difference is that now there was to be an effort to control and stimulate the growth. The goal was a gain of 25 percent in the gross national product in the next five years; to reach this target, the annual rate of growth must reach 4 percent by 1970, production per person must be increased by 3.4 percent, investment in industry increased by 7 percent per year in real terms, and exports expanded 5.25 percent per year. These ambitious goals were to be achieved by modernization of industrial plant and by increased industrial efficiency, by reduction in national defense costs, by restriant on aid to undeveloped countries, and by reallocation of public spending. The role of the National Board for Prices and Incomes was to be strengthened by "an early warning system" requiring notice to the Board of any proposed wage or price increases and deferment of action until a recommendation from the Board was received. To avoid a show-down with both industry and labor, the "voluntary" aspect was emphasized, together with "a common purpose" and "the national interest."

In general terms, the Government was committed to technological modernization and expansion of production by considered measures. Regional planning became more detailed, and "Little Neddies" (industrial development councils) were established for modernization of local industry. The Government undertook to implement the recommendations of the Devlin report (August 1965), which attacked restrictive practices on the docks arising from casual labor, which, in turn, had produced a series of unofficial strikes. In December the Plowden report recommended that the state become part owner of the largest airframe firm, and in January 1966 an Industrial Reorganization Corporation was created to assist and encourage industrial mergers and nationalization generally.

On all these developments Wilson sought to capitalize politically. At the party conference at the end of September 1965, rebellion from the left was repelled, though resistance to the "early-warning" procedure for increased wages claims won 40 percent of the vote, and Cousins's estrangement from the rest of the Cabinet was in the making. Wilson met more easily criticism of official policy on immigration from Commonwealth lands (further restrictions were proposed) and on diplomatic support of American policy in Vietnam. And no doubt Wilson's rise in the opinion polls was in part due to the position he took in the Rhodesian crisis, a position which seemed to many Englishmen to represent both wisdom and principle. In May of 1965 the Rhodesian Front Party had won a sweeping electoral victory (in all parliamentary seats in the predominantly European constituencies). This led to increased pressure on Ian Smith, the premier, to push for independence, if necessary unilaterally. Such action would, of course, be in defiance of British sovereignty. The British response was that any constitutional settlement must have black support and a guarantee, eventually, of majority rule. Conferences in London and Rhodesia got nowhere, and on November 11, despite warnings from London of economic sanctions, Smith unilaterally proclaimed Rhodesian independence. The British Government sought to renew negotiations and imposed sanctions, step by step (no further purchase of tobacco, sugar, etc., from Rhodesia, and an embargo on oil destined for Rhodesia). By the end of January 1966 all trade between Great Britain and Rhodesia and been interdicted.

Wilson was clearly in charge; no member of Wilson's cabinet resigned between the 1964 and 1966 elections. Heath was in a quite different situation. In general his reputation had suffered. His remarks about the

National Plan as "the biggest gimmick the Government has thus far produced", and even his more positive and more intelligent comment that the policy of the Government had run counter to the philosophy of the Plan, had little effect. What was more significant, politically, was that Heath could not end the divisions within his own party. There was no agreement in the shadow cabinet on an incomes policy, nor on defense spending. Earlier differences on colonial and Commonwealth questions surfaced once more in the Rhodesian question. Heath endorsed the general policy of the Government but could not carry Lord Salisbury and his supporters with him. Heath's difficulties became a matter of mirth when Angus Maude, Conservative spokesman on Commonwealth affairs, in an article in *Spectator* in January 1966, said that to the public the Conservative Party was "a meaningless irrelevance." At Heath's request, Maude resigned from the shadow cabinet. More valuable to the Conservative cause was a party statement entitled *Putting Britain Right Ahead,* a document of some distinction because it dealt with the future and not the past. Its provisions have even been called "radical": tax reform in the interests of an expanding economy, a reassertaion of the commitment to enter the European Economic Community, reform of trade union practices in industrial disputes, and certain changes in the welfare state which would reduce state costs and limit services to those who needed it.

1966: The Make or Break Year for Labor

As the new year opened, it was reasonably certain that an election was just ahead. Wilson declared that 1966 would be "a make or break" year for Labor. In the Commons the Government's overall majority was now down to three. Wilson must surely have a stronger hold on the Commons before proceeding with legislation on prices and incomes, and to wait until spring was past would most likely mean postponement of the election until autumn. And it was to Wilson's advantage to have a poll before Heath had established himself. A significant by-election in Hull in January emphasized Labor's potential strength. A swing of but one percent would have transferred the seat to the Conservatives. But Labor held it with a large majority—a swing of 4.5 percent in its favor. This poll may have influenced Wilson's judgment (though later he remarks to the contrary). But in the event, on February 28 he announced a general election for March 31.

The General Election, March 1966

The campaign was not spirited—there had been too much political talk for the past year. But the manifestos were of more than normal interest. Labor's *Time for Decision* reads: "We are asking for a mandate to carry through the radical reconstruction of our national life which we began eighteen months ago." And it predicted a 25 percent increase in the standard of living under the next parliament if Labor won. Such slogans as "You *know* Labor Government works" and references to "the thirteen wasted years" of Conservatism were designed for popular consumption. The Conservative *Action not Words,* a new version of *Putting Britain Right Ahead,* referred to itself as "the party of the pacemakers," suggesting that they were, in fact, the party of "change." The incomes policy was not a major issue in the debate—it was much too complex to explain to the electorate. On this matter, as on others, Labor was able, in the words of one scholar, to conceal divisions within its own ranks "behind a real and symbolic unity." The Conservative slogan of "9–5–1" attracted attention for its summary of the economic achievement under Labor in 1965—a 9 percent increase in wages, a 5 percent rise in prices, and a 1 percent gain in production. But the lesson was hardly crystal clear, particularly to a wage earner. Coverage by the press reflected general ennui, in this case perhaps reenforced by jealousy of the dominance of television among the media. "Give Wilson a good majority so that this time there can be no alibis," read the large type of the *Daily Mirror* on election morning. For most voters, the choice did indeed come down to a question of Wilson or Heath.

All the indicators, including the offers of bookmakers, predicted a Labor victory, but hardly of the magnitude it proved to be. The first constituency (Cheltenham) to declare showed a 2.9 percent swing for Labor; then Exeter, for the first time in electoral history, reported a Labor win. This settled the matter. The final figures were 363 for Labor and 253 for the Conservatives. The Labor majority over all other parties was now 97, and the party was almost assured of four to five years in power. The Conservatives did not regain a single seat lost in 1964. Heath, himself, barely held his seat, and Thorneycroft, the Conservative spokesman on foreign affairs, was defeated. Labor's popular vote of 47.9 percent (as against the Conservative 41.9 percent) was the largest margin of victory of either party since 1945. The Liberals, now led by the popular Jo Grimond and hopeful that their stance of independence of Labor would bring recognition, won 12 seats with 8.5 percent of the votes. Analysis of election results indicates that significant changes in the class basis of parties were taking place. In 1966 Labor lost working-class votes but attracted a greatly increased middle-class vote. And the new Labor members of the Commons were not, generally speaking, of working-class background.

Following the election came important Cabinet changes: Roy Jenkins, who had demonstrated unusual ability as minister of Aviation, went to the Home Office; Richard Marsh (an official of the National Union of Public Employees) became minister of Power, replacing Fred Lee, who went to the Colonial Office; George Thompson, a strong advocate for entry into the Common Market, became chancellor of the Duchy of Lancaster, reenforcing the position of George Brown, who was assigned a special role in European economic relations. Shortly before the election, Barbara Castle had been designated minister of Transport.

Briefly, after the election, the situation, both political and economic, seemed under control. Wilson had been the first prime minister in the century to increase his majority in the Commons while leading his party to a second victory. This result seemed to reenforce the insistence of Labor that the economy was in good order. The Speech from the Throne opening the new Parliament carried a strong note of optimism. During the campaign the chancellor of the Exchequer gave assurances that there was "no need for severe increases in taxation." And in his new budget, Callaghan's only significant move was the introduction of the Selective Employment Tax, to be paid by employers for each of their employees. In reality it was a tax on service industries, passed on to those served, since the act called for remission of the tax in the manufacturing industries. Further optimism was indicated in the publication, July 1, of a bill to nationalize iron and steel.

Prices and Incomes Again

But only briefly did Labor's victory overshadow the faltering economic policy of 1964–66. That optimism had little foundation was soon evident. On May 16 the National Union of Seamen went on strike for a wage increase and a forty-hour week, referred to in the *Annual Register* as "the worst industrial dispute in Britain since 1926." The Government declared a state of emergency, and Wilson was able to substantiate his allegations that Communist influence operated within the union. Demands were somewhat moderated, and the issues were settled July 1. But the prolonged strike with its final wage settlement of a 10 percent increase constituted a challenge to the new incomes policy. But this was only one of many cases. Shortly after, Wilson told the Commons, "The time has come to call a halt."

On July 4 the Prices and Incomes Bill was published—this required review by the Board of all increases in wages, prices, or dividends, in effect delaying settlements as much as four months. In protest, the day before, Frank Cousins, minister of Technology, long known to be opposed to this measure, resigned. He declared that the bill made trade unionism "an adjunct of Government," with voluntarism meaning for trade unionism "freedom only to do as it is told by the Government." He returned to his post as general secretary of the Transport and General Workers' Union. Further trouble came from the miners; the union membership, contrary to recommendations from their leaders, refused to approve the bill. In view of this atmosphere, the language of the bill was modified to emphasize its "voluntary" character and now provided for a six-month freeze on incomes, to be followed by an additional six months of "severe restraint." If the Government chose to act against a breach of the "freeze," it would have to act through an Order in Council. After one of the most tumultous parliamentary debates on record (with Brown, the head of D.E.A., hardly permitted to speak) the bill became law August 12.

Devaluation or deflation? In the meantime had come the most serious sterling crisis since 1949; in July the pound dropped to its lowest point in twenty months. An unfavorable balance of payments was predicted through 1967. The Government had a choice of devaluation of the currency or deflation of the economy. The Cabinet was sharply divided, with strong support for devaluation coming from Brown, Crosland, Jenkins, and Crossman. Protracted Cabinet meetings on July 19–20 led to the decision—a deflationary budget with much heavier taxation and with slashes in public expenditure. Wilson reported to the Commons: "We need . . . a more purposive use of labour for the sake of increased exports and giving effect to other national priorities. This redeployment can be achieved only by cuts in the present inflated level of demand, both in the private and public sectors." This procedure had been recommended by the Treasury. But to George Brown and the D.E.A. it spelled the destruction of the National Plan, which had been based upon an expansionist economy. Brown threatened to resign and in August did exchange posts with the foreign secretary, Michael Stewart.

Thereafter Wilson and his supporters suffered considerably in credibility. Unemployment, increased by the sluggish economy, doubled by the end of the year. In October H. R. F. Catherwood declared that the original goal of 25 percent gain in the *g.n.p.* in five years could not survive these measures of July 1966. Later, the historian, Robert Rhodes James, observed that the election of 1966 had been won "on a false prospectus." Wilson, himself, looking back several years later concluded that in July 1966 "the suddenness and devastating character of the crisis had undeniably thrown us off course." Perhaps it was the turning point of the administration; Wilson does not rule this out. Thereafter the incomes and prices policy was on the defensive.

To be sure, all this was not at once evident. In September there was, surprisingly, a surplus in international payments, and the year indicated a temporary growth in exports of six percent. Trade unionism accepted the "wage freeze" and the "restraint" in economic if not in political terms. Even with Cousins leading the opposition, the Labor Party Conference in October supported the Government's wages policy, 3,836,000 to 2,515,000. It was a dramatic moment: the Labor Party, which owed its life to trade unionism, decreed that collective bargaining was subject to Governmental regulation. On the other hand, it was the Conservatives in their party conference who proclaimed the principle of freedom for trade unions to negotiate wage agreements. Of course, as we shall see, both attitudes were subject to change.

The immediate results of the "freeze period" were somewhat more favorable than might have been expected. For a time, prices were stabilized, strikes decreased in number, and only a few compulsory orders were issued by the Government. But the economy showed no sign of advancement. And the alienation of trade union membership from its leadership and the divergence of the Labor Party Conference from the Government had begun.

It is a story which will be repeated with variations. The 1966 legislation on prices and incomes ran its course by July 1, 1967. A new law continued Government authority to delay wage increases. An ominous feature was that this was the first legislation on this subject to lack support from the Trades Union Congress. Its Executive Committee refused to endorse it, and in September the Congress by a large majority supported a resolution condemning the Government for its "intervention in collective bargaining." The decisions of July 1966 still haunted Cabinet and Commons; once again, the prospect of devaluation was in the air, but in July 1967, Callaghan said flatly that it offered no remedy. In August the prime minister assumed personal control of the D.E.A. and at the party conference wisely talked about the future rather than of the past. He secured support from the conference for application for membership in the Common Market—a marked change of sentiment within the party from that of five years before.

But brave words did not prevent tensions within the business community, at home and abroad, from reaching the near panic stage by mid November. On the 18th, the Government reversed itself and announced devaluation of the pound sterling from $2.80 to $2.40, a drop of 14.3 percent. This action came not because of concern for the dangers of speculation in sterling but rather because it was finally recognized that this was the only measure which would strengthen industrial production and reduce unemployment. But it was not Wilson's manner to be candid, and his pronouncements, ignoring the inconsistencies of his policy, did him no good. Over television he declared that devaluation did not mean "that the pound here in Britain, in your pocket or purse or in your bank, has been devalued." To be sure, this sentence was taken out of context by his critics (he did, in fact, add that some prices would rise) and used unfairly against him, but in attempting to play down the significance of devaluation he invited just such treatment.

At the same time came new leadership at the Exchequer. Callaghan was replaced by Roy Jenkins, who had continued to demonstrate his administrative ability at the Home Office. In the crisis of July 1966 he had supported George Brown and favored devaluation. Now, in November 1967, he said there was no alternative; to expand exports, prices at home must rise more than incomes.

Britain in Europe: Is it Still Non?

But at just this juncture Wilson met another defeat— this time at Brussels at the hands of the European Economic Community, or more specifically, at the hands of France. As has been mentioned, here was another turnabout for Labor, which had in 1962 opposed association with the Common Market and in 1964–65 had ignored the matter. But circumstances were rapidly changing. It was now fairly clear that Commonwealth trade with the E.E.C. was in a healthier state than its trade with the United Kingdom. And Wilson had made a commitment of some kind to the deputy leader of the party, George Brown, an ardent exponent of British membership in the Common Market. And so the proposal of British application for membership, with due concern for British and Commonwealth interests, figured prominently in the party manifesto before the election of 1966 and in the Queen's Address opening the new Parliament. Just as Macmillan had been moved to action in 1961 by the sorry condition of the economy, so now in November 1966 Wilson was persuaded that application ot the Common Market was a sound move both economically and politically. Encouragement was somewhat limited, as Wilson discovered in his tour (January and February 1967) of Common Market capitals; and there was strong opposition at home within his own party. But early in May the Cabinet gave approval. "This is a historic decision which will determine the future of Britain, of Europe and indeed of the world for decades to come," Wilson told the nation. With Heath's enthusiastic support from the Opposition front bench, after a three-day debate, the Cabinet action was approved in the Commons 488 to 62, but with 34 Labor members in opposition and 51 abstaining. The Lords quickly added their approval, and formal application to the Common Market was made May 11.

The British were optimistic. "We expect to get in," said Brown, enthusiastic over the prospects for industrial recovery. Callaghan forecast a favorable balance of payments for the rest of the year. The Labor Party Conference in October endorsed the Government action. And early response from Brussels seemed promising. But the shadow of de Gaulle again fell across the British application. He at once referred to "formidable obstacles" to British entrance. In due course, at a press conference on November 27, he gave an unqualified *Non*. He remarked acidly that Britain was merely trying to get other nations to solve her problems, and that the Common Market would suffer, not benefit, from British membership. Soon after, the French foreign minister, Couve de Murville, gave the formal French answer at the Council of Ministers: "We reject negotiation now because Britain's economy is not strong enough for her to join." Other countries, though favorable toward the British application, would not stand up against de Gaulle. Altogether, Wilson had bad luck on this matter—success might well have altered his situation.

We read in the *Annual Register* for 1967:

> The year ended with the country in a mixed and introspective mood. Devaluation had marked yet another setback in the postwar struggle to restore the nation's economic strength and was a blow to national self-esteem. It also eroded still further confidence in politicians of all parties since they—and Mr. Wilson most recently—had been the instruments of failure.... Yet for all the talk of national bankruptcy, prosperity was evident at all levels of society in the pre-Christmas shopping weeks. There was, however, an uneasy awareness that bleaker times might lie ahead, although there was also the hope that Government and people alike might seize the opportunities that devaluation offered in the year to come.

For the Labor Government, in particular, the future looked dark. Three years had elapsed since Labor had confidently taken office, but thus far she had failed in her chief aim—to strengthen the economy. The incomes policy, after some prospect of success, had brought no solutions, had contributed to rising industrial unrest, and had lost support within the party and within trade unionism. Frequent changes occurred in the Cabinet, and these usually from dissatisfaction with policy. More glaring were the setbacks of the party at the polls. By-elections throughout the year revealed a striking shift to the Conservative side. In municipal elections, Labor suffered a net loss of 586 seats. In county elections, the most dramatic Conservative victory was in the Greater London Council, where after the poll they enjoyed an 82-18 majority over Labor, which lost control for the first time since 1934. In February 1968 opinion polls throughout the land gave the Conservatives an 18 percent lead.

World Policy 1965–70

It is self-evident that devaluation and the general state of the economy contributed to a major decision of the Government on external affairs in January 1968. On the 16th, Wilson announced in the Commons that British withdrawal from Singapore, Malaysia, and the Persian Gulf would be complete by 1971. Just three years before, in December 1964, Wilson had insisted that the British role East of Suez would be maintained. In the interim, an issue consistently pushed aside in earlier years became the subject of constant debate in the press and on the platform. It was no longer a question of the nature of Empire and Commonwealth, nor of Britain's policy toward this nation or that, nor even of the character of national defense. These matters were absorbed in a fundamental problem: in the future what was to be Britain's role in the world?

Even before 1965 had run its course, it was generally recognized that political and economic questions in the Middle East, in Africa, and in Asia so far as they affected Britain could not be settled by military action. One consideration was quite simple; the peoples concerned never accepted defeat. Another, not so simple but equally self-evident: when issues concerned the Soveit Union's national interest, nothing could be gained by a British challenge to her as a military power. And finally, the British economy, it was now abundantly clear, could no longer maintain a defense establishment adequate in itself to protect the United Kingdom. In the future the thrust of British policy would be toward strengthening the United Nations, toward supporting NATO as the best guarantee against a European war, toward cooperation with the other states of western Europe, and toward control of the proliferation of nuclear arms.

For illustration of these generalizations we may turn in almost any direction. The British now sponsored peace missions to Vietnam, though still formally supporting American policy. Decisions as to defense measures, though usually reached amid controversy, moved steadily and surely toward more limited commitment and reduced spending. Sharp reductions in defense costs were announced in August 1965, and in December a white paper suggested a reduction of the Territorial Army (that is, the home forces) to about 70,000. In February 1966, after a policy review that lasted fifteen months, British forces overseas were reduced by one-third. At the same time a white paper issued by Defense Minister Healey declared that aircraft carriers would cease to be the chief strike force at sea.

As to the remaining British forces in the Middle East and in Southeast Asia, decisions were reached slowly and with difficulty. Britain had treaty commitments; she also had oil and business interests in the Persian Gulf area. On the other hand, there were circumstances over which Britain had little control—and these often dictated the course of events. According to plan, the military base at Aden was to be closed when the South Arabian Federation, sponsored by Britain, achieved independence in 1968. But conflict among the tribesmen of Yemen tore apart the Federation, and in 1965 the British Government through the High Commissioner resumed control. In 1967 all British troops were withdrawn and an independent People's Democratic Republic of South Yemen (including Aden) came into being. For Malaysia, a white paper in July 1967 envisaged gradual reduction of British forces there and in Singapore as well, with complete exodus by the mid seventies. However, with the end in 1968 of the conflict between Malaysia and Indonesia, the process of withdrawal moved more rapidly. Free interest loans and grants compensated for economic effects of military withdrawal. And provision was made for regular discussion of defense policy in cooperation with Britain, Australia, and New Zealand.

But Denis Healey, Defense secretary, in February 1969, reiterated the Wilson theme of a year before. The Defense white paper, he said, "set the seal on Britain's transformation from a world Power to a European Power." NATO, as Healey made clear, was now the basis of British security and national defense. In this area, any rise in the British contribution in men or money produced little controversy. In the electoral campaign of 1964 Labor pledged to renegotiate the Nassau Agreement of 1962 by which Britain secured control over her *Polaris* submarines. Briefly the Wilson Government considered an Atlantic Nuclear Force, but this proposition was not attractive to continental allies in NATO. And it was dropped. The Nassau Agreement remained in force. On this issue Wilson was at his political best in avoiding a revolt in Labor's left wing. For one thing, he took former unilateralists such as Cousins, Crossman, and Mrs. Castle into the Cabinet; they now shared responsibility for Government policy. The long argument of the fifties over strategic nuclear forces was not renewed. The Wilson Government made it clear that Britain would have an independent nuclear force for the immediate future. In late 1970 the fourth British *Polaris* submarine, H.M.S. *Revenge*, joined the fleet.

The Commonwealth

The Commonwealth grew in numbers if not in importance. With some of these additions are associated untoward events. Mauritius, after being a crown colony for 158 years, became independent in March 1968. But disorders marred the transition and British troops had to be quickly transferred from Singapore to keep order. The planned visit of Princess Alexandra, to grace the ceremony of independence, was called off. In the same year, Nauru, a small island in the southeast Pacific Ocean, since World War I administered by Britain, Australia, and New Zealand became independent as an associate member of the Commonwealth. And in South Africa, Swaziland, a high commission territory administered by Britain after World War II, became independent. Fiji, a group of 322 islands in the South Pacific which had been a crown colony since 1874, attained statehood in October 1970; in the same year was added Tonga, another group of islands which had been a British protectorate. Two years later Bangladesh, formely East Pakistan, attained independence following the Bengali revolt. This revolt was brought to a conclusion by the U.S.S.R. rather than by the United Kingdom. The Bahamas, and Grenada, crown colonies since 1783, became independent in 1973. Papua New Guinea, administered by Australia after World War I, became a state in its own right in 1975. All these lands accepted association in the Commonwealth. As a protest against Britain's decision to recognize Bangladesh as an independent country, Pakistan left the Commonwealth in 1972.

By 1969, twenty-eight lands were sending heads of state to the conferences of the Commonwealth. But no longer was it a group of powers, large and small, with common traditions and institutions and united in policy. At annual meetings, the heads of state raised their own particular problems; indeed, the greatest attention was often paid to the affairs of the smaller or more backward countries. Britain found that she had assumed obligations for which there was often very little return.

Among British possession Gibraltar had a unique story. For several years in the sixties the Spanish Government claimed sovereignty on the basis of the Treaty of Utrecht of 1713. A referendum in 1967 placed before the inhabitants a direct choice between accepting Spanish sovereignty or "voluntarily retaining the link with the United Kingdom with democratic local institutions and with the United Kingdom retaining its present responsibilities." Nearly all the registered voters exercised the option; 12,138 voted "for Britain" and 44 "for Spain." By a new constitution in 1969 the "Colony of Gibraltar" became the "City of Gibraltar."

Britain showed less and less inclination to intervene in Commonwealth lands struck by civil war and rebellion. So she stood aside during the civil war in Nigeria 1966–70; the federal forces finally forced "the Republic of Biafra" to surrender. This restraint on the part of the British won the admiration of the Third World. But it was another matter when Britain would not intervene, militarily, in Rhodesia.

Rhodesia. Of all the colonial problems, that of Rhodesia seemed most completely to defy efforts at solution. Year after year, from the time of declaration of Rhodesia's unilateral independence in November 1965, the essentials remained much the same. The basic fact, of course, was that the Europeans, comprising 5 percent of the population, dominated political and economic institutions. In 1965 Britain stated five principles as the basis for settlement of the qustion of Rhodesian independence; in 1966 a sixth principle or condition was added. In summary form these conditions were: (1) unimpeded progress toward majority rule to be maintained and guaranteed; (2) guarantees against retrogressive amendments to the constitution after it was in operation; (3) immediate improvement in the political status of the Africans; (4) progress toward ending racial discrimination; (5) any basis proposed for independence must be acceptable to the Rhodesian people as a whole; (6) insurance that, regardless of race, there would be no oppression of majority by minority or of minority by majority. Direct discussions between the Rhodesian prime minister, Ian Smith, and Wilson meeting in naval vessels off Gibraltar, got nowhere. Smith insisted and reiterated that his party, the Rhodesian Front, be in power while any new constitution was tested. In 1969 that party issued its own "constitution," a document which failed to meet the British conditions; but this document was overwhelmingly supported, in a referendum in Rhodesia, by the largely European electorate. It was crystal clear that Ian Smith had no intention of moving toward rule by the African majority. He seemed completely confident of the strength of his bargaining position. As a matter of fact, sanctions imposed by Great Britain and the United Nations were ineffective except for a curtailing of tobacco exports from Rhodesia. In sum, to use the language of the 1967 *Annual Register*, Rhodesia had ceased to be a crisis; instead it had become a long-term problem.

Powellism. By 1968 race had become a volatile matter in Britain as well. The issue in question was the size and character of colored immigration to Britain from Commonwealth lands. It was an area which could hardly have been considered a problem ten years before, when the British took for granted harmonious relationships within the multiracial Commonwealth. In 1951 the census showed the immigrant population (colored peoples born overseas) to be about 75,000. Ten years later that census figure was 336,000. And for an eighteen-month period in 1961–62, in the face of threatened limitations, the net arrivals in Britain from India, Pakistan, and the West Indies were

203,000, about as many as there had been between 1955 and 1960. The Immigration Act of 1962 established limited controls. The public was confused and so were the politicians—both caught between Commonwealth idealism and the potential problems to English society and economy from rising immigration. By 1966 the colored population in England and Wales reached an estimated figure of 929,000, of which 213,000 had been born in Britain. In 1966 legislation tightened restrictions, with permits of entry reduced from 20,000 a year to 8,500, with dependents admitted limited to wives and children.

As a political and social issue the matter leaped into prominence with the Commonwealth Immigration Act (March 1, 1968), which had been prompted by the action of the Kenya Government in refusing work permits to non-citizen Asian residents, who, possessing British passports, had then moved to Britain in large numbers. The new legislation, which was bipartisan, limited Asian immigrants from Kenya to 1,500 a year (equivalent to 7,000, including dependents). The debate during the legislative process was impassioned, and included an almost unprecedented nineteen-hour session in the Lords. As the bill proceeded toward enactment, masses of desperate Asians sought to leave Kenya bound for Britain before the law would prevent entry; it was a sorry story spread over the front pages of newspapers throughout the world.

Soon after, parliamentary debate over a racial relations bill got under way, but rational discussion was impeded by the impassioned argument over immigration. This reached something of a climax in an address on April 20 at Birmingham by Enoch Powell, now shadow minister of Defense for the Conservatives. His remarks on the consequences of continued immigration went far beyond the boundaries of reason, accuracy, and good taste. It must be read to appreciate its impact. "In fifteen or twenty years the black man will have the whip hand over the white man" in Britain, he asserted. "We must be mad . . . as a nation, to be permitting the annual inflow of some 50,000 dependents, who are for the most part the material of the future growth of the immigrant descended population." And the social problems which would follow! The English people would become "strangers in their own country," unable to secure hospital beds, find places for their children in school, their neighborhoods transformed "beyond recognition," the immigrant worker taking control in the factories. And the climax: "As I look ahead, I am filled with foreboding. . . . In numerical terms it will be of American proportions long before the end of the century. Only resolute and urgent action will avert it even now."

Edward Heath at once dismissed Powell from the shadow cabinet because of the "racialist" tone of the address. Powell had asserted that the Conservative Party supported "checking" further inflow and promoting further outflow; Heath had to set straight the record in this regard. At Birmingham, Heath made formal response to Powell and called for national, nonpartisan cooperation in dealing with immigration in the interests of all concerned.

Nonetheless, Powell had transformed the problem into a leading social and political issue. To the credit of the leadership of both parties, the Race Relations Bill became law; it dealt soberly and intelligently with such matters as discrimination in employment because of race. It should also be added, in fairness to Powell himself, that he had aired an important question which the politicians had often put aside, and he had dealt with it in terms that the public understood. It soon became apparent, from the numerous demonstrations and the flood of mail on the matter to Powell, that he had a large following in the land, including strong support from the right wing of his party. "Powellism"—his personality and his approach to national issues—had to be reckoned with in the future.

The Duncan Report

We may round out this examination of British external policy by reference to the Duncan report of 1969. A committee headed by Sir Val Duncan, a prominent industrialist, had been instructed in September 1968 to examine "the functions and scale of British representational effort overseas in the light of recent decisions on foreign and defence policy, and of the economic situation and needs of the country." In short, what sort of representation abroad should Britain have in the future?

By way of answer, Britain is frankly referred to as "a major power of second rank" and the primacy of commercial interests over political is asserted. Britain, the report asserted, should concentrate its attention on the rich trading areas of the world—Europe and North America. At once there were protests. The economist Wilfred Beckerman found such conclusions quite superficial and unenlightened. And *The Observer*, while welcoming the investigation, was disappointed by the limited perspective of the report and regretted its failure to recognize Britain's part in efforts to establish a more stable world order and to meet the problems raised by the emergence of the Third World. But the very fact that such matters should be subject of controversy is a commentary on that which is transpiring. As one historian, Joseph Frankel, observes: while in the recent past Britain has pursued global ambitions at the expense of immediate interests, the danger for the future is that she will "pursue narrowly conceived immediate interests to the neglect of global policies."

1969—"In Place of Strife"—A New Code of Industrial Relations?

In a final effort toward an effective prices and incomes policy, the Wilson Government in 1969 sought to legislate controls which would be enforced by penal sanctions over trade unions and their membership. This episode reached its climax in what the journalist, Peter Jenkins, calls "The Battle of Downing Street." To understand this development and assess its consequences we must briefly follow economic policy after devaluation of the pound in November 1967.

Devaluation, November 1967 and After. This devaluation was accompanied by retrenchment in domestic spending as well as in external policy already discussed. In the ensuing two years the budget was to be cut £716 million. The price of medical prescriptions was set at 2 shillings and sixpence, with some exemptions; free milk in secondary schools ended; the raising of the school-leaving age from 15 to 16 was postponed from 1971 to 1973; National Insurance dues were increased for both employers and employees; and housing and road building schedules were cut back. These measures constituted the first major shift of Labor from its long-held concept of "a welfare state for all" and was very much an about-face for Wilson, who had resigned from the Labor Government in 1951 because of his opposition to charges for prescriptions and dental work.

On the other hand, all this was very consistent with past attitudes and actions of the new chancellor of the Exchequer, Roy Jenkins. For the immediate future the decisions were his. In his first budget message, in March 1968, he declared before a crowded House that the country should profit by devaluation. Incomes must be held down, strikes reduced, public expenditures slashed. Taxes, especially indirect taxes, would be increased by £923 million. A special levy was imposed on income from investments; these rose to a high of 40 percent; this tax was in addition to existing income tax and surtax dues, and in some cases amounted to a one percent levy on capital itself. It was a clarion call for a lower standard of living. And Jenkins was much admired for his courage.

Perhaps devaluation *was* the part of wisdom. But it was decidedly unpopular. In by-elections that followed soon after the budget was presented, the Government lost three hitherto "safe seats" with an average swing over to the Conservative side of 18 percent. Cabinet changes reflected uncertainties, fears, and tensions. The Earl of Longford resigned his leadership of the House of Lords in protest against deferment of the school-leaving age. More significant was the resignation of the foreign secretary, George Brown, still Wilson's chief rival in the party. The administration, Brown charged, was "presidential," with the prime minister making decisions "over the heads of his ministers." Brown remained deputy leader of the party, with a place on the Party National Executive Committee. Michael Stewart returned to the Foreign Office.

A little later, in April 1968, numerous other Cabinet changes were made. Perhaps the most important for domestic policy were the increased roles of two left-wingers—the assignment to Richard Crossman of responsibility for reorganization of social services and the appointment of Mrs. Barbara Castle to the Labor Department, now renamed the Ministry of Employment and Productivity, with responsibility for the prices and incomes policy. It was already clear that Mrs. Castle's chief responsibility would be to seek cooperation from the trade unions.

But these new roles of Jenkins, Castle, and Crossman notwithstanding, it was abundantly clear as the year proceeded that the Government was in for trouble with the party, with the Trades Union Congress, and with the electorate. The heart of the matter is in the fortunes of the 1968 Prices and Incomes Bill, which placed a 3.5 percent ceiling on wages, dividends, and salary increases. And in the future there was to be at least a twelve-month interval (replacing seven) between any such increases. As in previous measures, the compliance was to be voluntary, generally speaking; but when recommended by the Prices and Incomes Board, the Government could enforce decisions of that Board.

Obstacles at once appeared. First there were the Labor back-benchers with 34 abstentions on the second reading (May 21) of the bill in the Commons. Results in parliamentary by-elections (extending Labor losses already noted earlier in the year) and in local elections reflected growing lack of confidence in the Government. A press campaign clamoring for Wilson's departure went too far; many of its assertions were successfully refuted, and it was Cecil King, chairman of the corporation owning the *Daily Mirror* and the *Sun*, who was dismissed. But fortune did not smile elsewhere. The party National Executive Committee barely (a 13–12 vote) supported the Prices and Incomes Bill, but the party conference at the end of September voted down the principle of statutory control of wages by a majority of 5 to 1. At the Trades Union Congress, an overwhelming majority of 7 to 1 supported a resolution rejecting "any further legislation the aim of which would be to curb basic trade union rights." Even "vetting" by trade unions themselves had declining support. Voluntary controls, exercised under the authority of the T.U.C., were supported by a very narrow majority. Trade union leadership was changing, but with what result was uncertain. In 1967 Hugh Scanlon became president of the Amalgamated Union of Engineers; and in January 1969

Victor Feather succeeded Woodcock as the general secretary of the Trades Union Congress. Later in that year, Cousins, the general secretary of the Transport and General Workers' Union, was replaced by Jack Jones.

Of more immediate importance were the early stages of inflation. As a result of devaluation and incomes policies, the cost of living for most factory workers was rising faster than wages. This gave rise to a rash of strikes, most of them "wildcat," that is, unofficial. The admirable British records on strikes during 1964–66 (better than that of the United States, Italy, France, or Japan) made all the more startling the sharp rise in 1968. During the first six months, we are told, more working days were lost in strikes than during any one year from 1963 to 1967. Many of these wildcat strikes were petty and local, but they were often troublesome for just this reason; at a brake factory, for example, there were some 57 disputes in eighteen months. Such strikes were often directed as much against trade union leadership as against industrial management. At the end of 1968 the rank and file of certain unions were talking of seeking wage increases of as much as 18 percent, while leadership of the T.U.C. thought in terms of 2.5 percent to 4.5 percent.

It so happened that in June 1968 appeared the report of the Royal Commission on Trade Unions and Employers, an inquiry into the law as it affected trade unionism, after three years study. The Donovan report, as it was generally called, pointed out that 95 percent of industrial strikes were unofficial and resulted from faulty industrial negotiations within trade unionism. A shift from national wage agreements in various industries to settlements between particular companies and local unions was urged. And an investigative Commission for Industrial Relations along with Labor Tribunals to settle disputes was proposed. Quite naturally the report was examined and judged in terms of the conditions in 1968. Trade unionists generally found it praiseworthy, but most employers and business associations found it of little value; it failed, they said, to deal with wildcat strikes. Labor and management were moving farther apart. Opinion polls showed business executives generally supporting a prices and incomes policy administered by the Government. But there was far less support, in one poll only a 31 percent vote, for the particular policies pursued by the Wilson Government. On the other hand, a goodly majority of trade union members thought that wages was a matter for unions and employers to settle.

As for Wilson and Mrs. Castle, they were determined to go well beyond the Donovan report. It was as clear to them as to anyone else that Labor's incomes policy had not thus far succeeded, that voluntary procedures with limited restraints had failed, and that wages had not been held down to levels commensurate with increased industrial production and foreign trade. The time had come, they decided, for genuine reform of industrial relations.

The White Paper. On January 17, 1969, the white paper *In Place of Strife* was published. Just how much the minister of Employment and Productivity (Mrs. Castle) was responsible for this and just how much the prime minister was we do not now know. It is likely that Wilson's mind returned to the seamen's strike in 1966, so costly to Government standing, and also to the prolonged unofficial strike in 1968 of dock workers in Liverpool and London. In any case, he promptly endorsed the proposal in a B.B.C. broadcast. And Jenkins promised his support. The most significant provision was that in case of an unofficial strike, without sanction of the established union, the Government could order a return to work in "a conciliatory pause" of twenty-eight days, while a settlement was sought. If the order was ignored, financial penalties were to be imposed. Under certain circumstances the Government could require a trade union to ballot its membership before leadership called an unofficial strike. In case of a dispute between unions which the T.U.C. could not settle, the matter was to be referred to a new agency, the Commission on Industrial Relations. Its recommendation could be enforced by the Government. The Commission, under the chairmanship of George Woodcock, was established March 1; until legislation was enacted, its operations were merely advisory.

For the moment, *In Place of Strife* was well received, judging from the press and public opinion polls. But as the implications were more fully realized in the trade union world, doubts arose, and, to use Mrs. Castle's words, also "a sense of alarm and outrage." The concept of voluntarism in trade unionism (the freedom to bargain for a working contract and the freedom to strike) would be modified by a penal element—a change which would not be temporary but permanent. Did not any man or woman have the right to refuse to work if he or she so chose? And it was uncertain just how the law would be enforced and penalties exacted.

Larger questions developed. How would legislation of *In Place of Strife* affect the relation of workers to their unions and the unions with the General Council of the T.U.C.? And how would this alter the relation of the working class to the Labor Party? But it was also clear from the beginning that Wilson and Mrs. Castle would have trouble closer at home—with the Cabinet and with Parliament, where the trade union element in the Labor Party membership numbered about 130. This problem was anticipated, for Wilson and Mrs. Castle bypassed the Cabinet Subcommittee on Industrial Relations and solicited support from the

T.U.C. and from the Employers' Confederation of British Industry before bringing the matter formally to the attention of the whole Cabinet.

Opposition grew as time passed. On March 3 the Commons approved the white paper as the basis for a bill but with almost half of the Labor back-benchers denying support. A more decisive vote came March 26, when the National Executive Committee of the Labor Party voted 16–5 against endorsing for legislation all of the proposals in the white paper. The "No" votes included James Callaghan, home secretary, and the *Economist* observed that the bill to reform trade unions might prove more troublesome to the Labor Party than it was worth to the country. On April 3, just after returning from a trip to Nigeria, Wilson restored discipline in the Cabinet by getting its unanimous consent to bring the bill before the Commons and its reaffirmation of the doctrine of collective responsibility within the Cabinet.

By this time strong sentiment against *In Place of Strife* had built up within the General Council of the T.U.C. The Council's offer to take action in accordance with the Donovan report brought Wilson's reply that this did not constitute "an equally effective alternative" to the Government proposal for enforcing discipline within trade unionism. Originally Wilson and Mrs. Castle counted on an Act of Parliament which would be activated in 1970; but now, pressed by Jenkins, Crossman, and others for immediate action, they decided to present to the Commons a shorter Industrial Relations Bill which could be implemented at once. The key provision, however, remained: this was the "conciliation pause", already explained.

And so on April 15, 1969 Roy Jenkins in his budget statement to the Commons declared: "We need to facilitate the smooth working of collective bargaining in industry and to help prevent the occurrence of unnecessary and damaging disputes.... The Government have, therefore, decided to implement without delay during the present session some of the more important provisions incorporated in the White Paper *In Place of Strife*." Jenkins also announced that the 1968 Prices and Incomes Act, requiring a delay of twelve months in wage settlements including increases, would not be renewed. In the debate he and Mrs. Castle declared that the 1968 Act had been a temporary measure and that with the Industrial Relations Bill, the Government would be able to return to the less stringent regulations of 1966, by which the Government could order a three-months delay on wage increases.

Reform of the House of Lords?

This change in tactics was prompted in part by the experience with another controversial measure, the House of Lords Reform Bill, on which the Government was about to admit defeat. And so we must now break our consideration of the Industrial Relations Bill to tell briefly the story of this Parliament bill. This goes back to the election manifesto of 1966, in which Labor had declared it would propose legislation which would protect measures passed by the Commons from being delayed or defeated in the Lords. In the course of the next year, the initiative came from the Lords chamber itself, with discussion leading to formation of a Cabinet Committee to study the whole question. At once this committee was flooded with proposals for reform, some even in the direction of both reforming the membership and strengthening the role of the Lords.

In opening the 1967–68 session of Parliament, the Queen's Address in October 1967 reads: "Legislation will be introduced to reduce the present powers of the House of Lords and to eliminate its present hereditary basis, thereby enabling it to develop within the framework of a modern Parliamentary system. My Government are prepared to enter into consultations appropriate to a constitutional change of such importance."

The second sentence was included on the initiative of the Opposition. All three parties were represented in the Inter-Party Conference which met at once. While considerable agreement was evident on proposals of changes in the membership and powers of the Lords, the possibilities for strong party control and of domination of party by faction raised doubts and uncertainties. The showdown came in June 1968 with the vote in the Lords on the Southern Rhodesian Sanctions Order which implemented sanctions in a United Nations resolution. By this time the Conservative Opposition in the Lords was prepared to join the shadow cabinet against that order. Roy Jenkins, in an address at Birmingham June 15, indicated that the Inter-Party Conference on Lords Reform would end if the Lords rejected the Sanctions order. And so they did on June 18 by a majority of nine votes. Two days later, Wilson declared that "the deliberate and calculated decision of the Conservative Party" to defeat the Order made impossible a continuation of all-party talks on Lords reform.

Wilson added that the Government would proceed with its own "comprehensive and radical" measure. But this was to have no greater success. In December 1968 a bill was introduced limiting hereditary membership and insuring that the Government of the day would have a working majority; no party would be able to control the Lords beyond the time of their control of the Commons. A complicated provision created two tiers of membership, one *voting* (hereditary peers of first creation and all life peers who regularly attended) and the other *non-voting* (the hereditary peers by succession). The newly constituted chamber would be able to delay an ordinary public bill for but six months. Though this measure by February had gone successfully through the second reading in the Lords (251–56) and through the Commons (285–136), it was increasingly evident that the details and their implications hopelessly divided the membership of each party. Labor back-benchers led by Michael Foot and Conservative back-benchers led by Enoch Powell (a strange combination) opposed the measure, on the grounds that it was being imposed upon them, and charged that it gave party leadership too much additional control over patronage. Also, there were differences over the timing— Conservatives hoped to postpone activation of any such legislation until after the next election. All these matters were aired in the committee stage, which, by nature of the bill, was in the Committee of the Whole House. For some eleven days, including "ghastly nights," the debate extended, much of it mere filibustering with little attention to serious discussion. Finally, on April 17, 1969 the prime minister announced that in order to make way for the Industrial Relations Bill the Government would not proceed further with the Parliament Bill. Its passage, he said, was doubtful, and the outcome of efforts at Lords reform a failure.

"The Battle of Downing Street"

Wilson's words in June 1968, already quoted, could not conceal the fact that Government policy on Lords reform had been defeated not by the Conservatives but by Labor and the trade unions. We reach much the same conclusion as we proceed with the fortunes of the Industrial Relations Bill in 1969.

At a meeting of the Parliamentary Labor Party (the Labor M.P.s) on April 17, Wilson dwelt on this "essential bill. Essential to our economic recovery. Essential to the balance of payments. Essential to full employment. It is an essential component of ensuring the economic success of the Government .... essential to its continuance in office. There can be no going back." Wilson quite properly in his own account protests that this oft-quoted passage omits his prior reference to his repeated invitation to the unions to provide their own remedy for unofficial strikes. At another party meeting a few days later, Mrs. Castle, according to Wilson, declared that it was the shadow of this bill which was making the T.U.C. recognize the problem and that if it were dropped "the T.U.C. would go back to sleep for five years more."

Nonetheless, opposition within the party and the labor community continued to mount. On May 6, Douglas Houghton, chairman of the Parliamentary Party, had warned that back-bench support for the Industrial Relations Bill should not be taken for granted. He declared:

"Ministers must not fall into the error of believing that their determination and resolve to force things through the party and the House is either desirable or possible.

The decisive factor, it would seem, was the attitude and the action of the Trades Union Congress. Wilson reiterated, in consultation with its officials and in an interview over the B.B.C., that the Government would proceed with the Industrial Relations Bill unless the T.U.C. came forward with an acceptable alternate proposal for enforcing discipline and order within the trade union movement. Early in June the Congress of the T.U.C. met at Croydon in special conference session—the second such in a hundred years—and approved the Council's proposals in their *Programme for Action*. This gave the General Council power to intervene in unions where there were unofficial strikes. But it was clear that the role of the T.U.C. and its Council would be merely that of assisting settlement of unofficial strikes, not of imposing sanctions. On the other hand, the special Congress voted overwhelmingly against the Government bill; on the statutory penal clauses (imposing financial penalties) the vote was 359,000 in favor and 8,252,000 opposed. And Scanlon of the Engineers warned of the consequences of any such legislation.

Wilson and Mrs. Castle found the *Programme for Action* unacceptable as an alternative to their bill, which they seemed determined to legislate. But now not for long. The position of the T.U.C. strengthened the opposition of the Parliamentary Labor Party to the bill. Indeed, it became highly doubtful that the measure would receive Commons' approval. And the Cabinet, itself, by this time, or a majority of it, did not wish to proceed. Wilson and Mrs. Castle gave way on the basis of a broad statement of intent from the Council of the T.U.C. that it would establish a committee to investigate unofficial strikes and, at its discretion, press the unions to order a return to work.

On June 18 Wilson announced to the Commons this agreement. "Surrender" declared the headlines in the *Daily Express* and the *Daily Mail*. Naturally Wilson himself placed the best possible interpretation on the outcome. He told the nation of the "solemn and binding undertaking unanimously agreed by the whole General Council of the T.U.C." But even in Wilson's own "personal record" in *The Labour Government (1964–1970)* the episode does not emerge as an achievement. He writes: "The issues in ... *In Place of Strife* had therefore been settled by a decision to introduce legislation to enact the positive provisions of the Donovan Report, and by our decision of 18th June to follow Donovan in not proceeding with punitive legislation."

In truth, the Government had failed in its endeavor to curb, by penal sanctions, the trade unions, and had also abandoned, at least for a time, its prices and incomes policy. However, neither the Labor Government nor the Labor Party fell apart. While, in long-range terms, the economy usually changes slowly, observable changes, in detail large or small, usually have immediate effects politically. Now, in midsummer 1969, the devaluation of 1967 began to pay off. A favorable balance of payments in foreign trade was announced for August and continued the remainder of the year. With autumn all indicators showed a steady, if slow, improvement in the standing of the Government with the public. The polls showed that the Conservative lead had dropped sharply, and in by-elections Labor lost no more seats. It would seem that, in part at any rate, this reflected a new respect among the middle classes and the business community generally for Harold Wilson's courage in attacking head-on the major problem of wildcat strikes.

And the outcome of the Industrial Relations Bill had not split wide open the labor world, as might well have happened with an attempt to force the measure through Parliament. Quite naturally, Wilson's address in September at the annual meeting of the Trades Union Congress, in which he appealed for continued wage restraint and implementation of the Council pledge, was received either in silence or with shouts of protest. And by a close vote the Congress opposed a renewal of the Prices and Incomes Act. Nevertheless, a resolution asserting the "necessity" of continued support of the Labor Party by the Congress was carried unanimously.

At the Labor Party Conference a month later, there was essential unity. Jenkins was optimistic about a growth in the economy of 3 to 4 percent and about the decline in unemployment. He called for a continuation of tough measures in taxation and met no challenge when he suggested heavier indirect taxation. But reaffirmation of an incomes policy in a party document *Agenda for a Generation* brought a strong protest vote from Scanlon's Engineers and from Jones's Transport and General Workers' Union. Nonetheless, at the end of the year the Government renewed its powers to delay wage increases; but even on this limited measure, 28 members abstained from the division in the Commons. Toward the end of the year Wilson reopened the Common Market issue; but on this matter the party was still sharply divided, and it was clear that no action would come until after another general election.

General Election, June 1970

By law, an election for members of Parliament was not required until the spring of 1971. And as 1969 moved toward its close, there was little indication that Wilson would choose an early date. Certainly he and his Cabinet had suffered a great decline in national confidence since those days in 1964 when they had taken office so confidently.

Year after year, the same problems loomed—the unfortunate state of the economy, the unfavorable balance of payments only briefly arrested, rising taxation, increasing unemployment, industrial disorder, stalemate in Rhodesia—with no solutions. Trade union cooperation in solving industrial problems had been limited and the trade unions were still the most important component of the Labor Party. During the years 1964–69, production had increased less than one-half of the 25 percent which the Government had predicted. Since 1945, Britain's economy had expanded only about one-half that of other industrial countries. The rise of the standard of living had been "minimal," well below that of the chief nations in the Common Market. And now in 1968–69 there was a sharp rise in prices, obviously connected with sharp wage increases demanded by labor and with the disorder in the trade union world. Wilfred Beckerman, an economist at the University of London, in his *The Labour Government's Economic Record, 1964–1970* (1972) declared that that record "cannot be termed anything but disappointing." To him and to many other economists, the major mistake was in delaying devaluation so long. In 1966 the Government was virtually guaranteed five years of power. Just who was responsible for delaying devaluation? This is doubtless a matter on which historians, as evidence accumulates, will dwell in the future.

Harold Wilson had been both a surprise and a disappointment. It was widely expected that as prime minister he would continue his association with left-wing elements in the party and would thus be prompt in writing off commitments abroad, would scale down appropriations for nuclear power and perhaps end the independent nuclear deterrent, and would extend the welfare state and the areas of nationalization. In fact, he often proved to be compromising, indecisive, inconsistent with previous attitudes and policies, chary of troublesome issues. Often he seemed to have little long-range purpose except to stay in office. But he was "no man of straw." In his leadership of the Cabinet and his control of the Commons, as well as his approach to the public, he proved to be a consummate politician. At a Labor Party Conference in 1963 he had said that "a lot of politics is presentation and what isn't is timing." And he practiced what he preached. This will appear in the seventies, for his career is far from over.

Achievements of the Labor Government. This analysis should not suggest that the Wilson Government in these years was without achievement. The Civil Service was subjected to its first comprehensive examination in well over a century. The Fulton report (June 1968) brought to light the artificial and often stultifying distinctions between the administrative, the executive, and the clerical grades in the service and deplored the absence of professionalism. A new Civil Service Department was created and steps taken toward the establishment a few years later of a Civil Service training college. In another area, education, the concept of the comprehensive school was extended in theory and practice, and the proportion of the gross national product assigned to education was increased. And there was legislation liberalizing social behavior: concerning homosexuality, abortion, divorce, Sunday entertainment, and censorship. Labor carried out its pledge (1966) to renationalize steel. In 1967, for the second time, ninety percent of the industry was brought together under the National Steel Corporation, which was three times as large as the next largest producer on the continent. Lord Melchett, a Conservative peer, was appointed chairman.

Barbara Castle's notable Transport Act of 1968 reflected courage and intelligence in dealing with financial deficits and inefficiency in the railway and road haulage. For the nationalized railways this legislation wiped out financial losses which had piled up from the past, transferred unremunerative traffic to road haulage, and provided compensation for services which were still socially desirable though unremunerative. The goal for British Railways was operation without deficits by 1974. Also, the Transport Act completely transformed road haulage in the endeavor to make maximum use of railways in handling freight previously carried on congested highways, to eliminate competition between the railways and road haulage, and, in general to render road haulage safer, more efficient, and more economical.

Such matters, important as they were, probably stirred the electorate, one way or another, very little. The public was much more conscious of the measures taken by the Government in Northern Ireland. In the background were centuries of animosity and discontent between Catholics and Protestants. Since 1922 Northern Ireland had been self-governing in domestic affairs, with its own Parliament and its own Cabinet, though responsibility for general law and order remained with the Government in Westminster. Now the issues were the claims to equality by the Catholic minority represented in the Catholic Civil Rights Movement— there had indeed been discrimination in such matters as assignment of housing and in employment. The Catholic position, in its extreme form, by mid 1969 was represented by Bernadette Devlin, a twenty-one-year-old student; in a by-election for a seat in the Parliament at Westminster she brought together various dissident groups and defeated the Ulster Unionist candidate. Her maiden speech in the Commons (April 22) was an impassioned attack on the policy of the Ulster government. On the other hand, the Protestant Unionist position in its extreme form was represented by the Rev. Ian Paisley, who led a revolt within the Unionist

Party against the moderate prime minister, Captain Terence O'Neill, who was striving for accommodation with the Catholics. In an effort to strengthen the moderate cause, O'Neill called for a general election for the Irish Parliament. O'Neill himself was almost defeated by Paisley, running as an independent, and he resigned. Control seemed to have passed to the militants on both sides, and this was soon manifested in sporadic riots and demonstrations which by August had become more organized and frequent in Londonderry and Belfast, with bomb attacks, street fighting, and houses burned by the hundreds.

The Government at Westminster won respect for its prompt, restrained, and apparently successful efforts at restoring order. Wilson, in response to the appeal from the new prime minister, Major James Chichester-Clark, sent regular army troops into Belfast. It was agreed that the existing reserve security forces (largely Protestant), known as the "B-Specials," were to be phased out. And the Royal Ulster Constabulary was to be replaced by a civilian police force, unarmed. It was understood that the Ulster Government would move promptly toward granting full civil liberties to Catholics. These matters were discussed at length with both sides by Callaghan, the home secretary, in a visit to Belfast in late August. In his delicate role as adviser, he was reassuring in London as well as in Belfast. But this chapter in Irish history had just opened.

The Irish situation was the exception—on most fronts the rating of Labor was uncertain. But so was that of the Conservatives. The critics of Wilson by no means flocked to the standard of Heath. A party in Opposition usually has more trouble preserving unity of purpose than one in office. And for Heath, who had never headed a Government, it was particularly difficult to establish himself in the party and with the public. Perhaps the most ominous threat still came from Enoch Powell. Support for him had increased, particularly from the business community. As chances of an early election increased, he came more and more to the fore. On immigration he now went even further than in 1968. In an address January 17, 1970, he declared that Britain faced the prospect of a fifth or a fourth of the population in certain areas being "replaced by distinctive communities of alien origin." Public funds, he said, should be spent not in social services for these immigrants but on their repatriation in their countries of origin. He called for open debate on these matters in the party and in the Commons. The very next day, after Powell's speech, Heath, in a B.B.C. interview, declared that Powell's words were "an example of man's inhumanity to man which is absolutely intolerable in a Christian civilized society."

Very likely Heath's peace of mind improved at the end of the month when the shadow cabinet met at the Selsdon Park Hotel in Surrey for a weekend discussion of party policy and strategy. It was agreed that the party should support increased indirect taxation (and, accordingly, reduced taxation on incomes) and reform of the legal position of the trade unions, should favor restriction on immigration, tighten laws against public demonstrations, and, most important of all, strengthen the agencies for the enforcement of law and order. Heath promptly reported to the nation over the B.B.C. Wilson, for his part, in his public addresses, delineated at length what he referred to as "the Selsdon Man" who was "designing a system of society for the ruthless and the pushing, the uncaring." And again: "This is not just a lurch to the right, it is an atavistic desire to reverse the course of 25 years of social revolution." The campaign had obviously begun.

The Poll. The first of many surprises in the 1970 election was that it came so soon. The explanation very likely is in the steadily improving political and economic climate for Labor. In February 1970 Britain enjoyed a favorable balance of trade for the sixth successive month, "a period such as we have not had in years," said Jenkins while in the United States. Tensions between the party and the trade union world were relaxing. There had been no effective prices and incomes controls since April 1969, and now in 1970 wages were rising faster than prices. In the public sector, wage settlements in January and February averaged a 12 percent increase. A bill requiring local school authorities to plan ahead in the development of the comprehensive school to replace the grammar school and the technical school attracted favorable attention from other than confirmed Conservatives on this issue. Altogether, from public opinion polls and from local elections it was evident that the big lead so long enjoyed by the Conservatives was gradually diminishing. Finally, at the end of April a poll favored Labor for the first time in three years. On May 12 a Gallup Poll indicated a 7 percent lead for Labor. Wilson apparently decided that he had more chance of victory immediately than if he delayed until autumn. On May 18, he announced a General Election for June 18.

There was agreement on one matter—the weather. It was the finest June in many years, with scarcely any rain during the weeks of the campaign. Otherwise it was a rather dull campaign. The manifestoes— the Conservative *A Better Tomorrow,* Labor's *Now Britain's Strong: Let's Make Her Great to Live In,* and the Liberal Party's *What a Life* attracted little attention. The Conservative document made for the best reading. The Liberal campaign got nowhere. Jo Grimond had hoped for an enlarged role for his party after Labor's victory in 1964. Discouraged, he resigned party leadership in 1967 and was succeeded by Jeremy Thorpe, whose energetic campaign in 1970 furthered the cause only in his own constituency, North Devon.

The election was really a personal contest between Wilson and Heath. Wilson mingled with the crowds, with such apparent success that Heath turned to the same technique, but much less successfully. Press conferences were frequent, with Wilson generally considered the more effective. And his party closed ranks behind him. For Heath there was always the possibility of trouble from Enoch Powell. His fiery speeches to "halt immigration now" were ignored by Heath as much as possible. At the time, it was widely concluded that Powell anticipated a Conservative defeat and was grooming himself for a bid for party leadership. Very likely in the campaign, Powell's role, though embarrassing, did Heath's cause little harm.

Public interest during the campaign was dominated by public opinion polls; they had come a long way since 1945 when there was but a single poll. Now there were half a dozen, with four of them published regularly in national newspapers. Results always made headlines. Confidence in their infallibility had developed. What reason was there to believe that they would be wrong in the election of 1970? When Wilson announced the election on May 18, all the polls indicated a Labor victory, with the margin over the Conservatives steadily growing. One poll indicated a Labor margin in the Commons of 70. During the last ten days, however, there was a wide divergence in the samples published. But to the end, most of the polls indicated a clear-cut Labor victory.

The result? The Government and the pollsters were all "demolished in ten minutes," said the *Economist* for June 27. The very first result, that from Guildford, showed a 6 percent swing to the Conservatives; minutes later there was a similar story from Cheltenham; soon a 9 percent shift was reported from the two Wolverhampton constituencies. The outcome was clear. Here it stands in relation to 1966:

	1966		1970	
	M.P.s	Popular vote	M.P.s	Popular vote
Labor	363	47.9%	287	43 %
Conservative	253	41.9%	330	46.4%
Liberal	12	8.5%	6	7.4%

The overall average swing to the Conservatives was 4.8 percent. Eighty-eight seats changed hands, leaving the Conservatives with a majority of 31 over all other parties. The lowest turnout (72 percent) of the electorate since the war hurt Labor the most. As to the Liberals, the analysts conclude that their candidacies did not seriously affect the fortunes of either of the major parties.

How to explain the Conservative victory? Developments during the last few days of the campaign may have contributed. On June 15 the newspapers carried the report of the first deficit in the balance of payments in nine months. Also, remarks during the campaign of Lord Cromer, Governor of the Bank of England from 1961–66, were given wide currency. On June 1 over a B.B.C program, *Panorama,* he declared: "There is no question that any government that comes into power is going to find a much more difficult financial position than the new government found in 1964." And a Labor sympathizer, Lord Kearton, who appeared on the same program, agreed. Undoubtedly there was a swing back to the Conservatives the last few days of the campaign. David Butler and Michael Pinto-Duschinsky, in their authoritative account of the election, conclude that it "provided one of the rare examples of an election that may have been decided by what happened during the campaign." But, as has often been observed, the wonder is not that the Labor Party lost, but rather, in view of its previous record, that it came so close to victory.

13 The Perils of Inflation

David McKie and
Chris Cook, eds.
*The Decade of
Disillusion:
British Politics in
the Sixties* (1972),
p. 6

The seventies start with a great deal less optimism, a great
deal more scepticism and suspicion, than did the sixties.
Perhaps, for that reason they are unlikely to end in so much
disappointment.

David Marquand
Sunday Times,
26 October 1975,
as quoted in
*Annual Register:
World Events in
1975* (1976), p. 5

No honest politician who bothers to listen to what his
constituents tell him, can seriously deny that the party
system of this country is now in greater disrepute than it
has been for decades.

Roy Jenkins
*Afternoon on the
Potomac?* (1972),
p. 23

Britain always has been primarily a European rather than
an imperial power. There is one school of thought that sees
us as having started in Europe and being now back on our
paternal doorstep again but after an imperial excursion
lasting for most of the past three centuries. In fact we have
never been away from Europe.

1970–1977

In examining British politics and economics in the final period of our survey, the historian becomes a reporter. Our information now comes largely from government reports, the proceedings of Parliament, and news articles and commentary in the daily and weekly press. Our narrative is surely tentative, lacking in objectivity, limited in perspective, and hesitant in prognostication. But it may have one merit; it probably well represents the material that came to the attention of an Englishman not himself actively engaged either in politics or industry, but anxious to keep well informed and concerned about the future of his land.

The Heath Administration 1970–74

After his defeat in the election of June 18, 1970, Harold Wilson went off to write, at considerable length, his own version of the "burdens of power," and Edward Heath moved into No. 10 Downing Street. His Cabinet appointments startled no one—familiar names in the positions of great responsibility. Iain Macleod went to the Exchequer, Sir Alec Douglas-Home to the Foreign Office, and Reginald Maulding to the Home Office. One selection was unexpected; Anthony Barber, minister of Health back in 1963–64, was appointed chancellor of

545

the Duchy of Lancaster and chief British representative in Common Market negotiations. But not for long: a month later he went to the Exchequer upon the sudden death of MacLeod, a very great loss, for he was the most experienced member of the new Government and was generally respected. Geoffrey Rippon replaced Barber as responsible for Common Market negotiations. Later, in October, came a thorough reorganization of administration agencies, presumably in the interests of efficiency, including a new Central Policy Review Staff to provide independent examination of departmental proposals.

Heath, himself, as the victor in the election, was a bit of a surprise. He capitalized on this mood and declared that his victory constituted a challenge. "We were returned to office to change the course and the history of this nation, nothing else. And it is this new course which the Government is now shaping," he told the Conservative Party Conference in October.

"An Ever Narrowing Base"

It may be said at the outset, as we begin the analysis of this administration, that the essential problems were domestic. Indeed, by this time the story of British external relations has become somewhat tiresome and uninspiring. The refrain is ever the same—an imperial past has been left behind; would there be a European future? A white paper in 1971 speaks of "an ever narrowing base." To be sure, this Conservative Government decided to keep something of a military presence east of Suez, along with Australia and New Zealand for the security of Malaysia and Singapore. And in the ever-changing situation in the Persian Gulf, treaties of friendship were made with the new Union of Arab Emirates, with some military personnel on loan for training local defense forces.

But these are mere details. The collective political role of the Commonwealth had ceased to have meaning. In 1971, at the meeting of Commonwealth prime ministers at Singapore, a formal declaration referred to the Commonwealth as "a voluntary association of independent sovereign states." With entrance into the Common Market, Britain renounced any special role in the Commonwealth. In 1971, the U.K. prime minister inquired: Are member nations "willing to make the effort to give a new relevance to this association?" The question mark remains. Furthermore, one reads into the conference in Bermuda in December 1971 between Prime Minister Heath and President Nixon a recognition that "the special relation" between their two lands had lost significance. Consultation would, of course, continue but not necessarily agreement. To all appearances, domestic problems had crowded out Britain's concern for her world role.

"Stagflation"

The story of domestic policy during the four years of
the Heath administration is tortuous and often bewildering. The problems, and the response of the Government as well, were perplexing; there
were many turnabouts in policy both by the Government and by the
Opposition. The nation, itself, we might almost say, kept changing its
mind.

By 1970, Britain's economic plight, affecting every individual in the
land, added up to *inflation*. This was evident in the last years of the
Wilson administration; it would continue year in and year out for as far
ahead as one could see. The unique feature of Britain's problem, however, was that wages were rising faster than prices. In the summer of
1970 the minister for Employment and Productivity had lectured the
leaders of the T.U.C. on this point: since the first of the year, wages had
risen at the rate of 12 percent per year, prices 6 percent, and production
less than 2 percent. The figures may have been approximate but the
lesson was clear.

Heath himself seemed the personification of energy and action. He
would reform the tax structure; he would have no truck with a statutory
incomes policy; rather, he would get to the heart of the matter—reform
industrial relations, that is, reform trade unions; he would do his utmost
to get Britain into the Common Market. The economy, he was convinced, would expand in an atmosphere of free enterprise. This last
suggestion raised many questions. Would there be some denationalization—coal, steel, railways, electricity, gas? Would sectors of certain
nationalized industries, if making profits, be resold to private hands?

But just as Heath at the start talked of the condition of Britain in broad
terms, so his panaceas, inevitably, were at first generalities. He sought to
create an atmosphere favorable to stimulating the country's productivity;
so he would reduce public spending, cut taxes, stimulate investment and
industrial expansion. But such steps are not taken overnight. White papers outlined the future, but no significant change came until the spring of
1971. Then taxes were slashed by £546 million, with simplification and
reduction of income taxes and with reform of corporation taxes so as to
free savings and profits for industrial investment. In July, the chancellor
of the Exchequer went further. Tax reductions were now extended to
purchase taxes and controls were reduced or lightened on credit and
installment buying. Barber hoped to stimulate the economy but also to
hold inflation to a 5 percent annual rate; he had persuaded industrial
leaders to agree on a 5 percent ceiling on price rises in the forthcoming
year. These measures were not without some favorable results. But the
economic revival was very modest; for one thing, much of the additional

consumption had been satisfied from goods already in stock. Price rises, though moderating the last six months of the year, never fell below the 6 percent annual rate. For the entire year, 1971, the consumer price index rose about 8 percent. The spiral of wages/cost-of-production/prices was at work. "Stagflation"—prices rising faster than demand—was at hand.

But Heath's problems had just begun. By 1971 circumstances had concentrated attention on another area—that of industrial relations. Inflationary wage demands, supported by strikes, stoppages, and slow-downs, seemed to most people to be at the heart of the matter. In 1970 British industry chalked up the worst record in strikes and stoppages since 1926. And 1971 produced a similar record; while, to be sure, the number of stoppages decreased, the total number of working days lost rose even higher. Early in the year the postal workers demanded increases of 15 to 20 percent. When offered 8 percent, they struck for six weeks, finally settling for about 9 percent. Curiously enough, the ingenuity of the British people, so often lacking in formal negotiations, came to the rescue; improvisation, cooperation, and good will made the result for the English people merely an inconvenience.

In the private sector, strikes of one kind or another continued through most of the year. In April demands of the locomotive engineers and firemen for a 15 to 25 percent increase in wages brought "a go-slow policy" for some ten days, completely disrupting railroad traffic and operations. The settlement by the British Railways Board with a 9.5 percent increase was regarded as a victory for the Government, which expressed disappointment that private management had not displayed equal firmness. On the other hand, Government officials were outraged at the two months halt in operations at the Ford plants, where the strike was finally ended with a 33 percent raise in wages over a two-year period. But the astonishing development was the purchase by the Government of the aero-engine division of Rolls Royce, Ltd., to prevent its financial crash. What would happen next?—a Conservative Government had nationalized a division of Rolls Royce, "the jewel of private enterprise," in the words of the *Annual Register*. Later in the year came other strikes in protest against the Industrial Relations Act and to this we now turn.

Industrial Relations Act

From its first days the Heath Government knew that some action on trade unions was essential and inevitable. The Conservative Manifesto in 1970 and the Queen's Speech opening the new Parliament both pledged action where Labor had failed. On December 3 was published the Industrial Relations Bill; its purpose was to define the obligations of trade unions, particularly in relation to unofficial strikes.

Wage agreements arrived at by collective bargaining were to be enforced by law, and a National Industrial Relations Court was created to deal with infractions. That court was also empowered to order a compulsory sixty-day "cooling-off period" in a threatened strike if a crisis developed and to order a secret ballot in a union where a strike loomed. The "closed shop" was barred. Infractions of this law made unions liable to damages up to £100,000.

Well before this bill became law came strikes in protest. For now the atmosphere of trade unionism had changed from the days of the Labor Government and was not only suspicious of statutory controls but positively opposed. Officials of the T.U.C. ceased to be cooperative. Newspaper advertisements paid for by the trade unions declaimed: "If it is a crime to fight for a better life we're guilty." There was a series of one-day strikes to demonstrate opposition. And on February 21, 1971, close to 100,000 trade union members, according to the estimate, marched from Hyde Park down to Trafalgar Square in protest. Controversy also raged in the Commons and the Lords. Nearly sixty days of parliamentary time (some 450 hours) were required to pass the bill through the legislative process. In March 1971 it was approved by the Commons after closure had ended debate. On August 5 it became part of the law of the land. The comment of the general secretary of the T.U.C. was: "The dust will not settle on this issue until the Act is repealed."

The Industrial Relations Act was activated by stages with full implementation in February 1972. Some of its provisions reflected reasoned detachment; a Code of Industrial Relations drafted by the secretary of state for Employment placed responsibility for harmonious relations of labor and staff on management and emphasized voluntarism in collective bargaining. Much more controversial was the National Industrial Relations Court, which began operations December 1, 1971, with power to adjudicate disputes between management and unions and to enforce the strike ballot and the "cooling-off period" before strikes.

At first sight, the provision for registration of all trade unions with the Government seemed innocuous. But as it happened, this requirement provided the initial impetus to opposition. Trade union leaders advised member unions of the T.U.C. to ignore this requirement, for to register would indicate acceptance and even approval of the statute. Leadership of the opposition was provided, not so much by the Council of the T.U.C., as by the militants—shop stewards and officials in the unions themselves. A major question arose—to what extent is a union responsible for the actions of its members? An important test case, which reflected the general atmosphere, was a dispute in April 1972 over wage demands of 200,000 railway workers. They sought a 16 percent increase; the Railway Board offered 12.5 percent; thereupon the union called for a "work to rule" procedure which meant following to the letter every detail in the regulations and no overtime. The result: in the Greater London area with its complex commuter schedules there was utter confusion. On application of the Government, the National Industrial Relations Court ordered a secret ballot among trade union members on the issues at stake. The Government had expected acceptance of the Board's offer by the rank and file, but the vote was 6 to 1 for further pressure from the union for its demands. Eventually, in June, the dispute was settled on terms more favorable to the workers than the original offer.

Other strikes, normal and legal in character, reflected the bitter feelings of other workers. From January 9 to February 23, 1972, 280,000 coal miners were on strike for wage demands (originally made the previous July). At the outset, some workers sought a wage increase of as much as 47 percent. The Coal Board had first offered 12 percent, with a productivity bonus added. Negotiations stalled with the miners demanding an average increase of 25 percent and the Board proffering 15 percent. The miners were "a just case for special treatment," ruled the special Court of Inquiry presided over by a Lord of Appeal, Lord Wilberforce, and public opinion seemed to echo this sentiment. Final settlement increased the average wage increase by about 20 percent. The Government had been forced to back down; members of the Cabinet were humiliated. This ruling was a blow to Heath's attack on inflation, for he had urged a general ceiling of 8 percent on wage increases. The miners' success led to aggressive demands from engineers, builders, and teachers.

A crisis was developing. Prices were rising—with an inflation rate of 7 to 8 percent a year—and wages rising faster. During the first six months of 1972 the rate of growth of the gross national product was but 1 percent. Unemployment, at 900,000, stood at the highest figure since the thirties; the balance of trade, internationally, showed an ever-increasing deficit. And experts in international exchange emphasized the plight of the pound and the tensions in the exchange market. In June the Government announced that the pound would be "floated" rather than held to a fixed parity and its trading rate at once dropped from $2.61 to $2.42. A leading banker is quoted as saying: "The market is telling the Government that if it doesn't solve the inflation problem, the economy is going to hell."

Another Prices and Incomes Policy. All these factors contributed to the decision of Heath and his ministers that a formal prices and incomes policy was essential—this despite the fact that in 1970 they had eschewed just such action. They hoped they could work out a voluntary policy. As early as March 1972 senior members of the Cabinet had met with representatives of industry and with the Council of the T.U.C. to discuss possible joint action. These talks were continued during the summer with a determined effort at agreement in October and November. But the results were never more than pious hopes and generalities. Indeed, much of the time was spent discussing the fate of the Industrial Relations Act. Heath's proposals for holding the line on both prices and incomes brought demands from trade union leaders of extension of price control to food and rent and less restraint on wage advances.

Government leaders finally concluded that there was no alternative to independent state action through statutory control. The 1970 Conservative manifesto had given an unqualified "no" to statutory controls. Heath himself had spoken of incomes and price controls as "statism" and as "immoral." Now (November 6) he announced to the Commons an immediate freeze for ninety days of all prices, incomes, rents, and dividends—this to be enforced by legislation which would be at once enacted, hopefully with the cooperation of trade unionism. These moves brought smiles to the faces of the Opposition and frowns to many a Conservative, some of the latter group insisting that party policy had been deserted. A white paper in January 1973 outlined the second phase with a Program for Controlling Inflation. This became operative in April with a Pay Board to supervise wage increases and a Price Commission to control prices. Annual wage increases would be limited to £1 per week plus 4 percent (with a maximum of £250). Dividend increases were to be kept at 5 percent per year. A code of rules and procedures, approved by Parliament, would guide those boards which were empowered to impose fines on recalcitrant individuals and unions.

The Common Market

This policy of statutory controls was being implemented at about the same time that Britain was admitted to the European Economic Community, now usually referred to as the European Community. Formal entry came January 1, 1973—a successful conclusion to long negotiations on the continent and to controversy at home extending for two years and a half—the achievement for which the Heath Government is most likely to be remembered. In the midst of it all, on January 1, 1971, the *Economist* declared that the decision on this matter "may set the course of British history for the rest of the century."

Shortly after the election of June 1970, negotiations began at Luxembourg in accordance with arrangements already made by the outgoing Labor Government. The first hurdle was the problem of working out terms of entry which would be acceptable to France and others of the Six. This involved enormous detail concerning the ground rules for a transitional period of five years, the contribution of the United Kingdom to the Common Market budget, and decision about such highly important matters as New Zealand's dairy products and Commonwealth sugar. In the negotiations at Brussels from October 1970 to May 1971, the chief British representative, Sir Geoffrey Rippon, rendered distinguished service. His greatest achievement, perhaps, was his success in reaching agreement on the budget, for, as first encountered, there was a wide gap between the proposals of the two sides. The climax of this phase was a critical meeting between Heath and Georges Pompidou, the French president, in May in the Elysée Palace in Paris. The result was a warm and unqualified endorsement by Pompidou of Britain's prospective membership. And shortly afterward, in Luxembourg, Rippon's entrance into the chamber where the ministers of the Six were convening was greeted with spontaneous applause.

On these deliberations and their outcome Heath reported to the Commons with the utmost confidence. But his white paper setting forth, much like an election campaign document, the arguments, political and economic, for British entry, was the signal for protracted debate in Parliament and throughout the land. Polls indicated that something like sixty percent of the British people at this time were opposed to British membership in the Common Market; chief concerns were the future of British institutions and possible rise in food costs. The debate in the Commons, July 21–26, "expositive and explorative," brought into the open not only outright opposition but sharp divisions within the political parties.

It was this division within Labor which provided the most drama. In 1967, Wilson, as prime minister, was directing British application for membership in the Common Market. At that time he had declared: "The Government's purpose derives above all from our conviction that Europe is now faced with the great opportunity of a great move forward in political unity and that we can—and indeed we must—play our full part of it." Now, early in 1971, Wilson took an unequivocal stand against British entry: he referred to the Common Market as "a rule-ridden bureaucracy" and "an agricultural welfare complex." On the other hand, in May 1971, the *Manchester Guardian* carried a full-page advertisement, supporting British membership and signed by one hundred Labor M.P.s, including eight members of the Shadow Cabinet. There was a head-on collision at a one-day conference of constituency party and trade union representatives on July 17 and at a meeting of the Parliamentary Labor Party July 19. Wilson declared the Rippon terms unsatisfactory and unacceptable to the Labor Party. On the other hand, George Thomson, the negotiator in 1968, declared that at that time the Labor Party would have accepted the Rippon terms, and in this he was supported by Roy Jenkins and Michael Stewart (who had been foreign secretary in the

Wilson Cabinet). Lord George Brown made a similar statement in the Lords. As to Wilson's rejection, Jenkins declared: "I beg the party not to follow this recipe for disappointment and decline, but to face problems realistically and to lift its eyes beyond the narrow short term political considerations of the moment."

No doubt Wilson was striving for unity, for the labor movement, as distinct from the Labor Party, was overwhelmingly anti-Common Market. This included the two largest unions. The executive committee of the party, strongly representative of the trade unions, voted 15–7 against entry; and the Party Conference did likewise, in October, by a 5 to 1 margin. The annual meeting of the Trades Union Congress (in September) also rejected membership.

On the other hand, Heath had his party, or much the larger part of it, behind him; the annual Conference approved membership in the Common Market by an 8 to 1 vote. In October came the crucial division in the Commons, with Heath permitting a "free party vote." After six days of debate, on the whole of high quality, a motion to approve "the Government's decision of principle to join the European Community on the basis of the arrangements which have been negotiated" was carried 356–244; 69 Laborites, including Jenkins and Thomson, supported the motion despite the party decision to vote against it; some 20 other Labor members abstained from voting. At Dover, bonfires were lighted, visible across the Channel at Calais where other fires were lighted in return.

On January 22, 1972, Britain (represented by Heath, Douglas-Home, and Rippon) signed in Brussels the Treaty of Accession to the European Community. Denmark, Ireland, and Norway signed on the same occasion. It was calculated that the enlarged Community of Ten would have a population of 257,000,000 with (as reckoned by 1970 statistics) 26 percent of world exports and 27.4 percent of world imports.

For Britain one constitutional step remained—the passage by Parliament of "enabling legislation" which set forth principles of membership and details of the accommodation of British law with Community law. The critical vote in the Commons came February 17; it was a tense moment, for this was a strict party vote, with responsibility resting on the Government to find the necessary votes. This, they just managed to do, 309 to 301, with some 15 Conservatives (including Enoch Powell) voting no and five others abstaining. The efforts of the Labor Party to delay membership were defeated; in October, a summit meeting of the countries forming the enlarged Community established broad principles of cooperation in monetary policy. On January 1, 1973, the United Kingdom was indeed a member, and a variety of cultural events celebrated the occasion. But Wilson had pledged that his party on return to power would renegotiate the terms of membership and hold a popular referendum. In this position he was overwhelmingly supported by the annual Labor Party Conference in October 1973.

"A Matter of Economic Survival"

Entrance into the European Community inevitably called attention to Britain's badly lagging economy. During the previous ten years, economic growth had averaged but 3.2 percent a year, far behind the achievement of other member countries. The economic dilemma which developed in 1973 and which brought a general election early in 1974 indicate how tentative was official action and how fragile the results. The Government still regarded labor, particularly the trade unions, as the chief obstacle to greater productivity and a stable economy. While the unions accepted the first part of the Government program, that is, the ninety-day freeze period, with fairly good grace, they confronted Phase Two, with its guideline for wage increase and its Board to enforce them, with a series of strikes affecting public services. During February 1973 there were protest strikes (one day) of 250,000 civil servants, including air traffic officers, custom officials, and hospital workers. Gas workers staged a five-and-one-half-week strike. On May Day, some 600,000 industrial workers staged one day of "national protest and stoppage" against the price and incomes policy.

Here and there the unions showed moderation and order was generally maintained; as Victor Feather rightly pointed out, the press played up the exceptions. But there can be no doubt that the breach between trade unionism and public opinion was widening. Militancy in labor was growing and Communist influence, while not controlling, was growing in the miners union. In September 1973 the T.U.C. Conference demanded repeal of the Industrial Relations Act and condemned "the anti trade union attitude and class prejudice of the Tory Government." And Feather, who had taken the lead in the transformation of the T.U.C. into a political instrument, retired as its general secretary. He was made a life peer. He had been much respected by those who differed with him. Lionel Murray, Oxford graduate and Feather's deputy, succeeded him at the T.U.C.

Thus, the trade union world was possessed of some responsible leadership. And the economy itself was not without encouraging signs. Ironically, during the course of 1973, generally considered a year of disaster, indexes showed improvement with an increase in exports early in the year, a modest decline in unemployment, some growth in capital investment, expansion of certain industries. On March 6, 1973, Barber, chancellor of the Exchequer, was optimistic in his budget address. Growth of g.n.p. was now at 5 percent and he hoped this would continue. In June 1973 the Opinion Research Center reported that, for the first time in two years, the Conservatives led Labor in voter preference; the majority appeared to think that the Government had done well. It was with some confidence that Heath, on October 3, announced Phase Three of the prices and incomes policy. Controls on prices were to continue, with regulations concerning wages somewhat eased. But pay increases were to be held to 7 percent per year with a margin for flexibility of one percent and special provision for "threshold pay" to meet cost of living rises. The Government well knew the success of this phase depended on the coal miners; they would set the tone and style of other workers.

Early in 1973 the miners had voted against a strike for wage claims, and union leadership seemed sympathetic toward official policy, relatively generous toward the miners, whose wages were now again on a level with the best-paid segments of the working class. And in wage negotiations the National Coal Board made an offer somewhat better than the formal limits in Phase Three. But at this point (in October) the Israeli-Arab War touched off what was to prove to be the most serious economic crisis since the thirties. The immediate problem was the power shortage following hard on the sharp reduction of oil shipments from Arab countries, with rising prices and still higher predicted. Britain hoped to weather this situation, since 70 percent of her electrical power was produced by coal. But the case, or at least the position, of the miners was now strengthened. And the spirit of its leadership was more militant. The miners refused to work overtime unless their pay demands were met. Now the Coal Board offered a 13 percent increase and later 16 percent plus a high productivity bonus, and this despite the guidelines of Phase Three. It was in vain; the locomotive engineers and the electrical engineers joined the ban against overtimes.

A Three-Day Work Week. December was a month of bewilderment and apprehension for the ordinary citizen. William Whitelaw, with a reputation as a negotiator in Northern Ireland, was brought back to London as secretary of state for Employment. On December 13 Heath spoke to the Commons and to the country. He called for economies of 30 percent in electricity, saying that coal supplies at power plants had been cut 40 percent. Except for essential industries and services, there would be but five work days between December 17 and 31 and after that a three-day work week—this, of course, to conserve energy. In London, darkness in December arrives at 4 P.M. After that, if shops were open they were lighted by candles; TV programs ended at 10:30 P.M.; the Christmas tree in Trafalgar Square was only briefly lighted. At once some 750,000 registered for unemployment benefits; steel officials estimated a 50 percent decrease in production. In an address on December 11, the president of the Confederation of British Industry called the situation "a matter of economic survival" and predicted that the energy crisis would extend through most of 1974. Sir Fred Catherwood, who had been the head of the National Economic Development Office, feared that the next two months would bring millions of lay-offs among the working class.

An emergency session of Parliament, January 9–10, brought no solution. The gap between the wage demands of the miners and the offers to them widened, 30 or 40 percent as against 16.5 percent. The leaders of the T.U.C. pledged that if the miners case was solved satisfactorily, other unions would not use this as a basis for their own claims; the Government, perhaps concluding that the T.U.C. could not speak for individual unions, found this unsatisfactory. The critical development may have been the decision of the miners union to have a strike ballot. This, taken February 4, showed 81 percent of the miners favorable to a strike. Further meetings of Government officials with union leaders brought no progress.

A general election had seemed likely. This impasse with the miners seemed to make it inevitable, for Heath decided that the issue should go to the country. He telegraphed the Queen, who was on tour in Australia, and announced February 7 immediate dissolution of Parliament and a general election to be held February 28. By law no election was required until June of 1975. The situation—a conflict of interest between the state and the trade unions—brought the election in February 1974. Heath's Government had failed in its endeavor to reestablish economic stability for the successful operation of a free enterprise capitalistic society. To no avail had its policy been reversed—a change from support of a free economy bent on industrial expansion to state controls to combat inflation.

On the Plus Side

This sad, some would say humiliating, record pushed out of mind, almost out of sight, the very respectable showing of the Heath Government in other areas. We have already underlined one achievement, that is, the entrance into the Common Market. Then there was immigration, a thorny problem with mixed results inevitable. In 1970 the Conservatives had pledged controls. Legislation in 1971 required for entry a work permit for a specific job; after five years the immigrant might settle permanently; the concept of single Commonwealth citizenship was retained. And by order of the home secretary, the schedule of entry for Kenyan Asians, holders of British passports, was speeded up. But in 1972 proposals for immigration control that would be less favorable, comparatively speaking, for citizens of Canada, Australia, and New Zealand were defeated. In August 1972 a sudden announcement of expulsions from Uganda of all Asians not possessing Ugandan citizenship brought some 25,000 to Britain by the end of the year. While social problems mounted, immigration, as a political issue, declined in importance.

The Local Government Act of 1972 produced the most thorough reorganization of local government since 1888; the distinction between county and county borough was replaced by metropolitan and nonmetropolitan areas. Some historic names lost significance; Rutland became a district of Leicestershire, and Cumberland and Westmorland went together in Cumbria; new names appeared, such as Avon. Local authorities were reduced in number from 1800 to 500. This statute became effective in April 1974. At the same time, a major reorganization of the National Health Service became operative. An expensive and inefficient array of authorities was replaced, in England, by fourteen regional authorities which supervised day-to-day activities in ninety health areas. The Heath Government also reorganized taxation and social welfare benefits. With a single tax assessment based on income, taxes due would be offset by credits for family status, pensions, and other social security benefits. And it may also be noted that "Decimalization Day" came February 15, 1971, and went by without serious incident. Now there were 100 pence in the pound. Careful organization and planning, along with education, rebuked the prophets of confusion.

The End of Stormont. In Northern Ireland the Heath Government wrestled valiantly with the problem; that much at least can be said. There was a policy and there was action and to many the steps taken seemed reasonable and worthy of success. The goal, as set from Westminster, was a government by consent in Ulster in which a Catholic minority could live freely and peacefully alongside a Protestant majority. But the magnitude and complexities of the problem grew. During 1970–71, riots and incidents produced something like a state of civil war. In 1971, 173 persons, including the first British soldier, were listed as victims of violence. In August of that year the prime minister, Chichester-Clark, at odds with the Unionist Party in Belfast and with Westminster over security measures, resigned, to be succeeded by Brian Faulkner, considered by many the best hope for settlement of the Irish question within the framework of Stormont (the Parliament). A year later, Faulkner and Heath were themselves at an impasse over security measures; Heath wisehd to keep complete control in London. In what he referred to as the most difficult decision he ever had to make, Heath announced the suspension of the provincial government in Ulster, with the Westminster Government to assume full control. At the time this measure seemed to point straight to disaster—the end of Stormont was exactly what the Catholic faction in Ulster desired. But the new policy under William Whitelaw, secretary of state for Northern Ireland, had promise. It was high time, for 1972 proved the most tragic year since the troubles began; of 679 deaths by violence, 467 of them came in 1972.

Whitelaw pledged to the Protestants that Northern Ireland would remain associated with the United Kingdom as long as the majority desired it. In March 1973, a white paper outlined the immediate future: authority in a new assembly in which Catholics would be represented in proportion to their numbers, with Catholics sharing committee chairmanships. The new regime seemed to get off to a good start. A large vote of about 72 percent of the electorate, in which the extremists on either side counted for little, elected the new assembly of 78 members. On December 30, 1973, direct rule from London ended. The new Executive of 11 members representing all factions was sworn in to office. Tripartite talks at Sunningdale in Berkshire between representatives of the U.K., of the Republic of Ireland, and of Northern Ireland agreed on a "Council of Ireland" to deal with common problems. The role of the Council was not clear, though the Dublin Government for the first time agreed that the status of Northern Ireland was to be changed only with the consent of the majority. More important, immediately, was the role of the new Executive, which was unacceptable to all factions. And it was ominous that violence, associated with the IRA Provisionals, reached to London in the Christmas shopping season—sixty persons were injured. And by 1974 some 200 British soldiers had died in Northern Ireland.

Rhodesia. As to Rhodesia, next to Northern Ireland, Britain's most difficult external problem in these years, prospects for solution at the start of the administration brightened. In 1970 Ian Smith, the prime minister, announced his willingness to resume talks. These proceeded slowly but by the end of 1971 Smith accepted the Five Principles which Britain for some years had made the basis of any settlement of the question of Rhodesian independence which had been moot since Rhodesia's unilateral declaration in 1965. Were these principles, as a basis for a new constitution, acceptable to the Rhodesians? This was the next question. A test of opinion was conducted under the direction of Lord Pearce over a period of two months early in 1972. The result: the great majority of whites found the conditions acceptable; most of the Africans did not. "In our opinion," the Pearce Commission reported, "the people of Rhodesia as a whole do not regard the proposals as acceptable as a basis of independence." To lead those Africans who found the conditions unacceptable, the African National Council had been formed in December 1971. But now this agency gave impetus to the Africans' own formula for transition to majority rule in "Zimbabwe." They had no trust in Smith; too often had they heard him say there would be no majority rule in Rhodesia while he was alive. And there was a renewal of civil disobedience which had died down after 1965.

But the winds of change were still blowing. In 1973 Rhodesia closed the Zambesi River border with Zambia; this incident was to prove to be the beginning of controversy and possibly conflict between the independent black African states and the white-dominated Rhodesia and South Africa. Would the stance of Ian Smith change? That was the problem.

Two Elections in Eight Months

As we approach the general election of February 1974 we must note the chief development in the Labor Party since 1970; this was the growth in the role and power of the left. During 1970–71 something of a vacuum developed—Wilson was not an active leader of the Opposition. Indeed, the *New Statesman* in May 1972 called for his resignation. But the chief factor was the growth of a powerful group in the Commons led by Michael Foot (a constituency member of the party National Executive with the highest individual vote ever recorded) and by Anthony Wedgwood Benn, and the growing political role of the Trades Union Congress. Ideologically this leftist movement manifested itself, particularly, in renewed emphasis upon public ownership of industry with increased worker control. Nationalization, indeed, had come alive again as a political issue. One who had opposed Gaitskell on "Clause Four" of the party constitution, back in 1959–60, now declared: "Today Clause Four is not just a theory and an aspiration. It is the only basis on which we can put new inspiration and vigour into the economic life of Britain." At the Labor annual conference, resolutions for further nationalization, often in opposition to recommendations from the Executive Committee, became stronger and more comprehensive.

However, the sharpest division within the party came, as already noted, on the question of membership in the Common Market. At first, with the application for entry by the Heath Government, Wilson draggd his feet. Then he opposed entry on terms as negotiated. Once Britain was on her way to entry, Wilson did not advocate outright withdrawal but insisted that there must be a popular referendum or a general election on the matter, and further controversy developed. Finally, in late March of 1972, party leadership voted to support "a consultative referendum" on British membership. "I cannot accept this constant shifting of ground," declared Roy Jenkins, always an ardent advocate for the Common Market, and he resigned as deputy party leader; he was joined by seven others from the shadow cabinet, including Harold Lever, chief spokesman on power, and George Thomson, who had negotiated with the Common Market on behalf of Labor.

For Wilson it should be added that very likely he could not have united the party in 1974 behind support for membership in the Common Market. Any such attempt would have been disastrous for party relations with the trade unions. As it was, by 1973 Wilson was restoring unity; he had persuaded the Labor Annual Conference to oppose merely the Conservative terms of entry; he had reasserted his leadership in the shadow cabinet to which Jenkins returned. One of the peacemakers was James Callaghan, party chairman and shadow foreign secretary, who now appeared as the person most likely to succeed Wilson should he step down in the near future. Callaghan's chief rivals for leadership were Denis Healey and Roy Jenkins, though the latter had little support in the trade unions.

The Election of February 28, 1974

The election of February 28, 1974, has many elements of special interest. For one thing, the campaign was very short—exactly three weeks, no more, from the day of Heath's dissolution of the privious Parliament. And the brevity of the campaign adds to its dramatic quality, for most students of British politics agree that it was this campaign itself which determined the outcome, and to a much greater extent than in the election of 1970. During these three weeks, it is concluded, more voters changed their minds (perhaps some of them more than once) than in any other election of our time.

The explanation does not seem to lie in basic differences in ideology or policy between the two major parties, nor in the effort of each party to sharply distinguish itself from the other. To be sure, Labor since 1970 had come forward with a massive program of state ownership or control of industry, whereas the Conservatives had rediscovered the virtues of free enterprise. The differences over the Common Market have already been emphasized. But it is not likely that these matters changed many votes in February 1974. Undoubtedly of more interest to the voters were the reversals of policies in which both parties had indulged. The Conservatives had abruptly ended Stormont, had virtually nationalized Rolls Royce, had enlarged public expenditures, had pressed into operation statutory controls of prices and incomes—all this contrary to well-known party statements in 1970 and even later. On the other hand, by 1973, Labor, in direct opposition to its own performance 1964–70, now rejected the terms of entry into the E.E.C. and was stoutly opposed to controls by law of incomes and prices.

Confronted with such inconsistency, it appears that the voter in appraising the situation confronting Britain early in 1974 was influenced by the issues of the moment and voted accordingly. But more significant is the fact that for many voters "the issues of the moment" changed in the course of the brief campaign. As it opened, the initiative was in the hands of the Conservatives. The election, at the start, was a kind of referendum on the demands and position of the miners, who in a sense cooperated with the Conservatives by deciding to continue their strike regardless of the election. When Heath called for an election he broadcast to the nation:

> There are some people involved in the mining dispute who have made it clear that what they want to do is to bring down the elected Government—not just this Government but any Government. They have made it clear they want to change our whole democratic way of life . . . . The great majority of you are fed up to the teeth with them and with the disruption they cause . . . . It's time for you to speak with your votes. It's time for your voice to be heard—the voice of the moderate and reasonable people of Britain: the voice of the majority. It's time for you to say to the extremists, the militants and to the plain and simple misguided: we've had enough.

And the party manifesto, *Firm Action for a Fair Britain*, dwelt on the dangers of "extremism" and in its closing sections declared "Who Rules Britain?" was the dominant question.

> The choice before the nation today, as never before, is a choice between moderation and extremism . . . . Labour today faces the nation committed to a left wing programme more dangerous and more extreme than ever before in its history . . . the moderates in Labour's ranks have lost control and the real power in the Labour Party has been taken over, for the first time ever, by the extreme left wing. And this in turn has been made possible by the dominance of a small group of power-hungry trade union leaders, whose creature the Labour Party has now become.

Heath seemed to be much more successful, as a politician, than in previous campaigns. His arguments impressed the voters. At the end of the first week both the private polls conducted by the parties and most of the public polls which were published throughout the daily and Sunday press indicated a substantial Conservative lead of from 6 to 9 percent.

Wilson, consummate politician that he was, did not allow the campaign debate to linger long on ground chosen by the opposition. He promptly diverted attention to the broader question of the condition of the economy, in particular to rising inflation. The party manifesto *Let Us Work Together—Labour's way out of the Crisis* reflected radical thought in Labor's ranks. It aimed at "a fundamental and irreversible shift in the balance of *power* and *wealth* in favour of working people and their families." Its tone, not so much its content, which had been put together in 1973, controlled the atmosphere of the second phase of the.campaign. And Wilson was able to use the words "social contract" as a key phrase. To defeat inflation, he said, the Government and the trade unions must work together. And he made much of an informal understanding with the T.U.C. in February 1973, in which the T.U.C. had agreed to work for voluntary wage restraints in return for stricter price controls, larger pensions, and complete freedom of collective bargaining. Of course, the Industrial Relations Act must be repealed. This "social contract" was, according to Wilson, the symbol of harmony, reconciliation, and getting back to work.

As the campaign progressed, various circumstances seemed to conspire in Labor's favor. On February 15, the campaign but a week old, the retail price index published in the press indicated a rise of 20 percent in food prices the previous twelve months. Then there was controversy over a so-called mixup of figures in the Pay Board's consideration of the miners' wages demand—it was alleged that the figures used represented the miners to their disadvantage. Heath denied the allegation but later said this was the circumstance which most affected the outcome of the election. Now Enoch Powell intervened—emerging from silence on February 23—to announce that he was voting Labor, since the Conservatives, in his view, had retracted on so many of its commitments; also, he declared, the English people, not the Government, should decide on British entrance into the Common Market. Then it was officially announced that in January the trade gap between exports and imports reached £383 million—a new record monthly deficit. And two days before the poll, Campbell Adamson, the Director General of the Confederation of British Industry, at a business conference and not realizing that his remarks were being taped by the B.B.C., declared that the Industrial Relations Act had failed and should be repealed.

These factors, or some of them, seem to explain the shift in the opinion polls and the final outcome of the election. Just the day before the vote *The Times* reported that an Opinion Research Centre poll revealed a decided change in the mood of the voters. Now, the significant issue was not *who rules Britain?* but rather, *how to get Britain back to work* in order to defeat inflation, particularly the rising food prices. By that time the lead of the Conservatives had been reduced to 2 to 5 percent, hardly conclusive. Still the press predicted a Conservative victory in parliamentary seats and Labor leaders were not optimistic, since their last private poll still revealed a one percent Conservative lead.

The outcome closely reflected the results of the final opinion polls. In popular vote the Conservatives achieved 37.8 percent and Labor 37.1 percent. But in members of parliament Labor emerged with 301 to 296 for the Conservatives. Perhaps the most dramatic revelation of the poll was the extraordinary success of "third parties," which elected 38 M.P.s and polled 25 percent of the popular vote. Obviously there was considerable discontent with the major parties. A Liberal election poster read: "*You* can change the face of Britain; take power—VOTE LIBERAL." Early in the campaign Jeremy Thorpe, party leader, had declared,"We are out for power, and if we do not get that, what we want is a large enough vote in this country, backed by a large enough number of Liberals in the Commons, to have an influence which no Government can disregard." By-elections in 1973 had shown startling Liberal gains, and in the February 1974 campaign, the polls indicated a 20–25 percent Liberal vote. The actual result was 19.3 percent, though returning but 14 M.P.s. The Scottish National Party was more spectacular, electing 7 M.P.s with but 5 percent of the popular vote. More ominous to some was the firm establishment of the National Front as the fourth party, polling for its 54 candidates an average vote of 3.3 percent, with no victories. Born in February of 1967, in protest of the accommodation of Conservatives and Labor on immigration legislation, the National Front brought together extreme rightist groups to whom race was the chief political and social problem.

A Minority Government

One matter was clear—Britain was to have a minority government, the first since 1931. But by which party remained uncertain for a few days. Heath, as the incumbent, sought to form a coalition with the Liberals and offered Cabinet seats to Thorpe and others. But the Liberals insisted on a definite commitment from the Conservatives that electoral reform would provide proportional representation and thus assure the Liberals of seats in the Commons commensurate with their popular vote. Thorpe rejected Heath's offer; Heath resigned. Wilson was summoned by the queen, who had returned from Australia the morning of the election. So Labor, with a plurality but not a majority in the Commons, returned to power. Indeed, the popular vote of Labor, slightly below the Conservatives, was their weakest showing at the polls since 1935. But Wilson had his Cabinet slate ready, constructed around the centrists, Callaghan as foreign secretary, Healey as chancellor of the Exchequer, and Edward Short (an M.P. since 1951 and member of the

Wilson Government, 1966–70) as lord president of the Council and leader of the Commons. Jenkins returned to the Home Office. Other appointments of special interest were the left-wingers, Michael Foot as secretary of state for Employment and Anthony Wedgwood Benn for Industry.

The tenure of this Cabinet and of this Parliament was short—only until October 1974—and crowded. The Queen's Speech opening the new Parliament March 6—no state carriage, no royal robes, no fanfare—set the tone. Action was demanded. In fact, there was briefly an era of "good feeling." Wilson promptly declared that votes of confidence in the Government would not be sought on routine matters and that he would not resign on the loss of a snap division. Heath and Thorpe were conciliatory, the latter commenting, "We are all minorities now."

Labor was aided by the circumstance that the three-day work week had not been disastrous; decline in production was much less than anticipated; again the British had met a great emergency. A return to a five-day work week was announced for March 8, with all restrictions on the use of electricity lifted. Michael Foot requested that the National Coal Board and the miners union settle the strike promptly—this was accomplished at once with the miners returning to the pits on March 11. The settlement followed the recommendations of the Pay Board —its first assignment— including a 25 percent wage increase to those who worked at the face. The T.U.C. renewed its pledge not to use this settlement as a lever for similar increases elsewhere. And thus the decisions of the Conservative Government had been reversed.

The economic program of the new Government was simple enough in its objectives—check the rising prices and restrain wage increases by voluntary procedures. Inflation was now running at 13.3 percent per year. February 1974 witnessed a deficit in international trade of a billion dollars; it was the highest yet for any one month. Healey's budget presented March 26 was designed to reduce home consumption of goods and to reduce sharply borrowing for the support of the public sector of business and social services. Coal, electricity, and steel must more nearly pay for themselves. But a larger budget was required and, accordingly, taxes were raised on cigarettes, alcohol, gasoline, postage; the Value Added Tax was extended and personal income taxes and corporation taxes increased. The rise in taxes hit just about everyone. But annual subsidies would hold down basic food costs.

But the trade unions were the central concern. The Trade Union and Labor Relations Bill was promptly introduced, had its second reading May 7, and became law August 31. With this ended the Conservative Government's Industrial Relations Act and with it the Pay Board, registration of trade unions, and the National Industrial Relations Court. Government officials promptly met with T.U.C. leaders to discuss the problems of wages, prices, rents, mortgages. In June, Wilson addressed the conference of the General and Municipal Workers Union on these and related matters. In July a Royal Commission on the Distribution of Income and Wealth was established with Lord Diamond (a treasury official in the Labor Government 1964–70) as its chairman. A new Conciliation and Arbitration Service was created. And the T.U.C. council issued (June 26) a statement, *Collective Bargaining and the Social Contract,* which set forth guidelines: "real income" must be protected if inflation continued; wage claims should be made but once a year; the lowest paid workers should have special treatment; particular attention must be given to agreements promoting industrial efficiency.

Wilson and the Cabinet welcomed this document, made increasing use of the phrase "the social contract" and sought to give it significance. But it was the Council of the T.U.C., and not the rank and file membership of the unions, which was the other party to "the contract." And it was never carefully defined. Even so, Labor insisted that it was the basis for cooperation between Government and trade unions in dealing with prices and incomes. Wilson, always on the initiative, in a broadcast October 14, even widened the application of "the social contract." It "is no mere paper agreement approved by politicians and trade unions. It is not concerned solely or even primarily with wages. It covers the whole range of national policies.... The only way the battle can be won is by the Government and the people uniting on a national policy."

But the idea of the "social contract" was put to many tests. Let us take some examples. The issue of private practice in National Health Service hospitals and wage claims of hospital personnel produced a controversy which lasted from July until September. Finally the Government accepted the recommendation of a committee of inquiry; this added £170 million per year to the Health Service budget. Then at the annual Trades Union Congress at Brighton in early September, membership was asked to endorse "the social contract" in political terms, as an alternative to the Conservative "confrontation" policy. Both Wilson and Callaghan were there. When it appeared that Hugh Scanlon would throw the million votes of the engineers union against such a motion, Callaghan gave a blunt warning: "Back the social contract or face mass unemployment on a scale unknown since the 1930s." Murray, the T.U.C. general secretary, appealed for unity; Scanlon went along and the endorsement of the "social contract" was carried overwhelmingly.

Polling October 10

Another general election was expected. Confrontations in the Commons became common; the Government was defeated some twenty times on proposed amendments to legislative bills. The

Labor Government, any Government, required independent control. Opinion polls in August showed Labor in the lead, but by a modest margin. So confident were the Conservatives of a prompt return to the poll booths that its election manifesto was issued on September 10. Labor followed on September 16; the central theme was "the social contract." But the surprise was an unqualified pledge that within a year after the election, a Labor Government would put before the electorate the question of acceptance of the present Common Market terms. The Liberals kept their options open: their manifesto committed the party "unashamedly . . . to breaking the two-party system"; as Thorpe sometimes put it, the party of management alternating with the party of trade unionism.

On September 18 Wilson announced that the election for a new Parliament would come October 10. The campaign need not detain us; for one thing, no careful study of it has yet been made. But clearly it lacked spirit—the parties bickered much of the time over statistics: what was the figure of inflation? just how much unemployment was there? Thorpe proposed a televised debate of the party leaders but this was rejected. Wilson campaigned on "the social contract," while Heath hammered away on the theme of national unity. Voter interest flagged, as shown in a turnout of 72.8 percent of the electorate, as against 78.7 percent the previous February.

The result was a Labor victory somewhat less than that predicted by the polls, with 319 seats, as against 276 for the Conservatives. A net gain of 18 gave Labor an overall majority of 3. In the popular vote, Labor's count was more respectable than in February; this time it was 39.3 percent, against 35.7 percent for the Conservatives. For the Liberals the October 1974 poll was a rude disappointment. They had seemed on the upgrade. But now, though fielding the largest number of candidates (619) since 1918, their members of Parliament were reduced to 13, with 125 forfeited deposits (as against 23 in February) and a shattered morale. We may note here that Jeremy Thorpe's leadership of the Liberals continued until May 1976. In by-elections Liberals were by then doing poorly. Suggestions of homosexuality weakened Thorpe's position in the Commons. He stood his ground for a while but resigned in May. Jo Grimond, the party leader from 1956–67, assumed a caretaker's role. Two months later David Steel was elected, defeating John Pardoe by a vote of 12, 541 to 7,032. In Steel's selection not only party M.P.s but local branches of the party participated in proportion to their performance in recent general elections.

Enter Mrs. Margaret Thatcher. The 1974 elections brought more immediate changes in the Conservative Party. Alec

Douglas-Home and Anthony Barber both made it known well before the October poll that they would not again stand. In due course, both received life peerages. As to party leadership, Heath apparently assumed he was to continue, but inevitably loss of two elections in one year brought out talk in Conservative circles of a need for a change. It was then suggested that when in Opposition, Conservative M.P.s should vote annually on party leadership, with balloting to continue until a clear decision was evident. This procedure was followed in February 1975. Immediately Mrs. Margaret Thatcher, formerly secretary of state for Education and now party spokesman on economic questions, challenged Heath. On the first ballot, the result was Heath 119 and Thatcher 130, with a third candidate, Hugh Fraser, receiving 16. Heath and Fraser stood down. A week later came the second ballot. Mrs. Thatcher's chief opponent now was William Whitelaw, a moderate in policy, now well known for his negotiations in Northern Ireland and probably the person in public estimation entitled to succeed Heath. But Mrs. Thatcher, with solid support from the right wing of the parliamentary party, and a brilliant campaigner, emerged an easy victor, with 146 votes to Whitelaw's 76. Mrs. Thatcher, the daughter of a working grocer, had won a science degree at Oxford, then studied law and was admitted to Lincoln's Inn. She entered the House of Commons in 1959. At 49, she was the first woman to lead a major party. Some old faces returned and some new appeared in her shadow cabinet: Geoffrey Howe for the Exchequer and George Younger for Defense; Foreign Affairs and the Commonwealth went to Reginald Maudling, whom Heath had defeated for party leadership in 1965. The new party chairman was Lord Thorneycroft, one-time chancellor of the Exchequer. These changes reflected a swing to the right and a reaction against tendencies in recent years to mute Conservative ideological differences with Labor.

Wilson made no changes in the major posts in the Cabinet. As the new Parliament met, the problems had not changed, the solutions suggested were familiar, even the language remained much the same. The years 1974–76 were, of course, dominated by economics. And the heart of the matter is still inflation. By the summer of 1975 the rate of inflation would rise to 25 percent per annum. The public sector—welfare services and nationalized transport and industries—offered to the government perhaps its most acute problem. To meet the ever-increasing costs of operation, including wage rises, the Government had to increase charges to the public as well as to increase borrowing to cover deficits.

The Government sought to set the tone of its program in the Queen's Speech to the new Parliament. The Government would seek "the fulfillment of the social contract as an essential element in its strategy for curbing inflation, reducing the balance of payment deficits, encouraging industrial investment and promoting social and economic justice." In a

national broadcast Wilson appealed for the support for the social contract "in the spirit and in the letter." He asked that the trade unions not
"seize more than their share of the national income" and added that the
Government would do its best to subsidize industry for greater productivity. And the new budget (November 12) provided £1,500 million to
industry. Taxes were increased; nationalized industries were encouraged
to raise their own prices to reduce deficit spending by the Government.
Healey, the chancellor of the Exchequer, warned: "At least in the next
few years the great majority of us cannot expect any appreciable increase
in our living standards."

Of course, the reaction to these statements and measures varied. But
Jack Jones of the normally aggressive Transport and General Workers
Union called for moderation in wage claims. "It is simply no good pressing actions that lead to the closure of firms we work for," he declared.
But elsewhere cooperation was uneven; crises over wage demands are
now found among white-collar workers, among the professions, teachers
and journalists, for example. But then, surprisingly enough, the
engineers, normally steering to the left, voted down exorbitant demands
first advanced, this as a gesture of "loyalty to Labor."

The most consistent pressures against Government policies came in the
Commons from within its own ranks, from those on the left, protesting
against assistance to industry and to cuts in social services. To satisfy, in
measure, the demands for further nationalization of industry, two measures were introduced early in 1975: the Industry Bill, which provided
for state purchase of shares in private companies and participation in
their management, and the Community Land Bill, which empowered
local authorities to purchase land subject to development. But for most
Cabinet members the current economic crisis took precedence over
ideological demands of the left.

We now break the narrative of domestic history—political and economic—to analyze significant developments in the outside world.

External Affairs, 1974–76

"Foreign and Commonwealth affairs played little
lively part" in 1975, says the *Annual Register* for that year. Indeed, the
tone is negative; the year brought continued cuts in the defense budget.
Upon Labor's return to office in March 1974, the Government undertook, in its own language, "the most extensive and thorough review of
our system of defense ever undertaken... in peacetime." Eight months
later, Roy Mason, the Defense secretary of state, told the Commons that
the proportion of the *g.n.p.* used for defense, which was then 5.5 percent,
should be reduced to 4.5 percent in the following ten years. "We can no

longer go on policing the world," he declared. Accordingly, the forces of the army, the navy and air command would all be pruned and expenditure for research and development reduced. But, he insisted, this would not affect Britain's role in NATO, which "is the linchpin of British security." And it was noted that the British contribution to NATO had been consistently larger in proportion to the economy than that of other European members.

Referendum on the Common Market

Foreign affairs in our day are as much concerned with the economy as with diplomatic and military policy. And so here we record a matter of great moment: British membership in the Common Market was confirmed by popular referendum. After formal entry in January 1973, the Labor Party committed itself to a renegotiation of the terms of entry. This hardly made for warm relations between London and Brussels on Labor's return to office in February 1974. Further puzzlement and even suspicion developed when in the October 1974 election Labor committed itself to a popular referendum, the results to be mandatory on the government. But though the party leaders were still divided, official policy relaxed somewhat. The referendum stated the question to be put to the voters thus: "Do you think the United Kingdom should stay in the European Community (Common Market)?" And the result was to be considered influential, but not binding.

Indeed, the whole question was hardly a party matter on which agreement was necessary. No doubt Wilson did not intend that it should be. When the Cabinet voted 16-7 in favor of remaining in the European Community, Wilson announced (March 17) that the Government recommended to the public a yes vote on the referendum. But by a vote of 18 to 11 the National Executive Committee of the Labor Party recommended withdrawal and a special party conference confirmed this with a 2 to 1 vote. A majority of the Labor members of the Commons were also against remaining in the Common Market but a white paper advocating continued membership was carried in the Commons by a 396 to 170 vote (more than double the majority of 112 which was recorded in the crucial vote in October 1971). In Labor's ranks 148 voted no, 138 voted aye, and 32 abstained. The Conservative Party took no tactical advantage of this split.

In the country at large, the discussion and debate was reasoned and non-political, and it was reported fairly by the press. There was general recognition that the policies of the European Community were changing in Britain's favor and no Commonwealth land now viewed British membership as disadvantageous. Roy Jenkins, Labor home secretary, now, as president of "Britain in Europe," led the forces for a yes vote on the referendum. But the figure who emerged as the man of the occasion was the former prime minister, Edward Heath. The result of the vote on June 5, 1975, was an overall majority of 67.2 percent yes vote and uniform in the various regions. The only majority no vote came from the Shetlands and the Eastern Isles, where Scandinavian fishermen predominated. If much of the yes vote was without great enthusiasm, it was with the thought that the Common Market was better than "going it alone." But, nonetheless, the result was a victory for Heath and the Conservatives and also an outstanding example of Wilson's successful handling of an issue on which his party was sharply divided. He had satisfied both left and right. In July 1975 he declared at a top-level meeting in Brussels that British commitment was now total. A year later, Callaghan reported enthusiastically on plans for a popularly elected European Assembly in which Britain would have 81 seats (as would West Germany, Italy, and France) out of a total of 410. A European Parliament, elected by universal suffrage! Here was a new chapter in the story of the E.E.C. But one is not surprised to find Britain dragging her feet—by February 1978 she had not yet passed the necessary legislation through Parliament.

Northern Ireland—"The Damnable Question"

There were startling though hardly decisive changes in the situation in Northern Ireland. The new Executive, formed at the end of 1973, lasted five months; then its Unionist members resigned. While the Catholic and Protestant department heads sought to work harmoniously, their power was limited; they had no control over internal security. A continuation of violence contibuted to the sweeping victory of the Unionists in the United Kingdom General Election in February 1974. Capture of 11 out of 12 seats reflected the strong Unionist opposition to the Sunningdale agreement as, so they said, likely to lead toward incorporation of Ulster in an Irish Republic, and in May the Ulster Workers Council staged widespread strikes against the Executive and the Council of Ireland. With the collapse of the Executive, the Assembly was prorogued and direct rule from Westminster renewed, If the people of Northern Ireland agreed on anything, it was that they wished to work out thier own form of government.

Meantime, there was increased pressure from Catholics in Dublin as well as in Ulster against the continued violence of the Irish Republican Army. This led to an announcement of a "cease-fire" from December 20, 1974 to January 2, 1975—and then extended two weeks. While the cease-fire had no significant effect, acts of violence were less numerous than during 1972 and 1973.

Having failed in the attempt to provide a political solution, Westminster turned to a constitutional convention in which, it was hoped, Northern Ireland could find its own solutions. By proportional representation the voters selected 78 members for this convention, which convened in May 1975. A Protestant coalition numbered 46 members; under the leadership of the Rev. Ian Paisley, it refused the Catholic minority any significant share in reaching decisions. Terrorism by the I.R.A. was renewed with increased attention to British targets—the Green Park Underground station in Piccadilly, hotels, restaurants, private homes. The Convention was recalled in February 1976; it had been hoped that a committee system could lead to power sharing, but to no avail. In March 1976 the Convention was dissolved and direct rule from Westminster continued. "The sad fact, the reality, was that the historical prejudices, deeply held, did not allow a solution to be reached," said Merlyn Rees, the British secretary for Northern Ireland. It was an obvious remark; but what else could be said? Some impetus for an independent republic of Northern Ireland developed, but Callaghan, in his first visit (July) to Belfast as prime minister, declared that it "will not cease to be a part of the United Kingdom unless it is a clear wish of the majority that the links should be severed." In September, 1976 Roy Mason replaced Rees as Secretary of State for Northern Ireland and general policy through 1977 continued much the same—direct rule from Westminster, under army protection, to be shifted over to police protection as rapidly as possible. Through all the turmoil of these years it is interesting to note that the industrial productivity of Northern Ireland had grown since 1968 or 1969 and industrial relations between management and labor were remarkably good.

Rhodesia to "Zimbabwe"?

As to the problems of Rhodesia, language used was often a reflection of the changes in process. It was not frequently "The New Rhodesia" and, indeed, very often "Zimbabwe," as the blacks expect to call their country if and when their majority rule is achieved. The important new factor was that by 1975, with full independence to the Portuguese colonies of Mozambique and Angola, the land-locked country of Rhodesia was virtually surrounded by independent black nations. But independence did not mean peace, particularly in Angola, where rival black factions were in conflict, and also in sections of Rhodesia, where guerrilla warfare was renewed. An ominous fact was that black forces training in Mozambique far outnumbered the small white army in Rhodesia. A closing of borders could destroy most of Rhodesia's trade. Little wonder that more whites were now emigrating from Rhodesia than were immigrating to it. South Africa read the signs of the time more readily than did Rhodesia. B. J. Vorster, the prime minister in Pretoria, found in President Kaunda of Zambia a person of common aims—a racial truce throughout the southern states in Africa and a common economic policy. The alternative, as both saw it, was prolonged and tragic racial conflict. It was now Vorster who used all the weight of his office to persuade Ian Smith to accept a negotiated settlement leading to majority rule in Rhodesia.

To reach such conclusion, the British Government in March 1976 outlined its suggestions for a prompt and orderly transition (within 18 to 24 months) and Callaghan promised British influence for the prompt removal of economic sanctions against Rhodesia and for financial aid to the new state. Ian Smith responded half-heartedly, perhaps hoping to buy more time; Callaghan observed that Smith "does not realize he no longer has much time to buy." In September, American initiative, through Secretary of State Kissinger, who visited Pretoria and the various black capitals, proposed a transitional regime providing for a consultative council, equally divided between blacks and whites but with a white chairman, and an executive council dominated by blacks. The whites were to have responsibility for maintaining law and order. And the British were to have general oversight. But these details remained very much a matter of negotiation for both blacks and whites. Differences were not resolved at a prolonged conference at Geneva attended by Smith and the leaders of the major African parties, with Ivor Richard, the British representative to the United Nations, presiding. Agreement could not come where fear and suspicion dominated. The conference stalled first on the matter of timing; Britain urged March 1, 1978, for the final turnover, and African leaders wanted it sooner. An accommodation of a sort seemed to be reached on this point, but then developed a deadlock, which could not be resolved over the control of the army and security forces and the chairmanship of the council. The Genevan conference ended, with no agreement, in mid-December. In January 1977 Richard offered further proposals, assigning to Britain (to be aided and supported, it was hoped, by the United States) a more active role in the transitional period. By this time, Ian Smith was again taking the initiative and was seeking the support of the moderate elements among the blacks, and he rejected out of hand British control during the period of transition.

In the course of 1977, Ian Smith, evasive as he remained, came to accept majority black rule as the final solution to the Rhodesian problem. Now the problem was determining the conditions under which transfer of power would take place. Smith's great concern was the guarantee of the rights of the whites, notably their representation in the legislative assembly. In the negotiations it was a question of just which black elements represented the black community and would be likely to control a black-majority government. Smith continued to shun British and American efforts to influence the process and dealt directly with the black nationalist leaders, notably a Methodist Bishop, Abel Muzorewa, and the Rev. Ndabaningi Sithole and Senator Jeremiah Chirau. The outcome was an agreement signed by Smith and these black leaders on March 3, 1978, calling for the installation of the black-majority government the last day of the year. Our story of Rhodesia has been told necessarily in narrative form; it has been an ever-changing tale. With the agreement of March 3, 1978, the immediate problem now became the attitude of the Patriotic Front, an alliance of black insurgents, backed by a guerrilla army and supported by the states adjoining Rhodesia. Led by Joshua Nkomo and Robert Mugabe, the Patriotic Front denounced the negotiations and the terms of transfer. Will guerrilla warfare become general civil war in Rhodesia? It is not likely that the struggle for black majority rule in Rhodesia is over.

Devolution in Scotland and Wales?

Back in 1967 Ludovic Kennedy wrote in *Spectator* for November 10: "It was primarily the British Empire that made and kept us British. Now it is gone and the word British is almost devoid of meaning."

What Kennedy had in mind was the growing sense of *regionalism* in the United Kingdom. The prime example is Scotland, where regionalism had become, for many, *separatism*. Always proud of its own history and its own institutions, Scotland was a natural bed for the growth of nationalism. Polls in the seventies indicated that perhaps 20 percent favored complete independence; but many more, perhaps a majority, desired a Scottish assembly. In Wales the nationalistic movement was less well organized, less widespread.

The English have been increasingly aware of the implications of Scottish and Welsh nationalism, and particularly during general elections to Parliament, for a Labor majority in the Commons has been dependent on its control of the electorate in Scotland and Wales. Official action began with a Royal Commission appointed in 1969. Its report in October 1973 ruled out self-government or a federation which would share sovereignty with Westminster. Devolution of many administrative functions was proposed. In September 1974 came a Labor Cabinet white paper proposing directly elected assemblies; the Scottish assembly would have legislative power, the Welsh only administrative.

By this time the matter had arrested general attention and we are assured that the sentence in the Queen's Speech to Parliament in October

1975 which aroused most discussion was the promise of the Government to "bring forward legislative proposals for the establishment of Scottish and Welsh Assemblies to exercise wide governmental responsibilities within the framework of the United Kingdom."

But, to the rage of the Scottish Nationalists, progress was very slow. A white paper outlined generalities but suggested that decisions be made without haste since the proposal involved a basic change in constitutional procedure. The bill finally introduced late in 1976 provided for assemblies (150 members in Scotland and 80 in Wales) with limited legislative power and control of expenditures for education, housing, transportation, industrial development. But these assemblies would have no control over taxation, defense, foreign policy, or North Sea oil. The details pleased neither the Scots or the Welsh, and each of the major parties at Westminster was divided within itself. The result was almost endless debate, and a host of amendments. One such, which survived, required support of 40 percent of the Scottish or Welsh electorate in a referendum. Finally the measure for Scotland was carried in the Commons early in 1978, only to confront long debate in the Lords. Its fairly prompt enactment into law and a similar measure for Wales were essential if Labor were to win the next general election.

The "Social Contract," 1974–76

In 1975 the chief fact of life for most people was inflation; by summer, we repeat, it was 25 percent per annum. And as the year opened, there was no official prices and incomes policy, other than the vague "social contract." With restraints voluntary, a variety of strikes, large and small, for conditions of work as well as for wages, kept the industrial world in disorder, especially among the miners, the railroad workers, the dockers, and hospital workers in the National Health Service. In February 1975 the miners rejected a Coal Board wage offer but finally settled for a 35 percent hike in pay. Coal prices shot up 30 percent and electricity 7.5 percent. On the day of the coal settlement, the largest railway union put in a similar wage claim, to maintain, they said, the proper relation to miners' wages.

But generally speaking, in government, business management, and trade union circles the tendency was toward moderation and accommodation. The key individual now seemed to be Jack Jones. At a rally of his Transport and General Workers Union he declared that "the present trend for wages to rise faster than prices spells economic danger." On June 25 the council of the T.U.C. set down the principle that in the ensuing year wage increases be kept to 10 percent, with a similar target for prices levels. Healey was enthusiastic. He at once drafted an anti-inflationary white paper; for the year, beginning August 1, pay rises were to be kept to £6 per week; salaries above £8500 were to be frozen. This proposal was accepted by all moderate elements in the trade union world and even by the miners, though with considerable dissent in Yorkshire and Scotland, where some union officials had in mind increases of as much as 60 percent.

By the end of 1975 results were somewhat mixed. The Central Statistical Office reported that the standard of living had dropped 7 percent during the year. Most people thought inflation was a worse evil than unemployment. Wilson said it had been "a hard year," yet it had been a remarkable achievement to have secured agreement between the Government and the trade unions "and I believe pretty well the whole British people about the things that have to be done to overcome inflation." There was basis for his statement. During the last six months of 1975, the annual rate of inflation fell to 13.6 percent, a reduction of nearly 50 percent. Figures on overseas trade were more favorable, and the rate of unemployment, about 4.5 percent, was lower than in most industrialized countries. Signs of improvement continued into 1976. Industrial disorder declined; during the first five months of 1976 less time was lost through strikes than during the whole of 1975. In March 1976 the British economy reflected the best balance of payments surplus in over five years. And for the year ending July 31, 1976, wage rises averaged 11.5 percent, not far from the target of 10 percent.

But there is another side, that of industrial production. The worldwide recession retarded Britain more than it did most other industrial lands; the hope and even the expectation of 5 percent rise in productivity during 1975 had not materialized; the level of production had not been above that of 1970; little or no growth was expected for 1976. To put the problem more starkly, in 1960 the return on capital investment industrially was 13 percent; in 1975 it was but 4 percent. But the Government now made a conscious effort to give priority to industrial development. In November 1975, Wilson, Healey, and Varley (secretary of state for Industry) met with representatives of management and labor at Chequers and announced a new economic policy, modifying principles generally accepted since 1945. The welfare programs were to take second place to industry. In February 1976 a white paper on *Public Expenditures* emphasized the cutback in expenditures for road transport, health, housing, environmental protection, civil service, and education, with increases in appropriations only to "Trade, Industry and Employment." The condition of the nationalized industries is reflected in the resignation early in 1976 of the chairman of the British Steel Corporation and also the chairman of the British Railways Board.

But in private industry a mood of some optimism prevailed. This in part rose from the development of new sources of energy, undersea oil and gas in the North Sea. Oil fields had first been discovered off Scotland in 1971; the first oil was brought ashore in 1975, at great expense, to be sure, but, nonetheless, a harbinger of things to come. And gas fields were discovered off the shores of East Anglia and Yorkshire. During 1976, Britain took 20 million tons of oil from the North Sea; this was expected to double in 1977, thereby taking care of two-fifths of Britain's requirement. Funds for research in deep water technology for the extraction of both oil and gas were included in the 1976 budgets upon recommendation of the Offshore Energy Technology Board. Late in 1976 it was announced that in peacetime five warships would be assigned to the oil and gas fields. Also in 1976 came the first commercial flights of the *Concorde,* a supersonic transport plane produced by an Anglo-French partnership over a period of twelve years. With its cruising speed of 1,300 miles per hour, the plane can reach any destination in twelve hours' time or less.

Labor Leadership: Wilson to Callaghan

One of the most important events of 1976 was the resignation, quite unexpected, on March 16, of Harold Wilson, then sixty years of age. His career is impressive—in Parliament for thirty-one years and on the front bench for nearly thirty. His tenure of eight years as prime minister was longer than that of any other in peace-time in this century. But it is much too soon to judge his career. Indeed, it is not over, for he remained in the Commons as a back-bencher from Huyton, Lancs.

On one matter, we may be sure; he was a very hard worker, a point worth making when we think of Stanley Baldwin and Ramsay MacDonald. "I have had to work 7 days a week, at least 12 to 14 hours a day," he remarked with some pride; and we may believe him. However, to many people he lacked credibility; in 1969 an opinion poll indicated that only 35 percent of those questioned took him at his word. This, of course, was at his low point in popularity, just after the failure of *In Place of Strife.* Everyone, even a prime minister, has a right to change his mind; but with Wilson this became something of a habit: on the Common Market, on statutory controls of prices and incomes, on nuclear weapons.

It would now seem that he will be remembered as an extraordinarily successful politician. He had a way of asserting and establishing his personal authority with Cabinet and Parliament, and, above all, with the party leadership, which he held together after Gaitskell's death and after *In Place of Strife*. He was at his best when he seemed to be at bay, fenced in. It is then that his speeches have quality; when he knows he is standing on secure ground his speeches are routine. He hardly deserved popularity, for he seldom accepted responsibility for mistakes and stood aloof from party controversy which he himself generated.

To what extent was he responsible for Britain's failure to rejuvenate her economy in the sixties and seventies, as did so many countries in western Europe? At the beginning of his career, Britain had just emerged as one of the great powers victorious in World War II, but in 1976 Britain, stripped of her important role in the world, was struggling to retain a respectable place in the European community. Under other inspiration might not the story have had a somewhat different ending? Today these are rhetorical questions. But Peter Jenkins had a point when he said that Wilson's timing of his resignation was "an invitation to continuity."

This is evident as we turn to his successor, James ("Sunny Jim") Callaghan, chosen by the Labor members of Parliament. Three ballots were required. On the first (March 24) a pack of six was in the running; Michael Foot led, but with only 90 votes out of 314. The others were Callaghan (84 votes), Jenkins, Benn, Healey, and Crosland, who finished in that order. After the second ballot the field was reduced to Callaghan, now in the lead with 141 votes, and Foot with 133. Neither had a majority. On the third ballot (April 5) Callaghan emerged as the clear winner, 176 to Foot's 137. Callaghan was selected partly on his own merits and partly for his centrist position. He had generally been loyal to Wilson, breaking with him only on *In Place of Strife*. He was well known as a peacemaker. But he was also a man of great experience, for, beginning in 1964, he had served successively in the Exchequer, in the Home Office, and in the Foreign and Commonwealth Office. He had not been successful at the Exchequer, but then who, in these years, had? He was more of an "Atlanticist" than a "Europeanist," though he gave solid support to the Common Market when it was up for referendum.

John Clare, who had worked with Callaghan on a book about Northern Ireland, *A House Divided*, says: "His great strength is in absorbing other people's ideas, filtering them through his own considerable common sense, rejecting what he feels public opinion will not bear and expressing what is left in a plain and confident manner. It is that very considerable talent that has got him where he is today." With good reason, therefore, he has been labeled a "consensus man." He appointed Foot (his chief rival for the prime ministership) lord president of the Council and leader of the House of Commons. Foot has been extraordinarily successful in maintaining discipline in the Parliamentary Party.

It was at once evident that Callaghan would continue the general policies of Wilson. Again, any action toward nationalization of the shipbuilding and aircraft industries was postponed. The first priority was the stimulation of British private business. Borrowing requirements for governmental expenditures in the public sector were to be reduced by twenty percent. And there were to be cuts in welfare and unemployment benefits; assistance on mortgages would be reduced, charges for dental work and eyeglasses increased, and library and museum hours shortened.

Perhaps the most important action was the renewal of the agreements on incomes and prices. In May 1976 a new "contract" was drafted. Callaghan, Healey, Jack Jones, and Lionel Murray (general secretary of the T.U.C.) agreed to limit wage increases for the coming year to an average of 4.5 percent. Later, in August, the Price Code provided new guidelines. It was hoped that by these measures inflation would again be halved.

A Tentative Assessment

These developments in 1975 and 1976 reveal a considerable change from preceding years in the atmosphere and practice of relationship among labor, industrial management, and government. For the second year, an agreement, which included the coal miners, was reached on control of wage increases. There were even suggestions of involving workers in business and factory management (notably in the report of the Bullock Committee in January 1977) as well as development of incentives to greater productivity for both management and labor. The goal was obvious: stability of prices and incomes with adequate profit for industrial growth. The Confederation of British Industry was sufficiently encouraged to predict that by the end of 1977 inflation would drop to 4 percent. The National Economic Development Council (Government, management, labor) received reports from thirty-nine Sectoral Working Parties and in August 1976 issued a new working paper which projected a growth in British productivity of 8 percent per year, on the average, through 1978. All that was, indeed, unprecedented optimism.

But there were warning signs as well. The more militant unions, notably Scanlon's engineers, were restless. Jack Jones said that after another twelve-month restraint on wage increases there must be a return to free collective bargaining. And if the economy did improve, even if not by a great deal, it then seemed unlikely that cooperation in the "social contract" sense would continue. In September 1976 some 38,000 seamen went on strike—the first challenge on a large scale to the wage-price understandings of 1975–76. There was a suggestion of finality in the remarks, in January 1977, of David Basnett, general secretary of the General and Municipal Workers Union. He said: "There cannot be a third round of wage restraints that involve the kind of cuts in living standards nor can there be a rigid formula for economic and social policies like the past two years preventing any flexibility at the local level."

The Plight of the Pound. In 1976, the problems of the economy were compounded by the monetary crisis. Early in 1975 the pound stood at $2.40. A few months later it had dropped to $2.30. And a decline toward a $2.00 pound had started. By March 1976 it had fallen below that to $1.92, and by June to $1.70. The chancellor of the Exchequer, Healey, said it was the result of speculation; but the real cause seems to have been English inflation, with little confidence in the outside world in the pound of the future. Many countries sold their reserves in pounds. And the Bank of England borrowing rate was 11.5 percent, far higher than in other industrial countries.

In June 1976 the Bank of England arranged with international bankers a six-months loan of $5,300,000,000. But to little avail. In the summer were broken almost all records of drought. The sky was blue but the land was parched. And the pound plummeted, by September to $1.65 and by October to just below $1.60. Healey knew no recourse other than to try to keep wages and prices under control, keep the money supply tight, and reduce budget deficits and public expenditures still further. He announced just such measures in December, and, on the basis of these efforts at stability, Britain received on January 3, 1977, from the International Monetary Fund the largest credit granted in its history— $3,900,000,000.

This loan apparently saved the Callaghan Government. But the prime minister still had to contend with dissent in his own party. Much of the left thought the answer to Britain's economic plight was to reduce sharply all imports. Also, they wished to give priority to easing unemployment, which they predicted would merely rise still higher with budget cuts in the public sector. They sought restoration of funds for the social services, and they were opposed to direct election by the voters of representatives to the European Parliament. But Callaghan was able to turn much of this aside; fortunately for him, Foot had moved closer to the center. Perhaps to appease the left, a measure to nationalize the aricraft and shipbuilding industries was passed through the Commons, only to meet delaying amendments in the Lords.

The Jubilee Year, 1977

Nineteen seventy-seven proved a more cheerful year than 1976; celebration of the twenty-fifth anniversary of the accession of Elizabeth II created an atmosphere which encouraged a more optimistic view of what lay ahead. Formal ceremonies began May 4 with addresses of the Lords and of the Commons in the venerable Westminster Hall. A month later came a crowded week of activity: a national service of Thanksgiving in St. Paul's Cathedral was attended by the royal family; a royal progress on the Thames revived a practice of the first Elizabeth; the heads of 33 of the 36 countries associated in the Commonwealth met in London in the biennial gathering; throughout the United Kingdom nearly every town had its parades, fairs, and dances. And during the year there was an endless succession of pageants, concerts, and sporting events. The queen and Prince Philip toured the British Isles and Commonwealth lands. Foreign visitors competed with the British for acquisition of the commemorative jubilee crown piece whose face value was 25 pence. John Grigg, who had suggested, twenty years before, that the royal family was out of touch with the times, now declared that Elizabeth II had been "unquestionably a good queen" and might yet prove to be a great one.

One turns with less enthusiasm and also with some temerity to the economic and political scene of the Jubilee year. There was a Labor point of view and a Conservative point of veiw, each with variations; there was the conflicting perspective of industrial management and of the trade unionists; self-interest tended to dominate the attitude of the individual toward society.

Quite naturally the Government sought to capitalize on the Jubilee mood. And so the prime minister in his New Year's message in 1977 found much basis for encouragement. "Let us put behind us . . . unnecessary disputes . . . . Let future historians look back on 1977 as a pendulum year in our history, the year when the people of Britain found themselves and began to climb back. Never let us forget that we are much better than we think we are! And, although we are not the biggest in the world, when we put our minds to it we should be the best!"

Then, and repeatedly thereafter, the emphasis was on industrial expansion—more "productive," more "efficient," and as "export minded" as possible. Jack Jones continued to support the "social contract", calling on labor to make 1977 "the year of the beaver." By March "Sunny Jim" Callaghan was telling the National Press Club that Britain was "certainly one of the fortunate countries in Europe." And the Sunday *Times* affirmed: "Compared to a year ago, the situation is markedly better financially, moderately improved industrially."

The index which attracted attention was that of the balance of international payments—substantial reduction in deficits during the first six months of the year, with a surplus as 1977 came to an end, this improvement deriving from increased tourist revenue, the strengthening of the pound sterling, and the output of North Sea oil, the latter accounting for perhaps 1 percent annually in the growth of the gross national product.

The year averaged out with an increase in the *g.n.p.* of 3 percent, considerably better than the previous year.

And the "social contract" operated, at least in principle, if not to the letter. No official pressure was exerted on the trade unions to force adherence to the suggested guidelines of no more than a 10 percent increase in wage agreements. But the Trades Union Congress in its annual meeting in September endorsed a policy of the "twelve-month settlement." Prices did rise somewhat faster than wages, but by the close of 1977 the annual rate of inflation had dropped to 13 percent with a mdoerate decline in unemployment.

But such progress was gradual and was, in the view of many, overshadowed by the many failures in public policy during 1976—in July 1977 the Government issued a report indicating that in 1976 wages had risen 8 percent and prices 16 percent. Such a consequence of wage restraints and general inflation made the electorate restless and lost Labor much of its usual support. This was dramatically apparent in municipal elections and by-elections in the course of 1977. Most notable was the poll to fill the Commons seat vacated by Roy Jenkins when he became President of the European Commission, the executive branch of the Common Market. A 17 percent swing brought the Conservatives an overwhelming victory. And public opinion polls demonstrated that the Conservatives had made inroads on the labor vote, that the Scottish electorate, normally Labor, was impatient with the slow progerss of devolution, and that the protest vote was growing within the ranks of the Liberal Party and the National Front.

Indeed, when the Labor overall majority was reduced, early in the year, to 3, a general election seemed imminent. However, the political situation was stabilized, March 22, by a collaborative agreement between Labor and the Liberals, whose 13 M.P.s were committed to support the Government on any vote of confidence in the Commons. In return, Labor agreed to consult the Liberals on proposed legislation and to give increased attention to Liberal concerns, particularly that of proportional representation in the forthcoming election of British membership in the European Parliament. At this point we pause to record the sudden death (February 1977) of Anthony Crosland, aged 58, the secretary of state at the Foreign and Commonwealth Office. Since 1964 he had occupied six different ministerial posts and had proved, in the language of the Conservative *Daily Telegraph,* both "an ornament and a pillar" of the Government. His place was now taken by David Owen, 38—a surprise, since it had been expected that the chancellor of the Exchequer, Denis Healey, would get the post.

Her Majesty's Loyal Opposition grew increasingly impatient with a Labor Government barely clinging to office. With the Lib-Lab agreement,

Mrs. Thatcher, Conservative leader, stepped up her attacks. In July she declared in the Commons that the Labor Government in office since 1974 represented "a total failure the like of which no other Government even under socialism has equalled." The press commented that she herself was moving to the right; she had, indeed, said that she opposed governmental control of prices and wages. And she called for curbs on immigration, particularly from Asia and the West Indies. On this latter issue she did have considerable popular support, though several members of her own shadow cabinet were quick to disassociate themselves from her uncompromising position. All of which moved Callaghan to declare that Mrs. Thatcher was providing "the most reactionary Conservative leadership ... since the First World War."

The next general election is not due by law until October 1979. But Callaghan will call for a poll at the time which seems most auspicious for his Government and his party. Certainly in January of 1978 Labor was in a much stronger position than a year before. The rate of inflation had fallen, at least temporarily, to just below 10 percent; the miners had agreed to accept the 10 percent guideline for annual increases in wages; the standard of living for most workers was rising without steep increases in pay; the pound sterling was holding on to its advantageous position in the money market, and there was at last a surplus in the international balance of payments. But Callaghan will be cautious. When the Liberals, in January 1978, in a special party meeting, voting overwhelmingly to retain ties with Labor in Parliament, there was no immediate political pressure. Callaghan is likely to wait until the final measures of devolution for Scotland and Wales are enacted and direct elections approved for British membership in the Parliament of the European Community.

In October 1977 the prime minister remarked to the Labor Party Conference that "the next two decades will be unlike anything this country has known since it first moved to become an industrial power two hundred years ago." Such rhetoric is representative of the mood of British leadership today. The inevitability of change, perhaps fundamental change, is accepted. But there will be choices to be made. Callaghan and Mrs. Thatcher both represent resourcefulness and initiative, and it will indeed make a difference which is at 10 Downing Street. The British trade union movement is militant but not dogmatic. Early in 1978 came the announcement of the retirement of Jack Jones, as secretary of the Transport and General Workers' Union. And he was in the queen's New Year's Honors list in recognition of his contribution to the nation. But what about his successor, Moss Evans, who is said to oppose continuation of the present voluntary ceiling of 10 percent on wage increases? Politically there is the strong protest vote in the Liberal Party and in the National

Front as well as the uncertainty concerning the constituencies in Wales and Scotland which in the past have voted Labor. The factors are many and diverse, but to the historian writing early in 1978, it appears that the coming general election, whether in 1978 or 1979, will be far more a key event than most national polls. It will determine whether Labor, perhaps increasingly influenced by its left wing, or the Conservatives apparently moving somewhat to the right, will be in power during much of the eighties, a decade likely to prove more decisive in determining Britain's future than were the sixties or the seventies.

14 A Society in Motion

Colin Buchanan
*The State of
Britain* (1972),
p. 87

What we do with the island will reflect our cultural
standards very accurately, our humanity to each other, our
concern for other life forms, our sense of the past, our
responsibility for the future. It is a neat tight little island
and to make something splendid of it would be a vastly
interesting thing to do.

Sir Geoffrey
Crowther
as quoted in
James D. Koerner,
*Reform in
Education:
England and the
United States*
(1968), p. 229

... a growing sense of astonishment that two countries
[Great Britain and the United States] which share the same
language, so many of the same cultural traditions and ways
of life, whose political, religious and social aspirations are
so largely identical, should have educational systems so
utterly different as to provide almost no basis for a
comparison between them.

William A.
Robson
*Welfare State and
Welfare Society:
Illusion and
Reality* (1976),
p. 179

There is no short cut to the welfare society from the
conflict, selfishness and lack of consensus which mark our
present condition.

1950 – 1977

In this last chapter we shall examine and describe briefly certain aspects of the British way of life, apart from party politics and the economy, as we find it in the last twenty-five years, but more especially in the sixties and seventies. In so doing we shall inevitably have in mind, as well, the British scene at the beginning of the century.

Many contrasts are evident. Perhaps the most obvious will be in the operation of *change*. Edwardian England was a dynamic period, but it witnessed no startling transformation. To those then alive, the English world was in its essentials much the same in 1910 as it had been in 1901 and, indeed, it required a world war to reveal just what change was taking place. In the early forties we have another cataclysm from which we date ideas and forces which, it would seem, have been gathering momentum ever since. "The collapse of British power" is a frequent theme of thoughtful writers on the fate of the British Empire and the Commonwealth. At home "an affluent society" with apparent abundance replaced briefly the austerity of the war years and after. The welfare state was supposed to have made England a land fit for heroes to live in, but "the affluent society" in time proved something of an illusion and the welfare state itself came up for cross-examination. But there are many other changes which are not only matters of interest and importance but

in which the English may well take pride: the rise of "new towns" to deal
with the problems of an urban society and to provide more gracious
living; the growth of ecumenism in religion; leadership in the arts. In
every-day experience the Britain of 1977 is a quite different world from
that of 1945: in housing, transport, education, manner of dress,
entertainment, and so on; in the fading out of the inhibited Britisher; the
growth of the world of sport; the blessing and the tyranny of television
and radio; perhaps a change in national character and outlook.

Land and People

The census of 1971 (one had been taken every ten
years since 1801, save for 1941) produced no great surprises; it demonstrated that Britain's population is fairly stable in numbers (with a small
rate of growth), predominantly middle-aged (but with the very young
and the very old gradually increasing proportionately), and overwhelmingly urban (with concentration in a few vast built-up areas but with a
tendency to return to the countryside). In 1901 the population of Great
Britain was 36,999,946; seventy years later it was 53,978,000. This
represented an increase from the 51,283,000 recorded in 1961. For the
rest of the century, an average growth of 0.2 percent per year is estimated.

By 1971 of major countries in Europe only Belgium and The Netherlands were more crowded than Britain. During most of the twentieth
century the movement from country to town, so striking throughout the
nineteenth century, tapered off. Between 1931 and 1951 the urban population remained fairly steady at 80 percent. However, by 1971 it had
dropped to 78.2 percent. The spectacular phenomenon of the twentieth
century has been the growth of the conurbation, defined as a group of
neighboring towns which, by peripheral development, has grown into "a
single built-up area with common industrial or commercial and social
interests." By 1971 the term was assigned to seven areas: Metropolitan
(Greater London), West Midlands (Birmingham), Southeast Lancashire
(Manchester), Merseyside (Liverpool), West Yorkshire (Leeds), Tyneside (Newcastle-upon-Tyne), Clydeside (Glasgow). Of these, Metropolitan London was in a class apart, with a population of over 7 million in an
area of 610 square miles. Since 1921 about 40 percent of the population
of England, proper, has lived in these conurbations, with some decline in
the postwar years (by 1971 it was 33 percent), as areas immediately
outside the official conurbations have developed as places of residence for
those working in the inner areas.

The face of England, rural as well as urban, is rapidly changing, though
the changes in the cities are more arresting. Those in London may be

taken as representative. The London trams ceased operation in 1952 after an honorable history of nearly a century. No one who saw them, no one who rode them, can forget how they lurched along the Thames embankment, screeched around curves, and fanned out from Thames-side for fifteen miles in all directions. But in traffic only a few years later they would have seemed incongruous. Enemy action during the blitz of World War II destroyed many venerable structures (or forced their transformation), notably the Wren churches in the City. A development plan of 1951 set forth twenty years of reconstruction and by the end of that period had changed certain sections of London almost beyond recognition. A new London Bridge was opened in March 1973; the old bridge was reconstructed in Arizona in the United States. Modern architecture was not to be denied, and increasingly streamlined glass structures pushed aloft, with more modest traditional buildings alongside preserving their identity and dignity as best they could. Since London could no longer spread outward, she pushed skyward. The Shell building, rising 351 feet on the south bank and erected in 1962 at a cost of £33 million, shocked most sensibilities; the Hilton Hotel in Park Lane and Vickers House on Millbank, erected in 1963 and each thirty-two stories high, were artistically more acceptable. By 1965 was completed the General Post Office telecommunications tower rising 580 feet, near the north end of Tottenham Court Road. In the City a veritable jungle of glass and masonry appeared; from afar the classic views of St. Paul's were obstructed; close at hand the cathedral seemed almost dwarfed by buildings without history and without meaning. In November 1972 was opened the new 26-story Stock Exchange Building. But happily, the stretches of green open space, large and small, which for centuries have given London character and charm, remain largely undisturbed. And the gardens—to which most Britishers have a great devotion—behind or in front of homes, old and new, and in the public squares and parks, continue to be a source of pride and delight. In the fifties the Savill Gardens constituted a notable development in the Royal Park at Windsor, and the 400-acre estate of Wakefield Place was added to the Royal Botanical Gardens at Kew. In 1972 some 400 square miles of uplands in mid-Wales was reserved for a national park. Concern for amenities in the country at large is also found in statutes that have authorized local authorities to preserve historic buildings, protect woodlands, and provide public footpaths into the uncultivated countryside. Voluntary organizations are active, most notably in the National Trust, founded in 1895, which by 1976 owned and preserved 400,000 acres of land and 200 historic buildings.

The department of State for the Environment is much concerned with problems of pollution. Plans are afoot for attacking some 2,000 miles of badly polluted riverways. Earlier, the fog of December 1952 which took 4,000 lives led to the Clean Air Act of 1956. In the seventies attention turned to the vast network of canals, about 4,000 miles of them, built in the eighteenth and nineteenth centuries, which are now being restored, either for recreational facilities (cruising, canoeing, fishing) or for commercial use.

Town Planning

Town planning is hardly a new idea; the phrase itself dates back at least to 1906; for, to the Victorians and the Edwardians, towns were as much of a problem as they are today. However, between the two world wars, any serious attempt at solution was pushed aside by more pressing issues at home and abroad. Only since 1945 has "planning" been regarded as essential for solving urban problems in the contemporary world. But its progress has been halting and uncertain. In certain cities—particularly Coventry, Exeter, Plymouth—war damage compelled prompt action. For the metropolitan area of Greater London, serious efforts at long-range planning date from Patrick Abercrombie's *Plan for Greater London*, prepared in 1944 under the authority of the Ministry of Town and Country Planning. The area was conceived of as four concentric circles or rings. The first was that of Inner London (the area of the London County), from which it was proposed to remove a million residents. The second ring, that of prewar suburbs, was to remain as it had been. In the third and fourth areas provision was made for the "overspill" from Inner London. The third area, known as the "Green Belt Ring" was to remain as it was, about three-quarters agricultural or woodland with scattered communities but with no additional housing development. In the fourth area provision was made for extending existing towns and for "new towns" as provided for in a statute of 1947 and later legislation. The population of Greater London in 1976 was just under seven and a-half million, a decrease of over one-half million since 1961 and back to the 1921 level. Otherwise the premises of the Abercrombie Plan proved wrong. It assumed that the tendency for southeast England to grow could be checked and that surplus industry and population would be moved to other parts of the country. Instead, the population of southeast England is still growing—a 6 percent increase between 1961 and 1971—and London is still at the heart of the area. By the sixties more than a million persons had been removed since 1945 from residence in the inner ring, but a large proportion of them had merely been reestablished in the new urban communities within commuting distance from the center. By 1965 over 300,000 living outside the conurbation commuted fifty miles or more five or six days a week.

New Towns. "New towns," sometimes called garden cities or satellite towns, soon became an accepted part of urban planning. Various legislative enactments were consolidated in statutes in 1965 and 1968 empowering the secretary of state for Environment and the secretaries of state for Scotland and for Wales to designate any area as a "new town." Since 1946, 33 "new towns" (with 1,800,000 residents by 1975) have been so designated, including 23 in England and Wales and 6 in Scotland, each making a conscious effort to coordinate industry, shops, homes, schools, and recreational facilities. Eleven developed as satellites of London and were designed primarily to relieve housing problems in the greater London area. A good example is Stevenage in Hertfordshire; in 1944 it was a town of 400, but by 1972 numbered 67,000 and was still growing. Even more spectacular was the village of Laindon in Essex, which has been swallowed up in Basildon New Town, with 129,000 residents by 1972. The largest "new town" seems to be Central Lancashire, which replaced Preston, Leyland, and Chorley along with some villages. By the mid-seventies, Central Lancashire had a population of 240,000; in part it was designed to coordinate economic development to replace the rapidly fading cotton industry in that area. "The new towns represent a notable achievement in positive land use. They are generally recognized as one of the most successful post-war experiments, both socially and industrially, and as a profitable long-term investment." These words of a Government "handbook" are likely to meet with general approval.

Planning has become regional. Late in 1963 a Government white paper presented a plan for the development of the Northeast, the area from York to the Scottish border. The proposals included construction of four new towns and two new universities at Durham and Newcastle-upon-Tyne, the reconstruction of Newcastle with a tunnel under the Tyne, and a Durham motorway. Similar proposals were made for central Scotland, with public service investment to be stepped up from a normal £40 million to £140 million for 1964–65. Then in March 1964 came a more elaborate Survey for the Southeast—all land below a line drawn from the Wash in the northeast to Bournemouth on the channel in Hampshire. This area represented 17 percent of the land surface of the United Kingdom in which lived 34 percent of the people. In the "Great Wen" of London, a part of this area, within 40 miles of Charing Cross were 12.5 million people, about one-fourth of the population of Great Britain. It was anticipated that by 1981 an additional 3.5 million will be seeking homes in the Southeast. The survey called for doubling the area of the Green Belt around London to prevent the continued expansion of the metropolitan area, the development of three new cities of considerable size (Bletchley in Buckinghamshire, Newbury in Berkshire, and a city in the Southampton-Portsmouth area in Hampshire), the expansion of towns around London (Ipswich, Northampton, Peterborough, Swindon), and new towns at Ashford in Kent and Stanstead in Sussex. This survey of 1964 was somewhat modified in 1967. The new strategy was to replace the centers of population growth along the main communication routes, which it was hoped, would induce industry and labor to leave London. Existing towns rather than "new towns" were to be developed.

By 1965 eight economic regions, as well as Scotland and Wales, had been outlined. In 1974 the Redcliffe-Maud Report (*Conduct in Local Government*) led to the establishment of economic councils in each of these areas; this is part of the plan for regional devolution. Special attention, as we have seen, was directed to Scotland and to Wales.

Traffic. In November 1963 Professor Colin Buchanan, professor of Transport at Imperial College, London, and adviser to the minister of Transport, presented a report, *Traffic in Towns,* which educated the public with its revolutionary analysis and recommendations. Buchanan confronted the extraordinary growth in motor traffic—2.5 million cars on British roads in 1953, almost 7.5 million ten years later. He proposed the integration of traffic planning and urban renewal, to handle as parts of the same environmental problem the needs of the private motorist, the traffic of industry and business, and the requirements of the pedestrian. As his prime example of the chaos which developed under a policy of *laissez-faire,* Buchanan cited Oxford Street in London, "which tries to discharge the two irreconcilable functions of being one of the most popular shopping centers in Europe as well as being a main traffic distributor for London." He presented pilot studies for widely different areas—for Leeds, Norwich, Newbury, and a section of London—which incorporated his recommendations, including the restriction of access to city centers and shopping areas, and the improvement of access roads.

Some of Buchanan's ideas are now in operation, particularly in the new towns. Thus, Stevenage has a shopping center designed for a city population of 80,000 with its pedestrian area from which vehicles are prohibited; Stevenage is often cited as Britain's finest contribution to recent city planning. Cumbernauld, one of the Scottish new towns housing people from Glasgow, has a city center on eight levels—a vast, many-purpose building with shopping area, offices, theatres, residences. Vehicular travel is limited to the lowest level. In London the traffic problem has thus far been met with expedients such as the dismantling of Hyde Park Corner and the construction of an underpass; in 1973, Oxford Street between Portman Street and Regent Street was barred to all traffic save taxis and busses, a measure which has succeeded dramatically despite early grumbling and apprehension. Buchanan's ideas may have helped preserve Christ Church Meadow in Oxford against proposals for access to Oxford from the East other than across Magdalen Bridge and up the High Street.

In 1974 the Covent Garden Market was moved across the Thames to Battersea. For 300 years it had shared an area of one hundred acres with residences, theatres, opera houses, and commercial premises. Covent Garden has lost its distinctive atmosphere but will be transformed into a quiet eddy of houses, theatres, shops, school, and a park which may in time develop a new flavor. For London more revolutionary changes may be in store. In February 1973 the Government announced preliminary plans for a six-lane road ringing London with a five-mile radius; it was calculated that it would require twenty years to complete. Some eight or ten plans have been drafted for Piccadilly Circus, others for the redevelopment of Victoria Street. Even more uncertain are proposals for transforming Whitehall into a new setting of public buildings free of traffic and a modernizing of Parliament Square. On such measure Britain, in continual economic crisis and struggling to reduce expenditures in the public sector, is likely to proceed slowly. Already, in 1975, was abandoned, for the time being at least, the plan to construct, with France, a railroad tunnel under the English Channel.

So bewildering was the changing scene that Raymond Williams in his *The Country and the City* (1973) was moved to remark: "the common image of the country is now an image of the past and the common image of the city an image of the future."

Border Lands

We have already examined the political atmosphere in Scotland and Wales, with the prospect of eventual devolution of constitutional authority from Westminster. Whatever the outcome may be, the political questions are not as complex as other aspects of national expression: language, tradition, culture. Indeed, social scientists hesitate to deal with England, Scotland, and Wales simultaneously. And Scotland itself is difficult to discuss as a whole. Each of the three sections—the highlands, the southern uplands, and the lowlands—has its own economic problems and, to a degree, its own social fabric.

But Scotland considers itself something apart from England, and the Scots resent representation of their land as merely a geographical expression. The coronation of Elizabeth II in 1953 aroused irritation, for there was, of course, no Elizabeth I in Scottish history. However, the balance was somewhat redressed when in 1969 the queen addressed the Assembly of the Church of Scotland on the four hundredth anniversary of the

Scottish Reformation. It was the first appearance of royalty in the Assembly since 1602. The strength of the separatist movement arises from the singular characteristics of Scottish institutions (religion, education, and law) and from its cultural heritage. The Edinburgh Festival is international in character but no less a matter of provincial pride. The best of Scottish literature and art have retained distinctive characteristics. But the use of the Gaelic language is limited to a few secluded areas.

The Welsh, like the Scots, are outraged if labeled "English." But Wales, like Scotland, is not all of a piece. Some seventy percent of the population live in the southeast, which is as heavily industrialized as any region in England. The rest of Wales remains largely pastoral. And religion is still somewhat divisive. The Church of England was finally disestablished in 1920 but efforts to bring together the unestablished Church in Wales and the Free Churches have failed. The strength of Welsh nationalism today springs from the current cultural revival and has limited expression in support for political devolution and limited autonomy. The fruits of this cultural revival are perhaps best found in village life in North Wales, with its choral groups, drama clubs, its local eisteddfod. The federated University of Wales through its five colleges has stimulated Celtic scholarship, studies in prehistory, and a linguistic and literary revival. The very popular national eisteddfod, an annual bardic festival, is held alternately in North Wales and South. Poets compete for the "Chair" and the "Crown." But perhaps the greatest attraction is the choral singing. We are assured that either a choral or mass rendition of the Welsh national anthem, "Land of my Fathers," provides an emotional experience almost beyond compare. But to conclude these remarks on a more practical level, despite the efforts of ardent nationalists, the use of the Welsh language continues to decline. The census of 1971 shows that about 21 percent of the population speak Welsh as their first language; ten years earlier the figure was 26 percent. Other surveys indicate that the use of Welsh by school children is proportionately less. A statute was necessary in 1967 to guarantee equal validity for the Welsh tongue with English in conduct of official business and legal matters. And there has been recurring controversy as to whether the annual eisteddfod should be conducted in Welsh alone or should be bilingual.

While any notion of "home rule all-round" for Scotland and Wales is not to be taken seriously, it is likely that their future in local politics, education, religion, language, and culture is largely in their own hands.

Government by Queen, Lords, and Commons

"Our best professional monarch for several, for perhaps many, generations" was the comment of *The Times* as Queen

Elizabeth II approached her Silver Jubilee Year, 1977. The American student of British affairs was all the more conscious of her role from the very considerable part she and the Duke of Edinburgh had in the bicentennial commemoration of the Declaration of Independence. The royal couple were in the United States (Philadelphia, Washington, D.C., New York, and Boston) at the climax of pageantry, July 6–11, 1976.

Kingsley Martin, no patriotic sentimentalist, observed in his *The Crown and the Establishment* (1962) that as Britain has declined in power the prestige of the Crown has increased. But Queen Elizabeth and Prince Philip have come to represent not only dignity, continuity, and stability, but energy, sound judgment, and intelligence as well. Prince Philip is well versed in technological and scientific matters and his advice and support are frequently sought. When Harold Wilson resigned as prime minister, he gave a farewell dinner at No. 10 for the Queen. He said: "I certainly advise my successor to do his homework before his audience or he will feel like an unprepared schoolboy."

Poets laureate C. Day Lewis and Sir John Betjeman did not take very seriously their obligation for verse on special occasions, the birth of Prince Andrew in 1960 and the queen's Jubilee in 1977. But general interest and pride in the royal family has increased. Prince Andrew, the royal couple's third child was the first born to a reigning sovereign of Britain since 1857. In 1964, a fourth child, Prince Edward, provided a family of three boys and one girl; in Britain only one family in twenty-five had as many as four young children. All have been educated in schools and not by private tutors. On July 1, 1969, Prince Charles was invested as Prince of Wales at Caernarvon Castle, a ceremony followed on radio and television throughout the world. A crowded House of Lords heard his maiden speech. It came in the course of a debate on a report on "Sports and Leisure" and it was, said Prince Charles, about a hundred years since a member of his family had spoken in the Lords. Princess Anne has had her own career; she developed style and competence in horsemanship, and participated in international riding competition. She was married to Captain Mark Phillips, November 14, 1973, in Westminster Abbey.

Constitutional Issues

If the monarchy continues serenely, there is much complaint elsewhere. What is wrong with Britain? Some observers find the answer in politics. From the early fifties it has been the fashion to write and talk about the weaknesses of parliamentary government in Britain. Some of the central issues are:

1. *The Role of the Cabinet.* Even the nature of problem is controversial. One position is represented by the question posed for debate in the Lords on May 17, 1950: "Resolved, that the growing power of the Cabinet is a danger to the democratic constitution of the country." Can it still be maintained that the Cabinet is, in practice, responsible to the House of Commons? Not once in the twentieth century has any Cabinet installed with majority support in the Commons ever lost control of that majority. And further, does not the Cabinet, through discipline over the parliamentary party, practically dictate legislation?

On the other hand, some conclude that the Cabinet has been downgraded, even denigrated. "Cabinet Government" is considered an obsolete term. Decisions, it is said, are not made by the Cabinet as a group and collective responsibility is a myth. An effective and dramatic expression of this interpretation is found in Richard Crossman, a member of the Wilson Cabinet 1964–70. His *The Diaries of a Cabinet Minister* have been published, beginning in 1976, despite an application for an injunction against publication initiated by the attorney general of the Labor Government in 1975. Crossman was convinced that, in Bagehot's terminology, the Cabinet had become a "dignified" rather than an "efficient" element in the British constitution. As a Cabinet minister, Crossman declared, he never influenced Government policy. Measures for dealing with the economic crisis, he said, were determined by Wilson and two or three others.

2. *The Power of the Prime Minister.* To replace the term "Cabinet Government" we find the phrase "Prime Ministerial Government." As the office is depicted by Crossman and others, the prime minister often seems more powerful than the president of the United States. Certainly the prestige and the potential, in an able man, has grown enormously in the twentieth century. Questions arise which cannot yet be answered. To what extent, for example, was the Suez policy in 1956 the decision of Eden and two or three others? Was the wholesale change in the Government in July 1962 carried through by the commanding prestige of Macmillan? In an earlier period it is likely that the result would have been another prime minister or some other party in power. In more recent years one finds Wilson, Heath, and Callaghan apparently dictating the policy of the Cabinet—fuller understanding awaits more revelation of the kind found in the Crossman diaries. To complicate matters still further, it may be that all Cabinet members, including the prime minister, are much of the time dominated by the permanent civil service.

3. *The Position of M.P.s.* After World War II the role of the back-benchers in the Commons became a matter of increasing inquiry. They had but few opportunities to speak, and then usually to an almost empty House. Their role in party decisions was limited. The chief whip, deputy chief whip, and junior whips maintained solidarity; the Government whips' office adjoins No. 10 Downing Street. Parliamentary debates have declined in importance. The voice of the M.P. in the Commons cannot compete with the press, television, and the public platform. Is not the civil servant, immune from party discipline, more important in formation and administration of policy? Is not the policymaker in a public corporation more powerful? So runs the bill of complaint.

4. *The Significance of Political Party.* Do elections matter? Does it really matter which party is in office? Are the parties offering alternatives, significant choices? Such were the questions raised by David Butler and Dennis Kavanagh after the election of February 1974. It was suggested that now the differences within parties were far more significant than those between them. Political issues were so blurred and party shifts so frequent in the sixties and seventies that such terms as "right," "center," and "left" meant little to the electorate. Is not such party control over the political process a form of tyranny?

5. *The Importance of the Voter.* Not since 1945 has any party won as much as 50 percent of the popular vote in a general election. The issue is sharpened in the reminder of *The Times* (June 6, 1975) that in the October 1974 poll 5,346,800 electors returned 13 members of Parliament, while 11,468,136 (less than 40 percent of the total vote cast) elected 319 members. To *The Times* it was "the outcome of a lottery" and a clear case for "electoral reform." As to the individual elector, what determines his vote: issues, party manifestoes, the merits of rival candidates in his district, the influence of public opinion polls? Is all reality reduced to "the image" projected to influence and attract him? Is there any reason to believe that governmental policy in Britain is a reflection of public opinion? The electors have little or no part in the selection of party candidates; they do not vote for members of a second chamber; on only one occasion has there been a referendum on a matter of public importance—on the Common Market in 1975—and that was not considered binding.

To state these questions is often to answer them. But commentary in the fifties and sixties was diversified. Those with experience often spoke superficially. Herbert Morrison, in *Government and Parliament* (1954), wrote a remarkable perceptive "survey from the inside" of what happened, but he was uncritical in discussing constitutional procedures. Likewise, L. S. Amery, in *Thoughts on the Constitution* (1947), made some interesting suggestions, but his conclusions were conventional. The important contributions are found in writings of a polemical nature. In Christopher Hollis's *Can Parliament Survive?* (1949) the question mark set the tone. G. W. Keeton answered this question in *The Passing of Parliament* (1952). In a lucid and carefully argued position he concluded: "Parliament . . . is predestined, if present tendencies continue, to become merely a ratifying body and a suitable forum for the ventilation of grievances." Michael Foot, in *Parliament in Danger!* (1959), began: "A curse on party politics . . . a gnawing cynicism about parliament itself—[such ideas] have provided, I believe, the dominant mood in British politics over recent years." Aneurin Bevan in his *In Place of Fear* (1952) called for "boldness" and "audacity." For him parliamentary power was the essential instrument for "transforming the structure of society." To many questions Peter G. Richards, in *Honourable Members: A Study of the British Backbencher* (1959), provided moderate and sensible answers. M.P.s are not "sheep or goats." They are generally esteemed; those belonging to the majority are usually more influential than are those with the Opposition, but the strength of members always varies according to circumstances. Brian Chapman, in *British Government Observed* (1963), declared that public policy is too often determined by "finding the least controversial course between conflicting interests" and considered that "institutional failures" explain many of the difficulties. His remedy was a "modernization" of Parliament with a better-paid, more self-assertive, and "more formidable kind of politician." An informed and effective analysis is found in Bernard Crick's *The Reform of Parliament* (1964), "an interpretation of what our system does and an advocacy that it should be reformed in certain directions." The reforms proposed include complete change in the composition and functions of the Lords and fundamental modifications of procedures in the Commons, particularly in the committee system, with a view to more control over ministers.

Some of these comments are now (1977) dated, but they reflect the changing character of both questions and answers. In 1968 Humphrey Berkeley in *The Power of the Prime Minister* argued that each elected Parliament should be given a fixed term, thus taking from the prime minister the power to control the timing of general elections. A study of political behavior in the process of change based on interviews over the period 1963–70 is the subject of David Butler and Donald Stokes, *Political Change in Britain* (1974). Richard Hodder-Williams in *Public Opinion Polls and British Politics* (1970) examined the relation between polls and representative democracy. The discussion is ongoing. Perhaps the most interesting feature is that these issues have been a matter of general as well as professional discussion and debate. And the same could not be said of constitutional questions early in the century.

Some Changes. Either as a result of this debate in and out of Westminster or as a result of changing circumstance, the years 1965–75 witnessed striking and significant change in many of Britain's political institutions. As Frank Stacey pointed out in his invaluable *British Government 1966–1975* (1975), some were efforts of "reform," and some of "reorganization," with little practical difference between these terms.

We have already discussed the abortive effort to "reform" both the membership and the functions of the House of Lords during 1968–69. A similar effort had been made through an all-party conference back in 1948, but also in vain. However, some significant changes have come. In 1958 life peerages were created. The first such included four women, and in general this provision has brought into the Lords many people of great experience and national prominence, including elder statesmen from the Commons. In January 1977 there were 279 life peers and peeresses. On the other hand, the Peerage Act of 1963, already mentioned, permitted hereditary peers to renounce their peerages and seek seats in the Commons.

Salaries have been raised, partly as a result of inflation, but they are still modest by American standards. In 1977 the prime minister received £20,000, Cabinet ministers £13,000, and junior ministers £5,500. M.P.s received a salary of £5750, with allowances for office expenses and for residence in London. Members of the Lords are only reimbursed for the expenses they incur while attending the House.

To the widespread cry for "more open government" some response has been made. In 1965 and again in 1975 the Conservative Party modified procedures for the selection of party leaders in Parliament. The effective decision was given to the Conservative members of the House of Commons who accept the discipline of the party whip—that is, those who are accepted as members in good standing of the Parliamentary Party. An overall majority was required. Essentially this same procedure has been followed by the Labor Party for some years.

Serious effort has been directed reforming legislative procedure, providing for more effective scrutiny by the Commons of budget estimates and the examination of delegated legislation. Bernard Crick had proposed that the "Specialist Committees" take charge during the committee stage of legislation and exercise some control. But there was strong op-

position, and limited experimentation indicated that "specialized sub-
committees" didn't fill the bill. The Wilson Labor Government, after
1966, experimented with "Select Committees" (Agriculture, Education
and Science, Scottish Affairs, Race Relations, and Immigration) formed
from membership of the Commons; this met with good results. In various other ways the back-bencher has been given a somewhat larger role,
particularly in initiating private member bills, dealing with matters which
otherwise might well have been hopelessly entwined in party politics.

Cabinet structure was substantially changed under Wilson and Heath.
The aim was greater efficiency, to be achieved by including all ministerial
heads of departments in a Cabinet of reasonable size. Inevitably this
experimentation produced some "giant departments," but it did provide
all departments with a spokesman in the Cabinet. Thus, the Department
of Environment, for example, included Planning and Local Government,
Transport, Housing and Construction, Sport and Recreation. Heath's
Government established a Central Policy Review Staff whose function
was to examine the general strategy of the Government's program and to
study projects with a view to evaluating the options available to the
Government.

Other changes have already been mentioned. Electoral reform was
limited to the statute of 1969, which lowered the voting age to 18 (and
also lowered to 18 the age of those qualified to marry without permission, to own land, to raise mortgages, and to make wills). But proportional representation, despite the outcry of the Liberals and their not
inconsiderable support elsewhere, seems no further advanced. Its proponents have no good answer to the argument that proportional representation in the British Parliament would encourage the formation of weak
minority or coalition governments. Nor has sentiment grown for the use
of the popular referendum. The issue of the Common Market was suitable for resolution in this manner because it was a matter on which all
parties were divided within their own ranks.

We have already had occasion to refer to Civil Service reform and to
the Local Government Acts of 1972 and 1974. In both areas earnest and
intelligent minds have been at work with good results, though these are
hardly areas to be dealt with summarily, for new problems are constantly
arising. Some weaknesses in local government practice were emphasized
in the "Bains Report" (1972), the findings of a study group entitled *Local
Authorities, Management and Structure*. A corporate rather than a departmental approach to problems was recommended. Long rivalry between county councils and borough councils led to some restoration of
the power of the boroughs. In 1965, a new body, the Greater London
Council replaced the London County Council; most services were restored to the individual boroughs.

The most far-reaching changes in the administration of justice since the Judicature Acts of 1873–75—such is the usual comment on the Courts Act of 1971. Implementing the recommendations of a Royal Commission under the chairmanship of Lord Beeching, this legislation abolished the Courts of Assize and the Quarter Sessions, which date back to the Middle Ages. A new court of record, the Crown Court, was granted jurisdiction of all cases on indictment, this to be exercised anywhere in England and Wales, at three levels, depending on the nature of the offense. Jurisdiction was to be exercised by High Court judges, circuit judges, and recorders. The Crown Court was to hear appeals from the magistrates' courts.

In 1965 the Murder Act was enacted, declaring that "no person shall suffer death for murder." This apparently ended a century of controversy. After World War II the matter came up persistently. In 1948 the home secretary said that there was almost no possibility that a person would be executed for a crime he didn't commit. In the early fifties several prominent cases raised in the minds of the public serious doubt that that conclusion was justified. There were some dozen hangings each year before 1957; persuasive books were written; public opinion polls indicated that the large majority favored a trial suspension of the penalty. The Act of 1965 retained the death penalty for a few offenses only, such as treason and mutiny. This act was provisional for four years; in 1969 it was confirmed by both houses as required. In 1973 and again in 1974 the Commons rejected efforts to restore the death sentence for murder, but each time by a lesser vote, for the activities of the Irish Republican Army had revived the issue.

Because of the persistent interest in the rights of the individual manifested by Labor politicians, particularly Roy Jenkins, Anthony Crosland, and Harold Lever, the Labor Government, 1964–70, in one way or another enacted significant legislation: the Abortion Act (1967), which legalized abortion if certain conditions were met; the Sexual Offences Act (1967), which legalized homosexual acts between consenting adults; and the Divorce Act (1969), which greatly broadened the theoretical grounds for divorce—with this statute, divorce would be granted if it were demonstrated that the marriage in question was completely shattered, and this to be established in ways indicated by the new law. The Theatres Act (1968) abolished the responsibility of censorship in the lord chancellor. In various directions the rights of women were broadened, especially with the Equal Pay Act and the Sex Discrimination Act, both of which became effective in 1975 and which together protected against discrimination in wages, education, housing, and other matters.

And in some quarters cries arose for a "Bill of Rights," required, so it was said, because of the long years of dominance of the judicial authorities by the executive. In this highly controversial area the Government proceeded cautiously, issuing a "discussion document" in 1976 which suggested ways of protecting civil liberties.

The Welfare State

The phrase "welfare state" defies definition. We may be literal-minded and suggest with William Robson, in his remarkable *Welfare State and Welfare Society: Illusion and Reality* (1976), that "a welfare state is one in which public policy is predominantly concerned with the welfare of its members," but then we encounter the question What is "welfare"? Or we may be more academic and use Derek Fraser's language (*The Evolution of the Welfare State*, 1973) and say that the term "represented the social consciousness of the British people in the middle of the twentieth century." This at least emphasizes that the term has had its own history. For most people early in the century it meant that public policy recognized poverty as a condition which could be ameliorated. The idea of the welfare state as providing social services for all came from Labor. Then, after World War II, the term came to represent not merely improvement of the condition of a particular class but establishment of equality of status. The term has thus come to be associated with the redistribution of the national income and with education, housing, health care, care of the handicapped, and even planning in order to improve the environment. Nearly every adult has national insurance to which, along with his employer and the state, he makes regular contributions. Thus, a system of national savings has been established, from which payments are made in time of need: sickness, unemployment, widowhood, old age, and so on. All this replaced the Keynesian ideal of "full employment" as the goal of economic and social endeavor.

But the evolution of the term "welfare state" will continue. We need, writes D. C. Marsh (*The Welfare State*, 1970) "a rational objective assessment of the main aims of social policy in relation to the kind of society we want ours to be, and of the methods of achieving them." He and other students of the question are aware that in recent years, in a comparatively affluent society, the significant element in the welfare state has become competition. There was more compassion for the needy in 1910 than in 1976, by which time there was more insistence upon the rights of the individual than upon his obligations. "Relative deprivation" was then a frequent cry.

The Standard of Living

To put all this in proper perspective, we may point out that in the twenty years following 1955 Britain developed a standard of living for nearly all its people which in food, shelter, clothing, housing, use of leisure time was much better than it had been at any previous time in her history. In the decade of the fifties, real wages increased more than 16 percent, and by 1960 the average adult manual worker received over £13 per week. Nearly half of England's working families had more than one wage earner, and the average income of workers' families was somewhat over £16 per week. Then in the decade 1961–71 average household incomes rose 94 percent; retail prices during the same period rose 57 percent. Extra income went, in many cases, for vacations; in 1960 only about 3 percent of all full-time manual workers had more than two weeks paid vacation; by 1972, 75 percent were entitled to three weeks or more. Also, additional income went for automobiles, entertainment, better housing, fuel, and light. During the years of rising retail prices, social security benefits kept pace. By 1973–74 the country was spending over £16 billion on social services, which worked out to about £287 a year per person.

It is not strange, therefore, that a visitor to England hears the casual observation that poverty has disappeared. But if we take Robson's definition of poverty as meaning "lack of access to a standard of life which provides the essentials for the maintenance of bodily and mental health, together with reasonable opportunities for family life and the upbringing of children," there is considerable "poverty," perhaps as much as 5 percent.

If the welfare state has sought a significant redistribution of national incomes, the actual facts are interesting. Professor Titmuss in his *Income Distribution and Social Change* (1962) declared: "there is more than a hint from a number of studies that income inequality has been increasing since 1949 whilst the ownership of wealth ... has probably become still more unequal and, in terms of family ownership, possibly strikingly more unequal, in recent years." As to ownership of capital wealth, there is much greater inequality in Britain than in most industrialized countries. Then, average figures on national income obviously tell us little about those at either end of the scale. Thus, though for 1961–62, average personal income on the Inland Revenue Report was £819 before tax, 42 percent of the people had incomes of under £500 a year before tax. At one extreme, about 1,000 men and women in London were sleeping in the open, according to a survey in 1961–62; at the other extreme, nearly half of the wealth in the country was owned by 2 percent of the people. Certain working-class family incomes seemed to remain at good levels, but were usually earned through overtime and often at the expense of family life. In 1962, 6 percent of households had incomes of over £40 per week, but a very large percentage of these had two or three or more earners. And a short period of unemployment because of a strike or change of employment could play havoc with family budgets geared to making payments on hire-purchase indebtedness. Since 1959 money incomes have risen much more rapidly than has the increase in national production; over a five-year period, incomes increased about 5.3 percent annually, and the domestic product per head about 2.3 percent. Thus, the actual standard of living has risen, but has risen slowly.

Nothing has been more striking in England in the postwar era than the revolution in housing. Subsidies of one kind or another have made home ownership possible for the average family. After 1953 about 300,000 houses were built each year, with the figure climbing to 382,000 in 1964. Then a white paper called for 500,000 houses a year by 1970. Results fell short; yet between 1945 and 1975 about 8.5 million new homes were built, with 43 percent of the population living in houses built since the war. Even so, many thousands were constantly registered with local authorities for new housing when available. By 1976 Britain's population of 56,000,000 lived in about 20.1 million dwellings, about half occupier owned. Of the other half, some two-thirds are owned and operated by local government authorities. Next to education, housing was the largest item in the local council budget. In the cities, slum clearance remained an essential problem; in 1964 one-half million dwellings were still classified as "slums."

Table 8   Summary of Public Expenditures on Social Services and Housing, Selected Fiscal Years, 1965–1977

| Services | (1 million) | | | |
	1965–66	1969–70	1973–74	1976–77
Education	1,636	2,299	4,078	7,423
National Health Service	1,319	1,762	3,055	6,234
Personal Social Services	109	233	554	1,208
School meals, milk and welfare foods	131	161	213	469
Social Security Benefits	2,499	3,656	5,718	11,527
Housing	953	1,219	2,621	5,195
Total Public Expenditure	6,647	9,320	16,238	32,056

Source: *Annual Abstract of Statistics,* 112 (1975): 54; 114 (1977): 54.

A Medical Service for All

The National Health Service has firmly established itself amid controversy. Harry Eckstein, one of the more reliable students of this agency, wrote in the mid-fifties: "Both the best and the worst one can say about it is that it has succeeded in supplying free medical and allied services indiscriminately to all, without making any appreciable differences in the quantity or quality of services supplied." In digesting this modest and somewhat ambiguous statement, one should bear in mind that prior to the Health Service, only about 20 million people (considerably less than half the population) were covered by any kind of health insurance.

Against this statement we should place the comment of another historian, some six years later. In 1961 Almont Lindsey wrote: "In the light of past accomplishments and future goals, the Health Service cannot very well be excluded from any list of notable achievements of the twentieth century. So much has it become a part of the British way of life, it is difficult for the average Englishman to imagine what it would be like without those services that have contributed so much to his physical and mental well-being." (In Lindsey's *Socialized Medicine in England and Wales* [1962] we have a reliable guide to the early history of the Service.) These two statements (that of Eckstein and of Lindsey) represent the transition from a National Health Service struggling in its infancy and somewhat uncertain of the future to one which in the sixties seemed to be achieving the original object "to secure improvement in the physical and mental health of the people."

Despite problems, the atmosphere of the fifties reflected confidence in the Service, as illustrated in a notable investigation, inaugurated in 1953, with its findings published in 1956. This was the Guillebaud Committee, composed not of experts, who might have had preconceived opinions, but of prominent and respected individuals quite independent of the medical profession itself. The minister of Health in a Conservative Government, Iain MacLeod, told the Commons that the inquiry would be impartial—and it was. He welcomed the report as a "vindication of the National Health Service as it now exists." The *British Medical Journal* called it an "impartial judgment" and admitted that "on the assumption that the state should provide a comprehensive medical service for the whole population the Report shows that by and large this country has not made such a bad job." The report, which was not completely satisfactory to either ardent friends or foes of the Service, put to rest charges, based on vague rumors, that the agency was extravagant, inefficient, and wasteful. The Guillebaud Committee concluded that there was no proof of widespread abuse, that the cost of health service per person had not increased, and that the overall cost compared favorably with that of medical service in the United States. Actually, in the years covered by the report, 1948–54, the Service consumed a declining proportion of the national wealth. In the half dozen years that followed, the service, while increasing somewhat in relative costs, never consumed as much as 4 percent of the gross national product, the percentage which seemed to be spent by most industrialized countries on medical service, and very much less than that spent in the United States. These general statements for Britain hold for the early sixties; while costs rose, they remained at about 3.6 percent of the gross national product. In 1962 the cost per person came to a little over £19.

The Guillebaud report was at once outdated in the degree to which it was unaware of the inadequacies of the program in 1956 and of the problems which lay ahead. A major problem, and the one that has been most in the public view, has been that of establishing adequate incomes for doctors—no problem born of the National Health Service, for prior to 1939 the majority of doctors received wholly inadequate remuneration. The problem of remuneration under the Health Service was first met in the implementation of the reports of the Spens Committee in 1948. The British Medical Association and the Ministry of Health agreed on "capitation fees," fixed payment per year for each patient registered with a doctor. This made it possible that the most sought-after doctors, and perhaps the best, would receive the highest incomes. In the course of the fifties, the maximum number of patients on the list of a general practitioner was cut from 4,000 to 3,500 and the average list declined from 2,600 to 2,300. About 98 percent of all general practitioners became associated with the service.

In February 1965 a Review Body on Doctors' Remuneration recommended a £5½ million pay increase for general practitioners, but most of it was set aside for their staffs and improving their surgeries (offices). The award added only £250 a year to average net income—bringing it to a little over £3,000—which was derided by the British Medical Association as amounting to no more than a penny a consultation. A "Doctors' Charter" proposed by the B.M.A. sought an average net income of about £4,300 a year, a maximum list of 2,000 patients, a five and one-half day work week, and six weeks' annual holiday. In the turmoil that ensued, the B.M.A. called upon the 23,000 general practitioners to submit undated resignations which would be activated if negotiations failed. Well over half responded. The threat of a revolt ended when the prime minister announced that the pay increase of £5½ million was unconditional. It was but a temporary solution. In 1966 the Government accepted the recommendations of the Kindersley Review Body for substantial increases for general practitioners, dentists, and hospital staffs. For the g.p.s this amounted to 30 percent, implemented in two stages. By 1972 the average g.p., with 2,500 National Health Service patients, earned about £6,000.

But by that time the unstable economy and the beginnings of inflation had brought other problems. The hospital building program launched in 1962 slowed down, as did construction plans for clinics, mental health centers, and nursing homes. Efforts to limit public spending led to cuts in the National Health Service budget, and this stimulated unrest in hopital staffs and other personnel, at best modestly remunerated, and a series of temporary strikes in 1974–75 for increased wages, improved work conditions, and as protest against "paying patients" in National Health Service hospitals.

This last issue became not only an occupational problem but a political dispute as well. In the face of bitter Conservative opposition, the Labor Government in 1975 announced that "pay beds" would be phased out of hospitals operated by the Service; then doctors would not be permitted to treat paying patients in those hospitals. A Royal Commission was appointed to assess the situation, including the problem of constantly rising costs. There was some suggestion that doctors in the National Health Service should not be permitted to take paying patients, but this clearly raised more problems than it solved. Differences were resolved by compromise. Legislation in 1976, in which the House of Lords had a significant role, provided for a gradual phasing out of "pay beds" in National Service hospitals; the operation of private medical practice was to be administered by a board independent of the National Service.

Education

The decades of the sixties and seventies will indeed be memorable in the history of education in Britain. First, there was a series of reports, remarkable for their thoroughness and professional knowledge, on schooling at all levels, setting the stage for discussion and action in the years that followed. A high point came in December 1972. The minister of Education, Mrs. Margaret Thatcher, outlined a ten-year program of growth, with public expenditures for elementary and secondary education increasing by 3 percent and for higher education by 5 percent. Mrs. Thatcher summarized the characteristics of the program: "First it provides an earlier start in education for all children whose parents want them to receive it. Secondly, it provides a larger and better trained teaching profession and for further improvement in the teacher/pupil ratio. Thirdly, it provides increased opportunities in higher education, both in numbers of places and in range of options."

Elementary Education. One of the least controversial areas during most of the twentieth century, elementary education received steadily increased attention during the sixties and seventies. A primary concern was the expansion of the school population (by 1971 the age group 5–8 was 22 percent larger than in 1964); with this went a shortage of trained teachers, crowded classrooms, and special problems of underprivileged children. These matters were discussed at length in 1967 in the Plowden Report to the Central Advisory Council for Education. This report inspired a program likely to be followed for the rest of the century. Nursery education, it was urged, should be available without charge; it was estimated that by 1982 some 700,000 places would be needed, as against the 300,000 available in 1973. The Plowden Report expressed special concern for the "slum" areas, which it designated as "educational priority" areas. The report was almost universally praised.

Secondary Education. In secondary education the issues in time became political and social as well as strictly educational. The Education Act of 1944 required the education of all children until the age of 15 and delegated to local councils the responsibility for establishing schools and courses of study. The impetus to change has often come from semi-official committees. One of the most influential was appointed by the Department of Education and headed by Sir Geoffrey Crowther (later Lord Crowther). Its report, issued in 1959, recommended raising the school-leaving age to 16 as soon as practicable. This recommendation finally became law in 1972–73, at the end of a period of declining numbers of the age group 15–18, and thus at a time when an additional year of compulsory education would exercise a minimum strain on the educational system.

Then in 1963 the Newsom Report (Sir John Newsom headed a committee appointed by the Central Advisory Council for Education) directed attention to children with less-than-average ability and performance and proposed a study of techniques for teaching handicapped children and experimentation with school organization. The final year in school, the report said, should provide job training, a sort of "initiation into the adult world of work and leisure." A few years later the Public Schools Commission, also with Newsom as its chairman, recommended gradual integration of independent "public" schools with state schools over the following twenty years. In the interim, about half of the pupils, selected on the basis of their "need," should come from state schools with fees paid by the state. The payment of fees by the parents was to be gradually phased out. This report settled little; it inspired a general debate on a controversial subject. The minority report of the Commission, written by John Vaisey, contended that these measures would merely extend a privileged system of education but now to be paid for out of state funds. Local educational authorities were reluctant to spend their allotments in this fashion. A related problem was that of "direct grant grammar schools" supported partly by fees from parents and partly from the Department of Education, with local educational authorities exercising no control whatsoever.

The central question in all these reports and the discussion they stimulated was what kinds of secondary education should be offered and what choices should be available to the student. Until the fifties this choice was the old grammar school, whose training was nonvocational and preparatory for universities and the professions, or the technical school, which was strictly vocational, or—a postwar development—"the secondary modern school," designed to provide a good all-round education neither strictly academic nor strictly technical. The local authority determined the basis of selection, but usually it was a matter of the child's record in the elementary school along with certain tests taken at the age of about eleven. The famous "eleven plus" exam has come in for much criticism, not so much for the examination itself as for the use to which it has been put in determining, once and for all, the kind of secondary education the child was to have. The Crowther Report denounced the exam and declared that this system was wasteful of talent—with half the ablest children leaving school as soon as possible. Another authority, H. C. Dent, wrote "Eleven Plus Misplacements." It was pointed out that many students who scored well in the "eleven plus" did not later fulfill the promise then shown, while other students did not develop interests and capabilities until well after the age of eleven. In the Commons in January 1965 the secretary of state for Education and Science pointed out how unevenly the system had operated. In England, he said, without contradiction, the range of children able to get into grammar schools varied from 8 percent to 34 percent, and in Wales the range was even wider. Certain statistics reinforced the problem—between 1950 and 1963 the proportion of fifteen- and sixteen-year-olds staying in school was up only 50 percent, while the proportion of those 17 and 18 years of age remaining in school doubled.

Some local authorities facilitated shifts from one type of school to another, and others reorganized the curriculum of the "modern school" to embrace some grammar school and some technical school–type training. The most radical change was offered in the appearance of the "comprehensive school," which offered all types of education and was open to all students regardless of performance in the "eleven plus." It is possible for a student in the comprehensive school to shift from one course of study to another as interest and capacity warrant. Those enthusiastic about the comprehensive school are able to cite excellent results. On the other hand, the grammar schools have demonstrably done an excellent job for university preparatory students.

The new Labor Government in January 1965 carried a resolution in the Commons "for reorganizing secondary education on a non-selective basis to suit local conditions in full consultation with teachers and parents." But a few years later, in 1969, the Labor Government requested that local authorities submit schemes for ending the eleven plus exam and for developing comprehensive schools. Only 22 out of 163 authorities responded, and the Government threatened to compel uniformity. This came to a halt with the advent of the Heath Government in 1970; the Conservatives wished to retain the grammar school, the public school, and the direct grant school as part of a diversified educational system. When Labor returned to power in 1974, the Government again raised the issue; by that time about half of the students in state-maintained secondary education attended comprehensive schools. Legislation now empowered the Government to compel transition to the comprehensive school. It was also announced that "direct grant schools" would be phased out. But it is likely that compulsion and uniformity, if they come, will come slowly; the shift to regional devolution in local affairs will encourage diversity.

The larger question is: can the momentum for change in educational philosophy and administration continue? The immediate problem is economic: where will funds come from to reduce size of classes still overcrowded, to develop nursery education, to provide adequate compensation for teachers in elementary and secondary education, and either to maintain or absorb public (independent) schools?

Higher Education. We have already noted the change in philosophical attitude toward higher education manifested in the years immediately after the war. But the impact of change was not fully felt until the fifties, when expansion of facilities and modification of curricula began to transform a segment of English life which, before 1939, had been almost impervious to social forces at work elsewhere.

Early in 1961 it was calculated that about 170,000 students (about 6 percent of the relevant age group) were in various types of higher education. Registration in universities alone reached 106,000, over twice the prewar figure. Funds available to the University Grants Committee steadily increased in the fifties, and by the end of the decade about four-fifths of all university students were receiving government aid, and the larger proportion of all university budgets was underwritten by the state. New institutions were somewhat slow to develop, or so it seemed ten years later. After Keele (the University of North Staffordshire) in 1949, no new universities were established until the University of Sussex at Brighton in 1961. Sussex began with 50 students, which by 1970, according to plan, grew to 3,000. Another notable development was the new Churchill College at Cambridge, established in 1960, with about two-thirds of its students in science and technology, and provisions for considerable post-graduate study. All of the older universities felt growing pains; Oxford and Cambridge doubled in size between 1938 and 1960. Altogether, it was a different atmosphere from that of prewar Britain, with its 17 universities and state aid of only £4 million per year.

The explosion, however, was yet to come. In October 1963 the Report on Higher Education from a committee headed by Lord Robbins, a noted economist, recommended massive expansion. A ten-year program set a target of 390,000 places in institutions of higher learning by 1973–74, including 218,000 in the universities alone. A total of some sixty universities was envisaged (as against 32 in 1963), including ten colleges of advanced technology and two postgraduate schools for business and management. Reorganization of Teachers Training Colleges was urged, with incorporation within the universities and with facilities for four years of study. The report was promptly accepted by the Government, with a useful debate in the Lords urging an increase in the number of places for postgraduate study to provide the staff for the rapidly expanding undergraduate program.

In 1963, shortly before the appearance of the Robbins Report, the University of York and the University of East Anglia (Norwich) were founded. A year later came Lancaster, the University of Essex at Colchester, the University of Kent at Canterbury, and the University of Warwick at Coventry. These new "redbrick" institutions broke pretty much from the educational traditions. They emphasized general education before specialization. In this respect Sussex proved to be the pacesetter: when the student chose his major area of study, he included subject matter common to related disciplines.

As the years passed, the target of the Robbins Report was more than reached. This may be expressed in several ways. In the sixties the number of university degree candidates doubled. By 1975 there were 480,000 students in higher or further education. Of these some 240,000 were full-time students in 44 universities. About 50 percent were studying the liberal arts and the social sciences, about 35 percent were pursuing science and technology, with the remainder taking pre-law, pre-medicine, or pre-theology courses of study. Public funds accounted for about 90 percent of the expenditures, with the universities alone receiving £426,000,000 annually. By the eighties it is estimated that the student population in universities will number 375,000. An experiment which may be regarded as an established institution is the Open University, a nonresidential university launched in 1971. By 1976 it had more than 40,000 students, most of them part-time, a very considerable number seeking university degrees. Instruction is through correspondence courses and summer schools, and through television and radio broadcasts at listening and study centers. The charges against students are low and merely supplement grants from the Department of Education and Science.

The Robbins Report inspired the appointment in 1964 of the Franks Commission (under Sir Oliver Franks, provost of Worcester College, Oxford) to inquire into "the part which Oxford plays and should play in the future in the system of higher education in the United Kingdom." The report two years later advocated stronger central administration, proposed liberalizing the admissions system, recommended a higher percentage of women students (they were then 1 in 6), and urged greater emphasis on technology and science. Sharp criticism was directed at All Souls College, which has no students, for its "infirmity of purpose." It is not surprising that these suggestions, while favorably received, have been but slowly implemented.

The program for higher education has been designed to produce technologists as well as scientists. Striking advance was made in institutions loosely described as "polytechnics," originally developed in connection with a particular industry or workplace. In 1966, some 30 of these institutions were brought together administratively under the rubric "New Polytechnics," by Anthony Crosland, minister of Education. Now public funds facilitated their growth. Ten Colleges of Advanced Technology (known as CATS) were elevated to university status in 1962 and transferred from the control of local authorities to the Ministry of Education.

Inevitably, the economic crisis of the seventies, especially the problem of inflation, has had its effects on higher education. White papers in 1976 indicated retrenchment in the immediate future. University budgets were frozen, new construction halted. And for the first time since the war, applications for places in universities direct from secondary schools dropped in numbers. Whether or not these conditions are merely temporary remains to be seen.

The significance of this expansion of higher education rests only to a degree in the figures, impressive as they may be. In truth, the percentage of those continuing formal education beyond the secondary level in Britain is likely to remain below not only that in the United States but also that in such countries as France, Sweden, and Canada as well. In assessing this fact, the Robbins Committee did well to point out that in Britain the ratio of wastage is very low, financial assistance is greater than is offered in most countries, and the British student receives far greater attention and stands a much better chance of receiving a degree,. In any case, the expansion is sufficient to produce social change that is incalculable. The son of a miner, the daughter of a bus driver, now has educational opportunity equal to that of a child from a family of means or position. The privileged position of the child sent to one of the famous public schools will soon be a matter of the past. The Robbins Report concluded that in innate ability there was very little difference among students according to social or economic status. The Newsom Report of 1963 revealed that the gap in reading and vocabulary skills according to economic status had noticeably narrowed, with relative improvement in the children of manual workers. The potential has always been present, but only recently has there been incentive and opportunity. The deliberate location of most of the new universities in or near cities or conurbations indicates that higher education is now closely associated with the realities of modern society.

Popular Culture

This book, while primarily concerned with political and economic history, has devoted conisderable attention to the "social" context as well. We have tried from time to time to take some note of the "culture" broadly conceived—moral and intellectual values, religious outlook, means of communication, cultivation of the arts, the use of leisure time. And we return briefly to this theme, "the quality of life," we might call it, as manifested in the closing decades of our period. If these few pages lead the reader to further examination on his own, their purpose will have been well served.

Religion

In religious observance and doctrine the significant changes since World War II, more especially since 1960, include (1) modifications in the government of the Church of England and a changing relation between church and state; (2) halting steps toward union of the Church of England with the Methodist Church; (3) reconciliation, in attitude, of the Church of England with the Roman Church; (4) the challenge to traditional Christian doctrine and ethics in the ranks of both clergy and laity; (5) the steady decline in church affiliation and attendance.

In 1970 the governmental authority of the Church of England was vested in the General Synod, providing an equal voice for bishops, clergy, and laity. This came at the end of more than a half century of discussion and debate. The Church of England had been governed by convocations of bishops and clergy, with no laity included, from the break with Rome in the sixteenth century down to the twentieth century. In 1919 came a separate house of laity with limited functions. In a few years the new General Synod has demonstrated its significance. In 1975 it accepted in principle the ordaining of women priests but deferred final decision. In 1974 Parliament authorized the General Synod to make changes in prayerbook and service if not contrary to the doctrine of the church. The Synod proposed that the church and not the state should have the final voice in the appointment of bishops. And in 1975 it pressed for the abolition of lay patronage in appointment of clergy. These appeared to be steps toward ultimate disestablishment of the church, but formal separation of church and state is not likely to come for some time.

Ecumenism. Ecumenism, at least as an ideal, has been in the air much of the time since 1945. When Archbishop Temple was enthroned at Canterbury in 1942, he spoke in his sermon of the ecumenical movement, "the great new fact of our time." It remained to be seen how deep this would run in theology and church organization and how much of it was due to mere irrelevance of the issues today. Church leaders, at least, took it very seriously. Christian unity, both within and without the Anglican Communion was one of the chief goals of Geoffrey Fisher, archbishop of Canterbury, 1945–61. The theme of the Lambeth Conference of 1958 was reconciliation. In 1960 Fisher made an apostolic visit to Rome and to Pope John XXIII, the first such meeting since the fourteenth century. In 1966 Fisher's successor, Archbishop Arthur Michael Ramsey, met with Pope Paul VI in a simple religious ceremony in the Sistine Chapel. "The world observes, history will remember," said the Pope. Since then groups representing both faiths have declared that they are in essential agreement on theology and faith. But church organization will pose almost insurmountable problems and no actual unity is in sight.

On the other hand, a union of the Church of England and the Methodist Church, discussed for many years, seemed about to become an actuality in the sixties. A negotiating committee of distinguished Anglicans and Methodists was authorized at the Lambeth Conference (1958); this commission presented in 1963 its "plan," which provided for an initial step in which the two churches would still be "distinct" but "in full communion," to be followed, after some years, by complete union. The prospect of favorable decision according to the timetable of "the plan" was sufficiently promising to justify noted historian Roger Lloyd's writing in his *The Church of England 1900–1965* (1966) that it would indeed be "surprising if in the end these proposals . . . came to nothing." Yet, as of 1976, that was the story. General approval was voiced by the clergy of both communions—at the Lambeth Conference in 1968 and at the Methodist Conference in 1969. In January 1969 it was agreed that a favorable vote of a 75 percent majority would be required in both the General Synod and the Methodist Conference. The Methodists met this requirement in both 1969 and 1970, but the General Synod mustered only a 69 percent favorable vote in 1969, and only 65 percent in 1971 and 1972. The bishops were overwhelmingly favorable; the opposition came from the laity. Indeed, on all matters of change—on theology and church organization and on divorce and abortion—the laity were, as Anthony Sampson suggests (*The New Anatomy of Britain,* 1971), more conservative and "more churchy" than the clergy.

It should be noted that in 1972, after years of negotiation, Congregationalists and Presbyterians joined in the United Reformed Church in England and Wales. Certainly the idea and the ideal of ecumenism was nurtured by the new Coventry Cathedral, consecrated May 25, 1962, in the presence of the queen. Alongside the ruins of the medieval St. Michael's, a casualty of the Blitz in 1940, now stands the new edifice, a remarkable achievement, designed by Sir Basil Spence and constructed in seven years' time at a cost of £1½ million. It includes a Chapel of Unity, which in 1965 was given a Congregational minister as its warden. The new Anglican cathedral is "a triumph for a church anxious to present its faith to the people in a contemporary way," declared the *Economist.* It has drawn an unending stream of visitors.

Theological doctrine, now a controversial theme in churches and out, has attracted considerable attention. The religious themes of C. S. Lewis (d. 1963) were well known to those of all or no religious persuasion, and the works of Dorothy Sayers (d. 1957), an interpreter of religion as well as gifted writer of mystery stories, were bestsellers. The world of theology was both stimulated and disturbed by *Soundings: Essays Concerning Christian Understanding* (1962), edited by Dr. A. R. Vidler, Dean of King's College, Cambridge, which called for a fresh approach to theology and asked: "what questions shall we face?" The next year came *Honest to God,* which is said to have sold a million copies in various languages. The author, John A. T. Robinson, the Bishop of Woolwich, concluded that the church had failed to interpret God in intelligible terms to modern man. Thus, the traditional notion of a personal God, and perhaps even the Incarnation and the Trinity, were in question.

On the public generally the impact of organized sectarian faith has considerably declined, as revealed by various polls of sabbath observance. In 1973 approximately 27,500,000 of the population of the United Kingdom had been baptized in the Church of England, but those "confirmed" numbered but 9,304,000 in 1976. In England and Wales there were about 4,000,000 Roman Catholics. The Methodists numbered 560,000 and were on the decline. No doubt much of the cause was apathy in a materialistic world. But also, in the not too distant past, churches and church-related societies had served many secular functions—education, charity, recreation—which have been transferred to other agencies.

Communication: The Press, Television, Radio

Britain is a land of newspaper readers; next to Sweden it has the largest number of subscribers in proportion to population. On the Underground in London, on the busses, on the railroads, in the parks, in hotel lounges, the visitor is aware of the ubiquity of the newspaper. Many papers distributed nationally have larger circulations than American dailies. For 1974 some average circulation figures for London dailies are: *Daily Mirror*, 4.2 million; the *Sun*, 3.3 million; *Daily Express*, 3.2 million; the *Daily Telegraph*, 1.4 million; *The Guardian*, 360,000; *The Times*, 350,000. The Sunday "nationals" have even larger circulation, led by *News of the World* with nearly 6 million. Estimated circulation of regional morning and evening papers in 1976 was about 5 million.

Yet, strange as it may seem, most papers have been financially in the red in the sixties and seventies. Since 1955 nine national papers have succumbed to rising costs and have folded. In 1974–75 several London papers (the *Observer, Daily Telegraph, Sunday Telegraph, The Times*) announced cuts of one-third in labor costs in order to survive. The provincial press is in a somewhat healthier state.

No other aspect of English society is more subject to change and evades more successfully any attempt to characterize it. Even the essential role of the press has changed since World War II. "The newspaper of opinion is a mirage long pursued by English journalism but only briefly achieved," remarks a thoughtful commentator, Anthony Smith, in *The British Press since the War* (1974). Of the national dailies only *The Times, The Telegraph*, and *The Guardian* (and to this we add the Sunday nationals—*The Observer, The Sunday Telegraph* and *The Sunday Times*) seek to win the minds of its readers. Even these papers are less "political" than they were earlier in the century when there were close links between proprietors and editors on the one hand and the government on the other. Elsewhere journalists show little interest in molding public opinion; they merely seek to determine the reading habits of the reading public, to pander to them, and to create an atmosphere favorable for advertising. Indeed, the newsroom, rather than the editorial room, exerts power and makes the important decisions.

Newspaper proprietorship is constantly changing character; now it seldom emerges from the world of journalism itself but comes from the outside. There is Lord Thomson, like Beaverbrook half a century earlier, a recent (1953) newcomer from Canada. He purchased *The Scotsman* (Edinburgh) and later, in 1959, the *Sunday Times*, and in 1966 *The Times* itself. He is now often regarded as the personification of the commercialized press of the postwar ear. Then there is Cecil King, a nephew of Lord Northcliffe, who acquired possession of the tabloid *Daily Mirror* in 1951 and went on in the next decade to construct the largest of the press empires. This included the *Sun*, which replaced his *Herald*. King had Labor's support and had designs for office in the Government which came to power in 1964. But he turned critic, and during the crisis over economic policy in 1968 he wrote his famous leader "Enough is Enough" for the *Sun* (May 10), which so enraged his fellow board members that they combined to oust him from his chairmanship. The latest of the "press barons" is Rupert Murdoch, who, fresh from Australia in the late sixties, soon became owner of the Sunday paper with the largest circulation, *The News of the World*, and subsequently purchased the ailing *Sun*, which he transformed into a tabloid largely devoted to sports and sex and more than doubled its circulation. Anthony Sampson has remarked: "Murdoch had knocked on the head the idea that the level of popular journalism might be gradually rising."

On the other hand, it is often maintained that the best of the weekly periodicals in England are superior to the best in the United States. Largest circulation is found among women's magazines and the *Radio Times* and the *TV Times*. In political and social opinion the leaders are the *Economist* (no political association), *New Statesman* (an outgrowth of the "radical" *Nation*, now with an independent socialist approach), *Spectator* (independent Conservative outlook), *Tribune* (left-wing Labor). For literary comment and criticism the best have been (and they are good indeed) the *Times Literary Supplement* and *The Listener*. Of the numerous journals that appear three or four times a year, some of the ventures launched since World War II have been boldly experimental and creative; they include *Horizon* (1940–50), the *Cambridge Journal* (1947–54), *Encounter*, *Past and Present* (a historical journal), and the *New Left Review*. In these journals we have a bridge back to the kind of commitment found in leftist writers in the thirties.

Television and radio ... We may characterize television and radio broadcasting in a different tone from that which we have used with the daily press. Indeed, the press has been overtaken; television and radio offer more to the discriminating public; they now provide a better forum for the presentation of ideas and the discussion of national issues.

Public broadcasting, as we have seen, dates back to 1922; the B.B.C. also inaugurated the world's first regular television service in 1936. After World War II, in the years of "affluence," television came to be more of a necessity in British households than central heating or plumbing. In 1959, 70 percent of households had the "telly"; by the mid sixties it was 90 percent; by 1975, 96 percent. No control over the programs of the B.B.C. is exercised by the government; and no advertising is carried. The domestic service of the B.B.C. is entirely financed by license fees on receiving sets. In 1974 the fee was £12 per year for color sets and £7 per year for black and white; about 18,000,000 licenses were issued in 1974, one-third of them for color sets.

Until 1955 broadcasting was a monopoly of the B.B.C., but then the argument "we are not a nation of intellectuals" won out over violent protest, in provision for commercial television. The Independent Television Authority was created, later changed to Independent Broadcasting Authority, and by 1964 was transmitting from twenty-two stations into 13 million homes. It is financed by rental payments from the program companies.

Special programs in the sixties or seventies, outstanding for their quality or listener success or both, include David Frost (a leading television personality of the sixties) with his satire on public figures in *That Was the Week that Was*, which eventually reached 12,000,000 viewers; the *Royal Palaces of Britain*, Christmas Day, 1966, with Kenneth Clark; *Civilization*, also with Kenneth Clark; a twenty-six–episode presentation of Galsworthy's *Forsyte Saga*; Thackeray's *Vanity Fair*; *Coronation Street*, a popular serial of everyday life, which in 1970 celebrated its tenth anniversary as the longest run on television; *The Search for the Nile*; two series on World War II; *Upstairs, Downstairs* (a popular serial of Edwardian England, World War I, and after); *America*, with Alistair Cooke, heralding the American bicentennial; *The Ascent of Man*, with Jacob Bronowski. Most of these programs were repeated in the United States with outstanding success. And no one who listened will ever forget the superb handling of the state funeral of Winston Churchill in 1965 by the B.B.C.'s incomparable Richard Dimbleby; his commentary during hours of solemn pageantry went to all quarters of the world.

Audio broadcasting is provided by the B.B.C. alone; its famous Third Program, launched in 1946, was devoted to broadcasts of intellectual and artistic distinction and is widely credited with raising popular taste. For the election of October 1974, thirteen one-hour programs were devoted to questions from voters and answers from candidates. In 1971–72 (and then repeated) came *The Long March of Everyman*, a series of twenty-six programs on the history of Britain since 1750. Entirely audio, the story was told through lectures, readings, folk songs, orchestral music.

Britain has become one of the six leading "external broadcasters" in the world; this service of the B.B.C. is financed by the government. External broadcasting began in 1932 as a link among Commonwealth nations. During the war the B.B.C. broadcast in forty-five languages, remembered in the Western world as one of the great voices of faith and humanity. The V for Victory signal—the letter V in Morse code followed by the central theme of Beethoven's Fifth Symphony—originated with the B.B.C. and was quickly accepted as the symbol of defiance in an embattled world. After the war the B.B.C. continued to broadcast news abroad, as well as reports on business, technology, finance, sports. The B.B.C. has few peers in its reputation for credibility; in its programming it is entirely independent of the government.

The Arts and Entertainment

One might well have expected that in times of economic crisis all possible resources would have been used to extend industrial production, eliminate unemployment, and reduce inflation. And, in particular, one would have expected that as national budgets reflected drastic cuts in defense sepnding and in funding social services, the Arts would also have been restricted. But on the contrary, in the sixties and seventies, official patronage, through grants from state funds, of both the fine arts and the performing arts has steadily increased and more than kept pace with inflation. Indeed, the figures are rather startling: in fiscal year 1969–70, £17 million; in 1971–72, £30.3 million; and in 1974–75, £52.7 million. In part this rise was due to admission charges, in 1970 and after, for entrance to museums and galleries.

Generally speaking, official aid was channeled through the Arts Council, which had been created by royal charter in 1946. This Council, from 1965 appointed by the secretary of state for Education and Science, had as its function, in official language: "to develop and improve the knowledge, understanding and practice of the arts, to increase their accessibility to the public, and to advise and co-operate with government departments, local authorities and other organizations." The Council controlled the funds allocated and made grants to orchestras, to opera, dance, and theatre companies, with more limited assistance to individual artists for particular projects.

Between 1956 and 1971 grants to the Arts Council steadily increased; by 1971 the Council was supporting 171 enterprises in London and 1,115 outside. Indeed, the Council transformed the theater in the provinces. Much of the impetus came from Jennie Lee, widow of Aneurin Bevan, who became parliamentary undersecretary for Education and Science in 1965. A building fund was created to supplement other resources for construction. Here are some of the results. In 1967, adjacent to the Royal Festival Hall on the south bank of the Thames, the Queen Elizabeth Hall and the Purcell Room, designed for smaller audiences, opened their doors. In 1969 came construction of a £1 million extension of the National Gallery in London. In 1976 the National Theatre Company, which for years had been playing to near capacity crowds in the "Old Vic" in Waterloo Road, moved to its new home on the south bank, with three separate theatres varying in size, stage facilities, and purpose. Completion was delayed by the series of national financial crises in the early seventies, but there it stands along the promenade, with the concert halls, Hayward Art Gallery, and National Film Theatre.

There is no end to what may be said of London theatre, art, and music. British films improved in quality after World War II and stimulated higher quality in Hollywood. However, in the sixties and seventies, patronage of the cinema steadily declined, and some would say the quality of the screen as well. Television had innumerable advantages and soon stole much of the cinema-going public. But there was no similar story in the other performing arts. Theatre charges remained fairly moderate in London. Head and shoulders above most of his fellow actors, Sir Laurence Olivier won a commanding position on both stage and screen, and from 1962 to 1973 was the Director of the National Theatre Company. Plays were produced in memorable version by the Royal Shakespeare Company at Stratford-upon-Avon and at the Aldwych Theatre in London.

Distinguished seasons of orchestral music have been presented by the London Philharmonic, the London Symphony, and other companies in London at the Royal Festival Hall and the new concert halls nearby; the Promenade Concerts have filled the vast space of the Albert Hall and recitals continued at Wigmore Hall. In Benjamin Britten (1913–76) Britain proudly acclaimed one of the most original and prolific composers of the twentieth century. Best known were his opera *Peter Grimes* (1945), with its scenes in the drab seaside villages of Suffolk, and *Turn of the Screw* (1970), based on the Henry James story. Opera is presented much of the year in London at the Royal Opera House, Covent Garden, and at Sadler's Wells; a summer season, with internationally known stars, has made celebrated Glyndebourne in Sussex.

English ballet gained a worldwide reputation through Sadler's Wells, incorporated in the Royal Ballet in 1957. In the thirties and during World War II and after the stars were the incomparable Margot Fonteyn and Robert Helpmann, the Australian; for years Helpmann was *premier danseur* with Sadler's Wells. His role as Margot Fonteyn's partner was taken over by Rudolf Nureyev, born in East Siberia in 1938, who made his Covent Garden debut in *Giselle*, in February 1962.

We may note briefly other matters. The first Commonwealth Festival of the Arts was held in 1965 in London, with smaller festivals in Glasgow, Liverpool, and Cardiff. It is safe to say that this festival and its successors contributed more to Commonwealth unity than did politics. The Edinburgh International Festival, over a period of three weeks, is famous and has inspired other arts festivals up and down the land. Shifting our ground somewhat, we mention that London has been and is a major center for the international art trade. In the sixties was reopened the refurbished Whitehall Banquetting Hall, created by Inigo Jones in the seventeenth century. Construction was finally completed (it began in

1904) of the gothic structure of the Metropolitan Cathedral of Christ the King in Liverpool; and Niklaus Pevsner has completed his *The Buildings of Britain*, thirty-seven volumes in all, a *tour de force* which is critical, enlightened, and comprehensive. In December 1976, the London Museum, formerly housed in Kensington Palace, opened new doors on Aldersgate. Two floors present 7,500 exhibits.

The Quality of Life

In its manifesto in 1964 a major political party pointed with pride to "the quality of life" which had been achieved in Britain. A dozen years later one is not likely to find this statement repeated, though the question it raises appears at every turn. This is what "popular culture" is all about. Here we shall suggest other areas where an answer may be found.

One might examine the use of leisure time—television and radio, the cinema, partying, reading, sports, and so on—with a view to making judgments. There is legalized betting on horses and greyhounds which came in 1960; since then the turnover in gambling has grown to a billion pounds per year and beyond. One would also have to examine and assess the cinema, increasingly dominated by violence, sex, and sadism. What was the impact of "pop music" and what the meaning of the idolization of the Beatles? The significance and popularity of satire and irony in fiction, in journalism, and on the stage, as though nothing were sacred or even significant, might attract attention—the astonishing success of "Beyond the Fringe" in the theatre, and of "That Was the Week That Was" and "Not So Much a Programme, More a Way of Life" on television, and the popularity in some circles of even stronger medicine in the periodical *Private Eye*. Or what is one to make of the restless teenagers following groups of fractious "Mods" and "Rockers" to seaside towns on holiday weekends (between 3,000 and 5,000 juveniles swarmed into Hastings over Bank Holiday in August 1964)? During the last sixties, student demonstrations, demanding student representation on academic councils and changes in courses and examinations, brought a halt to class schedules at the London School of Economics and elsewhere. At the University of Essex students broke up a high-level conference which was taking evidence on student problems. Crime of all kinds has increased; the police report for 1964 spoke of one million indictable offenses in England and Wales, of which only 40 percent were cleared up. The incidence of fatal accidents on highways in the sixties was said to be twice as many per motor car mile as in the United States. One might be offended at irreverence or indifferent manners—a case in point would be the jostling, the talking, the smoking, the photographing during prayers at the Remembrance Service for the dead of two World Wars at the Cenotaph in Whitehall.

On the other hand, the observer might note that these same traits of contemporary culture are found elsewhere, often more glaring. The rate of crime, for example, has been far less in London than in New York City. Much of the British scene, little changed in half a century, still beckons the visitor from abroad. More than half of the family dwellings have a garden plot. Along Green Park in London are the stalls with fruit, roses, and daily papers; Hyde Park Corner on a Sunday continues rich in "human eccentricity"; groups of school children still troop in and out of the cathedrals at Canterbury, at York, at Exeter, or wherever. To be sure, many an activity has been transformed. The supermarket finally hit Britain in the fifties and sixties, with startling change, best illustrated in the success story of the Marks and Spencer retail stores. Lord Marks' ambition "to glamorize women and children at prices they can afford to pay" was fully realized. Marks received the American (1962) "Retailer of the Year" award; his citation declared that he had been "largely responsible for the revolution in dress in the British Isles."

Our observation, of course, has no limits. It would include attention to public libraries—where nearly one-third of the population in the 1970s are registered users—and a purview of classrooms and laboratories in colleges and universities. And it would lead to respectful attention to the steady sale of books of quality at bookstalls on the street and in railway stations which would recall what the paperback revolution has done for a nation's reading habits. "One of the more democratic successes in our recent social history," wrote Richard Hoggart in 1970 of the role of Penguin in contemporary society. Again, one would recall a matchless and moving performance of Margot Fonteyn in *Giselle*, and more recently Rudolf Nureyev in *Sleeping Beauty*, or Laurence Olivier's *Othello*, or a summer production at the Glyndebourne Festival, or a crowded service at St. Paul's to hear a sermon by Martin Luther King.

But even to use the phrase "the quality of life" may seem mocking in the intellectual atmosphere of the sixties and seventies. Skepticism, irony, a sense of insufficiency, and irritable introspection dominate the examination of contemporary institutions. Penguin issued a special series called, "What's Wrong with ...?" Countless books have dealt with "British problems." Many people no longer consider the welfare state an achievement, a source of pride and satisfaction; rather, some people have said that it has made Britain a static and drab little world. Even in social reform, Britain, they say, prefers manners to efficiency, the amateur to the professional, the Establishment to technocracy.

When one turns to contemporary writing—fiction, poetry, drama—

one seldom fails to find other clues to the "quality of life." Many prewar novelists such as Henry Green, Elizabeth Bowen, Joyce Cary, Rebecca West, and Evelyn Waugh reached the peak of their powers after 1945. But by the sixties they had ceased to be topical, and as such had been replaced by a group of younger writers (among them Kingsley Amis, John Osborne, John Wain, Alan Sillitoe) who, for the most part, were born between the wars. Of course, there was still Angus Wilson, to many much more relevant. In 1962 he was referred to by a critic as "the best contemporary British novelist." And there is also Anthony Powell, who has come increasingly into his own.

In an age in which class distinctions are supposed to be disappearing, one of the most popular themes in fiction has been the study of conduct in a class-conscious society. A common character is a lad from a working-class background who goes to a university (usually Oxford) on a government grant and finds himself in unfamiliar situations controlled by ideas of class. He confronts the problem of his own identity in a world neither he nor anyone else understands. His way out is that of the author who creates him—usually the existential solution. In much of postwar writing we find recognition of the impossibility of finding final answers through reason, of the many-sidedness of truth, of the fallacy of the abstract, and of salvation in the comic, the absurd and the ironic. Therein, we are told, lies morality and commitment as well as freedom.

The British people can hardly, more than any others, escape the human predicament. That they are "a puzzled people" was the conclusion following a study made in 1947 of popular attitudes toward religion, ethics, and politics. World War II did not, like World War I, produce illusion, but its conviction, purpose, and objective, were not permanent. At the same time, writing in the seventies, it is well to remember that only a score of years ago, in the fifties, the mood of the City, the atmosphere of Whitehall, the spirit of Redbrick and Oxbridge was one of buoyancy and optimism. It may well be that intellectual currents can be as ephemeral as political.

Whither Britain?

Whither Britain? As we approach the conclusion of our examination of Britain's history in the first three-quarters of the twentieth century, we face this question which, though now banal, is inevitable. But, though repetitious, the question still comes as something of a shock. Recent developments have not taken the course the British themselves, along with most outsiders, would have predicted seventy-five, fifty, even twenty-five years ago. Little attention was given in the fifties to the occasional voice, such as that of Robert Gathorne-Hardy, declaring that the British absolutely refused to recognize their greatly reduced position in the world. Even a decade later the climate of thought in Britain is well reflected in Churchill's affirmation in 1963, on accepting honorary American citizenship: "Reject the view that Britain and the Commonwealth should now be relegated to a tame and minor role."

Ten or fifteen years later it is a different story. Reassessment of Britain's economy, her role in the world, and her way of life has absorbed the attention of journalists at home and abroad and, indeed, preoccupies the British mind generally. Books with titles such as *Decline and Fall? Britain's Crisis in the Sixties* (1969) by Paul Einzig, or *Who Killed the British Empire? An Inquest* (1975) by George Woodcock, have become commonplace. At long last, a realization of the facts of life and a combination of anxiety and resignation have replaced the optimism and pride of the postwar years.

The possible consequences for the "British outlook" and for the "British character" are hardly within our purview, but it may be useful to note some of the cautionary signs of the time. The *New Statesman* for April 3, 1964, in an article "Britain: A Nation of Gamblers?" referred to gambling as "one of the few growth industries." Then there was the opening sentence of the 1972 edition of the usually bland *Annual Register*: "An atmosphere of bitterness, lawlessness, and, at times, even of violence, permeated British society in the early months . . . . It was totally alien to the traditional pattern of British political and industrial life."

Conscience was touched. In his "Call to the Nation," October 15, 1975, the Archbishop of Canterbury (the Most Reverend Donald Coggan) spoke of the alarming rise of "materialism, selfishness and envy" among the British people. On November 25, 1976, in a sermon at Westminster Abbey, the Right Reverend Prof. Thomas F. Torrance, Moderator of the General Assembly of the Church of Scotland, posed a question: "Are there not elements in our sociological and parliamentary tradition which have gone sour on us and have been damaged by disintegrating forces from within?"

But there is another side. Britain's national morale and the probity of her leaders stand up well in comparison with other lands. In Britain there has been no McCarthyism and no Watergate. Pride still has its place; the subject matter of *The British Genius* is that of a small island state whose role in the world is entirely out of proportion to her area and her population; this book appeared in 1973.

And we must recognize that Britain's dominance of the industrial world in the century before World War I derived largely from her unique role as an industrial pioneer. This rested largely on her control of the world market as a source of raw materials and as an outlet for her own production. She was, indeed, the first industrialized nation. Now the entire world is well on its way toward an industrialized society, with national economies resting increasingly on home resources in materials and technological skill. Of all the leading capitalist countries, Britain is the only one whose share in the world's production and in the world market has gone steadily downhill since 1945. But she does remain the most urbanized and most industrialized among the larger states of western Europe, and many an economist would assert that there is no reason why she should not keep pace and even regain leadership in many areas.

And so, though Britain may have become less important to students of contemporary society, she does not necessarily face disaster. In the Jubilee year of 1977, the American *Saturday Review* devoted an issue (June 11) to "the British bequest to all nations and to all men, as peerless in recorded history." Thus, twentieth-century Britain is properly linked with the more distant past. In a little island with few resources but favored by geography and nature, the energy and ingenuity of the British people created not only a state and a nation but also a civilization. But if history teaches anything it is that no individual, no nation, no society can live in or on the past. In 1945 Churchill observed: "Ask what you please, look where you will, you cannot get to the bottom of the resources of Britain." Here, indeed, is the fundamental question. The writer now leaves the role of historian in these closing lines and suggests that Britain's resources must be tapped anew. Traditional ideas and institutions will not solve to any considerable degree the problems of political organization and of human rights, of the economy and trade unionism, of the welfare state, of Britain's role in the world. What is required is a new national purpose, a new dynamic. Only thus will we be able to speak in the future of the British genius which adapts successfully to change, which finds in pragmatism the philosophical and practical answer to all problems, and which avoids the violent solutions which would mean the destruction of the Britain both of the past and of the present.

Table 9 Governments and Prime Ministers since 1900

June 1895	Unionist	Marquess of Salisbury
July 1902	Unionist	Arthur J. Balfour
December 1905	Liberal	Sir Henry Campbell-Bannerman
April 1908	Liberal	Herbert H. Asquith
May 1915	Coalition	Herbert H. Asquith
December 1916	Coalition	David Lloyd George
October 1922	Conservative	A. Bonar Law
May 1923	Conservative	Stanley Baldwin
January 1924	Labor	J. Ramsay MacDonald
November 1924	Conservative	Stanley Baldwin
June 1929	Labor	J. Ramsay MacDonald
August 1931	National	J. Ramsay MacDonald
June 1935	National	Stanley Baldwin
May 1937	National	Neville Chamberlain
May 1940	Coalition	Winston S. Churchill
May 1945	Conservative	Winston S. Churchill
July 1945	Labor	Clement R. Attlee
October 1951	Conservative	Winston S. Churchill
April 1955	Conservative	Sir Anthony Eden
January 1957	Conservative	Harold Macmillan
October 1963	Conservative	Earl of Home (Sir Alec Douglas-Home)
October 1964	Labor	Harold Wilson
June 1970	Conservative	Edward Heath
March 1974	Labor	Harold Wilson
April 1976	Labor	James Callaghan

Select Bibliography

Much of the preparation of *Britain in Transition: The Twentieth Century* has paralleled the compilation of the author's *Modern England 1901–1970* (Conference on British Studies Bibliographical Handbooks) published by the Cambridge University Press in 1976. Hopefully this has worked to the advantage of both.

Modern England, 1901–1970 is the first comprehensive bibliography of published historical material, including printed sources (official documents, letters, diaries, autobiographies, and memoirs) as well as monographs, biographies, and articles. Some 2,500 items are included, for the most part published before January 1, 1974. Many items are briefly annotated and cross references help to bring together related material. Arrangement is by topics under fifteen headings, including "Science and Technology," "Religious History," and "History of the Fine Arts," as well as the more conventional categories of "Political History," "Foreign Relations," "Social History," and the rest.

Except for the most recent publications, all of the items listed below will be found in the bibliographical handbook. For a far wider selection of material and for areas of study not included in this text, the handbook itself should be consulted.

General Works

Various works, differing in character and length, deal with all or a very considerable portion of twentieth-century Britain.

Henry Pelling's *Modern Britain, 1885–1955* (1960) is a brief, readable narrative, largely political in emphasis. Another brief treatment, somewhat broader in scope, is provided in David Thomson's *England in the Twentieth Century, 1914–1963* (1965). Much more comprehensive is T. O. Lloyd's *Empire to Welfare State: English History, 1906–1967* (1970). W. N. Medlicott's *Contemporary England, 1914–1964* (1967) is an admirable work, reflecting in particular the author's mastery of diplomatic history, while A. J. P. Taylor's *English History, 1914–1945* (1965) is celebrated for its incisive brilliance. R. Rhodes James's *The British Revolution: British Politics, 1880–1939* (2 vols., 1976–77) is the most recent political survey and is abreast of recent scholarship. C. J. Bartlett's excellent *A History of Postwar Britain, 1945–1974* (1977) supersedes other efforts.

Politics tend to control Britain's story; certainly they dominate the bibliography. J. H. Grainger, *Character and Style in English Politics* (1969) is a thoughtful and stimulating essay. For general insights the most useful analysis is in R. T. McKenzie, *British Political Parties: the Distribution of Power within the Conservative and Labour Parties* (2d ed., 1963). Robert Blake's Ford Lectures at Oxford in 1968, *The Conservative Party from Peel to Churchill* (1970), opens up the subject in a lively manner. Roy Douglas, *The History of the Liberal Party, 1895– 1970* (1971) is useful for party organization, but is otherwise disappointing. A fine survey of "the revival, triumph, division and decline" of the Liberal Party is found in K. O. Morgan, *The Age of Lloyd George* (1971). For Labor the best "short history" is Carl F. Brand, *History of the Labour Party from 1914* (rev. ed., 1973). To complement it, read G. D. H. Cole, *History of the Labour Party from 1914* (1948). A very useful *Dictionary of Labour Biography* (1972, 1974, 1977), edited by J. M. Bellamy and J. Saville, is in progress. James Klugmann's massive *History of the Communist Party of Great Britain* (2 vols., 1969) is strongly partisan and might well be compared with Henry Pelling's more reliable *The British Communist Party* (1928), and a new work by Hugo Dewar, *Communist Politics in Britain: The CPGB from its Origins to the Second World War* (1976).

Beginning with the election of 1945 we have in the Nuffield Series a scholarly and comprehensive analysis of each general election down to 1974. R. B. McCallum and A. Readman were the authors of the study of the 1945 election; thereafter, D. E. Butler and associates. On political practice and results several useful guides range over the period. These include D. E. Butler, *The Electoral System in Britain since 1918* (2d ed., 1963); Michael Kinnear, *The British Voter: An Atlas and Survey since 1885* (1968); and Chris Cook and John Ramsden, eds., *By-elections in British Politics* (1973), a study of by-elections since 1918. Indispensable for electoral data of all kinds is David Butler and Jennie Freeman, *British Political Facts, 1900–1968* (1969).

No up-to-date work examines constitutional history in detail for the whole period. However, the theory and practice of Cabinet Government is well handled in J. P. Mackintosh, *The British Cabinet* (1962) and Hans Daalder, *Cabinet Reform in Britain, 1914–1963* (1963). D. N. Chester, ed., *The Organization of British Central Government, 1914–1956* (1957), and K. B. Smellie, *A History of Local Government* (4th ed., 1968), are still standard items. For Empire and Commonwealth, Nicholas Mansergh, *The Commonwealth Experience* (1969) is an utterly fascinating work and includes a useful bibliography. Also well worth reading is a popular survey by K. B. Bradley in his *The Living Commonwealth* (1961). For the history of various areas one should turn promptly to the volumes of the *Cambridge History of the British Empire*.

The best survey of economic history is Sidney Pollard's *The Development of the British Economy, 1914–1967* (2d ed., 1969). A treatment with nineteenth-century background is found in R. S. Sayers, *A History of Economic Change in England, 1880–1939* (1967). The relative retardation in Britain is the central theme of G. A. Phillip and R. T. Maddock, *The Growth of the British Economy 1918–1968* (1973). An introduction to the central themes in economic history together with an invaluable bibliography is found in D. H. Aldcroft and H. W. Richardson, *The British Economy, 1870–1939* (1969).

In diplomatic history, a recent publication of great value is J. A. S. Grenville, ed., *The Major International Treaties, 1914–1973: A History and Guide with Texts* (1974). A standard survey is William N. Medlicott, *British Policy since Versailles, 1919–1963* (3d ed., 1968). The "special relation," so-called, is examined in an authoritative manner in Basil Collier, *The Lion and the Eagle: Anglo-American Strategy, 1900–1950* (1972). A fascinating narrative of naval history through most of the period is found in A. J. Marder, *From the Dreadnought to Scapa Flow: The Royal Navy in the Fisher Era, 1904–1919* (5 vols., 1961–70) and *From the Dardanelles to Oran: Studies of the Royal Navy in War and Peace, 1915–1940* (1974).

For broad as well as intensive examination of social structure one should immediately consult D. C. March, *The Changing Social Structure of England and Wales 1871–1961* (rev. ed., 1965). More sociological in approach is Judith Ryder and Harold Silver, *Modern English Society . . . 1850–1970* (1970). Extraordinary detail is found in A. H. Halsey, ed., *Trends in British Society since 1900: A Guide to the Changing Social Structure of Britain* (1972). Donald Read's *The English Provinces* (1964) is an important examination of regionalism. Derek Fraser follows an important theme in his *The Evolution of the British Welfare State* (1973). A survey of educational change and reform for the years 1895–1965 is in G. A. N. Lowndes, *The Silent Social Revolution* (2d ed., 1969). Successful oral history is found in Melvin Bragg, *Speak for England* (1969), based on interviews with inhabitants of Wigton, Cumberland. Religious history may be followed in the masterful treatment of Horton Davies in his *Worship and Theology in England*, vol. 5, *The Ecumenical Century, 1900–1965* (1965). E. R. Norman, *Church and Society in England, 1770–1970* (1976) is concerned with the broader impact of religion. Roger Lloyd, *The Church of England, 1900–1965* (1966) is the best one-volume treatment. Essays concerned with the history of ideas are presented in C. B. Cox and A. E. Dyson, eds., *The Twentieth-Century Mind: Histories, Ideas and Literature in Britain* (3 vols., 1972).

Chapters 1–4 (1900–1914)

If the reader seeks a narrative account of "what happened" in these years together with Victorian background there is still nothing better than R. C. K. Ensor, *England, 1870–1914* (1936). More detail and considerably more interpretation are provided in another classic, vols. 5 and 6 of Elie Halévy, *History of the English People in the Nineteenth Century* (1926, 1934). A brief treatment, with an emphasis on foreign affairs, is in Doreen Collins, *Aspects of British Politics, 1904–1919* (1965). But for more depth one should turn to Donald Read, *Edwardian England, 1901–1915: Society and Politics* (1972) and to Paul Thompson, *The Edwardians: The Remaking of British Society* (1975), the latter in part based on interviews with people who lived in the Edwardian period.

When manuscript material became available in the archives a host of important studies of politics appeared. For the early history of the Labor Party one should turn to Philip Poirier, *The Advent of the British Labour Party* (1958); Frank Bealey and Henry Pelling, *Labour and Politics, 1900–1906* (1958); Roy Gregory, *The Miners and British Politics, 1906–1914* (1968). Colin Cross in *The Liberals in Power, 1905–1914* aims to be both "comprehensive" and "brief." By contrast, great detail will be found in Peter Rowland's two volumes on *The Last Liberal Governments* (1968, 1971). Important monographs include A. K. Russell, *The Liberal Landslide: General Election of 1906* (1973); Richard Semple, *Unionists Divided: Arthur Balfour, Joseph Chamberlain and the Unionist Free Traders* (1972); H. V. Emy, *Liberals, Radicals and Social Politics, 1892–1914* (1973); H. C. G. Mathew, *The Liberal Imperialists: The Ideas and Politics of a Post-Gladstonian Elite* (1973); Stephen Koss, *Non-Conformity in Modern British Politics* (1975); P. F. Clarke, *Lancashire and the New Liberalism* (1971). Neal Blewett, *The Peers, the Parties and the People: The General Elections of 1910* (1972) is detailed; a more lively account of the constitutional crisis of 1901–11 will be found in Roy Jenkins, *Mr. Balfour's Poodle* (1954). The flood of writing on the women's movement includes Andrew Rosen, *Rise Up, Women!* (1974) and David Morgan, *Suffragists and Liberals* (1975), which displace earlier studies.

Vital sources from the foreign office archives have made possible a rewriting of diplomatic history for the prewar period. Among the significant books are George W. Monger, *The End of Isolation: British Foreign Policy, 1900–1907* (1963) and S. R. Williamson, Jr., *The Politics of Grand Strategy: Britain and France Prepare for War, 1904–1914*

(1969), now the standard treatment. The eager student will be well rewarded with a reading of Zara S. Steiner, *The Foreign Office and Foreign Policy 1898–1914* (1969). E. L. Woodward's well-known *Great Britain and the German Navy* (1935) should now be read in conjunction with Peter Padfield *The Great Naval Race: The Anglo-German Naval Rivalry, 1900–1914* (1974). Max Beloff, *Imperial Sunset*, vol. 1, *Britain's Liberal Empire, 1897–1921* (1969) is a brilliant treatment; for developments after the Boer War, consult L. M. Thompson, *The Unification of South Africa, 1902–1910* (1960). A. T. Q. Stewart, *The Ulster Crisis* (1975) is now the best work on the Irish troubles, 1912–14.

Edwardian society has finally received the close analysis it requires and warrants. In addition to the very readable and informative essays in *Edwardian England, 1901–14* (1964) ed. by Simon Nowell-Smith, there is S. L. Hynes's significant *The Edwardian Turn of Mind* (1968). Early phases of social reform have won attention. We now have a comprehensive study in Bentley B. Gilbert's *National Insurance in Great Britain: The Origins of the Welfare State* (1966). For more general treatment, consult J. R. Hay, *The Origins of the Liberal Welfare Reforms, 1906–1914* (1975).

In the past ten to fifteen years good to excellent biographies of statesmen, politicians, and editors have been published, some to replace earlier writing, others an entirely new contribution to historiography. The definitive *Life of Joseph Chamberlain* launched by J. L. Garvin in 1932 has finally been completed with vols. 4–6 by Julian Amery (1951–69). John Wilson's *CB* (1973) is now the best work on Campbell-Bannerman, though J. A. Spender's two-volume work (1924) is still useful. When the Lloyd George Papers became available in the late sixties, historians rushed to the Beaverbrook Library. And Peter Rowland hurried off to the publisher his *David Lloyd George* (1976), which is the best biography thus far, but is likely to have rivals before long.

The official biography of Winston Churchill is in progress, begun by Randolph S. Churchill and continued by Martin Gilbert. Volume 5 (1977) carries the story to 1939. There are companion volumes of documents. And Robert Rhodes James has edited *Winston S. Churchill: His Complete Speeches, 1897–1963* (8 vols.) (1974). A useful one-volume life of Churchill by Henry Pelling (1974) is also available. Roy Jenkins's stylish *Asquith: Portrait of a Man and an Era* (1964) makes good reading, but the standard biography is now Stephen Koss's *Asquith* (1976). And in K. O. Morgan, *Keir Hardie* (1975) we have the kind of biography Hardie deserved.

Other important biographies include: Philip Magnus, *King Edward the Seventh* (1964); Robert Rhodes James, *Rosebery* (1963); two works on Arthur James Balfour, one by Kenneth Young (1963) and the other by Sydney Zebel (1973); Keith Robbins, *Sir Edward Grey* (1971); John Barlow's *Milner: Apostle of Empire* (1975); Dudley Sommer, *Haldane of Cloan* (1960); A. M. Gollin, *"The Observer" and J. L. Garvin, 1908–1914* (1960); Stephen Koss, *Fleet Street Radical: A. G. Gardiner and the*

"Daily News" (1973); A. F. Havighurst, *Radical Journalist: H. W. Massingham, 1860–1924* (1974).

Chapters 5 and 6 (1914–24)

The immediate background of Britain's entrance into World War I is examined in detail by an American historian, B. E. Schmitt, in *The Coming of War*, vol. 2 (1930) and by the Italian historian, Luigi Albertini, in *The Origins of the War of 1914* (3 vols., 1952–57). George Malcolm Thomson's, *The Twelve Days: 24 July to 4 August 1914* (1964) provides armchair reading of high quality. Excellent one-volume histories of the war are B. H. Liddell Hart, *A History of the World War, 1914–1918* (2d ed., 1934) and C. B. Falls, *The First World War* (1960). For complete coverage one should consult the *Official Histories*. Notable episodes are chronicled in Alan Moorehead, *Gallipoli* (1956) and Alistair Horne, *The Price of Glory: Verdun 1916* (1963). Geoffrey Bennett, *Naval Battles of the First World War* (1968) is the best one-volume treatment.

On the government as a war machine there is Lord Hankey's massive *Supreme Command, 1914–18* (2 vols., 1961); a briefer account is found in his *Government Control in War* (1945). Both should now be studied along with Stephen Roskill, *Hankey: Man of Secrets* (3 vols., 1970–74), based on Hankey's unedited diary and other papers. Government controls on the economy during the war have been closely studied. For general interest the most useful are S. J. Hurwitz, *State Intervention in Great Britain, 1914–1919* (1949); William Beveridge, *British Food Control* (1928); Francis W. Hirst, *The Consequences of the War to Great Britain* (1934). The last two are a part of the multivolume *Economic and Social History of the World War, British Series* ed. J. T. Shotwell. For the impact of the war on British society, see A. J. B. Marwick, *The Deluge: British Society and the First World War* (1965).

The domestic politics of the war are now being studied in depth. *British Strategy and Politics, 1914–1918* (1965) by Paul Guinn opens up all the issues. For the early years we find in Cameron Hazelhurst's *Politicians at War, July 1914 to May 1915* (1971) both scholarship and argument. Controversy rages among historians over the key event of Asquith's replacement by Lloyd George in December 1916. Lord Beaverbrook's presentation in *Politicians and the War 1914–1916* (1928) needs to be checked by A. J. P. Taylor's *Beaverbrook* (1972); Robert Blake, *The Unknown Prime Minister, The Life and Times of Bonar Law* (1955); J. E. Wrench, *Geoffrey Dawson and Our Times* (1955); and Randolph Churchill's *Lord Derby* (1960). Postwar politics can be followed in detail and with understanding in Maurice Cowling, *The Impact of Labour, 1920–24* (1970; in Michael Kinnear, *The Fall of Lloyd George: The Political Crisis of 1922* (1973); and in Chris Cook, *The Age of Alignment: Electoral Politics in Britain 1922–29* (1975). In these works and others the fortunes of the Liberal Party during and after the war have been examined in detail. One of the important contributions is Trevor Wilson, *The Downfall of the Liberal Party, 1914–1935* (1966).

The history of the Labor Party in this period may be followed in serveral excellent works: Ross McKibbin, *The Evolution of the Labour Party, 1910–1924* (1975); David Coates, *The Labour Party and the Struggle for Socialism* (1975); J. M. Winter, *Socialism and the Challenge of War: Ideas and Politics in Britain, 1912–1918* (1974).

On problems of peacemaking and postwar diplomacy important insights are afforded in several contemporary writings: Lord Riddell, *Intimate Diary of the Peace Conference and After, 1918–1923* (1933); Harold Nicolson, *Peacemaking, 1919* (1933); Lord Hankey, *The Supreme Control at the Paris Peace Conference, 1919* (1963); Trevor Wilson, ed., *The Political Diaries of C. P. Scott, 1911–1928* (1970). For insights afforded by perspective a half-century and more later, consult Kenneth J. Calder, *Britain and the Origins of the New Europe, 1914–1918* (1976). On Ireland, before, during, and after the war, George Dangerfield will enlighten and perhaps startle in his *The Damnable Question: A Study in Anglo-Irish Relations* (1976). On "reconstruction" in Britain we are fortunate in having P. B. Johnson, *Land Fit for Heroes: The Planning of British Reconstruction* (1968).

Biographies associated with these years include some with high standards of scholarship and literary quality. Some, not already mentioned, are Harold Nicolson, *King George the Fifth* (1952) and also his *Curzon: the Last Phase* (1934); G. K. A. Bell, Randall Davidson, *The Life of the Archbishop of Canterbury* (1952); R. F. Harrod, *Life of John Maynard Keynes* (1951); Philip Magnus, *Kitchener* (1958); Reginald Pound and Geoffrey Harmsworth, *Northcliffe* (1959). Among valuable autobiographies, memoirs and diaries for this period are: L. S. Amery, *My Political Life*, vol. 2, (1953); John Buchan, *Pilgrim's Way* (1940); Winston Churchill, *The World Crisis* (1923) and *The Aftermath* (1929); Stephen Gwynn, ed., *Anvil of War* (1936); David Lloyd George, *War Memoirs*, 4 vols. (1933–34); Stephen McKenna, *While I Remember* (1921); Beatrice Webb, *Diaries, 1912–1924* (1952); E. L. Woodward, *Short Journey* (1942).

Chapters 7 and 8 (1924–39)

The best known and still the most useful single volume on the interwar years is C. L. Mowat, *Britain Between the Wars, 1918–1939* (1955). And for social history, broadly defined, nothing yet has replaced Robert Graves and Alan Hodge, *The Long Week-end* (1940). John Montgomery, *The Twenties* (1957) is also a perceptive book. Provocative essays on various aspects of English life are found in John Raymond, ed., *The Baldwin Age* (1960), and over a broader span of years in Gillian Peele and Chris Cook, eds., *The Politics of Reappraisal, 1918–1939* (1975). For connections between literary currents and political and social problems, see J. K. Johnstone, *The Bloomsbury Group*

(1954) and S. L. Hynes, *The Auden Generation: Literature and Politics in the 1930s* (1976).

The political history of the period is being reconstructed. Older books still very valuable include Richard Lyman, *The First Labour Government, 1924* (1957); R. S. Bassett, *Nineteen Thirty-One: Political Crisis* (1958). R. K. Middlemas in *The Clydesiders: A Left Wing Struggle for Parliamentary Power* (1965) presents a highly significant aspect of Labor politics. The most recent treatment of the "Abdication Crisis" in 1936 is in Frances Donaldson, *Edward VIII* (1974). Ian Colvin's *The Chamberlain Cabinet* (1971) is based on Cabinet papers. Robert Paul Shay Jr. in *Rearmament in the Thirties: Politics and Profits* (1977), is scholarly and enlightening. However, perhaps the most rewarding approach to the many problems the politics of the twenties and thirties pose for historians is in recent biographies, notably on Stanley Baldwin by Keith Middlemas and James Barnes (1969), by H. Montgomery Hyde (1973), and by Kenneth Young (1976). Equally significant are R. Rhodes James, *Churchill: A Study in Failure, 1900–1939* (1970); a biography of Neville Chamberlain by Keith Feiling (1946); R. J. A. Skidelsky, *Oswald Mosley* (1975; Earl of Birkenhead, *Halifax* (1965); and at long last a full-scale biography of Ramsay MacDonald by David Marquand (1977).

In economic history, Derek H. Aldcroft's *The Inter-War Economy: Britain, 1919–1939* (1969) is the best book on the subject. But his conclusions should be compared with those of W. Arthur Lewis, *Economic Survey, 1919–1939* (1949) and A. J. Youngson, *Britain's Economic Growth, 1920–1966* (1967). A recent treatment, presented in more general terms, is Sean Glynn and John Oxborrow, *Interwar Britain: A Social and Economic History* (1976). The best studies of the General Strike of 1926 are by W. H. Crook (1931) and Julian Symons (1957); both include accounts by participants. Bentley Gilbert continues his examination of "social reform" in *British Social Policy, 1914–1939* (1970).

For foreign policy, from this period on, an excellent guide to "what happened" will be found in the annual volumes edited by Arnold J. Toynbee, published by the Royal Institute of International Affairs under the title *Survey of International Affairs* (1925–). Excellent narrative, carrying through this period, is found in F. S. Northedge, *The Troubled Giant: Britain among the Powers, 1916–1939* (1966). Highly impressionistic and somewhat uneven in quality, yet thoughtful and worth reading is Correlli Barnett's treatment of the same period, in *The Collapse of British Power* (1972). The standard treatment of of the navy is in S. W. Roskill, *Naval Policy between the Wars* (2 vols., 1968, 1976). An important subject is well handled in K. W. Watkins, *Britain Divided: The Effect of the Spanish Civil War on British Opinion* (1963). British policy in the 1930s, particularly toward Germany and Italy, is now a very controversial subject among historians. In *All Souls and Appeasement* (1961) A. L. Rowse indicts the Conservative Party with responsibility for the coming of war, while A. J. P. Taylor in *The Origins of the Second World War* (1961, and 2d ed., n.d.) seeks to exonerate Hitler of the charge of deliberately seeking war to achieve Nazi ambitions of expansion. More detail and even more argument is found in Keith Middlemas, *Diplomacy of Illusion: The British Government and Germany, 1937–39* (1972); Maurice Cowling, *The Impact of Hitler: British Politics and British Policy, 1933–1940* (1965); and S. K. Newman, *March 1939: The British Guarantee to Poland* (1976). Sidney Aster, *1939: The Making of the Second World War* (1973) is based largely on archival material available in 1970. For imperial questions between the wars one should consult W. K. Hancock, *Survey of Commonwealth Affairs*, vol. 1, *Problems of Nationality, 1918–1936* (1937) and vol. 2, *Problems of Economic Policy, 1918–1939* (1942), and Nicholas Mansergh, *Survey of British Commonwealth Affairs: Problems of External Policy, 1931–1939* (1952).

Autobiographies, memoirs, letters have poured forth from the presses. The more valuable are: L. S. Amery, *My Political Life*, vol. 3 (1955); Lord Citrine, *Men and Work* (1964); Duff Cooper, *Old Men Forget* (1953); P. J. Grigg, *Prejudice and Judgment* (1948); Thomas Jones, *Whitehall Diary*, ed. K. Middlemas (3 vols. 1969—71) on the years 1916—30, and also Jones' *A Diary with Letters, 1931–50* (1954); Lord Vansittart, *The Mist Procession* (1958). In his *History of Broadcasting in the United Kingdom* (3 vols., 1961–70) Asa Briggs carries the story to 1945. Excellent contemporary commentary on England in the thirties is found in David Low, *Years of Wrath: A Cartoon History, 1931–1945* (1946); Malcolm Muggeridge, *The Sun Never Sets* (1940) and J. B. Priestley, *English Journey* (1934).

Chapters 9 and 10 (1939–51)
World War II, 1939–45

B. H. Liddell Hart, *History of the Second World War* (1970) and Basil Collier, *A Short History of the Second World War* (1967) are perhaps the best one-volume treatments. The War Cabinet papers were the basis for the two volumes by Roger Parkinson: *Blood, Toil, Tears and Sweat: The War History from Dunkirk to Alamein* (1973) and *A Day's March Nearer Home: The War History from Alamein to VE Day* (1974). A fascinating approach both for the dilletante and for the serious student is through Winston Churchill's six-volume *The Second World War* (1948–53). His wartime speeches are conveniently collected in four volumes edited by Charles Eade. However, the serious student will wish to study Churchill's account along with the results of professional research. Preeminent is the official British history of the war which consists, in the main, of a Military Series edited by J. R. M. Butler and a Civil Series edited by Sir Keith Hancock. These two series constitute an outstanding historical achievement. In following the course of the way one will greatly benefit from consulting the volumes on *The United States in World War II* produced by the Office of Military History, Department of the Army. Of special interest would be W. F. Craven and J. L. Cate,

Army Air Forces in World War II (7 vols., 1948–58); G. A. Harrison, *Cross-Channel Attack* (1951); and F. C. Pogue, *The Supreme Command* (1954).

J. C. Masterman's *The Double Cross System* (1972) is admirable in every way as an account of the British intelligence activities, especially the story of German agents in the U.K. We do not yet have a reliable account of the manner in which the secret code of the German high command was broken and the significance thereof. This must await the release of British official documents. Meantime we have rather sensational accounts, somewhat contradictory, which cannot be checked for accuracy. These include F. W. Winterbotham, *The Ultra Secret* (1974); Anthony Cave Brown, *Bodyguard of Lies: The Vital Role of Deceptive Strategy in World War II* (1975); William Stevenson, *A Man Called Intrepid: The Secret War, 1939–45* (1976).

For the diplomatic history of the war we have "a record compiled from British archives," a part of the "official history" of the war. This is E. L. Woodward's *British Foreign Policy in the Second World War* (4 vols., 1970–76). More interpretative treatments are found in the volumes of the *Survey of International Affairs* already mentioned. Special aspects are treated in length: W. L. Langer and S. E. Gleason, *The Challenge to Isolation, 1937–1940* (1952) and *The Undeclared War, 1940–1941* (1953) concerns the immediate background of the war in the United States; J. L. Snell, *The Meaning of Yalta: Big Three Diplomacy and the Balance of Power* (1956) and *Wartime Origins of the East-West Dilemma over Germany* (1959); Herbert Feis, *Between War and Peace: The Potsdam Conference* (1960); Elizabeth Barker, *British Policy in Southeast Europe in the Second World War* (1976). For Britain and the atomic bomb consult R. W. Clark, *The Birth of the Bomb* (1961) and especially M. M. Gowing, *Britain and Atomic Energy, 1939–1945* (1964) which is continued by her *Independence and Deterrence: Britain and Atomic Energy, 1939–45* (1964) which is continued by her *Independence and Deterrence: Britain and Atomic Energy, 1945–1952* (2 vols., 1974).

Of special interest and value in studying the English people during the war are F. K. Mason, *Battle over Britain* (1969); Robert Wright, *Dowding and the Battle of Britain* (1969)—Dowding was in charge of Fighter Command. William Sansom, *Westminster in War* (1947) is one of the best contemporary accounts of the London Blitz. For the impact of the war on society, a controversial subject, for varying points of view consult A. J. B. Marwick, *Britain in the Century of Total War ... 1900–1967* (1968); Henry Pelling, *Britain and the Second World War* (1970); Norman Longmate, *How We Lived Then: A History of Every-day Life during the Second World War* (1971). For social change in progress significant works are: H. C. Dent, *Education in Transition* (1944); Bruce Truscot, *Red Brick University* (1943); E. Lipson, *A Planned Economy or Free Enterprise: The Lessons of History* (2nd ed., 1946); Lord Beveridge, *Power and Influence* (1953); F. A. Iremonger, *William Temple, Archbishop of Canterbury* (1948).

1945–51

As already mentioned, the general elections are examined individually in the Nuffield Series. In *Conservative Party in Opposition, 1945–51* (1964) J. D. Hoffman renders good service. On the complexities of the postwar economy, Andrew Shonfield, *British Economic Policy since the War* (1958) is of general interest. On international exchance, Eliot Zupnick, *Britain's Postwar Dollar Problem* (1957) is recommended. Various industries are treated at some length in G. D. N. Worswick and P. H. Ady, eds., *The British Economy, 1945–1950* (1952).

A considerable literature has appeared on nationalization and the welfare state. A brief clear story from 1945 to the late sixties is found in G. L. Reid and Kevin Allen, *Nationalized Industries* (1970). More adequate is *The Nationalization of British Industry, 1945–51* (1976) by Sir Norman Chester. Many writers have been concerned with results: William Warren Haynes, *Nationalization in Practice: The British Coal Industry* (1953); A. A. Rogow, *The Labour Government and British Industry, 1945–1951* (1955); W. A. Robson, *Nationalized Industries and Public Ownership* (1960). In other works there is assessment of the various agencies of the "welfare state"; all the more interesting because written soon after the event: Ernest Watkins, *The Cautious Revolution* (1950); M. Penelope Hall, *Social Services of Modern England* (1952); Harry Eckstein, *The English Health Service: Its Origins, Structure and Achievements* (1958). Richard Titmuss in *Essays on "The Welfare State"* (1958) provides thoughtful and informed comment. Writing on educational problems was prolific after the war; especially significant are H. C. Dent, *Growth in English Education, 1946–1952* (1954) and *Universities in Transition* (1961); John Vaizey, *The Costs of Education* (1958). Cartoon history is provided in [Michael] Cummings, *These Uproarious Years: A Pictorial Post-War History* (1954).

Publications on postwar foreign policy are not very satisfactory, since official documentary material available to scholars is limited. The best treatment, written with some perspective, is in F. S. Northedge, *British Foreign Policy: The Process of Readjustment, 1945–1961* (1962). Hugh Seton-Watson's *Neither War nor Peace* (1960) is stimulating, and M. A. Fitzsimmons, *Foreign Policy of the British Labour Government, 1945–1951* (1953) is a careful and useful work. Leon D. Epstein, *Uneasy Ally* (1954) examines Anglo-American relations during the years 1945–52. The volumes of the *Survey of International Relations* include George Kirk, *Middle East in the War* (1952) and *Middle East, 1945–1950* (1954). The Royal Institute of International Affairs also issued *Great Britain and Egypt* (1952) and *Great Britain and Palestine* (1946). Nicholas Mansergh, *Survey of British Commonwealth Affairs: Problems of War Time Cooperation and Post-War Change, 1939–1952* (1958) is outstanding. K. C. Wheare, *The Constitutional Structure of the Commonwealth* (1960) is standard. Much more recent is the magisterial work on Britain and India, *The Transfer of Power, 1942–1947*, by Nicholas Mansergh. By 1976, vols. 1, 2, and 6 had appeared.

Full-scale biographies of individuals prominent since 1939 are still limited. There is John W. Wheeler-Bennett, *King George VI: His Life and Reign* (1958); the Earl of Birkenhead, *The Prof. in Two Worlds: The Official Life of Professor F. A. Lindemann, Viscount Cherwell*; Alan Bullock, *The Life and Times of Ernest Bevin* (1960–67); thus far two volumes have carried this fine biography to 1945. On the other hand, memoirs and autobiographies are beginning to multiply; it must be added that they are of uneven value. Those of particular interest include: Hugh Dalton, *Call Back Yesterday: Memoirs, 1887–1931* (1953); *The Fateful Years: Memoirs, 1931–1945* (1957) and *High Tide and After: Memoirs, 1945–1960* (1962); Lord Pakenham, *Born to Believe* (1953); Emanuel Shinwell. *Conflict Without Malice* (1955); Rt. Hon. Earl of Woolton, *Memoirs* (1959); Herbert Morrison, *An Autobiography* (1960); Francis Williams, *A Prime Minister Remembers: The War and Post-War Memoirs of the Rt. Hon. Earl Attlee* (1961).

Chapter 11 (1951–64)

For a brief account of "what happened" consult Mary Proudfoot, *British Politics and Government, 1951–1970*. For insight and understanding see S. H. Beer's well-known book, *British Politics in the Collectivist Age* (1965). Another remarkable book is David Butler, *Political Change in Britain: The Evolution of Electoral Choice* (2d ed., 1974), "a prodigious feat" in the language of *The Guardian*. The task and the problems of Labor are analyzed in R. M. Punnett, *Front-bench Opposition* (1973); Christopher Driver, *The Disarmers* (1964), principally on the CND movement; and David Widgery, *The Left in Britain, 1956–68* (1976). *The Liberal Party* received well-deserved attention by J. S. Rasmussen (1965) in his study of "retrenchment and revival." For problems common to all parties there is a lively examination in R. J. Jackson, *Rebels and Whips* (1968).

As to economic history, a useful approach is through E. E. Hagen and S. F. T. White, *Great Britain: Quiet Revolution in Planning* (1966). And then one can grapple with the problems as presented in G. A. Dorfman, *Wage Politics in Britain, 1945–67* (1973); Jacques Leruez, *Economic Policy and Politics in Great Britain, 1945–1974* (1975); Leo Panitch, *Social Democracy and Industrial Militancy, 1945–1974* (1976). Miriam Camps, *Britain and the European Community, 1955–1963* (1964) is excellent on the "Common Market." For an analysis of British industry, we have two studies at the time: D. D. N. Worswick and P. H. Ady, *The British Economy in the Nineteen-Fifties* (1963); J. C. R. Dow, *The Management of the British Economy, 1945–60* (1964). Almont Lindsey, *Socialized Medicine in England and Wales: The National Health Service, 1948–1961* (1962) is the best book on the subject written during these years.

On foreign policy the volumes of the *Survey of International Affairs* continue to be indispensable. For analysis we are fortunate in having Elizabeth Barker, *Britain in a Divided Europe, 1945–1970* (1971) and Joseph Frankel, *British Foreign Policy, 1945–1973* (1975). Significant themes are followed by C. J. Bartlett in *Retreat: A Short History of British Defence Policy, 1945–1970* (1972) and by A. J. Pierre, *Nuclear Politics* ... *1939–1970* (1972). Anthony Nutting, *No End of a Lesson: The Story of Suez* (1967) is one of the best accounts; the war itself is the subject of A. J. Barker, *Suez* (1964). Documents are readily available in D. C. Watt, ed., *Documents on the Suez Crisis* (1957).

Nicholas Mansergh, ed., *Documents and Speeches on Commonwealth Affairs, 1952–1962* (1963) is standard. The *Survey of Commonwealth Affairs* is continued by J. D. B. Miller in his scholarly and articulate *Problems of Expansion and Attrition, 1953–1969* (1974). Informative treatments, often reflecting the perspective at the time written are: F. H. Underhill, *The British Commonwealth* (1956); C. E. Carrington, *The Liquidation of the British Empire* (1961); Kenneth Bradley, *The Living Commonwealth* (1961); W. B. Hamilton et al., *A Decade of the Commonwealth, 1955–1964* (1966); David Goldsworthy, *Colonial Issues in British Politics, 1945–1961* (1971).

Harry Hopkins, *The New Look: A Social History of the Forties and Fifties in Britain* (1963) is lively and popular presentation. The fashionable approach was introspective and clinical as in E. A. Johns, *The Social Structure of Modern Britain* (1965); Richard Titmuss, *Income Distribution and Social Change* (1962); W. L. Guttsman, *The British Political Elite* (1963); Michael Young, *Rise of the Meritocracy, 1870–2033* (1962). For city planning and "new towns" in these years, one should consult J. P. Coppock and H. C. Prince, *Greater London* (1964) and J. B. Cullingworth, *Town and Country Planning in England and Wales* (1964).

Thus far, biographies on the period have been of no great significance. Both Geoffrey McDermott, *Leader Lost: a Biography of Hugh Gaitskell* (1972) and Sidney Aster, *Anthony Eden* (1976) are, however, informative. Sir Anthony Eden's *Memoirs* have appeared in three volumes (1960–65)—they are rather thin. Harold Macmillan's massive six-volume autobiography is revealing as to Macmillan himself, but generally disappointing otherwise. In contrast we have R. A. Butler's fascinating and significant one-volume *The Art of the Possible* (1971), the Earl of Kilmuir (D. P. Maxwell Fyfe)'s *Political Adventure* (1964), and the Earl of Longford (Frank Pakenham)'s *Five Lives* (1964). J. C. Masterman's autobiography, *On The Chariot Wheel* (1975) is in a class by itself as he ranges over MI5, Oxford, and elsewhere.

Chapters 12 and 13 (1964–76)

Much of the bibliography referred to in the previous section carries over. Inevitably, much of the writing on this period proper is journalistic in character and tentative in tone. However, there are several works, of a general nature, well worth reading: Paul Einzig, *Decline and Fall? Britain's Crisis in the Sixties* (1969); Brian Lapping, *The Labour Government, 1964–70* (1970); Bernard Levin, *The Pendulum Years: Britain and the Sixties* (1970); David McKie and Chris Cook, eds., *The Decade of Disillusion: British Politics in the Sixties* (1972); R. Rhodes James, *Ambitions and Realities: British Politics, 1964–1970* (1972). Richard Hodder-Williams deals with a timely theme in *Public Opinion Polls and British Politics* (1970).

There are solid contributions to constitutional theory and practice. Frank Stacey's fine *The Government of Great Britain* (1968) is brought up to the present in its "sequel": *British Government 1966 to 1975: Years of Reform* (1975), a remarkably good book. Good service has also been rendered local government by Lord Redcliffe-Maud and Bruce Wood in *English Local Government Reformed* (1974) and by Peter G. Richards in *The Reformed Local Government System* (1975). Richards is also the author of *Parliament and Conscience* (1970), concerned with liberalization of the laws on divorce, homosexuality, abortion, and censorship. Janet P. Morgan in *The House of Lords and the Labour Government, 1964–1970* (1975) deals definitively with the only serious effort in our times to reform the House of Lords.

For these years we have already some highly interesting, even significant, testimony from leadership. Harold Wilson gives us at considerable length his version in *The Labour Government, 1964–1970* (1971), which perhaps tells us more about the author than about his times. George Brown, in his forthright way, gives another story of the sixties in his *In My Way* (1970). But rising in significance above either of them is Richard Crossman, *The Diaries of a Cabinet Minister* (3 vols., 1975–77) on the years 1964–70. These volumes, published despite official objection, carry out Crossman's desire to provide an "inside story" of the operations of the British government. It should prove interesting to read the Crossman diaries in conjunction with *The Cecil King Diary, 1965–1970* (1972), King being prominent in the newspaper world.

In 1965, Wilfred Beckerman, a well-known economist, with others ventured a forecast, *The British Economy in 1975*. They also assessed *The Labour Government's Economic Record, 1964–1970* (1972). Irving Richter in *Political Purpose in Trade Unions* (1973) examined practice since 1950. A work recently published, Michael Stewart's *Politics and Economic Policy since 1964* (1977) promises some enlightenment. Robert Boardman and A. J. R. Groom, eds., with essays by various writers, in *The Management of Britain's External Relations* (1973) reveal the changes in this area.

Colin Buchanan's *The State of Britain* (1972) is a neat summary of the history of planning measures. R. G. S. Brown, *The Changing National Health Service* (1973) is the best guide for this period. A statistical study of great value is provided in G. C. Fiegehen et al., *Poverty and Progress in Britain 1953–1973* (1977). But the reader interested in the general fortunes of "the welfare state" should consult William A. Robson, *Welfare State and Welfare Society* (1976) and D. C. Marsh, *The Welfare State* (1970). For some of the final contributions of Richard Titmuss in his examination of "welfare society," consult his essays in *Commitment to Welfare* (1968).

Chapter 14 (1950–77)

Much of the important bibliography associated with this chapter is referred to in the text. Consult also relevant items mentioned in the previous two sections.

Index

DATE DUE